PROGRAMMING IN

Custom Edition

Taken from:

C# for Programmers, Second Edition
by Harvey M. Deitel and Paul J. Deitel

and

Core C# and .NET
by Stephen C. Perry

Custom Publishing

New York   Boston   San Francisco
London   Toronto   Sydney   Tokyo   Singapore   Madrid
Mexico City   Munich   Paris   Cape Town   Hong Kong   Montreal

Cover image courtesy of PhotoDisc/Getty Images.

Taken from:

C# for Programmers, Second Edition
by Harvey M. Deitel and Paul J. Deitel
Copyright © 2006 by Pearson Education, Inc.
Published by Prentice Hall
Upper Saddle River, New Jersey 07458

Core C# and .NET
by Stephen C. Perry
Copyright © 2006 by Pearson Education, Inc.
Published by Prentice Hall

This special edition published in cooperation with Pearson Custom Publishing.

All trademarks, service marks, registered trademarks, and registered service marks are the property of their respective owners and are used herein for identification purposes only.

Printed and bound in the United States of America

10 9 8 7 6 5 4 3

2008820096

SB

**Pearson
Custom Publishing**
is a division of

www.pearsonhighered.com

ISBN 10: 0-558-05432-3
ISBN 13: 978-0-558-05432-8

This textbook, *Programming in C#*, combines selected content from two original textbooks specifically chosen for use in this course. Every attempt has been made to reflow content and renumber internal references to provide consistent pedagogy and ease of use.

Many thanks to Frank Miller and Rachelle Reese for their editorial review and selection of this textbook.

Dedication

C# for Programmers, Second Edition, by Harvey M. Deitel and Paul J. Deitel

To Janie Schwark of Microsoft
With sincere gratitude for the privilege and
the pleasure of working closely with you for so many years.

Harvey M. Deitel and Paul J. Deitel

Core C# and .NET, by Stephen C. Perry

To the people who taught me the essentials:
Shuford, how to tie my shoelaces,
Miss White, how to read,
Mrs. Price, how to study,
and Mom, who taught me how to dream.

Contents

14 Working with XML in .NET   569

Introduction to C# Applications

What's in a name?
That which we call a rose
by any other name
would smell as sweet.

—William Shakespeare

When faced with a decision,
I always ask, "What would
be the most fun?"

—Peggy Walker

"Take some more tea," the
March Hare said to Alice,
very earnestly. "I've had
nothing yet." Alice replied
in an offended tone, "So I
can't take more." "You mean
you can't take less," said the
Hatter, "it's very easy to take
more than nothing."

—Lewis Carroll

OBJECTIVES

In this chapter you will learn:

- To write simple C# applications using code rather than visual programming.

- To write statements that input and output data to the screen.

- To declare and use data of various types.

- To store and retrieve data from memory.

- To use arithmetic operators.

- To determine the order in which operators are applied.

- To write decision-making statements.

- To use relational and equality operators.

- To use message dialogs to display messages.

1.1 Introduction

We now introduce C# application programming, which facilitates a disciplined approach to application design. Most of the C# applications you will study in this book process information and display results. In this chapter, we introduce *console applications*—these input and output text in a *console window*. In Microsoft Windows 95/98/ME, the console window is the *MS-DOS prompt*. In other versions of Microsoft Windows, the console window is the *Command Prompt*.

We begin with several examples that simply display messages on the screen. We then demonstrate an application that obtains two numbers from a user, calculates their sum and displays the result. You will learn how to perform various arithmetic calculations and save the results for later use. Many applications contain logic that requires the application to make decisions—the last example in this chapter demonstrates decision-making fundamentals by showing you how to compare numbers and display messages based on the comparison results. For example, the application displays a message indicating that two numbers are equal only if they have the same value. We carefully analyze each example one line at a time.

1.2 A Simple C# Application: Displaying a Line of Text

Let us consider a simple application that displays a line of text. (Later in this section, we discuss how to compile and run an application.) The application and its output are shown in Fig. 1.1. The application illustrates several important C# language features. For your convenience, each program we present in this book includes line numbers, which are not part of actual C# code. In Section 1.3, we show how to display line numbers for your C# code in the IDE. We will soon see that line 10 does the real work of the application—namely, displaying the phrase Welcome to C# Programming! on the screen. We now consider each line of the application.

Line 1

```
// Fig. 1.1: Welcome1.cs
```

```
 1   // Fig. 1.1: Welcome1.cs
 2   // Text-printing application.
 3   using System;
 4
 5   public class Welcome1
 6   {
 7      // Main method begins execution of C# application
 8      public static void Main( string[] args )
 9      {
10         Console.WriteLine( "Welcome to C# Programming!" );
11      } // end method Main
12   } // end class Welcome1
```

```
Welcome to C# Programming!
```

Fig. 1.1 | Text-printing application.

begins with //, indicating that the remainder of the line is a *comment*. We begin every application with a comment indicating the figure number and the name of the file in which the application is stored.

A comment that begins with // is called a *single-line comment*, because it terminates at the end of the line on which it appears. A // comment also can begin in the middle of a line and continue until the end of that line (as in lines 7, 11 and 12).

Delimited comments such as

```
/* This is a delimited
   comment. It can be
   split over many lines */
```

can be spread over several lines. This type of comment begins with the delimiter /* and ends with the delimiter */. All text between the delimiters is ignored by the compiler. C# incorporated delimited comments and single-line comments from the C and C++ programming languages, respectively. In this book, we use only single-line comments in our programs.

Line 2

```
// Text-printing application.
```

is a single-line comment that describes the purpose of the application.

Line 3

```
using System;
```

is a *using directive* that helps the compiler locate a class that is used in this application. A great strength of C# is its rich set of predefined classes that you can reuse rather than "reinventing the wheel." These classes are organized under *namespaces*—named collections of related classes. Collectively, .NET's namespaces are referred to as the *.NET Framework Class Library (FCL)*. Each using directive identifies predefined classes that a C# application should be able to use. The using directive in line 3 indicates that this example uses classes from the System namespace, which contains the predefined Console class (discussed shortly) used in Line 10, and many other useful classes.

Common Programming Error 1.1

All using directives must appear before any other code (except comments) in a C# source code file; otherwise a compilation error occurs.

Error-Prevention Tip 1.1

Forgetting to include a using directive for a class used in your application typically results in a compilation error containing a message such as "The name 'Console' does not exist in the current context." When this occurs, check that you provided the proper using directives and that the names in the using directives are spelled correctly, including proper use of uppercase and lowercase letters.

For each new .NET class we use, we indicate the namespace in which it is located. This information is important because it helps you locate descriptions of each class in the *.NET documentation*. A Web-based version of this documentation can be found at

    msdn2.microsoft.com/en-us/library/ms229335

This can also be found in the Visual C# Express documentation under the **Help** menu. You can also place the cursor on the name of any .NET class or method, then press the *F1* key to get more information.

Line 4 is simply a blank line. Together, blank lines, space characters and tab characters are known as ***whitespace***. (Space characters and tabs are known specifically as ***whitespace characters***.) Whitespace is ignored by the compiler. In this and the next several chapters, we discuss conventions for using whitespace to enhance application readability.

Line 5

```
public class Welcome1
```

begins a *class declaration* for the class Welcome1. Every application consists of at least one class declaration that is defined by you—the programmer. These are known as ***user-defined classes***. The **class keyword** introduces a class declaration and is immediately followed by the *class name* (Welcome1). Keywords (sometimes called ***reserved words***) are reserved for use by C# and are always spelled with all lowercase letters. The complete list of C# keywords is shown in Fig. 1.2.

C# Keywords				
abstract	as	base	bool	break
byte	case	catch	char	checked
class	const	continue	decimal	default
delegate	do	double	else	enum
event	explicit	extern	false	finally
fixed	float	for	foreach	goto
if	implicit	in	int	interface
internal	is	lock	long	namespace
new	null	object	operator	out

Fig. 1.2 | C# keywords. (Part 1 of 2.)

C# Keywords				
override	*params*	*private*	*protected*	*public*
readonly	*ref*	*return*	*sbyte*	*sealed*
short	*sizeof*	*stackalloc*	*static*	*string*
struct	*switch*	*this*	*throw*	*true*
try	*typeof*	*uint*	*ulong*	*unchecked*
unsafe	*ushort*	*using*	*virtual*	*void*
volatile	*while*			

Fig. 1.2 | C# keywords. (Part 2 of 2.)

By convention, all class names begin with a capital letter and capitalize the first letter of each word they include (e.g., SampleClassName). This is frequently referred to as *Pascal casing*. A class name is an *identifier*—a series of characters consisting of letters, digits and underscores (_) that does not begin with a digit and does not contain spaces. Some valid identifiers are Welcome1, identifier, _value and m_inputField1. The name 7button is not a valid identifier because it begins with a digit, and the name input field is not a valid identifier because it contains a space. Normally, an identifier that does not begin with a capital letter is not the name of a class. C# is *case sensitive*—that is, uppercase and lowercase letters are distinct, so a1 and A1 are different (but both valid) identifiers. Identifiers may also be preceded by the @ character. This indicates that a word should be interpreted as an identifier, even if it is a keyword (e.g. @int). This allows C# code to use code written in other .NET languages where an identifier might have the same name as a C# keyword.

Good Programming Practice 1.1

By convention, always begin a class name's identifier with a capital letter and start each subsequent word in the identifier with a capital letter.

Common Programming Error 1.2

C# is case sensitive. Not using the proper uppercase and lowercase letters for an identifier normally causes a compilation error.

In Chapters 1–6, every class we define begins with the keyword *public*. For now, we will simply require this keyword. You will learn more about public and non-public classes in Chapter 7. When you save your public class declaration in a file, the file name is usually the class name followed by the .cs filename extension. For our application, the file name is Welcome1.cs.

Good Programming Practice 1.2

By convention, a file that contains a single public class should have a name that is identical to the class name (plus the .cs extension) in terms of both spelling and capitalization. Naming your files in this way makes it easier for other programmers (and you) to determine where the classes of an application are located.

A *left brace* (in line 6 in Fig. 1.1), {, begins the *body* of every class declaration. A corresponding *right brace* (in line 12), }, must end each class declaration. Note that lines 7–11 are indented. This indentation is one of the spacing conventions mentioned earlier. We define each spacing convention as a Good Programming Practice.

Error-Prevention Tip 1.2

Whenever you type an opening left brace, {, in your application, immediately type the closing right brace, }, then reposition the cursor between the braces and indent to begin typing the body. This practice helps prevent errors due to missing braces.

Good Programming Practice 1.3

*Indent the entire body of each class declaration one "level" of indentation between the left and right braces that delimit the body of the class. This format emphasizes the class declaration's structure and makes it easier to read. You can let the IDE format your code by selecting **Edit > Advanced > Format Document**.*

Good Programming Practice 1.4

*Set a convention for the indent size you prefer, then uniformly apply that convention. The **Tab** key may be used to create indents, but tab stops vary among text editors. We recommend using three spaces to form each level of indentation. We show how to do this in Section 1.3.*

Common Programming Error 1.3

It is a syntax error if braces do not occur in matching pairs.

Line 7

```
// Main method begins execution of C# application
```

is a comment indicating the purpose of lines 8–11 of the application. Line 8

```
public static void Main( string[] args )
```

is the starting point of every application. The *parentheses* after the identifier Main indicate that it is an application building block called a method. Class declarations normally contain one or more methods. Method names usually follow the same Pascal casing capitalization conventions used for class names. For each application, exactly one of the methods in a class must be called Main (which is typically defined as shown in line 8); otherwise, the application will not execute. Methods are able to perform tasks and return information when they complete their tasks. Keyword *void* (line 8) indicates that this method will not return any information after it completes its task. Later, we will see that many methods do return information. You will learn more about methods in Chapters 2 and 5. For now, simply mimic Main's first line in your applications.

The left brace in line 9 begins the *body of the method declaration*. A corresponding right brace must end the method's body (line 11 of Fig. 1.1). Note that line 10 in the body of the method is indented between the braces.

Good Programming Practice 1.5

As with class declarations, indent the entire body of each method declaration one "level" of indentation between the left and right braces that define the method body. This format makes the structure of the method stand out and makes the method declaration easier to read.

Line 10

```
Console.WriteLine( "Welcome to C# Programming!" );
```

instructs the computer to *perform an action*—namely, to print (i.e., display on the screen) the *string* of characters contained between the double quotation marks. A string is sometimes called a *character string*, a *message* or a *string literal*. We refer to characters between double quotation marks simply as *strings*. Whitespace characters in strings are not ignored by the compiler.

Class **Console** provides *standard input/output* capabilities that enable applications to read and display text in the console window from which the application executes. The **Console.WriteLine** *method* displays (or prints) a line of text in the console window. The string in the parentheses in line 10 is the *argument* to the method. Method Console.WriteLine performs its task by displaying (also called outputting) its argument in the console window. When Console.WriteLine completes its task, it positions the *screen cursor* (the blinking symbol indicating where the next character will be displayed) at the beginning of the next line in the console window. (This movement of the cursor is similar to what happens when a user presses the *Enter* key while typing in a text editor—the cursor moves to the beginning of the next line in the file.)

The entire line 10, including Console.WriteLine, the parentheses, the argument "Welcome to C# Programming!" in the parentheses and the *semicolon* (**;**), is called a *statement*. Each statement ends with a semicolon. When the statement in line 10 executes, it displays the message Welcome to C# Programming! in the console window. A method is typically composed of one or more statements that perform the method's task.

Common Programming Error 1.4

Omitting the semicolon at the end of a statement is a syntax error.

Some programmers find it difficult when reading or writing an application to match the left and right braces ({ and }) that delimit the body of a class declaration or a method declaration. For this reason, some programmers include a comment after each closing right brace (}) that ends a method declaration and after each closing right brace that ends a class declaration. For example, line 11

```
} // end method Main
```

specifies the closing right brace of method Main, and line 12

```
} // end class Welcome1
```

specifies the closing right brace of class Welcome1. Each of these comments indicates the method or class that the right brace terminates. Visual Studio can help you locate matching braces in your code. Simply place the cursor next to one brace and Visual Studio will highlight the other.

Good Programming Practice 1.6

Following the closing right brace of a method body or class declaration with a comment indicating the method or class declaration to which the brace belongs improves application readability.

1.3 Creating Your Simple Application in Visual C# Express

Now that we have presented our first console application (Fig. 1.1), we provide a step-by-step explanation of how to compile and execute it using Visual C# Express.

Creating the Console Application

After opening Visual C# 2005 Express, select **File > New Project…** to display the **New Project** dialog (Fig. 1.3), then select the **Console Application** template. In the dialog's **Name** field, type Welcome1. Click **OK** to create the project. The IDE now contains the open console application, as shown in Fig. 1.4. Note that the editor window already contains some code provided by the IDE. Some of this code is similar to that of Fig. 1.1. Some is not, and uses features that we have not yet discussed. The IDE inserts this extra code to help organize the application and to provide access to some common classes in the .NET Framework Class Library—at this point in the book, this code is neither required nor relevant to the discussion of this application; delete all of it.

The code coloring scheme used by the IDE is called *syntax-color highlighting* and helps you visually differentiate application elements. Keywords appear in blue, and other text is black. When present, comments are green. In this book, we syntax shade our code similarly—bold italic for keywords, italic for comments, bold gray for literals and constants, and black for other text. One example of a literal is the string passed to Console.WriteLine in line 10 of Fig. 1.1. You can customize the colors shown in the code editor by selecting **Tools > Options….** This displays the **Options** dialog (Fig. 1.5). Then click the plus sign, +, next to **Environment** and select **Fonts and Colors**. Here you can change the colors for various code elements.

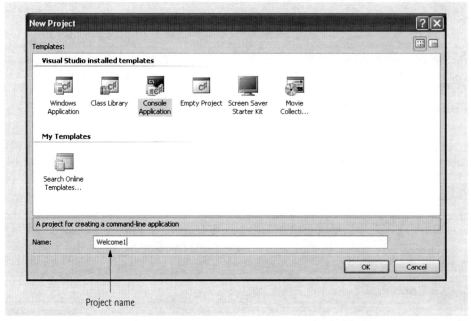

Fig. 1.3 | Creating a **Console Application** with the **New Project** dialog.

Editor window

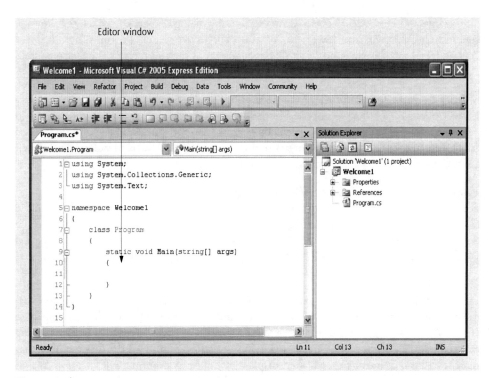

Fig. 1.4 | IDE with an open console application.

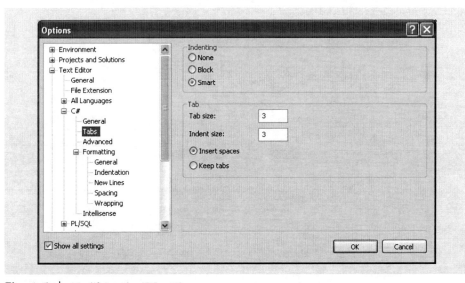

Fig. 1.5 | Modifying the IDE settings.

Modifying the Editor Settings to Display Line Numbers

Visual C# Express provides many ways to personalize your coding experience. In this step, you will change the settings so that your code matches that of this book. To have the IDE display line numbers, select **Tools > Options....** In the dialog that appears, click the **Show all settings** checkbox on the lower left of the dialog, then click the plus sign next to **Text Editor** in the left pane and select **All Languages.** On the right, check the **Line Numbers** check box. Keep the **Options** dialog open.

Setting Code Indentation to Three Spaces per Indent
In the **Options** dialog that you opened in the previous step (Fig. 1.5), click on the plus sign next to C# in the left pane and select **Tabs.** Enter **3** for both the **Tab Size** and **Indent Size** fields. Any new code you add will now use three spaces for each level of indentation. Click **OK** to save your settings, close the dialog and return to the editor window.

Changing the Name of the Application File
For applications we create in this book, we change the default name of the application file (i.e., Program.cs) to a more descriptive name. To rename the file, click Program.cs in the **Solution Explorer** window. This displays the application file's properties in the **Properties** window (Fig. 1.6). Change the **File Name** *property* to Welcome1.cs.

Writing Code
In the editor window (Fig. 1.4), type the code from Fig. 1.1. After you type (in line 10) the class name and a dot (i.e., Console.), a window containing a scrollbar is displayed (Fig. 1.7). This IDE feature, called *IntelliSense*, lists a class's **members**, which include method names. As you type characters, Visual C# Express highlights the first member that matches all the characters typed, then displays a tool tip containing a description of that member. You can either type the complete member name (e.g., WriteLine), double click the member name in the member list or press the *Tab* key to complete the name. Once the complete name is provided, the *IntelliSense* window closes.

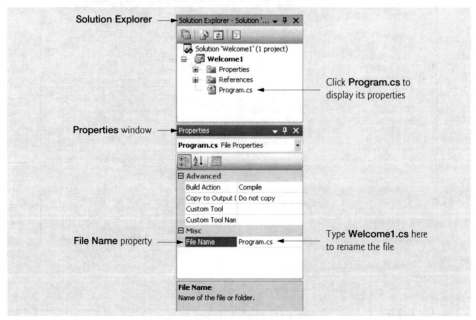

Fig. 1.6 | Renaming the program file in the **Properties** window.

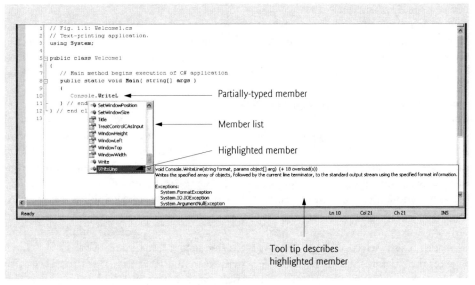

Fig. 1.7 | *IntelliSense* feature of Visual C# Express.

When you type the open parenthesis character, (, after `Console.WriteLine`, the ***Parameter Info*** window is displayed (Fig. 1.8). This window contains information about the method's parameters. As you will learn in Chapter 5, there can be several versions of a method—that is, a class can define several methods that have the same name as long as they have different numbers and/or types of parameters. These methods normally all perform similar tasks. The *Parameter Info* window indicates how many versions of the selected method are available and provides up and down arrows for scrolling through the different versions. For example, there are 19 versions of the `WriteLine` method—we use one of these 19 versions in our application. The *Parameter Info* window is one of the many features provided by the IDE to facilitate application development. In the next several chapters, you will learn more about the information displayed in these windows. The *Parameter Info* window is especially helpful when you want to see the different ways in which a method can be used. From the code in Fig. 1.1, we already know that we intend to display one string with `WriteLine`, so because you know exactly which version of `WriteLine` you want to use, you can simply close the *Parameter Info* window by pressing the *Esc* key.

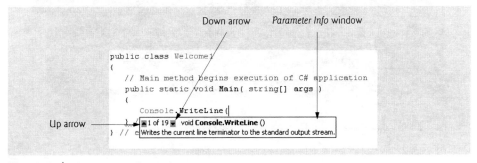

Fig. 1.8 | *Parameter Info* window.

Saving the Application

Select **File > Save All** to display the **Save Project** dialog (Fig. 1.9). In the **Location** text box, specify the directory where you want to save this project. We choose to save the project in the MyProjects directory on the C: drive. Select the **Create directory for solution** checkbox (to enable Visual Studio to create the directory if it does not already exist), and click **Save**.

Compiling and Running the Application

You are now ready to compile and execute your application. Depending on the type of application, the compiler may compile the code into files with a **.exe** (*executable*) *extension*, a **.dll** (*dynamic link library*) *extension* or one of several other extensions. Such files are called assemblies and are the packaging units for compiled C# code. These assemblies contain the Microsoft Intermediate Language (MSIL) code for the application.

To compile the application, select **Build > Build Solution**. If the application contains no syntax errors, your console application will compile into an executable file (named Welcome1.exe, in the project's directory). To execute this console application (i.e., Welcome1.exe), select **Debug > Start Without Debugging** (or type *<Ctrl> F5*), which invokes the Main method (Fig. 1.1). The statement in line 10 of Main displays Welcome to C# Programming!. Figure 1.10 shows the results of executing this application. Note that the results are displayed in a console window. Leave the application open in Visual C# Express; we will go back to it later in this section.

Fig. 1.9 | **Save Project** dialog.

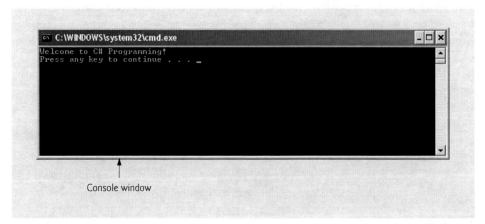

Console window

Fig. 1.10 | Executing the application shown in Fig. 1.1.

Running the Application from the Command Prompt

As we mentioned at the beginning of the chapter, you can execute applications outside the IDE in a **Command Prompt**. This is useful when you simply want to run an application rather than open it for modification. To open the **Command Prompt**, select **Start > All Programs > Accessories > Command Prompt**. [*Note:* Windows 2000 users should replace **All Programs** with **Programs**.] The window (Fig. 1.11) displays copyright information, followed by a prompt that indicates the current directory. By default, the prompt specifies the current user's directory on the local machine (in our case, C:\Documents and Settings\deitel). On your machine, the folder name deitel will be replaced with your username. Enter the command cd (which stands for "change directory"), followed by the /d flag (to change drives if necessary), then the directory where the application's .exe file is located (i.e., the Release directory of your application). For example, the command   cd /d C:\MyProjects\Welcome1\Welcome1\bin\Release   (Fig. 1.12) changes the current directory, to the Welcome1 application's Release directory on the C: drive. The next prompt displays the new directory. After changing to the proper directory, you can run the compiled application by entering the name of the .exe file (i.e., Welcome1). The application will run to completion, then the prompt will display again, awaiting the next command. To close the **Command Prompt**, type exit (Fig. 1.12) and press *Enter*.

Note that Visual C# 2005 Express maintains a Debug and a Release directory in each project's bin directory. The Debug directory contains a version of the application that can be used with the debugger. The Release directory contains an optimized version that you could provide to your clients. In the complete Visual Studio 2005, you can select the specific version you wish to build from the **Solution Configurations** drop-down list in the toolbars at the top of the IDE. The default is the Debug version.

[*Note:* Many environments show **Command Prompt** windows with black backgrounds and white text. We adjusted these settings in our environment to make our screen captures more readable.]

Syntax Errors, Error Messages and the Error List Window

Go back to the application in Visual C# Express. When you type a line of code and press the *Enter* key, the IDE responds either by applying syntax-color highlighting or by generating a *syntax error*, which indicates a violation of Visual C#'s rules for creating correct

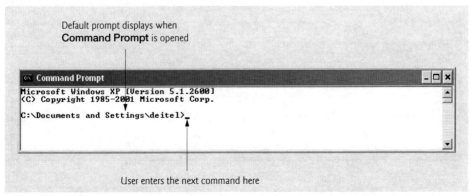

Fig. 1.11 | Executing the application shown in Fig. 1.1 from a **Command Prompt** window.

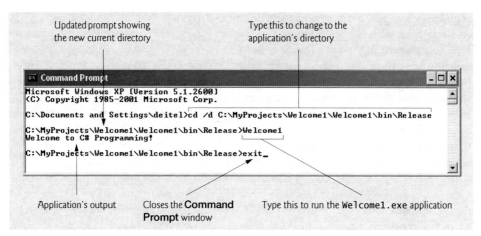

Updated prompt showing the new current directory

Type this to change to the application's directory

Application's output   Closes the **Command Prompt** window   Type this to run the **Welcome1.exe** application

Fig. 1.12 | Executing the application shown in Fig. 1.1 from a **Command Prompt** window.

applications (i.e., one or more statements are not written correctly). Syntax errors occur for various reasons, such as missing parentheses and misspelled keywords.

When a syntax error occurs, the IDE underlines the error in red and provides a description of the error in the ***Error List window*** (Fig. 1.13). If the **Error List** window is

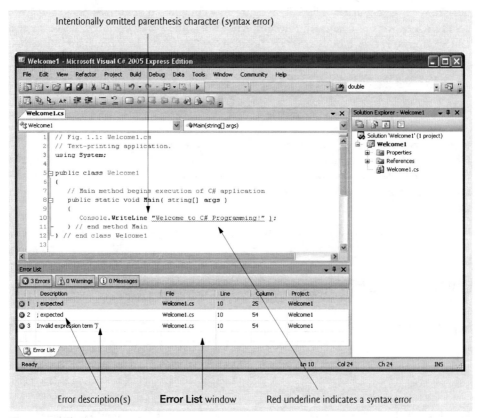

Intentionally omitted parenthesis character (syntax error)

Error description(s)   **Error List** window   Red underline indicates a syntax error

Fig. 1.13 | Syntax errors indicated by the IDE.

not visible in the IDE, select **View > Error List** to display it. In Figure 1.13, we intentionally omitted the first parenthesis in line 10. The first error contains the text "**; expected.**" and specifies that the error is in column 25 of line 10. This error message appears when the compiler thinks that the line contains a complete statement, followed by a semicolon, and the beginning of another statement. The second error contains the same text, but specifies that this error is in column 54 of line 10 because the compiler thinks that this is the end of the second statement. The third error has the text "**Invalid expression term ')'**" because the compiler is confused by the unmatched right parenthesis. Although we are attempting to include only one statement in line 10, the missing left parenthesis causes the compiler to incorrectly assume that there is more than one statement on that line, to misinterpret the right parenthesis and to generate *three* error messages.

 Error-Prevention Tip 1.3

One syntax error can lead to multiple entries in the **Error List** *window. Each error that you address could eliminate several subsequent error messages when you recompile your application. So when you see an error you know how to fix, correct it and recompile—this may make several other errors disappear.*

1.4 Modifying Your Simple C# Application

This section continues our introduction to C# programming with two examples that modify the example of Fig. 1.1 to print text on one line by using several statements and to print text on several lines by using only one statement.

Displaying a Single Line of Text with Multiple Statements

"Welcome to C# Programming!" can be displayed several ways. Class Welcome2, shown in Fig. 1.14, uses two statements to produce the same output as that shown in Fig. 1.1. From this point forward, we highlight the new and key features in each code listing, as shown in lines 10–11 of Fig. 1.14.

```
1   // Fig. 1.14: Welcome2.cs
2   // Printing one line of text with multiple statements.
3   using System;
4
5   public class Welcome2
6   {
7      // Main method begins execution of C# application
8      public static void Main( string[] args )
9      {
10         Console.Write( "Welcome to " );
11         Console.WriteLine( "C# Programming!" );
12      } // end method Main
13   } // end class Welcome2
```

```
Welcome to C# Programming!
```

Fig. 1.14 | Printing one line of text with multiple statements.

The application is almost identical to Fig. 1.1. We discuss only the changes here. Line 2

```
// Printing one line of text with multiple statements.
```

is a comment stating the purpose of this application. Line 5 begins the Welcome2 class declaration.

Lines 10–11 of method Main

```
Console.Write( "Welcome to " );
Console.WriteLine( "C# Programming!" );
```

display one line of text in the console window. The first statement uses Console's method *Write* to display a string. Unlike WriteLine, after displaying its argument, Write does not position the screen cursor at the beginning of the next line in the console window—the next character the application displays will appear immediately after the last character that Write displays. Thus, line 11 positions the first character in its argument (the letter "C") immediately after the last character that line 10 displays (the space character before the string's closing double-quote character). Each Write statement resumes displaying characters from where the last Write statement displayed its last character.

Displaying Multiple Lines of Text with a Single Statement

A single statement can display multiple lines by using newline characters, which indicate to Console methods Write and WriteLine when they should position the screen cursor to the beginning of the next line in the console window. Like space characters and tab characters, newline characters are whitespace characters. The application of Fig. 1.15 outputs four lines of text, using newline characters to indicate when to begin each new line.

Most of the application is identical to the applications of Fig. 1.1 and Fig. 1.14, so we discuss only the changes here. Line 2

```
// Printing multiple lines with a single statement.
```

is a comment stating the purpose of this application. Line 5 begins the Welcome3 class declaration.

```
1   // Fig. 1.15: Welcome3.cs
2   // Printing multiple lines with a single statement.
3   using System;
4
5   public class Welcome3
6   {
7      // Main method begins execution of C# application
8      public static void Main( string[] args )
9      {
10        Console.WriteLine( "Welcome\nto\nC#\nProgramming!" );
11     } // end method Main
12  } // end class Welcome3
```

```
Welcome
to
C#
Programming!
```

Fig. 1.15 | Printing multiple lines with a single statement.

Line 10

```
Console.WriteLine( "Welcome\nto\nC#\nProgramming!" );
```

displays four separate lines of text in the console window. Normally, the characters in a string are displayed exactly as they appear in the double quotes. Note, however, that the two characters \ and n (repeated three times in the statement) do not appear on the screen. The *backslash* (\) is called an *escape character*. It indicates to C# that a "special character" is in the string. When a backslash appears in a string of characters, C# combines the next character with the backslash to form an *escape sequence*. The escape sequence \n represents the *newline character*. When a newline character appears in a string being output with `Console` methods, the newline character causes the screen cursor to move to the beginning of the next line in the console window. Figure 1.16 lists several common escape sequences and describes how they affect the display of characters in the console window.

1.5 Formatting Text with `Console.Write` and `Console.WriteLine`

`Console` methods `Write` and `WriteLine` also have the capability to display formatted data. Figure 1.17 outputs the strings `"Welcome to"` and `"C# Programming!"` with `WriteLine`.

Line 10

```
Console.WriteLine( "{0}\n{1}", "Welcome to", "C# Programming!" );
```

calls method `Console.WriteLine` to display the application's output. The method call specifies three arguments. When a method requires multiple arguments, the arguments are separated with *commas* (,)—this is known as a *comma-separated list*.

Good Programming Practice 1.7

Place a space after each comma (,) in an argument list to make applications more readable.

Escape sequence	Description
\n	Newline. Positions the screen cursor at the beginning of the next line.
\t	Horizontal tab. Moves the screen cursor to the next tab stop.
\r	Carriage return. Positions the screen cursor at the beginning of the current line—does not advance the cursor to the next line. Any characters output after the carriage return overwrite the characters previously output on that line.
\\	Backslash. Used to place a backslash character in a string.
\"	Double quote. Used to place a double-quote character (") in a string. For example, `Console.Write( "\"in quotes\"" );` displays `"in quotes"`

Fig. 1.16 | Some common escape sequences.

```
1   // Fig. 1.17: Welcome4.cs
2   // Printing multiple lines of text with string formatting.
3   using System;
4
5   public class Welcome4
6   {
7      // Main method begins execution of C# application
8      public static void Main( string[] args )
9      {
10         Console.WriteLine( "{0}\n{1}", "Welcome to", "C# Programming!" );
11      } // end method Main
12   } // end class Welcome4
```

```
Welcome to
C# Programming!
```

Fig. 1.17 | Printing multiple lines of text with string formatting.

Remember that all statements end with a semicolon (;). Therefore, line 10 represents only one statement. Large statements can be split over many lines, but there are some restrictions.

Common Programming Error 1.5

Splitting a statement in the middle of an identifier or a string is a syntax error.

Method WriteLine's first argument is a *format string* that may consist of *fixed text* and *format items*. Fixed text is output by WriteLine as we demonstrated in Fig. 1.1. Each format item is a placeholder for a value. Format items also may include optional formatting information.

Format items are enclosed in curly braces and contain a sequence of characters that tell the method which argument to use and how to format it. For example, the format item {0} is a placeholder for the first additional argument (because C# starts counting from 0), {1} is a placeholder for the second, etc. The format string in line 10 specifies that Write-Line should output two arguments and that the first one should be followed by a newline character. So this example substitutes "Welcome to" for the {0} and "C# Programming!" for the {1}. The output shows that two lines of text are displayed. Note that because braces in a formatted string normally indicate a placeholder for text substitution, you must type two left braces ({{) or two right braces (}}) to insert a single left or right brace into a formatted string, respectively. We introduce additional formatting features as they are needed in our examples.

1.6 Another C# Application: Adding Integers

Our next application reads (or inputs) two *integers* (whole numbers, like –22, 7, 0 and 1024) typed by a user at the keyboard, computes the sum of the values and displays the result. This application must keep track of the numbers supplied by the user for the calculation later in the application. Applications remember numbers and other data in the computer's memory and access that data through application elements called *variables*.

The application of Fig. 1.18 demonstrates these concepts. In the sample output, we highlight data the user enters at the keyboard in bold.

Lines 1–2

```
// Fig. 1.18: Addition.cs
// Displaying the sum of two numbers input from the keyboard.
```

state the figure number, file name and purpose of the application.

Line 5

```
public class Addition
```

begins the declaration of class Addition. Remember that the body of each class declaration starts with an opening left brace (line 6), and ends with a closing right brace (line 26).

The application begins execution with method Main (lines 8–25). The left brace (line 9) marks the beginning of Main's body, and the corresponding right brace (line 25) marks the end of Main's body. Note that method Main is indented one level within the body of class Addition and that the code in the body of Main is indented another level for readability.

```
1   // Fig. 1.18: Addition.cs
2   // Displaying the sum of two numbers input from the keyboard.
3   using System;
4
5   public class Addition
6   {
7      // Main method begins execution of C# application
8      public static void Main( string[] args )
9      {
10        int number1; // declare first number to add
11        int number2; // declare second number to add
12        int sum; // declare sum of number1 and number2
13
14        Console.Write( "Enter first integer: " ); // prompt user
15        // read first number from user
16        number1 = Convert.ToInt32( Console.ReadLine() );
17
18        Console.Write( "Enter second integer: " ); // prompt user
19        // read second number from user
20        number2 = Convert.ToInt32( Console.ReadLine() );
21
22        sum = number1 + number2; // add numbers
23
24        Console.WriteLine( "Sum is {0}", sum ); // display sum
25      } // end method Main
26   } // end class Addition
```

```
Enter first integer: 45
Enter second integer: 72
Sum is 117
```

Fig. 1.18 | Displaying the sum of two numbers input from the keyboard.

Line 10

```
int number1; // declare first number to add
```

is a *variable declaration statement* (also called a *declaration*) that specifies the name and type of a variable (number1) that is used in this application. A variable's name enables the application to access the value of the variable in memory—the name can be any valid identifier. (See Section 1.2 for identifier naming requirements.) A variable's type specifies what kind of information is stored at that location in memory. Like other statements, declaration statements end with a semicolon (;).

The declaration in line 10 specifies that the variable named number1 is of type *int*—it will hold *integer* values (whole numbers such as 7, -11, 0 and 31914). The range of values for an int is -2,147,483,648 (int.MinValue) to +2,147,483,647 (int.MaxValue). We will soon discuss types *float*, *double* and *decimal*, for specifying real numbers, and type *char*, for specifying characters. Real numbers contain decimal points, as in 3.4, 0.0 and -11.19. Variables of type float and double store approximations of real numbers in memory. Variables of type decimal store real numbers precisely (to 28–29 significant digits), so decimal variables are often used with monetary calculations. Variables of type char represent individual characters, such as an uppercase letter (e.g., A), a digit (e.g., 7), a special character (e.g., * or %) or an escape sequence (e.g., the newline character, \n). Types such as int, float, double, decimal and char are often called *simple types*. Simple-type names are keywords and must appear in all lowercase letters.

The variable declaration statements at lines 11–12

```
int number2; // declare second number to add
int sum; // declare sum of number1 and number2
```

similarly declare variables number2 and sum to be of type int.

Variable declaration statements can be split over several lines, with the variable names separated by commas (i.e., a comma-separated list of variable names). Several variables of the same type may be declared in one declaration or in multiple declarations. For example, lines 10–12 can also be written as follows:

```
int number1, // declare first number to add
    number2, // declare second number to add
    sum; // declare sum of number1 and number2
```

Good Programming Practice I.8

Declare each variable on a separate line. This format allows a comment to be easily inserted next to each declaration.

Good Programming Practice I.9

Choosing meaningful variable names helps code to be self-documenting (i.e., one can understand the code simply by reading it rather than by reading documentation manuals or viewing an excessive number of comments).

Good Programming Practice 1.10

By convention, variable-name identifiers begin with a lowercase letter, and every word in the name after the first word begins with a capital letter. This naming convention is known as camel casing.

Line 14

```
Console.Write( "Enter first integer: " ); // prompt user
```

uses Console.Write to display the message "Enter first integer: ". This message is called a *prompt* because it directs the user to take a specific action.

Line 16

```
number1 = Convert.ToInt32( Console.ReadLine() );
```

works in two steps. First, it calls the Console's **ReadLine** method. This method waits for the user to type a string of characters at the keyboard and press the *Enter* key to submit the string to the application. Then, the string is used as an argument to the **Convert** class's **ToInt32** method, which converts this sequence of characters into data of an type int. As we mentioned earlier in this chapter, some methods perform a task then return the result of that task. In this case, method ToInt32 returns the int representation of the user's input.

Technically, the user can type anything as the input value. ReadLine will accept it and pass it off to the ToInt32 method. This method assumes that the string contains a valid integer value. In this application, if the user types a noninteger value, a runtime logic error will occur and the application will terminate. Chapter 10, Exception Handling, discusses how to make your applications more robust by enabling them to handle such errors and continue executing. This is also known as making your application *fault tolerant.*

In line 16, the result of the call to method ToInt32 (an int value) is placed in variable number1 by using the *assignment operator*, =. The statement is read as "number1 gets the value returned by Convert.ToInt32." Operator = is called a *binary operator* because it has two *operands*—number1 and the result of the method call Convert.ToInt32. This statement is called an *assignment statement* because it assigns a value to a variable. Everything to the right of the assignment operator, =, is always evaluated before the assignment is performed.

Good Programming Practice 1.11

Place spaces on either side of a binary operator to make it stand out and make the code more readable.

Line 18

```
Console.Write( "Enter second integer: " ); // prompt user
```

prompts the user to enter the second integer. Line 20

```
number2 = Convert.ToInt32( Console.ReadLine() );
```

reads a second integer and assigns it to the variable number2.

Line 22

```
sum = number1 + number2; // add numbers
```

is an assignment statement that calculates the sum of the variables number1 and number2 and assigns the result to variable sum by using the assignment operator, =. Most calculations are performed in assignment statements. When the application encounters the addition operator, it uses the values stored in the variables number1 and number2 to perform the calculation. In the preceding statement, the addition operator is a binary operator—its two *operands* are number1 and number2. Portions of statements that contain calculations are called *expressions*. In fact, an expression is any portion of a statement that has a value associated with it. For example, the value of the expression number1 + number2 is the sum of the numbers. Similarly, the value of the expression Console.ReadLine() is the string of characters typed by the user.

After the calculation has been performed, line 24

```
Console.WriteLine( "Sum is {0}", sum ); // display sum
```

uses method Console.WriteLine to display the sum. The format item {0} is a placeholder for the first argument after the format string. Other than the {0} format item, the remaining characters in the format string are all fixed text. So method WriteLine displays "Sum is ", followed by the value of sum (in the position of the {0} format item) and a newline.

Calculations can also be performed inside output statements. We could have combined the statements in lines 22 and 24 into the statement

```
Console.WriteLine( "Sum is {0}", ( number1 + number2 ) );
```

The parentheses around the expression number1 + number2 are not required—they are included to emphasize that the value of the expression number1 + number2 is output in the position of the {0} format item.

1.7 Memory Concepts

Variable names such as number1, number2 and sum actually correspond to *locations* in the computer's memory. Every variable has a *name*, a *type*, a *size* and a *value*.

In the addition application of Fig. 1.18, when the statement (line 16)

```
number1 = Convert.ToInt32( Console.ReadLine() );
```

executes, the number typed by the user is placed into a *memory location* to which the name number1 has been assigned by the compiler. Suppose that the user enters 45. The computer places that integer value into location number1, as shown in Fig. 1.19. Whenever a value is placed in a memory location, the value replaces the previous value in that location and the previous value is lost.

When the statement (line 20)

```
number2 = Convert.ToInt32( Console.ReadLine() );
```

executes, suppose that the user enters 72. The computer places that integer value into location number2. The memory now appears as shown in Fig. 1.20.

Fig. 1.19 | Memory location showing the name and value of variable number1.

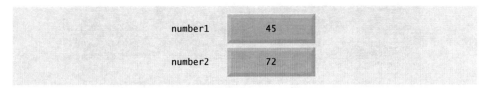

Fig. 1.20 | Memory locations after storing values for number1 and number2.

After the application of Fig. 1.18 obtains values for number1 and number2, it adds the values and places the sum into variable sum. The statement (line 22)

```
sum = number1 + number2; // add numbers
```

performs the addition, then replaces sum's previous value. After sum has been calculated, memory appears as shown in Fig. 1.21. Note that the values of number1 and number2 appear exactly as they did before they were used in the calculation of sum. These values were used, but not destroyed, as the computer performed the calculation—when a value is read from a memory location, the process is nondestructive.

1.8 Arithmetic

Most applications perform arithmetic calculations. The *arithmetic operators* are summarized in Fig. 1.22. Note the use of various special symbols not used in algebra. The *asterisk* (*) indicates multiplication, and the *percent sign* (%) is the *remainder operator* (called modulus in some languages), which we will discuss shortly. The arithmetic operators in Fig. 1.22 are binary operators—for example, the expression f + 7 contains the binary operator + and the two operands f and 7.

Integer division yields an integer quotient—for example, the expression 7 / 4 evaluates to 1, and the expression 17 / 5 evaluates to 3. Any fractional part in integer division is simply discarded (i.e., truncated)—no rounding occurs. C# provides the remainder operator, %, which yields the remainder after division. The expression x % y yields the remainder after x is divided by y. Thus, 7 % 4 yields 3, and 17 % 5 yields 2. This operator is most commonly used with integer operands, but can also be used with floats, doubles, and decimals. In later chapters, we consider several interesting applications of the remainder operator, such as determining whether one number is a multiple of another.

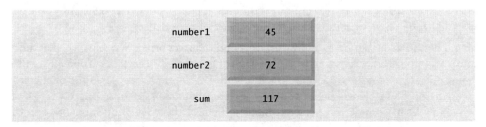

Fig. 1.21 | Memory locations after calculating and storing the sum of number1 and number2.

C# operation	Arithmetic operator	Algebraic expression	C# expression
Addition	+	$f + 7$	f + 7
Subtraction	–	$p - c$	p - c
Multiplication	*	$b \cdot m$	b * m
Division	/	x / y or $\frac{x}{y}$ or $x \div y$	x / y
Remainder	%	$r \bmod s$	r % s

Fig. 1.22 | Arithmetic operators.

Arithmetic expressions must be written in *straight-line form* to facilitate entering applications into the computer. Thus, expressions such as "a divided by b" must be written as a / b, so that all constants, variables and operators appear in a straight line. The following algebraic notation is generally not acceptable to compilers:

$$\frac{a}{b}$$

Parentheses are used to group terms in C# expressions in the same manner as in algebraic expressions. For example, to multiply a times the quantity b + c, we write

    a * (b + c)

If an expression contains *nested parentheses*, such as

    ((a + b) * c)

the expression in the innermost set of parentheses (a + b in this case) is evaluated first.

C# applies the operators in arithmetic expressions in a precise sequence determined by the following *rules of operator precedence*, which are generally the same as those followed in algebra (Fig. 1.23):

1. Multiplication, division and remainder operations are applied first. If an expression contains several such operations, the operators are applied from left to right. Multiplication, division and remainder operators have the same level of precedence.

2. Addition and subtraction operations are applied next. If an expression contains several such operations, the operators are applied from left to right. Addition and subtraction operators have the same level of precedence.

These rules enable C# to apply operators in the correct order. When we say that operators are applied from left to right, we are referring to their *associativity*. You will see that some operators associate from right to left. Figure 1.23 summarizes these rules of operator precedence. The table will be expanded as additional operators are introduced.

Now let us consider several expressions in light of the rules of operator precedence. Each example lists an algebraic expression and its C# equivalent. The following is an example of an arithmetic mean (average) of five terms:

Operator(s)	Operation(s)	Order of evaluation (associativity)
Evaluated first		
*	Multiplication	If there are several operators of this
/	Division	type, they are evaluated from left to
%	Remainder	right.
Evaluated next		
+	Addition	If there are several operators of this
-	Subtraction	type, they are evaluated from left to
		right.

Fig. 1.23 | Precedence of arithmetic operators.

Algebra: $m = \dfrac{a + b + c + d + e}{5}$

C#:   `m = ( a + b + c + d + e ) / 5;`

The parentheses are required because division has higher precedence than addition. The entire quantity (a + b + c + d + e) is to be divided by 5. If the parentheses are erroneously omitted, we obtain a + b + c + d + e / 5, which evaluates as

$$a + b + c + d + \dfrac{e}{5}$$

The following is an example of the equation of a straight line:

Algebra: $y = mx + b$

C#:   `y = m * x + b;`

No parentheses are required. The multiplication operator is applied first because multiplication has a higher precedence than addition. The assignment occurs last because it has a lower precedence than multiplication or addition.

The following example contains remainder (%), multiplication, division, addition and subtraction operations:

Algebra: $z = pr\,\%q + w/x - y$

C#:   `z = p * r % q + w / x - y;`

       ⑥ ① ② ④ ③ ⑤

The circled numbers under the statement indicate the order in which C# applies the operators. The multiplication, remainder and division operations are evaluated first in left-to-right order (i.e., they associate from left to right), because they have higher precedence than addition and subtraction. The addition and subtraction operations are evaluated next. These operations are also applied from left to right.

To develop a better understanding of the rules of operator precedence, consider the evaluation of a second-degree polynomial ($y = ax^2 + bx + c$):

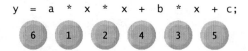

The circled numbers indicate the order in which C# applies the operators. The multiplication operations are evaluated first in left-to-right order (i.e., they associate from left to right), because they have higher precedence than addition. The addition operations are evaluated next and are applied from left to right. There is no arithmetic operator for exponentiation in C#, so x^2 is represented as x * x. Section 4.4 shows an alternative for performing exponentiation in C#.

Suppose that a, b, c and x in the preceding second-degree polynomial are initialized (given values) as follows: a = 2, b = 3, c = 7 and x = 5. Figure 1.24 illustrates the order in which the operators are applied.

As in algebra, it is acceptable to place unnecessary parentheses in an expression to make the expression clearer. These are called **redundant parentheses**. For example, the preceding assignment statement might be parenthesized to highlight its terms as follows:

    y = (a * x * x) + (b * x) + c;

Step 1.   y = 2 * 5 * 5 + 3 * 5 + 7;   (Leftmost multiplication)

           2 * 5 is 10

Step 2.   y = 10 * 5 + 3 * 5 + 7;   (Leftmost multiplication)

           10 * 5 is 50

Step 3.   y = 50 + 3 * 5 + 7;   (Multiplication before addition)

           3 * 5 is 15

Step 4.   y = 50 + 15 + 7;   (Leftmost addition)

           50 + 15 is 65

Step 5.   y = 65 + 7;   (Last addition)

           65 + 7 is 72

Step 6.   y = 72   (Last operation—place 72 in y)

Fig. 1.24 | Order in which a second-degree polynomial is evaluated.

1.9 Decision Making: Equality and Relational Operators

A *condition* is an expression that can be either *true* or *false*. This section introduces a simple version of C#'s *if statement* that allows an application to make a *decision* based on the value of a condition. For example, the condition "grade is greater than or equal to 60" determines whether a student passed a test. If the condition in an if statement is true, the body of the if statement executes. If the condition is false, the body does not execute. We will see an example shortly.

Conditions in if statements can be formed by using the *equality operators* (==, and !=) and *relational operators* (>, <, >= and <=) summarized in Fig. 1.25. The two equality operators (== and !=) each have the same level of precedence, the relational operators (>, <, >= and <=) each have the same level of precedence, and the equality operators have lower precedence than the relational operators. They all associate from left to right.

The application of Fig. 1.26 uses six if statements to compare two integers entered by the user. If the condition in any of these if statements is true, the assignment statement associated with that if statement executes. The application uses the Console class to prompt for and read two lines of text from the user, extracts the integers from that text with the ToInt32 method of class Convert, and stores them in variables number1 and number2. Then the application compares the numbers and displays the results of the comparisons that are true.

The declaration of class Comparison begins at line 6

```
public class Comparison
```

The class's Main method (lines 9–39) begins the execution of the application. Lines 11–12

```
int number1; // declare first number to compare
int number2; // declare second number to compare
```

declare the int variables used to store the values entered by the user.

Standard algebraic equality and relational operators	C# equality or relational operator	Sample C# condition	Meaning of C# condition
Equality operators			
=	==	x == y	x is equal to y
≠	!=	x != y	x is not equal to y
Relational operators			
>	>	x > y	x is greater than y
<	<	x < y	x is less than y
≥	>=	x >= y	x is greater than or equal to y
≤	<=	x <= y	x is less than or equal to y

Fig. 1.25 | Equality and relational operators.

Lines 14–16

```
// prompt user and read first number
Console.Write( "Enter first integer: " );
number1 = Convert.ToInt32( Console.ReadLine() );
```

prompt the user to enter the first integer and input the value. The input value is stored in variable number1.

```
1  // Fig. 1.26: Comparison.cs
2  // Comparing integers using if statements, equality operators,
3  // and relational operators.
4  using System;
5
6  public class Comparison
7  {
8     // Main method begins execution of C# application
9     public static void Main( string[] args )
10    {
11       int number1; // declare first number to compare
12       int number2; // declare second number to compare
13
14       //prompt user and read first number
15       Console.Write( "Enter first integer: " );
16       number1 = Convert.ToInt32( Console.ReadLine() );
17
18       //prompt user and read second number
19       Console.Write( "Enter second integer: " );
20       number2 = Convert.ToInt32( Console.ReadLine() );
21
22       if ( number1 == number2 )
23          Console.WriteLine( "{0} == {1}", number1, number2 );
24
25       if ( number1 != number2 )
26          Console.WriteLine( "{0} != {1}", number1, number2 );
27
28       if ( number1 < number2 )
29          Console.WriteLine( "{0} < {1}", number1, number2 );
30
31       if ( number1 > number2 )
32          Console.WriteLine( "{0} > {1}", number1, number2 );
33
34       if ( number1 <= number2 )
35          Console.WriteLine( "{0} <= {1}", number1, number2 );
36
37       if ( number1 >= number2 )
38          Console.WriteLine( "{0} >= {1}", number1, number2 );
39    } // end method Main
40 } // end class Comparison
```

Fig. 1.26 | Comparing integers using if statements, equality operators and relational operators. (Part 1 of 2.)

```
Enter first integer: 42
Enter second integer: 42
42 == 42
42 <= 42
42 >= 42
```

```
Enter first integer: 1000
Enter second integer: 2000
1000 != 2000
1000 < 2000
1000 <= 2000
```

```
Enter first integer: 2000
Enter second integer: 1000
2000 != 1000
2000 > 1000
2000 >= 1000
```

Fig. 1.26 | Comparing integers using if statements, equality operators and relational operators. (Part 2 of 2.)

Lines 18–20

```
// prompt user and read second number
Console.Write( "Enter second integer: " );
number2 = Convert.ToInt32( Console.ReadLine() );
```

perform the same task, except that the input value is stored in variable number2.
Lines 22–23

```
if ( number1 == number2 )
    Console.WriteLine( "{0} == {1}", number1, number2 );
```

compare the values of the variables number1 and number2 to determine whether they are equal. An if statement always begins with keyword if, followed by a condition in parentheses. An if statement expects one statement in its body. The indentation of the body statement shown here is not required, but it improves the code's readability by emphasizing that the statement in line 23 is part of the if statement that begins in line 22. Line 23 executes only if the numbers stored in variables number1 and number2 are equal (i.e., the condition is true). The if statements in lines 25–26, 28–29, 31–32, 34–35 and 37–38 compare number1 and number2 with the operators !=, <, >, <= and >=, respectively. If the condition in any of the if statements is true, the corresponding body statement executes.

 Common Programming Error 1.6

Forgetting the left and/or right parentheses for the condition in an if statement is a syntax error—the parentheses are required.

Common Programming Error 1.7

Confusing the equality operator, ==, with the assignment operator, =, can cause a logic error or a syntax error. The equality operator should be read as "is equal to," and the assignment operator should be read as "gets" or "gets the value of." To avoid confusion, some people read the equality operator as "double equals" or "equals equals."

Common Programming Error 1.8

It is a syntax error if the operators ==, !=, >= and <= contain spaces between their symbols, as in = =, ! =, > = and < =, respectively.

Common Programming Error 1.9

Reversing the operators !=, >= and <=, as in =!, => and =<, is a syntax error.

Good Programming Practice 1.12

Indent an if statement's body to make it stand out and to enhance application readability.

Note that there is no semicolon (;) at the end of the first line of each if statement. Such a semicolon would result in a logic error at execution time. For example,

```
if ( number1 == number2 ); // logic error
    Console.WriteLine( "{0} == {1}", number1, number2 );
```

would actually be interpreted by C# as

```
if ( number1 == number2 )
    ; // empty statement

Console.WriteLine( "{0} == {1}", number1, number2 );
```

where the semicolon in the line by itself—called the *empty statement*—is the statement to execute if the condition in the if statement is true. When the empty statement executes, no task is performed in the application. The application then continues with the output statement, which always executes, regardless of whether the condition is true or false, because the output statement is not part of the if statement.

Common Programming Error 1.10

Placing a semicolon immediately after the right parenthesis of the condition in an if statement is normally a logic error.

Note the use of whitespace in Fig. 1.26. Recall that whitespace characters, such as tabs, newlines and spaces, are normally ignored by the compiler. So statements may be split over several lines and may be spaced according to your preferences without affecting the meaning of an application. It is incorrect to split identifiers, strings, and multicharacter operators (like >=). Ideally, statements should be kept small, but this is not always possible.

Good Programming Practice 1.13

Place no more than one statement per line in an application. This format enhances readability.

Good Programming Practice 1.14

A lengthy statement can be spread over several lines. If a single statement must be split across lines, choose breaking points that make sense, such as after a comma in a comma-separated list, or after an operator in a lengthy expression. If a statement is split across two or more lines, indent all subsequent lines until the end of the statement.

Figure 1.27 shows the precedence of the operators introduced in this chapter. The operators are shown from top to bottom in decreasing order of precedence. All these operators, with the exception of the assignment operator, =, associate from left to right. Addition is left associative, so an expression like x + y + z is evaluated as if it had been written as (x + y) + z. The assignment operator, =, associates from right to left, so an expression like x = y = 0 is evaluated as if it had been written as x = (y = 0), which, as you will soon see, first assigns the value 0 to variable y and then assigns the result of that assignment, 0, to x.

Good Programming Practice 1.15

Refer to the operator precedence chart when writing expressions containing many operators. Confirm that the operations in the expression are performed in the order you expect. If you are uncertain about the order of evaluation in a complex expression, use parentheses to force the order, as you would do in algebraic expressions. Observe that some operators, such as assignment, =, associate from right to left rather than from left to right.

1.10 (Optional) Software Engineering Case Study: Examining the ATM Requirements Document

Now we begin our optional object-oriented design and implementation case study. The Software Engineering Case Study sections at the ends of this and the next several chapters will ease you into object orientation. We will develop software for a simple automated teller machine (ATM) system, providing you with a concise, carefully paced, complete design and implementation experience. In Chapters 2–7 and 9, we will perform the various steps of an object-oriented design (OOD) process using the UML, while relating these steps to the object-oriented concepts discussed in the chapters. This is not an exercise; rather, it is an end-to-end learning experience that concludes with a detailed walkthrough of the complete C# code that implements our design. It will begin to acquaint you with the kinds of substantial problems encountered in industry and their solutions.

Operators			Associativity	Type
*	/	%	left to right	multiplicative
+	-		left to right	additive
<	<=	> >=	left to right	relational
==	!=		left to right	equality
=			right to left	assignment

Fig. 1.27 | Precedence and associativity of operations discussed.

We begin our design process by presenting a *requirements document* that specifies the overall purpose of the ATM system and *what* it must do. Throughout the case study, we refer to the requirements document to determine precisely what functionality the system must include.

Requirements Document

A small local bank intends to install a new automated teller machine (ATM) to allow users (i.e., bank customers) to perform basic financial transactions (Fig. 1.28). For simplicity, each user can have only one account at the bank. ATM users should be able to view their account balance, withdraw cash (i.e., take money out of an account) and deposit funds (i.e., place money into an account).

The user interface of the automated teller machine contains the following hardware components:

- a screen that displays messages to the user
- a keypad that receives numeric input from the user
- a cash dispenser that dispenses cash to the user
- a deposit slot that receives deposit envelopes from the user

The cash dispenser begins each day loaded with 500 $20 bills. [*Note:* Owing to the limited scope of this case study, certain elements of the ATM described here simplify various aspects of a real ATM. For example, a real ATM typically contains a device that reads a user's account number from an ATM card, whereas this ATM asks the user to type an account number on the keypad (which you will simulate with your personal computer's keypad).

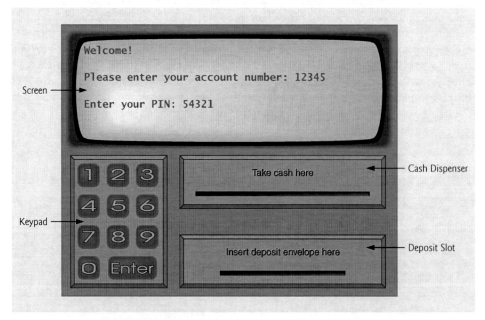

Fig. 1.28 | Automated teller machine user interface.

Also, a real ATM usually prints a paper receipt at the end of a session, but all output from this ATM appears on the screen.]

The bank wants you to develop software to perform the financial transactions initiated by bank customers through the ATM. The bank will integrate the software with the ATM's hardware at a later time. The software should simulate the functionality of the hardware devices (e.g., cash dispenser, deposit slot) in software components, but it need not concern itself with how these devices perform their duties. The ATM hardware has not been developed yet, so instead of writing your software to run on the ATM, you should develop a first version of the software to run on a personal computer. This version should use the computer's monitor to simulate the ATM's screen and the computer's keyboard to simulate the ATM's keypad.

An ATM session consists of authenticating a user (i.e., proving the user's identity) based on an account number and personal identification number (PIN), followed by creating and executing financial transactions. To authenticate a user and perform transactions, the ATM must interact with the bank's account information database. [*Note:* A database is an organized collection of data stored on a computer.] For each bank account, the database stores an account number, a PIN and a balance indicating the amount of money in the account. [*Note:* The bank plans to build only one ATM, so we do not need to worry about multiple ATMs accessing the database at the same time. Furthermore, we assume that the bank does not make any changes to the information in the database while a user is accessing the ATM. Also, any business system like an ATM faces reasonably complicated security issues that go well beyond the scope of a first- or second-semester programming course. We make the simplifying assumption, however, that the bank trusts the ATM to access and manipulate the information in the database without significant security measures.]

Upon approaching the ATM, the user should experience the following sequence of events (see Fig. 1.28):

1. The screen displays a welcome message and prompts the user to enter an account number.

2. The user enters a five-digit account number, using the keypad.

3. For authentication purposes, the screen prompts the user to enter the PIN (personal identification number) associated with the specified account number.

4. The user enters a five-digit PIN, using the keypad.

5. If the user enters a valid account number and the correct PIN for that account, the screen displays the main menu (Fig. 1.29). If the user enters an invalid account number or an incorrect PIN, the screen displays an appropriate message, then the ATM returns to *Step 1* to restart the authentication process.

After the ATM authenticates the user, the main menu (Fig. 1.29) displays a numbered option for each of the three types of transactions: balance inquiry (option 1), withdrawal (option 2) and deposit (option 3). The main menu also displays an option that allows the user to exit the system (option 4). The user then chooses either to perform a transaction (by entering 1, 2 or 3) or to exit the system (by entering 4). If the user enters an invalid option, the screen displays an error message, then redisplays the main menu.

If the user enters 1 to make a balance inquiry, the screen displays the user's account balance. To do so, the ATM must retrieve the balance from the bank's database.

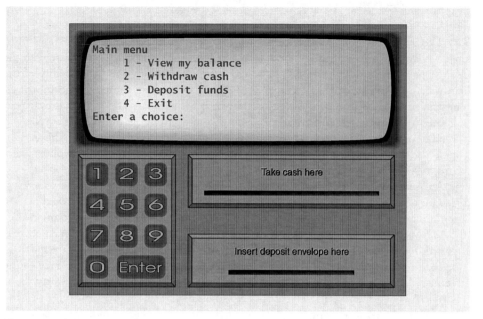

Fig. 1.29 | ATM main menu.

The following actions occur when the user enters 2 to make a withdrawal:

1. The screen displays a menu (shown in Fig. 1.30) containing standard withdrawal amounts: $20 (option 1), $40 (option 2), $60 (option 3), $100 (option 4) and $200 (option 5). The menu also contains option 6 that allows the user to cancel the transaction.

2. The user enters a menu selection (1–6) using the keypad.

3. If the withdrawal amount chosen is greater than the user's account balance, the screen displays a message stating this and telling the user to choose a smaller amount. The ATM then returns to *Step 1*. If the withdrawal amount chosen is less than or equal to the user's account balance (i.e., an acceptable withdrawal amount), the ATM proceeds to *Step 4*. If the user chooses to cancel the transaction (option 6), the ATM displays the main menu (Fig. 1.29) and waits for user input.

4. If the cash dispenser contains enough cash to satisfy the request, the ATM proceeds to *Step 5*. Otherwise, the screen displays a message indicating the problem and telling the user to choose a smaller withdrawal amount. The ATM then returns to *Step 1*.

5. The ATM debits (i.e., subtracts) the withdrawal amount from the user's account balance in the bank's database.

6. The cash dispenser dispenses the desired amount of money to the user.

7. The screen displays a message reminding the user to take the money.

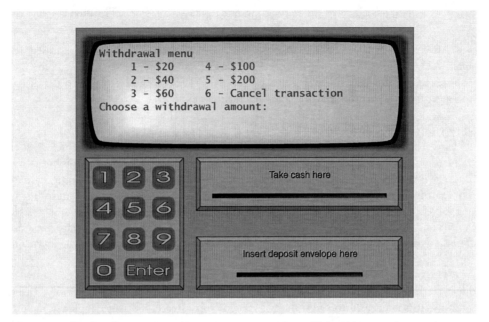

Fig. 1.30 | ATM withdrawal menu.

The following actions occur when the user enters 3 (from the main menu) to make a deposit:

1. The screen prompts the user to enter a deposit amount or to type 0 (zero) to cancel the transaction.

2. The user enters a deposit amount or 0, using the keypad. [*Note:* The keypad does not contain a decimal point or a dollar sign, so the user cannot type a real dollar amount (e.g., $147.25). Instead, the user must enter a deposit amount as a number of cents (e.g., 14725). The ATM then divides this number by 100 to obtain a number representing a dollar amount (e.g., 14725 ÷ 100 = 147.25).]

3. If the user specifies a deposit amount, the ATM proceeds to *Step 4*. If the user chooses to cancel the transaction (by entering 0), the ATM displays the main menu (Fig. 1.29) and waits for user input.

4. The screen displays a message telling the user to insert a deposit envelope into the deposit slot.

5. If the deposit slot receives a deposit envelope within two minutes, the ATM credits (i.e., adds) the deposit amount to the user's account balance in the bank's database. [*Note:* This money is not immediately available for withdrawal. The bank first must verify the amount of cash in the deposit envelope, and any checks in the envelope must clear (i.e., money must be transferred from the check writer's account to the check recipient's account). When either of these events occurs, the bank appropriately updates the user's balance stored in its database. This occurs independently of the ATM system.] If the deposit slot does not receive a deposit envelope within two minutes, the screen displays a message that the

system has canceled the transaction due to inactivity. The ATM then displays the main menu and waits for user input.

After the system successfully executes a transaction, the system should redisplay the main menu (Fig. 1.29) so that the user can perform additional transactions. If the user chooses to exit the system (by entering option 4), the screen should display a thank you message, then display the welcome message for the next user.

Analyzing the ATM System

The preceding statement presented a simplified requirements document. Typically, such a document is the result of a detailed process of *requirements gathering* that might include interviews with potential users of the system and specialists in fields related to the system. For example, a systems analyst who is hired to prepare a requirements document for banking software (e.g., the ATM system described here) might interview people who have used ATMs and financial experts to gain a better understanding of *what* the software must do. The analyst would use the information gained to compile a list of *system requirements* to guide systems designers.

The process of requirements gathering is a key task of the first stage of the software life cycle. The *software life cycle* specifies the stages through which software evolves from the time it is conceived to the time it is retired from use. These stages typically include analysis, design, implementation, testing and debugging, deployment, maintenance and retirement. Several software life cycle models exist, each with its own preferences and specifications for when and how often software engineers should perform the various stages. *Waterfall models* perform each stage once in succession, whereas *iterative models* may repeat one or more stages several times throughout a product's life cycle.

The analysis stage of the software life cycle focuses on precisely defining the problem to be solved. When designing any system, one must certainly *solve the problem right*, but of equal importance, one must *solve the right problem*. Systems analysts collect the requirements that indicate the specific problem to solve. Our requirements document describes our simple ATM system in sufficient detail that you do not need to go through an extensive analysis stage—it has been done for you.

To capture what a proposed system should do, developers often employ a technique known as *use case modeling*. This process identifies the *use cases* of the system, each of which represents a different capability that the system provides to its clients. For example, ATMs typically have several use cases, such as "View Account Balance," "Withdraw Cash," "Deposit Funds," "Transfer Funds Between Accounts" and "Buy Postage Stamps." The simplified ATM system we build in this case study requires only the first three use cases (Fig. 1.31).

Each use case describes a typical scenario in which the user uses the system. You have already read descriptions of the ATM system's use cases in the requirements document; the lists of steps required to perform each type of transaction (i.e., balance inquiry, withdrawal and deposit) actually described the three use cases of our ATM—"View Account Balance," "Withdraw Cash" and "Deposit Funds."

Use Case Diagrams

We now introduce the first of several UML diagrams in our ATM case study. We create a *use case diagram* to model the interactions between a system's clients (in this case study,

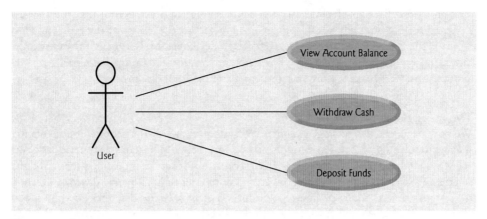

Fig. 1.31 | Use case diagram for the ATM system from the user's perspective.

bank customers) and the system. The goal is to show the kinds of interactions users have with a system without providing the details—these are shown in other UML diagrams (which we present throughout the case study). Use case diagrams are often accompanied by informal text that describes the use cases in more detail—like the text that appears in the requirements document. Use case diagrams are produced during the analysis stage of the software life cycle. In larger systems, use case diagrams are simple but indispensable tools that help system designers focus on satisfying the users' needs.

Figure 1.31 shows the use case diagram for our ATM system. The stick figure represents an ***actor***, which defines the roles that an external entity—such as a person or another system—plays when interacting with the system. For our automated teller machine, the actor is a User who can view an account balance, withdraw cash and deposit funds using the ATM. The User is not an actual person, but instead comprises the roles that a real person—when playing the part of a User—can play while interacting with the ATM. Note that a use case diagram can include multiple actors. For example, the use case diagram for a real bank's ATM system might also include an actor named Administrator who refills the cash dispenser each day.

We identify the actor in our system by examining the requirements document, which states, "ATM users should be able to view their account balance, withdraw cash and deposit funds." The actor in each of the three use cases is simply the User who interacts with the ATM. An external entity—a real person—plays the part of the User to perform financial transactions. Figure 1.31 shows one actor, whose name, User, appears below the actor in the diagram. The UML models each use case as an oval connected to an actor with a solid line.

Software engineers (more precisely, systems designers) must analyze the requirements document or a set of use cases, and design the system before programmers implement it in a particular programming language. During the analysis stage, systems designers focus on understanding the requirements document to produce a high-level specification that describes *what* the system is supposed to do. The output of the design stage—a ***design specification***—should specify *how* the system should be constructed to satisfy these requirements. In the next several Software Engineering Case Study sections, we perform the steps of a simple OOD process on the ATM system to produce a design specification containing a collection of UML diagrams and supporting text. Recall that the UML is designed for use with any OOD process. Many such processes exist, the best known of which is the Rational Unified Process™ (RUP) developed by Rational Software Corporation (now a division of IBM). RUP is a rich process for designing "industrial strength" applications. For this case study, we present a simplified design process.

Designing the ATM System

We now begin the design stage of our ATM system. A *system* is a set of components that interact to solve a problem. For example, to perform the ATM system's designated tasks, our ATM system has a user interface (Fig. 1.28), contains software that executes financial transactions and interacts with a database of bank account information. *System structure* describes the system's objects and their interrelationships. *System behavior* describes how the system changes as its objects interact with one another. Every system has both structure and behavior—designers must specify both. There are several distinct types of system structures and behaviors. For example, the interactions among objects in the system differ from those between the user and the system, yet both constitute a portion of the system behavior.

The UML 2 specifies 13 diagram types for documenting system models. Each diagram type models a distinct characteristic of a system's structure or behavior—six diagram types relate to system structure; the remaining seven relate to system behavior. We list here only the six types of diagrams used in our case study—one of which (the class diagram) models system structure; the remaining five model system behavior.

1. *Use case diagrams*, such as the one in Fig. 1.31, model the interactions between a system and its external entities (actors) in terms of use cases (system capabilities, such as "View Account Balance," "Withdraw Cash" and "Deposit Funds").

2. *Class diagrams*, which you will study in Section 2.11, model the classes, or "building blocks," used in a system. Each noun, or "thing," described in the requirements document is a candidate to be a class in the system (e.g., "account," "keypad"). Class diagrams help us specify the structural relationships between parts of the system. For example, the ATM system class diagram will, among other things, specify that the ATM is physically composed of a screen, a keypad, a cash dispenser and a deposit slot.

3. *State machine diagrams*, which you will study in Section 4.9, model the ways in which an object changes state. An object's *state* is indicated by the values of all the object's attributes at a given time. When an object changes state, it may subsequently behave differently in the system. For example, after validating a user's PIN, the ATM transitions from the "user not authenticated" state to the "user authenticated" state, at which point the ATM allows the user to perform financial transactions (e.g., view account balance, withdraw cash, deposit funds).

4. *Activity diagrams*, which you will also study in Section 4.9, model an object's *activity*—the object's workflow (sequence of events) during program execution. An activity diagram models the actions the object performs and specifies the order in which it performs these actions. For example, an activity diagram shows that the ATM must obtain the balance of the user's account (from the bank's account information database) before the screen can display the balance to the user.

5. *Communication diagrams* (called collaboration diagrams in earlier versions of the UML) model the interactions among objects in a system, with an emphasis on *what* interactions occur. You will learn in Section 6.14 that these diagrams show which objects must interact to perform an ATM transaction. For example, the ATM must communicate with the bank's account information database to retrieve an account balance.

6. *Sequence diagrams* also model the interactions among the objects in a system, but unlike communication diagrams, they emphasize *when* interactions occur. You will learn in Section 6.14 that these diagrams help show the order in which interactions occur in executing a financial transaction. For example, the screen prompts the user to enter a withdrawal amount before cash is dispensed.

In Section 2.11, we continue designing our ATM system by identifying the classes from the requirements document. We accomplish this by extracting key nouns and noun phrases from the requirements document. Using these classes, we develop our first draft of the class diagram that models the structure of our ATM system.

Internet and Web Resources

The following URLs provide information on object-oriented design with the UML.

www-306.ibm.com/software/rational/uml/
Lists frequently asked questions about the UML, provided by IBM Rational.

www.douglass.co.uk/documents/softdocwiz.com.UML.htm
Links to the Unified Modeling Language Dictionary, which defines all terms used in the UML.

www.agilemodeling.com/essays/umlDiagrams.htm
Provides in-depth descriptions and tutorials on each of the 13 UML 2 diagram types.

www-306.ibm.com/software/rational/offerings/design.html
IBM provides information about Rational software available for designing systems, and downloads of 30-day trial versions of several products, such as IBM Rational Rose® XDE (eXtended Development Environment) Developer.

www.embarcadero.com/products/describe/index.html
Provides a 15-day trial license for the Embarcadero Technologies® UML modeling tool Describe.™

www.borland.com/together/index.html
Provides a free 30-day license to download a trial version of Borland® Together® ControlCenter™—a software development tool that supports the UML.

www.ilogix.com/rhapsody/rhapsody.cfm
Provides a free 30-day license to download a trial version of I-Logix Rhapsody®—a UML 2-based model-driven development environment.

argouml.tigris.org
Contains information and downloads for ArgoUML, a free open-source UML tool.

www.objectsbydesign.com/books/booklist.html
Lists books on the UML and object-oriented design.

www.objectsbydesign.com/tools/umltools_byCompany.html
Lists software tools that use the UML, such as IBM Rational Rose, Embarcadero Describe, Sparx Systems Enterprise Architect, I-Logix Rhapsody and Gentleware Poseidon for UML.

`www.ootips.org/ood-principles.html`
Provides answers to the question "What makes a good object-oriented design?"
`www.cetus-links.org/oo_uml.html`
Introduces the UML and provides links to numerous UML resources.

Recommended Readings
The following books provide information on object-oriented design with the UML.

Ambler, S. *The Elements of the UML 2.0 Style*. New York: Cambridge University Press, 2005.

Booch, G. *Object-Oriented Analysis and Design with Applications, Third Edition*. Boston: Addison-Wesley, 2004.

Eriksson, H., et al. *UML 2 Toolkit*. New York: John Wiley, 2003.

Kruchten, P. *The Rational Unified Process: An Introduction*. Boston: Addison-Wesley, 2004.

Larman, C. *Applying UML and Patterns: An Introduction to Object-Oriented Analysis and Design, Second Edition*. Upper Saddle River, NJ: Prentice Hall, 2002.

Roques, P. *UML in Practice: The Art of Modeling Software Systems Demonstrated Through Worked Examples and Solutions*. New York: John Wiley, 2004.

Rosenberg, D., and K. Scott. *Applying Use Case Driven Object Modeling with UML: An Annotated e-Commerce Example*. Reading, MA: Addison-Wesley, 2001.

Rumbaugh, J., I. Jacobson, and G. Booch. *The Complete UML Training Course*. Upper Saddle River, NJ: Prentice Hall, 2000.

Rumbaugh, J., I. Jacobson, and G. Booch. *The Unified Modeling Language Reference Manual*. Reading, MA: Addison-Wesley, 1999.

Rumbaugh, J., I. Jacobson, and G. Booch. *The Unified Software Development Process*. Reading, MA: Addison-Wesley, 1999.

Software Engineering Case Study Self-Review Exercises

1.1   Suppose we enabled a user of our ATM system to transfer money between two bank accounts. Modify the use case diagram of Fig. 1.31 to reflect this change.

1.2   _____ model the interactions among objects in a system with an emphasis on *when* these interactions occur.
   a) Class diagrams
   b) Sequence diagrams
   c) Communication diagrams
   d) Activity diagrams

1.3   Which of the following choices lists stages of a typical software life cycle in sequential order?
   a) design, analysis, implementation, testing
   b) design, analysis, testing, implementation
   c) analysis, design, testing, implementation
   d) analysis, design, implementation, testing

Answers to Software Engineering Case Study Self-Review Exercises

1.1   Figure 1.32 contains a use case diagram for a modified version of our ATM system that also allows users to transfer money between accounts.

1.2   b.

1.3   d.

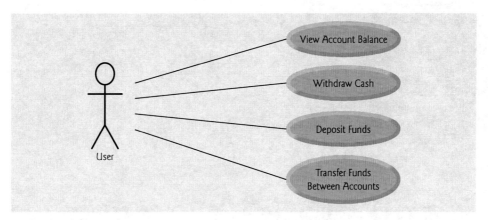

Fig. 1.32 | Use case diagram for a modified version of our ATM system that also allows users to transfer money between accounts.

1.11 Wrap-Up

You learned many important features of C# in this chapter, including displaying data on the screen in a command prompt, inputting data from the keyboard, performing calculations and making decisions. The applications presented here introduced you to basic programming concepts. As you will see in Chapter 2, C# applications typically contain just a few lines of code in method Main—these statements normally create the objects that perform the work of the application. In Chapter 2, you will learn how to implement your own classes and use objects of those classes in applications.

2

Introduction to Classes and Objects

*Nothing can have value
without being an object of
utility.*
—Karl Marx

*Your public servants serve
you right.*
—Adlai E. Stevenson

*Knowing how to answer one
who speaks,
To reply to one who sends a
message.*
—Amenemope

*You will see something new.
Two things. And I call them
Thing One and Thing Two.*
—Dr. Theodor Seuss Geisel

OBJECTIVES

In this chapter you will learn:

■ What classes, objects, methods and instance variables
are.

■ How to declare a class and use it to create an object.

■ How to implement a class's behaviors as methods.

■ How to implement a class's attributes as instance
variables and properties.

■ How to call an object's methods to make the methods
perform their tasks.

■ The differences between instance variables of a class and
local variables of a method.

■ How to use a constructor to ensure that an object's data
is initialized when the object is created.

■ The differences between value types and reference types.

2.1 Introduction

In Chapter 1, you began to use concepts of object-oriented programming to create simple applications that displayed messages to the user, obtained information from the user, performed calculations and made decisions. One common feature of every application in Chapter 1 was that all the statements that performed tasks were located in method `Main`. Typically, the applications you develop in this book will consist of two or more classes, each containing one or more methods. If you become part of a development team in industry, you might work on applications that contain hundreds, or even thousands, of classes. In this chapter, we present a simple framework for organizing object-oriented applications in C#.

First, we explain the concept of classes using a real-world example. Then we present five complete working applications to demonstrate how to create and use your own classes. The first four of these examples begin our case study on developing a grade-book class that instructors can use to maintain student test scores. This case study is enhanced over the next several chapters, culminating with the version presented in Chapter 6, Arrays. The last example in the chapter introduces the type `decimal` and uses it to declare monetary amounts in the context of a bank account class that maintains a customer's balance.

2.2 Classes, Objects, Methods, Properties and Instance Variables

Let's begin with a simple analogy to help you understand classes and their contents. Suppose you want to drive a car and make it go faster by pressing down on its accelerator pedal. What must happen before you can do this? Well, before you can drive a car, someone has to design it. A car typically begins as engineering drawings, similar to the blueprints used to design a house. These engineering drawings include the design for an accelerator pedal to make the car go faster. The pedal "hides" the complex mechanisms that actually make the car go faster, just as the brake pedal "hides" the mechanisms that slow the car and the steering wheel "hides" the mechanisms that turn the car. This enables people with little or no knowledge of how engines work to drive a car easily.

Unfortunately, you cannot drive the engineering drawings of a car. Before you can drive a car, the car must be built from the engineering drawings that describe it. A completed car will have an actual accelerator pedal to make the car go faster, but even that's not enough—the car will not accelerate on its own, so the driver must press the accelerator pedal.

Now let's use our car example to introduce the key programming concepts of this section. Performing a task in an application requires a method. The *method* describes the mechanisms that actually perform its tasks. The method hides from its user the complex tasks that it performs, just as the accelerator pedal of a car hides from the driver the complex mechanisms of making the car go faster. In C#, we begin by creating an application unit called a *class* to house (among other things) a method, just as a car's engineering drawings house (among other things) the design of an accelerator pedal. In a class, you provide one or more methods that are designed to perform the class's tasks. For example, a class that represents a bank account might contain one method to deposit money in an account, another to withdraw money from an account and a third to inquire what the current account balance is.

Just as you cannot drive an engineering drawing of a car, you cannot "drive" a class. Just as someone has to build a car from its engineering drawings before you can actually drive a car, you must build an *object* of a class before you can get an application to perform the tasks the class describes. That is one reason C# is known as an object-oriented programming language.

When you drive a car, pressing its gas pedal sends a message to the car to perform a task—make the car go faster. Similarly, you send *messages* to an object—each message is known as a *method call* and tells a method of the object to perform its task.

Thus far, we have used the car analogy to introduce classes, objects and methods. In addition to the capabilities a car provides, it also has many *attributes*, such as its color, the number of doors, the amount of gas in its tank, its current speed and its total miles driven (i.e., its odometer reading). Like the car's capabilities, these attributes are represented as part of a car's design in its engineering diagrams. As you drive a car, these attributes are always associated with the car. Every car maintains its own attributes. For example, each car knows how much gas is in its own gas tank, but not how much is in the tanks of other cars. Similarly, an object has attributes that are carried with the object as it is used in an application. These attributes are specified as part of the object's class. For example, a bank account object has a balance attribute that represents the amount of money in the account. Each bank account object knows the balance in the account it represents, but not the balances of the other accounts in the bank. Attributes are specified by the class's *instance variables*.

Notice that these attributes are not necessarily accessible directly. The car manufacturer does not want drivers to take apart the car's engine to observe the amount of gas in its tank. Instead, the driver can check the meter on the dashboard. The bank does not want its customers to walk into the vault to count the amount of money in an account. Instead, the customers talk to a bank teller. Similarly, you do not need to have access to an object's instance variables in order to use them. You can use the *properties* of an object. Properties contain *get accessors* for reading the values of variables, and *set accessors* for storing values into them.

The remainder of this chapter presents examples that demonstrate the concepts we introduced here in the context of the car analogy. The first four examples, summarized below, incrementally build a GradeBook class:

1. The first example presents a GradeBook class with one method that simply displays a welcome message when it is called. We show how to *create an object* of that class and call the method so that it displays the welcome message.

2. The second example modifies the first by allowing the method to receive a course name as an "argument" and by displaying the name as part of the welcome message.

3. The third example shows how to store the course name in a GradeBook object. For this version of the class, we also show how to use properties to set the course name and obtain the course name.

4. The fourth example demonstrates how the data in a GradeBook object can be initialized when the object is created—the initialization is performed by the class's constructor.

The last example in the chapter presents an Account class that reinforces the concepts presented in the first four examples and introduces the decimal type—a decimal number can contain a decimal point, as in 0.0345, –7.23 and 100.7, and is used for precise calculations, especially those involving monetary values. For this purpose, we present an Account class that represents a bank account and maintains its decimal balance. The class contains a method to credit a deposit to the account, thus increasing the balance, and a property to retrieve the balance and ensure that all values assigned to the balance are non-negative. The class's constructor initializes the balance of each Account object as the object is created. We create two Account objects and make deposits into each to show that each object maintains its own balance. The example also demonstrates how to input and display decimal numbers.

2.3 Declaring a Class with a Method and Instantiating an Object of a Class

We begin with an example that consists of classes GradeBook (Fig. 2.1) and GradeBook-Test (Fig. 2.2). Class GradeBook (declared in file GradeBook.cs) will be used to display a message on the screen (Fig. 2.2) welcoming the instructor to the grade-book application. Class GradeBookTest (declared in the file GradeBookTest.cs) is a testing class in which the Main method will create and use an object of class GradeBook. By convention, we declare classes GradeBook and GradeBookTest in separate files, such that each file's name matches the name of the class it contains.

To start, select **File > New Project...** to open the **New Project** dialog, then create a GradeBook **Console Application**. Delete all the code provided automatically by the IDE and replace it with the code in Fig. 2.1.

Class GradeBook
The GradeBook *class declaration* (Fig. 2.1) contains a DisplayMessage method (lines 8–11) that displays a message on the screen. Line 10 of the class displays the message. Recall that a class is like a blueprint—we need to make an object of this class and call its method to get line 10 to execute and display its message. (We do this in Fig. 2.2.)

```
 I    // Fig. 2.1: GradeBook.cs
 2    // Class declaration with one method.
 3    using System;
 4
 5    public class GradeBook
 6    {
 7       // display a welcome message to the GradeBook user
 8       public void DisplayMessage()
 9       {
10          Console.WriteLine( "Welcome to the Grade Book!" );
11       } // end method DisplayMessage
12    } // end class GradeBook
```

Fig. 2.1 | Class declaration with one method.

The class declaration begins in line 5. The keyword public is an *access modifier*. For now, we simply declare every class public. Every class declaration contains keyword class followed by the class's name. Every class's body is enclosed in a pair of left and right braces ({ and }), as in lines 6 and 12 of class GradeBook.

In Chapter 1, each class we declared had one method named Main. Class GradeBook also has one method—DisplayMessage (lines 8–11). Recall that Main is a special method that is always called automatically when you execute an application. Most methods do not get called automatically. As you will soon see, you must call method DisplayMessage to tell it to perform its task.

The method declaration begins with keyword public to indicate that the method is "available to the public"—that is, it can be called from outside the class declaration's body by methods of other classes. Keyword void—known as the method's *return type*—indicates that this method will not return (i.e., give back) any information to its *calling method* when it completes its task. When a method that specifies a return type other than void is called and completes its task, the method returns a result to its calling method. For example, when you go to an automated teller machine (ATM) and request your account balance, you expect the ATM to give you back a value that represents your balance. If you have a method Square that returns the square of its argument, you would expect the statement

```
int result = Square( 2 );
```

to return 4 from method Square and assign 4 to variable result. If you have a method Maximum that returns the largest of three integer arguments, you would expect the statement

```
int biggest = Maximum( 27, 114, 51 );
```

to return the value 114 from method Maximum and assign the value to variable biggest. You have already used methods that return information—for example, in Chapter 1 you used Console *method* ReadLine to input a string typed by the user at the keyboard. When ReadLine inputs a value, it returns that value for use in the application.

The name of the method, DisplayMessage, follows the return type (line 8). By convention, method names begin with an uppercase first letter, and all subsequent words in the name begin with a capital letter. The parentheses after the method name indicate that this is a method. An empty set of parentheses, as shown in line 8, indicates that this method does not require additional information to perform its task. Line 8 is commonly referred to as the ***method header***. Every method's body is delimited by left and right braces, as in lines 9 and 11.

The body of a method contains statement(s) that perform the method's task. In this case, the method contains one statement (line 10) that displays the message "Welcome to the Grade Book!", followed by a newline in the console window. After this statement executes, the method has completed its task.

Next, we'd like to use class GradeBook in an application. As you learned in Chapter 1, method Main begins the execution of every application. Class GradeBook cannot begin an application because it does not contain Main. This was not a problem in Chapter 1, because every class you declared had a Main method. To fix this problem for the Grade-Book, we must either declare a separate class that contains a Main method or place a Main method in class GradeBook. To help you prepare for the larger applications you will encounter later in this book and in industry, we use a separate class (GradeBookTest in this example) containing method Main to test each new class we create in this chapter.

Adding a Class to a Visual C# Project

For each example in this chapter, you will add a class to your console application. To do this, right click the project name in the **Solution Explorer** and select **Add > New Item...** from the pop-up menu. In the **Add New Item** dialog that appears, select **Code File** and enter the name of your new file—in this case, GradeBookTest.cs. A new, blank file will be added to your project. Add the code from Fig. 2.2 to this file.

Class GradeBookTest

The GradeBookTest class declaration (Fig. 2.2) contains the Main method that controls our application's execution. Any class that contains a Main method (as shown in line 7) can be used to execute an application. This class declaration begins in line 4 and ends in line 15. The class contains only a Main method, which is typical of many classes that simply begin an application's execution.

```
 1   // Fig. 2.2: GradeBookTest.cs
 2   // Create a GradeBook object and call its DisplayMessage method.
 3
 4   public class GradeBookTest
 5   {
 6      // Main method begins program execution
 7      public static void Main( string[] args )
 8      {
 9         // create a GradeBook object and assign it to myGradeBook
10         GradeBook myGradeBook = new GradeBook();
11
12         // call myGradeBook's DisplayMessage method
13         myGradeBook.DisplayMessage();
14      } // end Main
15   } // end class GradeBookTest
```

```
Welcome to the Grade Book!
```

Fig. 2.2 | Create a GradeBook object and call its DisplayMessage method.

Lines 7–14 declare method Main. A key part of enabling the method Main to begin the application's execution is the static keyword (line 7), which indicates that Main is a static method. A static method is special because it can be called without first creating an object of the class (in this case, GradeBookTest) in which the method is declared. We explain static methods in Chapter 5, Methods: A Deeper Look.

In this application, we'd like to call class GradeBook's DisplayMessage method to display the welcome message in the console window. Typically, you cannot call a method that belongs to another class until you create an object of that class, as shown in line 10. We begin by declaring variable myGradeBook. Note that the variable's type is GradeBook—the class we declared in Fig. 2.1. Each new class you create becomes a new type in C# that can be used to declare variables and create objects. New class types will be accessible to all classes in the same project. You can declare new class types as needed; this is one reason why C# is known as an *extensible language*.

Variable myGradeBook (line 10) is initialized with the result of the *object creation expression* new GradeBook(). The new operator creates a new object of the class specified to the right of the keyword (i.e., GradeBook). The parentheses to the right of the Grade-Book are required. As you will learn in Section 2.9, those parentheses in combination with a class name represent a call to a constructor, which is similar to a method, but is used only at the time an object is created to initialize the object's data. In that section you will see that data can be placed in parentheses to specify initial values for the object's data. For now, we simply leave the parentheses empty.

We can now use myGradeBook to call its method DisplayMessage. Line 13 calls the method DisplayMessage (lines 8–11 of Fig. 2.1) using variable myGradeBook followed by a *dot operator* (.), the method name DisplayMessage and an empty set of parentheses. This call causes the DisplayMessage method to perform its task. This method call differs from the method calls in Chapter 1 that displayed information in a console window— each of those method calls provided arguments that specified the data to display. At the beginning of line 13, "myGradeBook." indicates that Main should use the GradeBook object that was created on line 10. The empty parentheses in line 8 of Fig. 2.1 indicate that method DisplayMessage does not require additional information to perform its task. For this reason, the method call (line 13 of Fig. 2.2) specifies an empty set of parentheses after the method name to indicate that no arguments are being passed to method DisplayMe-ssage. When method DisplayMessage completes its task, method Main continues executing at line 14. This is the end of method Main, so the application terminates.

UML Class Diagram for Class GradeBook
Figure 2.3 presents a *UML class diagram* for class GradeBook of Fig. 2.1. UML is a graphical language used by programmers to represent their object-oriented systems in a standardized

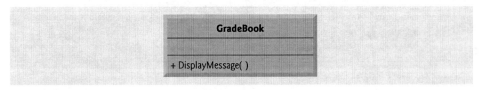

Fig. 2.3 | UML class diagram indicating that class GradeBook has a public DisplayMessage operation.

manner. In the UML, each class is modeled in a class diagram as a rectangle with three compartments. The top compartment contains the name of the class centered horizontally in boldface type. The middle compartment contains the class's attributes, which correspond to instance variables and properties in C#. In Fig. 2.3, the middle compartment is empty because the version of class GradeBook in Fig. 2.1 does not have any attributes. The bottom compartment contains the class's operations, which correspond to methods in C#. The UML models operations by listing the operation name followed by a set of parentheses. Class GradeBook has one method, DisplayMessage, so the bottom compartment of Fig. 2.3 lists one operation with this name. Method DisplayMessage does not require additional information to perform its tasks, so there are empty parentheses following DisplayMessage in the class diagram, just as they appeared in the method's declaration in line 8 of Fig. 2.1. The plus sign (+) in front of the operation name indicates that DisplayMessage is a public operation in the UML (i.e., a public method in C#). The plus sign is sometimes called the *public visibility symbol.* We will often use UML class diagrams to summarize a class's attributes and operations.

2.4 Declaring a Method with a Parameter

In our car analogy from Section 2.2, we discussed the fact that pressing a car's gas pedal sends a message to the car to perform a task—make the car go faster. But how fast should the car accelerate? As you know, the farther down you press the pedal, the faster the car accelerates. So the message to the car actually includes both the task to be performed and additional information that helps the car perform the task. This additional information is known as a *parameter*—the value of the parameter helps the car determine how fast to accelerate. Similarly, a method can require one or more parameters that represent additional information it needs to perform its task. A method call supplies values—called arguments—for each of the method's parameters. For example, the Console.WriteLine method requires an argument that specifies the data to be displayed in a console window. Similarly, to make a deposit into a bank account, a Deposit method specifies a parameter that represents the deposit amount. When the Deposit method is called, an argument value representing the deposit amount is assigned to the method's parameter. The method then makes a deposit of that amount, by increasing the account's balance.

Our next example declares class GradeBook (Fig. 2.4) with a DisplayMessage method that displays the course name as part of the welcome message. (See the sample execution in Fig. 2.5.) The new DisplayMessage method requires a parameter that represents the course name to output.

Before discussing the new features of class GradeBook, let's see how the new class is used from the Main method of class GradeBookTest (Fig. 2.5). Line 12 creates an object of class GradeBook and assigns it to variable myGradeBook. Line 15 prompts the user to enter a course name. Line 16 reads the name from the user and assigns it to the variable nameOfCourse, using Console method ReadLine to perform the input. The user types the course name and presses *Enter* to submit the course name to the application. Note that pressing *Enter* inserts a newline character at the end of the characters typed by the user. Method ReadLine reads characters typed by the user until the newline character is encountered, then returns a string containing the characters up to, but not including, the newline. The newline character is discarded.

```
 1   // Fig. 2.4: GradeBook.cs
 2   // Class declaration with a method that has a parameter.
 3   using System;
 4
 5   public class GradeBook
 6   {
 7      // display a welcome message to the GradeBook user
 8      public void DisplayMessage( string courseName )
 9      {
10         Console.WriteLine( "Welcome to the grade book for\n{0}!",
11            courseName );
12      } // end method DisplayMessage
13   } // end class GradeBook
```

Fig. 2.4 | Class declaration with a method that has a parameter.

```
 1   // Fig. 2.5: GradeBookTest.cs
 2   // Create GradeBook object and pass a string to
 3   // its DisplayMessage method.
 4   using System;
 5
 6   public class GradeBookTest
 7   {
 8      // Main method begins program execution
 9      public static void Main( string[] args )
10      {
11         // create a GradeBook object and assign it to myGradeBook
12         GradeBook myGradeBook = new GradeBook();
13
14         // prompt for and input course name
15         Console.WriteLine( "Please enter the course name:" );
16         string nameOfCourse = Console.ReadLine(); // read a line of text
17         Console.WriteLine(); // output a blank line
18
19         // call myGradeBook's DisplayMessage method
20         // and pass nameOfCourse as an argument
21         myGradeBook.DisplayMessage( nameOfCourse );
22      } // end Main
23   } // end class GradeBookTest
```

```
Please enter the course name:
CS101 Introduction to C# Programming

Welcome to the grade book for
CS101 Introduction to C# Programming!
```

Fig. 2.5 | Create GradeBook object and pass a string to its DisplayMessage method.

Line 21 calls myGradeBook's DisplayMessage method. The variable nameOfCourse in parentheses is the argument that is passed to method DisplayMessage so that the method can perform its task. Variable nameOfCourse's value in Main becomes the value of method DisplayMessage's parameter courseName in line 8 of Fig. 2.4. When you execute this application, notice that method `DisplayMessage` outputs the name you type as part of the welcome message (Fig. 2.5).

Software Engineering Observation 2.1

Normally, objects are created with new. One exception is a string literal that is contained in quotes, such as "hello". String literals are references to string objects that are implicitly created by C#.

More on Arguments and Parameters

When you declare a method, you must specify in the method's declaration whether the method requires data to perform its task. To do so, you place additional information in the method's *parameter list*, which is located in the parentheses that follow the method name. The parameter list may contain any number of parameters, including none at all. Empty parentheses following the method name (as in Fig. 2.1, line 8) indicate that a method does not require any parameters. In Fig. 2.4, `DisplayMessage`'s parameter list (line 8) declares that the method requires one parameter. Each parameter must specify a type and an identifier. In this case, the type `string` and the identifier `courseName` indicate that method `DisplayMessage` requires a `string` to perform its task. At the time the method is called, the argument value in the call is assigned to the corresponding parameter (in this case, `courseName`) in the method header. Then, the method body uses the parameter `courseName` to access the value. Lines 10–11 of Fig. 2.4 display parameter `courseName`'s value, using the `{0}` format item in `WriteLine`'s first argument. Note that the parameter variable's name (Fig. 2.4, line 8) can be the same or different from the argument variable's name (Fig. 2.5, line 21).

A method can specify multiple parameters by separating each parameter from the next with a comma. The number of arguments in a method call must match the number of parameters in the parameter list of the called method's declaration. Also, the types of the arguments in the method call must be consistent with the types of the corresponding parameters in the method's declaration. (As you will learn in subsequent chapters, an argument's type and its corresponding parameter's type are not always required to be identical.) In our example, the method call passes one argument of type `string` (`nameOfCourse` is declared as a `string` in line 16 of Fig. 2.5), and the method declaration specifies one parameter of type `string` (line 8 in Fig. 2.4). So the type of the argument in the method call exactly matches the type of the parameter in the method header.

Common Programming Error 2.1

A compilation error occurs if the number of arguments in a method call does not match the number of parameters in the method declaration.

Common Programming Error 2.2

A compilation error occurs if the types of the arguments in a method call are not consistent with the types of the corresponding parameters in the method declaration.

Updated UML Class Diagram for Class GradeBook

The UML class diagram of Fig. 2.6 models class `GradeBook` of Fig. 2.4. Like Fig. 2.4, this `GradeBook` class contains `public` operation `DisplayMessage`. However, this version of `DisplayMessage` has a parameter. The UML models a parameter a bit differently from C#

by listing the parameter name, followed by a colon and the parameter type in the parentheses following the operation name. The UML has several data types that are similar to the C# types. For example, UML types String and Integer correspond to C# types string and int, respectively. Unfortunately, the UML does not provide types that correspond to every C# type. For this reason, and to avoid confusion between UML types and C# types, we use only C# types in our UML diagrams. Class Gradebook's method DisplayMessage (Fig. 2.4) has a string parameter named courseName, so Fig. 2.6 lists courseName : string between the parentheses following DisplayMessage.

Notes on using Directives

Notice the using directive in Fig. 2.5 (line 4). This indicates to the compiler that the application uses classes in the System namespace, like the Console class. Why do we need a using directive to use class Console, but not class GradeBook? There is a special relationship between classes that are compiled in the same project, like classes GradeBook and GradeBookTest. By default, such classes are considered to be in the same namespace. A using directive is not required when one class in a namespace uses another in the same namespace—such as when class GradeBookTest uses class GradeBook. You will see in Section 7.14 how to declare your own namespaces with the namespace keyword. For simplicity, our examples in this chapter do not declare a namespace. Any classes that are not explicitly placed in a namespace are implicitly placed in the so-called *global namespace*.

Actually, the using directive in line 4 is not required if we always refer to class Console as System.Console, which includes the full namespace and class name. This is known as the class's *fully qualified class name*. For example, line 15 could be written as

```
System.Console.WriteLine( "Please enter the course name:" );
```

Most C# programmers consider using fully qualified names to be cumbersome, and instead prefer to use using directives. The code generated by the Visual C# Form Designer uses fully qualified names.

2.5 Instance Variables and Properties

In Chapter 1, we declared all of an application's variables in the application's Main method. Variables declared in the body of a particular method are known as *local variables* and can be used only in that method. When a method terminates, the values of its local variables are lost. Recall from Section 2.2 that an object has attributes that are carried with the object as it is used in an application. Such attributes exist before a method is called on an object and after the method completes execution.

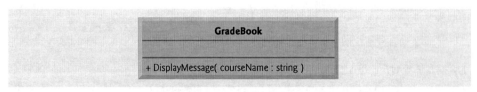

Fig. 2.6 | UML class diagram indicating that class GradeBook has a public DisplayMessage operation with a courseName parameter of type string.

Attributes are represented as variables in a class declaration. Such variables are called *fields* and are declared inside a class declaration but outside the bodies of the class's method declarations. When each object of a class maintains its own copy of an attribute, the field that represents the attribute is also known as an instance variable—each object (instance) of the class has a separate instance of the variable in memory. [*Note:* In Chapter 7, Classes and Objects: A Deeper Look, we discuss another type of field called a static variable, where all objects of the same class share one copy of the variable.]

A class normally consists of one or more properties that manipulate the attributes that belong to a particular object of the class. The example in this section demonstrates a GradeBook class that contains a courseName instance variable to represent a particular GradeBook object's course name, and a CourseName property to manipulate courseName.

GradeBook Class with an Instance Variable and a Property

In our next application (Figs. 2.7–2.8), class GradeBook (Fig. 2.7) maintains the course name as an instance variable so that it can be used or modified at any time during an application's execution. The class also contains one method—DisplayMessage (lines 24–30)—and one property—CourseName (line 11–21). Properties are used to manipulate an object's attributes. For example, in that chapter, we used a Label's Text property to specify the text to display on the Label. In this example, we use a property in code rather than in the **Properties** window of the IDE. To do this, we first declare a property as a member of the GradeBook class. As you will soon see, the GradeBook's CourseName property can be used to store a course name in a GradeBook (in instance variable courseName) or retrieve the GradeBook's course name (from instance variable courseName). Method DisplayMessage—which now specifies no parameters—still displays a welcome message that includes the course name. However, the method now uses the CourseName property to obtain the course name from instance variable courseName.

A typical instructor teaches more than one course, each with its own course name. Line 8 declares courseName as a variable of type string. Line 8 is a declaration for an instance variable because the variable is declared in the body of the class (lines 7–31) but outside the bodies of the class's method (lines 24–30) and property (lines 11–21). Every instance (i.e., object) of class GradeBook contains one copy of each instance variable. For example, if there are two GradeBook objects, each object has its own copy of courseName (one per object). All the methods and properties of class GradeBook can directly manipulate its instance variable courseName, but it is considered good practice for methods of a class to use that class's properties to manipulate instance variables (as we do in line 29 of method DisplayMessage). The software engineering reasons for this will soon become clear.

```
1   // Fig. 2.7: GradeBook.cs
2   // GradeBook class that contains a courseName instance variable,
3   // and a property to get and set its value.
4   using System;
5
6   public class GradeBook
7   {
8      private string courseName; // course name for this GradeBook
```

Fig. 2.7 | GradeBook class that contains a private instance variable, courseName and a public property to get and set its value. (Part 1 of 2.)

```
 9
10    // property to get and set the course name
11    public string CourseName
12    {
13       get
14       {
15          return courseName;
16       } // end get
17       set
18       {
19          courseName = value;
20       } // end set
21    } // end property CourseName
22
23    // display a welcome message to the GradeBook user
24    public void DisplayMessage()
25    {
26       // use property CourseName to get the
27       // name of the course that this GradeBook represents
28       Console.WriteLine( "Welcome to the grade book for\n{0}!",
29          CourseName ); // display property CourseName
30    } // end method DisplayMessage
31 } // end class GradeBook
```

Fig. 2.7 | GradeBook class that contains a private instance variable, courseName and a public property to get and set its value. (Part 2 of 2.)

Access Modifiers public and private

Most instance variable declarations are preceded with the keyword private (as in line 8). Like public, keyword private is an access modifier. Variables or methods declared with access modifier private are accessible only to methods of the class in which they are declared. Thus, variable courseName can be used only in property CourseName and method DisplayMessage of class GradeBook.

Software Engineering Observation 2.2

Precede every field and method declaration with an access modifier. As a rule of thumb, instance variables should be declared private and methods and properties should be declared public. If the access modifier is omitted before a member of a class, the member is implicitly declared private by default. (We will see that it is appropriate to declare certain methods private, if they will be accessed only by other methods of the class.)

Good Programming Practice 2.1

We prefer to list the fields of a class first, so that, as you read the code, you see the names and types of the variables before you see them used in the methods of the class. It is possible to list the class's fields anywhere in the class outside its method declarations, but scattering them can make code difficult to read.

Good Programming Practice 2.2

Placing a blank line between method and property declarations enhances application readability.

Declaring instance variables with access modifier private is known as ***information hiding***. When an application creates (instantiates) an object of class GradeBook, variable courseName is encapsulated (hidden) in the object and can be accessed only by methods and properties of the object's class. In class GradeBook, the property CourseName manipulates the instance variable courseName.

Setting and Getting the Values of private *Instance Variables*

How can we allow a program to manipulate a class's private instance variables but ensure that they remain in a valid state? We need to provide controlled ways for programmers to "get" (i.e., retrieve) the value in an instance variable and "set" (i.e., modify) the value in an instance variable. For these purposes, programmers using languages other than C# normally use methods known as *get* and *set* methods. These methods typically are made public, and provide ways for the client to access or modify private data. Historically, these methods begin with the words "Get" and "Set"—in our class GradeBook, for example, if we were to use such methods they might be called GetCourseName and SetCourseName, respectively.

Although you can define methods like GetCourseName and SetCourseName, C# properties provide a more elegant solution. Next, we show how to declare and use properties.

GradeBook Class with a Property

The GradeBook class's CourseName ***property declaration*** is located in lines 11–21 of Fig. 2.7. The property begins in line 11 with an access modifier (in this case, public), followed by the type that the property represents (string) and the property's name (Course-Name). Property names are normally capitalized.

Properties contain ***accessors*** that handle the details of returning and modifying data. A property declaration can contain a get accessor, a set accessor or both. The get accessor (lines 13–16) enables a client to read the value of private instance variable courseName; the set accessor (lines 17–20) enables a client to modify courseName.

After defining a property, you can use it like a variable in your code. For example, you can assign a value to a property using the = (assignment) operator. This executes the code in the property's set accessor to set the value of the corresponding instance variable. Similarly, referencing the property to use its value (for example, to display it on the screen) executes the code in the property's get accessor to obtain the corresponding instance variable's value. We show how to use properties shortly. By convention, we name each property with the capitalized name of the instance variable that it manipulates (e.g., CourseName is the property that represents instance variable courseName)—C# is case sensitive, so these are distinct identifiers.

get and set Accessors

Let us look more closely at property CourseName's get and set accessors (Fig. 2.7). The get accessor (lines 13–16) begins with the identifier ***get*** and is delimited by braces. The accessor's body contains a ***return statement***, which consists of the keyword ***return*** followed by an expression. The expression's value is returned to the client code that uses the property. In this example, the value of courseName is returned when the property Course-Name is referenced. For example, the following statement

```
string theCourseName = gradeBook.CourseName;
```

where gradeBook is an object of class GradeBook, executes property CourseName's get accessor, which returns the value of instance variable courseName. That value is then stored in variable theCourseName. Note that property CourseName can be used as simply as if it were an instance variable. The property notation allows the client to think of the property as the underlying data. Again, the client cannot directly manipulate instance variable courseName because it is private.

The set accessor (lines 17–20) begins with the identifier *set* and is delimited by braces. When the property CourseName appears in an assignment statement, as in

```
gradeBook.CourseName = "CS100 Introduction to Computers";
```

the text "CS100 Introduction to Computers" is passed to an implicit parameter named value, and the set accessor executes. Notice that value is implicitly declared and initialized in the set accessor—it is a compilation error to declare a local variable value in this body. Line 19 stores this value in instance variable courseName. Note that set accessors do not return any data when they complete their tasks.

The statements inside the property in lines 15 and 19 (Fig. 2.7) each access course-Name even though it was declared outside the property. We can use instance variable courseName in the methods and properties of class GradeBook because courseName is an instance variable of the class. The order in which methods and properties are declared in a class does not determine when they are called at execution time, so you can declare method DisplayMessage (which uses property CourseName) before you declare property CourseName. Within the property itself, the get and set accessors can appear in any order, and either accessor can be omitted. In Chapter 7, we discuss how to omit either a set or get accessor to create so-called "read-only" and "write-only" properties, respectively.

Using Property CourseName in Method DisplayMessage
Method DisplayMessage (lines 24–30 of Fig. 2.7) does not receive any parameters. Lines 28–29 output a welcome message that includes the value of instance variable courseName. We do not reference courseName directly. Instead, we access property CourseName (line 29), which executes the property's get accessor, returning the value of courseName.

GradeBookTest Class That Demonstrates Class GradeBook
Class GradeBookTest (Fig. 2.8) creates a GradeBook object and demonstrates property CourseName. Line 11 creates a GradeBook object and assigns it to local variable myGrade-Book of type GradeBook. Lines 14–15 display the initial course name using the object's CourseName property—this executes the property's get accessor, which returns the value of courseName.

Note that the first line of the output shows an empty name (marked by ' '). Unlike local variables, which are not automatically initialized, every field has a *default initial value*—a value provided by C# when you do not specify the initial value. Thus, fields are not required to be explicitly initialized before they are used in an application—unless they must be initialized to values other than their default values. The default value for an instance variable of type string (like courseName) is null. When you display a string variable that contains the value null, no text is displayed on the screen. We will discuss the significance of null in Section 2.8.

```
1   // Fig. 2.8: GradeBookTest.cs
2   // Create and manipulate a GradeBook object.
3   using System;
4
5   public class GradeBookTest
6   {
7       // Main method begins program execution
8       public static void Main( string[] args )
9       {
10          // create a GradeBook object and assign it to myGradeBook
11          GradeBook myGradeBook = new GradeBook();
12
13          // display initial value of CourseName
14          Console.WriteLine( "Initial course name is: '{0}'\n",
15              myGradeBook.CourseName );
16
17          // prompt for and read course name
18          Console.WriteLine( "Please enter the course name:" );
19          string theName = Console.ReadLine(); // read a line of text
20          myGradeBook.CourseName = theName; // set name using a property
21          Console.WriteLine(); // output a blank line
22
23          // display welcome message after specifying course name
24          myGradeBook.DisplayMessage();
25      } // end Main
26  } // end class GradeBookTest
```

```
Initial course name is: ''

Please enter the course name:
CS101 Introduction to C# Programming

Welcome to the grade book for
CS101 Introduction to C# Programming!
```

Fig. 2.8 | Create and manipulate a GradeBook object.

Line 18 prompts the user to enter a course name. Local string variable theName (declared in line 19) is initialized with the course name entered by the user, which is returned by the call to ReadLine. Line 20 assigns theName to object myGradeBook's CourseName property. When a value is assigned to CourseName, the value specified (in this case, theName) is assigned to implicit parameter value of CourseName's set accessor (lines 17–20, Fig. 2.7). Then parameter value is assigned by the set accessor to instance variable courseName (line 19 of Fig. 2.7). Line 21 (Fig. 2.8) displays a blank line, then line 24 calls myGradeBook's DisplayMessage method to display the welcome message containing the course name.

2.6 UML Class Diagram with a Property

Figure 2.9 contains an updated UML class diagram for the version of class GradeBook in Fig. 2.7. We model properties in the UML as attributes—the property (in this case, CourseName) is listed as a public attribute—as indicated by the plus (+) sign—preceded by the word "property" in *guillemets* (« and »). Using descriptive words in guillemets (called

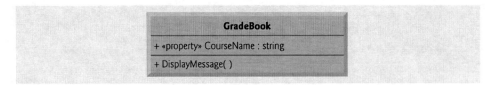

Fig. 2.9 | UML class diagram indicating that class GradeBook has a public CourseName property of type string and one public method.

stereotypes in the UML) helps distinguish properties from other attributes and operations. The UML indicates the type of the property by placing a colon and a type after the property name. The get and set accessors of the property are implied, so they are not listed in the UML diagram. Class GradeBook also contains one public method DisplayMessage, so the class diagram lists this operation in the third compartment. Recall that the plus (+) sign is the public visibility symbol.

In the preceding section, you learned how to declare a property in C# code. You saw that we typically name a property the same as the instance variable it manipulates, but with a capital first letter (e.g., property CourseName manipulates instance variable courseName). A class diagram helps you design a class, so it is not required to show every implementation detail of the class. Since, an instance variable that is manipulated by a property is really an implementation detail of that property, our class diagram does not show the courseName instance variable. A programmer implementing the GradeBook class based on this class diagram would create the instance variable courseName as part of the implementation process (as we did in Fig. 2.7).

In some cases, you may find it necessary to model the private instance variables of a class that are not properties. Like properties, instance variables are attributes of a class and are modeled in the middle compartment of a class diagram. The UML represents instance variables as attributes by listing the attribute name, followed by a colon and the attribute type. To indicate that an attribute is private, a class diagram would list the *private visibility symbol*—a minus sign (–)—before the attribute's name. For example, the instance variable courseName in Fig. 2.7 would be modeled as "- courseName : string" to indicate that it is a private attribute of type string.

2.7 Software Engineering with Properties and set and get Accessors

Using properties as described earlier in this chapter would seem to violate the notion of private data. Although providing a property with get and set accessors may appear to be the same as making its corresponding instance variable public, this is not the case. A public instance variable can be read or written by any property or method in the program. If an instance variable is private, the client code can access the instance variable only indirectly through the class's non-private properties or methods. This allows the class to control the manner in which the data is set or returned. For example, get and set accessors can translate between the format of the data used by the client and the format stored in the private instance variable.

Consider a Clock class that represents the time of day as a private int instance variable time, containing the number of seconds since midnight. Suppose the class provides a

Time property of type string to manipulate this instance variable. Although get accessors typically return data exactly as it is stored in an object, they need not expose the data in this "raw" format. When a client refers to a Clock object's Time property, the property's get accessor could use instance variable time to determine the number of hours, minutes and seconds since midnight, then return the time as a string of the form "HH:MM:SS". Similarly, suppose a Clock object's Time property is assigned a string of the form "HH:MM:SS". The method Convert.ToInt32 is presented in Section 1.6, the Time property's set accessor could convert this string to an int number of seconds since midnight and store the result in the Clock object's private instance variable time. The Time property's set accessor can also provide *data validation* capabilities that scrutinize attempts to modify the instance variable's value to ensure that the value it receives represents a valid time (e.g., "12:30:45" is valid but "42:85:70" is not). We demonstrate data validation in Section 2.10. So, although a property's accessors enable clients to manipulate private data, they carefully control those manipulations, and the object's private data remains safely encapsulated (i.e., hidden) in the object. This is not possible with public instance variables, which can easily be set by clients to invalid values.

Properties of a class should also be used by the class's own methods to manipulate the class's private instance variables, even though the methods can directly access the private instance variables. Accessing an instance variable via a property's accessors—as in the body of method DisplayMessage (Fig. 2.7, lines 28–29)—creates a more robust class that is easier to maintain and less likely to malfunction. If we decide to change the representation of instance variable courseName in some way, the declaration of method DisplayMessage does not require modification—only the bodies of property CourseName's get and set accessors that directly manipulate the instance variable will need to change. For example, suppose we want to represent the course name as two separate instance variables—courseNumber (e.g., "CS101") and courseTitle (e.g., "Introduction to C# Programming"). The DisplayMessage method can still use property CourseName's get accessor to obtain the full course name to display as part of the welcome message. In this case, the get accessor would need to build and return a string containing the courseNumber, followed by the courseTitle. Method DisplayMessage would continue to display the complete course title "CS101 Introduction to C# Programming," because it is unaffected by the change to the class's instance variables.

Software Engineering Observation 2.3

Accessing private data through set and get accessors not only protects the instance variables from receiving invalid values, but also hides the internal representation of the instance variables from that class's clients. Thus, if representation of the data changes (often to reduce the amount of required storage or to improve performance), only the properties' implementations need to change—the clients' implementations need not change as long as the services provided by the properties are preserved.

2.8 Value Types vs. Reference Types

Types in C# are divided into two categories—*value types* and *reference types*. C#'s simple types are all value types. A variable of a value type (such as int) simply contains a value of that type. For example, Fig. 2.10 shows an int variable named count that contains the value 7.

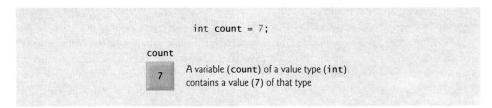

Fig. 2.10 | Value type variable.

By contrast, a variable of a reference type (sometimes called a *reference*) contains the address of a location in memory where the data referred to by that variable is stored. Such a variable is said to *refer to an object* in the program. Line 11 of Fig. 2.8 creates a Grade-Book object, places it in memory and stores the object's memory address in reference variable myGradeBook of type GradeBook as shown in Fig. 2.11. Note that the GradeBook object is shown with its courseName instance variable.

Reference type instance variables (such as myGradeBook in Fig. 2.11) are initialized by default to the value *null*. string is a reference type. For this reason, string variable courseName is shown in Fig. 2.11 with an empty box representing the null-valued variable in memory.

A client of an object must use a reference to the object to *invoke* (i.e., call) the object's methods and access the object's properties. In Fig. 2.8, the statements in Main use variable myGradeBook, which contains the GradeBook object's reference, to send messages to the GradeBook object. These messages are calls to methods (like DisplayMessage) or references to properties (like CourseName) that enable the program to interact with GradeBook objects. For example, the statement (in line 20 of Fig. 2.8)

```
myGradeBook.CourseName = theName; // set name using a property
```

uses the reference myGradeBook to set the course name by assigning a value to property CourseName. This sends a message to the GradeBook object to invoke the CourseName property's set accessor. The message includes as an argument the value "CS101 Introduction to C# Programming" that CourseName's set accessor requires to perform its task. The set accessor uses this information to set the courseName instance variable. In Section 5.14, we discuss value types and reference types in detail.

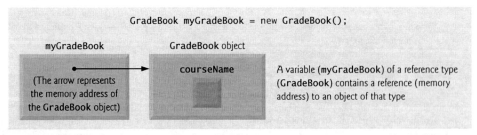

Fig. 2.11 | Reference type variable.

Software Engineering Observation 2.4

A variable's declared type (e.g., int, double or GradeBook) indicates whether the variable is of a value or a reference type. If a variable's type is not one of the thirteen simple types, or an enum or a struct type (which we discuss in Section 5.10), then it is a reference type. For example, Account account1 indicates that account1 is a variable that can refer to an Account object.

2.9 Initializing Objects with Constructors

As mentioned in Section 2.5, when an object of class GradeBook (Fig. 2.7) is created, its instance variable courseName is initialized to null by default. What if you want to provide a course name when you create a GradeBook object? Each class you declare can provide a *constructor* that can be used to initialize an object of a class when the object is created. In fact, C# requires a constructor call for every object that is created. The new operator calls the class's constructor to perform the initialization. The constructor call is indicated by the class name, followed by parentheses. For example, line 11 of Fig. 2.8 first uses new to create a GradeBook object. The empty parentheses after "new GradeBook" indicate a call without arguments to the class's constructor. By default, the compiler provides a *default constructor* with no parameters in any class that does not explicitly include a constructor, so *every* class has a constructor.

When you declare a class, you can provide your own constructor to specify custom initialization for objects of your class. For example, you might want to specify a course name for a GradeBook object when the object is created, as in

```
GradeBook myGradeBook =
    new GradeBook( "CS101 Introduction to C# Programming" );
```

In this case, the argument "CS101 Introduction to C# Programming" is passed to the GradeBook object's constructor and used to initialize the courseName. Each time you create a different GradeBook object, you can provide a different course name. The preceding statement requires that the class provide a constructor with a string parameter. Figure 2.12 contains a modified GradeBook class with such a constructor.

```
1   // Fig. 2.12: GradeBook.cs
2   // GradeBook class with a constructor to initialize the course name.
3   using System;
4
5   public class GradeBook
6   {
7      private string courseName; // course name for this GradeBook
8
9      // constructor initializes courseName with string supplied as argument
10     public GradeBook( string name )
11     {
12        CourseName = name; // initialize courseName using property
13     } // end constructor
14
```

Fig. 2.12 | GradeBook class with a constructor to initialize the course name. (Part 1 of 2.)

```
15      // property to get and set the course name
16      public string CourseName
17      {
18          get
19          {
20              return courseName;
21          } // end get
22          set
23          {
24              courseName = value;
25          } // end set
26      } // end property CourseName
27
28      // display a welcome message to the GradeBook user
29      public void DisplayMessage()
30      {
31          // use property CourseName to get the
32          // name of the course that this GradeBook represents
33          Console.WriteLine( "Welcome to the grade book for\n{0}!",
34              CourseName );
35      } // end method DisplayMessage
36  } // end class GradeBook
```

Fig. 2.12 | GradeBook class with a constructor to initialize the course name. (Part 2 of 2.)

Lines 10–13 declare the constructor for class GradeBook. A constructor must have the same name as its class. Like a method, a constructor specifies in its parameter list the data it requires to perform its task. Unlike a method, a constructor doesn't specify a return type. When you create a new object (with new), you place this data in the parentheses that follow the class name. Line 10 indicates that class GradeBook's constructor has a parameter called name of type string. In line 12 of the constructor's body, the name passed to the constructor is assigned to instance variable courseName via the set accessor of property CourseName.

Figure 2.13 demonstrates initializing GradeBook objects using this constructor. Lines 12–13 create and initialize a GradeBook object. The constructor of class GradeBook is called with the argument "CS101 Introduction to C# Programming" to initialize the course name. The object creation expression to the right of = in lines 12–13 returns a reference to the new object, which is assigned to variable gradeBook1. Lines 14–15 repeat this process for another GradeBook object, this time passing the argument "CS102 Data Structures in C#" to initialize the course name for gradeBook2. Lines 18–21 use each object's CourseName property to obtain the course names and show that they were indeed initialized when the objects were created. In the introduction to Section 2.5, you learned that each instance (i.e., object) of a class contains its own copy of the class's instance variables. The output confirms that each GradeBook maintains its own copy of instance variable courseName.

Like methods, constructors also can take arguments. However, an important difference between constructors and methods is that constructors cannot return values—in fact, they cannot specify a return type (not even void). Normally, constructors are declared public. If a class does not include a constructor, the class's instance variables are initialized to their default values. If you declare any constructors for a class, C# will not create a default constructor for that class.

```
 1   // Fig. 2.13: GradeBookTest.cs
 2   // GradeBook constructor used to specify the course name at the
 3   // time each GradeBook object is created.
 4   using System;
 5
 6   public class GradeBookTest
 7   {
 8      // Main method begins program execution
 9      public static void Main( string[] args )
10      {
11         // create GradeBook object
12         GradeBook gradeBook1 = new GradeBook( // invokes constructor
13            "CS101 Introduction to C# Programming" );
14         GradeBook gradeBook2 = new GradeBook( // invokes constructor
15            "CS102 Data Structures in C#" );
16
17         // display initial value of courseName for each GradeBook
18         Console.WriteLine( "gradeBook1 course name is: {0}",
19            gradeBook1.CourseName );
20         Console.WriteLine( "gradeBook2 course name is: {0}",
21            gradeBook2.CourseName );
22      } // end Main
23   } // end class GradeBookTest
```

```
gradeBook1 course name is: CS101 Introduction to C# Programming
gradeBook2 course name is: CS102 Data Structures in C#
```

Fig. 2.13 | GradeBook constructor used to specify the course name at the time each GradeBook object is created.

Error-Prevention Tip 2.1

Unless default initialization of your class's instance variables is acceptable, provide a constructor to ensure that your class's instance variables are properly initialized with meaningful values when each new object of your class is created.

Adding the Constructor to Class GradeBook's UML Class Diagram

The UML class diagram of Fig. 2.14 models class GradeBook of Fig. 2.12, which has a constructor that has a courseName parameter of type string. Like operations, the UML models constructors in the third compartment of a class in a class diagram. To distinguish a constructor from a class's operations, the UML places the word "constructor" between guillemets (« and ») before the constructor's name. It is customary to list constructors before other operations in the third compartment.

2.10 Floating-Point Numbers and Type decimal

In our next application, we depart temporarily from our GradeBook case study to declare a class called Account that maintains the balance of a bank account. Most account balances are not whole numbers (e.g., 0, −22 and 1024). For this reason, class Account represents the account balance as a real number (i.e., a number with a decimal point, such as 7.33, 0.0975 or 1000.12345). C# provides three simple types for storing real numbers in memory—float,

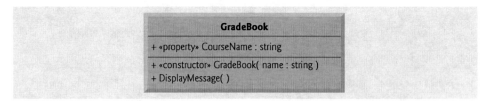

Fig. 2.14 | UML class diagram indicating that class GradeBook has a constructor with a name parameter of type string.

double, and decimal. Types float and double are called *floating-point* types. The primary difference between them and decimal is that decimal variables store a limited range of real numbers precisely, whereas floating-point variables store only approximations of real numbers, but across a much greater range of values. Also, double variables can store numbers with larger magnitude and finer detail (i.e., more digits to the right of the decimal point—also known as the number's *precision*) than float variables. A key application of type decimal is representing monetary amounts.

Real Number Precision and Memory Requirements
Variables of type float represent *single-precision floating-point numbers* and have seven significant digits. Variables of type double represent *double-precision floating-point numbers*. These require twice as much memory as float variables and provide 15–16 significant digits—approximately double the precision of float variables. Furthermore, variables of type decimal require twice as much memory as double variables and provide 28–29 significant digits. For the range of values required by most applications, variables of type float should suffice for approximations, but you can use double or decimal to "play it safe." In some applications, even variables of type double and decimal will be inadequate—such applications are beyond the scope of this book.

Most programmers represent floating-point numbers with type double. In fact, C# treats all real numbers you type in an application's source code (such as 7.33 and 0.0975) as double values by default. Such values in the source code are known as *floating-point literals*. To type a *decimal literal*, you must type the letter "M" or "m" at the end of a real number (for example, 7.33M is a decimal literal rather than a double). Integer literals are implicitly converted into type float, double or decimal when they are assigned to a variable of one of these types.

Although floating-point numbers are not always 100% precise, they have numerous applications. For example, when we speak of a "normal" body temperature of 98.6, we do not need to be precise to a large number of digits. When we read the temperature on a thermometer as 98.6, it may actually be 98.5999473210643. Calling this number simply 98.6 is fine for most applications involving body temperatures. Due to the imprecise nature of floating-point numbers, type decimal is preferred over the floating-point types whenever the calculations need to be exact, as with monetary calculations. In cases where approximation is enough, double is preferred over type float because double variables can represent floating-point numbers more accurately. For this reason, we use type decimal throughout the book for dealing with monetary amounts and type double for other real numbers.

Real numbers also arise as a result of division. In conventional arithmetic, for example, when we divide 10 by 3, the result is 3.3333333..., with the sequence of 3s repeating infinitely. The computer allocates only a fixed amount of space to hold such a value, so clearly the stored floating-point value can be only an approximation.

Common Programming Error 2.3

Using floating-point numbers in a manner that assumes they are represented precisely can lead to logic errors.

Account *Class with an Instance Variable of Type* decimal

Our next application (Figs. 2.15–2.16) contains an oversimplified class named Account (Fig. 2.15) that maintains the balance of a bank account. A typical bank services many accounts, each with its own balance, so line 7 declares an instance variable named balance of type decimal. Variable balance is an instance variable because it is declared in the body of the class (lines 6–36) but outside the class's method and property declarations (lines 10–13, 16–19 and 22–35). Every instance (i.e., object) of class Account contains its own copy of balance.

Class Account contains a constructor, a method, and a property. Since it is common for someone opening an account to place money in the account immediately, the constructor (lines 10–13) receives a parameter initialBalance of type decimal that represents the account's starting balance. Line 12 assigns initialBalance to the property Balance, invoking Balance's set accessor to initialize the instance variable balance.

Method Credit (lines 16–19) does not return any data when it completes its task, so its return type is void. The method receives one parameter named amount—a decimal value that is added to the property Balance. Line 18 uses both the get and set accessors of Balance. The expression Balance + amount invokes property Balance's get accessor to obtain the current value of instance variable balance, then adds amount to it. We then assign the result to instance variable balance by invoking the Balance property's set accessor (thus replacing the prior balance value).

Property Balance (lines 22–35) provides a get accessor, which allows clients of the class (i.e., other classes that use this class) to obtain the value of a particular Account object's balance. The property has type decimal (line 22). Balance also provides an enhanced set accessor.

In Section 2.5, we introduced properties whose set accessors allow clients of a class to modify the value of a private instance variable. In Fig. 2.7, class GradeBook defines property CourseName's set accessor to assign the value received in its parameter value to instance variable courseName (line 19). This CourseName property does not ensure that courseName contains only valid data.

The application of Figs. 2.15–2.16 enhances the set accessor of class Account's property Balance to perform this validation (also known as ***validity checking***). Line 32 (Fig. 2.15) ensures that value is non-negative. If the value is greater than or equal to 0, the amount stored in value is assigned to instance variable balance in line 33. Otherwise, balance is left unchanged.

AccountTest *Class to Use Class* Account

Class AccountTest (Fig. 2.16) creates two Account objects (lines 10–11) and initializes them respectively with 50.00M and -7.53M (the decimal literals representing the real numbers

```
1    // Fig. 2.15: Account.cs
2    // Account class with a constructor to
3    // initialize instance variable balance.
4
5    public class Account
6    {
7       private decimal balance; // instance variable that stores the balance
8
9       // constructor
10      public Account( decimal initialBalance )
11      {
12         Balance = initialBalance; // set balance using property
13      } // end Account constructor
14
15      // credit (add) an amount to the account
16      public void Credit( decimal amount )
17      {
18         Balance = Balance + amount; // add amount to balance
19      } // end method Credit
20
21      // a property to get and set the account balance
22      public decimal Balance
23      {
24         get
25         {
26            return balance;
27         } // end get
28         set
29         {
30            // validate that value is greater than or equal to 0;
31            // if it is not, balance is left unchanged
32            if ( value >= 0 )
33               balance = value;
34         } // end set
35      } // end property Balance
36   } // end class Account
```

Fig. 2.15 | Account class with a constructor to initialize instance variable balance.

50.00 and -7.53). Note that the Account constructor (lines 10–13 of Fig. 2.15) references property Balance to initialize balance. In previous examples, the benefit of referencing the property in the constructor was not evident. Now, however, the constructor takes advantage of the validation provided by the set accessor of the Balance property. The constructor simply assigns a value to Balance rather than duplicating the set accessor's validation code. When line 11 of Fig. 2.16 passes an initial balance of -7.53 to the Account constructor, the constructor passes this value to the set accessor of property Balance, where the actual initialization occurs. This value is less than 0, so the set accessor does not modify balance, leaving this instance variable with its default value of 0.

Lines 14–17 in Fig. 2.16 output the balance in each Account by using the Account's Balance property. When Balance is used for account1 (line 15), the value of account1's balance is returned by the get accessor in line 26 of Fig. 2.15 and displayed by the Console.WriteLine statement (Fig. 2.16, lines 14–15). Similarly, when property Balance is called for account2 from line 17, the value of the account2's balance is returned from line 26 of Fig. 2.15 and displayed by the Console.WriteLine statement (Fig. 2.16, lines 16–17). Note that the balance of account2 is 0 because the constructor ensured that the account could not begin with a negative balance. The value is output by WriteLine with the format item {0:C}, which formats the account balance as a monetary amount. The : after the 0 indicates that the next character represents a *format specifier*, and the C format specifier after the : specifies a monetary amount (C is for currency). The cultural settings on the user's machine determine the format for displaying monetary amounts. For example, in the United States, 50 displays as $50.00. In Germany, 50 displays as 50,00€. Figure 2.17 lists a few other format specifiers in addition to C.

```csharp
1   // Fig. 2.16: AccountTest.cs
2   // Create and manipulate an Account object.
3   using System;
4
5   public class AccountTest
6   {
7      // Main method begins execution of C# application
8      public static void Main( string[] args )
9      {
10        Account account1 = new Account( 50.00M ); // create Account object
11        Account account2 = new Account( -7.53M ); // create Account object
12
13        // display initial balance of each object using a property
14        Console.WriteLine( "account1 balance: {0:C}",
15           account1.Balance ); // display Balance property
16        Console.WriteLine( "account2 balance: {0:C}\n",
17           account2.Balance ); // display Balance property
18
19        decimal depositAmount; // deposit amount read from user
20
21        // prompt and obtain user input
22        Console.Write( "Enter deposit amount for account1: " );
23        depositAmount = Convert.ToDecimal( Console.ReadLine() );
24        Console.WriteLine( "adding {0:C} to account1 balance\n",
25           depositAmount );
26        account1.Credit( depositAmount ); // add to account1 balance
27
28        // display balances
29        Console.WriteLine( "account1 balance: {0:C}",
30           account1.Balance );
31        Console.WriteLine( "account2 balance: {0:C}\n",
32           account2.Balance );
33
34        // prompt and obtain user input
35        Console.Write( "Enter deposit amount for account2: " );
36        depositAmount = Convert.ToDecimal( Console.ReadLine() );
37        Console.WriteLine( "adding {0:C} to account2 balance\n",
38           depositAmount );
39        account2.Credit( depositAmount ); // add to account2 balance
```

Fig. 2.16 | Create and manipulate an Account object. (Part 1 of 2.)

```
40
41          // display balances
42          Console.WriteLine( "account1 balance: {0:C}", account1.Balance );
43          Console.WriteLine( "account2 balance: {0:C}", account2.Balance );
44      } // end Main
45  } // end class AccountTest
```

```
account1 balance: $50.00
account2 balance: $0.00

Enter deposit amount for account1: 49.99
adding $49.99 to account1 balance

account1 balance: $99.99
account2 balance: $0.00

Enter deposit amount for account2: 123.21
adding $123.21 to account2 balance

account1 balance: $99.99
account2 balance: $123.21
```

Fig. 2.16 | Create and manipulate an Account object. (Part 2 of 2.)

Format Specifier	Description
C or c	Formats the string as currency. Precedes the number with an appropriate currency symbol ($ in the US). Separates digits with an appropriate separator character (comma in the US) and sets the number of decimal places to two by default.
D or d	Formats the string as a decimal. Displays number as an integer.
N or n	Formats the string with commas and a default of two decimal places.
E or e	Formats the number using scientific notation with a default of six decimal places.
F or f	Formats the string with a fixed number of decimal places (two by default).
G or g	General. Formats the number normally with decimal places or using scientific notation, depending on context. If a format item does not contain a format specifier, format G is assumed implicitly.
X or x	Formats the string as hexadecimal.

Fig. 2.17 | string format specifiers.

Line 19 declares local variable depositAmount to store each deposit amount entered by the user. Unlike the instance variable balance in class Account, the local variable depositAmount in Main is *not* initialized to 0 by default. However, this variable does not need to be initialized here because its value will be determined by the user's input.

Line 22 prompts the user to enter a deposit amount for account1. Line 23 obtains the input from the user by calling the Console class's ReadLine method, and then passing the string entered by the user to the Convert class's **ToDecimal** method, which returns the decimal value in this string. Lines 24–25 display the deposit amount. Line 26 calls object account1's Credit method and supplies depositAmount as the method's argument. When the method is called, the argument's value is assigned to parameter amount of method Credit (lines 16–19 of Fig. 2.15), then method Credit adds that value to the balance (line 18 of Fig. 2.15). Lines 29–32 (Fig. 2.16) output the balances of both Accounts again to show that only account1's balance changed.

Line 35 prompts the user to enter a deposit amount for account2. Line 36 obtains the input from the user by calling Console class's ReadLine method, and passing the return value to the Convert class's ToDecimal method. Lines 37–38 display the deposit amount. Line 39 calls object account2's Credit method and supplies depositAmount as the method's argument, then method Credit adds that value to the balance. Finally, lines 42–43 output the balances of both Accounts again to show that only account2's balance changed.

set and get Accessors with Different Access Modifiers

By default, the get and set accessors of a property have the same access as the property—for example, for a public property, the accessors are public. It is possible to declare the get and set accessors with different access modifiers. In this case, one of the accessors must implicitly have the same access as the property and the other must be declared with a more restrictive access modifier than the property. For example, in a public property, the get accessor might be public and the set accessor might be private. We demonstrate this feature in Section 7.6.

Error-Prevention Tip 2.2

The benefits of data integrity are not automatic simply because instance variables are made private—you must provide appropriate validity checking and report the errors.

Error-Prevention Tip 2.3

set accessors that set the values of private data should verify that the intended new values are proper; if they are not, the set accessors should leave the instance variables unchanged and generate an error. We demonstrate how to gracefully generate errors in Chapter 10, Exception Handling.

UML Class Diagram for Class Account

The UML class diagram in Fig. 2.18 models class Account of Fig. 2.15. The diagram models the Balance property as a UML attribute of type decimal (because the corresponding C#

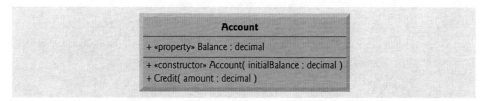

Fig. 2.18 | UML class diagram indicating that class Account has a public Balance property of type decimal, a constructor and a method.

property had type decimal). The diagram models class Account's constructor with a parameter initialBalance of type decimal in the third compartment of the class. The diagram models operation Credit in the third compartment with an amount parameter of type decimal (because the corresponding method has an amount parameter of C# type decimal).

2.11 (Optional) Software Engineering Case Study: Identifying the Classes in the ATM Requirements Document

Now we begin designing the ATM system that we introduced in Chapter 1. In this section, we identify the classes that are needed to build the ATM system by analyzing the nouns and noun phrases that appear in the requirements document. We introduce UML class diagrams to model the relationships between these classes. This is an important first step in defining the structure of our system.

Identifying the Classes in a System

We begin our object-oriented design (OOD) process by identifying the classes required to build the ATM system. We will eventually describe these classes using UML class diagrams and implement these classes in C#. First, we review the requirements document of Section 1.10 and find key nouns and noun phrases to help us identify classes that comprise the ATM system. We may decide that some of these nouns and noun phrases are attributes of other classes in the system. We may also conclude that some of the nouns and noun phrases do not correspond to parts of the system and thus should not be modeled at all. Additional classes may become apparent to us as we proceed through the design process. Figure 2.19 lists the nouns and noun phrases in the requirements document.

We create classes only for the nouns and noun phrases that have significance in the ATM system. We do not need to model "bank" as a class, because the bank is not a part of the ATM system—the bank simply wants us to build the ATM. "User" and "customer" also represent entities outside of the system—they are important because they interact with our ATM system, but we do not need to model them as classes in the ATM system. Recall that we modeled an ATM user (i.e., a bank customer) as the actor in the use case diagram of Fig. 1.31.

Nouns and noun phrases in the requirements document		
bank	money / funds	account number
ATM	screen	PIN
user	keypad	bank database
customer	cash dispenser	balance inquiry
transaction	$20 bill / cash	withdrawal
account	deposit slot	deposit
balance	deposit envelope	

Fig. 2.19 | Nouns and noun phrases in the requirements document.

We do not model "$20 bill" or "deposit envelope" as classes. These are physical objects in the real world, but they are not part of what is being automated. We can adequately represent the presence of bills in the system using an attribute of the class that models the cash dispenser. (We assign attributes to classes in Section 3.12.) For example, the cash dispenser maintains a count of the number of bills it contains. The requirements document does not say anything about what the system should do with deposit envelopes after it receives them. We can assume that simply acknowledging the receipt of an envelope—an *operation* performed by the class that models the deposit slot—is sufficient to represent the presence of an envelope in the system. (We assign operations to classes in Section 5.15.)

In our simplified ATM system, representing various amounts of "money," including the "balance" of an account, as attributes of other classes seems most appropriate. Likewise, the nouns "account number" and "PIN" represent significant pieces of information in the ATM system. They are important attributes of a bank account. They do not, however, exhibit behaviors. Thus, we can most appropriately model them as attributes of an account class.

Though the requirements document frequently describes a "transaction" in a general sense, we do not model the broad notion of a financial transaction at this time. Instead, we model the three types of transactions (i.e., "balance inquiry," "withdrawal" and "deposit") as individual classes. These classes possess specific attributes needed to execute the transactions they represent. For example, a withdrawal needs to know the amount of money the user wants to withdraw. A balance inquiry, however, does not require any additional data. Furthermore, the three transaction classes exhibit unique behaviors. A withdrawal involves dispensing cash to the user, whereas a deposit involves receiving a deposit envelope from the user. [*Note:* In Section 9.9, we "factor out" common features of all transactions into a general "transaction" class using the object-oriented concepts of abstract classes and inheritance.]

We determine the classes for our system based on the remaining nouns and noun phrases from Fig. 2.19. Each of these refers to one or more of the following:

- ATM
- screen
- keypad
- cash dispenser
- deposit slot
- account
- bank database
- balance inquiry
- withdrawal
- deposit

The elements of this list are likely to be classes we will need to implement our system, although it's too early in our design process to claim that this list is complete.

We can now model the classes in our system based on the list we have created. We capitalize class names in the design process—a UML convention—as we will do when we write the actual C# code that implements our design. If the name of a class contains more than one word, we run the words together and capitalize each word (e.g., MultipleWordName). Using these conventions, we create classes ATM, Screen, Keypad, CashDispenser, DepositSlot, Account, BankDatabase, BalanceInquiry, Withdrawal and Deposit. We construct our system using all of these classes as building blocks. Before we begin building the system, however, we must gain a better understanding of how the classes relate to one another.

Modeling Classes

The UML enables us to model, via *class diagrams*, the classes in the ATM system and their interrelationships. Figure 2.20 represents class ATM. In the UML, each class is modeled as a rectangle with three compartments. The top compartment contains the name of the class, centered horizontally and appearing in boldface. The middle compartment contains the class's attributes. (We discuss attributes in Section 3.12 and Section 4.9.) The bottom compartment contains the class's operations (discussed in Section 5.15). In Fig. 2.20, the middle and bottom compartments are empty, because we have not yet determined this class's attributes and operations.

Class diagrams also show the relationships between the classes of the system. Figure 2.21 shows how our classes ATM and Withdrawal relate to one another. For the moment, we choose to model only this subset of the ATM classes for simplicity. We present a more complete class diagram later in this section. Notice that the rectangles representing classes in this diagram are not subdivided into compartments. The UML allows the suppression of class attributes and operations in this manner, when appropriate, to create more readable diagrams. Such a diagram is said to be an *elided diagram*—one in which some information, such as the contents of the second and third compartments, is not modeled. We will place information in these compartments in Section 3.12 and Section 5.15.

In Fig. 2.21, the solid line that connects the two classes represents an *association*—a relationship between classes. The numbers near each end of the line are *multiplicity* values, which indicate how many objects of each class participate in the association. In this case, following the line from one end to the other reveals that, at any given moment, one ATM object participates in an association with either zero or one Withdrawal objects—zero if the current user is not performing a transaction or has requested a different type of transaction, and one if the user has requested a withdrawal. The UML can model many types of multiplicity. Figure 2.22 explains the multiplicity types.

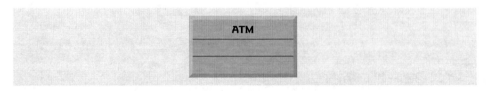

Fig. 2.20 | Representing a class in the UML using a class diagram.

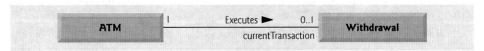

Fig. 2.21 | Class diagram showing an association among classes.

Symbol	Meaning
0	None
1	One
m	An integer value
0..1	Zero or one
m, n	m or n
$m..n$	At least m, but not more than n
*	Any nonnegative integer (zero or more)
0..*	Zero or more (identical to *)
1..*	One or more

Fig. 2.22 | Multiplicity types.

An association can be named. For example, the word Executes above the line connecting classes ATM and Withdrawal in Fig. 2.21 indicates the name of that association. This part of the diagram reads "one object of class ATM executes zero or one objects of class Withdrawal." Note that association names are directional, as indicated by the filled arrowhead—so it would be improper, for example, to read the preceding association from right to left as "zero or one objects of class Withdrawal execute one object of class ATM."

The word currentTransaction at the Withdrawal end of the association line in Fig. 2.21 is a *role name*, which identifies the role the Withdrawal object plays in its relationship with the ATM. A role name adds meaning to an association between classes by identifying the role a class plays in the context of an association. A class can play several roles in the same system. For example, in a college personnel system, a person may play the role of "professor" when relating to students. The same person may take on the role of "colleague" when participating in a relationship with another professor, and "coach" when coaching student athletes. In Fig. 2.21, the role name currentTransaction indicates that the Withdrawal object participating in the Executes association with an object of class ATM represents the transaction currently being processed by the ATM. In other contexts, a Withdrawal object may take on other roles (e.g., the previous transaction). Notice that we do not specify a role name for the ATM end of the Executes association. Role names are often omitted in class diagrams when the meaning of an association is clear without them.

In addition to indicating simple relationships, associations can specify more complex relationships, such as objects of one class being composed of objects of other classes. Consider a real-world automated teller machine. What "pieces" does a manufacturer put together to build a working ATM? Our requirements document tells us that the ATM is composed of a screen, a keypad, a cash dispenser and a deposit slot.

In Fig. 2.23, the *solid diamonds* attached to the association lines of class ATM indicate that class ATM has a *composition* relationship with classes Screen, Keypad, CashDispenser and DepositSlot. Composition implies a whole/part relationship. The class that has the composition symbol (the solid diamond) on its end of the association line is the whole (in this case, ATM), and the classes on the other end of the association lines are the parts—in this case, classes Screen, Keypad, CashDispenser and DepositSlot. The compositions in

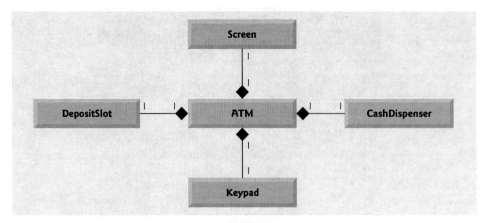

Fig. 2.23 | Class diagram showing composition relationships.

Fig. 2.23 indicate that an object of class ATM is formed from one object of class Screen, one object of class CashDispenser, one object of class Keypad and one object of class DepositSlot—the ATM "has a" screen, a keypad, a cash dispenser and a deposit slot. The *"has-a" relationship* defines composition. (We will see in the Software Engineering Case Study section in Chapter 9 that the "is-a" relationship defines inheritance.)

According to the UML specification, composition relationships have the following properties:

1. Only one class in the relationship can represent the whole (i.e., the diamond can be placed on only one end of the association line). For example, either the screen is part of the ATM or the ATM is part of the screen, but the screen and the ATM cannot both represent the whole in the relationship.

2. The parts in the composition relationship exist only as long as the whole, and the whole is responsible for the creation and destruction of its parts. For example, the act of constructing an ATM includes manufacturing its parts. Furthermore, if the ATM is destroyed, its screen, keypad, cash dispenser and deposit slot are also destroyed.

3. A part may belong to only one whole at a time, although the part may be removed and attached to another whole, which then assumes responsibility for the part.

The solid diamonds in our class diagrams indicate composition relationships that fulfill these three properties. If a "has-a" relationship does not satisfy one or more of these criteria, the UML specifies that hollow diamonds be attached to the ends of association lines to indicate *aggregation*—a weaker form of composition. For example, a personal computer and a computer monitor participate in an aggregation relationship—the computer "has a" monitor, but the two parts can exist independently, and the same monitor can be attached to multiple computers at once, thus violating the second and third properties of composition.

Figure 2.24 shows a class diagram for the ATM system. This diagram models most of the classes that we identified earlier in this section, as well as the associations between them that we can infer from the requirements document. [*Note:* Classes BalanceInquiry and Deposit participate in associations similar to those of class Withdrawal, so we have chosen

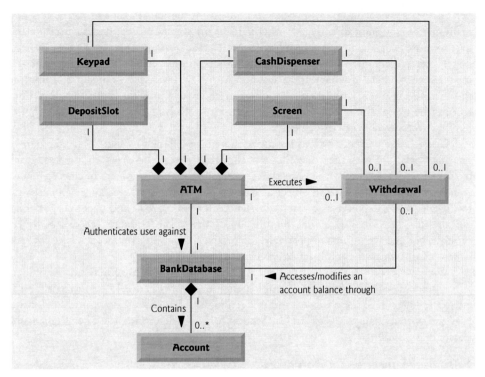

Fig. 2.24 | Class diagram for the ATM system model.

to omit them from this diagram for simplicity. In Chapter 9, we expand our class diagram to include all the classes in the ATM system.]

Figure 2.24 presents a graphical model of the structure of the ATM system. This class diagram includes classes BankDatabase and Account, and several associations that were not present in either Fig. 2.21 or Fig. 2.23. The class diagram shows that class ATM has a *one-to-one relationship* with class BankDatabase—one ATM object authenticates users against one BankDatabase object. In Fig. 2.24, we also model the fact that the bank's database contains information about many accounts—one object of class BankDatabase participates in a composition relationship with zero or more objects of class Account. Recall from Fig. 2.22 that the multiplicity value 0..* at the Account end of the association between class BankDatabase and class Account indicates that zero or more objects of class Account take part in the association. Class BankDatabase has a *one-to-many relationship* with class Account—the BankDatabase can contain many Accounts. Similarly, class Account has a *many-to-one relationship* with class BankDatabase—there can be many Accounts in the BankDatabase. Recall from Fig. 2.22 that the multiplicity value * is identical to 0..*.]

Figure 2.24 also indicates that if the user is performing a withdrawal, "one object of class Withdrawal accesses/modifies an account balance through one object of class Bank-Database." We could have created an association directly between class Withdrawal and class Account. The requirements document, however, states that the "ATM must interact with the bank's account information database" to perform transactions. A bank account contains sensitive information, and systems engineers must always consider the security of personal data when designing a system. Thus, only the BankDatabase can access and manipulate an account directly. All other parts of the system must interact with the database to retrieve or update account information (e.g., an account balance).

The class diagram in Fig. 2.24 also models associations between class Withdrawal and classes Screen, CashDispenser and Keypad. A withdrawal transaction includes prompting the user to choose a withdrawal amount and receiving numeric input. These actions require the use of the screen and the keypad, respectively. Dispensing cash to the user requires access to the cash dispenser.

Classes BalanceInquiry and Deposit, though not shown in Fig. 2.24, take part in several associations with the other classes of the ATM system. Like class Withdrawal, each of these classes associates with classes ATM and BankDatabase. An object of class Balance-Inquiry also associates with an object of class Screen to display the balance of an account to the user. Class Deposit associates with classes Screen, Keypad and DepositSlot. Like withdrawals, deposit transactions require use of the screen and the keypad to display prompts and receive inputs, respectively. To receive a deposit envelope, an object of class Deposit associates with an object of class DepositSlot.

We have identified the classes in our ATM system, although we may discover others as we proceed with the design and implementation. In Section 3.12, we determine the attributes for each of these classes, and in Section 4.9, we use these attributes to examine how the system changes over time. In Section 5.15, we determine the operations of the classes in our system.

Software Engineering Case Study Self-Review Exercises

2.1   Suppose we have a class Car that represents a car. Think of some of the different pieces that a manufacturer would put together to produce a whole car. Create a class diagram (similar to Fig. 2.23) that models some of the composition relationships of class Car.

2.2   Suppose we have a class File that represents an electronic document in a stand-alone, non-networked computer represented by class Computer. What sort of association exists between class Computer and class File?

  a) Class Computer has a one-to-one relationship with class File.
  b) Class Computer has a many-to-one relationship with class File.
  c) Class Computer has a one-to-many relationship with class File.
  d) Class Computer has a many-to-many relationship with class File.

2.3   State whether the following statement is *true* or *false*. If *false*, explain why: A UML class diagram in which a class's second and third compartments are not modeled is said to be an elided diagram.

2.4   Modify the class diagram of Fig. 2.24 to include class Deposit instead of class Withdrawal.

Answers to Software Engineering Case Study Self-Review Exercises

2.1   Figure 2.25 presents a class diagram that shows some of the composition relationships of a class Car.

2.2   c. In a computer network, this relationship could be many-to-many.

2.3   True.

2.4   Figure 2.26 presents a class diagram for the ATM including class Deposit instead of class Withdrawal (as in Fig. 2.24). Note that class Deposit does not associate with class CashDispenser, but does associate with class DepositSlot.

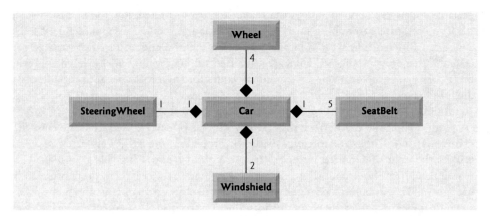

Fig. 2.25 | Class diagram showing some composition relationships of a class Car.

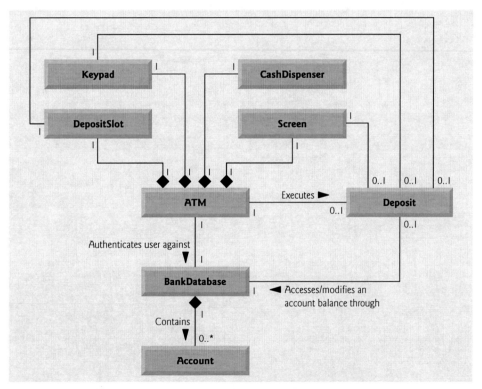

Fig. 2.26 | Class diagram for the ATM system model including class Deposit.

2.12 Wrap-Up

In this chapter, you learned the basic object-oriented concepts of classes, objects, methods, instance variables and properties—these will be used in most substantial C# applications you create. You learned how to declare instance variables of a class to maintain data for each object of the class, how to declare methods that operate on that data, and how to declare properties to obtain and set that data. We demonstrated how to call a method to tell it to perform its task and how to pass information to methods as arguments. We discussed the difference between a local variable of a method and an instance variable of a class and that only instance variables are initialized automatically. You also learned how to use a class's constructor to specify the initial values for an object's instance variables. We discussed some of the differences between value types and reference types. You learned about the value types float, double and decimal for storing real numbers.

Throughout the chapter, we showed how the UML can be used to create class diagrams that model the constructors, methods, properties and attributes of classes. You learned the value of declaring instance variables private, and using public properties to manipulate them. For example, we demonstrated how set accessors in properties can be used to validate an object's data and ensure that the object is maintained in a consistent state. In the next chapter we begin our introduction to control statements, which specify the order in which an application's actions are performed. You will use these in your methods to specify how they should perform their tasks.

3

Control Statements: Part I

Let's all move one place on.
—Lewis Carroll

The wheel is come full circle.
—William Shakespeare

How many apples fell on Newton's head before he took the hint!
—Robert Frost

All the evolution we know of proceeds from the vague to the definite.
—Charles Sanders Peirce

OBJECTIVES

In this chapter you will learn:

■ To use the `if` and `if...else` selection statements to choose between alternative actions.

■ To use the `while` repetition statement to execute statements in an application repeatedly.

■ To use counter-controlled repetition and sentinel-controlled repetition.

■ To use the increment, decrement and compound assignment operators.

3.1 Introduction

In this chapter, we introduce C#'s if, if...else and while control statements. We devote a portion of the chapter (and Chapters 4 and 6) to further developing the GradeBook class introduced in Chapter 2. In particular, we add a method to the GradeBook class that uses control statements to calculate the average of a set of student grades. Another example demonstrates additional ways to combine control statements to solve a similar problem. We introduce C#'s compound assignment operators and explore its increment and decrement operators. Finally, we present an overview of C#'s simple types.

3.2 Control Structures

Normally, statements in an application are executed one after the other in the order in which they are written. This process is called *sequential execution*. Various C# statements, which we will soon discuss, enable you to specify that the next statement to execute is not necessarily the next one in sequence. This is called *transfer of control*.

During the 1960s, it became clear that the indiscriminate use of transfers of control was the root of much difficulty experienced by software development groups. The blame was pointed at the *goto statement* (used in most programming languages of the time), which allows programmers to specify a transfer of control to one of a very wide range of possible destinations in an application (creating what is often called "spaghetti code"). The notion of so-called *structured programming* became almost synonymous with "goto elimination." We recommend that you avoid C#'s goto statement.

The research of Bohm and Jacopini[1] had demonstrated that applications could be written without goto statements. The challenge of the era for programmers was to shift their styles to "goto-less programming." Not until the 1970s did programmers start taking

---

1. Bohm, C., and G. Jacopini, "Flow Diagrams, Turing Machines, and Languages with Only Two Formation Rules," *Communications of the ACM*, Vol. 9, No. 5, May 1966, pp. 336–371.

structured programming seriously. The results were impressive. Software development groups reported shorter development times, more frequent on-time delivery of systems and more frequent within-budget completion of software projects. The key to these successes was that structured applications were clearer, easier to debug and modify, and more likely to be bug free in the first place.

Bohm and Jacopini's work demonstrated that all applications could be written in terms of only three control structures—the *sequence structure*, the *selection structure* and the *repetition structure*. The term "control structures" comes from the field of computer science. When we introduce C#'s implementations of control structures, we will refer to them in the terminology of the *C# Language Specification* as "control statements."

Sequence Structure in C#

The sequence structure is built into C#. Unless directed otherwise, the computer executes C# statements one after the other in the order in which they are written—that is, in sequence. The UML *activity diagram* in Fig. 3.1 illustrates a typical sequence structure in which two calculations are performed in order. C# lets you have as many actions as you want in a sequence structure. As you will soon see, anywhere a single action may be placed, you may place several actions in sequence.

An activity diagram models the *workflow* (also called the *activity*) of a portion of a software system. Such workflows may include a portion of an algorithm, such as the sequence structure in Fig. 3.1. Activity diagrams are composed of special-purpose symbols, such as *action-state symbols* (rectangles with their left and right sides replaced with arcs curving outward), *diamonds* and *small circles*. These symbols are connected by *transition arrows*, which represent the flow of the activity—that is, the order in which the actions should occur.

Activity diagrams help you develop and represent algorithms. Activity diagrams clearly show how control structures operate. Consider the activity diagram for the sequence structure in Fig. 3.1. It contains two *action states* that represent actions to perform. Each action state contains an *action expression*—for example, "add grade to total" or "add 1 to counter"—that specifies a particular action to perform. Other actions might include calculations or input/output operations. The arrows in the activity diagram represent *transitions*, which indicate the order in which the actions represented by the action states occur. The portion of the application that implements the activities illustrated by the diagram in Fig. 3.1 first adds grade to total, then adds 1 to counter.

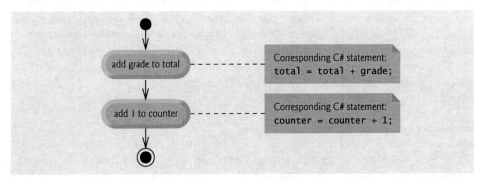

Fig. 3.1 | Sequence structure activity diagram.

The *solid circle* located at the top of the activity diagram represents the activity's *initial state*—the beginning of the workflow before the application performs the modeled actions. The *solid circle surrounded by a hollow circle* that appears at the bottom of the diagram represents the *final state*—the end of the workflow after the application performs its actions.

Figure 3.1 also includes rectangles with the upper-right corners folded over. These are UML *notes* (like comments in C#)—explanatory remarks that describe the purpose of symbols in the diagram. Figure 3.1 uses UML notes to show the C# code associated with each action state in the activity diagram. A *dotted line* connects each note with the element that the note describes. Activity diagrams normally do not show the C# code that implements the activity. We use notes for this purpose here to illustrate how the diagram relates to C# code. For more information on the UML, see our optional case study, which appears in the Software Engineering Case Study sections at the ends of Chapters 1–7 and 9, and visit www.uml.org.

Selection Structures in C#

C# has three types of selection structures, which from this point forward, we shall refer to as *selection statements*. These are discussed in this chapter and Chapter 4. The **if** *statement* either performs (selects) an action if a condition is true or skips the action if the condition is false. The **if...else** statement performs an action if a condition is true or performs a different action if the condition is false. The switch statement (Chapter 4) performs one of many different actions, depending on the value of an expression.

The if statement is called a *single-selection statement* because it selects or ignores a single action (or, as we will soon see, a single group of actions). The if...else statement is called a *double-selection statement* because it selects between two different actions (or groups of actions). The switch statement is called a *multiple-selection statement* because it selects among many different actions (or groups of actions).

Repetition Structures in C#

C# provides four repetition structures, which from this point forward, we shall refer to as *repetition statements* (also called *iteration statements* or *loops*). Repetition statements enable applications to perform statements repeatedly, depending on the value of a *loop-continuation condition*. The repetition statements are the while, do...while, for and foreach statements. (Chapter 4 presents the do...while and for statements. Chapter 6 discusses the foreach statement.) The while, for and foreach statements perform the action (or group of actions) in their bodies zero or more times—if the loop-continuation condition is initially false, the action (or group of actions) will not execute. The do...while statement performs the action (or group of actions) in its body one or more times.

The words if, else, switch, while, do, for and foreach are C# keywords. Keywords cannot be used as identifiers, such as variable names. A complete list of C# keywords appears in Fig. 1.2.

Summary of Control Statements in C#

C# has only three kinds of structured control statements: the sequence statement, selection statement (three types) and repetition statement (four types). Every application is formed by combining as many sequence, selection and repetition statements as is appropriate for the algorithm the application implements. As with the sequence statement in Fig. 3.1, we can model each control statement as an activity diagram. Each diagram contains an initial state and a final state that represent a control statement's entry point and exit point, respectively. *Single-entry/single-exit control statements* make it easy to build applications—the control statements are "attached" to one another by connecting the exit point of one to the entry point of the next. This procedure is similar to the way in which a child stacks building blocks, so we call it *control-statement stacking*. You will learn that there is only one other way in which control statements may be connected: *control-statement nesting*, in which a control statement appears inside another control statement. Thus, algorithms in C# applications are constructed from only three kinds of structured control statements, combined in only two ways. This is the essence of simplicity.

3.3 if Single-Selection Statement

Applications use selection statements to choose among alternative courses of action. For example, suppose that the passing grade on an exam is 60. The statement

```
if ( grade >= 60 )
    Console.WriteLine( "Passed" );
```

determines whether the condition grade >= 60 is true or false. If the condition is true, "Passed" is printed, and the next statement in order is performed. If the condition is false, no printing occurs and the next statement in order is performed.

Figure 3.2 illustrates the single-selection if statement. This activity diagram contains what is perhaps the most important symbol in an activity diagram—the diamond, or *decision symbol*, which indicates that a decision is to be made. The workflow will continue along a path determined by the symbol's associated *guard conditions*, which can be true or false. Each transition arrow emerging from a decision symbol has a guard condition (specified in square brackets next to the transition arrow). If a guard condition is true, the workflow enters the action state to which the transition arrow points. In Fig. 3.2, if the grade is greater than or equal to 60, the application prints "Passed" then transitions to the final state of this activity. If the grade is less than 60, the application immediately transitions to the final state without displaying a message.

The if statement is a single-entry/single-exit control statement. You will see that the activity diagrams for the remaining control statements also contain initial states, transition arrows, action states that indicate actions to perform and decision symbols (with associated guard conditions) that indicate decisions to be made, and final states.

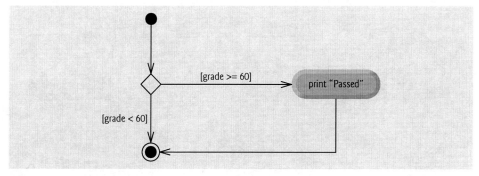

Fig. 3.2 | if single-selection statement UML activity diagram.

3.4 if...else Double-Selection Statement

The if single-selection statement performs an indicated action only when the condition is true; otherwise, the action is skipped. The if...else double-selection statement allows you to specify an action to perform when the condition is true and a different action when the condition is false. For example, the statement

```
if ( grade >= 60 )
    Console.WriteLine( "Passed" );
else
    Console.WriteLine( "Failed" );
```

prints "Passed" if the grade is greater than or equal to 60, but prints "Failed" if it is less than 60. In either case, after printing occurs, the next statement in sequence is performed.

Figure 3.3 illustrates the flow of control in the if...else statement. Once again, the symbols in the UML activity diagram (besides the initial state, transition arrows and final state) represent action states and a decision.

Conditional Operator (?:)

C# provides the *conditional operator* (?:), which can be used in place of an if...else statement. This is C#'s only *ternary operator*—this means that it takes three operands. Together, the operands and the ?: symbols form a *conditional expression.* The first operand (to the left of the ?) is a *boolean* expression (i.e., an expression that evaluates to a bool-type value—*true* or *false*), the second operand (between the ? and :) is the value of the conditional expression if the boolean expression is true and the third operand (to the right of the :) is the value of the conditional expression if the boolean expression is false. For example, the statement

```
Console.WriteLine( grade >= 60 ? "Passed" : "Failed" );
```

prints the value of WriteLine's conditional-expression argument. The conditional expression in this statement evaluates to the string "Passed" if the boolean expression grade >= 60 is true and evaluates to the string "Failed" if the boolean expression is false. Thus, this statement with the conditional operator performs essentially the same function as the if...else statement shown earlier in this section. You will see that conditional expressions can be used in some situations where if...else statements cannot.

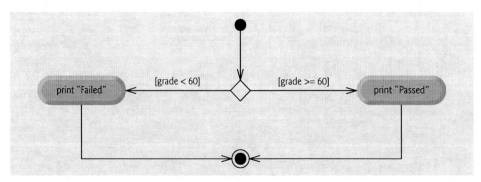

Fig. 3.3 | if...else double-selection statement UML activity diagram.

Good Programming Practice 3.1

Conditional expressions are more difficult to read than if...else statements and should be used to replace only simple if...else statements that choose between two values.

Good Programming Practice 3.2

When a conditional expression is inside a larger expression, it's good practice to parenthesize the conditional expression for clarity. Adding parentheses may also prevent operator precedence problems that could cause syntax errors.

Nested if...else Statements

An application can test multiple cases by placing if...else statements inside other if...else statements to create *nested if...else statements*. For example, the following nested if...else statement prints A for exam grades greater than or equal to 90, B for grades in the range 80 to 89, C for grades in the range 70 to 79, D for grades in the range 60 to 69 and F for all other grades:

```
if ( grade >= 90 )
   Console.WriteLine( "A" );
else
   if ( grade >= 80 )
      Console.WriteLine( "B" );
   else
      if ( grade >= 70 )
         Console.WriteLine( "C" );
      else
         if ( grade >= 60 )
            Console.WriteLine( "D" );
         else
            Console.WriteLine( "F" );
```

If grade is greater than or equal to 90, the first four conditions will be true, but only the statement in the if-part of the first if...else statement will execute. After that statement executes, the else-part of the "outermost" if...else statement is skipped. Most C# programmers prefer to write the preceding if...else statement as

```
if ( grade >= 90 )
   Console.WriteLine( "A" );
else if ( grade >= 80 )
   Console.WriteLine( "B" );
else if ( grade >= 70 )
   Console.WriteLine( "C" );
else if ( grade >= 60 )
   Console.WriteLine( "D" );
else
   Console.WriteLine( "F" );
```

The two forms are identical except for the spacing and indentation, which the compiler ignores. The latter form is popular because it avoids deep indentation of the code to the right—such indentation often leaves little room on a line of code, forcing lines to be split and decreasing the readability of your code.

Dangling-else Problem

The C# compiler always associates an else with the immediately preceding if unless told to do otherwise by the placement of braces ({ and }). This behavior can lead to what is referred to as the *dangling-else problem*. For example,

```
if ( x > 5 )
   if ( y > 5 )
      Console.WriteLine( "x and y are > 5" );
else
   Console.WriteLine( "x is <= 5" );
```

appears to indicate that if x is greater than 5, the nested if statement determines whether y is also greater than 5. If so, the string "x and y are > 5" is output. Otherwise, it appears that if x is not greater than 5, the else part of the if...else outputs the string "x is <= 5".

Beware! This nested if...else statement does not execute as it appears. The compiler actually interprets the statement as

```
if ( x > 5 )
   if ( y > 5 )
      Console.WriteLine( "x and y are > 5" );
   else
      Console.WriteLine( "x is <= 5" );
```

in which the body of the first if is a nested if...else. The outer if statement tests whether x is greater than 5. If so, execution continues by testing whether y is also greater than 5. If the second condition is true, the proper string—"x and y are > 5"—is displayed. However, if the second condition is false, the string "x is <= 5" is displayed, even though we know that x is greater than 5.

To force the nested if...else statement to execute as it was originally intended, we must write it as follows:

```
if ( x > 5 )
{
   if ( y > 5 )
      Console.WriteLine( "x and y are > 5" );
}
else
   Console.WriteLine( "x is <= 5" );
```

The braces ({}) indicate to the compiler that the second if statement is in the body of the first if and that the else is associated with the *first* if.

Blocks

The if statement normally expects only one statement in its body. To include several statements in the body of an if (or the body of an else for an if...else statement), enclose the statements in braces ({ and }). A set of statements contained within a pair of braces is called a *block*. A block can be placed anywhere in an application that a single statement can be placed.

The following example includes a block in the else-part of an if...else statement:

```
if ( grade >= 60 )
    Console.WriteLine( "Passed" );
else
{
    Console.WriteLine( "Failed" );
    Console.WriteLine( "You must take this course again." );
}
```

In this case, if grade is less than 60, the application executes both statements in the body of the else and prints

```
Failed.
You must take this course again.
```

Note the braces surrounding the two statements in the else clause. These braces are important. Without the braces, the statement

```
Console.WriteLine( "You must take this course again." );
```

would be outside the body of the else-part of the if...else statement and would execute regardless of whether the grade was less than 60.

Good Programming Practice 3.3

Always using braces in an if...else (or other) statement helps prevent their accidental omission, especially when adding statements to the if-part or the else-part at a later time. To avoid omitting one or both of the braces, some programmers type the beginning and ending braces of blocks before typing the individual statements within the braces.

Just as a block can be placed anywhere a single statement can be placed, it is also possible to have an empty statement. Recall from Section 1.9 that the empty statement is represented by placing a semicolon (;) where a statement would normally be.

Common Programming Error 3.1

Placing a semicolon after the condition in an if or if...else statement leads to a logic error in single-selection if statements and a syntax error in double-selection if...else statements (when the if-part contains an actual body statement).

3.5 while Repetition Statement

A *repetition statement* allows you to specify that an application should repeat an action while some condition remains true. As an example of C#'s *while repetition statement*, consider a code segment designed to find the first power of 3 larger than 100. Suppose int variable product is initialized to 3. When the following while statement finishes executing, product contains the result:

```
int product = 3;

while ( product <= 100 )
    product = 3 * product;
```

When this while statement begins execution, the value of variable product is 3. Each repetition of the while statement multiplies product by 3, so product takes on the subsequent values 9, 27, 81 and 243 successively. When variable product becomes 243, the while statement condition—product <= 100—becomes false. This terminates the repetition, so the final value of product is 243. At this point, application execution continues with the next statement after the while statement.

Common Programming Error 3.2

Not providing in the body of a while statement an action that eventually causes the condition in the while to become false normally results in a logic error called an **infinite loop***, in which the loop never terminates.*

The UML activity diagram in Fig. 3.4 illustrates the flow of control that corresponds to the preceding while statement. This diagram also introduces the UML's *merge symbol*. The UML represents both the merge symbol and the decision symbol as diamonds. The merge symbol joins two flows of activity into one. In this diagram, the merge symbol joins the transitions from the initial state and the action state, so they both flow into the decision that determines whether the loop should begin (or continue) executing. The decision and merge symbols can be distinguished by the number of "incoming" and "outgoing" transition arrows. A decision symbol has one transition arrow pointing to the diamond and two or more transition arrows pointing out from the diamond to indicate possible transitions from that point. Each transition arrow pointing out of a decision symbol has a guard condition next to it. A merge symbol has two or more transition arrows pointing to the diamond and only one transition arrow pointing from the diamond, to indicate multiple activity flows merging to continue the activity. None of the transition arrows associated with a merge symbol have guard conditions.

Figure 3.4 clearly shows the repetition of the while statement discussed earlier in this section. The transition arrow emerging from the action state points back to the merge, from which program flow transitions back to the decision that is tested at the beginning of each repetition of the loop. The loop continues to execute until the guard condition product > 100 becomes true. Then the while statement exits (reaches its final state), and control passes to the next statement in sequence in the application.

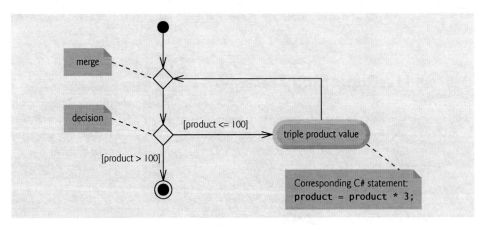

Fig. 3.4 | while repetition statement UML activity diagram.

3.6 Formulating Algorithms: Counter-Controlled Repetition

To illustrate how algorithms are developed, we modify the GradeBook class of Chapter 2 to solve two variations of a problem that averages student grades. Consider the following problem statement:

> *A class of 10 students took a quiz. The grades (integers in the range 0 to 100) for this quiz are available to you. Determine the class average on the quiz.*

The class average is equal to the sum of the grades divided by the number of students. The algorithm for solving this problem on a computer must input each grade, keep track of the total of all grades input, perform the averaging calculation and print the result.

We use *counter-controlled repetition* to input the grades one at a time. This technique uses a variable called a *counter* (or *control variable*) to control the number of times a set of statements will execute. In this example, repetition terminates when the counter exceeds 10. This section presents a version of class GradeBook (Fig. 3.5) that implements the algorithm in a C# method. The section then presents an application (Fig. 3.6) that demonstrates the algorithm in action.

Implementing Counter-Controlled Repetition in Class GradeBook
Class GradeBook (Fig. 3.5) contains a constructor (lines 11–14) that assigns a value to the class's instance variable courseName (declared in line 8) by using property CourseName. Lines 17–27 and 30–35 declare property CourseName and method DisplayMessage, respectively. Lines 38–64 declare method DetermineClassAverage, which implements the class-averaging algorithm.

Lines 40–43 declare local variables total, gradeCounter, grade and average to be of type int. Variable grade stores the user input.

Note that the declarations (in lines 40–43) appear in the body of method DetermineClassAverage. Recall that variables declared in a method body are local variables and can be used only from the line of their declaration in the method to the closing right brace of the method declaration. A local variable's declaration must appear before the variable is used in that method. A local variable cannot be accessed outside the method in which it is declared.

```
1   // Fig. 3.5: GradeBook.cs
2   // GradeBook class that solves class-average problem using
3   // counter-controlled repetition.
4   using System;
5
6   public class GradeBook
7   {
8      private string courseName; // name of course this GradeBook represents
9
10     // constructor initializes courseName
11     public GradeBook( string name )
12     {
13        CourseName = name; // initializes courseName by using property
14     } // end constructor
```

Fig. 3.5 | GradeBook class that solves class-average problem using counter-controlled repetition. (Part 1 of 2.)

```
15
16      // property to get and set the course name
17      public string CourseName
18      {
19         get
20         {
21            return courseName;
22         } // end get
23         set
24         {
25            courseName = value; // set should validate
26         } // end set
27      } // end property CourseName
28
29      // display a welcome message to the GradeBook user
30      public void DisplayMessage()
31      {
32         // property CourseName gets the name of the course
33         Console.WriteLine( "Welcome to the grade book for\n{0}!\n",
34            CourseName );
35      } // end method DisplayMessage
36
37      // determine class average based on 10 grades entered by user
38      public void DetermineClassAverage()
39      {
40         int total; // sum of the grades entered by user
41         int gradeCounter; // number of the grade to be entered next
42         int grade; // grade value entered by the user
43         int average; // average of the grades
44
45         // initialization phase
46         total = 0; // initialize the total
47         gradeCounter = 1; // initialize the loop counter
48
49         // processing phase
50         while ( gradeCounter <= 10 ) // loop 10 times
51         {
52            Console.Write( "Enter grade: " ); // prompt the user
53            grade = Convert.ToInt32( Console.ReadLine() ); // read grade
54            total = total + grade; // add the grade to total
55            gradeCounter = gradeCounter + 1; // increment the counter by 1
56         } // end while
57
58         // termination phase
59         average = total / 10; // integer division yields integer result
60
61         // display total and average of grades
62         Console.WriteLine( "\nTotal of all 10 grades is {0}", total );
63         Console.WriteLine( "Class average is {0}", average );
64      } // end method DetermineClassAverage
65   } // end class GradeBook
```

Fig. 3.5 | GradeBook class that solves class-average problem using counter-controlled repetition. (Part 2 of 2.)

In the versions of class GradeBook in this chapter, we simply read and process a set of grades. The averaging calculation is performed in method DetermineClassAverage using local variables—we do not preserve any information about student grades in instance variables of the class. In later versions of the class (in Chapter 6, Arrays), we maintain the grades in memory using an instance variable that refers to a data structure known as an array. This allows a GradeBook object to perform various calculations on the same set of grades without requiring the user to enter the grades multiple times.

We say that a variable is *definitely assigned* when the variable is assigned in every possible flow of control. Notice that each local variable declared in lines 40-43 is definitely assigned before it is used in calculations. The assignments (in lines 46–47) initialize total to 0 and gradeCounter to 1. Variables grade and average (for the user input and calculated average, respectively) need not be initialized here—their values are assigned as they are input or calculated later in the method.

Common Programming Error 3.3

Using the value of a local variable before it is definitely assigned results in a compilation error. All local variables must be definitely assigned before their values are used in expressions.

Error-Prevention Tip 3.1

Initialize each counter and total, either in its declaration or in an assignment statement. Totals are normally initialized to 0. Counters are normally initialized to 0 or 1, depending on how they are used (we will show examples of each).

Line 50 indicates that the while statement should continue looping as long as the value of gradeCounter is less than or equal to 10. While this condition remains true, the while statement repeatedly executes the statements between the braces that delimit its body (lines 51–56).

Line 52 displays the prompt "Enter grade: " in the console window. Line 53 reads the grade entered by the user and assigns it to variable grade. Then line 54 adds the new grade entered by the user to the total and assigns the result to total, which replaces its previous value.

Line 55 adds 1 to gradeCounter to indicate that the application has processed a grade and is ready to input the next grade from the user. Incrementing gradeCounter eventually causes gradeCounter to exceed 10. At that point the while loop terminates because its condition (line 50) becomes false.

When the loop terminates, line 59 performs the averaging calculation and assigns its result to the variable average. Line 62 uses Console's WriteLine method to display the text "Total of all 10 grades is " followed by variable total's value. Line 63 then uses WriteLine to display the text "Class average is " followed by variable average's value. Method DetermineClassAverage returns control to the calling method (i.e., Main in GradeBookTest of Fig. 3.6) after reaching line 64.

Class GradeBookTest

Class GradeBookTest (Fig. 3.6) creates an object of class GradeBook (Fig. 3.5) and demonstrates its capabilities. Lines 9–10 of Fig. 3.6 create a new GradeBook object and assign it to variable myGradeBook. The string in line 10 is passed to the GradeBook constructor (lines 11–14 of Fig. 3.5). Line 12 calls myGradeBook's DisplayMessage method to display

```
1  // Fig. 3.6: GradeBookTest.cs
2  // Create GradeBook object and invoke its DetermineClassAverage method.
3  public class GradeBookTest
4  {
5     public static void Main( string[] args )
6     {
7        // create GradeBook object myGradeBook and
8        // pass course name to constructor
9        GradeBook myGradeBook = new GradeBook(
10          "CS101 Introduction to C# Programming" );
11
12       myGradeBook.DisplayMessage(); // display welcome message
13       myGradeBook.DetermineClassAverage(); // find average of 10 grades
14    } // end Main
15 } // end class GradeBookTest
```

```
Welcome to the grade book for
CS101 Introduction to C# Programming!

Enter grade: 88
Enter grade: 79
Enter grade: 95
Enter grade: 100
Enter grade: 48
Enter grade: 88
Enter grade: 92
Enter grade: 83
Enter grade: 90
Enter grade: 85

Total of all 10 grades is 848
Class average is 84
```

Fig. 3.6 | Create GradeBook object and invoke its DetermineClassAverage method.

a welcome message to the user. Line 13 then calls myGradeBook's DetermineClassAverage method to allow the user to enter 10 grades, for which the method then calculates and prints the average—the method performs the algorithm shown in Fig. 3.5.

Notes on Integer Division and Truncation

The averaging calculation performed by method DetermineClassAverage in response to the method call at line 13 in Fig. 3.6 produces an integer result. The application's output indicates that the sum of the grade values in the sample execution is 848, which when divided by 10, should yield the floating-point number 84.8. However, the result of the calculation total / 10 (line 59 of Fig. 3.5) is the integer 84, because total and 10 are both integers. Dividing two integers results in *integer division*—any fractional part of the calculation is lost (i.e., *truncated*, not rounded). We will see how to obtain a floating-point result from the averaging calculation in the next section.

Common Programming Error 3.4

Assuming that integer division rounds (rather than truncates) can lead to incorrect results. For example, 7 ÷ 4, which yields 1.75 in conventional arithmetic, truncates to 1 in integer arithmetic, rather than rounding to 2.

3.7 Formulating Algorithms: Sentinel-Controlled Repetition

Let us generalize Section 3.6's class-average problem. Consider the following problem:

> *Develop a class-averaging application that processes grades for an arbitrary number of students each time it is run.*

In the previous class-average example, the problem statement specified the number of students, so the number of grades (10) was known in advance. In this example, no indication is given of how many grades the user will enter during the application's execution. The application must process an arbitrary number of grades.

One way to solve this problem is to use a special value called a *sentinel value* (also called a *signal value*, a *dummy value* or a *flag value*) to indicate "end of data entry." This is called *sentinel-controlled repetition*. The user enters grades until all legitimate grades have been entered. The user then types the sentinel value to indicate that no more grades will be entered.

Clearly, a sentinel value must be chosen that cannot be confused with an acceptable input value. Grades on a quiz are nonnegative integers, so –1 is an acceptable sentinel value for this problem. Thus, a run of the class-average application might process a stream of inputs such as 95, 96, 75, 74, 89 and –1. The application would then compute and print the class average for the grades 95, 96, 75, 74 and 89. Since –1 is the sentinel value, it should not enter into the averaging calculation.

Implementing Sentinel-Controlled Repetition in Class GradeBook

Figure 3.7 shows the C# class GradeBook containing method DetermineClassAverage that uses sentinel-controlled repetition. Although each grade is an integer, the averaging calculation is likely to produce a number with a decimal point—in other words, a real number or floating-point number. The type int cannot represent such a number, so this class uses type double to do so.

The while statement (lines 54–62) is followed in sequence by an if...else statement (lines 66–77). Much of the code in this application is identical to the code in Fig. 3.5, so we concentrate on the new features and issues.

Line 42 declares double variable average. This variable allows us to store the calculated class average as a floating-point number. Line 46 initializes gradeCounter to 0, because no grades have been entered yet. Remember that this application uses sentinel-controlled repetition to input the grades from the user. To keep an accurate record of the number of grades entered, the application increments gradeCounter only when the user inputs a valid grade value.

Program Logic for Sentinel-Controlled Repetition vs. Counter-Controlled Repetition

Compare the program logic for sentinel-controlled repetition in this application with that for counter-controlled repetition in Fig. 3.5. In counter-controlled repetition, each repetition of the while statement (e.g., lines 50–56 of Fig. 3.5) reads a value from the user, for the specified number of repetitions. In sentinel-controlled repetition, the application reads the first value (lines 50–51 of Fig. 3.7) before reaching the while. This value determines whether the application's flow of control should enter the body of the while. If the condition of the while is false, the user entered the sentinel value, so the body of the while does not execute (because no grades were entered). If, on the other hand, the condition is

```
1   // Fig. 3.7: GradeBook.cs
2   // GradeBook class that solves class-average problem using
3   // sentinel-controlled repetition.
4   using System;
5
6   public class GradeBook
7   {
8      private string courseName; // name of course this GradeBook represents
9
10     // constructor initializes courseName
11     public GradeBook( string name )
12     {
13        CourseName = name; // initialize courseName by using property
14     } // end constructor
15
16     // property to get and set the course name
17     public string CourseName
18     {
19        get
20        {
21           return courseName;
22        } // end get
23        set
24        {
25           courseName = value; // set should validate
26        } // end set
27     } // end property CourseName
28
29     // display a welcome message to the GradeBook user
30     public void DisplayMessage()
31     {
32        Console.WriteLine( "Welcome to the grade book for\n{0}!\n",
33           CourseName );
34     } // end method DisplayMessage
35
36     // determine the average of an arbitrary number of grades
37     public void DetermineClassAverage()
38     {
39        int total; // sum of grades
40        int gradeCounter; // number of grades entered
41        int grade; // grade value
42        double average; // number with decimal point for average
43
44        // initialization phase
45        total = 0; // initialize total
46        gradeCounter = 0; // initialize loop counter
47
48        // processing phase
49        // prompt for input and read grade from user
50        Console.Write( "Enter grade or -1 to quit: " );
51        grade = Convert.ToInt32( Console.ReadLine() );
```

Fig. 3.7 | GradeBook class that solves class-average problem using sentinel-controlled repetition. (Part I of 2.)

```
52
53          // loop until sentinel value read from user
54          while ( grade != -1 )
55          {
56              total = total + grade; // add grade to total
57              gradeCounter = gradeCounter + 1; // increment counter
58
59              // prompt for input and read next grade from user
60              Console.Write( "Enter grade or -1 to quit: " );
61              grade = Convert.ToInt32( Console.ReadLine() );
62          } // end while
63
64          // termination phase
65          // if user entered at least one grade...
66          if ( gradeCounter != 0 )
67          {
68              // calculate average of all grades entered
69              average = ( double ) total / gradeCounter;
70
71              // display total and average (with two digits of precision)
72              Console.WriteLine( "\nTotal of the {0} grades entered is {1}",
73                  gradeCounter, total );
74              Console.WriteLine( "Class average is {0:F2}", average );
75          } // end if
76          else // no grades were entered, so output error message
77              Console.WriteLine( "No grades were entered" );
78      } // end method DetermineClassAverage
79  } // end class GradeBook
```

Fig. 3.7 | GradeBook class that solves class-average problem using sentinel-controlled repetition. (Part 2 of 2.)

true, the body begins execution, and the loop adds the grade value to the total (line 56) and adds 1 to gradeCounter (line 57). Then lines 60–61 in the loop's body input the next value from the user. Next, program control reaches the closing right brace of the body at line 62, so execution continues with the test of the while's condition (line 54). The condition uses the most recent grade input by the user to determine whether the loop's body should execute again. Note that the value of variable grade is always input from the user immediately before the application tests the while condition. This allows the application to determine whether the value just input is the sentinel value *before* the application processes that value (i.e., adds it to the total). If the sentinel value is input, the loop terminates; the application does *not* add –1 to the total.

Good Programming Practice 3.4

In a sentinel-controlled loop, the prompts requesting data entry should explicitly remind the user of the sentinel value.

After the loop terminates, the if...else statement at lines 66–77 executes. The condition at line 66 determines whether any grades were input. If none were input, the else part (lines 76–77) of the if...else statement executes and displays the message "No grades were entered", and the method returns control to the calling method.

Explicitly and Implicitly Converting Between Simple Types

If at least one grade was entered, line 69 of Fig. 3.7 calculates the average of the grades. Recall from Fig. 3.5 that integer division yields an integer result. Even though variable average is declared as a double (line 42), the calculation

```
average = total / gradeCounter;
```

loses the fractional part of the quotient before the result of the division is assigned to average. This occurs because total and gradeCounter are both integers, and integer division yields an integer result. To perform a floating-point calculation with integer values, we must temporarily treat these values as floating-point numbers for use in the calculation. C# provides the *unary cast operator* to accomplish this task. Line 69 uses the *(double)* cast operator—a unary operator—to create a *temporary* floating-point copy of its operand total (which appears to the right of the operator). Using a cast operator in this manner is called *explicit conversion*. The value stored in total is still an integer.

The calculation now consists of a floating-point value (the temporary double version of total) divided by the integer gradeCounter. C# knows how to evaluate only arithmetic expressions in which the operands' types are identical. To ensure that the operands are of the same type, C# performs an operation called *promotion* (or *implicit conversion*) on selected operands. For example, in an expression containing values of the types int and double, the int values are promoted to double values for use in the expression. In this example, the value of gradeCounter is promoted to type double, then floating-point division is performed and the result of the calculation is assigned to average. As long as the (double) cast operator is applied to any variable in the calculation, the calculation will yield a double result. Later in this chapter, we discuss all the simple types. You will learn more about the promotion rules in Section 5.7.

Common Programming Error 3.5

The cast operator can be used to convert between simple numeric types, such as int and double, and between related reference types (as we discuss in Chapter 9, Polymorphism, Interfaces & Operator Overloading). Casting to the wrong type may cause compilation errors or runtime errors.

Cast operators are available for all simple types. (We'll discuss cast operators for reference types in Chapter 9.) The cast operator is formed by placing parentheses around the name of a type. Cast operators associate from right to left and have the same precedence as other unary operators, such as unary + and unary -. This precedence is one level higher than that of the *multiplicative operators* *, / and %. We indicate the cast operator with the notation (*type*) in our precedence charts, to indicate that any type name can be used to form a cast operator.

Line 74 outputs the class average using Console's WriteLine method. In this example, we decided that we'd like to display the class average rounded to the nearest hundredth and output the average with exactly two digits to the right of the decimal point. The format specifier F in WriteLine's format item (line 74) indicates that variable average's value should be displayed as a real number. The number after the format specifier F represents the number of decimal places (in this case, 2) that should be output to the right of the decimal point in the floating-point number—also known as the number's *precision*. Any floating point value output with F2 will be rounded to the hundredths position—for example, 123.457 would be rounded to 123.46, and 27.333 would be rounded to 27.33.

In this application, the three grades entered during the sample execution of class Grade-BookTest (Fig. 3.8) total 263, which yields the average 87.66666.... The format item rounds the average to the hundredths position, and the average is displayed as 87.67.

3.8 Formulating Algorithms: Nested Control Statements

In this case study, we *nest* one control statement within another. Consider the following problem statement:

> *A college offers a course that prepares students for the state licensing exam for real estate brokers. Last year, 10 of the students who completed this course took the exam. The college wants to know how well its students did on the exam. You have been asked to write an application to summarize the results. You have been given a list of these 10 students. Next to each name is written a 1 if the student passed the exam or a 2 if the student failed.*
>
> *Your application should analyze the results of the exam as follows:*
>
> > *1. Input each test result (i.e., a 1 or a 2). Display the message "Enter result" on the screen each time the application requests another test result.*
> >
> > *2. Count the number of test results of each type.*
> >
> > *3. Display a summary of the test results indicating the number of students who passed and the number who failed.*
> >
> > *4. If more than eight students passed the exam, print the message "Raise tuition."*

```
1   // Fig. 3.8: GradeBookTest.cs
2   // Create GradeBook object and invoke its DetermineClassAverage method.
3   public class GradeBookTest
4   {
5      public static void Main( string[] args )
6      {
7         // create GradeBook object myGradeBook and
8         // pass course name to constructor
9         GradeBook myGradeBook = new GradeBook(
10           "CS101 Introduction to C# Programming" );
11
12        myGradeBook.DisplayMessage(); // display welcome message
13        myGradeBook.DetermineClassAverage(); // find average of grades
14     } // end Main
15  } // end class GradeBookTest
```

```
Welcome to the grade book for
CS101 Introduction to C# Programming!

Enter grade or -1 to quit: 96
Enter grade or -1 to quit: 88
Enter grade or -1 to quit: 79
Enter grade or -1 to quit: -1

Total of the 3 grades entered is 263
Class average is 87.67
```

Fig. 3.8 | Create GradeBook object and invoke its DetermineClassAverage method.

After reading the problem statement, we make the following observations:

1. The application must process test results for 10 students. A counter-controlled loop can be used because the number of test results is known in advance.

2. Each test result has a numeric value—either a 1 or a 2. Each time the application reads a test result, the application must determine whether the number is a 1 or a 2. We test for a 1 in our algorithm. If the number is not a 1, we assume that it is a 2.

3. Two counters are used to keep track of the exam results—one to count the number of students who passed the exam and one to count the number of students who failed the exam.

4. After the application has processed all the results, it must determine whether more than eight students passed the exam.

The C# class that implements the algorithm is shown in Fig. 3.9, and two sample executions appear in Fig. 3.10.

```
1   // Fig. 3.9: Analysis.cs
2   // Analysis of examination results, using nested control statements.
3   using System;
4
5   public class Analysis
6   {
7      public void ProcessExamResults()
8      {
9         // initializing variables in declarations
10        int passes = 0; // number of passes
11        int failures = 0; // number of failures
12        int studentCounter = 1; // student counter
13        int result; // one exam result from user
14
15        // process 10 students using counter-controlled repetition
16        while ( studentCounter <= 10 )
17        {
18           // prompt user for input and obtain value from user
19           Console.Write( "Enter result (1 = pass, 2 = fail): " );
20           result = Convert.ToInt32( Console.ReadLine() );
21
22           // if...else nested in while
23           if ( result == 1 ) // if result 1,
24              passes = passes + 1;
25           else // else result is not 1, so
26              failures = failures + 1; // increment failures
27
28           // increment studentCounter so loop eventually terminates
29           studentCounter = studentCounter + 1;
30        } // end while
31
32        // termination phase; prepare and display results
33        Console.WriteLine( "Passed: {0}\nFailed: {1}", passes, failures );
```

Fig. 3.9 | Analysis of examination results, using nested control statements. (Part 1 of 2.)

```
34
35            // determine whether more than 8 students passed
36            if ( passes > 8 )
37                Console.WriteLine( "Raise Tuition" );
38        } // end method ProcessExamResults
39    } // end class Analysis
```

Fig. 3.9 | Analysis of examination results, using nested control statements. (Part 2 of 2.)

Lines 10–13 of Fig. 3.9 declare the variables that method ProcessExamResults of class Analysis uses to process the examination results. Several of these declarations use C#'s ability to incorporate variable initialization into declarations (passes is assigned 0, failures is assigned 0 and studentCounter is assigned 1). Looping applications may require initialization at the beginning of each repetition—such reinitialization would normally be performed by assignment statements rather than in declarations.

The while statement (lines 16–30) loops 10 times. During each repetition, the loop inputs and processes one exam result. Notice that the if...else statement (lines 23–26) for processing each result is nested in the while statement. If the result is 1, the if...else statement increments passes; otherwise, it assumes the result is 2 and increments failures. Line 29 increments studentCounter before the loop condition is tested again at line 16. After 10 values have been input, the loop terminates and line 33 displays the number of passes and the number of failures. The if statement at lines 36–37 determines whether more than eight students passed the exam and, if so, outputs the message "Raise Tuition".

Error-Prevention Tip 3.2

Initializing local variables when they are declared helps you avoid compilation errors that might arise from attempts to use uninitialized data. While C# does not require that local variable initializations be incorporated into declarations, it does require that local variables be initialized before their values are used in an expression.

AnalysisTest *Class That Demonstrates Class* Analysis

Class AnalysisTest (Fig. 3.10) creates an Analysis object (line 7) and invokes the object's ProcessExamResults method (line 8) to process a set of exam results entered by the user. Figure 3.10 shows the input and output from two sample executions of the application. During the first sample execution, the condition at line 36 of method ProcessExamResults in Fig. 3.9 is true—more than eight students passed the exam, so the application outputs a message indicating that the tuition should be raised.

```
 1    // Fig. 3.10: AnalysisTest.cs
 2    // Test application for class Analysis.
 3    public class AnalysisTest
 4    {
 5       public static void Main( string[] args )
 6       {
 7           Analysis application = new Analysis(); // create Analysis object
 8           application.ProcessExamResults(); // call method to process results
 9       } // end Main
10    } // end class AnalysisTest
```

Fig. 3.10 | Test application for class Analysis. (Part 1 of 2.)

```
Enter result (1 = pass, 2 = fail): 1
Enter result (1 = pass, 2 = fail): 2
Enter result (1 = pass, 2 = fail): 1
Enter result (1 = pass, 2 = fail): 1
Enter result (1 = pass, 2 = fail): 1
Enter result (1 = pass, 2 = fail): 1
Enter result (1 = pass, 2 = fail): 1
Enter result (1 = pass, 2 = fail): 1
Enter result (1 = pass, 2 = fail): 1
Enter result (1 = pass, 2 = fail): 1
Passed: 9
Failed: 1
Raise Tuition
```

```
Enter result (1 = pass, 2 = fail): 1
Enter result (1 = pass, 2 = fail): 2
Enter result (1 = pass, 2 = fail): 2
Enter result (1 = pass, 2 = fail): 2
Enter result (1 = pass, 2 = fail): 1
Enter result (1 = pass, 2 = fail): 1
Enter result (1 = pass, 2 = fail): 1
Enter result (1 = pass, 2 = fail): 1
Enter result (1 = pass, 2 = fail): 2
Enter result (1 = pass, 2 = fail): 2
Passed: 5
Failed: 5
```

Fig. 3.10 | Test application for class `Analysis`. (Part 2 of 2.)

3.9 Compound Assignment Operators

C# provides several *compound assignment operators* for abbreviating assignment expressions. Any statement of the form

>   *variable* = *variable   operator   expression*;

where *operator* is one of the binary operators +, -, *, / or % (or others we discuss later in the text) can be written in the form

>   *variable   operator*= *expression*;

For example, you can abbreviate the statement

>   c = c + 3;

with the *addition compound assignment operator*, +=, as

>   c += 3;

The += operator adds the value of the expression on the right of the operator to the value of the variable on the left of the operator and stores the result in the variable on the left of the operator. Thus, the assignment expression c += 3 adds 3 to c. Figure 3.11 shows the arithmetic compound assignment operators, sample expressions using the operators and explanations of what the operators do.

Assignment operator	Sample expression	Explanation	Assigns
Assume: **int** c = 3, d = 5, e = 4, f = 6, g = 12;			
+=	c += 7	c = c + 7	10 to c
-=	d -= 4	d = d - 4	1 to d
*=	e *= 5	e = e * 5	20 to e
/=	f /= 3	f = f / 3	2 to f
%=	g %= 9	g = g % 9	3 to g

Fig. 3.11 | Arithmetic compound assignment operators.

3.10 Increment and Decrement Operators

C# provides two unary operators for adding 1 to or subtracting 1 from the value of a numeric variable. These are the unary *increment operator*, **++**, and the unary *decrement operator*, **--**, respectively, which are summarized in Fig. 3.12. An application can increment by 1 the value of a variable called c using the increment operator, **++**, rather than the expression c = c + 1 or c += 1. An increment or decrement operator that is prefixed to (placed before) a variable is referred to as the *prefix increment operator* or *prefix decrement operator*, respectively. An increment or decrement operator that is postfixed to (placed after) a variable is referred to as the *postfix increment operator* or *postfix decrement operator*, respectively.

Incrementing (or decrementing) a variable with the prefix increment (or prefix decrement) operator causes it to be incremented (or decremented) by 1, and then the new value of the variable is used in the expression in which it appears. Incrementing (or decrementing) the variable with the postfix increment (or postfix decrement) operator causes the current value of the variable to be used in the expression in which it appears, and then the variable's value is incremented (or decremented) by 1.

Operator	Called	Sample expression	Explanation
++	prefix increment	++a	Increment a by 1, then use the new value of a in the expression in which a resides.
++	postfix increment	a++	Use the current value of a in the expression in which a resides, then increment a by 1.
--	prefix decrement	--b	Decrement b by 1, then use the new value of b in the expression in which b resides.
--	postfix decrement	b--	Use the current value of b in the expression in which b resides, then decrement b by 1.

Fig. 3.12 | Increment and decrement operators.

Good Programming Practice 3.5

Unlike binary operators, the unary increment and decrement operators should (by convention) be placed next to their operands, with no intervening spaces.

Figure 3.13 demonstrates the difference between the prefix increment and postfix increment versions of the ++ increment operator. The decrement operator (--) works similarly. Note that this example contains only one class, with method Main performing all the class's work. In this chapter and in Chapter 2, you have seen examples consisting of two classes—one class containing methods that perform useful tasks and one containing method Main, which creates an object of the other class and calls its methods. In this example, we simply want to show the mechanics of the ++ operator, so we use only one class declaration containing method Main. Occasionally, when it makes no sense to try to create a reusable class to demonstrate a simple concept, we will use a mechanical example contained entirely within the Main method of a single class.

Line 12 initializes the variable c to 5, and line 13 outputs c's initial value. Line 14 outputs the value of the expression c++. This expression performs the postfix increment operation on

```
1   // Fig. 3.13: Increment.cs
2   // Prefix increment and postfix increment operators.
3   using System;
4
5   public class Increment
6   {
7      public static void Main( string[] args )
8      {
9         int c;
10
11        // demonstrate postfix increment operator
12        c = 5; // assign 5 to c
13        Console.WriteLine( c ); // print 5
14        Console.WriteLine( c++ ); // print 5 again, then increment
15        Console.WriteLine( c ); // print 6
16
17        Console.WriteLine(); // skip a line
18
19        // demonstrate prefix increment operator
20        c = 5; // assign 5 to c
21        Console.WriteLine( c ); // print 5
22        Console.WriteLine( ++c ); // increment then print 6
23        Console.WriteLine( c ); // print 6 again
24     } // end Main
25  } // end class Increment
```

```
5
5
6

5
6
6
```

Fig. 3.13 | Prefix increment and postfix increment operators.

the variable c, so c's original value (5) is output, then c's value is incremented. Thus, line 14 outputs c's initial value (5) again. Line 15 outputs c's new value (6) to prove that the variable's value was indeed incremented in line 14.

Line 20 resets c's value to 5, and line 21 outputs c's value. Line 22 outputs the value of the expression ++c. This expression performs the prefix increment operation on c, so its value is incremented, then the new value (6) is output. Line 23 outputs c's value again to show that the value of c is still 6 after line 22 executes.

The arithmetic compound assignment operators and the increment and decrement operators can be used to simplify statements. For example, the three assignment statements in Fig. 3.9 (lines 24, 26 and 29)

```
passes = passes + 1;
failures = failures + 1;
studentCounter = studentCounter + 1;
```

can be written more concisely with compound assignment operators as

```
passes += 1;
failures += 1;
studentCounter += 1;
```

and even more concisely with prefix increment operators as

```
++passes;
++failures;
++studentCounter;
```

or with postfix increment operators as

```
passes++;
failures++;
studentCounter++;
```

When incrementing or decrementing a variable in a statement by itself, the prefix increment and postfix increment forms have the same effect, and the prefix decrement and postfix decrement forms have the same effect. It is only when a variable appears in the context of a larger expression that the prefix increment and postfix increment have different effects (and similarly for the prefix decrement and postfix decrement).

Common Programming Error 3.6

Attempting to use the increment or decrement operator on an expression other than one to which a value can be assigned is a syntax error. For example, writing ++(x + 1) is a syntax error because (x + 1) is not a variable.

Figure 3.14 shows the precedence and associativity of the operators we have introduced to this point. The operators are shown from top to bottom in decreasing order of precedence. The second column describes the associativity of the operators at each level of precedence. The conditional operator (?:); the unary operators prefix increment (++), prefix decrement (--), plus (+) and minus (-); the cast operators; and the assignment operators =, +=, -=, *=, /= and %= associate from right to left. All the other operators in the operator precedence chart in Fig. 3.14 associate from left to right. The third column names the groups of operators.

Operators					Associativity	Type
.	new	++*(postfix)*	--*(postfix)*		left to right	highest precedence
++	--	+	-	*(type)*	right to left	unary prefix
*	/	%			left to right	multiplicative
+	-				left to right	additive
<	<=	>	>=		left to right	relational
==	!=				left to right	equality
?:					right to left	conditional
=	+=	-=	*=	/=	%=	right to left	assignment

Fig. 3.14 | Precedence and associativity of the operators discussed so far.

3.11 Simple Types

There are thirteen *simple types* in C#. Like its predecessor languages C and C++, C# requires all variables to have a type. For this reason, C# is referred to as a *strongly typed language*.

In C and C++, programmers frequently have to write separate versions of applications to support different computer platforms, because the simple types are not guaranteed to be identical from computer to computer. For example, an int value on one machine might be represented by 16 bits (2 bytes) of memory, while an int value on another machine might be represented by 32 bits (4 bytes) of memory. In C#, int values are always 32 bits (4 bytes). In fact, *all* C# numeric types have fixed sizes.

Size of each type is in bits (there are eight bits to a byte) and its range of values. Because the designers of C# want it to be maximally portable, they use internationally recognized standards for both character formats (Unicode; for more information, visit www.unicode.org) and floating-point numbers (IEEE 754; for more information, visit grouper.ieee.org/groups/754/).

Recall from Section 2.5 that variables of simple types declared outside of a method as fields of a class are automatically assigned default values unless explicitly initialized. Instance variables of types char, byte, sbyte, short, ushort, int, uint, long, ulong, float, double, and decimal are all given the value 0 by default. Instance variables of type bool are given the value false by default. Similarly, reference type instance variables are initialized by default to the value null.

3.12 (Optional) Software Engineering Case Study: Identifying Class Attributes in the ATM System

In Section 2.11, we began the first stage of an object-oriented design (OOD) for our ATM system—analyzing the requirements document and identifying the classes needed to implement the system. We listed the nouns and noun phrases in the requirements document and identified a separate class for each one that plays a significant role in the ATM system. We then modeled the classes and their relationships in a UML class diagram (Fig. 2.24). Classes have attributes (data) and operations (behaviors). Class attributes are implemented in C# programs as instance variables and properties, and class operations are implemented as methods and properties. In this section, we determine many of the attributes needed in the ATM system. In Section 4.9, we examine how these attributes represent an object's state. In Section 5.15, we determine the operations for our classes.

Identifying Attributes

Consider the attributes of some real-world objects: A person's attributes include height, weight and whether the person is left-handed, right-handed or ambidextrous. A radio's attributes include its station setting, its volume setting and its AM or FM setting. A car's attributes include its speedometer and odometer readings, the amount of gas in its tank and what gear it is in. A personal computer's attributes include its manufacturer (e.g., Dell, Gateway, Sun, Apple or IBM), type of screen (e.g., LCD or CRT), main memory size and hard disk size.

We can identify many attributes of the classes in our system by looking for descriptive words and phrases in the requirements document. For each one we find that plays a significant role in the ATM system, we create an attribute and assign it to one or more of the classes identified in Section 2.11. We also create attributes to represent any additional data that a class may need as such needs become clear throughout the design process.

Figure 3.15 lists the words or phrases from the requirements document that describe each class. For example, the requirements document describes the steps taken to obtain a "withdrawal amount," so we list "amount" next to class Withdrawal.

Figure 3.15 leads us to create one attribute of class ATM. Class ATM maintains information about the state of the ATM. The phrase "user is authenticated" describes a state of the ATM (we discuss states in detail in Section 4.9), so we include userAuthenticated as a bool *attribute* (i.e., an attribute that has a value of either true or false). This attribute indicates whether the ATM has successfully authenticated the current user—userAuthenticated must be true for the system to allow the user to perform transactions and access account information. This attribute helps ensure the security of the data in the system.

Class	Descriptive words and phrases
ATM	user is authenticated
BalanceInquiry	account number
Withdrawal	account number amount
Deposit	account number amount
BankDatabase	[no descriptive words or phrases]
Account	account number PIN balance

Fig. 3.15 | Descriptive words and phrases from the ATM requirements document. (Part 1 of 2.)

Class	Descriptive words and phrases
Screen	[no descriptive words or phrases]
Keypad	[no descriptive words or phrases]
CashDispenser	begins each day loaded with 500 $20 bills
DepositSlot	[no descriptive words or phrases]

Fig. 3.15 | Descriptive words and phrases from the ATM requirements document. (Part 2 of 2.)

Classes BalanceInquiry, Withdrawal and Deposit share one attribute. Each transaction involves an "account number" that corresponds to the account of the user making the transaction. We assign integer attribute accountNumber to each transaction class to identify the account to which an object of the class applies.

Descriptive words and phrases in the requirements document also suggest some differences in the attributes required by each transaction class. The requirements document indicates that to withdraw cash or deposit funds, users must enter a specific "amount" of money to be withdrawn or deposited, respectively. Thus, we assign to classes Withdrawal and Deposit an attribute amount to store the value supplied by the user. The amounts of money related to a withdrawal and a deposit are defining characteristics of these transactions that the system requires for them to take place. Recall that C# represents monetary amounts with type decimal. Note that class BalanceInquiry does not need additional data to perform its task—it requires only an account number to indicate the account whose balance should be retrieved.

Class Account has several attributes. The requirements document states that each bank account has an "account number" and a "PIN," which the system uses for identifying accounts and authenticating users. We assign to class Account two integer attributes: accountNumber and pin. The requirements document also specifies that an account maintains a "balance" of the amount of money in the account, and that the money the user deposits does not become available for a withdrawal until the bank verifies the amount of cash in the deposit envelope and any checks in the envelope clear. An account must still record the amount of money that a user deposits, however. Therefore, we decide that an account should represent a balance using two decimal attributes—availableBalance and totalBalance. Attribute availableBalance tracks the amount of money that a user can withdraw from the account. Attribute totalBalance refers to the total amount of money that the user has "on deposit" (i.e., the amount of money available, plus the amount of cash deposits waiting to be verified or the amount of checks waiting to be cleared). For example, suppose an ATM user deposits $50.00 in cash into an empty account. The totalBalance attribute would increase to $50.00 to record the deposit, but the availableBalance would remain at $0 until a bank employee counts the amount of cash in the envelope and confirms the total. [*Note:* We assume that the bank updates the availableBalance attribute of an Account soon after the ATM transaction occurs, in response to confirming that $50 worth of cash was found in the deposit envelope. We assume that this update occurs through a transaction that a bank employee performs using a bank system other than the ATM. Thus, we do not discuss this transaction in our case study.]

Class CashDispenser has one attribute. The requirements document states that the cash dispenser "begins each day loaded with 500 $20 bills." The cash dispenser must keep track of the number of bills it contains to determine whether enough cash is on hand to satisfy withdrawal requests. We assign to class CashDispenser integer attribute count, which is initially set to 500.

For real problems in industry, there is no guarantee that requirements documents will be rich enough and precise enough for the object-oriented systems designer to determine all the attributes, or even all the classes. The need for additional classes, attributes and behaviors may become clear as the design process proceeds. As we progress through this case study, we too will continue to add, modify and delete information about the classes in our system.

Modeling Attributes

The class diagram in Fig. 3.16 lists some of the attributes for the classes in our system—the descriptive words and phrases in Fig. 3.15 helped us identify these attributes. For simplicity, Fig. 3.16 does not show the associations among classes—we showed these in Fig. 2.24. Systems designers commonly do this. Recall that in the UML, a class's attributes are placed in the middle compartment of the class's rectangle. We list each attribute's name and type separated by a colon (:), followed in some cases by an equal sign (=) and an initial value.

Consider the userAuthenticated attribute of class ATM:

```
userAuthenticated : bool = false
```

This attribute declaration contains three pieces of information about the attribute. The *attribute name* is userAuthenticated. The *attribute type* is bool. In C#, an attribute can be represented by a simple type, such as bool, int, double or decimal, or a class type—as discussed in Chapter 2. We have chosen to model only simple-type attributes in Fig. 3.16—we discuss the reasoning behind this decision shortly.

We can also indicate an initial value for an attribute. Attribute userAuthenticated in class ATM has an initial value of false. This indicates that the system initially does not consider the user to be authenticated. If an attribute has no initial value specified, only its name and type (separated by a colon) are shown. For example, the accountNumber attribute of class BalanceInquiry is an int. Here we show no initial value, because the value of this attribute is a number that we do not yet know. This number will be determined at execution time based on the account number entered by the current ATM user.

Figure 3.16 does not contain attributes for classes Screen, Keypad and DepositSlot. These are important components of our system for which our design process simply has not yet revealed any attributes. We may discover some, however, in the remaining phases of design or when we implement these classes in C#. This is perfectly normal.

Software Engineering Observation 3.1

Early in the design process, classes often lack attributes (and operations). Such classes should not be eliminated, however, because attributes (and operations) may become evident in the later phases of design and implementation.

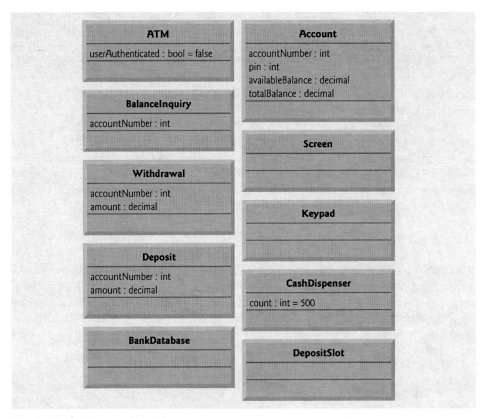

Fig. 3.16 | Classes with attributes.

Note that Fig. 3.16 also does not include attributes for class BankDatabase. We have chosen to include only simple-type attributes in Fig. 3.16 (and in similar class diagrams throughout the case study). A class-type attribute is modeled more clearly as an association (in particular, a composition) between the class with the attribute and the attribute's own class. For example, the class diagram in Fig. 2.24 indicates that class BankDatabase participates in a composition relationship with zero or more Account objects. From this composition, we can determine that when we implement the ATM system in C#, we will be required to create an attribute of class BankDatabase to hold zero or more Account objects. Similarly, we will assign attributes to class ATM that correspond to its composition relationships with classes Screen, Keypad, CashDispenser and DepositSlot. These composition-based attributes would be redundant if modeled in Fig. 3.16, because the compositions modeled in Fig. 2.24 already convey the fact that the database contains information about zero or more accounts and that an ATM is composed of a screen, keypad, cash dispenser and deposit slot. Software developers typically model these whole/part relationships as composition associations rather than as attributes required to implement the relationships.

The class diagram in Fig. 3.16 provides a solid basis for the structure of our model, but the diagram is not complete. In Section 4.9, we identify the states and activities of the objects in the model, and in Section 5.15 we identify the operations that the objects perform. As we present more of the UML and object-oriented design, we will continue to strengthen the structure of our model.

Software Engineering Case Study Self-Review Exercises

3.1 We typically identify the attributes of the classes in our system by analyzing the _____ in the requirements document.
a) nouns and noun phrases
b) descriptive words and phrases
c) verbs and verb phrases
d) All of the above.

3.2 Which of the following is not an attribute of an airplane?
a) length
b) wingspan
c) fly
d) number of seats

3.3 Describe the meaning of the following attribute declaration of class CashDispenser in the class diagram in Fig. 3.16:

```
count : int = 500
```

Answers to Software Engineering Case Study Self-Review Exercises

3.1 b.

3.2 c. Fly is an operation or behavior of an airplane, not an attribute.

3.3 This declaration indicates that attribute count is an int with an initial value of 500; count keeps track of the number of bills available in the CashDispenser at any given time.

3.13 Wrap-Up

Only three types of control structures—sequence, selection and repetition—are needed to develop any problem-solving algorithm. We demonstrated the if single-selection statement, the if...else double-selection statement and the while repetition statement. We used control-statement stacking to compute the total and the average of a set of student grades with counter-controlled and sentinel-controlled repetition, and we used control-statement nesting to analyze and make decisions based on a set of exam results. We introduced C#'s compound assignment operators, as well as its increment and decrement operators. Finally, we discussed the simple types. In Chapter 4, Control Statements: Part 2, we continue our discussion of control statements, introducing the for, do...while and switch statements.

4

Control Statements: Part 2

OBJECTIVES

In this chapter you will learn:

- The essentials of counter-controlled repetition.

- To use the for and do...while repetition statements to execute statements in an application repeatedly.

- To understand multiple selection using the switch selection statement.

- To use the break and continue program control statements to alter the flow of control.

- To use the logical operators to form complex conditional expressions in control statements.

Not everything that can be counted counts, and not every thing that counts can be counted.
—Albert Einstein

Who can control his fate?
—William Shakespeare

The used key is always bright.
—Benjamin Franklin

Intelligence ... is the faculty of making artificial objects, especially tools to make tools.
—Henri Bergson

Every advantage in the past is judged in the light of the final issue.
—Demosthenes

4.1 Introduction

In this chapter, we demonstrate all but one of C#'s remaining structured control statements—the `for`, `do...while` and `switch` statements. Through a series of short examples using `while` and `for`, we explore the essentials of counter-controlled repetition. We devote a portion of the chapter (and Chapter 6) to expanding the `GradeBook` class presented in Chapters 2 and 3. In particular, we create a version of class `GradeBook` that uses a `switch` statement to count the number of A, B, C, D and F grade equivalents in a set of numeric grades entered by the user. We introduce the `break` and `continue` program control statements. We discuss C#'s logical operators, which enable you to use more complex conditional expressions in control statements.

4.2 Essentials of Counter-Controlled Repetition

This section uses the `while` *repetition statement* introduced in Chapter 3 to formalize the elements required to perform counter-controlled repetition. Counter-controlled repetition requires

1. a *control variable* (or loop counter)

2. the *initial value* of the control variable

3. the *increment* (or *decrement*) by which the control variable is modified each time through the loop (also known as each *iteration of the loop*)

4. the *loop-continuation condition* that determines whether looping should continue.

To see these elements of counter-controlled repetition, consider the application of Fig. 4.1, which uses a loop to display the numbers from 1 through 10. Note that Fig. 4.1 contains only one method, `Main`, which does all of the class's work. For most applications in Chapters 2 and 3, we have encouraged the use of two separate files—one that declares a reusable class (e.g., `Account`) and one that instantiates one or more objects of that class (e.g., `AccountTest`) and demonstrates their functionality. Occasionally, however, it is more appropriate simply to create one class whose `Main` method concisely illustrates a basic concept. Throughout this chapter, we use several one-class examples like Fig. 4.1 to demonstrate the mechanics of various C# control statements.

```
1   // Fig. 4.1: WhileCounter.cs
2   // Counter-controlled repetition with the while repetition statement.
3   using System;
4
5   public class WhileCounter
6   {
7      public static void Main( string[] args )
8      {
9         int counter = 1; // declare and initialize control variable
10
11        while ( counter <= 10 ) // loop-continuation condition
12        {
13           Console.Write( "{0}  ", counter );
14           counter++; // increment control variable
15        } // end while
16
17        Console.WriteLine(); // output a newline
18     } // end Main
19  } // end class WhileCounter
```

```
1  2  3  4  5  6  7  8  9  10
```

Fig. 4.1 | Counter-controlled repetition with the while repetition statement.

In method Main of Fig. 4.1 (lines 7–18), the elements of counter-controlled repetition are defined in lines 9, 11 and 14. Line 9 declares the control variable (counter) as an int, reserves space for it in memory and sets its initial value to 1.

Line 13 in the while statement displays control variable counter's value during each iteration of the loop. Line 14 increments the control variable by 1 for each iteration of the loop. The loop-continuation condition in the while (line 11) tests whether the value of the control variable is less than or equal to 10 (the final value for which the condition is true). Note that the application performs the body of this while even when the control variable is 10. The loop terminates when the control variable exceeds 10 (i.e., counter becomes 11).

Common Programming Error 4.1

Because floating-point values may be approximate, controlling loops with floating-point variables may result in imprecise counter values and inaccurate termination tests.

Error-Prevention Tip 4.1

Control counting loops with integers.

Good Programming Practice 4.1

Place blank lines above and below repetition and selection control statements, and indent the statement bodies to enhance readability.

The application in Fig. 4.1 can be made more concise by initializing counter to 0 in line 9 and incrementing counter in the while condition with the prefix increment operator as follows:

```
while ( ++counter <= 10 ) // loop-continuation condition
    Console.Write( "{0}  ", counter );
```

This code saves a statement (and eliminates the need for braces around the loop's body), because the while condition performs the increment before testing the condition. (Recall from Section 3.10 that the precedence of ++ is higher than that of <=.) Coding in such a condensed fashion might make code more difficult to read, debug, modify and maintain.

Software Engineering Observation 4.1

"Keep it simple" is good advice for most of the code you will write.

4.3 for Repetition Statement

Section 4.2 presented the essentials of counter-controlled repetition. The while statement can be used to implement any counter-controlled loop. C# also provides the *for repetition statement*, which specifies the elements of counter-controlled-repetition in a single line of code. Figure 4.2 reimplements the application in Fig. 4.1 using the for statement.

The application's Main method operates as follows: when the for statement (lines 11–12) begins executing, control variable counter is declared and initialized to 1. (Recall from Section 4.2 that the first two elements of counter-controlled repetition are the control variable and its initial value.) Next, the application checks the loop-continuation condition, counter <= 10, which is between the two required semicolons. Because the initial value of counter is 1, the condition initially is true. Therefore, the body statement (line 12) displays control variable counter's value, which is 1. After executing the loop's body, the application increments counter in the expression counter++, which appears to the right of the second semicolon. Then the loop-continuation test is performed again to determine whether the application should continue with the next

```
 1   // Fig. 4.2: ForCounter.cs
 2   // Counter-controlled repetition with the for repetition statement.
 3   using System;
 4
 5   public class ForCounter
 6   {
 7      public static void Main( string[] args )
 8      {
 9         // for statement header includes initialization,
10         // loop-continuation condition and increment
11         for ( int counter = 1; counter <= 10; counter++ )
12            Console.Write( "{0}  ", counter );
13
14         Console.WriteLine(); // output a newline
15      } // end Main
16   } // end class ForCounter
```

```
1 2  3  4  5  6  7  8  9  10
```

Fig. 4.2 | Counter-controlled repetition with the for repetition statement.

iteration of the loop. At this point, the control variable value is 2, so the condition is still true (the final value is not exceeded)—and the application performs the body statement again (i.e., the next iteration of the loop). This process continues until the numbers 1 through 10 have been displayed and the counter's value becomes 11, causing the loop-continuation test to fail and repetition to terminate (after 10 repetitions of the loop body at line 12). Then the application performs the first statement after the for—in this case, line 14.

Note that Fig. 4.2 uses (in line 11) the loop-continuation condition counter <= 10. If you incorrectly specified counter < 10 as the condition, the loop would iterate only nine times—a common logic error called an *off-by-one error*.

Common Programming Error 4.2

Using an incorrect relational operator or an incorrect final value of a loop counter in the loop-continuation condition of a repetition statement causes an off-by-one error.

Good Programming Practice 4.2

Using the final value in the condition of a while *or* for *statement with the* <= *relational operator helps avoid off-by-one errors. For a loop that prints the values 1 to 10, the loop-continuation condition should be* counter <= 10, *rather than* counter < 10 *(which causes an off-by-one error) or* counter < 11 *(which is correct). Many programmers prefer so-called zero-based counting, in which to count 10 times,* counter *would be initialized to zero and the loop-continuation test would be* counter < 10.

Figure 4.3 takes a closer look at the for statement in Fig. 4.2. The for's first line (including the keyword for and everything in parentheses after for)—line 11 in Fig. 4.2—is sometimes called the *for statement header*, or simply the *for header*. Note that the for header "does it all"—it specifies each of the items needed for counter-controlled repetition with a control variable. If there is more than one statement in the body of the for, braces are required to define the body of the loop.

The general format of the for statement is

> **for** (*initialization*; *loopContinuationCondition*; *increment*)
>   *statement*

where the *initialization* expression names the loop's control variable and provides its initial value, the *loopContinuationCondition* is the condition that determines whether looping

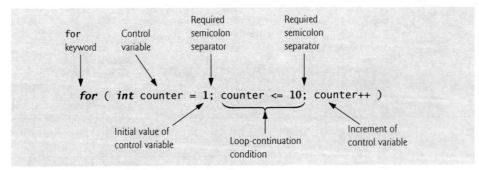

Fig. 4.3 | for statement header components.

should continue and the *increment* modifies the control variable's value (whether an increment or decrement), so that the loop-continuation condition eventually becomes false. The two semicolons in the for header are required. Note that we don't include a semicolon after *statement* because the semicolon is already assumed to be included in the notion of a *statement*.

Common Programming Error 4.3

Using commas instead of the two required semicolons in a for header is a syntax error.

In most cases, the for statement can be represented with an equivalent while statement as follows:

initialization;

while (*loopContinuationCondition*)
{
    statement
    increment;
}

In Section 4.7, we discuss a case in which a for statement cannot be represented with an equivalent while statement.

Typically, for statements are used for counter-controlled repetition, and while statements are used for sentinel-controlled repetition. However, while and for can each be used for either repetition type.

If the *initialization* expression in the for header declares the control variable (i.e., the control variable's type is specified before the variable name, as in Fig. 4.2), the control variable can be used only in that for statement—it will not exist outside the for statement. This restricted use of the name of the control variable is known as the variable's ***scope***. The scope of a variable defines where it can be used in an application. For example, a local variable can be used only in the method that declares the variable and only from the point of declaration through the end of the method. Scope is discussed in detail in Chapter 5, Methods: A Deeper Look.

Common Programming Error 4.4

When a for statement's control variable is declared in the initialization section of the for's header, using the control variable after the for's body is a compilation error.

All three expressions in a for header are optional. If the *loopContinuationCondition* is omitted, C# assumes that the loop-continuation condition is always true, thus creating an infinite loop. You can omit the *initialization* expression if the application initializes the control variable before the loop—in this case, the scope of the control variable will not be limited to the loop. You can omit the *increment* expression if the application calculates the increment with statements in the loop's body or if no increment is needed. The increment expression in a for acts as if it were a stand-alone statement at the end of the for's body. Therefore, the expressions

```
counter = counter + 1
counter += 1
++counter
counter++
```

are equivalent increment expressions in a for statement. Many programmers prefer counter++ because it is concise and because a for loop evaluates its increment expression after its body executes—so the postfix increment form seems more natural. In this case, the variable being incremented does not appear in a larger expression, so the prefix and postfix increment operators have the same effect.

Performance Tip 4.1

There is a slight performance advantage to using the prefix increment operator, but if you choose the postfix increment operator because it seems more natural (as in a for header), optimizing compilers will generate MSIL code that uses the more efficient form anyway.

Good Programming Practice 4.3

In many cases, the prefix and postfix increment operators are both used to add 1 to a variable in a statement by itself. In these cases, the effect is exactly the same, except that the prefix increment operator has a slight performance advantage. Given that the compiler typically optimizes your code to help you get the best performance, use the idiom (prefix or postfix) with which you feel most comfortable in these situations.

Common Programming Error 4.5

Placing a semicolon immediately to the right of the right parenthesis of a for header makes that for's body an empty statement. This is normally a logic error.

Error-Prevention Tip 4.2

Infinite loops occur when the loop-continuation condition in a repetition statement never becomes false. To prevent this situation in a counter-controlled loop, ensure that the control variable is incremented (or decremented) during each iteration of the loop. In a sentinel-controlled loop, ensure that the sentinel value is eventually input.

The initialization, loop-continuation condition and increment portions of a for statement can contain arithmetic expressions. For example, assume that x = 2 and y = 10; if x and y are not modified in the body of the loop, then the statement

```
for ( int j = x; j <= 4 * x * y; j += y / x )
```

is equivalent to the statement

```
for ( int j = 2; j <= 80; j += 5 )
```

The increment of a for statement may also be negative, in which case it is a decrement, and the loop counts downward.

If the loop-continuation condition is initially false, the application does not execute the for statement's body. Instead, execution proceeds with the statement following the for.

Applications frequently display the control variable value or use it in calculations in the loop body, but this use is not required. The control variable is commonly used to control repetition without being mentioned in the body of the for.

Error-Prevention Tip 4.3

Although the value of the control variable can be changed in the body of a for loop, avoid doing so, because this practice can lead to subtle errors.

The for statement's UML activity diagram is similar to that of the while statement (Fig. 3.4). Figure 4.4 shows the activity diagram of the for statement in Fig. 4.2. The diagram makes it clear that initialization occurs only once before the loop-continuation test is evaluated the first time, and that incrementing occurs each time through the loop after the body statement executes.

4.4 Examples Using the for Statement

The following examples show techniques for varying the control variable in a for statement. In each case, we write the appropriate for header. Note the change in the relational operator for loops that decrement the control variable.

a) Vary the control variable from 1 to 100 in increments of 1.

```
for ( int i = 1; i <= 100; i++ )
```

b) Vary the control variable from 100 to 1 in decrements of 1.

```
for ( int i = 100; i >= 1; i-- )
```

c) Vary the control variable from 7 to 77 in increments of 7.

```
for ( int i = 7; i <= 77; i += 7 )
```

d) Vary the control variable from 20 to 2 in decrements of 2.

```
for ( int i = 20; i >= 2; i -= 2 )
```

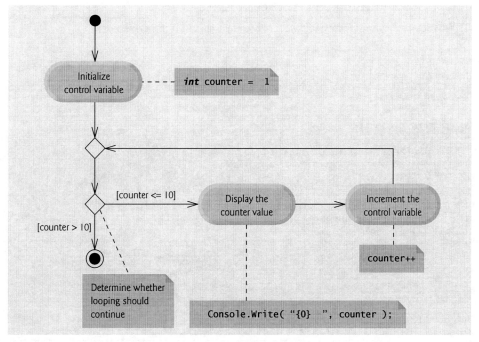

Fig. 4.4 | UML activity diagram for the for statement in Fig. 4.2.

e) Vary the control variable over the following sequence of values: 2, 5, 8, 11, 14, 17, 20.

```
for ( int i = 2; i <= 20; i += 3 )
```

f) Vary the control variable over the following sequence of values: 99, 88, 77, 66, 55, 44, 33, 22, 11, 0.

```
for ( int i = 99; i >= 0; i -= 11 )
```

Common Programming Error 4.6

Not using the proper relational operator in the loop-continuation condition of a loop that counts downward (e.g., using i <= 1 instead of i >= 1 in a loop counting down to 1) is a logic error.

Application: Summing the Even Integers from 2 to 20

We now consider two sample applications that demonstrate simple uses of for. The application in Fig. 4.5 uses a for statement to sum the even integers from 2 to 20 and store the result in an int variable called total.

The *initialization* and *increment* expressions can be comma-separated lists of expressions that enable you to use multiple initialization expressions or multiple increment expressions. For example, the body of the for statement in lines 12–13 of Fig. 4.5 could be merged into the increment portion of the for header by using a comma as follows:

```
for ( int number = 2; number <= 20; total += number, number += 2 )
    ; // empty statement
```

Good Programming Practice 4.4

Limit the size of control statement headers to a single line if possible.

```
1   // Fig. 4.5: Sum.cs
2   // Summing integers with the for statement.
3   using System;
4
5   public class Sum
6   {
7      public static void Main( string[] args )
8      {
9         int total = 0; // initialize total
10
11         // total even integers from 2 through 20
12         for ( int number = 2; number <= 20; number += 2 )
13            total += number;
14
15         Console.WriteLine( "Sum is {0}", total ); // display results
16      } // end Main
17   } // end class Sum
```

```
Sum is 110
```

Fig. 4.5 | Summing integers with the for statement.

Good Programming Practice 4.5

Place only expressions involving the control variables in the initialization and increment sections of a for statement. Manipulations of other variables should appear either before the loop (if they execute only once, like initialization statements) or in the body of the loop (if they execute once per iteration of the loop, like increment or decrement statements).

Application: Compound Interest Calculations

The next application uses the for statement to compute compound interest. Consider the following problem:

> *A person invests $1,000 in a savings account yielding 5% interest, compounded yearly. Assuming that all the interest is left on deposit, calculate and print the amount of money in the account at the end of each year for 10 years. Use the following formula to determine the amounts:*
>
> $$a = p\,(1 + r)^n$$
>
> *where*
>
> > *p* is the original amount invested (i.e., the principal)
> > *r* is the annual interest rate (e.g., use 0.05 for 5%)
> > *n* is the number of years
> > *a* is the amount on deposit at the end of the *n*th year.

This problem involves a loop that performs the indicated calculation for each of the 10 years the money remains on deposit. The solution is the application shown in Fig. 4.6. Lines 9–11 in method Main declare decimal variables amount and principal, and double variable rate. Lines 10–11 also initialize principal to 1000 (i.e., $1000.00) and rate to 0.05. C# treats real number constants like 0.05 as type double. Similarly, C# treats whole number constants like 7 and 1000 as type int. When principal is initialized to 1000, the value 1000 of type int is promoted to a decimal type implicitly—no cast is required.

Line 14 outputs the headers for the application's two columns of output. The first column displays the year, and the second column displays the amount on deposit at the end of that year. Note that we use the format item {1,20} to output the string "Amount on deposit". The integer 20 after the comma indicates that the value output should be displayed with a *field width* of 20—that is, WriteLine displays the value with at least 20 character positions. If the value to be output is less than 20 character positions wide (17 characters in this example), the value is *right justified* in the field by default (in this case the value is preceded by three blanks). If the year value to be output were more than four character positions wide, the field width would be extended to the right to accommodate the entire value—this would push the amount field to the right, upsetting the neat columns of our tabular output. To indicate that output should be *left justified*, simply use a negative field width.

The for statement (lines 17–25) executes its body 10 times, varying control variable year from 1 to 10 in increments of 1. This loop terminates when control variable year becomes 11. (Note that year represents *n* in the problem statement.)

Classes provide methods that perform common tasks on objects. In fact, most methods must be called on a specific object. For example, to output a greeting in Fig. 2.2, we called method DisplayMessage on the myGradeBook object. Many classes also provide methods that perform common tasks and do not need to be called on objects. Such methods are called ***static* methods**. For example, C# does not include an exponentiation operator, so

```
1   // Fig. 4.6: Interest.cs
2   // Compound-interest calculations with for.
3   using System;
4
5   public class Interest
6   {
7      public static void Main( string[] args )
8      {
9         decimal amount; // amount on deposit at end of each year
10        decimal principal = 1000; // initial amount before interest
11        double rate = 0.05; // interest rate
12
13        // display headers
14        Console.WriteLine( "{0}{1,20}", "Year", "Amount on deposit" );
15
16        // calculate amount on deposit for each of ten years
17        for ( int year = 1; year <= 10; year++ )
18        {
19           // calculate new amount for specified year
20           amount = principal *
21              ( ( decimal ) Math.Pow( 1.0 + rate, year ) );
22
23           // display the year and the amount
24           Console.WriteLine( "{0,4}{1,20:C}", year, amount );
25        } // end for
26     } // end Main
27  } // end class Interest
```

```
Year    Amount on deposit
   1           $1,050.00
   2           $1,102.50
   3           $1,157.63
   4           $1,215.51
   5           $1,276.28
   6           $1,340.10
   7           $1,407.10
   8           $1,477.46
   9           $1,551.33
  10           $1,628.89
```

Fig. 4.6 | Compound-interest calculations with for.

the designers of C#'s Math class defined static method Pow for raising a value to a power. You can call a static method by specifying the class name followed by the dot (.) operator and the method name, as in

ClassName.methodName(arguments)

Note that Console methods Write and WriteLine are static methods. In Chapter 5, you will learn how to implement static methods in your own classes.

We use static method Pow of class Math to perform the compound interest calculation in Fig. 4.6. Math.Pow(x, y) calculates the value of x raised to the yth power. The method receives two double arguments and returns a double value. Lines 20–21 perform the calculation $a = p(1 + r)^n$, where a is the amount, p is the principal, r is the rate and n is the year. Notice that in this calculation, we need to multiply a decimal value (principal) by a double value (the return value of Math.Pow). C# will not implicitly convert double to a decimal type, or vice versa, because of the possible loss of information in either conversion, so line 21 contains a (decimal) cast operator that explicitly converts the double return value of Math.Pow to a decimal.

After each calculation, line 24 outputs the year and the amount on deposit at the end of that year. The year is output in a field width of four characters (as specified by {0,4}). The amount is output as a currency value with the format item {1,20:C}. The number 20 in the format item indicates that the value should be output right justified with a field width of 20 characters. The format specifier C specifies that the number should be formatted as currency.

Notice that we declared the variables amount and principal to be of type decimal rather than double. Recall that we introduced type decimal for monetary calculations in Section 2.10. We also use decimal in Fig. 4.6 for this purpose. You may be curious as to why we do this. We are dealing with fractional parts of dollars and thus need a type that allows decimal points in its values. Unfortunately, floating-point numbers of type double (or float) can cause trouble in monetary calculations. Two double dollar amounts stored in the machine could be 14.234 (which would normally be rounded to 14.23 for display purposes) and 18.673 (which would normally be rounded to 18.67 for display purposes). When these amounts are added, they produce the internal sum 32.907, which would normally be rounded to 32.91 for display purposes. Thus, your output could appear as

```
   14.23
+ 18.67
 -------
   32.91
```

but a person adding the individual numbers as displayed would expect the sum to be 32.90. You have been warned!

Good Programming Practice 4.6

Do not use variables of type double (or float) to perform precise monetary calculations; use type decimal instead. The imprecision of floating-point numbers can cause errors that will result in incorrect monetary values.

Note that the body of the for statement contains the calculation 1.0 + rate, which appears as an argument to the Math.Pow method. In fact, this calculation produces the same result each time through the loop, so repeating the calculation in every iteration of the loop is wasteful.

Performance Tip 4.2

In loops, avoid calculations for which the result never changes—such calculations should typically be placed before the loop. [Note: Optimizing compilers will typically place such calculations outside loops in the compiled code.]

4.5 do...while Repetition Statement

The **do...while** *repetition statement* is similar to the while statement. In the while, the application tests the loop-continuation condition at the beginning of the loop, before executing the loop's body. If the condition is false, the body never executes. The do...while statement tests the loop-continuation condition *after* executing the loop's body; therefore, the body always executes at least once. When a do...while statement terminates, execution continues with the next statement in sequence. Figure 4.7 uses a do...while (lines 11–15) to output the numbers 1–10.

Line 9 declares and initializes control variable counter. Upon entering the do...while statement, line 13 outputs counter's value, and line 14 increments counter. Then the application evaluates the loop-continuation test at the bottom of the loop (line 15). If the condition is true, the loop continues from the first body statement in the do...while (line 13). If the condition is false, the loop terminates, and the application continues with the next statement after the loop.

Figure 4.8 contains the UML activity diagram for the do...while statement. This diagram makes it clear that the loop-continuation condition is not evaluated until after the loop performs the action state at least once. Compare this activity diagram with that of the while statement (Fig. 3.4). It is not necessary to use braces in the do...while repetition statement if there is only one statement in the body. However, most programmers include the braces, to avoid confusion between the while and do...while statements. For example,

> **while** (*condition*)

is normally the first line of a while statement. A do...while statement with no braces around a single-statement body appears as:

```
1   // Fig. 4.7: DoWhileTest.cs
2   // do...while repetition statement.
3   using System;
4
5   public class DoWhileTest
6   {
7      public static void Main( string[] args )
8      {
9         int counter = 1; // initialize counter
10
11         do
12         {
13            Console.Write( "{0}  ", counter );
14            counter++;
15         } while ( counter <= 10 ); // end do...while
16
17         Console.WriteLine(); // outputs a newline
18      } // end Main
19   } // end class DoWhileTest
```

```
1 2 3 4 5 6 7 8 9 10
```

Fig. 4.7 | do...while repetition statement.

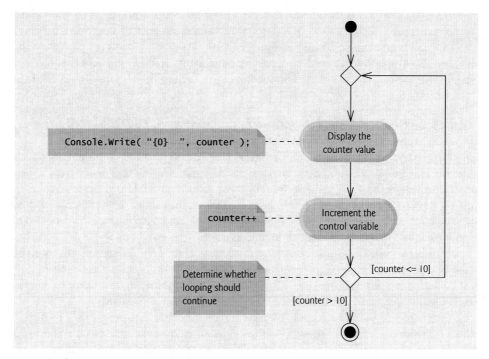

Fig. 4.8 | do...while repetition statement UML activity diagram.

```
do
    statement
while ( condition );
```

which can be confusing. A reader may misinterpret the last line—while(*condition*);— as a while statement containing an empty statement (the semicolon by itself). Thus, a do...while statement with one body statement is usually written as follows:

```
do
{
    statement
} while ( condition );
```

Error-Prevention Tip 4.4

Always include braces in a do...while statement, even if they are not necessary. This helps eliminate ambiguity between while statements and do...while statements containing only one statement.

4.6 switch Multiple-Selection Statement

We discussed the if single-selection statement and the if...else double-selection statement in Chapter 3. C# provides the ***switch multiple-selection*** statement to perform different actions based on the possible values of an expression. Each action is associated with the value of a *constant integral expression* or a *constant string expression* that the variable or expression on which the switch is based may assume. A constant integral expression is any expression involving character and integer constants that evaluates to an integer value (i.e., values of type sbyte, byte, short, ushort, int, uint, long, ulong, and char). A constant string expression is any expression composed of string literals that always results in the same string.

GradeBook Class with switch Statement to Count A, B, C, D and F Grades.
Figure 4.9 contains an enhanced version of the GradeBook class introduced in Chapter 2 and further developed in Chapter 3. The version of the class we now present not only calculates the average of a set of numeric grades entered by the user, but uses a switch statement to determine whether each grade is the equivalent of an A, B, C, D or F and to increment the appropriate grade counter. The class also displays a summary of the number of students who received each grade. Figure 4.10 shows sample input and output of the GradeBookTest application that uses class GradeBook to process a set of grades.

Like earlier versions of the class, class GradeBook (Fig. 4.9) declares instance variable courseName (line 7), property CourseName (lines 24–34) to access courseName and method DisplayMessage (lines 37–42) to display a welcome message to the user. The class also contains a constructor (lines 18–21) that initializes the course name.

Class GradeBook also declares instance variables total (line 8) and gradeCounter (line 9), which keep track of the sum of the grades entered by the user and the number of grades entered, respectively. Lines 10–14 declare counter variables for each grade category. Class GradeBook maintains total, gradeCounter and the five letter-grade counters as

```
1   // Fig. 4.9: GradeBook.cs
2   // GradeBook class uses switch statement to count A, B, C, D and F grades.
3   using System;
4
5   public class GradeBook
6   {
7       private string courseName; // name of course this GradeBook represents
8       private int total; // sum of grades
9       private int gradeCounter; // number of grades entered
10      private int aCount; // count of A grades
11      private int bCount; // count of B grades
12      private int cCount; // count of C grades
13      private int dCount; // count of D grades
14      private int fCount; // count of F grades
15
16      // constructor initializes courseName;
17      // int instance variables are initialized to 0 by default
18      public GradeBook( string name )
19      {
20          CourseName = name; // initializes courseName
21      } // end constructor
22
```

Fig. 4.9 | GradeBook class that uses a switch statement to count A, B, C, D and F grades. (Part 1 of 3.)

```
23      // property that gets and sets the course name
24      public string CourseName
25      {
26         get
27         {
28            return courseName;
29         } // end get
30         set
31         {
32            courseName = value;
33         } // end set
34      } // end property CourseName
35
36      // display a welcome message to the GradeBook user
37      public void DisplayMessage()
38      {
39         // CourseName gets the name of the course
40         Console.WriteLine( "Welcome to the grade book for\n{0}!\n",
41            CourseName );
42      } // end method DisplayMessage
43
44      // input arbitrary number of grades from user
45      public void InputGrades()
46      {
47         int grade; // grade entered by user
48         string input; // text entered by the user
49
50         Console.WriteLine( "{0}\n{1}",
51            "Enter the integer grades in the range 0-100.",
52            "Type <Ctrl> z and press Enter to terminate input:" );
53
54         input = Console.ReadLine(); // read user input
55
56         // loop until user enters the end-of-file indicator (<Ctrl> z)
57         while ( input != null )
58         {
59            grade = Convert.ToInt32( input ); // read grade off user input
60            total += grade; // add grade to total
61            gradeCounter++; // increment number of grades
62
63            // call method to increment appropriate counter
64            IncrementLetterGradeCounter( grade );
65
66            input = Console.ReadLine(); // read user input
67         } // end while
68      } // end method InputGrades
69
70      // add 1 to appropriate counter for specified grade
71      private void IncrementLetterGradeCounter( int grade )
72      {
```

Fig. 4.9 | GradeBook class that uses a switch statement to count A, B, C, D and F grades. (Part 2 of 3.)

```
73          // determine which grade was entered
74          switch ( grade / 10 )
75          {
76             case 9: // grade was in the 90s
77             case 10: // grade was 100
78                aCount++; // increment aCount
79                break; // necessary to exit switch
80             case 8: // grade was between 80 and 89
81                bCount++; // increment bCount
82                break; // exit switch
83             case 7: // grade was between 70 and 79
84                cCount++; // increment cCount
85                break; // exit switch
86             case 6: // grade was between 60 and 69
87                dCount++; // increment dCount
88                break; // exit switch
89             default: // grade was less than 60
90                fCount++; // increment fCount
91                break; // exit switch
92          } // end switch
93       } // end method IncrementLetterGradeCounter
94
95       // display a report based on the grades entered by the user
96       public void DisplayGradeReport()
97       {
98          Console.WriteLine( "\nGrade Report:" );
99
100         // if user entered at least one grade...
101         if ( gradeCounter != 0 )
102         {
103            // calculate average of all grades entered
104            double average = ( double ) total / gradeCounter;
105
106            // output summary of results
107            Console.WriteLine( "Total of the {0} grades entered is {1}",
108               gradeCounter, total );
109            Console.WriteLine( "Class average is {0:F2}", average );
110            Console.WriteLine( "{0}A: {1}\nB: {2}\nC: {3}\nD: {4}\nF: {5}",
111               "Number of students who received each grade:\n",
112               aCount, // display number of A grades
113               bCount, // display number of B grades
114               cCount, // display number of C grades
115               dCount, // display number of D grades
116               fCount ); // display number of F grades
117         } // end if
118         else // no grades were entered, so output appropriate message
119            Console.WriteLine( "No grades were entered" );
120      } // end method DisplayGradeReport
121   } // end class GradeBook
```

Fig. 4.9 | GradeBook class that uses a switch statement to count A, B, C, D and F grades. (Part 3 of 3.)

instance variables so that these variables can be used or modified in any of the class's methods. Note that the class's constructor (lines 18–21) sets only the course name—the remaining seven instance variables are ints and are initialized to 0 by default.

Class GradeBook contains three additional methods—InputGrades, IncrementLetterGradeCounter and DisplayGradeReport. Method InputGrades (lines 45–68) reads an arbitrary number of integer grades from the user using sentinel-controlled repetition and updates instance variables total and gradeCounter. Method InputGrades calls method IncrementLetterGradeCounter (lines 71–93) to update the appropriate letter-grade counter for each grade entered. Class GradeBook also contains method DisplayGradeReport (lines 96–120), which outputs a report containing the total of all grades entered, the average of the grades and the number of students who received each letter grade. Let's examine these methods in more detail.

Lines 47–48 in method InputGrades declare variables grade and input, which will store the user's input first as a string (in the variable input) then convert it to an int to store in the variable grade. Lines 50–52 prompt the user to enter integer grades and to type *<Ctrl> z* then press *Enter* to terminate the input. The notation *<Ctrl> z* means to simultaneously press both the *Ctrl* key and the *z* key when typing in a Command Prompt. *<Ctrl> z* is the Windows key sequence for typing the ***end-of-file indicator***. This is one way to inform an application that there is no more data to input. (The end-of-file indicator is a system-dependent keystroke combination. On many non-Windows systems, end-of-file is entered by typing *<Ctrl> d*.) [*Note:* Windows typically displays the characters ^Z in a Command Prompt when the end-of-file indicator is typed, as shown in the output of Fig. 4.10.]

Line 54 uses the ReadLine method to get the first line that the user entered and store it in variable input. The while statement (lines 57–67) processes this user input. The condition at line 57 checks if the value of input is a null reference. The Console class's ReadLine method will only return null if the user typed an end-of-file indicator. As long as the end-of-file indicator has not been typed, input will not contain a null reference, and the condition will pass.

Line 59 converts the string in input to an int type. Line 60 adds grade to total. Line 61 increments gradeCounter. The class's DisplayGradeReport method uses these variables to compute the average of the grades. Line 64 calls the class's IncrementLetterGradeCounter method (declared in lines 71–93) to increment the appropriate letter-grade counter, based on the numeric grade entered.

Method IncrementLetterGradeCounter contains a switch statement (lines 74–92) that determines which counter to increment. In this example, we assume that the user enters a valid grade in the range 0–100. A grade in the range 90–100 represents A, 80–89 represents B, 70–79 represents C, 60–69 represents D and 0–59 represents F. The switch statement consists of a block that contains a sequence of **case** *labels* and an optional **default** *label*. These are used in this example to determine which counter to increment based on the grade.

When the flow of control reaches the switch, the application evaluates the expression in the parentheses (grade / 10) following keyword switch. This is called the ***switch expression***. The application compares the value of the switch expression with each case label. The switch expression in line 74 performs integer division, which truncates the fractional part of the result. Thus, when we divide any value in the range 0–100 by 10, the result is always a value from 0 to 10. We use several of these values in our case labels. For example, if the user enters the integer 85, the switch expression evaluates to int value 8. The switch compares 8 with each case. If a match occurs (case 8: at line 80), the application executes the statements for that case. For the integer 8, line 81 increments bCount, because a grade in the 80s is a B. The **break** *statement* (line 82) causes program control to proceed with the first statement after the switch—in this application, we reach the end of method IncrementLetterGradeCounter's body, so control returns to line 66 in method InputGrades (the first line after the call to IncrementLetterGradeCounter). This line uses the ReadLine method to read the next line entered by the user and assign it to the variable input. Line 67 marks the end of the body of the while loop that inputs grades (lines 57–67), so control flows to the while's condition (line 57) to determine whether the loop should continue executing based on the value just assigned to the variable input.

The cases in our switch explicitly test for the values 10, 9, 8, 7 and 6. Note the case labels at lines 76–77 that test for the values 9 and 10 (both of which represent the grade A). Listing case labels consecutively in this manner with no statements between them enables the cases to perform the same set of statements—when the switch expression evaluates to 9 or 10, the statements in lines 78–79 execute. The switch statement does not provide a mechanism for testing ranges of values, so every value to be tested must be listed in a separate case label. Note that each case can have multiple statements. The switch statement differs from other control statements in that it does not require braces around multiple statements in each case.

In C, C++, and many other programming languages that use the switch statement, the break statement is not required at the end of a case. Without break statements, each time a match occurs in the switch, the statements for that case and subsequent cases execute until a break statement or the end of the switch is encountered. This is often referred to as "falling through" to the statements in subsequent cases. This frequently leads to logic errors when you forget the break statement. For this reason, C# has a "no fall through" rule for cases in a switch—after the statements in a case execute, you are required to include a statement that terminates the case, such as a break, a return, or a throw. (We discuss the throw statement in Chapter 10.)

Common Programming Error 4.7

Forgetting a break statement when one is needed in a switch is a syntax error.

If no match occurs between the switch expression's value and a case label, the statements after the default label (lines 90–91) execute. We use the default label in this example to process all switch-expression values that are less than 6—that is, all failing grades. If no match occurs and the switch does not contain a default label, program control simply continues with the first statement after the switch statement.

GradeBookTest *Class That Demonstrates Class* GradeBook

Class GradeBookTest (Fig. 4.10) creates a GradeBook object (lines 10–11). Line 13 invokes the object's DisplayMessage method to output a welcome message to the user. Line 14 invokes the object's InputGrades method to read a set of grades from the user and keep track of the sum of all the grades entered and the number of grades. Recall that method InputGrades also calls method IncrementLetterGradeCounter to keep track of the number of students who received each letter grade. Line 15 invokes method Display-GradeReport of class GradeBook, which outputs a report based on the grades entered. Line 101 of class GradeBook (Fig. 4.9) determines whether the user entered at least one grade—this avoids dividing by zero. If so, line 104 calculates the average of the grades. Lines 107–116 then output the total of all the grades, the class average and the number of students who received each letter grade. If no grades were entered, line 119 outputs an appropriate message. The output in Fig. 4.10 shows a sample grade report based on 9 grades.

```
 1   // Fig. 4.10: GradeBookTest.cs
 2   // Create GradeBook object, input grades and display grade report.
 3
 4   public class GradeBookTest
 5   {
 6      public static void Main( string[] args )
 7      {
 8         // create GradeBook object myGradeBook and
 9         // pass course name to constructor
10         GradeBook myGradeBook = new GradeBook(
11            "CS101 Introduction to C# Programming" );
12
13         myGradeBook.DisplayMessage(); // display welcome message
14         myGradeBook.InputGrades(); // read grades from user
15         myGradeBook.DisplayGradeReport(); // display report based on grades
16      } // end Main
17   } // end class GradeBookTest
```

```
Welcome to the grade book for
CS101 Introduction to C# Programming!

Enter the integer grades in the range 0-100.
Type <Ctrl> z and press Enter to terminate input:
99
92
45
100
57
63
76
14
92
^Z

Grade Report:
Total of the 9 grades entered is 638
Class average is 70.89
Number of students who received each grade:
A: 4
B: 0
C: 1
D: 1
F: 3
```

Fig. 4.10 | Create GradeBook object, input grades and display grade report.

Note that class GradeBookTest (Fig. 4.10) does not directly call GradeBook method IncrementLetterGradeCounter (lines 71–93 of Fig. 4.9). This method is used exclusively by method InputGrades of class GradeBook to update the appropriate letter-grade counter as each new grade is entered by the user. Method IncrementLetterGradeCounter exists solely to support the operations of class GradeBook's other methods and thus is declared private. Recall from Chapter 2 that methods declared with access modifier private can be called only by other methods of the class in which the private methods are declared. Such methods are commonly referred to as *utility methods* or *helper methods*, because they can be called only by other methods of that class and are used to support the operation of those methods.

switch Statement UML Activity Diagram

Figure 4.11 shows the UML activity diagram for the general switch statement. Every set of statements after a case label must end its execution in a break or return statement to terminate the switch statement after processing the case. Typically, you will use break statements. Figure 4.11 emphasizes this by including break statements in the activity diagram.

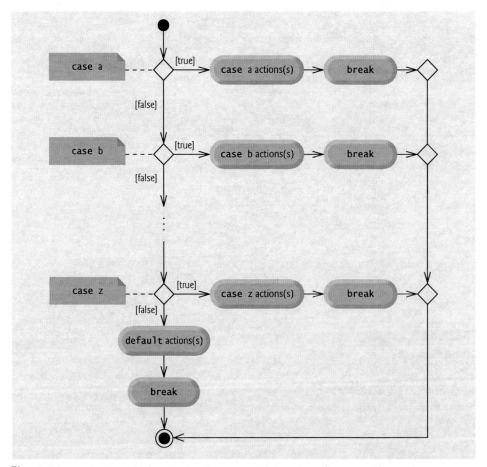

Fig. 4.11 | switch multiple-selection statement UML activity diagram with break statements.

The diagram makes it clear that the break statement at the end of a case causes control to exit the switch statement immediately.

Software Engineering Observation 4.2

Provide a default label in switch statements. Cases not explicitly tested in a switch that lacks a default label are ignored. Including a default label focuses you on the need to process exceptional conditions.

Good Programming Practice 4.7

Although each case and the default label in a switch can occur in any order, place the default label last for clarity.

When using the switch statement, remember that the expression after each case can be only a constant integral expression or a constant string expression—that is, any combination of constants that evaluates to a constant value of an integral or string type. An integer constant is simply an integer value (e.g., –7, 0 or 221). In addition, you can use *character constants*—specific characters in single quotes, such as 'A', '7' or '$'—which represent the integer values of characters. A string constant is a sequence of characters in double quotes, such as "Welcome to C# Programming!".

The expression in each case also can be a *constant*—a variable that contains a value which does not change for the entire application. Such a variable is declared with the keyword const (discussed in Chapter 5, Methods: A Deeper Look). C# also has a feature called enumerations, which we also present in Chapter 5. Enumeration constants can also be used in case labels. In Chapter 9, Polymorphism, Interfaces & Operator Overloading, we present a more elegant way to implement switch logic—we use a technique called polymorphism to create applications that are often clearer, easier to maintain and easier to extend than applications using switch logic.

4.7 break and continue Statements

In addition to selection and repetition statements, C# provides statements break and continue to alter the flow of control. The preceding section showed how break can be used to terminate a switch statement's execution. This section discusses how to use break to terminate any repetition statement.

break Statement

The break statement, when executed in a while, for, do...while, switch, or foreach, causes immediate exit from that statement. Execution continues with the first statement after the control statement. Common uses of the break statement are to escape early from a repetition statement or to skip the remainder of a switch (as in Fig. 4.9). Figure 4.12 demonstrates a break statement exiting a for.

When the if nested at line 13 in the for statement (lines 11–17) determines that count is 5, the break statement at line 14 executes. This terminates the for statement, and the application proceeds to line 19 (immediately after the for statement), which displays a message indicating the value of the control variable when the loop terminated. The loop fully executes its body only four times instead of 10 because of the break.

```
 1   // Fig. 4.12: BreakTest.cs
 2   // break statement exiting a for statement.
 3   using System;
 4
 5   public class BreakTest
 6   {
 7      public static void Main( string[] args )
 8      {
 9         int count; // control variable also used after loop terminates
10
11         for ( count = 1; count <= 10; count++ ) // loop 10 times
12         {
13            if ( count == 5 ) // if count is 5,
14               break; // terminate loop
15
16            Console.Write( "{0} ", count );
17         } // end for
18
19         Console.WriteLine( "\nBroke out of loop at count = {0}", count );
20      } // end Main
21   } // end class BreakTest
```

```
1 2 3 4
Broke out of loop at count = 5
```

Fig. 4.12 | break statement exiting a for statement.

continue Statement

The **continue statement**, when executed in a while, for, do...while, or foreach, skips the remaining statements in the loop body and proceeds with the next iteration of the loop. In while and do...while statements, the application evaluates the loop-continuation test immediately after the continue statement executes. In a for statement, the increment expression executes, then the application evaluates the loop-continuation test.

Figure 4.13 uses the continue statement in a for to skip the statement at line 14 when the nested if (line 11) determines that the value of count is 5. When the continue statement executes, program control continues with the increment of the control variable in the for statement (line 9).

In Section 4.3, we stated that the while statement can be used in most cases in place of for. The one exception occurs when the increment expression in the while follows a continue statement. In this case, the increment does not execute before the application evaluates the repetition-continuation condition, so the while does not execute in the same manner as the for.

Software Engineering Observation 4.3

Some programmers feel that break and continue statements violate structured programming. Since the same effects are achievable with structured programming techniques, these programmers prefer not to use break or continue statements.

```
 1   // Fig. 4.13: ContinueTest.cs
 2   // continue statement terminating an iteration of a for statement.
 3   using System;
 4
 5   public class ContinueTest
 6   {
 7      public static void Main( string[] args )
 8      {
 9         for ( int count = 1; count <= 10; count++ ) // loop 10 times
10         {
11            if ( count == 5 ) // if count is 5,
12               continue; // skip remaining code in loop
13
14            Console.Write( "{0} ", count );
15         } // end for
16
17         Console.WriteLine( "\nUsed continue to skip printing 5" );
18      } // end Main
19   } // end class ContinueTest
```

```
1 2 3 4 6 7 8 9 10
Used continue to skip printing 5
```

Fig. 4.13 | continue statement terminating an iteration of a for statement.

Software Engineering Observation 4.4

There is a tension between achieving quality software engineering and achieving the best-performing software. Often, one of these goals is achieved at the expense of the other. For all but the most performance-intensive situations, apply the following rule of thumb: First, make your code simple and correct; then make it fast and small, but only if necessary.

4.8 Logical Operators

The if, if...else, while, do...while and for statements each require a condition to determine how to continue an application's flow of control. So far, we have studied only *simple conditions*, such as count <= 10, number != sentinelValue and total > 1000. Simple conditions are expressed in terms of the relational operators >, <, >= and <=, and the equality operators == and !=. Each expression tests only one condition. To test multiple conditions in the process of making a decision, we performed these tests in separate statements or in nested if or if...else statements. Sometimes, control statements require more complex conditions to determine an application's flow of control.

C# provides *logical operators* to enable you to form more complex conditions by combining simple conditions. The logical operators are && (conditional AND), || (conditional OR), & (boolean logical AND), | (boolean logical inclusive OR), ∧ (boolean logical exclusive OR) and ! (logical negation).

Conditional AND (&&) Operator

Suppose that we wish to ensure at some point in an application that two conditions are *both* true before we choose a certain path of execution. In this case, we can use the && (*conditional AND*) operator, as follows:

```
if ( gender == FEMALE && age >= 65 )
    seniorFemales++;
```

This if statement contains two simple conditions. The condition gender == FEMALE compares variable gender to constant FEMALE. This might be evaluated, for example, to determine whether a person is female. The condition age >= 65 might be evaluated to determine whether a person is a senior citizen. The if statement considers the combined condition

```
gender == FEMALE && age >= 65
```

which is true if and only if *both* simple conditions are true. If the combined condition is true, the if statement's body increments seniorFemales by 1. If either or both of the simple conditions are false, the application skips the increment. Some programmers find that the preceding combined condition is more readable when redundant parentheses are added, as in:

```
( gender == FEMALE ) && ( age >= 65 )
```

The table in Fig. 4.14 summarizes the && operator. The table shows all four possible combinations of false and true values for *expression1* and *expression2*. Such tables are called **truth tables**. C# evaluates all expressions that include relational operators, equality operators or logical operators to bool values—which are either true or false.

Conditional OR (||) Operator
Now suppose that we wish to ensure that *either or both* of two conditions are true before we choose a certain path of execution. In this case, we use the || (*conditional OR*) operator, as in the following application segment:

```
if ( ( semesterAverage >= 90 ) || ( finalExam >= 90 ) )
    Console.WriteLine ( "Student grade is A" );
```

This statement also contains two simple conditions. The condition semesterAverage >= 90 is evaluated to determine whether the student deserves an A in the course because of a solid performance throughout the semester. The condition finalExam >= 90 is evaluated to determine whether the student deserves an A in the course because of an outstanding performance on the final exam. The if statement then considers the combined condition

```
( semesterAverage >= 90 ) || ( finalExam >= 90 )
```

and awards the student an A if either or both of the simple conditions are true. The only time the message "Student grade is A" is *not* printed is when both of the simple conditions

expression1	expression2	expression1 && expression2
false	false	false
false	true	false
true	false	false
true	true	true

Fig. 4.14 | && (conditional AND) operator truth table.

are false. Figure 4.15 is a truth table for operator conditional OR (| |). Operator && has a higher precedence than operator | |. Both operators associate from left to right.

Short-Circuit Evaluation of Complex Conditions

The parts of an expression containing && or | | operators are evaluated only until it is known whether the condition is true or false. Thus, evaluation of the expression

```
( gender == FEMALE ) && ( age >= 65 )
```

stops immediately if gender is not equal to FEMALE (i.e., at that point, it is certain that the entire expression is false) and continues if gender *is* equal to FEMALE (i.e., the entire expression could still be true if the condition age >= 65 is true). This feature of conditional AND and conditional OR expressions is called *short-circuit evaluation.*

 Common Programming Error 4.8

In expressions using operator &&, a condition—which we refer to as the dependent condition—may require another condition to be true for the evaluation of the dependent condition to be meaningful. In this case, the dependent condition should be placed after the other condition, or an error might occur. For example, in the expression (i != 0) && (10 / i == 2), the second condition must appear after the first condition, or a divide-by-zero error might occur.

Boolean Logical AND (&) and Boolean Logical OR (|) Operators

The *boolean logical AND* (**&**) and *boolean logical inclusive OR* (**|**) operators work identically to the && (conditional AND) and | | (conditional OR) operators, with one exception—the boolean logical operators always evaluate both of their operands (i.e., they do not perform short-circuit evaluation). Therefore, the expression

```
( gender == 1 ) & ( age >= 65 )
```

evaluates age >= 65 regardless of whether gender is equal to 1. This is useful if the right operand of the boolean logical AND or boolean logical inclusive OR operator has a required *side effect*—a modification of a variable's value. For example, the expression

```
( birthday == true ) | ( ++age >= 65 )
```

guarantees that the condition ++age >= 65 will be evaluated. Thus, the variable age is incremented in the preceding expression, regardless of whether the overall expression is true or false.

expression1	expression2	expression1 | | expression2
false	false	false
false	true	true
true	false	true
true	true	true

Fig. 4.15 | | | (conditional OR) operator truth table.

Error-Prevention Tip 4.5

For clarity, avoid expressions with side effects in conditions. The side effects may look clever, but they can make it harder to understand code and can lead to subtle logic errors.

Boolean Logical Exclusive OR (∧)

A complex condition containing the ***boolean logical exclusive OR*** (∧) operator (also called the ***logical XOR operator***) is `true` *if and only if one of its operands is `true` and the other is `false`.* If both operands are `true` or both are `false`, the entire condition is `false`. Figure 4.16 is a truth table for the boolean logical exclusive OR operator (∧). This operator is also guaranteed to evaluate both of its operands.

Logical Negation (!) Operator

The `!` (*logical negation*) operator enables you to "reverse" the meaning of a condition. Unlike the logical operators `&&`, `||`, `&`, `|` and ∧, which are binary operators that combine two conditions, the logical negation operator is a unary operator that has only a single condition as an operand. The logical negation operator is placed before a condition to choose a path of execution if the original condition (without the logical negation operator) is `false`, as in the code segment

```
if ( ! ( grade == sentinelValue ) )
    Console.WriteLine( "The next grade is {0}", grade );
```

which executes the `WriteLine` call only if `grade` is not equal to `sentinelValue`. The parentheses around the condition `grade == sentinelValue` are needed because the logical negation operator has a higher precedence than the equality operator.

In most cases, you can avoid using logical negation by expressing the condition differently with an appropriate relational or equality operator. For example, the previous statement may also be written as follows:

```
if ( grade != sentinelValue )
    Console.WriteLine( "The next grade is {0}", grade );
```

This flexibility can help you express a condition in a more convenient manner. Figure 4.17 is a truth table for the logical negation operator.

Logical Operators Example

Figure 4.18 demonstrates the logical operators and boolean logical operators by producing their truth tables. The output shows the expression that was evaluated and the `bool` result

expression1	expression2	expression1 ∧ expression2
false	false	false
false	true	true
true	false	true
true	true	false

Fig. 4.16 | ∧ (boolean logical exclusive OR) operator truth table.

expression	!expression
false	true
true	false

Fig. 4.17 | ! (logical negation) operator truth table.

```
1   // Fig. 4.18: LogicalOperators.cs
2   // Logical operators.
3   using System;
4
5   public class LogicalOperators
6   {
7      public static void Main( string[] args )
8      {
9         // create truth table for && (conditional AND) operator
10        Console.WriteLine( "{0}\n{1}: {2}\n{3}: {4}\n{5}: {6}\n{7}: {8}\n",
11           "Conditional AND (&&)", "false && false", ( false && false ),
12           "false && true", ( false && true ),
13           "true && false", ( true && false ),
14           "true && true", ( true && true ) );
15
16        // create truth table for || (conditional OR) operator
17        Console.WriteLine( "{0}\n{1}: {2}\n{3}: {4}\n{5}: {6}\n{7}: {8}\n",
18           "Conditional OR (||)", "false || false", ( false || false ),
19           "false || true", ( false || true ),
20           "true || false", ( true || false ),
21           "true || true", ( true || true ) );
22
23        // create truth table for & (boolean logical AND) operator
24        Console.WriteLine( "{0}\n{1}: {2}\n{3}: {4}\n{5}: {6}\n{7}: {8}\n",
25           "Boolean logical AND (&)", "false & false", ( false & false ),
26           "false & true", ( false & true ),
27           "true & false", ( true & false ),
28           "true & true", ( true & true ) );
29
30        // create truth table for | (boolean logical inclusive OR) operator
31        Console.WriteLine( "{0}\n{1}: {2}\n{3}: {4}\n{5}: {6}\n{7}: {8}\n",
32           "Boolean logical inclusive OR (|)",
33           "false | false", ( false | false ),
34           "false | true", ( false | true ),
35           "true | false", ( true | false ),
36           "true | true", ( true | true ) );
37
38        // create truth table for ^ (boolean logical exclusive OR) operator
39        Console.WriteLine( "{0}\n{1}: {2}\n{3}: {4}\n{5}: {6}\n{7}: {8}\n",
40           "Boolean logical exclusive OR (^)",
41           "false ^ false", ( false ^ false ),
42           "false ^ true", ( false ^ true ),
43           "true ^ false", ( true ^ false ),
44           "true ^ true", ( true ^ true ) );
```

Fig. 4.18 | Logical operators. (Part 1 of 2.)

```
45
46          // create truth table for ! (logical negation) operator
47          Console.WriteLine( "{0}\n{1}: {2}\n{3}: {4}",
48            "Logical negation (!)", "!false", ( !false ),
49            "!true", ( !true ) );
50       } // end Main
51    } // end class LogicalOperators
```

```
Conditional AND (&&)
false && false: False
false && true: False
true && false: False
true && true: True

Conditional OR (||)
false || false: False
false || true: True
true || false: True
true || true: True

Boolean logical AND (&)
false & false: False
false & true: False
true & false: False
true & true: True

Boolean logical inclusive OR (|)
false | false: False
false | true: True
true | false: True
true | true: True

Boolean logical exclusive OR (^)
false ^ false: False
false ^ true: True
true ^ false: True
true ^ true: False

Logical negation (!)
!false: True
!true: False
```

Fig. 4.18 | Logical operators. (Part 2 of 2.)

of that expression. Lines 10–14 produce the truth table for && (conditional AND). Lines 17–21 produce the truth table for || (conditional OR). Lines 24–28 produce the truth table for & (boolean logical AND). Lines 31–36 produce the truth table for | (boolean logical inclusive OR). Lines 39–44 produce the truth table for ^ (boolean logical exclusive OR). Lines 47–49 produce the truth table for ! (logical negation).

Figure 4.19 shows the precedence and associativity of the C# operators introduced so far. The operators are shown from top to bottom in decreasing order of precedence.

Operators						Associativity	Type
.	new	++ *(postfix)*	-- *(postfix)*			left to right	highest precedence
++	--	+	-	!	*(type)*	right to left	unary prefix
*	/	%				left to right	multiplicative
+	-					left to right	additive
<	<=	>	>=			left to right	relational
==	!=					left to right	equality
&						left to right	boolean logical AND
^						left to right	boolean logical exclusive OR
							left to right	boolean logical inclusive OR
&&						left to right	conditional AND
||						left to right	conditional OR
?:						right to left	conditional
=	+=	-=	*=	/=	%=	right to left	assignment

Fig. 4.19 | Precedence/associativity of the operators discussed so far.

4.9 (Optional) Software Engineering Case Study: Identifying Objects' States and Activities in the ATM System

In Section 3.12, we identified many of the class attributes needed to implement the ATM system and added them to the class diagram in Fig. 3.16. In this section, we show how these attributes represent an object's state. We identify some key states that our objects may occupy and discuss how objects change state in response to various events occurring in the system. We also discuss the workflow, or *activities*, that various objects perform in the ATM system. We present the activities of BalanceInquiry and Withdrawal transaction objects in this section.

State Machine Diagrams

Each object in a system goes through a series of discrete states. An object's state at a given point in time is indicated by the values of the object's attributes at that time. *State machine diagrams* model key states of an object and show under what circumstances the object changes state. Unlike the class diagrams presented in earlier case study sections, which focused primarily on the *structure* of the system, state machine diagrams model some of the *behavior* of the system.

Figure 4.20 is a simple state machine diagram that models two of the states of an object of class ATM. The UML represents each state in a state machine diagram as a *rounded rectangle* with the name of the state placed inside it. A *solid circle* with an attached stick arrowhead designates the *initial state*. Recall that we modeled this state information as the bool attribute userAuthenticated in the class diagram of Fig. 3.16. This attribute is initialized to false, or the "User not authenticated" state, according to the state machine diagram.

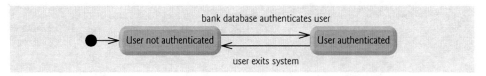

Fig. 4.20 | State machine diagram for some of the states of the ATM object.

The arrows with stick arrowheads indicate ***transitions*** between states. An object can transition from one state to another in response to various events that occur in the system. The name or description of the event that causes a transition is written near the line that corresponds to the transition. For example, the ATM object changes from the "User not authenticated" state to the "User authenticated" state after the bank database authenticates the user. Recall from the requirements document that the database authenticates a user by comparing the account number and PIN entered by the user with those of the corresponding account in the database. If the database indicates that the user has entered a valid account number and the correct PIN, the ATM object transitions to the "User authenticated" state and changes its userAuthenticated attribute to the value true. When the user exits the system by choosing the "exit" option from the main menu, the ATM object returns to the "User not authenticated" state in preparation for the next ATM user.

Software Engineering Observation 4.5

Software designers do not generally create state machine diagrams showing every possible state and state transition for all attributes—there are simply too many of them. State machine diagrams typically show only the most important or complex states and state transitions.

Activity Diagrams

Like a state machine diagram, an activity diagram models aspects of system behavior. Unlike a state machine diagram, an activity diagram models an object's workflow (sequence of events) during application execution. An activity diagram models the actions to perform and in what order the object will perform them. Recall that we used UML activity diagrams to illustrate the flow of control for the control statements presented in Chapter 3 and Chapter 4.

The activity diagram in Fig. 4.21 models the actions involved in executing a Balance-Inquiry transaction. We assume that a BalanceInquiry object has already been initialized and assigned a valid account number (that of the current user), so the object knows which balance to retrieve. The diagram includes the actions that occur after the user selects a balance inquiry from the main menu and before the ATM returns the user to the main menu—a BalanceInquiry object does not perform or initiate these actions, so we do not model them here. The diagram begins with the retrieval of the available balance of the user's account from the database. Next, the BalanceInquiry retrieves the total balance of the account. Finally, the transaction displays the balances on the screen.

The UML represents an action in an activity diagram as an action state, which is modeled by a rectangle with its left and right sides replaced by arcs curving outward. Each action state contains an action expression—for example, "get available balance of user's account from database"—that specifies an action to perform. An arrow with a stick arrowhead connects two action states, indicating the order in which the actions represented by the action states occur. The solid circle (at the top of Fig. 4.21) represents the activity's initial state—the beginning of the workflow before the object performs the modeled

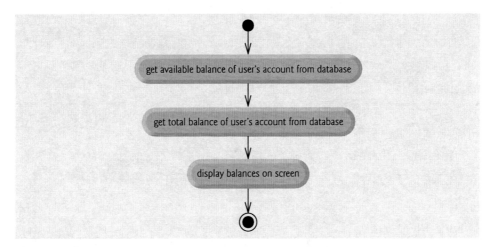

Fig. 4.21 | Activity diagram for a `BalanceInquiry` transaction.

actions. In this case, the transaction first executes the "get available balance of user's account from database" action expression. Second, the transaction retrieves the total balance. Finally, the transaction displays both balances on the screen. The solid circle enclosed in an open circle (at the bottom of Fig. 4.21) represents the final state—the end of the workflow after the object performs the modeled actions.

Figure 4.22 shows an activity diagram for a `Withdrawal` transaction. We assume that a `Withdrawal` object has been assigned a valid account number. We do not model the user selecting a withdrawal from the main menu or the ATM returning the user to the main menu, because these are not actions performed by a `Withdrawal` object. The transaction first displays a menu of standard withdrawal amounts (Fig. 1.30) and an option to cancel the transaction. The transaction then inputs a menu selection from the user. The activity flow now arrives at a decision symbol. This point determines the next action based on the associated guard conditions. If the user cancels the transaction, the system displays an appropriate message. Next, the cancellation flow reaches a merge symbol, where this activity flow joins the transaction's other possible activity flows (which we discuss shortly). Note that a merge can have any number of incoming transition arrows, but only one outgoing transition arrow. The decision at the bottom of the diagram determines whether the transaction should repeat from the beginning. When the user has canceled the transaction, the guard condition "cash dispensed or user canceled transaction" is true, so control transitions to the activity's final state.

If the user selects a withdrawal amount from the menu, amount (an attribute of class `Withdrawal` originally modeled in Fig. 3.16) is set to the value chosen by the user. The transaction next gets the available balance of the user's account (i.e., the availableBalance attribute of the user's `Account` object) from the database. The activity flow then arrives at another decision. If the requested withdrawal amount exceeds the user's available balance, the system displays an appropriate error message informing the user of the problem. Control then merges with the other activity flows before reaching the decision at the bottom of the diagram. The guard condition "cash not dispensed and user did not cancel" is true, so the activity flow returns to the top of the diagram, and the transaction prompts the user to input a new amount.

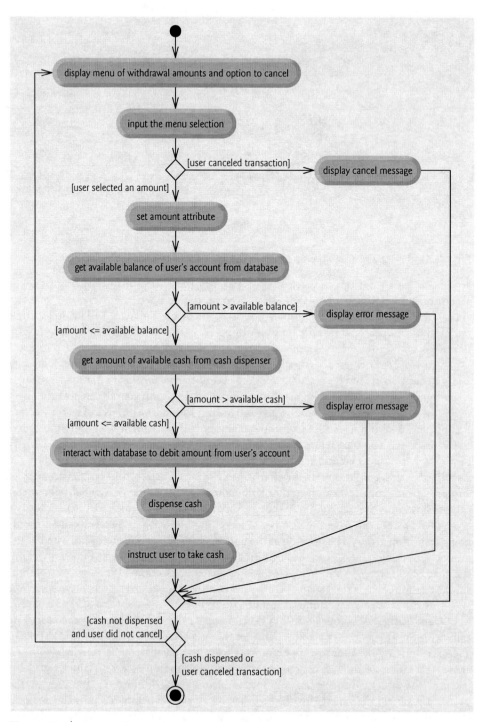

Fig. 4.22 | Activity diagram for a Withdrawal transaction.

If the requested withdrawal amount is less than or equal to the user's available balance, the transaction tests whether the cash dispenser has enough cash to satisfy the withdrawal request. If it does not, the transaction displays an appropriate error message and passes through the merge before reaching the final decision. Cash was not dispensed, so the activity flow returns to the beginning of the activity diagram, and the transaction prompts the user to choose a new amount. If sufficient cash is available, the transaction interacts with the database to debit the withdrawal amount from the user's account (i.e., subtract the amount from *both* the availableBalance and totalBalance attributes of the user's Account object). The transaction then dispenses the desired amount of cash and instructs the user to take the cash.

The main flow of activity next merges with the two error flows and the cancellation flow. In this case, cash was dispensed, so the activity flow reaches the final state.

We have taken the first steps in modeling the behavior of the ATM system and have shown how an object's attributes affect the object's activities. In Section 5.15, we investigate the operations of our classes to create a more complete model of the system's behavior.

Software Engineering Case Study Self-Review Exercises

4.1 State whether the following statement is *true* or *false*, and if *false*, explain why: State machine diagrams model structural aspects of a system.

4.2 An activity diagram models the _____ that an object performs and the order in which it performs them.
- a) actions
- b) attributes
- c) states
- d) state transitions

4.3 Based on the requirements document, create an activity diagram for a deposit transaction.

Answers to Software Engineering Case Study Self-Review Exercises

4.1 False. State machine diagrams model some of the behaviors of a system.

4.2 a.

4.3 Figure 4.23 presents an activity diagram for a deposit transaction. The diagram models the actions that occur after the user chooses the deposit option from the main menu and before the ATM returns the user to the main menu. Recall that part of receiving a deposit amount from the user involves converting an integer number of cents to a dollar amount. Also recall that crediting a deposit amount to an account involves increasing only the totalBalance attribute of the user's Account object. The bank updates the availableBalance attribute of the user's Account object only after confirming the amount of cash in the deposit envelope and after the enclosed checks clear—this occurs independently of the ATM system.

4.10 Wrap-Up

Chapter 3 discussed the if, if...else and while control statements. In this chapter, we discussed the for, do...while and switch control statements. (We will discuss the foreach statement in Chapter 6). You learned that any algorithm can be developed using combinations of sequence (i.e., statements listed in the order in which they should execute), the three selection statements—if, if...else and switch—and the four repetition statements—while,

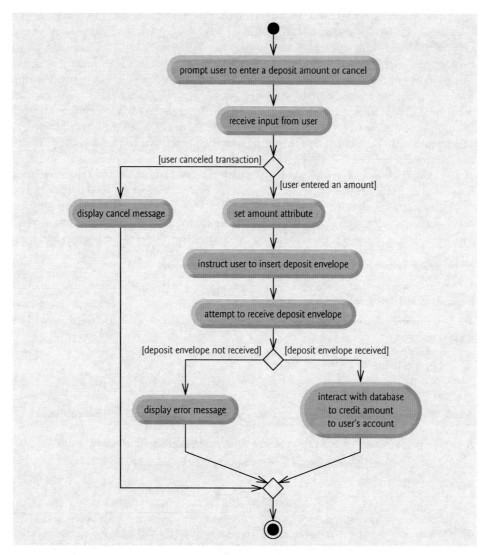

Fig. 4.23 | Activity diagram for a `Deposit` transaction.

do...while, for and foreach. You saw that the for and do...while statements are simply more convenient ways to express certain types of repetition. Similarly, we showed that the switch statement is a convenient notation for multiple selection, rather than using nested if...else statements. We discussed how you can combine various control statements by stacking and nesting them. We showed how to use the break and continue statements to alter the flow of control in repetition statements. You also learned about the logical operators, which enable you to use more complex conditional expressions in control statements.

In Chapter 2, we introduced the basic concepts of objects, classes and methods. Chapters 3 and 4 provided a thorough introduction to the control statements that you use to specify application logic in methods. In Chapter 5, we examine methods in greater depth.

5

Methods:
A Deeper Look

Form ever follows function.
—Louis Henri Sullivan

E pluribus unum.
(One composed of many.)
—Virgil

O! call back yesterday, bid
time return.
—William Shakespeare

Call me Ishmael.
—Herman Melville

When you call me that,
smile!
—Owen Wister

Answer me in one word.
—William Shakespeare

There is a point at which
methods devour themselves.
—Frantz Fanon

Life can only be understood
backwards; but it must be
lived forwards.
—Soren Kierkegaard

OBJECTIVES

In this chapter you will learn:

- How static methods and variables are associated with an entire class rather than specific instances of the class.

- How the method call/return mechanism is supported by the method call stack and activation records.

- How to use random-number generation to implement game-playing applications.

- To understand how the visibility of declarations is limited to specific regions of applications.

- What method overloading is and how to create overloaded methods.

- What recursive methods are.

- The differences between passing method arguments by value and by reference.

5.1 Introduction

We introduced methods in Chapter 2. In this chapter, we study methods in more depth. We emphasize how to declare and use methods to facilitate the design, implementation, operation and maintenance of large applications.

You will see that it is possible for certain methods, called static methods, to be called without the need for an object of the class to exist. You will learn how to declare a method with more than one parameter. You will also learn how C# is able to keep track of which method is currently executing, how value-type and reference-type arguments are passed to methods, how local variables of methods are maintained in memory and how a method knows where to return after it completes execution.

We discuss *simulation* techniques with random-number generation and develop a version of the casino dice game called craps that uses most of the programming techniques you have learned to this point in the book. In addition, you will learn to declare values that cannot change (i.e., constants). You will also learn to write methods that call themselves—this is called *recursion*.

Many of the classes you will use or create while developing applications will have more than one method of the same name. This technique, called *method overloading*, is used to implement methods that perform similar tasks but with different types or different numbers of arguments.

5.2 Packaging Code in C#

Three common ways of packaging code are methods, classes and namespaces. C# applications are written by combining new methods and classes that you write with predefined methods and classes available in the *.NET Framework Class Library* (also referred to as the *FCL*) and in various other class libraries. Related classes are often grouped into namespaces and compiled into class libraries so that they can be reused in other applications. You will learn how to create your own namespaces and class libraries in Chapter 7. The FCL provides many predefined classes that contain methods for performing common mathematical calculations, string manipulations, character manipulations, input/output operations, database operations, networking operations, file processing, error checking and many other useful operations.

Good Programming Practice 5.1

Familiarize yourself with the classes and methods provided by the FCL (msdn2.microsoft.com/en-us/library/ms229335). In Section 5.8, we present an overview of several common namespaces.

Software Engineering Observation 5.1

Don't try to "reinvent the wheel." When possible, reuse FCL classes and methods. This reduces application development time and avoids introducing programming errors.

Software Engineering Observation 5.2

To promote software reusability, every method should be limited to performing a single, well-defined task, and the name of the method should express that task effectively. Such methods make applications easier to write, debug, maintain and modify.

Error-Prevention Tip 5.1

A small method that performs one task is easier to test and debug than a larger method that performs many tasks.

Software Engineering Observation 5.3

If you cannot choose a concise name that expresses a method's task, your method might be attempting to perform too many diverse tasks. It is usually best to break such a method into several smaller methods.

5.3 static Methods, static Variables and Class Math

Although most methods execute on specific objects in response to method calls, this is not always the case. Sometimes a method performs a task that does not depend on the contents of any object. Such a method applies to the class in which it is declared as a whole and is known as a static method. It is not uncommon for a class to contain a group of static methods to perform common tasks. For example, recall that we used static method Pow of class Math to raise a value to a power in Fig. 4.6. To declare a method as static, place the keyword static before the return type in the method's declaration. You call any static method by specifying the name of the class in which the method is declared, followed by the dot (.) operator and the method name, as in

ClassName.*methodName*(*arguments*)

We use various methods of the Math class here to present the concept of static methods. Class Math (from the System namespace) provides a collection of methods that enable you to perform common mathematical calculations. For example, you can calculate the square root of 900.0 with the static method call

```
Math.Sqrt( 900.0 )
```

The preceding expression evaluates to 30.0. Method Sqrt takes an argument of type double and returns a result of type double. To output the value of the preceding method call in the console window, you might write the statement

```
Console.WriteLine( Math.Sqrt( 900.0 ) );
```

In this statement, the value that Sqrt returns becomes the argument to method Write-Line. Note that we did not create a Math object before calling method Sqrt. Also note that *all* of Math's methods are static—therefore, each is called by preceding the name of the method with the class name Math and the dot (.) operator. Similarly, Console method WriteLine is a static method of class Console, so we invoke the method by preceding its name with the class name Console and the dot (.) operator.

Method arguments may be constants, variables or expressions. If c = 13.0, d = 3.0 and f = 4.0, then the statement

```
Console.WriteLine( Math.Sqrt( c + d * f ) );
```

calculates and prints the square root of 13.0 + 3.0 * 4.0 = 25.0—namely, 5.0. Figure 5.1 summarizes several Math class methods. In the figure, x and y are of type double.

Method	Description	Example
Abs(x)	absolute value of x	Abs(23.7) is 23.7 Abs(0.0) is 0.0 Abs(-23.7) is 23.7
Ceiling(x)	rounds x to the smallest integer not less than x	Ceiling(9.2) is 10.0 Ceiling(-9.8) is -9.0
Cos(x)	trigonometric cosine of x (x in radians)	Cos(0.0) is 1.0
Exp(x)	exponential method e^x	Exp(1.0) is 2.71828 Exp(2.0) is 7.38906
Floor(x)	rounds x to the largest integer not greater than x	Floor(9.2) is 9.0 Floor(-9.8) is -10.0
Log(x)	natural logarithm of x (base e)	Log(Math.E) is 1.0 Log(Math.E * Math.E) is 2.0
Max(x, y)	larger value of x and y	Max(2.3, 12.7) is 12.7 Max(-2.3, -12.7) is -2.3
Min(x, y)	smaller value of x and y	Min(2.3, 12.7) is 2.3 Min(-2.3, -12.7) is -12.7

Fig. 5.1 | Math class methods. (Part 1 of 2.)

Method	Description	Example
Pow(x, y)	x raised to the power y (i.e., x^y)	Pow(2.0, 7.0) is 128.0 Pow(9.0, 0.5) is 3.0
Sin(x)	trigonometric sine of x (x in radians)	Sin(0.0) is 0.0
Sqrt(x)	square root of x	Sqrt(900.0) is 30.0
Tan(x)	trigonometric tangent of x (x in radians)	Tan(0.0) is 0.0

Fig. 5.1 | Math class methods. (Part 2 of 2.)

Math Class Constants PI and E

Class Math also declares two static variables that represent commonly used mathematical constants: **Math.PI** and **Math.E**. The constant Math.PI (3.14159265358979323846) is the ratio of a circle's circumference to its diameter. The constant Math.E (2.7182818284590452354) is the base value for natural logarithms (calculated with static Math method Log). These variables are declared in class Math with the modifiers public and const. Making them public allows other programmers to use these variables in their own classes. Any variable declared with keyword **const** is a constant—its value cannot be changed after the constant is declared. Both PI and E are declared const because their values never change. Also, any constant is implicitly static (so it is a syntax error to declare a constant with keyword static explicitly). Making these constants static allows them to be accessed via the class name Math and the dot (.) operator, just like class Math's methods. Recall from Section 3.5 that when each object of a class maintains its own copy of an attribute, the variable that represents the attribute is also known as an instance variable—each object (instance) of the class has a separate instance of the variable in memory. There are variables for which each object of a class does *not* have a separate instance of the variable. That is the case with static variables. When objects of a class containing static variables are created, all the objects of that class share one copy of the class's static variables. Together the static variables and instance variables represent the *fields* of a class. You will learn more about static variables in Section 7.10.

Why Is Method Main Declared static?

Why must Main be declared static? During application startup when no objects of the class have been created, the Main method must be called to begin program execution. The Main method is sometimes called the application's *entry point*. Declaring Main as static allows the execution environment to invoke Main without creating an instance of the class. Method Main is often declared with the header:

```
public static void Main( string args[] )
```

When you execute your application from the command line, you type the application name, as in

ApplicationName argument1 argument2 ...

In the preceding command, *argument1* and *argument2* are the ***command-line arguments*** to the application that specify a list of `strings` (separated by spaces) the execution environment will pass to the `Main` method of your application. Such arguments might be used to specify options (e.g., a file name) to run the application. As you will learn in Chapter 6, Arrays, your application can access those command-line arguments and use them to customize the application.

Additional Comments about Method `Main`

The header of a `Main` method does not need to appear exactly as we've shown. Applications that do not take command-line arguments may omit the `string[] args` parameter. The `public` keyword may also be omitted. In addition, you can declare `Main` with return type `int` (instead of `void`) to enable `Main` to return an error code with the `return` statement. A `Main` method declared with any one of these headers can be used as the application's entry point—but you can declare only one such `Main` method in each class.

In earlier chapters, most applications had one class that contained only `Main` and some examples had a second class that was used by `Main` to create and manipulate objects. Actually, any class can contain a `Main` method. In fact, each of our two-class examples could have been implemented as one class. For example, in the application in Fig. 4.9 and Fig. 4.10, method `Main` (lines 6–16 of Fig. 4.10) could have been taken as is and placed in class `GradeBook` (Fig. 4.9). The application results would be identical to those of the two-class version. You can place a `Main` method in every class you declare. Some programmers take advantage of this to build a small test application into each class they declare. However, if you declare more than one `Main` method among the classes of your project, you will need to indicate to the IDE which one you would like to be the application's entry point. You can do this by clicking the menu **Project > [ProjectName] Properties...** (where **[ProjectName]** is the name of your project) and selecting the class containing the `Main` method that should be the entry point from the **Startup object** list box.

5.4 Declaring Methods with Multiple Parameters

Chapters 2–4 presented classes containing simple methods that had at most one parameter. Methods often require more than one piece of information to perform their tasks. We now consider how to write your own methods with multiple parameters.

The application in Fig. 5.2 and Fig. 5.3 uses a user-defined method called `Maximum` to determine and return the largest of three `double` values that are input by the user. When the application begins execution, class `MaximumFinderTest`'s `Main` method (lines 6–10 of Fig. 5.3) creates an object of class `MaximumFinder` (line 8) and calls the object's `DetermineMaximum` method (line 9) to produce the application's output. In class `MaximumFinder` (Fig. 5.2), lines 11–15 of method `DetermineMaximum` prompt the user to enter three `double` values and read them from the user. Line 18 calls method `Maximum` (declared in lines 25–38) to determine the largest of the three `double` values passed as arguments to the method. When method `Maximum` returns the result to line 18, the application assigns `Maximum`'s return value to local variable `result`. Then line 21 outputs the maximum value. At the end of this section, we'll discuss the use of operator + in line 21.

Consider the declaration of method `Maximum` (lines 25–38). Line 25 indicates that the method returns a `double` value, that the method's name is `Maximum` and that the method requires three `double` parameters (x, y and z) to accomplish its task. When a method has

```
 1   // Fig. 5.2: MaximumFinder.cs
 2   // User-defined method Maximum.
 3   using System;
 4
 5   public class MaximumFinder
 6   {
 7      // obtain three floating-point values and determine maximum value
 8      public void DetermineMaximum()
 9      {
10         // prompt for and input three floating-point values
11         Console.WriteLine( "Enter three floating-point values,\n"
12            + " pressing 'Enter' after each one: " );
13         double number1 = Convert.ToDouble( Console.ReadLine() );
14         double number2 = Convert.ToDouble( Console.ReadLine() );
15         double number3 = Convert.ToDouble( Console.ReadLine() );
16
17         // determine the maximum value
18         double result = Maximum( number1, number2, number3 );
19
20         // display maximum value
21         Console.WriteLine( "Maximum is: " + result );
22      } // end method DetermineMaximum
23
24      // returns the maximum of its three double parameters
25      public double Maximum( double x, double y, double z )
26      {
27         double maximumValue = x; // assume x is the largest to start
28
29         // determine whether y is greater than maximumValue
30         if ( y > maximumValue )
31            maximumValue = y;
32
33         // determine whether z is greater than maximumValue
34         if ( z > maximumValue )
35            maximumValue = z;
36
37         return maximumValue;
38      } // end method Maximum
39   } // end class MaximumFinder
```

Fig. 5.2 | User-defined method `Maximum`.

more than one parameter, the parameters are specified as a comma-separated list. When
`Maximum` is called in line 18 of Fig. 5.2, the parameter x is initialized with the value of the
argument `number1`, the parameter y is initialized with the value of the argument `number2`
and the parameter z is initialized with the value of the argument `number3`. There must be
one argument in the method call for each parameter (sometimes called a *formal parameter*) in the method declaration. Also, each argument must be consistent with the type of
the corresponding parameter. For example, a parameter of type `double` can receive values
like 7.35 (a `double`), 22 (an `int`) or –0.03456 (a `double`), but not `strings` like "hello".
Section 5.7 discusses the argument types that can be provided in a method call for each
parameter of a simple type.

```
1   // Fig. 5.3: MaximumFinderTest.cs
2   // Application to test class MaximumFinder.
3   public class MaximumFinderTest
4   {
5      // application starting point
6      public static void Main( string[] args )
7      {
8         MaximumFinder maximumFinder = new MaximumFinder();
9         maximumFinder.DetermineMaximum();
10     } // end Main
11  } // end class MaximumFinderTest
```

```
Enter three floating-point values,
   pressing 'Enter' after each one:
3.33
2.22
1.11
Maximum is: 3.33
```

```
Enter three floating-point values,
   pressing 'Enter' after each one:
2.22
3.33
1.11
Maximum is: 3.33
```

```
Enter three floating-point values,
   pressing 'Enter' after each one:
1.11
2.22
867.5309
Maximum is: 867.5309
```

Fig. 5.3 | Application to test class MaximumFinder.

To determine the maximum value, we begin with the assumption that parameter x contains the largest value, so line 27 (Fig. 5.2) declares local variable maximumValue and initializes it with the value of parameter x. Of course, it is possible that parameter y or z contains the largest value, so we must compare each of these values with maximumValue. The if statement at lines 30–31 determines whether y is greater than maximumValue. If so, line 31 assigns y to maximumValue. The if statement at lines 34–35 determines whether z is greater than maximumValue. If so, line 35 assigns z to maximumValue. At this point, the largest of the three values resides in maximumValue, so line 37 returns that value to line 18. When program control returns to the point in the application where Maximum was called, Maximum's parameters x, y and z are no longer accessible in memory. Note that methods can return at most one value; the returned value can be a reference to an object that contains many values.

Note that `result` is a local variable in method `DetermineMaximum` because it is declared in the block that represents the method's body. Variables should be declared as fields of a class (i.e., as either instance variables or `static` variables of the class) only if they are required for use in more than one method of the class or if the application should save their values between calls to the class's methods.

Common Programming Error 5.1

Declaring method parameters of the same type as `float x, y` *instead of* `float x, float y` *is a syntax error—a type is required for each parameter in the parameter list.*

Software Engineering Observation 5.4

A method that has many parameters may be performing too many tasks. Consider dividing the method into smaller methods that perform the separate tasks. As a guideline, try to fit the method header on one line if possible.

Implementing Method `Maximum` *by Reusing Method* `Math.Max`

Recall from Fig. 5.1 that class `Math` has a `Max` method that can determine the larger of two values. The entire body of our maximum method could also be implemented with nested calls to `Math.Max`, as follows:

```
return Math.Max( x, Math.Max( y, z ) );
```

The leftmost call to `Math.Max` specifies arguments x and `Math.Max( y, z )`. Before any method can be called, all its arguments must be evaluated to determine their values. If an argument is a method call, the method call must be performed to determine its return value. So, in the preceding statement, `Math.Max( y, z )` is evaluated first to determine the maximum of y and z. Then the result is passed as the second argument to the other call to `Math.Max`, which returns the larger of its two arguments. Using `Math.Max` in this manner is a good example of software reuse—we find the largest of three values by reusing `Math.Max`, which finds the larger of two values. Note how concise this code is compared to lines 27–37 of Fig. 5.2.

Assembling Strings with String Concatenation

C# allows `string` objects to be created by assembling smaller `strings` into larger `strings` using operator + (or the compound assignment operator +=). This is known as ***string concatenation***. When both operands of operator + are `string` objects, operator + creates a new `string` object in which a copy of the characters of the right operand are placed at the end of a copy of the characters in the left operand. For example, the expression `"hello "` + `"there"` creates the `string` `"hello there"` without disturbing the original strings.

In line 21 of Fig. 5.2, the expression `"Maximum is: "` + `result` uses operator + with operands of types `string` and `double`. Every value of a simple type in C# has a `string` representation. When one of the + operator's operands is a `string`, the other is implicitly converted to a `string`, then the two are concatenated. In line 21, the `double` value is implicitly converted to its `string` representation and placed at the end of the `string` `"Maximum is: "`. If there are any trailing zeros in a `double` value, these will be discarded when the number is converted to a `string`. Thus, the number 9.3500 would be represented as 9.35 in the resulting `string`.

For values of simple types used in `string` concatenation, the values are converted to strings. If a `boolean` is concatenated with a `string`, the `bool` is converted to the `string` "True" or "False" (note that each is capitalized). All objects have a `ToString` method that returns a `string` representation of the object. When an object is concatenated with a `string`, the object's `ToString` method is implicitly called to obtain the `string` representation of the object.

Line 21 of Fig. 5.2 could also be written using `string` formatting as

```
Console.WriteLine( "Maximum is: {0}", result );
```

As with `string` concatenation, using a format item to substitute an object into a `string` implicitly calls the object's `ToString` method to obtain the object's `string` representation. You will learn more about method `ToString` in Chapter 6, Arrays.

When a large `string` literal is typed into an application's source code, you can break that `string` into several smaller `strings` and place them on multiple lines for readability. The `strings` can be reassembled using either string concatenation or string formatting.

Common Programming Error 5.2

It is a syntax error to break a `string` literal across multiple lines in an application. If a `string` does not fit on one line, split the `string` into several smaller `strings` and use concatenation to form the desired `string`.

Common Programming Error 5.3

Confusing the + operator used for string concatenation with the + operator used for addition can lead to strange results. The + operator is left-associative. For example, if integer variable y has the value 5, the expression "y + 2 = " + y + 2 results in the string "y + 2 = 52", not "y + 2 = 7", because first the value of y (5) is concatenated with the string "y + 2 = ", then the value 2 is concatenated with the new larger string "y + 2 = 5". The expression "y + 2 = " + (y + 2) produces the desired result "y + 2 = 7".

5.5 Notes on Declaring and Using Methods

You have seen three ways to call a method:

1. Using a method name by itself to call a method of the same class—such as `Maximum( number1, number2, number3 )` in line 18 of Fig. 5.2.

2. Using a variable that contains a reference to an object, followed by the dot (.) operator and the method name to call a non-static method of the referenced object—such as the method call in line 9 of Fig. 5.3, `maximumFinder.DetermineMaximum()`, which calls a method of class `MaximumFinder` from the `Main` method of `MaximumFinderTest`.

3. Using the class name and the dot (.) operator to call a `static` method of a class—such as `Math.Sqrt( 900.0 )` in Section 5.3.

Note that a `static` method can call only other `static` methods of the same class directly (i.e., using the method name by itself) and can manipulate only `static` variables in the same class directly. To access the class's non-static members, a `static` method must use a reference to an object of the class. Recall that `static` methods relate to a class as a whole, whereas non-`static` methods are associated with a specific instance (object) of the class and may manipulate the instance variables of that object. Many objects of a class, each with its own copies of the instance variables, may exist at the same time. Suppose a `static` method were to invoke a non-`static` method directly. How would the method know which object's instance variables to manipulate? What would happen if no objects of the class existed at the time the non-`static` method was invoked? Thus, C# does not allow a `static` method to access non-`static` members of the same class directly.

There are three ways to return control to the statement that calls a method. If the method does not return a result, control returns when the program flow reaches the method-ending right brace or when the statement

> **return**;

is executed. If the method returns a result, the statement

> **return** *expression*;

evaluates the *expression*, then returns the result (and control) to the caller.

Common Programming Error 5.4

Declaring a method outside the body of a class declaration or inside the body of another method is a syntax error.

Common Programming Error 5.5

Omitting the return type *in a method declaration is a syntax error.*

Common Programming Error 5.6

Placing a semicolon after the right parenthesis enclosing the parameter list of a method declaration is a syntax error.

Common Programming Error 5.7

Redeclaring a method parameter as a local variable in the method's body is a compilation error.

Common Programming Error 5.8

Forgetting to return a value from a method that should return a value is a compilation error. If a return type other than void *is specified, the method must contain a* return *statement that returns a value consistent with the method's* return *type. Returning a value from a method whose return type has been declared* void *is a compilation error.*

5.6 Method Call Stack and Activation Records

To understand how C# performs method calls, we first need to consider a data structure (i.e., collection of related data items) known as a *stack*. You can think of a stack as analogous to a pile of dishes. When a dish is placed on the pile, it is normally placed at the top (referred to as *pushing* the dish onto the stack). Similarly, when a dish is removed from the pile, it is always removed from the top (referred to as *popping* the dish off the stack). Stacks are known as *last-in-first-out (LIFO) data structures*—the last item pushed (inserted) on the stack is the first item popped off (removed from) the stack.

When an application calls a method, the called method must know how to return to its caller, so the return address of the calling method is pushed onto the *program execution stack* (sometimes referred to as the *method call stack*). If a series of method calls occurs, the successive return addresses are pushed onto the stack in last-in-first-out order so that each method can return to its caller.

The program execution stack also contains the memory for the local variables used in each invocation of a method during an application's execution. This data, stored as a portion of the program execution stack, is known as the *activation record* or *stack frame* of the method call. When a method call is made, the activation record for that method call is pushed onto the program execution stack. When the method returns to its caller, the activation record for this method call is popped off the stack, and those local variables are no longer known to the application. If a local variable holding a reference to an object is the only variable in the application with a reference to that object, when the activation record containing that local variable is popped off the stack, the object can no longer be accessed by the application and will eventually be deleted from memory during "garbage collection." We'll discuss garbage collection in Section 7.9.

Of course, the amount of memory in a computer is finite, so only a certain amount of memory can be used to store activation records on the program execution stack. If more method calls occur than can have their activation records stored on the program execution stack, an error known as a *stack overflow* occurs.

5.7 Argument Promotion and Casting

Another important feature of method calls is *argument promotion*—implicitly converting an argument's value to the type that the method expects to receive in its corresponding parameter. For example, an application can call Math method Sqrt with an integer argument even though the method expects to receive a double argument (but, as we will soon see, not vice versa). The statement

```
Console.WriteLine( Math.Sqrt( 4 ) );
```

correctly evaluates Math.Sqrt(4) and prints the value 2.0. The method declaration's parameter list causes C# to convert the int value 4 to the double value 4.0 before passing the value to Sqrt. Attempting these conversions may lead to compilation errors if C#'s *promotion rules* are not satisfied. The promotion rules specify which conversions are allowed—that is, which conversions can be performed without losing data. In the Sqrt example above, an int is converted to a double without changing its value. However, converting a double to an int truncates the fractional part of the double value—thus, part of the value is lost. Also, double variables can hold values much larger (and much smaller) than int variables, so assigning a double to an int can cause a loss of information when the double value doesn't fit in the int. Converting large integer types to small integer types (e.g., long to int) can also result in changed values.

The promotion rules apply to expressions containing values of two or more simple types and to simple-type values passed as arguments to methods. Each value is promoted to the appropriate type in the expression. (Actually, the expression uses a temporary copy of each value—the types of the original values remain unchanged.) Figure 5.4 lists the

Type	Conversion types
bool	no possible implicit conversions to other simple types
byte	*ushort*, *short*, *uint*, *int*, *ulong*, *long*, *decimal*, *float* or *double*
char	*ushort*, *int*, *uint*, *long*, *ulong*, *decimal*, *float* or *double*
decimal	no possible implicit conversions to other simple types
double	no possible implicit conversions to other simple types
float	*double*
int	*long*, *decimal*, *float* or *double*
long	*decimal*, *float* or *double*
sbyte	*short*, *int*, *long*, *decimal*, *float* or *double*
short	*int*, *long*, *decimal*, *float* or *double*
uint	*ulong*, *long*, *decimal*, *float* or *double*
ulong	*decimal*, *float* or *double*
ushort	*uint*, *int*, *ulong*, *long*, *decimal*, *float* or *double*

Fig. 5.4 | Implicit conversions between simple types.

simple types alphabetically and the types to which each can be promoted. Note that values of all simple types can also be implicitly converted to type `object`.

By default, C# does not allow you to implicitly convert values between simple types if the target type cannot represent the value of the original type (e.g., the `int` value 2000000 cannot be represented as a `short`, and any floating-point number with digits after its decimal point cannot be represented in an integer type such as `long`, `int` or `short`). Therefore, to prevent a compilation error in cases where information may be lost due to an implicit conversion between simple types, the compiler requires you to use a cast operator (introduced in Section 3.7) to explicitly force the conversion. This enables you to "take control" from the compiler. You essentially say, "I know this conversion might cause loss of information, but for my purposes here, that's fine." Suppose you create a method `Square` that calculates the square of an integer and thus requires an `int` argument. To call `Square` with a `double` argument named `doubleValue`, you would write the method call as `Square( (int) doubleValue )`. This method call explicitly casts (converts) the value of `doubleValue` to an integer for use in method `Square`. Thus, if `doubleValue`'s value is 4.5, the method receives the value 4 and returns 16, not 20.25 (which does, unfortunately, result in the loss of information).

Common Programming Error 5.9

Converting a simple-type value to a value of another simple type may change the value if the promotion is not allowed. For example, converting a floating-point value to an integral value may introduce truncation errors (loss of the fractional part) in the result.

5.8 The Framework Class Library

Many predefined classes are grouped into categories of related classes called namespaces. Together, these namespaces are referred to as the .NET Framework Class Library, or the FCL.

Throughout the text, using directives allow us to use library classes from the FCL without specifying their fully-qualified names. For example, the declaration

using System;

allows an application to use the class names from the System namespace without fully qualifying their names. This allows you to use the *unqualified class name* Console, rather than the fully qualified class name System.Console, in your code. A great strength of C# is the large number of classes in the namespaces of the FCL. Some key FCL namespaces are described in Fig. 5.5, which represents only a small portion of the reusable classes in the FCL. When learning C#, spend a portion of your time browsing the namespaces and classes in the .NET documentation (msdn2.microsoft.com/en-us/library/ms229335).

The set of namespaces available in the FCL is quite large. In addition to the namespaces summarized in Fig. 5.5, the FCL contains namespaces for complex graphics, advanced graphical user interfaces, printing, advanced networking, security, database processing, multimedia, accessibility (for people with disabilities) and many other capabilities. The preceding URL for the .NET documentation provides an overview of the Framework Class Library's namespaces.

Namespace	Description
System.Windows.Forms	Contains the classes required to create and manipulate GUIs. (Various classes in this namespace are discussed in Chapter 11, Graphical User Interface Concepts: Part 1, and Chapter 12, Graphical User Interface Concepts: Part 2.)
System.IO	Contains classes that enable programs to input and output data.
System.Data	Contains classes that enable programs to access and manipulate databases (i.e., organized collections of data).
System.Web	Contains classes used for creating and maintaining Web applications, which are accessible over the Internet.
System.Xml	Contains classes for creating and manipulating XML data. Data can be read from or written to XML files.
System.Collections System.Collections.Generic	Contains classes that define data structures for maintaining collections of data.
System.Net	Contains classes that enable programs to communicate via computer networks like the Internet.

Fig. 5.5 | FCL namespaces (a subset). (Part 1 of 2.)

Namespace	Description
System.Text	Contains classes and interfaces that enable programs to manipulate characters and strings.
System.Threading	Contains classes that enable programs to perform several tasks at the same time.
System.Drawing	Contains classes that enable programs to perform basic graphics processing, such as displaying shapes and arcs.

Fig. 5.5 | FCL namespaces (a subset). (Part 2 of 2.)

You can locate additional information about a predefined C# class's methods in the Framework Class Library Reference. When you visit this site, you will see an alphabetical listing of all the namespaces in the FCL. Locate the namespace and click its link to see an alphabetical listing of all its classes, with a brief description of each. Click a class's link to see a more complete description of the class. Click the **Methods** link in the left-hand column to see a listing of the class's methods.

Good Programming Practice 5.2

The online .NET Framework documentation is easy to search and provides many details about each class. As you learn each class in this book, you should review the class in the online documentation for additional information.

5.9 Case Study: Random-Number Generation

In this and the next section, we develop a nicely structured game-playing application with multiple methods. The application uses most of the control statements presented thus far in the book and introduces several new programming concepts.

There is something in the air of a casino that invigorates people—from the high rollers at the plush mahogany-and-felt craps tables to the quarter poppers at the one-armed bandits. It is the *element of chance*, the possibility that luck will convert a pocketful of money into a mountain of wealth. The element of chance can be introduced in an application via an object of class Random (of namespace System). Objects of class *Random* can produce random byte, int and double values. In the next several examples, we use objects of class Random to produce random numbers.

A new random-number generator object can be created as follows:

```
Random randomNumbers = new Random();
```

The random-number generator object can then be used to generate random byte, int and double values—we discuss only random int values here. For more information on the Random class, see msdn2.microsoft.com/en-us/library/ts6se2ek.

Consider the following statement:

```
int randomValue = randomNumbers.Next();
```

Method `Next` of class `Random` generates a random `int` value in the range 0 to +2,147,483,646, inclusive. If the `Next` method truly produces values at random, then every value in that range should have an equal chance (or probability) of being chosen each time method `Next` is called. The values returned by `Next` are actually *pseudorandom numbers*—a sequence of values produced by a complex mathematical calculation. The calculation uses the current time of day (which, of course, changes constantly) to *seed* the random-number generator such that each execution of an application yields a different sequence of random values.

The range of values produced directly by method `Next` often differs from the range of values required in a particular C# application. For example, an application that simulates coin tossing might require only 0 for "heads" and 1 for "tails." An application that simulates the rolling of a six-sided die might require random integers in the range 1–6. A video game that randomly predicts the next type of spaceship (out of four possibilities) that will fly across the horizon might require random integers in the range 1–4. For cases like these, class `Random` provides other versions of method `Next`. One receives an `int` argument and returns a value from 0 up to, but not including, the argument's value. For example, you might use the statement

```
int randomValue = randomNumbers.Next( 6 );
```

which returns 0, 1, 2, 3, 4 or 5. The argument 6—called the *scaling factor*—represents the number of unique values that `Next` should produce (in this case, six—0, 1, 2, 3, 4 and 5). This manipulation is called *scaling* the range of values produced by `Random` method `Next`.

Suppose we wanted to simulate a six-sided die that has the numbers 1–6 on its faces, not 0–5. Scaling the range of values alone is not enough. So we *shift* the range of numbers produced. We could do this by adding a *shifting value*—in this case 1—to the result of method `Next`, as in

```
face = 1 + randomNumbers.Next( 6 );
```

The shifting value (1) specifies the first value in the desired set of random integers. The preceding statement assigns to `face` a random integer in the range 1–6.

The third alternative of method `Next` provides a more intuitive way to express both shifting and scaling. This method receives two `int` arguments and returns a value from the first argument's value up to, but not including, the second argument's value. We could use this method to write a statement equivalent to our previous statement, as in

```
face = randomNumbers.Next( 1, 7 );
```

Rolling a Six-Sided Die

To demonstrate random numbers, let us develop an application that simulates 20 rolls of a six-sided die and displays the value of each roll. Figure 5.6 shows two sample outputs, which confirm that the results of the preceding calculation are integers in the range 1–6 and that each run of the application can produce a different sequence of random numbers. The `using` directive in line 3 enables us to use class `Random` without fully qualifying its name. Line 9 creates the Random object randomNumbers to produce random values. Line 16 executes 20 times in a loop to roll the die. The if statement (lines 21–22) in the loop starts a new line of output after every five numbers, so the results can be presented on multiple lines.

```csharp
1   // Fig. 5.6: RandomIntegers.cs
2   // Shifted and scaled random integers.
3   using System;
4
5   public class RandomIntegers
6   {
7      public static void Main( string[] args )
8      {
9         Random randomNumbers = new Random(); // random number generator
10        int face; // stores each random integer generated
11
12        // loop 20 times
13        for ( int counter = 1; counter <= 20; counter++ )
14        {
15           // pick random integer from 1 to 6
16           face = randomNumbers.Next( 1, 7 );
17
18           Console.Write( "{0}  ", face ); // display generated value
19
20           // if counter is divisible by 5, start a new line of output
21           if ( counter % 5 == 0 )
22              Console.WriteLine();
23        } // end for
24     } // end Main
25  } // end class RandomIntegers
```

```
3   3   3   1   1
2   1   2   4   2
2   3   6   2   5
3   4   6   6   1
```

```
6   2   5   1   3
5   2   1   6   5
4   1   6   1   3
3   1   4   3   4
```

Fig. 5.6 | Shifted and scaled random integers.

Rolling a Six-Sided Die 6000 Times

To show that the numbers produced by Next occur with approximately equal likelihood, let us simulate 6000 rolls of a die (Fig. 5.7). Each integer from 1 to 6 should appear approximately 1000 times.

```
1   // Fig. 5.7: RollDie.cs
2   // Roll a six-sided die 6000 times.
3   using System;
4
5   public class RollDie
6   {
7      public static void Main( string[] args )
8      {
9         Random randomNumbers = new Random(); // random number generator
10
11        int frequency1 = 0; // count of 1s rolled
12        int frequency2 = 0; // count of 2s rolled
13        int frequency3 = 0; // count of 3s rolled
14        int frequency4 = 0; // count of 4s rolled
15        int frequency5 = 0; // count of 5s rolled
16        int frequency6 = 0; // count of 6s rolled
17
18        int face; // stores most recently rolled value
19
20        // summarize results of 6000 rolls of a die
21        for ( int roll = 1; roll <= 6000; roll++ )
22        {
23           face = randomNumbers.Next( 1, 7 ); // number from 1 to 6
24
25           // determine roll value 1-6 and increment appropriate counter
26           switch ( face )
27           {
28              case 1:
29                 frequency1++; // increment the 1s counter
30                 break;
31              case 2:
32                 frequency2++; // increment the 2s counter
33                 break;
34              case 3:
35                 frequency3++; // increment the 3s counter
36                 break;
37              case 4:
38                 frequency4++; // increment the 4s counter
39                 break;
40              case 5:
41                 frequency5++; // increment the 5s counter
42                 break;
43              case 6:
44                 frequency6++; // increment the 6s counter
45                 break;
46           } // end switch
47        } // end for
```

Fig. 5.7 | Roll a six-sided die 6000 times. (Part I of 2.)

```
48
49          Console.WriteLine( "Face\tFrequency" ); // output headers
50          Console.WriteLine( "1\t{0}\n2\t{1}\n3\t{2}\n4\t{3}\n5\t{4}\n6\t{5}",
51             frequency1, frequency2, frequency3, frequency4,
52             frequency5, frequency6 );
53       } // end Main
54    } // end class RollDie
```

```
Face      Frequency
1         1039
2         994
3         991
4         970
5         978
6         1028
```

```
Face      Frequency
1         985
2         985
3         1001
4         1017
5         1002
6         1010
```

Fig. 5.7 | Roll a six-sided die 6000 times. (Part 2 of 2.)

As the two sample outputs show, the values produced by method Next enable the application to realistically simulate rolling a six-sided die. The application uses nested control statements (the switch is nested inside the for) to determine the number of times each side of the die occurred. The for statement (lines 21–47) iterates 6000 times. During each iteration, line 23 produces a random value from 1 to 6. This face value is then used as the switch expression (line 26) in the switch statement (lines 26–46). Based on the face value, the switch statement increments one of the six counter variables during each iteration of the loop. (In Chapter 6, Arrays, we show an elegant way to replace the entire switch statement in this application with a single statement.) Note that the switch statement has no default label because we have a case label for every possible die value that the expression in line 23 can produce. Run the application several times and observe the results. You'll see that every time you execute this application, it produces different results.

5.9.1 Scaling and Shifting Random Numbers

Previously, we demonstrated the statement

```
face = randomNumbers.Next( 1, 7 );
```

which simulates the rolling of a six-sided die. This statement always assigns to variable face an integer in the range $1 \leq$ face < 7. The width of this range (i.e., the number of consecutive integers in the range) is 6, and the starting number in the range is 1. Referring to the preceding statement, we see that the width of the range is determined by the difference between the two integers passed to Random method Next, and the starting number of the range is the value of the first argument. We can generalize this result as

```
number = randomNumbers.Next( shiftingValue, shiftingValue + scalingFactor );
```

where *shiftingValue* specifies the first number in the desired range of consecutive integers and *scalingFactor* specifies how many numbers are in the range.

It is also possible to choose integers at random from sets of values other than ranges of consecutive integers. For this purpose, it is simpler to use the version of the Next method that takes only one argument. For example, to obtain a random value from the sequence 2, 5, 8, 11 and 14, you could use the statement

```
number = 2 + 3 * randomNumbers.Next( 5 );
```

In this case, randomNumberGenerator.Next(5) produces values in the range 0–4. Each value produced is multiplied by 3 to produce a number in the sequence 0, 3, 6, 9 and 12. We then add 2 to that value to shift the range of values and obtain a value from the sequence 2, 5, 8, 11 and 14. We can generalize this result as

```
number = shiftingValue +
    differenceBetweenValues * randomNumbers.Next( scalingFactor );
```

where *shiftingValue* specifies the first number in the desired range of values, *difference-BetweenValues* represents the difference between consecutive numbers in the sequence and *scalingFactor* specifies how many numbers are in the range.

5.9.2 Random-Number Repeatability for Testing and Debugging

As we mentioned earlier in Section 5.9, the methods of class Random actually generate pseudorandom numbers based on complex mathematical calculations. Repeatedly calling any of Random's methods produces a sequence of numbers that appears to be random. The calculation that produces the pseudorandom numbers uses the time of day as a *seed value* to change the sequence's starting point. Each new Random object seeds itself with a value based on the computer system's clock at the time the object is created, enabling each execution of an application to produce a different sequence of random numbers.

When debugging an application, it is sometimes useful to repeat the exact same sequence of pseudorandom numbers during each execution of the application. This repeatability enables you to prove that your application is working for a specific sequence of random numbers before you test the application with different sequences of random numbers. When repeatability is important, you can create a Random object as follows:

```
Random randomNumbers = new Random( seedValue );
```

The seedValue argument (type int) seeds the random-number calculation. If the same seedValue is used every time, the Random object produces the same sequence of random numbers.

Error-Prevention Tip 5.2

While an application is under development, create the Random object with a specific seed value to produce a repeatable sequence of random numbers each time the application executes. If a logic error occurs, fix the error and test the application again with the same seed value—this allows you to reconstruct the same sequence of random numbers that caused the error. Once the logic errors have been removed, create the Random object without using a seed value, causing the Random object to generate a new sequence of random numbers each time the application executes.

5.10 Case Study: A Game of Chance (Introducing Enumerations)

One popular game of chance is the dice game known as "craps," which is played in casinos and back alleys throughout the world. The rules of the game are straightforward:

> *You roll two dice. Each die has six faces, which contain one, two, three, four, five and six spots, respectively. After the dice have come to rest, the sum of the spots on the two upward faces is calculated. If the sum is 7 or 11 on the first throw, you win. If the sum is 2, 3 or 12 on the first throw (called "craps"), you lose (i.e., "the house" wins). If the sum is 4, 5, 6, 8, 9 or 10 on the first throw, that sum becomes your "point." To win, you must continue rolling the dice until you "make your point" (i.e., roll that same point value). You lose by rolling a 7 before making your point.*

The application in Fig. 5.8 and Fig. 5.9 simulates the game of craps, using methods to define the logic of the game. In the Main method of class CrapsTest (Fig. 5.9), line 7 creates an object of class Craps (Fig. 5.8), and line 8 calls its Play method to start the game. The Play method (Fig. 5.8, lines 24–70) calls the RollDice method (Fig. 5.8, lines 73–85) as needed to roll the two dice and compute their sum. The four sample outputs in Fig. 5.9 show winning on the first roll, losing on the first roll, winning on a subsequent roll and losing on a subsequent roll, respectively.

```
1   // Fig. 5.8: Craps.cs
2   // Craps class simulates the dice game craps.
3   using System;
4
5   public class Craps
6   {
7      // create random number generator for use in method RollDice
8      private Random randomNumbers = new Random();
9
10     // enumeration with constants that represent the game status
11     private enum Status { CONTINUE, WON, LOST }
12
13     // enumeration with constants that represent common rolls of the dice
14     private enum DiceNames
15     {
16        SNAKE_EYES = 2,
17        TREY = 3,
18        SEVEN = 7,
19        YO_LEVEN = 11,
20        BOX_CARS = 12
21     }
22
23     // plays one game of craps
24     public void Play()
25     {
26        // gameStatus can contain CONTINUE, WON or LOST
27        Status gameStatus = Status.CONTINUE;
28        int myPoint = 0; // point if no win or loss on first roll
29
```

Fig. 5.8 | Craps class simulates the dice game craps. (Part 1 of 3.)

```
30          int sumOfDice = RollDice(); // first roll of the dice
31
32          // determine game status and point based on first roll
33          switch ( ( DiceNames ) sumOfDice )
34          {
35              case DiceNames.SEVEN: // win with 7 on first roll
36              case DiceNames.YO_LEVEN: // win with 11 on first roll
37                  gameStatus = Status.WON;
38                  break;
39              case DiceNames.SNAKE_EYES: // lose with 2 on first roll
40              case DiceNames.TREY: // lose with 3 on first roll
41              case DiceNames.BOX_CARS: // lose with 12 on first roll
42                  gameStatus = Status.LOST;
43                  break;
44              default: // did not win or lose, so remember point
45                  gameStatus = Status.CONTINUE; // game is not over
46                  myPoint = sumOfDice; // remember the point
47                  Console.WriteLine( "Point is {0}", myPoint );
48                  break;
49          } // end switch
50
51          // while game is not complete
52          while ( gameStatus == Status.CONTINUE ) // game not WON or LOST
53          {
54              sumOfDice = RollDice(); // roll dice again
55
56              // determine game status
57              if ( sumOfDice == myPoint ) // win by making point
58                  gameStatus = Status.WON;
59              else
60                  // lose by rolling 7 before point
61                  if ( sumOfDice == ( int ) DiceNames.SEVEN )
62                      gameStatus = Status.LOST;
63          } // end while
64
65          // display won or lost message
66          if ( gameStatus == Status.WON )
67              Console.WriteLine( "Player wins" );
68          else
69              Console.WriteLine( "Player loses" );
70      } // end method Play
71
72      // roll dice, calculate sum and display results
73      public int RollDice()
74      {
75          // pick random die values
76          int die1 = randomNumbers.Next( 1, 7 ); // first die roll
77          int die2 = randomNumbers.Next( 1, 7 ); // second die roll
78
79          int sum = die1 + die2; // sum of die values
80
```

Fig. 5.8 | Craps class simulates the dice game craps. (Part 2 of 3.)

```
81            // display results of this roll
82            Console.WriteLine( "Player rolled {0} + {1} = {2}",
83               die1, die2, sum );
84            return sum; // return sum of dice
85         } // end method RollDice
86      } // end class Craps
```

Fig. 5.8 | Craps class simulates the dice game craps. (Part 3 of 3.)

```
 1   // Fig. 5.9: CrapsTest.cs
 2   // Application to test class Craps.
 3   public class CrapsTest
 4   {
 5      public static void Main( string[] args )
 6      {
 7         Craps game = new Craps();
 8         game.Play(); // play one game of craps
 9      } // end Main
10   } // end class CrapsTest
```

```
Player rolled 2 + 5 = 7
Player wins
```

```
Player rolled 2 + 1 = 3
Player loses
```

```
Player rolled 4 + 6 = 10
Point is 10
Player rolled 1 + 3 = 4
Player rolled 1 + 3 = 4
Player rolled 2 + 3 = 5
Player rolled 4 + 4 = 8
Player rolled 6 + 6 = 12
Player rolled 4 + 4 = 8
Player rolled 4 + 5 = 9
Player rolled 2 + 6 = 8
Player rolled 6 + 6 = 12
Player rolled 6 + 4 = 10
Player wins
```

```
Player rolled 2 + 4 = 6
Point is 6
Player rolled 3 + 1 = 4
Player rolled 5 + 5 = 10
Player rolled 6 + 1 = 7
Player loses
```

Fig. 5.9 | Application to test class Craps.

Let's discuss the declaration of class Craps in Fig. 5.8. In the rules of the game, the player must roll two dice on the first roll, and must do the same on all subsequent rolls. We declare method RollDice (lines 73–85) to roll the dice and compute and print their sum. Method RollDice is declared once, but it is called from two places (lines 30 and 54) in method Play, which contains the logic for one complete game of craps. Method Roll-Dice takes no arguments, so it has an empty parameter list. Each time it is called, RollDice returns the sum of the dice, so the return type int is indicated in the method header (line 73). Although lines 76 and 77 look the same (except for the die names), they do not necessarily produce the same result. Each of these statements produces a random value in the range 1–6. Note that randomNumbers (used in lines 76 and 77) is not declared in the method. Rather it is declared as a private instance variable of the class and initialized in line 8. This enables us to create one Random object that is reused in each call to RollDice.

The game is reasonably involved. The player may win or lose on the first roll, or may win or lose on any subsequent roll. Method Play (lines 24–70) uses local variable gameStatus (line 27) to keep track of the overall game status, local variable myPoint (line 28) to store the "point" if the player does not win or lose on the first roll and local variable sumOfDice (line 30) to maintain the sum of the dice for the most recent roll. Note that myPoint is initialized to 0 to ensure that the application will compile. If you do not initialize myPoint, the compiler issues an error, because myPoint is not assigned a value in every branch of the switch statement—thus, the application could try to use myPoint before it is definitely assigned a value. By contrast, gameStatus does not require initialization because it *is* assigned a value in every branch of the switch statement—thus, it is guaranteed to be initialized before it is used. However, as good programming practice, we initialize it anyway.

Note that local variable gameStatus is declared to be of a new type called Status, which we declared in line 11. Type Status is declared as a private member of class Craps, because Status will be used only in that class. Status is a user-defined type called an *enumeration*, which declares a set of constants represented by identifiers. An enumeration is introduced by the keyword **enum** and a type name (in this case, Status). As with a class, braces ({ and }) delimit the body of an enum declaration. Inside the braces is a comma-separated list of *enumeration constants*. The enum constant names must be unique, but their underlying values need not be.

Good Programming Practice 5.3

Use only uppercase letters in the names of constants. This makes the constants stand out in an application and reminds you that enumeration constants are not variables.

Variables of type Status should be assigned only one of the three constants declared in the enumeration. When the game is won, the application sets local variable gameStatus to Status.WON (lines 37 and 58). When the game is lost, the application sets local variable gameStatus to Status.LOST (lines 42 and 62). Otherwise, the application sets local variable gameStatus to Status.CONTINUE (line 45) to indicate that the dice must be rolled again.

Good Programming Practice 5.4

Using enumeration constants (like Status.WON, Status.LOST and Status.CONTINUE) rather than literal integer values (such as 0, 1 and 2) can make code easier to read and maintain.

Line 30 in method Play calls RollDice, which picks two random values from 1 to 6, displays the value of the first die, the value of the second die and the sum of the dice, and returns the sum of the dice. Method Play next enters the switch statement at lines 33–49, which uses the sumOfDice value from line 30 to determine whether the game has been won or lost, or whether it should continue with another roll.

The sums of the dice that would result in a win or loss on the first roll are declared in the DiceNames enumeration in lines 14–21. These are used in the cases of the switch statement. The identifier names use casino parlance for these sums. Notice that in the DiceNames enumeration, a value is explicitly assigned to each identifier name. When the enum is declared, each constant in the enum declaration contains an underlying constant value of type int. If you do not assign a value to an identifier in the enum declaration, the compiler will do so. If the first enum constant is unassigned, the compiler gives it the value 0. If any other enum constant is unassigned, the compiler gives it a value equal to one more than the value of the preceding enum constant. For example, in the Status enumeration, the compiler implicitly assigns 0 to Status.WON, 1 to Status.CONTINUE and 2 to Status.LOST.

You could also declare an enum's underlying type to be byte, sbyte, short, ushort, int, uint, long or ulong by writing

private enum MyEnum : *typeName* { *CONSTANT1*, *CONSTANT2*, ... }

where *typeName* represents one of the integral simple types.

If you need to compare a simple-type value to the underlying value of an enumeration constant, you must use a cast operator to make the two types match. In the switch statement at lines 33–49, we use the cast operator to convert the int value in sumOfDice to type DiceNames and compare it to each of the constants in DiceNames. Lines 35–36 determine whether the player won on the first roll with SEVEN (7) or YO_LEVEN (11). Lines 39–41 determine whether the player lost on the first roll with SNAKE_EYES (2), TREY (3) or BOX_CARS (12). After the first roll, if the game is not over, the default case (lines 44–48) saves sumOfDice in myPoint (line 46) and displays the point (line 47).

If we are still trying to "make our point" (i.e., the game is continuing from a prior roll), the loop in lines 52–63 executes. Line 54 rolls the dice again. If sumOfDice matches myPoint in line 57, line 58 sets gameStatus to Status.WON, and the loop terminates because the game is complete. In line 61, we use the cast operator (int) to obtain the underlying value of DiceNames.SEVEN so that we can compare it to sumOfDice. If sumOfDice is equal to SEVEN (7), line 62 sets gameStatus to Status.LOST, and the loop terminates because the game is over. When the game completes, lines 66–69 display a message indicating whether the player won or lost and the application terminates.

Note the use of the various program-control mechanisms we have discussed. The Craps class uses two methods—Play (called from CrapsTest.Main) and RollDice (called twice from Play)—and the switch, while, if...else and nested if control statements. Note also the use of multiple case labels in the switch statement to execute the same statements for sums of SEVEN and YO_LEVEN (lines 35–36) and for sums of SNAKE_EYES, TREY and BOX_CARS (lines 39–41).

5.11 **Scope of Declarations**

You have seen declarations of various C# entities, such as classes, methods, properties, variables and parameters. Declarations introduce names that can be used to refer to such C# entities. The *scope* of a declaration is the portion of the application that can refer to the declared entity by its unqualified name. Such an entity is said to be "in scope" for that portion of the application. This section introduces several important scope issues. For more scope information, see *Section 1.7, Scopes,* of the *C# Language Specification.*

The basic scope rules are as follows:

1. The scope of a parameter declaration is the body of the method in which the declaration appears.

2. The scope of a local-variable declaration is from the point at which the declaration appears to the end of the block containing the declaration.

3. The scope of a local-variable declaration that appears in the initialization section of a for statement's header is the body of the for statement and the other expressions in the header.

4. The scope of a method, property or field of a class is the entire body of the class. This enables non-static methods and properties of a class to use any of the class's fields, methods and properties, regardless of the order in which they are declared. Similarly, static methods and properties can use any of the static members of the class.

Any block may contain variable declarations. If a local variable or parameter in a method has the same name as a field, the field is hidden until the block terminates execution. In Chapter 7, we discuss how to access hidden fields.

Error-Prevention Tip 5.3

Use different names for fields and local variables to help prevent subtle logic errors that occur when a method is called and a local variable of the method hides a field of the same name in the class.

The application in Fig. 5.10 and Fig. 5.11 demonstrates scoping issues with fields and local variables. When the application begins execution, class ScopeTest's Main method (Fig. 5.11, lines 6–10) creates an object of class Scope (line 8) and calls the object's Begin method (line 9) to produce the application's output (shown in Fig. 5.11).

```
1   // Fig. 5.10: Scope.cs
2   // Scope class demonstrates instance and local variable scopes.
3   using System;
4
5   public class Scope
6   {
7       // instance variable that is accessible to all methods of this class
8       private int x = 1;
9
10      // method Begin creates and initializes local variable x
11      // and calls methods UseLocalVariable and UseInstanceVariable
12      public void Begin()
13      {
14          int x = 5; // method's local variable x hides instance variable x
15
16          Console.WriteLine( "local x in method Begin is {0}", x );
17
```

Fig. 5.10 | Scope class demonstrates instance and local variable scopes. (Part 1 of 2.)

```
18          // UseLocalVariable has its own local x
19          UseLocalVariable();
20
21          // UseInstanceVariable uses class Scope's instance variable x
22          UseInstanceVariable();
23
24          // UseLocalVariable reinitializes its own local x
25          UseLocalVariable();
26
27          // class Scope's instance variable x retains its value
28          UseInstanceVariable();
29
30          Console.WriteLine( "\nlocal x in method Begin is {0}", x );
31       } // end method Begin
32
33       // create and initialize local variable x during each call
34       public void UseLocalVariable()
35       {
36          int x = 25; // initialized each time UseLocalVariable is called
37
38          Console.WriteLine(
39             "\nlocal x on entering method UseLocalVariable is {0}", x );
40          x++; // modifies this method's local variable x
41          Console.WriteLine(
42             "local x before exiting method UseLocalVariable is {0}", x );
43       } // end method UseLocalVariable
44
45       // modify class Scope's instance variable x during each call
46       public void UseInstanceVariable()
47       {
48          Console.WriteLine( "\ninstance variable x on entering {0} is {1}",
49             "method UseInstanceVariable", x );
50          x *= 10; // modifies class Scope's instance variable x
51          Console.WriteLine( "instance variable x before exiting {0} is {1}",
52             "method UseInstanceVariable", x );
53       } // end method UseInstanceVariable
54    } // end class Scope
```

Fig. 5.10 | Scope class demonstrates instance and local variable scopes. (Part 2 of 2.)

```
 1    // Fig. 5.11: ScopeTest.cs
 2    // Application to test class Scope.
 3    public class ScopeTest
 4    {
 5       // application starting point
 6       public static void Main( string[] args )
 7       {
 8          Scope testScope = new Scope();
 9          testScope.Begin();
10       } // end Main
11    } // end class ScopeTest
```

Fig. 5.11 | Application to test class Scope. (Part 1 of 2.)

```
local x in method Begin is 5

local x on entering method UseLocalVariable is 25
local x before exiting method UseLocalVariable is 26

instance variable x on entering method UseInstanceVariable is 1
instance variable x before exiting method UseInstanceVariable is 10

local x on entering method UseLocalVariable is 25
local x before exiting method UseLocalVariable is 26

instance variable x on entering method UseInstanceVariable is 10
instance variable x before exiting method UseInstanceVariable is 100

local x in method Begin is 5
```

Fig. 5.11 | Application to test class Scope. (Part 2 of 2.)

In class Scope (Fig. 5.11), line 8 declares and initializes the instance variable x to 1. This instance variable is hidden in any block (or method) that declares local variable named x. Method Begin (lines 12–31) declares local variable x (line 14) and initializes it to 5. This local variable's value is output to show that instance variable x (whose value is 1) is hidden in method Begin. The application declares two other methods—UseLocal-Variable (lines 34–43) and UseInstanceVariable (lines 46–53)—that each take no arguments and do not return results. Method Begin calls each method twice (lines 19–28). Method UseLocalVariable declares local variable x (line 36). When UseLocalVariable is first called (line 19), it creates local variable x and initializes it to 25 (line 36), outputs the value of x (lines 38–39), increments x (line 40) and outputs the value of x again (lines 41–42). When UseLocalVariable is called a second time (line 25), it re-creates local variable x and re-initializes it to 25, so the output of each UseLocalVariable call is identical.

Method UseInstanceVariable does not declare any local variables. Therefore, when it refers to x, instance variable x (line 8) of the class is used. When method UseInstance-Variable is first called (line 22), it outputs the value (1) of instance variable x (lines 48–49), multiplies the instance variable x by 10 (line 50) and outputs the value (10) of instance variable x again (lines 51–52) before returning. The next time method UseInstanceVariable is called (line 28), the instance variable has its modified value, 10, so the method outputs 10, then 100. Finally, in method Begin, the application outputs the value of local variable x again (line 30) to show that none of the method calls modified Begin's local variable x, because the methods all referred to variables named x in other scopes.

5.12 Method Overloading

Methods of the same name can be declared in the same class, as long as they have different sets of parameters (determined by the number, types and order of the parameters). This is called *method overloading*. When an *overloaded method* is called, the C# compiler selects the appropriate method by examining the number, types and order of the arguments in the call. Method overloading is commonly used to create several methods with the same name that perform the same or similar tasks, but on different types or different numbers of arguments. For example, Math methods Min and Max (summarized in Section 5.3) are overloaded with 11 versions. These find the minimum and maximum, respectively, of two values of each of the 11 numeric simple types. Our next example demonstrates declaring and invoking overloaded methods. You will see examples of overloaded constructors in Chapter 7.

Declaring Overloaded Methods

In class MethodOverload (Fig. 5.12), we include two overloaded versions of a method called Square—one that calculates the square of an int (and returns an int) and one that calculates the square of a double (and returns a double). Although these methods have the same name and similar parameter lists and bodies, you can think of them simply as *different* methods. It may help to think of the method names as "Square of int" and "Square of double," respectively. When the application begins execution, class MethodOverloadTest's Main method (Fig. 5.13, lines 5–9) creates an object of class MethodOverload (line 7) and calls the object's TestOverloadedMethods method (line 8) to produce the application's output (Fig. 5.13).

In Fig. 5.12, line 10 invokes method Square with the argument 7. Literal integer values are treated as type int, so the method call in line 10 invokes the version of Square at lines 15–20 that specifies an int parameter. Similarly, line 11 invokes method Square

```
1   // Fig. 5.12: MethodOverload.cs
2   // Overloaded method declarations.
3   using System;
4
5   public class MethodOverload
6   {
7      // test overloaded square methods
8      public void TestOverloadedMethods()
9      {
10        Console.WriteLine( "Square of integer 7 is {0}", Square( 7 ) );
11        Console.WriteLine( "Square of double 7.5 is {0}", Square( 7.5 ) );
12     } // end method TestOverloadedMethods
13
14     // square method with int argument
15     public int Square( int intValue )
16     {
17        Console.WriteLine( "Called square with int argument: {0}",
18           intValue );
19        return intValue * intValue;
20     } // end method Square with int argument
21
22     // square method with double argument
23     public double Square( double doubleValue )
24     {
25        Console.WriteLine( "Called square with double argument: {0}",
26           doubleValue );
27        return doubleValue * doubleValue;
28     } // end method Square with double argument
29  } // end class MethodOverload
```

Fig. 5.12 | Overloaded method declarations.

```
 1    // Fig. 5.13: MethodOverloadTest.cs
 2    // Application to test class MethodOverload.
 3    public class MethodOverloadTest
 4    {
 5       public static void Main( string[] args )
 6       {
 7          MethodOverload methodOverload = new MethodOverload();
 8          methodOverload.TestOverloadedMethods();
 9       } // end Main
10    } // end class MethodOverloadTest
```

```
Called square with int argument: 7
Square of integer 7 is 49
Called square with double argument: 7.5
Square of double 7.5 is 56.25
```

Fig. 5.13 | Application to test class `MethodOverload`.

with the argument 5.5. Literal real number values are treated as type `double`, so the method call in line 11 invokes the version of `Square` at lines 23–28 that specifies a `double` parameter. Each method first outputs a line of text to prove that the proper method was called in each case.

Notice that the overloaded methods in Fig. 5.12 perform the same calculation, but with two different types. C#'s new generics feature provides a mechanism for writing a single "generic method" that can perform the same tasks as an entire set of overloaded methods.

Distinguishing Between Overloaded Methods

The compiler distinguishes overloaded methods by their *signature*—a combination of the method's name, and the number, types and order of its parameters. The signature also includes the way those parameters are passed, which can be modified by the `ref` and `out` keywords that we discuss in Section 5.14. If the compiler looked only at method names during compilation, the code in Fig. 5.12 would be ambiguous—the compiler would not know how to distinguish between the two `Square` methods (lines 15–20 and 23–28). Internally, the compiler uses signatures to determine whether the methods in a class are unique in that class.

For example, in Fig. 5.12, the compiler will use the method signatures to distinguish between the "Square of `int`" method (the `Square` method that specifies an `int` parameter) and the "Square of `double`" method (the `Square` method that specifies a `double` parameter). If `Method1`'s declaration begins as

>   `void Method1( int a, float b )`

then that method will have a different signature than the method declared beginning with

>   `void Method1( float a, int b )`

The order of the parameter types is important—the compiler considers the preceding two `Method1` headers to be distinct.

Return Types of Overloaded Methods

In discussing the logical names of methods used by the compiler, we did not mention the return types of the methods. This is because method *calls* cannot be distinguished by return type. The application in Fig. 5.14 illustrates the compiler errors generated when two methods have the same signature, but different return types. Overloaded methods can have the same or different return types if the methods have different parameter lists. Also, overloaded methods need not have the same number of parameters.

 Common Programming Error 5.10

Declaring overloaded methods with identical parameter lists is a compilation error regardless of whether the return types are different.

5.13 Recursion

The applications we have discussed thus far are generally structured as methods that call one another in a disciplined, hierarchical manner. For some problems, however, it is useful to have a method call itself. A *recursive method* is a method that calls itself, either directly or indirectly through another method.

```
1   // Fig. 5.14: MethodOverload.cs
2   // Overloaded methods with identical signatures
3   // cause compilation errors, even if return types are different.
4   public class MethodOverloadError
5   {
6      // declaration of method Square with int argument
7      public int Square( int x )
8      {
9         return x * x;
10     }
11
12     // second declaration of method Square with int argument
13     // causes compilation error even though return types are different
14     public double Square( int y )
15     {
16        return y * y;
17     }
18  } // end class MethodOverloadError
```

Error List					
ⓧ 1 Error ⚠ 0 Warnings ⓘ 0 Messages					
Description	File	Line	Column	Project	
ⓧ 1 Type 'MethodOverloadError' already defines a member called 'Square' with the same parameter types	MethodOverloadError	14	18	MethodOverloadError	

Error List   Find Results

Fig. 5.14 | Overloaded methods with identical signatures cause compilation errors, even if return types are different.

We consider recursion conceptually first. Then we examine an application containing a recursive method. Recursive problem-solving approaches have a number of elements in common. When a recursive method is called to solve a problem, the method actually is capable of solving only the simplest case(s), or ***base case(s)***. If the method is called with a base case, the method returns a result. If the method is called with a more complex problem, the method divides the problem into two conceptual pieces: a piece that the method knows how to do and a piece that the method does not know how to do. To make recursion feasible, the latter piece must resemble the original problem, but be a slightly simpler or slightly smaller version of it. Because this new problem looks like the original problem, the method calls a fresh copy of itself to work on the smaller problem; this is referred to as a ***recursive call*** and is also called the ***recursion step***. The recursion step normally includes a `return` statement, because its result will be combined with the portion of the problem the method knew how to solve to form a result that will be passed back to the original caller.

The recursion step executes while the original call to the method is still active (i.e., while it has not finished executing). The recursion step can result in many more recursive calls, as the method divides each new subproblem into two conceptual pieces. For the recursion to terminate eventually, each time the method calls itself with a slightly simpler version of the original problem, the sequence of smaller and smaller problems must converge on the base case. At that point, the method recognizes the base case and returns a result to the previous copy of the method. A sequence of returns ensues until the original method call returns the result to the caller. This process sounds complex compared with the conventional problem solving we have performed to this point.

Recursive Factorial Calculations

As an example of recursion concepts at work, let us write a recursive application to perform a popular mathematical calculation. Consider the factorial of a nonnegative integer n, written $n!$ (and pronounced "n factorial"), which is the product

$$n \cdot (n-1) \cdot (n-2) \cdot \ldots \cdot 1$$

$1!$ is equal to 1 and $0!$ is defined to be 1. For example, $5!$ is the product $5 \cdot 4 \cdot 3 \cdot 2 \cdot 1$, which is equal to 120.

The factorial of an integer, `number`, greater than or equal to 0 can be calculated iteratively (nonrecursively) using the `for` statement as follows:

```
factorial = 1;

for ( int counter = number; counter >= 1; counter-- )
   factorial *= counter;
```

A recursive declaration of the factorial method is arrived at by observing the following relationship:

$$n! = n \cdot (n-1)!$$

For example, $5!$ is clearly equal to $5 \cdot 4!$, as is shown by the following equations:

$$5! = 5 \cdot 4 \cdot 3 \cdot 2 \cdot 1$$
$$5! = 5 \cdot (4 \cdot 3 \cdot 2 \cdot 1)$$
$$5! = 5 \cdot (4!)$$

The evaluation of 5! would proceed as shown in Fig. 5.15. Figure 5.15(a) shows how the succession of recursive calls proceeds until 1! is evaluated to be 1, which terminates the recursion. Figure 5.15(b) shows the values returned from each recursive call to its caller until the value is calculated and returned.

Figure 5.16 uses recursion to calculate and print the factorials of the integers from 0 to 10. The recursive method Factorial (lines 16–24) first tests to determine whether a terminating condition (line 19) is true. If number is less than or equal to 1 (the base case), Factorial returns 1, no further recursion is necessary and the method returns. If number is greater than 1, line 23 expresses the problem as the product of number and a recursive call to Factorial evaluating the factorial of number - 1, which is a slightly simpler problem than the original calculation, Factorial(number).

Method Factorial (lines 16–24) receives a parameter of type long and returns a result of type long. As can be seen in Fig. 5.16, factorial values become large quickly. We chose type long (which can represent relatively large integers) so that the application could calculate factorials greater than 20!. Unfortunately, the Factorial method produces large values so quickly that factorial values soon exceed even the maximum value that can be stored in a long variable. Due to the restrictions on the integral types, variables of type float, double, and decimal might ultimately be needed to calculate factorials of larger numbers. This situation points to a weakness in many programming languages—the languages are not easily extended to handle the unique requirements of various applications. As you know, C# is an extensible language that allows you to create a type that supports arbitrarily large integers if you wish. You could create a HugeInteger class, for example, that could enable an application to calculate the factorials of arbitrarily large numbers.

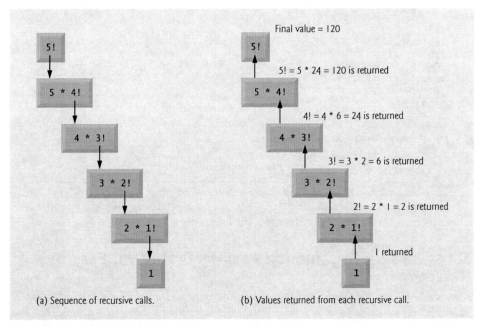

(a) Sequence of recursive calls.

(b) Values returned from each recursive call.

Fig. 5.15 | Recursive evaluation of 5!.

```
1   // Fig. 5.16: FactorialTest.cs
2   // Recursive Factorial method.
3   using System;
4
5   public class FactorialTest
6   {
7      public static void Main( string[] args )
8      {
9         // calculate the factorials of 0 through 10
10        for ( long counter = 0; counter <= 10; counter++ )
11           Console.WriteLine( "{0}! = {1}",
12              counter, Factorial( counter ) );
13     } // end method Main
14
15     // recursive declaration of method Factorial
16     public static long Factorial( long number )
17     {
18        // base case
19        if ( number <= 1 )
20           return 1;
21        // recursion step
22        else
23           return number * Factorial( number - 1 );
24     } // end method Factorial
25  } // end class FactorialTest
```

```
0! = 1
1! = 1
2! = 2
3! = 6
4! = 24
5! = 120
6! = 720
7! = 5040
8! = 40320
9! = 362880
10! = 3628800
```

Fig. 5.16 | Recursive Factorial method.

Common Programming Error 5.11

Either omitting the base case or writing the recursion step incorrectly so that it does not converge on the base case will cause infinite recursion, eventually exhausting memory. This error is analogous to the problem of an infinite loop in an iterative (nonrecursive) solution.

5.14 Passing Arguments: Pass-by-Value vs. Pass-by-Reference

Two ways to pass arguments to functions in many programming languages are *pass-by-value* and *pass-by-reference*. When an argument is passed by value (the default in C#), a *copy* of the argument's value is made and passed to the called function. Changes to the copy do not affect the original variable's value in the caller. This prevents the accidental side effects that so greatly hinder the development of correct and reliable software systems. Each argument that has been passed in the programs in this chapter so far has been passed by value. When an argument is passed by reference, the caller gives the method the ability to access and modify the caller's original variable.

Performance Tip 5.1

Pass-by-reference is good for performance reasons, because it can eliminate the pass-by-value overhead of copying large amounts of data.

Software Engineering Observation 5.5

Pass-by-reference can weaken security, because the called function can corrupt the caller's data.

To pass an object by reference into a method, simply provide as an argument in the method call the variable that refers to the object. Then, in the method body, reference the object using the parameter name. The parameter refers to the original object in memory, so the called method can access the original object directly.

Previously, we discussed the difference between value types and reference types. One of the major differences between them is that value-type variables store values, so specifying a value-type variable in a method call passes a copy of that variable's value to the method. Reference-type variables store references to objects, so specifying a reference-type variable as an argument passes the method a copy of the actual reference that refers to the object. Even though the reference itself is passed by value, the method can still use the reference it receives to modify the original object in memory. Similarly, when returning information from a method via a `return` statement, the method returns a copy of the value stored in a value-type variable or a copy of the reference stored in a reference-type variable. When a reference is returned, the calling method can use that reference to interact with the referenced object. So, in effect, objects are always passed by reference.

What if you would like to pass a variable by reference so the called method can modify the variable's value? To do this, C# provides keywords ***ref*** and ***out***. Applying the `ref` keyword to a parameter declaration allows you to pass a variable to a method by reference—the called method will be able to modify the original variable in the caller. The `ref` keyword is used for variables that already have been initialized in the calling method. Normally, when a method call contains an uninitialized variable as an argument, the compiler generates an error. Preceding a parameter with keyword `out` creates an ***output parameter***. This indicates to the compiler that the argument will be passed into the called method by reference and that the called method will assign a value to the original variable in the caller. If the method does not assign a value to the output parameter in every possible path of execution, the compiler generates an error. This also prevents the compiler from generating an error message for an uninitialized variable that is passed as an argument to a method. A method can return only one value to its caller via a return statement, but can return many values by specifying multiple output parameters.

You can also pass a reference-type variable by reference, which allows you to modify the passed reference-type variable so that it references a new object. Passing a reference by reference is a tricky but powerful technique that we discuss in Section 6.8.

The application in Figs. 5.17 and 5.18 uses the `ref` and `out` keywords to manipulate integer values. Class `ReferenceAndOutputParameters` (Fig. 5.17) contains three methods that calculate the square of an integer. Method SquareRef (lines 37–40) multiplies its parameter x by itself and assigns the new value to x. SquareRef's parameter x is declared as ref int, which indicates that the argument passed to this method must be an integer that is passed by reference. Because the argument is passed by reference, the assignment at line 39 modifies the original argument's value in the caller.

Method SquareOut (lines 44–48) assigns its parameter the value 6 (line 46), then squares that value. SquareOut's parameter is declared as out int, which indicates that the argument passed to this method must be an integer that is passed by reference and that the argument does not need to be initialized in advance.

```
1    // Fig. 5.17: ReferenceAndOutputParameters.cs
2    // Reference, output and value parameters.
3    using System;
4
5    class ReferenceAndOutputParameters
6    {
7       // call methods with reference, output and value parameters
8       public void DemonstrateReferenceAndOutputParameters()
9       {
10          int y = 5; // initialize y to 5
11          int z; // declares z, but does not initialize it
12
13          // display original values of y and z
14          Console.WriteLine( "Original value of y: {0}", y );
15          Console.WriteLine( "Original value of z: uninitialized\n" );
16
17          // pass y and z by reference
18          SquareRef( ref y ); // must use keyword ref
19          SquareOut( out z ); // must use keyword out
20
21          // display values of y and z after they are modified by
22          // methods SquareRef and SquareOut, respectively
23          Console.WriteLine( "Value of y after SquareRef: {0}", y );
24          Console.WriteLine( "Value of z after SquareOut: {0}\n", z );
25
26          // pass y and z by value
27          Square( y );
28          Square( z );
29
30          // display values of y and z after they are passed to method Square
31          // to demonstrate arguments passed by value are not modified
32          Console.WriteLine( "Value of y after Square: {0}", y );
33          Console.WriteLine( "Value of z after Square: {0}", z );
34       } // end method DemonstrateReferenceAndOutputParameters
35
36       // uses reference parameter x to modify caller's variable
37       void SquareRef( ref int x )
38       {
39          x = x * x; // squares value of caller's variable
40       } // end method SquareRef
41
```

Fig. 5.17 | Reference, output and value parameters. (Part 1 of 2.)

```
42        // uses output parameter x to assign a value
43        // to an uninitialized variable
44        void SquareOut( out int x )
45        {
46           x = 6; // assigns a value to caller's variable
47           x = x * x; // squares value of caller's variable
48        } // end method SquareOut
49
50        // parameter x receives a copy of the value passed as an argument,
51        // so this method cannot modify the caller's variable
52        void Square( int x )
53        {
54           x = x * x;
55        } // end method Square
56     } // end class ReferenceAndOutputParameters
```

Fig. 5.17 | Reference, output and value parameters. (Part 2 of 2.)

```
1     // Fig. 5.18: ReferenceAndOutputParamtersTest.cs
2     // Application to test class ReferenceAndOutputParameters.
3     class ReferenceAndOutputParamtersTest
4     {
5        static void Main( string[] args )
6        {
7           ReferenceAndOutputParameters test =
8              new ReferenceAndOutputParameters();
9           test.DemonstrateReferenceAndOutputParameters();
10        } // end Main
11     } // end class ReferenceAndOutputParamtersTest
```

```
Original value of y: 5
Original value of z: uninitialized

Value of y after SquareRef: 25
Value of z after SquareOut: 36

Value of y after Square: 25
Value of z after Square: 36
```

Fig. 5.18 | Application to test class ReferenceAndOutputParameters.

Method Square (lines 52–55) multiplies its parameter x by itself and assigns the new value to x. When this method is called, a copy of the argument is passed to the parameter x. Thus, even though parameter x is modified in the method, the original value in the caller is not modified.

Method DemonstrateReferenceAndOutputParameters (lines 8–34) invokes methods SquareRef, SquareOut and Square. This method begins by initializing variable y to 5 and declaring, but not initializing, variable z. Lines 18–19 call methods SquareRef and SquareOut. Notice that when you pass a variable to a method with a reference parameter, you must precede the argument with the same keyword (ref or out) that was used to declare the reference parameter. Lines 23–24 display the values of y and z after the calls to SquareRef and SquareOut. Notice that y has been changed to 25 and z has been set to 36.

Lines 27–28 call method Square with y and z as arguments. In this case, both variables are passed by value—only copies of their values are passed to Square. As a result, the values of y and z remain 25 and 36, respectively. Lines 32–33 output the values of y and z to show that they were not modified.

Common Programming Error 5.12

The ref and out arguments in a method call must match the parameters specified in the method declaration; otherwise, a compilation error occurs.

Software Engineering Observation 5.6

By default, C# does not allow you to choose whether to pass each argument by value or by reference. Value-types are passed by value. Objects are not passed to methods; rather, references to objects are passed to methods. The references themselves are passed by value. When a method receives a reference to an object, the method can manipulate the object directly, but the reference value cannot be changed to refer to a new object. In Section 6.8, you'll see that references also can be passed by reference.

5.15 (Optional) Software Engineering Case Study: Identifying Class Operations in the ATM System

In the "Software Engineering Case Study" sections at the ends of Chapters 2–4, we performed the first few steps in the object-oriented design of our ATM system. In Chapter 2, we identified the classes that we will likely need to implement, and we created our first class diagram. In Chapter 3, we described some attributes of our classes. In Chapter 4, we examined our objects' states and modeled their state transitions and activities. In this section, we determine some of the class operations (or behaviors) needed to implement the ATM system.

Identifying Operations

An operation is a service that objects of a class provide to clients of the class. Consider the operations of some real-world objects. A radio's operations include setting its station and volume (typically invoked by a person adjusting the radio's controls). A car's operations include accelerating (invoked by the driver pressing the accelerator pedal), decelerating (invoked by the driver pressing the brake pedal or releasing the gas pedal), turning, and shifting gears. Software objects can offer operations as well—for example, a software graphics object might offer operations for drawing a circle, drawing a line and drawing a square. A spreadsheet software object might offer operations like printing the spreadsheet, totaling the elements in a row or column and graphing information in the spreadsheet as a bar chart or pie chart.

We can derive many of the operations of the classes in our ATM system by examining the verbs and verb phrases in the requirements document. We then relate each of these to particular classes in our system (Fig. 5.19). The verb phrases in Fig. 5.19 help us determine the operations of our classes.

Modeling Operations

To identify operations, we examine the verb phrases listed for each class in Fig. 5.19. The "executes financial transactions" phrase associated with class ATM implies that class ATM instructs transactions to execute. Therefore, classes BalanceInquiry, Withdrawal and Deposit

Class	Verbs and verb phrases
ATM	executes financial transactions
BalanceInquiry	[none in the requirements document]
Withdrawal	[none in the requirements document]
Deposit	[none in the requirements document]
BankDatabase	authenticates a user, retrieves an account balance, credits an account, debits an account
Account	retrieves an account balance, credits a deposit amount to an account, debits a withdrawal amount to an account
Screen	displays a message to the user
Keypad	receives numeric input from the user
CashDispenser	dispenses cash, indicates whether it contains enough cash to satisfy a withdrawal request
DepositSlot	receives a deposit envelope

Fig. 5.19 | Verbs and verb phrases for each class in the ATM system.

each need an operation to provide this service to the ATM. We place this operation (which we have named Execute) in the third compartment of the three transaction classes in the updated class diagram of Fig. 5.20. During an ATM session, the ATM object will invoke the Execute operation of each transaction object to tell it to execute.

The UML represents operations (which are implemented as methods in C#) by listing the operation name, followed by a comma-separated list of parameters in parentheses, a colon and the return type:

operationName(parameter1, parameter2, …, parameterN) : returnType

Each parameter in the comma-separated parameter list consists of a parameter name, followed by a colon and the parameter type:

parameterName : parameterType

For the moment, we do not list the parameters of our operations—we will identify and model the parameters of some of the operations shortly. For some of the operations, we do not yet know the return types, so we also omit them from the diagram. These omissions are perfectly normal at this point. As our design and implementation proceed, we will add the remaining return types.

Operations of Class BankDatabase and Class Account

Figure 5.19 lists the phrase "authenticates a user" next to class BankDatabase—the database is the object that contains the account information necessary to determine whether the account number and PIN entered by a user match those of an account at the bank. Therefore, class BankDatabase needs an operation that provides an authentication service to the ATM. We place the operation AuthenticateUser in the third compartment of class BankDatabase (Fig. 5.20). However, an object of class Account, not class BankDatabase,

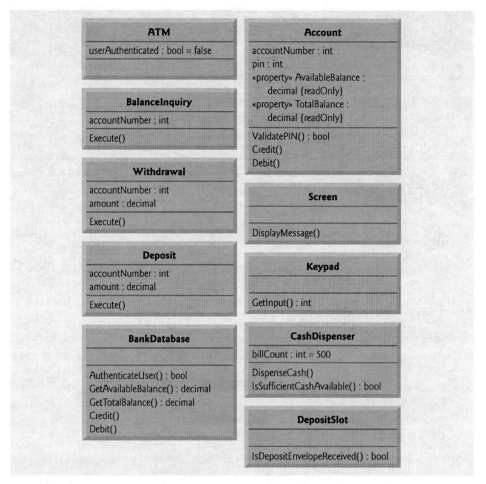

Fig. 5.20 | Classes in the ATM system with attributes and operations.

stores the account number and PIN that must be accessed to authenticate a user, so class Account must provide a service to validate a PIN obtained through user input against a PIN stored in an Account object. Therefore, we add a ValidatePIN operation to class Account. Note that we specify a return type of bool for the AuthenticateUser and ValidatePIN operations. Each operation returns a value indicating either that the operation was successful in performing its task (i.e., a return value of true) or that it was not successful (i.e., a return value of false).

Figure 5.19 lists several additional verb phrases for class BankDatabase: "retrieves an account balance," "credits an account" and "debits an account." Like "authenticates a user," these remaining phrases refer to services that the database must provide to the ATM, because the database holds all the account data used to authenticate a user and perform ATM transactions. However, objects of class Account actually perform the operations to which these phrases refer. Thus, class BankDatabase and class Account both need operations that correspond to each of these phrases. Recall from Section 2.11 that, because a bank account contains sensitive information, we do not allow the ATM to access accounts directly. The database acts as an intermediary between the ATM and the account data, preventing unauthorized access. As we will see in Section 6.14, class ATM invokes the operations of class BankDatabase, each of which in turn invokes corresponding operations (which are get accessors of read-only properties) in class Account.

The phrase "retrieves an account balance" suggests that classes BankDatabase and Account each need an operation that gets the balance. However, recall that Fig. 3.16 specified two attributes in class Account to represent a balance—availableBalance and totalBalance. A balance inquiry requires access to both balance attributes so that it can display them to the user, but a withdrawal needs to check only the value of available-Balance. To allow objects in the system to obtain these balance attributes individually from a specific Account object in the BankDatabase, we add operations GetAvailable-Balance and GetTotalBalance to the third compartment of class BankDatabase (Fig. 5.20). We specify a return type of decimal for each of these operations, because the balances that they retrieve are of type decimal.

Once the BankDatabase knows which Account to access, the BankDatabase must be able to obtain each balance attribute individually from that Account. For this purpose, we could add operations GetAvailableBalance and GetTotalBalance to the third compartment of class Account (Fig. 5.20). However, in C#, simple operations such as getting the value of an attribute are typically performed by a property's get accessor (at least when that particular class "owns" the underlying attribute). This design is for a C# application, so rather than modeling operations GetAvailableBalance and GetTotalBalance, we model decimal properties AvailableBalance and TotalBalance in class Account. Properties are placed in the second compartment of a class diagram. These properties replace the availableBalance and total-Balance attributes that we modeled for class Account in Fig. 3.16. Recall from Chapter 2 that a property's accessors are implied—thus, they are not modeled in a class diagram. Figure 5.19 does not mention the need to set the balances, so Fig. 5.20 shows properties Available-Balance and TotalBalance as read-only properties (i.e., they have only get accessors). To indicate a read-only property in the UML, we follow the property's type with "{readOnly}."

You may be wondering why we modeled AvailableBalance and TotalBalance *properties* in class Account, but modeled GetAvailableBalance and GetTotalBalance *operations* in class BankDatabase. Since there can be many Account objects in the BankDatabase, the ATM must specify which Account to access when invoking BankDatabase operations GetAvailableBalance and GetTotalBalance. The ATM does this by passing an account number argument to each BankDatabase operation. The get accessors of the properties you have seen in C# code cannot receive arguments. Thus, we modeled GetAvailableBalance and GetTotalBalance as operations in class BankDatabase so that we could specify parameters to which the ATM can pass arguments. Also, the underlying balance attributes are not owned by the BankDatabase, so get accessors are not appropriate here. We discuss the parameters for the BankDatabase operations shortly.

The phrases "credits an account" and "debits from an account" indicate that classes BankDatabase and Account must perform operations to update an account during deposits and withdrawals, respectively. We therefore assign Credit and Debit operations to classes BankDatabase and Account. You may recall that crediting an account (as in a deposit) adds an amount only to the Account's total balance. Debiting an account (as in a withdrawal), on the other hand, subtracts the amount from both the total and available balances. We hide these implementation details inside class Account. This is a good example of encapsulation and information hiding.

If this were a real ATM system, classes BankDatabase and Account would also provide a set of operations to allow another banking system to update a user's account balance after either confirming or rejecting all or part of a deposit. Operation ConfirmDepositAmount, for example, would add an amount to the Account's available balance, thus making deposited funds available for withdrawal. Operation RejectDepositAmount would subtract an amount from the Account's total balance to indicate that a specified amount, which had recently been deposited through the ATM and added to the Account's total balance, was invalidated (or checks may have "bounced"). The bank would invoke operation RejectDepositAmout after determining either that the user failed to include the correct amount of cash or that any checks did not clear (i.e., they "bounced"). While adding these operations would make our system more complete, we do not include them in our class diagrams or implementation because they are beyond the scope of the case study.

Operations of Class *Screen*

Class Screen "displays a message to the user" at various times in an ATM session. All visual output occurs through the screen of the ATM. The requirements document describes many types of messages (e.g., a welcome message, an error message, a thank-you message) that the screen displays to the user. The requirements document also indicates that the screen displays prompts and menus to the user. However, a prompt is really just a message describing what the user should input next, and a menu is essentially a type of prompt consisting of a series of messages (i.e., menu options) displayed consecutively. Therefore, rather than provide class Screen with an individual operation to display each type of message, prompt and menu, we simply create one operation that can display any message specified by a parameter. We place this operation (DisplayMessage) in the third compartment of class Screen in our class diagram (Fig. 5.20). Note that we do not worry about the parameter of this operation at this time—we model the parameter momentarily.

Operations of Class *Keypad*

From the phrase "receives numeric input from the user" listed by class Keypad in Fig. 5.19, we conclude that class Keypad should perform a GetInput operation. Because the ATM's keypad, unlike a computer keyboard, contains only the numbers 0–9, we specify that this operation returns an integer value. Recall from the requirements document that in different situations, the user may be required to enter a different type of number (e.g., an account number, a PIN, the number of a menu option, a deposit amount as a number of cents). Class Keypad simply obtains a numeric value for a client of the class—it does not determine whether the value meets any specific criteria. Any class that uses this operation must verify that the user entered appropriate numbers and, if not, display error messages via class Screen). [*Note:* When we implement the system, we simulate the ATM's keypad with a computer keyboard, and for simplicity, we assume that the user does not enter nonnumeric input using keys on the computer keyboard that do not appear on the ATM's keypad.

Operations of Class *CashDispenser* and Class *DepositSlot*

Figure 5.19 lists "dispenses cash" for class CashDispenser. Therefore, we create operation DispenseCash and list it under class CashDispenser in Fig. 5.20. Class CashDispenser also "indicates whether it contains enough cash to satisfy a withdrawal request." Thus, we include IsSufficientCashAvailable, an operation that returns a value of type bool, in class CashDispenser. Figure 5.19 also lists "receives a deposit envelope" for class Deposit-Slot. The deposit slot must indicate whether it received an envelope, so we place the operation IsEnvelopeReceived, which returns a bool value, in the third compartment of class DepositSlot. [*Note:* A real hardware deposit slot would most likely send the ATM a signal to indicate that an envelope was received. We simulate this behavior, however, with an operation in class DepositSlot that class ATM can invoke to find out whether the deposit slot received an envelope.]

Operations of Class ATM

We do not list any operations for class ATM at this time. We are not yet aware of any services that class ATM provides to other classes in the system. When we implement the system in C#, however, operations of this class, and additional operations of the other classes in the system, may become apparent.

Identifying and Modeling Operation Parameters

So far, we have not been concerned with the parameters of our operations—we have attempted to gain only a basic understanding of the operations of each class. Let's now take a closer look at some operation parameters. We identify an operation's parameters by examining what data the operation requires to perform its assigned task.

Consider the AuthenticateUser operation of class BankDatabase. To authenticate a user, this operation must know the account number and PIN supplied by the user. Thus we specify that operation AuthenticateUser takes int parameters userAccountNumber and userPIN, which the operation must compare to the account number and PIN of an Account object in the database. We prefix these parameter names with user to avoid confusion between the operation's parameter names and the attribute names that belong to class Account. We list these parameters in the class diagram in Fig. 5.21, which models only class BankDatabase. [*Note:* It is perfectly normal to model only one class in a class diagram. In this case, we are most concerned with examining the parameters of this particular class, so we omit the other classes. In class diagrams later in the case study, parameters are no longer the focus of our attention, so we omit the parameters to save space. Remember, however, that the operations listed in these diagrams still have parameters.]

Recall that the UML models each parameter in an operation's comma-separated parameter list by listing the parameter name, followed by a colon and the parameter type. Figure 5.21 thus specifies, for example, that operation AuthenticateUser takes two parameters—userAccountNumber and userPIN, both of type int.

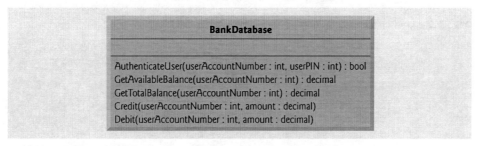

Fig. 5.21 | Class BankDatabase with operation parameters.

Class BankDatabase operations GetAvailableBalance, GetTotalBalance, Credit and Debit also each require a userAccountNumber parameter to identify the account to which the database must apply the operations, so we include these parameters in the class diagram. In addition, operations Credit and Debit each require a decimal parameter amount to specify the amount of money to be credited or debited, respectively.

The class diagram in Fig. 5.22 models the parameters of class Account's operations. Operation ValidatePIN requires only a userPIN parameter, which contains the user-specified PIN to be compared with the PIN associated with the account. Like their counterparts in class BankDatabase, operations Credit and Debit in class Account each require a decimal parameter amount that indicates the amount of money involved in the operation. Note that class Account's operations do not require an account number parameter—each of these operations can be invoked only on the Account object in which they are executing, so including a parameter to specify an Account is unnecessary.

Figure 5.23 models class Screen with a parameter specified for operation Display-Message. This operation requires only string parameter message, which indicates the text to be displayed.

The class diagram in Fig. 5.24 specifies that operation DispenseCash of class Cash-Dispenser takes decimal parameter amount to indicate the amount of cash (in dollars) to be dispensed. Operation IsSufficientCashAvailable also takes decimal parameter amount to indicate the amount of cash in question.

Note that we do not discuss parameters for operation Execute of classes Balance-Inquiry, Withdrawal and Deposit, operation GetInput of class Keypad and operation IsEnvelopeReceived of class DepositSlot. At this point in our design process, we cannot determine whether these operations require additional data to perform their tasks, so we leave their parameter lists empty. As we progress through the case study, we may decide to add parameters to these operations.

```
                    Account
────────────────────────────────────────
accountNumber : int
pin : int
«property» AvailableBalance : decimal {readOnly}
«property» TotalBalance : decimal {readOnly}
────────────────────────────────────────
ValidatePIN(userPIN: int) : bool
Credit(amount : decimal)
Debit(amount : decimal)
```

Fig. 5.22 | Class Account with operation parameters.

```
                    Screen
────────────────────────────────────────

────────────────────────────────────────
DisplayMessage(message : string)
```

Fig. 5.23 | Class Screen with an operation parameter.

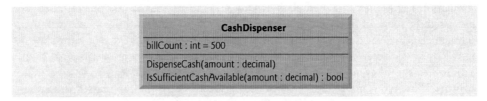

Fig. 5.24 | Class `CashDispenser` with operation parameters.

In this section, we have determined many of the operations performed by the classes in the ATM system. We have identified the parameters and return types of some of the operations. As we continue our design process, the number of operations belonging to each class may vary—we might find that new operations are needed or that some current operations are unnecessary—and we might determine that some of our class operations need additional parameters and different return types. Again, all of this is perfectly normal.

Software Engineering Case Study Self-Review Exercises

5.1 Which of the following is not a behavior?
    a) reading data from a file
    b) printing output
    c) text output
    d) obtaining input from the user

5.2 If you were to add to the ATM system an operation that returns the amount attribute of class `Withdrawal`, how and where would you specify this operation in the class diagram of Fig. 5.20?

5.3 Describe the meaning of the following operation listing that might appear in a class diagram for an object-oriented design of a calculator:

```
Add( x : int, y : int ) : int
```

Answers to Software Engineering Case Study Self-Review Exercises

5.1 c.

5.2 An operation that retrieves the amount attribute of class `Withdrawal` would typically be implemented as a get accessor of a property of class `Withdrawal`. The following would replace attribute amount in the attribute (i.e., second) compartment of class `Withdrawal`:

```
«property» Amount : decimal
```

5.3 This is an operation named `Add` that takes `int` parameters x and y and returns an `int` value. This operation would most likely sum its parameters x and y and return the result.

5.16 Wrap-Up

In this chapter, we discussed the difference between non-`static` and `static` methods, and we showed how to call `static` methods by preceding the method name with the name of the class in which it appears and the dot (.) operator. You saw that the `Math` class in the Framework Class Library provides many `static` methods to perform mathematical calculations. We presented several commonly used FCL namespaces. You learned how to use operator + to perform `string` concatenations. You also learned how to declare constant values in two ways—with the `const` keyword and with `enum` types. We demonstrated simulation techniques and used class Random to generate sets of random numbers. We discussed the scope of fields and local variables in a class. You saw how to overload methods in a class by providing methods with the same name but different signatures. We discussed how recursive methods call themselves, breaking larger problems into smaller subproblems until eventually the original problem is solved. You learned the differences between value types and reference types with respect to how they are passed to methods, and how to use the ref and out keywords to pass arguments by reference.

In Chapter 6, you will learn how to maintain lists and tables of data in arrays. You will see a more elegant implementation of the application that rolls a die 6000 times and two enhanced versions of our GradeBook case study. You will also learn how to access an application's command-line arguments that are passed to method Main when a console application begins execution.

6

Arrays

OBJECTIVES

In this chapter you will learn:

- To use arrays to store data in and retrieve data from lists and tables of values.

- To declare arrays, initialize arrays and refer to individual elements of arrays.

- To use the **foreach** statement to iterate through arrays.

- To pass arrays to methods.

- To declare and manipulate multidimensional arrays.

- To write methods that use variable-length argument lists.

- To read command-line arguments into an application.

6.1 Introduction

This chapter introduces the important topic of *data structures*—collections of related data items. *Arrays* are data structures consisting of related data items of the same type. Arrays are fixed-length entities—they remain the same length once they are created, although an array variable may be reassigned such that it refers to a new array of a different length.

After discussing how arrays are declared, created and initialized, we present a series of examples that demonstrate several common array manipulations. We also present a case study that uses arrays to simulate shuffling and dealing playing cards for use in card game applications. The chapter demonstrates C#'s last structured control statement—the `foreach` repetition statement—which provides a concise notation for accessing the data in arrays. Two sections of the chapter enhance the `GradeBook` case study from Chapters 2–4. In particular, we use arrays to enable the class to maintain a set of grades in memory and analyze student grades from multiple exams. These and other examples demonstrate the ways in which arrays allow you to organize and manipulate data.

6.2 Arrays

An array is a group of variables (called *elements*) containing values that all have the same type. Recall that types are divided into two categories—value types and reference types. Arrays are reference types. As you will see, what we typically think of as an array is actually a reference to an array instance in memory. The elements of an array can be either value types or reference types (including other arrays, as we will see in Section 6.10). To refer to a particular element in an array, we specify the name of the reference to the array and the position number of the element in the array. The position number of the element is called the element's *index*.

Figure 6.1 shows a logical representation of an integer array called c. This array contains 12 elements. An application refers to any one of these elements with an *array-access expression* that includes the name of the array, followed by the index of the particular element in *square brackets* ([]). The first element in every array has *index zero* and is sometimes called the *zeroth element.* Thus, the elements of array c are c[0], c[1], c[2] and so on. The highest index in array c is 11, which is one less than the number of elements in the array, because indices begin at 0. Array names follow the same conventions as other variable names.

An index must be a nonnegative integer and can be an expression. For example, if we assume that variable a is 5 and variable b is 6, then the statement

```
c[ a + b ] += 2;
```

adds 2 to array element c[11]. Note that an indexed array name is an array-access expression. Such expressions can be used on the left side of an assignment to place a new value into an array element. The array index must be a value of type int, uint, long or ulong, or a value of a type that can be implicitly promoted to one of these types.

Let's examine array c in Fig. 6.1 more closely. The *name* of the array is c. Every array instance knows its own length and provides access to this information with the Length property. For example, the expression c.Length uses array c's Length property to determine the length of the array. Note that the Length property of an array cannot be changed, because it does not provide a set accessor. The array's 12 elements are referred to as c[0], c[1], c[2], ..., c[11]. It is an error to refer to elements outside this range, such as c[-1] or c[12]. The value of c[0] is -45, the value of c[1] is 6, the value of c[2] is 0, the value of c[7] is 62 and the value of c[11] is 78. To calculate the sum of the values contained in the first three elements of array c and store the result in variable sum, we would write

```
sum = c[ 0 ] + c[ 1 ] + c[ 2 ];
```

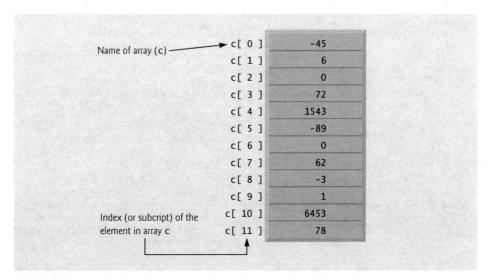

Fig. 6.1 | A 12-element array.

To divide the value of c[6] by 2 and assign the result to the variable x, we would write

```
x = c[ 6 ] / 2;
```

6.3 Declaring and Creating Arrays

Array instances occupy space in memory. Like objects, arrays are created with keyword new. To create an array instance, you specify the type and the number of array elements and the number of elements as part of an *array-creation expression* that uses keyword new. Such an expression returns a reference that can be stored in an array variable. The following declaration and array-creation expression create an array object containing 12 int elements and store the array's reference in variable c:

```
int[] c = new int[ 12 ];
```

This expression can be used to create the array shown in Fig. 6.1 (but not the initial values in the array—we'll show how to initialize the elements of an array momentarily). This task also can be performed in two steps as follows:

```
int[] c; // declare the array variable
c = new int[ 12 ]; // create the array; assign to array variable
```

In the declaration, the square brackets following the variable type int indicate that c is a variable that will refer to an array of ints (i.e., c will store a reference to an array object). In the assignment statement, the array variable c receives the reference to a new array object of 12 int elements. When an array is created, each element of the array receives a default value—0 for the numeric simple-type elements, false for bool elements and null for references. As we will soon see, we can provide specific, nondefault initial element values when we create an array.

Common Programming Error 6.1

In an array declaration, specifying the number of elements in the square brackets of the declaration (e.g., int[12] c;) is a syntax error.

An application can create several arrays in a single declaration. The following declaration reserves 100 elements for string array b and 27 elements for string array x:

```
string[] b = new string[ 100 ], x = new string[ 27 ];
```

In this declaration, string[] applies to each variable in the declaration. For readability, we prefer to declare only one variable per declaration, as in:

```
string[] b = new string[ 100 ]; // create string array b
string[] x = new string[ 27 ]; // create string array x
```

Good Programming Practice 6.1

For readability, declare only one variable per declaration. Keep each declaration on a separate line and include a comment describing the variable being declared.

An application can declare arrays of value-type elements or reference-type elements. For example, every element of an int array is an int value, and every element of a string array is a reference to a string object.

6.4 Examples Using Arrays

This section presents several examples that demonstrate declaring arrays, creating arrays, initializing arrays and manipulating array elements.

Creating and Initializing an Array

The application of Fig. 6.2 uses keyword new to create an array of 10 int elements that are initially 0 (the default for int variables).

Line 9 declares array—a reference capable of referring to an array of int elements. Line 12 creates the 10-element array object and assigns its reference to variable array. Line 14 outputs the column headings. The first column contains the index (0–9) of each array element, and the second column contains the default value (0) of each array element and has a field width of 8.

The for statement in lines 17–18 outputs the index number (represented by counter) and the value (represented by array[counter]) of each array element. Note that the loop control variable counter is initially 0—index values start at 0, so using zero-based counting allows the loop to access every element of the array. The for statement's loop-continuation

```
1   // Fig. 6.2: InitArray.cs
2   // Creating an array.
3   using System;
4
5   public class InitArray
6   {
7      public static void Main( string[] args )
8      {
9         int[] array; // declare array named array
10
11        // create the space for array and initialize to default zeros
12        array = new int[ 10 ]; // 10 int elements
13
14        Console.WriteLine( "{0}{1,8}", "Index", "Value" ); // headings
15
16        // output each array element's value
17        for ( int counter = 0; counter < array.Length; counter++ )
18           Console.WriteLine( "{0,5}{1,8}", counter, array[ counter ] );
19     } // end Main
20  } // end class InitArray
```

```
Index    Value
    0        0
    1        0
    2        0
    3        0
    4        0
    5        0
    6        0
    7        0
    8        0
    9        0
```

Fig. 6.2 | Creating an array.

condition uses the property array.Length (line 17) to obtain the length of the array. In this example, the length of the array is 10, so the loop continues executing as long as the value of control variable counter is less than 10. The highest index value of a 10-element array is 9, so using the less-than operator in the loop-continuation condition guarantees that the loop does not attempt to access an element beyond the end of the array (i.e., during the final iteration of the loop, counter is 9). We will soon see what happens when such an out-of-range index is encountered at execution time.

Using an Array Initializer

An application can create an array and initialize its elements with an *array initializer*, which is a comma-separated list of expressions (called an *initializer list*) enclosed in braces. In this case, the array length is determined by the number of elements in the initializer list. For example, the declaration

```
int[] n = { 10, 20, 30, 40, 50 };
```

creates a five-element array with index values 0, 1, 2, 3 and 4. Element n[0] is initialized to 10, n[1] is initialized to 20 and so on. This declaration does not require new to create the array object. When the compiler encounters an array declaration that includes an initializer list, the compiler counts the number of initializers in the list to determine the size of the array, then sets up the appropriate new operation "behind the scenes."

The application in Fig. 6.3 initializes an integer array with 10 values (line 10) and displays the array in tabular format. The code for displaying the array elements (lines 15–16) is identical to that in Fig. 6.2 (lines 17–18).

Calculating a Value to Store in Each Array Element

Some applications calculate the value to be stored in each array element. The application in Fig. 6.4 creates a 10-element array and assigns to each element one of the even integers from 2 to 20 (2, 4, 6, ..., 20). Then the application displays the array in tabular format. The for statement at lines 13–14 calculates an array element's value by multiplying the current value of the for loop's control variable counter by 2, then adding 2.

Line 9 uses the modifier const to declare the constant ARRAY_LENGTH, whose value is 10. Constants must be initialized when they are declared and cannot be modified thereafter. Note that constants, like the enum constants introduced in Section 5.10, are declared with all capital letters by convention, to make them stand out in the code.

```
1   // Fig. 6.3: InitArray.cs
2   // Initializing the elements of an array with an array initializer.
3   using System;
4
5   public class InitArray
6   {
7      public static void Main( string[] args )
8      {
9         // initializer list specifies the value for each element
10        int[] array = { 32, 27, 64, 18, 95, 14, 90, 70, 60, 37 };
11
12        Console.WriteLine( "{0}{1,8}", "Index", "Value" ); // headings
```

Fig. 6.3 | Initializing the elements of an array with an array initializer. (Part 1 of 2.)

```
13
14              // output each array element's value
15              for ( int counter = 0; counter < array.Length; counter++ )
16                  Console.WriteLine( "{0,5}{1,8}", counter, array[ counter ] );
17          } // end Main
18      } // end class InitArray
```

```
Index    Value
    0       32
    1       27
    2       64
    3       18
    4       95
    5       14
    6       90
    7       70
    8       60
    9       37
```

Fig. 6.3 | Initializing the elements of an array with an array initializer. (Part 2 of 2.)

Good Programming Practice 6.2

*Constants also are called **named constants**. Such variables often make applications more read-able than applications that use literal values (e.g., 10)—a named constant such as ARRAY_LENGTH clearly indicates its purpose, whereas a literal value could have different meanings based on the context in which it is used. Another advantage to using named constants is that if the value of the constant must be changed, it is necessary to change it only in the declaration, thus reducing the cost of maintaining the code.*

```
1   // Fig. 6.4: InitArray.cs
2   // Calculating values to be placed into the elements of an array.
3   using System;
4
5   public class InitArray
6   {
7       public static void Main( string[] args )
8       {
9           const int ARRAY_LENGTH = 10; // create a named constant
10          int[] array = new int[ ARRAY_LENGTH ]; // create array
11
12          // calculate value for each array element
13          for ( int counter = 0; counter < array.Length; counter++ )
14              array[ counter ] = 2 + 2 * counter;
15
16          Console.WriteLine( "{0}{1,8}", "Index", "Value" ); // headings
17
18          // output each array element's value
19          for ( int counter = 0; counter < array.Length; counter++ )
20              Console.WriteLine( "{0,5}{1,8}", counter, array[ counter ] );
21      } // end Main
22  } // end class InitArray
```

Fig. 6.4 | Calculating values to be placed into the elements of an array. (Part 1 of 2.)

```
Index    Value
    0        2
    1        4
    2        6
    3        8
    4       10
    5       12
    6       14
    7       16
    8       18
    9       20
```

Fig. 6.4 | Calculating values to be placed into the elements of an array. (Part 2 of 2.)

Common Programming Error 6.2

Assigning a value to a named constant after it has been initialized is a compilation error.

Common Programming Error 6.3

Attempting to declare a named constant without initializing it is a compilation error.

Summing the Elements of an Array

Often, the elements of an array represent a series of values to be used in a calculation. For example, if the elements of an array represent exam grades, an instructor may wish to total the elements of the array and use that total to calculate the class average for the exam. The GradeBook examples later in the chapter (Fig. 6.15 and Fig. 6.20) use this technique.

The application in Fig. 6.5 sums the values contained in a 10-element integer array. The application declares, creates and initializes the array at line 9. The for statement performs the calculations. [*Note:* The values supplied as array initializers are often read into an application, rather than specified in an initializer list. For example, an application could input the values from a user or from a file on disk. Reading the data into an application makes the application more reusable, because it can be used with different sets of data.]

Using Bar Charts to Display Array Data Graphically

Many applications present data to users in a graphical manner. For example, numeric values are often displayed as bars in a bar chart. In such a chart, longer bars represent proportionally larger numeric values. One simple way to display numeric data graphically is with a bar chart that shows each numeric value as a bar of asterisks (*).

Instructors often like to examine the distribution of grades on an exam. An instructor might graph the number of grades in each of several categories to visualize the grade distribution for the exam. Suppose the grades on an exam were 87, 68, 94, 100, 83, 78, 85, 91, 76 and 87. Note that there was one grade of 100, two grades in the 90s, four grades in the 80s, two grades in the 70s, one grade in the 60s and no grades below 60. Our next application (Fig. 6.6) stores this grade distribution data in an array of 11 elements, each corresponding to a category of grades. For example, array[0] indicates the number of grades in the range 0–9, array[7] indicates the number of grades in the range 70–79 and

```
1   // Fig. 6.5: SumArray.cs
2   // Computing the sum of the elements of an array.
3   using System;
4
5   public class SumArray
6   {
7      public static void Main( string[] args )
8      {
9         int[] array = { 87, 68, 94, 100, 83, 78, 85, 91, 76, 87 };
10        int total = 0;
11
12        // add each element's value to total
13        for ( int counter = 0; counter < array.Length; counter++ )
14           total += array[ counter ];
15
16        Console.WriteLine( "Total of array elements: {0}", total );
17     } // end Main
18  } // end class SumArray
```

```
Total of array elements: 849
```

Fig. 6.5 | Computing the sum of the elements of an array.

```
1   // Fig. 6.6: BarChart.cs
2   // Bar chart printing application.
3   using System;
4
5   public class BarChart
6   {
7      public static void Main( string[] args )
8      {
9         int[] array = { 0, 0, 0, 0, 0, 0, 1, 2, 4, 2, 1 };
10
11        Console.WriteLine( "Grade distribution:" );
12
13        // for each array element, output a bar of the chart
14        for ( int counter = 0; counter < array.Length; counter++ )
15        {
16           // output bar labels ( "00-09: ", ..., "90-99: ", "100: " )
17           if ( counter == 10 )
18              Console.Write( "  100: " );
19           else
20              Console.Write( "{0:D2}-{1:D2}: ",
21                 counter * 10, counter * 10 + 9 );
22
23           // print bar of asterisks
24           for ( int stars = 0; stars < array[ counter ]; stars++ )
25              Console.Write( "*" );
26
```

Fig. 6.6 | Bar chart printing application. (Part 1 of 2.)

```
27              Console.WriteLine(); // start a new line of output
28          } // end outer for
29      } // end Main
30  } // end class BarChart
```

```
Grade distribution:
00-09:
10-19:
20-29:
30-39:
40-49:
50-59:
60-69: *
70-79: **
80-89: ****
90-99: **
  100: *
```

Fig. 6.6 | Bar chart printing application. (Part 2 of 2.)

array[10] indicates the number of 100 grades. The two versions of class GradeBook later in the chapter (Fig. 6.15 and Fig. 6.20) contain code that calculates these grade frequencies based on a set of grades. For now, we manually create array by examining the set of grades and initializing the elements of array to the number of values in each range (line 9).

The application reads the numbers from the array and graphs the information as a bar chart. Each grade range is followed by a bar of asterisks indicating the number of grades in that range. To label each bar, lines 17–21 output a grade range (e.g., "70-79: ") based on the current value of counter. When counter is 10, line 18 outputs "   100: " to align the colon with the other bar labels. When counter is not 10, line 20 uses the format items {0:D2} and {1:D2} to output the label of the grade range. The format specifier D indicates that the value should be formatted as an integer, and the number after the D indicates how many digits this formatted integer must contain. The 2 indicates that values with fewer than two digits should begin with a leading 0.

The nested for statement (lines 24–25) outputs the bars. Note the loop-continuation condition at line 24 (stars < array[counter]). Each time the application reaches the inner for, the loop counts from 0 up to one less than array[counter], thus using a value in array to determine the number of asterisks to display. In this example, array[0]– array[5] contain 0s because no students received a grade below 60. Thus, the application displays no asterisks next to the first six grade ranges.

Using the Elements of an Array as Counters

Sometimes, applications use counter variables to summarize data, such as the results of a survey. In Fig. 5.8, we used separate counters in our die-rolling application to track the number of times each face of a six-sided die appeared as the application rolled the die 6000 times. An array version of the application in Fig. 5.8 is shown in Fig. 6.7.

Fig. 6.7 uses array frequency (line 10) to count the occurrences of each side of the die. *The single statement in line 14 of this application replaces lines 23–46 of Fig. 5.8.* Line 14 uses the random value to determine which frequency element to increment during each iteration of the loop. The calculation in line 14 produces random numbers from 1 to 6,

```
1   // Fig. 6.7: RollDie.cs
2   // Roll a six-sided die 6000 times.
3   using System;
4
5   public class RollDie
6   {
7      public static void Main( string[] args )
8      {
9         Random randomNumbers = new Random(); // random number generator
10        int[] frequency = new int[ 7 ]; // array of frequency counters
11
12        // roll die 6000 times; use die value as frequency index
13        for ( int roll = 1; roll <= 6000; roll++ )
14           ++frequency[ randomNumbers.Next( 1, 7 ) ];
15
16        Console.WriteLine( "{0}{1,10}", "Face", "Frequency" );
17
18        // output each array element's value
19        for ( int face = 1; face < frequency.Length; face++ )
20           Console.WriteLine( "{0,4}{1,10}", face, frequency[ face ] );
21     } // end Main
22  } // end class RollDie
```

```
Face Frequency
   1       956
   2       981
   3      1001
   4      1030
   5      1035
   6       997
```

Fig. 6.7 | Roll a six-sided die 6000 times.

so array frequency must be large enough to store six counters. We use a seven-element array in which we ignore frequency[0]—it is more logical to have the face value 1 increment frequency[1] than frequency[0]. Thus, each face value is used as an index for array frequency. We also replaced lines 50–52 of Fig. 5.8 by looping through array frequency to output the results (Fig. 6.7, lines 19–20).

Using Arrays to Analyze Survey Results

Our next example uses arrays to summarize the results of data collected in a survey:

> Forty students were asked to rate the quality of the food in the student cafeteria on a scale of 1 to 10 (where 1 means awful and 10 means excellent). Place the 40 responses in an integer array and summarize the results of the poll.

This is a typical array-processing application (see Fig. 6.8). We wish to summarize the number of responses of each type (i.e., 1 through 10). The array responses (lines 10–12) is a 40-element int array of the students' responses to the survey. We use 11-element array frequency (line 13) to count the number of occurrences of each response. Each element of the array is used as a counter for one of the survey responses and is initialized to 0 by default. As in Fig. 6.7, we ignore frequency[0].

```
 1  // Fig. 6.8: StudentPoll.cs
 2  // Poll analysis application.
 3  using System;
 4
 5  public class StudentPoll
 6  {
 7     public static void Main( string[] args )
 8     {
 9        // array of survey responses
10        int[] responses = { 1, 2, 6, 4, 8, 5, 9, 7, 8, 10, 1, 6, 3, 8, 6,
11           10, 3, 8, 2, 7, 6, 5, 7, 6, 8, 6, 7, 5, 6, 6, 5, 6, 7, 5, 6,
12           4, 8, 6, 8, 10 };
13        int[] frequency = new int[ 11 ]; // array of frequency counters
14
15        // for each answer, select responses element and use that value
16        // as frequency index to determine element to increment
17        for ( int answer = 0; answer < responses.Length; answer++ )
18           ++frequency[ responses[ answer ] ];
19
20        Console.WriteLine( "{0}{1,10}", "Rating", "Frequency" );
21
22        // output each array element's value
23        for ( int rating = 1; rating < frequency.Length; rating++ )
24           Console.WriteLine( "{0,6}{1,10}", rating, frequency[ rating ] );
25     } // end Main
26  } // end class StudentPoll
```

```
Rating Frequency
    1        2
    2        2
    3        2
    4        2
    5        5
    6       11
    7        5
    8        7
    9        1
   10        3
```

Fig. 6.8 | Poll analysis application.

The for loop at lines 17–18 takes the responses one at a time from array responses and increments one of the 10 counters in the frequency array (frequency[1] to frequency[10]). The key statement in the loop is line 18, which increments the appropriate frequency counter, depending on the value of responses[answer].

Let's consider several iterations of the for loop. When control variable answer is 0, the value of responses[answer] is the value of responses[0] (i.e., 1 in line 10), so the application interprets ++frequency[responses[answer]] as

```
++frequency[ 1 ]
```

which increments the value in frequency array element 1. To evaluate the expression, start with the value in the innermost set of square brackets, answer. Once you know answer's value (which is the value of the loop control variable in line 17), plug it into the expression and evaluate the next outer set of square brackets—i.e., responses[answer], which is a value selected from the responses array in lines 10–12. Then use the resulting value as the index for the frequency array to specify which counter to increment (line 18).

When answer is 1, responses[answer] is the value of responses[1], which is 2, so the application interprets ++frequency[responses[answer]] as

```
++frequency[ 2 ]
```

which increments the frequency array element 2.

When answer is 2, responses[answer] is the value of responses[2], which is 6, so the application interprets ++frequency[responses[answer]] as

```
++frequency[ 6 ]
```

which increments frequency array element 6, and so on. Regardless of the number of responses processed in the survey, the application requires only an 11-element array (in which we ignore element 0) to summarize the results, because all the response values are between 1 and 10, inclusive, and the index values for an 11-element array are 0 through 10.

If the data in the responses array had contained invalid values, such as 13, the application would have attempted to add 1 to frequency[13], which is outside the bounds of the array. In many programming languages, like C and C++, writing outside the bounds of an array is actually allowed and would overwrite arbitrary information in memory, often causing disastrous results. C# does not allow this—accessing any array element forces a check on the array index to ensure that it is valid (i.e., it must be greater than or equal to 0 and less than the length of the array). This is called ***bounds checking***. If an application uses an invalid index, the Common Language Runtime generates an exception (specifically, an ***IndexOutOfRangeException***) to indicate that an error occurred in the application at execution time. The condition in a control statement could determine whether an index is valid before allowing it to be used in an *array-access expression*, thus avoiding the exception.

Error-Prevention Tip 6.1

An exception indicates that an error has occurred in an application. You often can write code to recover from an exception and continue application execution, rather than abnormally terminating the application. Exception handling is discussed in Chapter 10.

Error-Prevention Tip 6.2

When writing code to loop through an array, ensure that the array index remains greater than or equal to 0 and less than the length of the array. The loop-continuation condition should prevent the accessing of elements outside this range.

6.5 Case Study: Card Shuffling and Dealing Simulation

The examples in the chapter thus far have used arrays containing value-type elements. This section uses random-number generation and an array of reference-type elements—namely, objects representing playing cards—to develop a class that simulates card shuffling and dealing. This class can then be used to implement applications that play card games.

We first develop class Card (Fig. 6.9), which represents a playing card that has a face (e.g., "Ace", "Deuce", "Three", ..., "Jack", "Queen", "King") and a suit (e.g., "Hearts", "Diamonds", "Clubs", "Spades"). Next, we develop the DeckOfCards class (Fig. 6.10), which creates a deck of 52 playing cards in which each element is a Card object. Then we build a test application (Fig. 6.11) that demonstrates class DeckOfCards's card shuffling and dealing capabilities.

Class Card

Class Card (Fig. 6.9) contains two string instance variables—face and suit—that are used to store references to the face value and suit name for a specific Card. The constructor for the class (lines 9–13) receives two strings that it uses to initialize face and suit. Method ToString (lines 16–19) creates a string consisting of the face of the card, the string " of " and the suit of the card. Recall from Chapter 5 that the + operator can be used to concatenate (i.e., combine) several strings to form one larger string. Card's ToString method can be invoked explicitly to obtain a string representation of a Card object (e.g., "Ace of Spades"). The ToString method of an object is called implicitly in many cases when the object is used where a string is expected (e.g., when WriteLine outputs the object with a format item or when the object is concatenated to a string using the + operator). For this behavior to occur, ToString must be declared with the header exactly as shown in line 16 of Fig. 6.9. We will explain the purpose of the override keyword in more detail when we discuss inheritance in Chapter 8.

Class DeckOfCards

Class DeckOfCards (Fig. 6.10) declares an instance-variable array named deck that contains Card objects (line 7). Like simple-type array declarations, the declaration of an array of objects includes the type of the elements in the array, followed by square brackets and the name of the

```
1   // Fig. 6.9: Card.cs
2   // Card class represents a playing card.
3   public class Card
4   {
5      private string face; // face of card ("Ace", "Deuce", ...)
6      private string suit; // suit of card ("Hearts", "Diamonds", ...)
7
8      // two-parameter constructor initializes card's face and suit
9      public Card( string cardFace, string cardSuit )
10     {
11        face = cardFace; // initialize face of card
12        suit = cardSuit; // initialize suit of card
13     } // end two-parameter Card constructor
14
15     // return string representation of Card
16     public override string ToString()
17     {
18        return face + " of " + suit;
19     } // end method ToString
20  } // end class Card
```

Fig. 6.9 | Card class represents a playing card.

array variable (e.g., Card[] deck). Class DeckOfCards also declares int instance variable currentCard (line 8), representing the next Card to be dealt from the deck array, and named constant NUMBER_OF_CARDS (line 9), indicating the number of Cards in the deck (52).

```csharp
1    // Fig. 6.10: DeckOfCards.cs
2    // DeckOfCards class represents a deck of playing cards.
3    using System;
4
5    public class DeckOfCards
6    {
7       private Card[] deck; // array of Card objects
8       private int currentCard; // index of next Card to be dealt
9       private const int NUMBER_OF_CARDS = 52; // constant number of Cards
10      private Random randomNumbers; // random number generator
11
12      // constructor fills deck of Cards
13      public DeckOfCards()
14      {
15         string[] faces = { "Ace", "Deuce", "Three", "Four", "Five", "Six",
16            "Seven", "Eight", "Nine", "Ten", "Jack", "Queen", "King" };
17         string[] suits = { "Hearts", "Diamonds", "Clubs", "Spades" };
18
19         deck = new Card[ NUMBER_OF_CARDS ]; // create array of Card objects
20         currentCard = 0; // set currentCard so first Card dealt is deck[ 0 ]
21         randomNumbers = new Random(); // create random number generator
22
23         // populate deck with Card objects
24         for ( int count = 0; count < deck.Length; count++ )
25            deck[ count ] =
26               new Card( faces[ count % 13 ], suits[ count / 13 ] );
27      } // end DeckOfCards constructor
28
29      // shuffle deck of Cards with one-pass algorithm
30      public void Shuffle()
31      {
32         // after shuffling, dealing should start at deck[ 0 ] again
33         currentCard = 0; // reinitialize currentCard
34
35         // for each Card, pick another random Card and swap them
36         for ( int first = 0; first < deck.Length; first++ )
37         {
38            // select a random number between 0 and 51
39            int second = randomNumbers.Next( NUMBER_OF_CARDS );
40
41            // swap current Card with randomly selected Card
42            Card temp = deck[ first ];
43            deck[ first ] = deck[ second ];
44            deck[ second ] = temp;
45         } // end for
46      } // end method Shuffle
47
```

Fig. 6.10 | DeckOfCards class represents a deck of playing cards. (Part 1 of 2.)

```
48        // deal one Card
49        public Card DealCard()
50        {
51           // determine whether Cards remain to be dealt
52           if ( currentCard < deck.Length )
53              return deck[ currentCard++ ]; // return current Card in array
54           else
55              return null; // return null to indicate that all Cards were dealt
56        } // end method DealCard
57     } // end class DeckOfCards
```

Fig. 6.10 | DeckOfCards class represents a deck of playing cards. (Part 2 of 2.)

The class's constructor instantiates the deck array (line 19) to be of size NUMBER_OF_CARDS. When first created, the elements of the deck array are null by default, so the constructor uses a for statement (lines 24–26) to fill the deck array with Cards. The for statement initializes control variable count to 0 and loops while count is less than deck.Length, causing count to take on each integer value from 0 to 51 (the indices of the deck array). Each Card is instantiated and initialized with two strings—one from the faces array (which contains the strings "Ace" through "King") and one from the suits array (which contains the strings "Hearts", "Diamonds", "Clubs" and "Spades"). The calculation count % 13 always results in a value from 0 to 12 (the 13 indices of the faces array in lines 15–16), and the calculation count / 13 always results in a value from 0 to 3 (the four indices of the suits array in line 17). When the deck array is initialized, it contains the Cards with faces "Ace" through "King" in order for each suit.

Method Shuffle (lines 30–46) shuffles the Cards in the deck. The method loops through all 52 Cards (array indices 0 to 51). For each Card, a number between 0 and 51 is picked randomly to select another Card. Next, the current Card object and the randomly selected Card object are swapped in the array. This exchange is performed by the three assignments in lines 42–44. The extra variable temp temporarily stores one of the two Card objects being swapped. The swap cannot be performed with only the two statements

```
deck[ first ] = deck[ second ];
deck[ second ] = deck[ first ];
```

If deck[first] is the "Ace" of "Spades" and deck[second] is the "Queen" of "Hearts", then after the first assignment, both array elements contain the "Queen" of "Hearts" and the "Ace" of "Spades" is lost—hence, the extra variable temp is needed. After the for loop terminates, the Card objects are randomly ordered. Only 52 swaps are made in a single pass of the entire array, and the array of Card objects is shuffled.

Method DealCard (lines 49–56) deals one Card in the array. Recall that currentCard indicates the index of the next Card to be dealt (i.e., the Card at the top of the deck). Thus, line 52 compares currentCard to the length of the deck array. If the deck is not empty (i.e., currentCard is less than 52), line 53 returns the top Card and increments current-Card to prepare for the next call to DealCard—otherwise, null is returned.

Shuffling and Dealing Cards

The application of Fig. 6.11 demonstrates the card dealing and shuffling capabilities of class DeckOfCards (Fig. 6.10). Line 10 creates a DeckOfCards object named myDeckOf-Cards. Recall that the DeckOfCards constructor creates the deck with the 52 Card objects

```
 1    // Fig. 6.11: DeckOfCardsTest.cs
 2    // Card shuffling and dealing application.
 3    using System;
 4
 5    public class DeckOfCardsTest
 6    {
 7       // execute application
 8       public static void Main( string[] args )
 9       {
10          DeckOfCards myDeckOfCards = new DeckOfCards();
11          myDeckOfCards.Shuffle(); // place Cards in random order
12
13          // print all 52 Cards in the order in which they are dealt
14          for ( int i = 0; i < 13; i++ )
15          {
16             // deal and print 4 Cards
17             Console.WriteLine( "{0,-20}{1,-20}{2,-20}{3,-20}",
18                myDeckOfCards.DealCard(), myDeckOfCards.DealCard(),
19                myDeckOfCards.DealCard(), myDeckOfCards.DealCard() );
20          } // end for
21       } // end Main
22    } // end class DeckOfCardsTest
```

Ten of Hearts	Ace of Diamonds	Jack of Spades	Queen of Diamonds
Six of Clubs	Seven of Hearts	Deuce of Spades	Seven of Diamonds
Queen of Spades	King of Hearts	Nine of Hearts	Deuce of Clubs
Eight of Clubs	Five of Diamonds	Three of Hearts	Five of Hearts
Three of Spades	Four of Diamonds	Six of Hearts	Nine of Diamonds
Queen of Clubs	Deuce of Diamonds	Queen of Hearts	Four of Clubs
Seven of Spades	Four of Hearts	Three of Diamonds	Seven of Clubs
Ten of Clubs	Ten of Spades	Jack of Diamonds	Jack of Clubs
Nine of Clubs	Six of Diamonds	Eight of Hearts	Eight of Spades
King of Spades	Three of Clubs	King of Diamonds	Six of Spades
Jack of Hearts	Ace of Clubs	Five of Spades	Nine of Spades
Deuce of Hearts	Five of Clubs	Ten of Diamonds	Ace of Hearts
Ace of Spades	Four of Spades	Eight of Diamonds	King of Clubs

Fig. 6.11 | Card shuffling and dealing application.

in order by suit and face. Line 11 invokes myDeckOfCards's Shuffle method to rearrange the Card objects. The for statement in lines 14–20 deals all 52 Cards in the deck and prints them in four columns of 13 Cards each. Lines 17–19 deal and print four Card objects, each obtained by invoking myDeckOfCards's DealCard method. When WriteLine outputs a Card with string formatting, the Card's ToString method (declared in lines 16–19 of Fig. 6.9) is invoked implicitly. Because the field width is negative, the result is output *left* justified in a field of width 20.

6.6 foreach Statement

In previous examples, we demonstrated how to use counter-controlled for statements to iterate through the elements in an array. In this section, we introduce the **foreach state-ment**, which iterates through the elements of an entire array or collection. This section discusses how to use the foreach statement to loop through an array. The syntax of a foreach statement is:

> **foreach** (*type identifier* **in** *arrayName*)
>   *statement*

where *type* and *identifier* are the type and name (e.g., int number) of the *iteration variable*, and *arrayName* is the array through which to iterate. The type of the iteration variable must match the type of the elements in the array. As the next example illustrates, the iteration variable represents successive values in the array on successive iterations of the foreach statement.

Figure 6.12 uses the foreach statement (lines 13–14) to calculate the sum of the integers in an array of student grades. The type specified is int, because array contains int values—therefore, the loop will select one int value from the array during each iteration. The foreach statement iterates through successive values in the array one-by-one. The foreach header can be read concisely as "for each iteration, assign the next element of array to int variable number, then execute the following statement." Thus, for each iteration, identifier number represents the next int value in the array. Lines 13–14 are equivalent to the following counter-controlled repetition used in lines 13–14 of Fig. 6.5 to total the integers in array:

> **for** (**int** counter = 0; counter < array.Length; counter++)
>   total += array[counter];

The foreach statement simplifies the code for iterating through an array. Note, however, that the foreach statement can be used only to access array elements—it cannot be used to modify elements. Any attempt to change the value of the iteration variable in the

```
1   // Fig. 6.12: ForEachTest.cs
2   // Using foreach statement to total integers in an array.
3   using System;
4
5   public class ForEachTest
6   {
7      public static void Main( string[] args )
8      {
9         int[] array = { 87, 68, 94, 100, 83, 78, 85, 91, 76, 87 };
10        int total = 0;
11
12        // add each element's value to total
13        foreach ( int number in array )
14           total += number;
15
16        Console.WriteLine( "Total of array elements: {0}", total );
17     } // end Main
18  } // end class ForEachTest
```

```
Total of array elements: 849
```

Fig. 6.12 | Using foreach statement to total integers in an array.

body of a foreach statement will cause a compilation error. If your application needs to modify elements, use the for statement.

The foreach statement can be used in place of the for statement whenever code looping through an array does not require access to the counter indicating the index of the current array element. For example, totaling the integers in an array requires access only to the element values—the index of each element is irrelevant. However, if an application must use a counter for some reason other than simply to loop through an array (e.g., to print an index number next to each array element value, as in the examples earlier in this chapter), use the for statement.

6.7 Passing Arrays and Array Elements to Methods

To pass an array argument to a method, specify the name of the array without any brackets. For example, if array hourlyTemperatures is declared as

```
double[] hourlyTemperatures = new double[ 24 ];
```

then the method call

```
ModifyArray( hourlyTemperatures );
```

passes the reference of array hourlyTemperatures to method ModifyArray. Every array object "knows" its own length (and makes it available via its Length property). Thus, when we pass an array object's reference to a method, we need not pass the array length as an additional argument.

For a method to receive an array reference through a method call, the method's parameter list must specify an array parameter. For example, the method header for method ModifyArray might be written as

```
void ModifyArray( double[] b )
```

indicating that ModifyArray receives the reference of an array of doubles in parameter b. The method call passes array hourlyTemperature's reference, so when the called method uses the array variable b, it refers to the same array object as hourlyTemperatures in the calling method.

When an argument to a method is an entire array or an individual array element of a reference type, the called method receives a copy of the reference. However, when an argument to a method is an individual array element of a value type, the called method receives a copy of the element's value. To pass an individual array element to a method, use the indexed name of the array as an argument in the method call. If you want to pass a value-type array element to a method by reference, you must use the ref keyword as shown in Section 5.14, Passing Arguments: Pass-by-Value vs. Pass-by-Reference.

Figure 6.13 demonstrates the difference between passing an entire array and passing a value-type array element to a method. The foreach statement at lines 17–18 outputs the five elements of array (an array of int values). Line 20 invokes method ModifyArray, passing array as an argument. Method ModifyArray (lines 37–41) receives a copy of array's reference and uses the reference to multiply each of array's elements by 2. To prove that array's elements (in Main) were modified, the foreach statement at lines 24–25 outputs the five elements of array again. As the output shows, method Modify-Array doubled the value of each element.

```
1   // Fig. 6.13: PassArray.cs
2   // Passing arrays and individual array elements to methods.
3   using System;
4
5   public class PassArray
6   {
7      // Main creates array and calls ModifyArray and ModifyElement
8      public static void Main( string[] args )
9      {
10        int[] array = { 1, 2, 3, 4, 5 };
11
12        Console.WriteLine(
13           "Effects of passing reference to entire array:\n" +
14           "The values of the original array are:" );
15
16        // output original array elements
17        foreach ( int value in array )
18           Console.Write( "   {0}", value );
19
20        ModifyArray( array ); // pass array reference
21        Console.WriteLine( "\n\nThe values of the modified array are:" );
22
23        // output modified array elements
24        foreach ( int value in array )
25           Console.Write( "   {0}", value );
26
27        Console.WriteLine(
28           "\n\nEffects of passing array element value:\n" +
29           "array[3] before ModifyElement: {0}", array[ 3 ] );
30
31        ModifyElement( array[ 3 ] ); // attempt to modify array[ 3 ]
32        Console.WriteLine(
33           "array[3] after ModifyElement: {0}", array[ 3 ] );
34     } // end Main
35
36     // multiply each element of an array by 2
37     public static void ModifyArray( int[] array2 )
38     {
39        for ( int counter = 0; counter < array2.Length; counter++ )
40           array2[ counter ] *= 2;
41     } // end method ModifyArray
42
43     // multiply argument by 2
44     public static void ModifyElement( int element )
45     {
46        element *= 2;
47        Console.WriteLine(
48           "Value of element in ModifyElement: {0}", element );
49     } // end method ModifyElement
50  } // end class PassArray
```

Fig. 6.13 | Passing arrays and individual array elements to methods. (Part 1 of 2.)

```
Effects of passing reference to entire array:
The values of the original array are:
   1    2    3    4    5

The values of the modified array are:
   2    4    6    8    10

Effects of passing array element value:
array[3] before ModifyElement: 8
Value of element in ModifyElement: 16
array[3] after ModifyElement: 8
```

Fig. 6.13 | Passing arrays and individual array elements to methods. (Part 2 of 2.)

Figure 6.13 next demonstrates that when a copy of an individual value-type array element is passed to a method, modifying the copy in the called method does not affect the original value of that element in the calling method's array. To show the value of array[3] before invoking method ModifyElement, lines 27–29 output the value of array[3] which is 8. Line 31 calls method ModifyElement and passes array[3] as an argument. Remember that array[3] is actually one int value (8) in array. Therefore, the application passes a copy of the value of array[3]. Method ModifyElement (lines 44–49) multiplies the value received as an argument by 2, stores the result in its parameter element, then outputs the value of element (16). Since method parameters, like local variables, cease to exist when the method in which they are declared completes execution, the method parameter element is destroyed when method ModifyElement terminates. Thus, when the application returns control to Main, lines 32–33 output the unmodified value of array[3] (i.e., 8).

6.8 Passing Arrays by Value and by Reference

In C#, a variable that "stores" an object, such as an array, does not actually store the object itself. Instead, such a variable stores a reference to the object (i.e., the location in the computer's memory where the object itself is stored). The distinction between reference-type variables and value-type variables raises some subtle issues that you must understand to create secure, stable programs.

As you know, when an application passes an argument to a method, the called method receives a copy of that argument's value. Changes to the local copy in the called method do not affect the original variable in the caller. If the argument is of a reference type, the method makes a copy of the reference, not a copy of the actual object that is referenced. The local copy of the reference also refers to the original object in memory, which means that changes to the object in the called method affect the original object in memory.

Performance Tip 6.1

Passing arrays and other objects by reference makes sense for performance reasons. If arrays were passed by value, a copy of each element would be passed. For large, frequently passed arrays, this would waste time and would consume considerable storage for the copies of the arrays—both of these problems cause poor performance.

In Section 5.14, you learned that C# allows variables to be passed by reference with keyword ref. You can also use keyword ref to pass a reference-type variable by reference, which allows the called method to modify the original variable in the caller and make that variable refer to a different object in memory. This is a subtle capability, which if misused, can lead to problems. For instance, when a reference-type object like an array is passed with ref, the called method actually gains control over the reference itself, allowing the called method to replace the original reference in the caller with a different object, or even with null. Such behavior can lead to unpredictable effects, which can be disastrous in mission-critical applications. The application in Fig. 6.14 demonstrates the subtle difference between passing a reference by value and passing a reference by reference with keyword ref.

Lines 11 and 14 declare two integer array variables, firstArray and firstArrayCopy. Line 11 initializes firstArray with the values 1, 2 and 3. The assignment statement on line 14 copies the reference stored in firstArray to variable firstArrayCopy, causing these variables to reference the same array object in memory. We make the copy of the reference so that we can determine later whether reference firstArray gets overwritten. The for statement at lines 23–24 prints the contents of firstArray before it is passed to method FirstDouble (line 27) so that we can verify that the array is passed by reference (i.e., the called method indeed changes the array's contents).

The for statement in method FirstDouble (lines 83–84) multiplies the values of all the elements in the array by 2. Line 87 creates a new array containing the values 11, 12 and 13, and assigns the array's reference to parameter array in an attempt to overwrite reference firstArray in the caller—this, of course, does not happen, because the reference was

```
1    // Fig. 6.14: ArrayReferenceTest.cs
2    // Testing the effects of passing array references
3    // by value and by reference.
4    using System;
5
6    public class ArrayReferenceTest
7    {
8       public static void Main( string[] args )
9       {
10         // create and initialize firstArray
11         int[] firstArray = { 1, 2, 3 };
12
13         // copy the reference in variable firstArray
14         int[] firstArrayCopy = firstArray;
15
16         Console.WriteLine(
17            "Test passing firstArray reference by value" );
18
19         Console.Write( "\nContents of firstArray " +
20            "before calling FirstDouble:\n\t" );
21
22         // print contents of firstArray
23         for ( int i = 0; i < firstArray.Length; i++ )
24            Console.Write( "{0} ", firstArray[ i ] );
25
```

Fig. 6.14 | Passing an array reference by value and by reference. (Part 1 of 3.)

```
26          // pass variable firstArray by value to FirstDouble
27          FirstDouble( firstArray );
28
29          Console.Write( "\n\nContents of firstArray after " +
30             "calling FirstDouble\n\t" );
31
32          // print contents of firstArray
33          for ( int i = 0; i < firstArray.Length; i++ )
34             Console.Write( "{0} ", firstArray[ i ] );
35
36          // test whether reference was changed by FirstDouble
37          if ( firstArray == firstArrayCopy )
38             Console.WriteLine(
39                "\n\nThe references refer to the same array" );
40          else
41             Console.WriteLine(
42                "\n\nThe references refer to different arrays" );
43
44          // create and initialize secondArray
45          int[] secondArray = { 1, 2, 3 };
46
47          // copy the reference in variable secondArray
48          int[] secondArrayCopy = secondArray;
49
50          Console.WriteLine( "\nTest passing secondArray " +
51             "reference by reference" );
52
53          Console.Write( "\nContents of secondArray " +
54             "before calling SecondDouble:\n\t" );
55
56          // print contents of secondArray before method call
57          for ( int i = 0; i < secondArray.Length; i++ )
58             Console.Write( "{0} ", secondArray[ i ] );
59
60          // pass variable secondArray by reference to SecondDouble
61          SecondDouble( ref secondArray );
62
63          Console.Write( "\n\nContents of secondArray " +
64             "after calling SecondDouble:\n\t" );
65
66          // print contents of secondArray after method call
67          for ( int i = 0; i < secondArray.Length; i++ )
68             Console.Write( "{0} ", secondArray[ i ] );
69
70          // test whether reference was changed by SecondDouble
71          if ( secondArray == secondArrayCopy )
72             Console.WriteLine(
73                "\n\nThe references refer to the same array" );
74          else
75             Console.WriteLine(
76                "\n\nThe references refer to different arrays" );
77       } // end method Main
```

Fig. 6.14 | Passing an array reference by value and by reference. (Part 2 of 3.)

```
78
79       // modify elements of array and attempt to modify reference
80       public static void FirstDouble( int[] array )
81       {
82          // double each element's value
83          for ( int i = 0; i < array.Length; i++ )
84             array[ i ] *= 2;
85
86          // create new object and assign its reference to array
87          array = new int[] { 11, 12, 13 };
88       } // end method FirstDouble
89
90       // modify elements of array and change reference array
91       // to refer to a new array
92       public static void SecondDouble( ref int[] array )
93       {
94          // double each element's value
95          for ( int i = 0; i < array.Length; i++ )
96             array[ i ] *= 2;
97
98          // create new object and assign its reference to array
99          array = new int[] { 11, 12, 13 };
100      } // end method SecondDouble
101   } // end class ArrayReferenceTest
```

```
Test passing firstArray reference by value

Contents of firstArray before calling FirstDouble:
      1 2 3

Contents of firstArray after calling FirstDouble
      2 4 6

The references refer to the same array

Test passing secondArray reference by reference

Contents of secondArray before calling SecondDouble:
      1 2 3

Contents of secondArray after calling SecondDouble:
      11 12 13

The references refer to different arrays
```

Fig. 6.14 | Passing an array reference by value and by reference. (Part 3 of 3.)

passed by value. After method FirstDouble executes, the for statement at lines 33–34 prints the contents of firstArray, demonstrating that the values of the elements have been changed by the method (and confirming that in C# arrays are always passed by reference). The if...else statement at lines 37–42 uses the == operator to compare references firstArray (which we just attempted to overwrite) and firstArrayCopy. The expression in line 37 evaluates to true if the operands of operator == reference the same object. In this case, the object represented by firstArray is the array created in line 11—not the array created in method FirstDouble (line 87)—so the original reference stored in first-Array was not modified.

Lines 45–76 perform similar tests, using array variables secondArray and second-ArrayCopy, and method SecondDouble (lines 92–100). Method SecondDouble performs the same operations as FirstDouble, but receives its array argument using keyword ref. In this case, the reference stored in secondArray after the method call is a reference to the array created in line 99 of SecondDouble, demonstrating that a variable passed with keyword ref can be modified by the called method so that the variable in the caller actually points to a different object—in this case, an array created in SecondDouble. The if...else statement in lines 71–76 confirms that secondArray and secondArrayCopy no longer refer to the same array.

Software Engineering Observation 6.1

When a method receives a reference-type parameter by value, a copy of the object's reference is passed. This prevents a method from overwriting references passed to that method. In the vast majority of cases, protecting the caller's reference from modification is the desired behavior. If you encounter a situation where you truly want the called procedure to modify the caller's reference, pass the reference-type parameter using keyword ref—but, again, such situations are rare.

Software Engineering Observation 6.2

In C#, objects (including arrays) are passed by reference by default. So, a called method receiving a reference to an object in a caller can change the caller's object.

6.9 Case Study: Class GradeBook Using an Array to Store Grades

This section further evolves class GradeBook, introduced in Chapter 2 and expanded in Chapters 3–4. Recall that this class represents a grade book used by an instructor to store and analyze a set of student grades. Previous versions of the class process a set of grades entered by the user, but do not maintain the individual grade values in instance variables of the class. Thus, repeat calculations require the user to re-enter the same grades. One way to solve this problem would be to store each grade entered in an individual instance of the class. For example, we could create instance variables grade1, grade2, ..., grade10 in class GradeBook to store 10 student grades. However, the code to total the grades and determine the class average would be cumbersome, and the class would not be able to process any more than 10 grades at a time. In this section, we solve this problem by storing grades in an array.

Storing Student Grades in an Array in Class GradeBook

The version of class GradeBook (Fig. 6.15) presented here uses an array of integers to store the grades of several students on a single exam. This eliminates the need to repeatedly input the same set of grades. Array grades is declared as an instance variable in line 8—therefore, each GradeBook object maintains its own set of grades. The class's constructor (lines 11–15) has two parameters—the name of the course and an array of grades. When an application (e.g., class GradeBookTest in Fig. 6.16) creates a GradeBook object, the application passes an existing int array to the constructor, which assigns the array's reference to instance variable grades (line 14). The size of array grades is determined by the class that passes the array to the constructor. Thus, a GradeBook object can process a variable number of grades—as many as are in the array in the caller. The grade values in the passed array could have been input from a user at the keyboard or read from a file on disk. In our test application, we simply initialize an array with a set of grade values (Fig. 6.16, line 9). Once the grades are stored in instance variable grades of class Grade-Book, all the class's methods can access the elements of grades as needed to perform various calculations.

```csharp
1   // Fig. 6.15: GradeBook.cs
2   // Grade book using an array to store test grades.
3   using System;
4
5   public class GradeBook
6   {
7       private string courseName; // name of course this GradeBook represents
8       private int[] grades; // array of student grades
9
10      // two-parameter constructor initializes courseName and grades array
11      public GradeBook( string name, int[] gradesArray )
12      {
13          CourseName = name; // initialize courseName
14          grades = gradesArray; // initialize grades array
15      } // end two-parameter GradeBook constructor
16
17      // property that gets and sets the course name
18      public string CourseName
19      {
20          get
21          {
22              return courseName;
23          } // end get
24          set
25          {
26              courseName = value;
27          } // end set
28      } // end property CourseName
29
30      // display a welcome message to the GradeBook user
31      public void DisplayMessage()
32      {
33          // CourseName property gets the name of the course
34          Console.WriteLine( "Welcome to the grade book for\n{0}!\n",
35              CourseName );
36      } // end method DisplayMessage
37
38      // perform various operations on the data
39      public void ProcessGrades()
40      {
41          // output grades array
42          OutputGrades();
43
```

Fig. 6.15 | Grade book using an array to store test grades. (Part 1 of 3.)

```
44          // call method GetAverage to calculate the average grade
45          Console.WriteLine( "\nClass average is {0:F2}", GetAverage() );
46
47          // call methods GetMinimum and GetMaximum
48          Console.WriteLine( "Lowest grade is {0}\nHighest grade is {1}\n",
49             GetMinimum(), GetMaximum() );
50
51          // call OutputBarChart to print grade distribution chart
52          OutputBarChart();
53       } // end method ProcessGrades
54
55       // find minimum grade
56       public int GetMinimum()
57       {
58          int lowGrade = grades[ 0 ]; // assume grades[ 0 ] is smallest
59
60          // loop through grades array
61          foreach ( int grade in grades )
62          {
63             // if grade lower than lowGrade, assign it to lowGrade
64             if ( grade < lowGrade )
65                lowGrade = grade; // new lowest grade
66          } // end for
67
68          return lowGrade; // return lowest grade
69       } // end method GetMinimum
70
71       // find maximum grade
72       public int GetMaximum()
73       {
74          int highGrade = grades[ 0 ]; // assume grades[ 0 ] is largest
75
76          // loop through grades array
77          foreach ( int grade in grades )
78          {
79             // if grade greater than highGrade, assign it to highGrade
80             if ( grade > highGrade )
81                highGrade = grade; // new highest grade
82          } // end for
83
84          return highGrade; // return highest grade
85       } // end method GetMaximum
86
87       // determine average grade for test
88       public double GetAverage()
89       {
90          int total = 0; // initialize total
91
92          // sum grades for one student
93          foreach ( int grade in grades )
94             total += grade;
95
```

Fig. 6.15 | Grade book using an array to store test grades. (Part 2 of 3.)

```
 96          // return average of grades
 97          return ( double ) total / grades.Length;
 98       } // end method GetAverage
 99
100       // output bar chart displaying grade distribution
101       public void OutputBarChart()
102       {
103          Console.WriteLine( "Grade distribution:" );
104
105          // stores frequency of grades in each range of 10 grades
106          int[] frequency = new int[ 11 ];
107
108          // for each grade, increment the appropriate frequency
109          foreach ( int grade in grades )
110             ++frequency[ grade / 10 ];
111
112          // for each grade frequency, print bar in chart
113          for ( int count = 0; count < frequency.Length; count++ )
114          {
115             // output bar label ( "00-09: ", ..., "90-99: ", "100: " )
116             if ( count == 10 )
117                Console.Write( "  100: " );
118             else
119                Console.Write( "{0:D2}-{1:D2}: ",
120                   count * 10, count * 10 + 9 );
121
122             // print bar of asterisks
123             for ( int stars = 0; stars < frequency[ count ]; stars++ )
124                Console.Write( "*" );
125
126             Console.WriteLine(); // start a new line of output
127          } // end outer for
128       } // end method OutputBarChart
129
130       // output the contents of the grades array
131       public void OutputGrades()
132       {
133          Console.WriteLine( "The grades are:\n" );
134
135          // output each student's grade
136          for ( int student = 0; student < grades.Length; student++ )
137             Console.WriteLine( "Student {0,2}: {1,3}",
138                student + 1, grades[ student ] );
139       } // end method OutputGrades
140    } // end class GradeBook
```

Fig. 6.15 | Grade book using an array to store test grades. (Part 3 of 3.)

Method ProcessGrades (lines 39–53) contains a series of method calls that result in the output of a report summarizing the grades. Line 42 calls method OutputGrades to print the contents of array grades. Lines 136–138 in method OutputGrades use a for statement to output the student grades. A for statement, rather than a foreach, must be used in this case, because lines 137–138 use counter variable student's value to output each grade next to a particular student number (see Fig. 6.16). Although array indices start at 0, an instructor would typically number students starting at 1. Thus, lines 137–138 output student + 1 as the student number to produce grade labels "Student 1: ", "Student 2: " and so on.

Method ProcessGrades next calls method GetAverage (line 45) to obtain the average of the grades in the array. Method GetAverage (lines 88–98) uses a foreach statement to total the values in array grades before calculating the average. The iteration variable in the foreach's header (e.g., int grade) indicates that for each iteration, int variable grade takes on a value in array grades. Note that the averaging calculation in line 97 uses grades.Length to determine the number of grades being averaged.

Lines 48–49 in method ProcessGrades call methods GetMinimum and GetMaximum to determine the lowest and highest grades of any student on the exam, respectively. Each of these methods uses a foreach statement to loop through array grades. Lines 61–66 in method GetMinimum loop through the array, and lines 64–65 compare each grade to low-Grade. If a grade is less than lowGrade, lowGrade is set to that grade. When line 68 executes, lowGrade contains the lowest grade in the array. Method GetMaximum (lines 72–85) works the same way as method GetMinimum.

Finally, line 52 in method ProcessGrades calls method OutputBarChart to print a distribution chart of the grade data using a technique similar to that in Fig. 6.6. In that example, we manually calculated the number of grades in each category (i.e., 0–9, 10–19, ..., 90–99 and 100) by simply looking at a set of grades. In this example, lines 109–110 use a technique similar to that in Fig. 6.7 and Fig. 6.8 to calculate the frequency of grades in each category. Line 106 declares and creates array frequency of 11 ints to store the frequency of grades in each grade category. For each grade in array grades, lines 109–110 increment the appropriate element of the frequency array. To determine which element to increment, line 110 divides the current grade by 10 using integer division. For example, if grade is 85, line 110 increments frequency[8] to update the count of grades in the range 80–89. Lines 113–127 next print the bar chart (see Fig. 6.6) based on the values in array frequency. Like lines 24–25 of Fig. 6.6, lines 123–124 of Fig. 6.15 use a value in array frequency to determine the number of asterisks to display in each bar.

Class GradeBookTest That Demonstrates Class GradeBook

The application of Fig. 6.16 creates an object of class GradeBook (Fig. 6.15) using int array gradesArray (declared and initialized in line 9). Lines 11–12 pass a course name and gradesArray to the GradeBook constructor. Line 13 displays a welcome message, and line 14 invokes the GradeBook object's ProcessGrades method. The output reveals the summary of the 10 grades in myGradeBook.

Software Engineering Observation 6.3

*A **test harness** (or test application) is responsible for creating an object of the class being tested and providing it with data. This data could come from any of several sources. Test data can be placed directly into an array with an array initializer, it can come from the user at the keyboard, it can come from a file or it can come from a network. After passing this data to the class's constructor to instantiate the object, the test harness should call the object to test its methods and manipulate its data. Gathering data in the test harness like this allows the class to manipulate data from several sources.*

```
 1   // Fig. 6.16: GradeBookTest.cs
 2   // Create GradeBook object using an array of grades.
 3   public class GradeBookTest
 4   {
 5      // Main method begins application execution
 6      public static void Main( string[] args )
 7      {
 8         // one-dimensional array of student grades
 9         int[] gradesArray = { 87, 68, 94, 100, 83, 78, 85, 91, 76, 87 };
10
11         GradeBook myGradeBook = new GradeBook(
12            "CS101 Introduction to C# Programming", gradesArray );
13         myGradeBook.DisplayMessage();
14         myGradeBook.ProcessGrades();
15      } // end Main
16   } // end class GradeBookTest
```

```
Welcome to the grade book for
CS101 Introduction to C# Programming!

The grades are:

Student  1:  87
Student  2:  68
Student  3:  94
Student  4: 100
Student  5:  83
Student  6:  78
Student  7:  85
Student  8:  91
Student  9:  76
Student 10:  87


Class average is 84.90
Lowest grade is 68
Highest grade is 100

Grade distribution:
00-09:
10-19:
20-29:
30-39:
40-49:
50-59:
60-69: *
70-79: **
80-89: ****
90-99: **
  100: *
```

Fig. 6.16 | Create GradeBook object using an array of grades.

6.10 Multidimensional Arrays

Multidimensional arrays with two dimensions are often used to represent *tables of values* consisting of information arranged in *rows* and *columns*. To identify a particular table element, we must specify two indices. By convention, the first identifies the element's row and the second its column. Arrays that require two indices to identify a particular element are called *two-dimensional arrays*. (Multidimensional arrays can have more than two dimensions, but arrays with more than two dimensions are beyond the scope of this book.) C# supports two types of two-dimensional arrays—*rectangular arrays* and *jagged arrays*.

Rectangular Arrays

Rectangular arrays are used to represent tables of information in the form of rows and columns, where each row has the same number of columns. Figure 6.17 illustrates a rectangular array named a containing three rows and four column—a three-by-four array. In general, an array with *m* rows and *n* columns is called an *m-by-n array*.

Every element in array a is identified in Fig. 6.17 by an array-access expression of the form a[*row*, *column*]; a is the name of the array, and *row* and *column* are the indices that uniquely identify each element in array a by row and column number. Note that the names of the elements in row 0 all have a first index of 0, and the names of the elements in column 3 all have a second index of 3.

Like one-dimensional arrays, multidimensional arrays can be initialized with array initializers in declarations. A rectangular array b with two rows and two columns could be declared and initialized with *nested array initializers* as follows:

```
int[ , ] b = { { 1, 2 }, { 3, 4 } };
```

The initializer values are grouped by row in braces. So 1 and 2 initialize b[0, 0] and b[0, 1], respectively, and 3 and 4 initialize b[1, 0] and b[1, 1], respectively. The compiler counts the number of nested array initializers (represented by sets of two inner braces within the outer braces) in the array declaration to determine the number of rows in array b. The compiler counts the initializer values in the nested array initializer for a row to determine the number of columns (two) in that row. The compiler will generate an error if the number of initializers in each row is not the same, because every row of a rectangular array must have the same length.

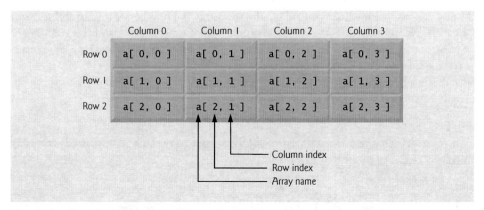

Fig. 6.17 | Rectangular array with three rows and four columns.

Jagged Arrays

A *jagged array* is maintained as a one-dimensional array in which each element refers to a one-dimensional array. The manner in which jagged arrays are represented makes them quite flexible, because the lengths of the rows in the array need not be the same. For example, jagged arrays could be used to store a single student's exam grades across multiple classes, where the number of exams may vary from class to class.

We can access the elements in a jagged array by an array-access expression of the form *arrayName*[*row*][*column*]—similar to the array-access expression for rectangular arrays, but with a separate set of square brackets for each dimension. A jagged array with three rows of different lengths could be declared and initialized as follows:

```
int[][] jagged = { new int[] { 1, 2 },
                   new int[] { 3 },
                   new int[] { 4, 5, 6 } };
```

In this statement, 1 and 2 initialize jagged[0][0] and jagged[0][1], respectively; 3 initializes jagged[1][0]; and 4, 5 and 6 initialize jagged[2][0], jagged[2][1] and jagged[2][2], respectively. Therefore, array jagged in the preceding declaration is actually composed of four separate one-dimensional arrays—one that represents the rows, one containing the values in the first row ({ 1, 2 }), one containing the value in the second row ({ 3 }) and one containing the values in the third row ({ 4, 5, 6 }). Thus, array jagged itself is an array of three elements, each reference to a one-dimensional array of int values.

Observe the differences between the array-creation expressions for rectangular arrays and jagged arrays. Two sets of square brackets follow the type of jagged, indicating that this is an array of int arrays. Furthermore, in the array initializer, C# requires the keyword new to create an array object for each row. Figure 6.18 illustrates the array reference jagged after it has been declared and initialized.

Creating Two-Dimensional Arrays with Array-Creation Expressions

A rectangular array can be created with an array-creation expression. For example, the following lines declare array b and assign it a reference to a three-by-four rectangular array:

```
int[ , ] b;
b = new int[ 3, 4 ];
```

In this case, we use the literal values 3 and 4 to specify the number of rows and number of columns, respectively, but this is not required—applications can also use variables and expressions to specify array dimensions. As with one-dimensional arrays, the elements of a rectangular array are initialized when the array object is created. x

A jagged array cannot be completely created with a single array creation expression. The following statement is a syntax error:

```
int[][] c = new int[ 2 ][ 5 ]; // error
```

Instead, each one-dimensional array in the jagged array must be initialized separately. A jagged array can be created as follows:

```
int[][] c;
c = new int[ 2 ][ ]; // create 2 rows
c[ 0 ] = new int[ 5 ]; // create 5 columns for row 0
c[ 1 ] = new int[ 3 ]; // create 3 columns for row 1
```

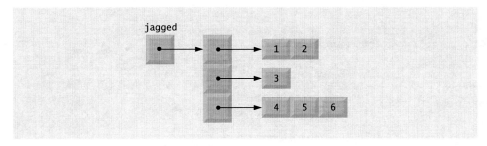

Fig. 6.18 | Jagged array with three rows of different lengths.

The preceding statements create a jagged array with two rows. Row 0 has five columns, and row 1 has three columns.

Two-Dimensional Array Example: Displaying Element Values

Figure 6.19 demonstrates initializing rectangular and jagged arrays with array initializers and using nested for loops to *traverse* the arrays (i.e., visit every element of each array).

Class InitArray's Main method declares two arrays. The declaration of rectangular (line 12) uses nested array initializers to initialize row 0 of the array to the values 1, 2 and 3, and the row 1 to the values 4, 5 and 6. The declaration of jagged (lines 17–19) uses

```
1   // Fig. 6.19: InitArray.cs
2   // Initializing rectangular and jagged arrays.
3   using System;
4
5   public class InitArray
6   {
7      // create and output rectangular and jagged arrays
8      public static void Main( string[] args )
9      {
10        // with rectangular arrays,
11        // every column must be the same length.
12        int[ , ] rectangular = { { 1, 2, 3 }, { 4, 5, 6 } };
13
14        // with jagged arrays,
15        // we need to use "new int[]" for every row,
16        // but every column does not need to be the same length.
17        int[][] jagged = { new int[] { 1, 2 },
18                           new int[] { 3 },
19                           new int[] { 4, 5, 6 } };
20
21        OutputArray( rectangular ); // displays array rectangular by row
22        Console.WriteLine(); // output a blank line
23        OutputArray( jagged ); // displays array jagged by row
24     } // end Main
```

Fig. 6.19 | Initializing jagged and rectangular arrays. (Part 1 of 2.)

```
25
26      // output rows and columns of a rectangular array
27      public static void OutputArray( int[ , ] array )
28      {
29         Console.WriteLine( "Values in the rectangular array by row are" );
30
31         // loop through array's rows
32         for ( int row = 0; row < array.GetLength( 0 ); row++ )
33         {
34            // loop through columns of current row
35            for ( int column = 0; column < array.GetLength( 1 ); column++ )
36               Console.Write( "{0}  ", array[ row, column ] );
37
38            Console.WriteLine(); // start new line of output
39         } // end outer for
40      } // end method OutputArray
41
42      // output rows and columns of a jagged array
43      public static void OutputArray( int[][] array )
44      {
45         Console.WriteLine( "Values in the jagged array by row are" );
46
47         // loop through array's rows
48         for ( int row = 0; row < array.Length; row++ )
49         {
50            // loop through columns of current row
51            for ( int column = 0; column < array[ row ].Length; column++ )
52               Console.Write( "{0}  ", array[ row ][ column ] );
53
54            Console.WriteLine(); // start new line of output
55         } // end outer for
56      } // end method OutputArray
57   } // end class InitArray
```

```
Values in the rectangular array by row are
1  2  3
4  5  6

Values in the jagged array by row are
1  2
3
4  5  6
```

Fig. 6.19 | Initializing jagged and rectangular arrays. (Part 2 of 2.)

nested initializers of different lengths. In this case, the initializer uses the keyword new to create a one-dimensional array for each row. Row 0 is initialized to have two elements with values 1 and 2, respectively. Row 1 is initialized to have one element with value 3. Row 2 is initialized to have three elements with the values 4, 5 and 6, respectively.

Method OutputArray has been overloaded with two versions. The first version (lines 27–40) specifies the array parameter as int[,] array to indicate that it takes a rectangular array. The second version (lines 43–56) takes a jagged array, because its array parameter is listed as int[][] array.

Line 21 invokes method OutputArray with argument rectangular, so the version of OutputArray at lines 27–40 is called. The for statement (lines 32–39) outputs the rows of a rectangular array. The loop-continuation condition of each for statement (lines 32 and 35) uses the rectangular array's GetLength method to obtain the length of each dimension. The dimensions are numbered starting from 0. So the method call GetLength(0) on array returns the size of the first dimension of the array (the number of rows), and the call GetLength(1) returns the size of the second dimension (the number of columns).

Line 23 invokes method OutputArray with argument jagged, so the version of OutputArray at lines 43–56 is called. The for statement (lines 48–55) outputs the rows of a jagged array. In the loop-continuation condition of the outer for statement (line 48), we use the property array.Length to determine the number of rows in the array. In the inner for statement (line 51), we use the property array[row].Length to determine the number of columns in the current row of the array. This condition enables the loop to determine the exact number of columns in each row.

Common Multidimensional-Array Manipulations Performed with for Statements
Many common array manipulations use for statements. As an example, the following for statement sets all the elements in row 2 of rectangular array a in Fig. 6.17 to 0:

```
for ( int column = 0; column < a.GetLength( 1 ); column++)
    a[ 2, column ] = 0;
```

We specified row 2; therefore, we know that the first index is always 2 (0 is the first row, and 1 is the second row). This for loop varies only the second index (i.e., the column index). The preceding for statement is equivalent to the assignment statements

```
a[ 2, 0 ] = 0;
a[ 2, 1 ] = 0;
a[ 2, 2 ] = 0;
a[ 2, 3 ] = 0;
```

The following nested for statement totals the values of all the elements in array a:

```
int total = 0;

for ( int row = 0; row < a.GetLength( 0 ); row++ )
{
    for ( int column = 0; column < a.GetLength( 1 ); column++ )
        total += a[ row, column ];
} // end outer for
```

These nested for statements total the array elements one row at a time. The outer for statement begins by setting the row index to 0 so that row 0's elements can be totaled by the inner for statement. The outer for then increments row to 1 so that row 1's elements can be totaled. Then the outer for increments row to 2 so that row 2's elements can be totaled. The variable total can be displayed when the outer for statement terminates. In the next example, we show how to process a rectangular array in a more concise manner using foreach statements.

6.11 Case Study: Class GradeBook Using a Rectangular Array

In Section 6.9, we presented class GradeBook (Fig. 6.15), which used a one-dimensional array to store student grades on a single exam. In most courses, students take several exams. Instructors are likely to want to analyze grades across the entire course, both for a single student and for the class as a whole.

Storing Student Grades in a Rectangular Array in Class GradeBook

Figure 6.20 contains a version of class GradeBook that uses a rectangular array grades to store the grades of a number of students on multiple exams. Each row of the array represents a single student's grades for the entire course, and each column represents the grades for the whole class on one of the exams the students took during the course. An application such as GradeBookTest (Fig. 6.21) passes the array as an argument to the GradeBook constructor. In this example, we use a 10-by-3 array containing 10 students' grades on three exams. Five methods perform array manipulations to process the grades. Each method is similar to its counterpart in the earlier one-dimensional array version of class GradeBook (Fig. 6.15). Method GetMinimum (lines 54–68) determines the lowest grade of any student for the semester. Method GetMaximum (lines 71–85) determines the highest grade of any student for the

```
1   // Fig. 6.20: GradeBook.cs
2   // Grade book using rectangular array to store grades.
3   using System;
4
5   public class GradeBook
6   {
7      private string courseName; // name of course this grade book represents
8      private int[ , ] grades; // rectangular array of student grades
9
10     // two-parameter constructor initializes courseName and grades array
11     public GradeBook( string name, int[ , ] gradesArray )
12     {
13        CourseName = name; // initialize courseName
14        grades = gradesArray; // initialize grades array
15     } // end two-parameter GradeBook constructor
16
17     // property that gets and sets the course name
18     public string CourseName
19     {
20        get
21        {
22           return courseName;
23        } // end get
24        set
25        {
26           courseName = value;
27        } // end set
28     } // end property CourseName
29
```

Fig. 6.20 | Grade book using rectangular array to store grades. (Part 1 of 4.)

```
30      // display a welcome message to the GradeBook user
31      public void DisplayMessage()
32      {
33         // CourseName property gets the name of the course
34         Console.WriteLine( "Welcome to the grade book for\n{0}!\n",
35            CourseName );
36      } // end method DisplayMessage
37
38      // perform various operations on the data
39      public void ProcessGrades()
40      {
41         // output grades array
42         OutputGrades();
43
44         // call methods GetMinimum and GetMaximum
45         Console.WriteLine( "\n{0} {1}\n{2} {3}\n",
46            "Lowest grade in the grade book is", GetMinimum(),
47            "Highest grade in the grade book is", GetMaximum() );
48
49         // output grade distribution chart of all grades on all tests
50         OutputBarChart();
51      } // end method ProcessGrades
52
53      // find minimum grade
54      public int GetMinimum()
55      {
56         // assume first element of grades array is smallest
57         int lowGrade = grades[ 0, 0 ];
58
59         // loop through elements of rectangular grades array
60         foreach ( int grade in grades )
61         {
62            // if grade less than lowGrade, assign it to lowGrade
63            if ( grade < lowGrade )
64               lowGrade = grade;
65         } // end foreach
66
67         return lowGrade; // return lowest grade
68      } // end method GetMinimum
69
70      // find maximum grade
71      public int GetMaximum()
72      {
73         // assume first element of grades array is largest
74         int highGrade = grades[ 0, 0 ];
75
76         // loop through elements of rectangular grades array
77         foreach ( int grade in grades )
78         {
79            // if grade greater than highGrade, assign it to highGrade
80            if ( grade > highGrade )
81               highGrade = grade;
82         } // end foreach
```

Fig. 6.20 | Grade book using rectangular array to store grades. (Part 2 of 4.)

```
83
84          return highGrade; // return highest grade
85    } // end method GetMaximum
86
87       // determine average grade for particular student
88       public double GetAverage( int student )
89       {
90          // get the number of grades per student
91          int amount = grades.GetLength( 1 );
92          int total = 0; // initialize total
93
94          // sum grades for one student
95          for ( int exam = 0; exam < amount; exam++ )
96             total += grades[ student, exam ];
97
98          // return average of grades
99          return ( double ) total / amount;
100      } // end method GetAverage
101
102      // output bar chart displaying overall grade distribution
103      public void OutputBarChart()
104      {
105         Console.WriteLine( "Overall grade distribution:" );
106
107         // stores frequency of grades in each range of 10 grades
108         int[] frequency = new int[ 11 ];
109
110         // for each grade in GradeBook, increment the appropriate frequency
111         foreach ( int grade in grades )
112         {
113            ++frequency[ grade / 10 ];
114         } // end foreach
115
116         // for each grade frequency, print bar in chart
117         for ( int count = 0; count < frequency.Length; count++ )
118         {
119            // output bar label ( "00-09: ", ..., "90-99: ", "100: " )
120            if ( count == 10 )
121               Console.Write( "  100: " );
122            else
123               Console.Write( "{0:D2}-{1:D2}: ",
124                  count * 10, count * 10 + 9 );
125
126            // print bar of asterisks
127            for ( int stars = 0; stars < frequency[ count ]; stars++ )
128               Console.Write( "*" );
129
130            Console.WriteLine(); // start a new line of output
131         } // end outer for
132      } // end method OutputBarChart
133
```

Fig. 6.20 | Grade book using rectangular array to store grades. (Part 3 of 4.)

```
134     // output the contents of the grades array
135     public void OutputGrades()
136     {
137        Console.WriteLine( "The grades are:\n" );
138        Console.Write( "              " ); // align column heads
139
140        // create a column heading for each of the tests
141        for ( int test = 0; test < grades.GetLength( 1 ); test++ )
142           Console.Write( "Test {0}  ", test + 1 );
143
144        Console.WriteLine( "Average" ); // student average column heading
145
146        // create rows/columns of text representing array grades
147        for ( int student = 0; student < grades.GetLength( 0 ); student++ )
148        {
149           Console.Write( "Student {0,2}", student + 1 );
150
151           // output student's grades
152           for ( int grade = 0; grade < grades.GetLength( 1 ); grade++ )
153              Console.Write( "{0,8}", grades[ student, grade ] );
154
155           // call method GetAverage to calculate student's average grade;
156           // pass row number as the argument to GetAverage
157           Console.WriteLine( "{0,9:F2}", GetAverage( student ) );
158        } // end outer for
159     } // end method OutputGrades
160  } // end class GradeBook
```

Fig. 6.20 | Grade book using rectangular array to store grades. (Part 4 of 4.)

semester. Method GetAverage (lines 88–100) determines a particular student's semester average. Method OutputBarChart (lines 103–132) outputs a bar chart of the distribution of all student grades for the semester. Method OutputGrades (lines 135–159) outputs the two-dimensional array in tabular format, along with each student's semester average.

Methods GetMinimum, GetMaximum and OutputBarChart each loop through array grades using the foreach statement—for example, the foreach statement from method GetMinimum (lines 60–65). To find the lowest overall grade, this foreach statement iterates through rectangular array grades and compares each element to variable lowGrade. If a grade is less than lowGrade, lowGrade is set to that grade.

When the foreach statement traverses the elements of the grades array, it looks at each element of the first row in order by index, then each element of the second row in order by index and so on. The foreach statement at lines 60–65 traverses the elements of grade in the same order as the following equivalent code, expressed with nested for statements:

```
for ( int row = 0; row < grades.GetLength( 0 ); row++ )
   for ( int column = 0; column < grades.GetLength( 1 ); column++ )
   {
      if ( grades[ row, column ] < lowGrade )
         lowGrade = grades[ row, column ];
   }
```

When the foreach statement completes, lowGrade contains the lowest grade in the rectangular array. Method GetMaximum works similarly to method GetMinimum.

Method OutputBarChart in Fig. 6.20 displays the grade distribution as a bar chart. Note that the syntax of the foreach statement (lines 111–114) is identical for one-dimensional and two-dimensional arrays.

Method OutputGrades (lines 135–159) uses nested for statements to output values of the array grades, in addition to each student's semester average. The output in Fig. 6.21 shows the result, which resembles the tabular format of an instructor's physical grade book. Lines 141–142 print the column headings for each test. We use the for statement rather than the foreach statement here so that we can identify each test with a number. Similarly, the for statement in lines 147–158 first outputs a row label using a counter variable to identify each student (line 149). Although array indices start at 0, note that lines 142 and 149 output test + 1 and student + 1, respectively, to produce test and student numbers starting at 1 (see Fig. 6.21). The inner for statement in lines 152–153 uses the outer for statement's counter variable student to loop through a specific row of array grades and output each student's test grade. Finally, line 157 obtains each student's semester average by passing the row index of grades (i.e., student) to method GetAverage.

Method GetAverage (lines 88–100) takes one argument—the row index for a particular student. When line 157 calls GetAverage, the argument is int value student, which specifies the particular row of rectangular array grades. Method GetAverage calculates the sum of the array elements on this row, divides the total by the number of test results and returns the floating-point result as a double value (line 99).

Class GradeBookTest That Demonstrates Class GradeBook

The application in Fig. 6.21 creates an object of class GradeBook (Fig. 6.20) using the two-dimensional array of ints named gradesArray (declared and initialized in lines 9–18).

```
1   // Fig. 6.21: GradeBookTest.cs
2   // Create GradeBook object using a rectangular array of grades.
3   public class GradeBookTest
4   {
5       // Main method begins application execution
6       public static void Main( string[] args )
7       {
8           // rectangular array of student grades
9           int[ , ] gradesArray = { { 87, 96, 70 },
10                                    { 68, 87, 90 },
11                                    { 94, 100, 90 },
12                                    { 100, 81, 82 },
13                                    { 83, 65, 85 },
14                                    { 78, 87, 65 },
15                                    { 85, 75, 83 },
16                                    { 91, 94, 100 },
17                                    { 76, 72, 84 },
18                                    { 87, 93, 73 } };
19
```

Fig. 6.21 | Create GradeBook object using a rectangular array of grades. (Part 1 of 2.)

```
20            GradeBook myGradeBook = new GradeBook(
21               "CS101 Introduction to C# Programming", gradesArray );
22            myGradeBook.DisplayMessage();
23            myGradeBook.ProcessGrades();
24         } // end Main
25      } // end class GradeBookTest
```

```
Welcome to the grade book for
CS101 Introduction to C# Programming!

The grades are:

            Test 1  Test 2  Test 3   Average
Student  1     87      96      70     84.33
Student  2     68      87      90     81.67
Student  3     94     100      90     94.67
Student  4    100      81      82     87.67
Student  5     83      65      85     77.67
Student  6     78      87      65     76.67
Student  7     85      75      83     81.00
Student  8     91      94     100     95.00
Student  9     76      72      84     77.33
Student 10     87      93      73     84.33

Lowest grade in the grade book is 65
Highest grade in the grade book is 100

Overall grade distribution:
00-09:
10-19:
20-29:
30-39:
40-49:
50-59:
60-69: ***
70-79: ******
80-89: ***********
90-99: *******
  100: ***
```

Fig. 6.21 | Create GradeBook object using a rectangular array of grades. (Part 2 of 2.)

Lines 20–21 pass a course name and gradesArray to the GradeBook constructor. Lines 22–23 then invoke myGradeBook's DisplayMessage and ProcessGrades methods to display a welcome message and obtain a report summarizing the students' grades for the semester, respectively.

6.12 Variable-Length Argument Lists

Variable-length argument lists allow you to create methods that receive an arbitrary number of arguments. A one-dimensional array-type argument preceded by the keyword **params** in a method's parameter list indicates that the method receives a variable number of arguments with the type of the array's elements. This use of a params modifier can occur only in the last entry of the parameter list. While you can use method overloading and array passing to accomplish much of what is accomplished with "varargs"—another name for variable-length argument lists—using the params modifier is more concise.

Figure 6.22 demonstrates method Average (lines 8–17), which receives a variable-length sequence of doubles (line 8). C# treats the variable-length argument list as a one-dimensional array whose elements are all of the same type. Hence, the method body can manipulate the parameter numbers as an array of doubles. Lines 13–14 use the foreach loop to walk through the array and calculate the total of the doubles in the array. Line 16 accesses numbers.Length to obtain the size of the numbers array for use in the averaging calculation. Lines 31, 33 and 35 in Main call method Average with two, three and four arguments, respectively. Method Average has a variable-length argument list, so it can average as many double arguments as the caller passes. The output reveals that each call to method Average returns the correct value.

```
1   // Fig. 6.22: VarargsTest.cs
2   // Using variable-length argument lists.
3   using System;
4
5   public class VarargsTest
6   {
7      // calculate average
8      public static double Average( params double[] numbers )
9      {
10        double total = 0.0; // initialize total
11
12        // calculate total using the foreach statement
13        foreach ( double d in numbers )
14           total += d;
15
16        return total / numbers.Length;
17     } // end method Average
18
19     public static void Main( string[] args )
20     {
21        double d1 = 10.0;
22        double d2 = 20.0;
23        double d3 = 30.0;
24        double d4 = 40.0;
25
26        Console.WriteLine(
27           "d1 = {0:F1}\nd2 = {1:F1}\nd3 = {2:F1}\nd4 = {3:F1}\n",
28           d1, d2, d3, d4 );
29
30        Console.WriteLine( "Average of d1 and d2 is {0:F1}",
31           Average( d1, d2 ) );
32        Console.WriteLine( "Average of d1, d2 and d3 is {0:F1}",
33           Average( d1, d2, d3 ) );
34        Console.WriteLine( "Average of d1, d2, d3 and d4 is {0:F1}",
35           Average( d1, d2, d3, d4 ) );
36     } // end Main
37  } // end class VarargsTest
```

Fig. 6.22 | Using variable-length argument lists. (Part 1 of 2.)

```
d1 = 10.0
d2 = 20.0
d3 = 30.0
d4 = 40.0

Average of d1 and d2 is 15.0
Average of d1, d2 and d3 is 20.0
Average of d1, d2, d3 and d4 is 25.0
```

Fig. 6.22 | Using variable-length argument lists. (Part 2 of 2.)

Common Programming Error 6.4

Using the params modifier with a parameter in the middle of a method parameter list is a syntax error. The params modifier may be used only with the last parameter of the parameter list.

6.13 Using Command-Line Arguments

On many systems, it is possible to pass arguments from the command line (these are known as *command-line arguments*) to an application by including a parameter of type string[] (i.e., an array of strings) in the parameter list of Main, exactly as we have done in every application in the book. By convention, this parameter is named args (Fig. 6.23, line 7). When an application is executed from the Command Prompt, the execution environment passes the command-line arguments that appear after the application name to

```
1   // Fig. 6.23: InitArray.cs
2   // Using command-line arguments to initialize an array.
3   using System;
4
5   public class InitArray
6   {
7      public static void Main( string[] args )
8      {
9         // check number of command-line arguments
10        if ( args.Length != 3 )
11           Console.WriteLine(
12              "Error: Please re-enter the entire command, including\n" +
13              "an array size, initial value and increment." );
14        else
15        {
16           // get array size from first command-line argument
17           int arrayLength = Convert.ToInt32( args[ 0 ] );
18           int[] array = new int[ arrayLength ]; // create array
19
20           // get initial value and increment from command-line argument
21           int initialValue = Convert.ToInt32( args[ 1 ] );
22           int increment = Convert.ToInt32( args[ 2 ] );
23
24           // calculate value for each array element
25           for ( int counter = 0; counter < array.Length; counter++ )
26              array[ counter ] = initialValue + increment * counter;
```

Fig. 6.23 | Using command-line arguments to initialize an array. (Part 1 of 2.)

```
27
28              Console.WriteLine( "{0}{1,8}", "Index", "Value" );
29
30              // display array index and value
31              for ( int counter = 0; counter < array.Length; counter++ )
32                  Console.WriteLine( "{0,5}{1,8}", counter, array[ counter ] );
33          } // end else
34      } // end Main
35  } // end class InitArray
```

```
C:\Examples\ch08\fig08_21>InitArray.exe
Error: Please re-enter the entire command, including
an array size, initial value and increment.
```

```
C:\Examples\ch08\fig08_21>InitArray.exe 5 0 4
Index   Value
    0       0
    1       4
    2       8
    3      12
    4      16
```

```
C:\Examples\ch08\fig08_21>InitArray.exe 10 1 2
Index   Value
    0       1
    1       3
    2       5
    3       7
    4       9
    5      11
    6      13
    7      15
    8      17
    9      19
```

Fig. 6.23 | Using command-line arguments to initialize an array. (Part 2 of 2.)

the application's Main method as strings in the one-dimensional array args. The number of arguments passed from the command line is obtained by accessing the array's Length property. For example, the command "MyApplication a b" passes two command-line arguments to application MyApplication. Note that command-line arguments are separated by white space, not commas. When the preceding command executes, the Main method entry point receives the two-element array args (i.e., args.Length is 2) in which args[0] contains the string "a" and args[1] contains the string "b". Common uses of command-line arguments include passing options and file names to applications.

Figure 6.23 uses three command-line arguments to initialize an array. When the application executes, if args.Length is not 3, the application prints an error message and terminates (lines 10–13). Otherwise, lines 16–32 initialize and display the array based on the values of the command-line arguments.

The command-line arguments become available to Main as strings in args. Line 17 gets args[0]—a string that specifies the array size—and converts it to an int value, which the application uses to create the array in line 18. The static method ToInt32 of class Convert converts its string argument to an int.

Lines 21–22 convert the args[1] and args[2] command-line arguments to int values and store them in initialValue and increment, respectively. Lines 25–26 calculate the value for each array element.

The output of the first sample execution indicates that the application received an insufficient number of command-line arguments. The second sample execution uses command-line arguments 5, 0 and 4 to specify the size of the array (5), the value of the first element (0) and the increment of each value in the array (4), respectively. The corresponding output indicates that these values create an array containing the integers 0, 4, 8, 12 and 16. The output from the third sample execution illustrates that the command-line arguments 10, 1 and 2 produce an array whose 10 elements are the nonnegative odd integers from 1 to 19.

6.14 (Optional) Software Engineering Case Study: Collaboration Among Objects in the ATM System

When two objects communicate with each other to accomplish a task, they are said to *collaborate*. A *collaboration* consists of an object of one class sending a *message* to an object of another class. Messages are sent in C# via method calls. In this section, we concentrate on the collaborations (interactions) among the objects in our ATM system.

In Section 5.15, we determined many of the operations of the classes in our system. In this section, we concentrate on the messages that invoke these operations. To identify the collaborations in the system, we return to the requirements document of Section 1.10. Recall that this document specifies the activities that occur during an ATM session (e.g., authenticating a user, performing transactions). The steps used to describe how the system must perform each of these tasks are our first indication of the collaborations in our system. As we proceed through this and the remaining Software Engineering Case Study sections, we may discover additional collaborations.

Identifying the Collaborations in a System

We begin to identify the collaborations in the system by carefully reading the sections of the requirements document that specify what the ATM should do to authenticate a user and to perform each transaction type. For each action or step described in the requirements document, we decide which objects in our system must interact to achieve the desired result. We identify one object as the sending object (i.e., the object that sends the message) and another as the receiving object (i.e., the object that offers that operation to clients of the class). We then select one of the receiving object's operations (identified in Section 5.15) that must be invoked by the sending object to produce the proper behavior. For example, the ATM displays a welcome message when idle. We know that an object of class Screen displays a message to the user via its DisplayMessage operation. Thus, we decide that the system can display a welcome message by employing a collaboration between the ATM and the Screen in which the ATM sends a DisplayMessage message to the Screen by invoking the DisplayMessage operation of class Screen. [*Note:* To avoid repeating the phrase "an object of class...," we refer to each object simply by using its class name preceded by an article (e.g., "a," "an" or "the")—for example, "the ATM" refers to an object of class ATM.]

Figure 6.24 lists the collaborations that can be derived from the requirements document. For each sending object, we list the collaborations in the order in which they are discussed in the requirements document. We list each collaboration involving a unique sender, message and recipient only once, even though the collaboration may occur several times during an ATM session. For example, the first row in Fig. 6.24 indicates that the ATM collaborates with the Screen whenever the ATM needs to display a message to the user.

Let's consider the collaborations in Fig. 6.24. Before allowing a user to perform any transactions, the ATM must prompt the user to enter an account number, then to enter a PIN. It accomplishes each of these tasks by sending a DisplayMessage message to the Screen. Both of these actions refer to the same collaboration between the ATM and the Screen, which is already listed in Fig. 6.24. The ATM obtains input in response to a prompt by sending a GetInput message to the Keypad. Next the ATM must determine whether the user-specified account number and PIN match those of an account in the database. It does so by sending an AuthenticateUser message to the BankDatabase. Recall that the Bank-Database cannot authenticate a user directly—only the user's Account (i.e., the Account that contains the account number specified by the user) can access the user's PIN to

An object of class...	sends the message...	to an object of class...
ATM	DisplayMessage	Screen
	GetInput	Keypad
	AuthenticateUser	BankDatabase
	Execute	BalanceInquiry
	Execute	Withdrawal
	Execute	Deposit
BalanceInquiry	GetAvailableBalance	BankDatabase
	GetTotalBalance	BankDatabase
	DisplayMessage	Screen
Withdrawal	DisplayMessage	Screen
	GetInput	Keypad
	GetAvailableBalance	BankDatabase
	IsSufficientCashAvailable	CashDispenser
	Debit	BankDatabase
	DispenseCash	CashDispenser
Deposit	DisplayMessage	Screen
	GetInput	Keypad
	IsDepositEnvelopeReceived	DepositSlot
	Credit	BankDatabase
BankDatabase	ValidatePIN	Account
	AvailableBalance (get)	Account
	TotalBalance (get)	Account
	Debit	Account
	Credit	Account

Fig. 6.24 | Collaborations in the ATM system.

authenticate the user. Figure 6.24 therefore lists a collaboration in which the Bank-Database sends a `ValidatePIN` message to an `Account`.

After the user is authenticated, the ATM displays the main menu by sending a series of `DisplayMessage` messages to the `Screen` and obtains input containing a menu selection by sending a `GetInput` message to the `Keypad`. We have already accounted for these collaborations. After the user chooses a type of transaction to perform, the ATM executes the transaction by sending an `Execute` message to an object of the appropriate transaction class (i.e., a `BalanceInquiry`, a `Withdrawal` or a `Deposit`). For example, if the user chooses to perform a balance inquiry, the ATM sends an `Execute` message to a `BalanceInquiry`.

Further examination of the requirements document reveals the collaborations involved in executing each transaction type. A `BalanceInquiry` retrieves the amount of money available in the user's account by sending a `GetAvailableBalance` message to the `BankDatabase`, which sends a `get` message to an `Account`'s `AvailableBalance` property to access the available balance. Similarly, the `BalanceInquiry` retrieves the amount of money on deposit by sending a `GetTotalBalance` message to the `BankDatabase`, which sends a `get` message to an `Account`'s `TotalBalance` property to access the total balance on deposit. To display both measures of the user's balance at the same time, the `BalanceInquiry` sends `DisplayMessage` messages to the `Screen`.

A `Withdrawal` sends `DisplayMessage` messages to the `Screen` to display a menu of standard withdrawal amounts (i.e., $20, $40, $60, $100, $200). The `Withdrawal` sends a `GetInput` message to the `Keypad` to obtain the user's menu selection. Next, the `Withdrawal` determines whether the requested withdrawal amount is less than or equal to the user's account balance. The `Withdrawal` obtains the amount of money available in the user's account by sending a `GetAvailableBalance` message to the `BankDatabase`. The `Withdrawal` then tests whether the cash dispenser contains enough cash by sending an `IsSufficientCashAvailable` message to the `CashDispenser`. A `Withdrawal` sends a `Debit` message to the `BankDatabase` to decrease the user's account balance. The Bank-Database in turn sends the same message to the appropriate `Account`. Recall that debiting an `Account` decreases both the total balance and the available balance. To dispense the requested amount of cash, the `Withdrawal` sends a `DispenseCash` message to the `CashDispenser`. Finally, the `Withdrawal` sends a `DisplayMessage` message to the `Screen`, instructing the user to take the cash.

A `Deposit` responds to an `Execute` message first by sending a `DisplayMessage` message to the `Screen` to prompt the user for a deposit amount. The `Deposit` sends a `GetInput` message to the `Keypad` to obtain the user's input. The `Deposit` then sends a `DisplayMessage` message to the `Screen` to tell the user to insert a deposit envelope. To determine whether the deposit slot received an incoming deposit envelope, the `Deposit` sends an `IsDepositEnvelopeReceived` message to the `DepositSlot`. The `Deposit` updates the user's account by sending a `Credit` message to the `BankDatabase`, which subsequently sends a `Credit` message to the user's `Account`. Recall that crediting an `Account` increases the total balance but not the available balance.

Interaction Diagrams

Now that we have identified a set of possible collaborations between the objects in our ATM system, let us graphically model these interactions. The UML provides several types of *interaction diagrams* that model the behavior of a system by modeling how objects interact with one another. The *communication diagram* emphasizes *which objects* participate in collaborations. [*Note:* Communication diagrams were called *collaboration diagrams* in earlier versions of the UML.] Like the communication diagram, the *sequence diagram* shows collaborations among objects, but it emphasizes *when* messages are sent between objects.

Communication Diagrams

Figure 6.25 shows a communication diagram that models the ATM executing a BalanceInquiry. Objects are modeled in the UML as rectangles containing names in the form objectName : ClassName. In this example, which involves only one object of each type, we disregard the object name and list only a colon followed by the class name. Specifying the name of each object in a communication diagram is recommended when modeling multiple objects of the same type. Communicating objects are connected with solid lines, and messages are passed between objects along these lines in the direction shown by arrows with filled arrowheads. The name of the message, which appears next to the arrow, is the name of an operation (i.e., a method) belonging to the receiving object—think of the name as a service that the receiving object provides to sending objects (its "clients").

The filled arrow in Fig. 6.25 represents a message—or *synchronous call*—in the UML and a method call in C#. This arrow indicates that the flow of control is from the sending object (the ATM) to the receiving object (a BalanceInquiry). Since this is a synchronous call, the sending object cannot send another message, or do anything at all, until the receiving object processes the message and returns control (and possibly a return value) to the sending object. The sender just waits. For example, in Fig. 6.25, the ATM calls method Execute of a BalanceInquiry and cannot send another message until Execute finishes and returns control to the ATM. [*Note:* If this were an *asynchronous call*, represented by a stick arrowhead, the sending object would not have to wait for the receiving object to return control—it would continue sending additional messages immediately following the asynchronous call. Such calls are beyond the scope of this book.]

Sequence of Messages in a Communication Diagram

Figure 6.26 shows a communication diagram that models the interactions among objects in the system when an object of class BalanceInquiry executes. We assume that the object's accountNumber attribute contains the account number of the current user. The collaborations in Fig. 6.26 begin after the ATM sends an Execute message to a BalanceInquiry (i.e., the interaction modeled in Fig. 6.25). The number to the left of a message name indicates the order in which the message is passed. The *sequence of messages* in a communication diagram progresses in numerical order from least to greatest. In this diagram, the numbering starts with message 1 and ends with message 3. The BalanceInquiry first sends a GetAvailableBalance message to the BankDatabase (message 1), then sends a GetTotalBalance message to the BankDatabase (message 2). Within the parentheses following a message name, we can specify a comma-separated list of the names of the

Fig. 6.25 | Communication diagram of the ATM executing a balance inquiry.

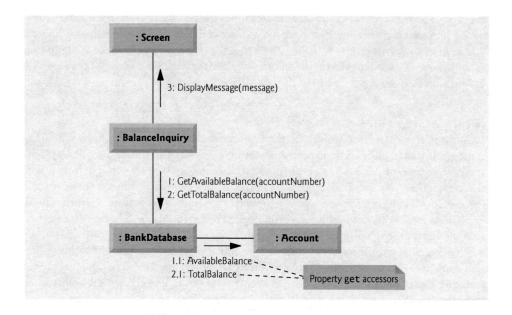

Fig. 6.26 | Communication diagram for executing a `BalanceInquiry`.

arguments sent with the message (i.e., arguments in a C# method call)—the `BalanceInquiry` passes attribute `accountNumber` with its messages to the `BankDatabase` to indicate which `Account`'s balance information to retrieve. Recall from Fig. 5.22 that operations `GetAvailableBalance` and `GetTotalBalance` of class `BankDatabase` each require a parameter to identify an account. The `BalanceInquiry` next displays the available balance and the total balance to the user by passing a `DisplayMessage` message to the `Screen` (message 3) that includes a parameter indicating the `message` to be displayed.

Note that Fig. 6.26 models two additional messages passing from the `BankDatabase` to an `Account` (message 1.1 and message 2.1). To provide the ATM with the two balances of the user's `Account` (as requested by messages 1 and 2), the `BankDatabase` must send get messages to the `Account`'s `AvailableBalance` and `TotalBalance` properties. A message passed within the handling of another message is called a ***nested message***. The UML recommends using a decimal numbering scheme to indicate nested messages. For example, message 1.1 is the first message nested in message 1—the `BankDatabase` sends the get message to the `Account`'s `AvailableBalance` property during `BankDatabase`'s processing of a `GetAvailableBalance` message. [*Note:* If the `BankDatabase` needed to pass a second nested message while processing message 1, the second message would be numbered 1.2.] A message may be passed only when all the nested messages from the previous message have been passed. For example, the `BalanceInquiry` passes message 3 to the `Screen` only after messages 2 and 2.1 have been passed, in that order.

The nested numbering scheme used in communication diagrams helps clarify precisely when and in what context each message is passed. For example, if we numbered the five messages in Fig. 6.26 using a flat numbering scheme (i.e., 1, 2, 3, 4, 5), someone looking at the diagram might not be able to determine that `BankDatabase` passes the get message to an Account's AvailableBalance property (message 1.1) *during* the BankDatabase's processing of message 1, as opposed to *after* completing the processing of message 1. The nested decimal numbers make it clear that the get message (message 1.1) is passed to an Account's AvailableBalance property within the handling of the GetAvailableBalance message (message 1) by the BankDatabase.

Sequence Diagrams

Communication diagrams emphasize the participants in collaborations but model their timing a bit awkwardly. A sequence diagram helps model the timing of collaborations more clearly. Figure 6.27 shows a sequence diagram modeling the sequence of interactions that occur when a Withdrawal executes. The dotted line extending down from an object's rectangle is that object's *lifeline*, which represents the progression of time. Actions typically occur along an object's lifeline in chronological order from top to bottom—an action near the top happens before one near the bottom.

Message passing in sequence diagrams is similar to message passing in communication diagrams. An arrow with a filled arrowhead extending from the sending object to the receiving object represents a message between two objects. The arrowhead points to an activation on the receiving object's lifeline. An *activation*, shown as a thin vertical rectangle, indicates that an object is executing. When an object returns control, a return message, represented as a dashed line with a stick arrowhead, extends from the activation of the object returning control to the activation of the object that initially sent the message. To eliminate clutter, we omit the return-message arrows—the UML allows this practice to make diagrams more readable. Like communication diagrams, sequence diagrams can indicate message parameters between the parentheses following a message name.

The sequence of messages in Fig. 6.27 begins when a Withdrawal prompts the user to choose a withdrawal amount by sending a DisplayMessage message to the Screen. The Withdrawal then sends a GetInput message to the Keypad, which obtains input from the user. We have already modeled the control logic involved in a Withdrawal in the activity diagram of Fig. 4.22, so we do not show this logic in the sequence diagram of Fig. 6.27. Instead, we model the best-case scenario, in which the balance of the user's account is greater than or equal to the chosen withdrawal amount, and the cash dispenser contains a sufficient amount of cash to satisfy the request. For information on how to model control logic in a sequence diagram, please refer to the Web resources and recommended readings listed at the end of Section 1.10.

After obtaining a withdrawal amount, the Withdrawal sends a GetAvailableBalance message to the BankDatabase, which in turn sends a get message to the Account's AvailableBalance property. Assuming that the user's account has enough money available to permit the transaction, the Withdrawal next sends an IsSufficientCashAvailable message to the CashDispenser. Assuming that there is enough cash available, the Withdrawal decreases the balance of the user's account (both the total balance and the available balance) by sending a Debit message to the BankDatabase. The BankDatabase responds by sending a Debit message to the user's Account. Finally, the Withdrawal sends a DispenseCash message to the CashDispenser and a DisplayMessage message to the Screen, telling the user to remove the cash from the machine.

We have identified collaborations among objects in the ATM system and modeled some of these collaborations using UML interaction diagrams—communication diagrams

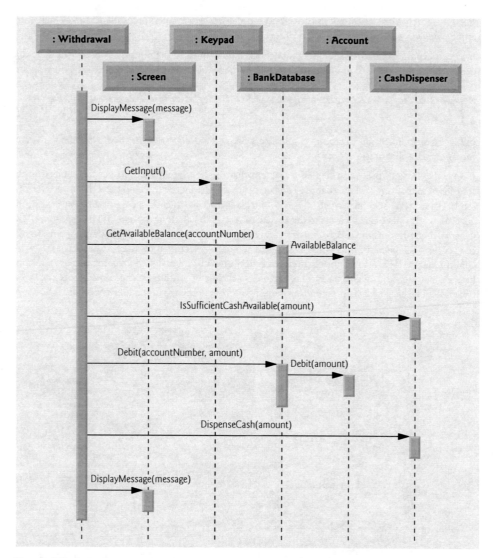

Fig. 6.27 | Sequence diagram that models a `Withdrawal` executing.

and sequence diagrams. In the next Software Engineering Case Study section (Section 7.17), we enhance the structure of our model to complete a preliminary object-oriented design, then we begin implementing the ATM system in C#.

Software Engineering Case Study Self-Review Exercises

6.1   A(n) _____ consists of an object of one class sending a message to an object of another class.

    a) association
    b) aggregation
    c) collaboration
    d) composition

6.2 Which form of interaction diagram emphasizes *what* collaborations occur? Which form emphasizes *when* collaborations occur?

6.3 Create a sequence diagram that models the interactions among objects in the ATM system that occur when a Deposit executes successfully. Explain the sequence of messages modeled by the diagram.

Answers to Software Engineering Case Study Self-Review Exercises

6.1 c.

6.2 Communication diagrams emphasize *what* collaborations occur. Sequence diagrams emphasize *when* collaborations occur.

6.3 Figure 6.28 presents a sequence diagram that models the interactions between objects in the ATM system that occur when a Deposit executes successfully. Figure 6.28 indicates that a Deposit first sends a DisplayMessage message to the Screen (to ask the user to enter a deposit amount). Next, the Deposit sends a GetInput message to the Keypad to receive the amount the user will be depositing. The Deposit then prompts the user (to insert a deposit envelope) by sending a DisplayMessage message to the Screen. The Deposit next sends an IsDepositEnvelopeReceived message to the DepositSlot to confirm that the deposit envelope has been received by the ATM. Finally, the Deposit increases the total balance (but not the available balance) of the user's Account by sending a Credit message to the Bank-Database. The BankDatabase responds by sending the same message to the user's Account.

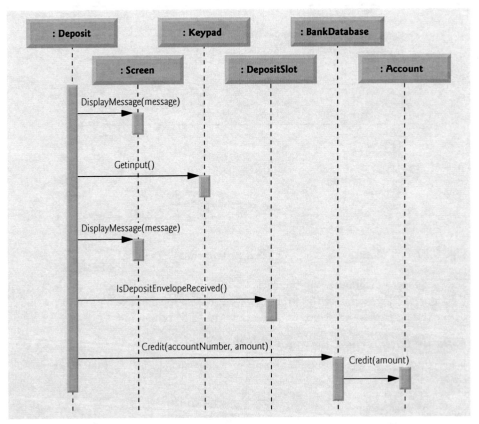

Fig. 6.28 | Sequence diagram that models a Deposit executing.

6.15 Wrap-Up

This chapter began our introduction to data structures, exploring the use of arrays to store data in and retrieve data from lists and tables of values. The chapter examples demonstrated how to declare arrays, initialize arrays and refer to individual elements of arrays. The chapter introduced the foreach statement as an additional means (besides the for statement) for iterating through arrays. We showed how to pass arrays to methods and how to declare and manipulate multidimensional arrays. Finally, the chapter showed how to write methods that use variable-length argument lists and how to read arguments passed to an application from the command line.

We have now introduced the basic concepts of classes, objects, control statements, methods and arrays. In Chapter 7, we take a deeper look at classes and objects.

7

Classes and Objects: A Deeper Look

OBJECTIVES

In this chapter you will learn:

- Encapsulation and data hiding.
- The concepts of data abstraction and abstract data types (ADTs).
- To use keyword `this`.
- To use indexers to access members of a class.
- To use `static` variables and methods.
- To use `readonly` fields.
- To take advantage of C#'s memory management features.
- How to create a class library.
- When to use the `internal` access modifier.

7.1 Introduction

In our discussions of object-oriented applications in the preceding chapters, we introduced many basic concepts and terminology that relate to C# object-oriented programming (OOP). We also discussed our application development methodology: We selected appropriate variables and methods for each application and specified the manner in which an object of our class collaborated with objects of classes in the .NET Framework Class Library to accomplish the application's overall goals.

In this chapter, we take a deeper look at building classes, controlling access to members of a class and creating constructors. We discuss composition—a capability that allows a class to have references to objects of other classes as members. We reexamine the use of properties and explore indexers as an alternative notation for accessing the members of a class. The chapter also discusses static class members and readonly instance variables in detail. We investigate issues such as software reusability, data abstraction and encapsulation. Finally, we explain how to organize classes in assemblies to help manage large applications and promote reuse, then show a special relationship between classes in the same assembly.

Chapter 8, Object-Oriented Programming: Inheritance, and Chapter 9, Polymorphism, Interfaces & Operator Overloading, introduce two additional key object-oriented programming technologies.

7.2 Time Class Case Study

Time1 *Class Declaration*

Our first example consists of two classes—Time1 (Fig. 7.1) and Time1Test (Fig. 7.2). Class Time1 represents the time of day. Class Time1Test is a testing class in which the Main method creates an object of class Time1 and invokes its methods. The output of this application appears in Fig. 7.2.

Class Time1 contains three private instance variables of type int (Fig. 7.1, lines 5–7)— hour, minute and second—that represent the time in universal-time format (24-hour clock format, in which hours are in the range 0–23). Class Time1 contains public methods Set-Time (lines 11–16), ToUniversalString (lines 19–23) and ToString (lines 26–31). These methods are the public *services* or the public *interface* that the class provides to its clients.

In this example, class Time1 does not declare a constructor, so the class has a default constructor that is supplied by the compiler. Each instance variable implicitly receives the default value 0 for an int. Note that when instance variables are declared in the class body they can be initialized using the same initialization syntax as a local variable.

```
1   // Fig. 7.1: Time1.cs
2   // Time1 class declaration maintains the time in 24-hour format.
3   public class Time1
4   {
5      private int hour;   // 0 - 23
6      private int minute; // 0 - 59
7      private int second; // 0 - 59
8
9      // set a new time value using universal time; ensure that
10     // the data remains consistent by setting invalid values to zero
11     public void SetTime( int h, int m, int s )
12     {
13        hour = ( ( h >= 0 && h < 24 ) ? h : 0 ); // validate hour
14        minute = ( ( m >= 0 && m < 60 ) ? m : 0 ); // validate minute
15        second = ( ( s >= 0 && s < 60 ) ? s : 0 ); // validate second
16     } // end method SetTime
17
18     // convert to string in universal-time format (HH:MM:SS)
19     public string ToUniversalString()
20     {
21        return string.Format( "{0:D2}:{1:D2}:{2:D2}",
22           hour, minute, second );
23     } // end method ToUniversalString
24
25     // convert to string in standard-time format (H:MM:SS AM or PM)
26     public override string ToString()
27     {
28        return string.Format( "{0}:{1:D2}:{2:D2} {3}",
29           ( ( hour == 0 || hour == 12 ) ? 12 : hour % 12 ),
30           minute, second, ( hour < 12 ? "AM" : "PM" ) );
31     } // end method ToString
32  } // end class Time1
```

Fig. 7.1 | Time1 class declaration maintains the time in 24-hour format.

Method SetTime (lines 11–16) is a public method that declares three int parameters and uses them to set the time. A conditional expression tests each argument to determine whether the value is in a specified range. For example, the hour value (line 13) must be greater than or equal to 0 and less than 24, because universal-time format represents hours as integers from 0 to 23 (e.g., 1 PM is hour 13 and 11 PM is hour 23; midnight is hour 0 and noon is hour 12). Similarly, both minute and second values (lines 14 and 15) must be greater than or equal to 0 and less than 60. Any out-of-range values are set to 0 to ensure that a Time1 object always contains consistent data—that is, the object's data values are always kept in range, even if the values provided as arguments to method SetTime are incorrect. In this example, 0 is a consistent value for hour, minute and second.

A value passed to SetTime is a correct value if that value is in the allowed range for the member it is initializing. So, any number in the range 0–23 would be a correct value for the hour. A correct value is always a consistent value. However, a consistent value is not necessarily a correct value. If SetTime sets hour to 0 because the argument received was out of range, then SetTime is taking an incorrect value and making it consistent, so the object remains in a consistent state at all times. In this case, the application might want to indicate that the object is incorrect. In Chapter 10, Exception Handling, you will learn techniques that enable your classes to indicate when incorrect values are received.

Software Engineering Observation 7.1

Methods and properties that modify the values of private variables should verify that the intended new values are proper. If they are not, they should place the private variables in an appropriate consistent state.

Method ToUniversalString (lines 19–23) takes no arguments and returns a string in universal-time format, consisting of six digits—two for the hour, two for the minute and two for the second. For example, if the time were 1:30:07 PM, method ToUniversalString would return 13:30:07. The return statement (lines 21–22) uses static method **Format** of class string to return a string containing the formatted hour, minute and second values, each with two digits and, where needed, a leading 0 (specified with the D2 format specifier—which pads the integer with 0s if it has less than two digits). Method Format is similar to the string formatting in method Console.Write, except that Format returns a formatted string rather than displaying it in a console window. The formatted string is returned by method ToUniversalString.

Method ToString (lines 26–31) takes no arguments and returns a string in standard-time format, consisting of the hour, minute and second values separated by colons and followed by an AM or PM indicator (e.g., 1:27:06 PM). Like method ToUniversalString, method ToString uses static string method Format to format the minute and second as two-digit values with leading 0s, if necessary. Line 29 uses a conditional operator (?:) to determine the value for hour in the string—if the hour is 0 or 12 (AM or PM), it appears as 12—otherwise, the hour appears as a value from 1 to 11. The conditional operator in line 30 determines whether AM or PM will be returned as part of the string.

Recall from Section 5.4 that all objects in C# have a ToString method that returns a string representation of the object. We chose to return a string containing the time in standard-time format. Method ToString is called implicitly when an object's string representation is output with a format item in a call to Console.Write. Remember that to specify the string representation of a class, we need to declare method ToString with keyword override—the reason for this will become clear when we discuss inheritance in Chapter 8.

Using Class Time1

As you learned in Chapter 2, each class you declare represents a new type in C#. Therefore, after declaring class Time1, we can use it as a type in declarations such as

```
Time1 sunset; // sunset can hold a reference to a Time1 object
```

The Time1Test application class (Fig. 7.2) uses class Time1. Line 10 creates a Time1 object and assigns it to local variable time. Note that new invokes class Time1's default constructor, since Time1 does not declare any constructors. Lines 13–17 output the time, first in universal-time format (by invoking time's ToUniversalString method in line 14), then in standard-time format (by explicitly invoking time's ToString method in line 16) to confirm that the Time1 object was initialized properly.

```csharp
1   // Fig. 7.2: Time1Test.cs
2   // Time1 object used in an application.
3   using System;
4
5   public class Time1Test
6   {
7      public static void Main( string[] args )
8      {
9         // create and initialize a Time1 object
10        Time1 time = new Time1(); // invokes Time1 constructor
11
12        // output string representations of the time
13        Console.Write( "The initial universal time is: " );
14        Console.WriteLine( time.ToUniversalString() );
15        Console.Write( "The initial standard time is: " );
16        Console.WriteLine( time.ToString() );
17        Console.WriteLine(); // output a blank line
18
19        // change time and output updated time
20        time.SetTime( 13, 27, 6 );
21        Console.Write( "Universal time after SetTime is: " );
22        Console.WriteLine( time.ToUniversalString() );
23        Console.Write( "Standard time after SetTime is: " );
24        Console.WriteLine( time.ToString() );
25        Console.WriteLine(); // output a blank line
26
27        // set time with invalid values; output updated time
28        time.SetTime( 99, 99, 99 );
29        Console.WriteLine( "After attempting invalid settings:" );
30        Console.Write( "Universal time: " );
31        Console.WriteLine( time.ToUniversalString() );
32        Console.Write( "Standard time: " );
33        Console.WriteLine( time.ToString() );
34     } // end Main
35  } // end class Time1Test
```

Fig. 7.2 | Time1 object used in an application. (Part 1 of 2.)

```
The initial universal time is: 00:00:00
The initial standard time is: 12:00:00 AM

Universal time after SetTime is: 13:27:06
Standard time after SetTime is: 1:27:06 PM

After attempting invalid settings:
Universal time: 00:00:00
Standard time: 12:00:00 AM
```

Fig. 7.2 | Time1 object used in an application. (Part 2 of 2.)

Line 20 invokes method SetTime of the time object to change the time. Then lines 21–25 output the time again in both formats to confirm that the time was set correctly.

To illustrate that method SetTime maintains the object in a consistent state, line 28 calls method SetTime with invalid arguments of 99 for the hour, minute and second. Lines 29–33 output the time again in both formats to confirm that SetTime maintains the object's consistent state, then the application terminates. The last two lines of the application's output show that the time is reset to midnight—the initial value of a Time1 object—after an attempt to set the time with three out-of-range values.

Notes on the Time1 Class Declaration
Consider several issues of class design with respect to class Time1. The instance variables hour, minute and second are each declared private. The actual data representation used within the class is of no concern to the class's clients. For example, it would be perfectly reasonable for Time1 to represent the time internally as the number of seconds since midnight or the number of minutes and seconds since midnight. Clients could use the same public methods and properties to get the same results without being aware of this.

Software Engineering Observation 7.2
Classes simplify programming because the client can use only the public members exposed by the class. Such members are usually client oriented rather than implementation oriented. Clients are neither aware of, nor involved in, a class's implementation. Clients generally care about what the class does but not how the class does it. (Clients do, of course, care that the class operates correctly and efficiently.)

Software Engineering Observation 7.3
Interfaces change less frequently than implementations. When an implementation changes, implementation-dependent code must change accordingly. Hiding the implementation reduces the possibility that other application parts will become dependent on class-implementation details.

7.3 Controlling Access to Members
The access modifiers public and private control access to a class's variables and methods. (In Section 7.15 and Chapter 8, we will introduce the additional access modifiers internal and protected, respectively.) As we stated in Section 7.2, the primary purpose of

`public` methods is to present to the class's clients a view of the services the class provides (the class's public interface). Clients of the class need not be concerned with how the class accomplishes its tasks. For this reason, a class's `private` variables and methods (i.e., the class's implementation details) are not directly accessible to the class's clients.

Figure 7.3 demonstrates that `private` class members are not directly accessible outside the class. Lines 9–11 attempt to access directly `private` instance variables hour, minute and second of Time1 object time. When this application is compiled, the compiler generates error messages stating that these `private` members are not accessible. [*Note:* This application assumes that the Time1 class from Fig. 7.1 is used.]

Common Programming Error 7.1

An attempt by a method that is not a member of a class to access a private member of that class is a compilation error.

Notice that members of a class—for instance, methods and instance variables—do not need to be explicitly declared `private`. If a class member is not declared with an access modifier, it has `private` access by default. We always explicitly declare `private` members.

7.4 Referring to the Current Object's Members with the this Reference

Every object can access a reference to itself with keyword this (also called the this *reference*). When a non-`static` method is called for a particular object, the method's body implicitly uses keyword this to refer to the object's instance variables and other methods. As

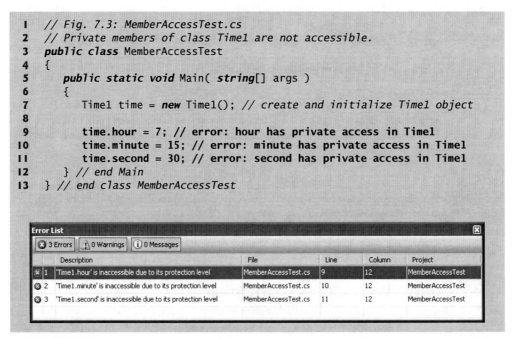

```
1  // Fig. 7.3: MemberAccessTest.cs
2  // Private members of class Time1 are not accessible.
3  public class MemberAccessTest
4  {
5     public static void Main( string[] args )
6     {
7        Time1 time = new Time1(); // create and initialize Time1 object
8
9        time.hour = 7; // error: hour has private access in Time1
10       time.minute = 15; // error: minute has private access in Time1
11       time.second = 30; // error: second has private access in Time1
12    } // end Main
13 } // end class MemberAccessTest
```

	Description	File	Line	Column	Project
1	'Time1.hour' is inaccessible due to its protection level	MemberAccessTest.cs	9	12	MemberAccessTest
2	'Time1.minute' is inaccessible due to its protection level	MemberAccessTest.cs	10	12	MemberAccessTest
3	'Time1.second' is inaccessible due to its protection level	MemberAccessTest.cs	11	12	MemberAccessTest

Fig. 7.3 | Private members of class Time1 are not accessible.

you will see in Fig. 7.4, you can also use keyword this *explicitly* in a non-static method's body. Section 7.5 and Section 7.6 show two more interesting uses of keyword this. Section 7.10 explains why keyword this cannot be used in a static method.

We now demonstrate implicit and explicit use of the this reference to enable class ThisTest's Main method to display the private data of a class SimpleTime object (Fig. 7.4). For the sake of brevity, we declare two classes in one file—class ThisTest is declared in lines 5–12, and class SimpleTime is declared in lines 15–48.

Class SimpleTime (lines 15–48) declares three private instance variables—hour, minute and second (lines 17–19). The constructor (lines 24–29) receives three int arguments to initialize a SimpleTime object. Note that for the constructor we used parameter names that are identical to the class's instance variable names (lines 17–19). We don't recommend this practice, but we did it here to hide the corresponding instance variables so that we could illustrate explicit use of the this reference. Recall from Section 5.11 that if a method contains a local variable with the same name as a field, that method will refer to the local variable rather than the field. In this case, the local variable hides the field in the method's scope. However, the method can use the this reference to refer to the hidden instance variable explicitly, as shown in lines 26–28 for SimpleTime's hidden instance variables.

Method BuildString (lines 32–37) returns a string created by a statement that uses the this reference explicitly and implicitly. Line 35 uses the this reference explicitly to

```
 1   // Fig. 7.4: ThisTest.cs
 2   // this used implicitly and explicitly to refer to members of an object.
 3   using System;
 4
 5   public class ThisTest
 6   {
 7      public static void Main( string[] args )
 8      {
 9         SimpleTime time = new SimpleTime( 15, 30, 19 );
10         Console.WriteLine( time.BuildString() );
11      } // end Main
12   } // end class ThisTest
13
14   // class SimpleTime demonstrates the "this" reference
15   public class SimpleTime
16   {
17      private int hour; // 0-23
18      private int minute; // 0-59
19      private int second; // 0-59
20
21      // if the constructor uses parameter names identical to
22      // instance variable names the "this" reference is
23      // required to distinguish between names
24      public SimpleTime( int hour, int minute, int second )
25      {
26         this.hour = hour; // set "this" object's hour instance variable
27         this.minute = minute; // set "this" object's minute
28         this.second = second; // set "this" object's second
29      } // end SimpleTime constructor
```

Fig. 7.4 | this used implicitly and explicitly to refer to members of an object. (Part 1 of 2.)

```
30
31        // use explicit and implicit "this" to call ToUniversalString
32        public string BuildString()
33        {
34           return string.Format( "{0,24}: {1}\n{2,24}: {3}",
35              "this.ToUniversalString()", this.ToUniversalString(),
36              "ToUniversalString()", ToUniversalString() );
37        } // end method BuildString
38
39        // convert to string in universal-time format (HH:MM:SS)
40        public string ToUniversalString()
41        {
42           // "this" is not required here to access instance variables,
43           // because method does not have local variables with same
44           // names as instance variables
45           return string.Format( "{0:D2}:{1:D2}:{2:D2}",
46              this.hour, this.minute, this.second );
47        } // end method ToUniversalString
48     } // end class SimpleTime
```

```
this.ToUniversalString(): 15:30:19
    ToUniversalString(): 15:30:19
```

Fig. 7.4 | this used implicitly and explicitly to refer to members of an object. (Part 2 of 2.)

call method ToUniversalString. Line 36 uses the this reference implicitly to call the same method. Note that both lines perform the same task. Programmers typically do not use the this reference explicitly to reference other methods in the current object. Also, note that line 46 in method ToUniversalString explicitly uses the this reference to access each instance variable. This is not necessary here, because the method does not have any local variables that hide the instance variables of the class.

Common Programming Error 7.2

It is often a logic error when a method contains a parameter or local variable that has the same name as an instance variable of the class. In such a case, use reference this if you wish to access the instance variable of the class—otherwise, the method parameter or local variable will be referenced.

Error-Prevention Tip 7.1

Avoid method parameter names or local variable names that conflict with field names. This helps prevent subtle, hard-to-locate bugs.

Class ThisTest (Fig. 7.4, lines 5–12) demonstrates class SimpleTime. Line 9 creates an instance of class SimpleTime and invokes its constructor. Line 10 invokes the object's BuildString method, then displays the results.

Performance Tip 7.1

C# conserves memory by maintaining only one copy of each method per class—this method is invoked by every object of the class. Each object, on the other hand, has its own copy of the class's instance variables (i.e., non-static variables). Each method of the class implicitly uses the this reference to determine the specific object of the class to manipulate.

7.5 Indexers

Chapter 2 introduced properties as a way to access a class's private data in a controlled manner via the properties' get and set accessors. Sometimes a class encapsulates lists of data such as arrays. Such a class can use keyword this to define property-like class members called *indexers* that allow array-style indexed access to lists of elements. With "conventional" C# arrays, the index must be an integer value. A benefit of indexers is that you can define both integer indices and non-integer indices. For example, you could allow client code to manipulate data using strings as indices that represent the data items' names or descriptions. When manipulating "conventional" C# array elements, the array element access operator always returns a value of the same type—i.e., the type of the array. Indexers are more flexible—they can return any type, even one that is different from the type of the underlying data.

Although an indexer's element access operator is used like an array element access operator, indexers are defined like properties in a class. Unlike properties, for which you can choose an appropriate property name, indexers must be defined with keyword this. Indexers have the general form:

```
accessModifier returnType this[ IndexType1 name1, IndexType2 name2, ... ]
{
    get
    {
        // use name1, name2, ... here to get data
    }
    set
    {
        // use name1, name2, ... here to set data
    }
}
```

The *IndexType* parameters specified in the brackets ([]) are accessible to the get and set accessors. These accessors define how to use the index (or indices) to retrieve or modify the appropriate data member. As with properties, the indexer's get accessor must return a value of type *returnType* and the set accessor can use the implicit parameter value to reference the value that should be assigned to the element.

Common Programming Error 7.3

Declaring indexers as static is a syntax error.

The application of Figs. 7.5–7.6 contains two classes—class Box represents a box with a length, a width and a height, and class BoxTest demonstrates class Box's indexers.

The private data members of class Box are string array names (line 6), which contains the names (i.e., "length", "width" and "height") for the dimensions of a Box, and double array dimensions (line 7), which contains the size of each dimension. Each element in array names corresponds to an element in array dimensions (e.g., dimensions[2] contains the height of the Box).

Box defines two indexers (lines 18–33 and lines 36–59) that each return a double value representing the size of the dimension specified by the indexer's parameter. Indexers can be overloaded like methods. The first indexer uses an int index to manipulate an element in the dimensions array. The second indexer uses a string index representing the name of the dimension to manipulate an element in the dimensions array. Each indexer returns -1 if its

```
 1   // Fig. 7.5: Box.cs
 2   // Box class definition represents a box with length,
 3   // width and height dimensions with indexers.
 4   public class Box
 5   {
 6      private string[] names = { "length", "width", "height" };
 7      private double[] dimensions = new double[ 3 ];
 8
 9      // constructor
10      public Box( double length, double width, double height )
11      {
12         dimensions[ 0 ] = length;
13         dimensions[ 1 ] = width;
14         dimensions[ 2 ] = height;
15      }
16
17      // indexer to access dimensions by integer index number
18      public double this[ int index ]
19      {
20         get
21         {
22            // validate index to get
23            if ( ( index < 0 ) || ( index >= dimensions.Length ) )
24               return -1;
25            else
26               return dimensions[ index ];
27         } // end get
28         set
29         {
30            if ( index >= 0 && index < dimensions.Length )
31               dimensions[ index ] = value;
32         } // end set
33      } // end numeric indexer
34
35      // indexer to access dimensions by their string names
36      public double this[ string name ]
37      {
38         get
39         {
40            // locate element to get
41            int i = 0;
42            while ( ( i < names.Length ) &&
43               ( name.ToLower() != names[ i ] ) )
44               i++;
45
46            return ( i == names.Length ) ? -1 : dimensions[ i ];
47         } // end get
48         set
49         {
50            // locate element to set
51            int i = 0;
```

Fig. 7.5 | Box class definition represents a box with length, width and height dimensions with indexers. (Part 1 of 2.)

```
52              while ( ( i < names.Length ) &&
53                 ( name.ToLower() != names[ i ] ) )
54                 i++;
55
56              if ( i != names.Length )
57                 dimensions[ i ] = value;
58           } // end set
59        } // end string indexer
60     } // end class Box
```

Fig. 7.5 | Box class definition represents a box with length, width and height dimensions with indexers. (Part 2 of 2.)

get accessor encounters an invalid subscript. Each indexer's set accessor assigns value to the appropriate element of dimensions only if the index is valid. Normally, you would have an indexer throw an exception if it receives an invalid index. We discuss how to throw exceptions in Chapter 10, Exception Handling.

Notice that the string indexer uses a while structure to search for a matching string in the names array (lines 42–44 and lines 52–54). If a match is found, the indexer manipulates the corresponding element in array dimensions (lines 46 and 57).

Class BoxTest (Fig. 7.6) manipulates the private data members of class Box through Box's indexers. Local variable box is declared at line 10, and initialized to a new instance of class Box. We use the Box constructor to initialize box with dimensions of 30, 30, and 30. Lines 14–16 use the indexer declared with parameter int to obtain the three dimensions of box, and display them with WriteLine. The expression box[0] (line 14) implicitly calls the get accessor of the indexer to obtain the value of box's private instance variable dimensions[0]. Similarly, the assignment to box[0] in line 20 implicitly calls the set accessor in lines 28–32 of Fig. 7.5. The set accessor implicitly sets its value parameter to 10, then sets dimensions[0] to value (10). Lines 24 and 28–30 in Fig. 7.6 take similar actions, using the overloaded indexer with a string parameter to manipulate the same data.

```
1    // Fig. 7.6: BoxTest.cs
2    // Indexers provide access to a Box object's members.
3    using System;
4
5    public class BoxTest
6    {
7       public static void Main( string[] args )
8       {
9          // create a box
10         Box box = new Box( 30, 30, 30 );
11
12         // show dimensions with numeric indexers
13         Console.WriteLine( "Created a box with the dimensions:" );
14         Console.WriteLine( "box[ 0 ] = {0}", box[ 0 ] );
15         Console.WriteLine( "box[ 1 ] = {0}", box[ 1 ] );
16         Console.WriteLine( "box[ 2 ] = {0}", box[ 2 ] );
17
```

Fig. 7.6 | Indexers provide access to an object's members. (Part 1 of 2.)

```
18          // set a dimension with the numeric indexer
19          Console.WriteLine( "\nSetting box[ 0 ] to 10...\n" );
20          box[ 0 ] = 10;
21
22          // set a dimension with the string indexer
23          Console.WriteLine( "Setting box[ \"width\" ] to 20...\n" );
24          box[ "width" ] = 20;
25
26          // show dimensions with string indexers
27          Console.WriteLine( "Now the box has the dimensions:" );
28          Console.WriteLine( "box[ \"length\" ] = {0}", box[ "length" ] );
29          Console.WriteLine( "box[ \"width\" ] = {0}", box[ "width" ] );
30          Console.WriteLine( "box[ \"height\" ] = {0}", box[ "height" ] );
31      } // end method Main
32  } // end class BoxTest
```

```
Created a box with the dimensions:
box[ 0 ] = 30
box[ 1 ] = 30
box[ 2 ] = 30

Setting box[ 0 ] to 10...

Setting box[ "width" ] to 20...

Now the box has the dimensions:
box[ "length" ] = 10
box[ "width" ] = 20
box[ "height" ] = 30
```

Fig. 7.6 | Indexers provide access to an object's members. (Part 2 of 2.)

7.6 Time Class Case Study: Overloaded Constructors

As you know, you can declare your own constructor to specify how objects of a class should be initialized. Next, we demonstrate a class with several *overloaded constructors* that enable objects of that class to be initialized in different ways. To overload constructors, simply provide multiple constructor declarations with different signatures. Recall from Section 5.12 that the compiler differentiates signatures by the number, types and order of the parameters in each signature.

Class Time2 with Overloaded Constructors

By default, instance variables hour, minute and second of class Time1 (Fig. 7.1) are initialized to their default values of 0 (which is midnight in universal time). Class Time1 does not enable the class's clients to initialize the time with specific non-zero values. Class Time2 (Fig. 7.7) contains five overloaded constructors for conveniently initializing its objects in a variety of ways. The constructors ensure that each Time2 object begins in a consistent state. In this application, four of the constructors invoke a fifth constructor, which in turn calls method SetTime. Method SetTime invokes the set accessors of properties Hour, Minute and Second, which ensure that the value supplied for hour is in the range 0 to 23 and that the values for minute and second are each in the range 0 to 59. If a value is out

```
 1   // Fig. 7.7: Time2.cs
 2   // Time2 class declaration with overloaded constructors.
 3   public class Time2
 4   {
 5      private int hour; // 0 - 23
 6      private int minute; // 0 - 59
 7      private int second; // 0 - 59
 8
 9      // Time2 parameterless constructor: initializes each instance variable
10      // to zero; ensures that Time2 objects start in a consistent state
11      public Time2() : this( 0, 0, 0 ) { }
12
13      // Time2 constructor: hour supplied, minute and second defaulted to 0
14      public Time2( int h ) : this( h, 0, 0 ) { }
15
16      // Time2 constructor: hour and minute supplied, second defaulted to 0
17      public Time2( int h, int m ) : this( h, m, 0 ) { }
18
19      // Time2 constructor: hour, minute and second supplied
20      public Time2( int h, int m, int s )
21      {
22         SetTime( h, m, s ); // invoke SetTime to validate time
23      } // end Time2 three-parameter constructor
24
25      // Time2 constructor: another Time2 object supplied
26      public Time2( Time2 time )
27         : this( time.Hour, time.Minute, time.Second ) { }
28
29      // set a new time value using universal time; ensure that
30      // the data remains consistent by setting invalid values to zero
31      public void SetTime( int h, int m, int s )
32      {
33         Hour = h; // set the Hour property
34         Minute = m; // set the Minute property
35         Second = s; // set the Second property
36      } // end method SetTime
37
38      // Properties for getting and setting
39      // property that gets and sets the hour
40      public int Hour
41      {
42         get
43         {
44            return hour;
45         } // end get
46         // make writing inaccessible outside the class
47         private set
48         {
49            hour = ( ( value >= 0 && value < 24 ) ? value : 0 );
50         } // end set
51      } // end property Hour
```

Fig. 7.7 | Time2 class declaration with overloaded constructors. (Part 1 of 2.)

```
52
53      // property that gets and sets the minute
54      public int Minute
55      {
56         get
57         {
58            return minute;
59         } // end get
60         // make writing inaccessible outside the class
61         private set
62         {
63            minute = ( ( value >= 0 && value < 60 ) ? value : 0 );
64         } // end set
65      } // end property Minute
66
67      // property that gets and sets the second
68      public int Second
69      {
70         get
71         {
72            return second;
73         } // end get
74         // make writing inaccessible outside the class
75         private set
76         {
77            second = ( ( value >= 0 && value < 60 ) ? value : 0 );
78         } // end set
79      } // end property Second
80
81      // convert to string in universal-time format (HH:MM:SS)
82      public string ToUniversalString()
83      {
84         return string.Format(
85            "{0:D2}:{1:D2}:{2:D2}", Hour, Minute, Second );
86      } // end method ToUniversalString
87
88      // convert to string in standard-time format (H:MM:SS AM or PM)
89      public override string ToString()
90      {
91         return string.Format( "{0}:{1:D2}:{2:D2} {3}",
92            ( ( Hour == 0 || Hour == 12 ) ? 12 : Hour % 12 ),
93            Minute, Second, ( Hour < 12 ? "AM" : "PM" ) );
94      } // end method ToString
95   } // end class Time2
```

Fig. 7.7 | Time2 class declaration with overloaded constructors. (Part 2 of 2.)

of range, it is set to 0 by the corresponding property (once again ensuring that each instance variable remains in a consistent state). The compiler invokes the appropriate constructor by matching the number and types of the arguments specified in the constructor call with the number and types of the parameters specified in each constructor declaration. Note that class Time2 also provides properties for each instance variable.

Class Time2's Constructors

Line 11 declares a *parameterless constructor*—a constructor invoked without arguments. Note that this constructor has an empty body, as indicated by the empty set of curly braces after the constructor header. Instead, we introduce a use of the this reference that is allowed only in the constructor's header. In line 11, the usual constructor header is followed by a colon (:), then the keyword this. The this reference is used in method-call syntax (along with the three int arguments) to invoke the Time2 constructor that takes three int arguments (lines 20–23). The parameterless constructor passes values of 0 for the hour, minute and second to the constructor with three int parameters. The use of the this reference as shown here is called a *constructor initializer.* Constructor initializers are a popular way to reuse initialization code provided by one of the class's constructors rather than defining similar code in another constructor's body. We use this syntax in four of the five Time2 constructors to make the class easier to maintain. If we needed to change how objects of class Time2 are initialized, only the constructor that the class's other constructors call would need to be modified. Even that constructor might not need modification—it simply calls the SetTime method to perform the actual initialization, so it is possible that the changes the class might require would be localized to this method.

Line 14 declares a Time2 constructor with a single int parameter representing the hour, which is passed with 0 for the minute and second to the constructor at lines 20–23. Line 17 declares a Time2 constructor that receives two int parameters representing the hour and minute, which are passed with 0 for the second to the constructor at lines 20–23. Like the parameterless constructor, each of these constructors invokes the constructor at lines 20–23 to minimize code duplication. Lines 20–23 declare the Time2 constructor that receives three int parameters representing the hour, minute and second. This constructor calls SetTime to initialize the instance variables to consistent values. SetTime, in turn, invokes the set accessors of properties Hour, Minute and Second.

Common Programming Error 7.4

A constructor can call methods of the class. Be aware that the instance variables might not yet be in a consistent state, because the constructor is in the process of initializing the object. Using instance variables before they have been initialized properly is a logic error.

Lines 26–27 declare a Time2 constructor that receives a Time2 reference to another Time2 object. In this case, the values from the Time2 argument are passed to the three-parameter constructor at lines 20–23 to initialize the hour, minute and second. Note that line 27 could have directly accessed the hour, minute and second instance variables of the constructor's time argument with the expressions time.hour, time.minute and time.second—even though hour, minute and second are declared as private variables of class Time2.

Software Engineering Observation 7.4

When one object of a class has a reference to another object of the same class, the first object can access all the second object's data and methods (including those that are private).

Notes Regarding Class Time2's Methods, Properties and Constructors

Note that Time2's properties are accessed throughout the body of the class. In particular, method SetTime assigns values to properties Hour, Minute and Second in lines 33–35, and methods ToUniversalString and ToString use properties Hour, Minute and Second in line 85 and lines 92–93, respectively. In each case, these methods could have accessed the class's private data directly without using the properties. However, consider changing the representation of the time from three int values (requiring 12 bytes of memory) to a single int value representing the total number of seconds that have elapsed since midnight (requiring only 4 bytes of memory). If we make such a change, only the bodies of the methods that access the private data directly would need to change—in particular, the individual properties Hour, Minute and Second. There would be no need to modify the bodies of methods SetTime, ToUniversalString or ToString, because they do not access the private data directly. Designing the class in this manner reduces the likelihood of programming errors when altering the class's implementation.

Similarly, each Time2 constructor could be written to include a copy of the appropriate statements from method SetTime. Doing so may be slightly more efficient, because the extra constructor call and the call to SetTime are eliminated. However, duplicating statements in multiple methods or constructors makes changing the class's internal data representation more difficult and error-prone. Having the Time2 constructors call the three-parameter constructor (or even call SetTime directly) requires any changes to the implementation of SetTime to be made only once.

Software Engineering Observation 7.5

When implementing a method of a class, use the class's properties to access the class's private data. This simplifies code maintenance and reduces the likelihood of errors.

Also notice that class Time2 takes advantage of access modifiers to ensure that clients of the class must use the appropriate methods and properties to access private data. In particular, the properties Hour, Minute and Second declare private set accessors (lines 47, 61 and 75, respectively) to restrict the use of the set accessors to members of the class. We declare these private for the same reasons that we declare the instance variables private— to simplify code maintenance and ensure that the data remains in a consistent state. Although the methods in class Time2 still have all the advantages of using the set accessors to perform validation, clients of the class must use the SetTime method to modify this data. The get accessors of properties Hour, Minute and Second are implicitly declared public because their properties are declared public—when there is no access modifier before a get or set accessor, the accessor inherits the access modifier preceding the property name.

Using Class Time2's Overloaded Constructors

Class Time2Test (Fig. 7.8) creates six Time2 objects (lines 9–14) to invoke the overloaded Time2 constructors. Line 9 shows that the parameterless constructor (line 11 of Fig. 7.7) is invoked by placing an empty set of parentheses after the class name when allocating a Time2 object with new. Lines 10–14 of the application demonstrate passing arguments to the other Time2 constructors. C# invokes the appropriate overloaded constructor by matching the number and types of the arguments specified in the constructor call with the number and types of the parameters specified in each constructor declaration. Line 10 invokes the constructor at line 14 of Fig. 7.7. Line 11 invokes the constructor at line 17 of Fig. 7.7. Lines 12–13 invoke the constructor at lines 20–23 of Fig. 7.7. Line 14 invokes the constructor at lines 26–27 of Fig. 7.7. The application displays the string representation of each initialized Time2 object to confirm that each was initialized properly.

```
 1   // Fig. 7.8: Time2Test.cs
 2   // Overloaded constructors used to initialize Time2 objects.
 3   using System;
 4
 5   public class Time2Test
 6   {
 7      public static void Main( string[] args )
 8      {
 9         Time2 t1 = new Time2(); // 00:00:00
10         Time2 t2 = new Time2( 2 ); // 02:00:00
11         Time2 t3 = new Time2( 21, 34 ); // 21:34:00
12         Time2 t4 = new Time2( 12, 25, 42 ); // 12:25:42
13         Time2 t5 = new Time2( 27, 74, 99 ); // 00:00:00
14         Time2 t6 = new Time2( t4 ); // 12:25:42
15
16         Console.WriteLine( "Constructed with:\n" );
17         Console.WriteLine( "t1: all arguments defaulted" );
18         Console.WriteLine( "   {0}", t1.ToUniversalString() ); // 00:00:00
19         Console.WriteLine( "   {0}\n", t1.ToString() ); // 12:00:00 AM
20
21         Console.WriteLine(
22            "t2: hour specified; minute and second defaulted" );
23         Console.WriteLine( "   {0}", t2.ToUniversalString() ); // 02:00:00
24         Console.WriteLine( "   {0}\n", t2.ToString() ); // 2:00:00 AM
25
26         Console.WriteLine(
27            "t3: hour and minute specified; second defaulted" );
28         Console.WriteLine( "   {0}", t3.ToUniversalString() ); // 21:34:00
29         Console.WriteLine( "   {0}\n", t3.ToString() ); // 9:34:00 PM
30
31         Console.WriteLine( "t4: hour, minute and second specified" );
32         Console.WriteLine( "   {0}", t4.ToUniversalString() ); // 12:25:42
33         Console.WriteLine( "   {0}\n", t4.ToString() ); // 12:25:42 PM
34
35         Console.WriteLine( "t5: all invalid values specified" );
36         Console.WriteLine( "   {0}", t5.ToUniversalString() ); // 00:00:00
37         Console.WriteLine( "   {0}\n", t5.ToString() ); // 12:00:00 AM
38
39         Console.WriteLine( "t6: Time2 object t4 specified" );
40         Console.WriteLine( "   {0}", t6.ToUniversalString() ); // 12:25:42
41         Console.WriteLine( "   {0}", t6.ToString() ); // 12:25:42 PM
42      } // end Main
43   } // end class Time2Test
```

```
Constructed with:

t1: all arguments defaulted
   00:00:00
   12:00:00 AM

t2: hour specified; minute and second defaulted
   02:00:00
   2:00:00 AM                                    (continued...)
```

Fig. 7.8 | Overloaded constructors used to initialize Time2 objects. (Part 1 of 2.)

```
t3: hour and minute specified; second defaulted
   21:34:00
   9:34:00 PM

t4: hour, minute and second specified
   12:25:42
   12:25:42 PM

t5: all invalid values specified
   00:00:00
   12:00:00 AM

t6: Time2 object t4 specified
   12:25:42
   12:25:42 PM
```

Fig. 7.8 | Overloaded constructors used to initialize Time2 objects. (Part 2 of 2.)

7.7 Default and Parameterless Constructors

Every class must have at least one constructor. Recall from Section 2.9 that if you do not provide any constructors in a class's declaration, the compiler creates a default constructor that takes no arguments when it is invoked. In Section 8.4.1, you will learn that the default constructor implicitly performs a special task.

The compiler will not create a default constructor for a class that explicitly declares at least one constructor. In this case, if you want to be able to invoke the constructor with no arguments, you must declare a parameterless constructor—as in line 11 of Fig. 7.7. Like a default constructor, a parameterless constructor is invoked with empty parentheses. Note that the Time2 parameterless constructor explicitly initializes a Time2 object by passing to the three-parameter constructor 0 for each parameter. Since 0 is the default value for int instance variables, the parameterless constructor in this example could actually omit the constructor initializer. In this case, each instance variable would receive its default value when the object is created. If we omit the parameterless constructor, clients of this class would not be able to create a Time2 object with the expression new Time2().

Common Programming Error 7.5

If a class has constructors, but none of the public constructors are parameterless constructors, and an application attempts to call a parameterless constructor to initialize an object of the class, a compilation error occurs. A constructor can be called with no arguments only if the class does not have any constructors (in which case the default constructor is called) or if the class has a public parameterless constructor.

Common Programming Error 7.6

Only constructors can have the same name as the class. Declaring a method, property or field with the same name as the class is a compilation error.

7.8 Composition

A class can have references to objects of other classes as members. Such a capability is called *composition* and is sometimes referred to as a ***has-a relationship***. For example, an object of class AlarmClock needs to know the current time and the time when it is supposed to sound its alarm, so it is reasonable to include two references to Time objects as members of the AlarmClock object.

Software Engineering Observation 7.6

One form of software reuse is composition, in which a class has as members references to objects of other classes.

Our example of composition contains three classes—Date (Fig. 7.9), Employee (Fig. 7.10) and EmployeeTest (Fig. 7.11). Class Date (Fig. 7.9) declares instance variables month, day and year (lines 7–9) to represent a date. The constructor receives three int parameters. Line 15 implicitly invokes the set accessor of property Month (lines 41–50) to validate the month—an out-of-range value is set to 1 to maintain a consistent state. Line 16 similarly uses property Year to set the year—but notice that the set accessor of Year (lines 28–31) assumes that the value for year is correct and does not validate it. Line 17 uses property Day (lines 54–78), which validates and assigns the value for day based on the current month and year (by using properties Month and Year in turn to obtain the values of month and year). Note that the order of initialization is important because the set accessor of property Day validates the value for day based on the assumption that month and year are correct. Line 66 determines whether the day is correct based on the number of days in the particular Month. If the day is not correct, lines 69–70 determine whether the Month is February, the day is 29 and the Year is a leap year. Otherwise, if the parameter value does not contain a correct value for day, line 75 sets day to 1 to maintain the Date in a consistent state. Note that line 18 in the constructor outputs the this reference as a string. Since this is a reference to the current Date object, the object's ToString method (lines 81–84) is called implicitly to obtain the object's string representation.

Class Employee (Fig. 7.10) has instance variables firstName, lastName, birthDate and hireDate. Members birthDate and hireDate (lines 7–8) are references to Date objects, demonstrating that a class can have as instance variables references to objects of other classes. The Employee constructor (lines 11–18) takes four parameters—first, last, dateOfBirth and dateOfHire. The objects referenced by parameters dateOfBirth and dateOfHire are assigned to the Employee object's birthDate and hireDate instance variables, respectively. Note that when class Employee's ToString method is called, it returns a string containing the string representations of the two Date objects. Each of these strings is obtained with an implicit call to the Date class's ToString method.

```csharp
1   // Fig. 7.9: Date.cs
2   // Date class declaration.
3   using System;
4
5   public class Date
6   {
7       private int month; // 1-12
8       private int day; // 1-31 based on month
9       private int year; // any year (could validate)
10
```

Fig. 7.9 | Date class declaration. (Part 1 of 3.)

```
11    // constructor: use property Month to confirm proper value for month;
12    // use property Day to confirm proper value for day
13    public Date( int theMonth, int theDay, int theYear )
14    {
15       Month = theMonth; // validate month
16       Year = theYear; // could validate year
17       Day = theDay; // validate day
18       Console.WriteLine( "Date object constructor for date {0}", this );
19    } // end Date constructor
20
21    // property that gets and sets the year
22    public int Year
23    {
24       get
25       {
26          return year;
27       } // end get
28       private set // make writing inaccessible outside the class
29       {
30          year = value; // could validate
31       } // end set
32    } // end property Year
33
34    // property that gets and sets the month
35    public int Month
36    {
37       get
38       {
39          return month;
40       } // end get
41       private set // make writing inaccessible outside the class
42       {
43          if ( value > 0 && value <= 12 ) // validate month
44             month = value;
45          else // month is invalid
46          {
47             Console.WriteLine( "Invalid month ({0}) set to 1.", value );
48             month = 1; // maintain object in consistent state
49          } // end else
50       } // end set
51    } // end property Month
52
53    // property that gets and sets the day
54    public int Day
55    {
56       get
57       {
58          return day;
59       } // end get
60       private set // make writing inaccessible outside the class
61       {
62          int[] daysPerMonth =
63             { 0, 31, 28, 31, 30, 31, 30, 31, 31, 30, 31, 30, 31 };
```

Fig. 7.9 | Date class declaration. (Part 2 of 3.)

```
64
65            // check if day in range for month
66            if ( value > 0 && value <= daysPerMonth[ Month ] )
67               day = value;
68            // check for leap year
69            else if ( Month == 2 && value == 29 &&
70               ( Year % 400 == 0 || ( Year % 4 == 0 && Year % 100 != 0 ) ) )
71               day = value;
72            else
73            {
74               Console.WriteLine( "Invalid day ({0}) set to 1.", value );
75               day = 1; // maintain object in consistent state
76            } // end else
77         } // end set
78      } // end property Day
79
80      // return a string of the form month/day/year
81      public override string ToString()
82      {
83         return string.Format( "{0}/{1}/{2}", Month, Day, Year );
84      } // end method ToString
85   } // end class Date
```

Fig. 7.9 | Date class declaration. (Part 3 of 3.)

```
1    // Fig. 7.10: Employee.cs
2    // Employee class with references to other objects.
3    public class Employee
4    {
5       private string firstName;
6       private string lastName;
7       private Date birthDate;
8       private Date hireDate;
9
10      // constructor to initialize name, birth date and hire date
11      public Employee( string first, string last,
12         Date dateOfBirth, Date dateOfHire )
13      {
14         firstName = first;
15         lastName = last;
16         birthDate = dateOfBirth;
17         hireDate = dateOfHire;
18      } // end Employee constructor
19
20      // convert Employee to string format
21      public override string ToString()
22      {
23         return string.Format( "{0}, {1}  Hired: {2}  Birthday: {3}",
24            lastName, firstName, hireDate, birthDate );
25      } // end method ToString
26   } // end class Employee
```

Fig. 7.10 | Employee class with references to other objects.

Class `EmployeeTest` (Fig. 7.11) creates two `Date` objects (lines 9–10) to represent an `Employee`'s birthday and hire date, respectively. Line 11 creates an `Employee` and initializes its instance variables by passing to the constructor two `string`s (representing the `Employee`'s first and last names) and two `Date` objects (representing the birthday and hire date). Line 13 implicitly invokes the `Employee`'s `ToString` method to display the values of its instance variables and demonstrate that the object was initialized properly.

7.9 Garbage Collection and Destructors

Every object you create uses various system resources, such as memory. In many programming languages, these system resources are reserved for the object's use until they are explicitly released. If all the references to the object that manages the resource are lost before the resource is explicitly released, the application can no longer access the resource to release it. This is known as a *resource leak*.

We need a disciplined way to give resources back to the system when they are no longer needed, thus avoiding resource leaks. The Common Language Runtime (CLR) performs automatic memory management by using a *garbage collector* to reclaim the memory occupied by objects that are no longer in use, so the memory can be used for other objects. When there are no more references to an object, the object becomes *eligible for destruction*. Every object has a special member, called a *destructor*, that is invoked by the garbage collector to perform *termination housekeeping* on an object just before the garbage collector reclaims the object's memory. A destructor is declared like a parameterless constructor, except that its name is the class name, preceded by a tilde (~), and it has no access modifier in its header. After the garbage collector calls the object's destructor, the object becomes *eligible for garbage collection*. The memory for such an object can be reclaimed by the garbage collector. *Memory leaks*, which are common in other languages like C and C++ (because memory is not automatically reclaimed in those languages), are

```
1    // Fig. 7.11: EmployeeTest.cs
2    // Composition demonstration.
3    using System;
4
5    public class EmployeeTest
6    {
7       public static void Main( string[] args )
8       {
9          Date birth = new Date( 7, 24, 1949 );
10         Date hire = new Date( 3, 12, 1988 );
11         Employee employee = new Employee( "Bob", "Blue", birth, hire );
12
13         Console.WriteLine( employee );
14      } // end Main
15   } // end class EmployeeTest
```

```
Date object constructor for date 7/24/1949
Date object constructor for date 3/12/1988
Blue, Bob  Hired: 3/12/1988  Birthday: 7/24/1949
```

Fig. 7.11 | Composition demonstration.

less likely in C# (but some can still happen in subtle ways). Other types of resource leaks can occur. For example, an application could open a file on disk to modify the file's contents. If the application does not close the file, no other application can modify (or possibly even use) the file until the application that opened the file completes.

A problem with the garbage collector is that it is not guaranteed to perform its tasks at a specified time. Therefore, the garbage collector may call the destructor any time after the object becomes eligible for destruction, and may reclaim the memory any time after the destructor executes. In fact, neither may happen before an application terminates. Thus, it is unclear if, or when, the destructor will be called. For this reason, most programmers should avoid using destructors. In Section 7.10, we demonstrate a situation in which we use a destructor. We will also demonstrate some of the static methods of class *GC* (in namespace System), which allow us to exert some control over the garbage collector and when destructors are called.

Software Engineering Observation 7.7

A class that uses system resources, such as files on disk, should provide a method to eventually release the resources. Many FCL classes provide Close or Dispose methods for this purpose.

7.10 static Class Members

Every object has its own copy of all the instance variables of the class. In certain cases, only one copy of a particular variable should be shared by all objects of a class. A static *variable* is used in such cases. A static variable represents *classwide information*—all objects of the class share the same piece of data. The declaration of a static variable begins with the keyword static.

Let's motivate static data with an example. Suppose that we have a video game with Martians and other space creatures. Each Martian tends to be brave and willing to attack other space creatures when it is aware that there are at least four other Martians present. If fewer than five Martians are present, each Martian becomes cowardly. Thus each Martian needs to know the martianCount. We could endow class Martian with martian-Count as an instance variable. If we do this, every Martian will have a separate copy of the instance variable, and every time we create a new Martian, we will have to update the instance variable martianCount in every Martian. This wastes space on redundant copies, wastes time updating the separate copies and is error prone. Instead, we declare martian-Count to be static, making martianCount classwide data. Every Martian can access the martianCount as if it were an instance variable of class Martian, but only one copy of the static martianCount is maintained. This saves space. We save time by having the Martian constructor increment the static martianCount—there is only one copy, so we do not have to increment separate copies of martianCount for each Martian object.

Software Engineering Observation 7.8

Use a static variable when all objects of a class must use the same copy of the variable.

The scope of a static variable is the body of its class. A class's public static members can be accessed by qualifying the member name with the class name and the dot (.) operator, as in Math.PI. A class's private static class members can be accessed only through the methods and properties of the class. Actually, static class members exist even when no objects of the class exist—they are available as soon as the class is loaded into memory at execution time. To access a private static member from outside its class, a public static method or property can be provided.

Common Programming Error 7.7

It is a compilation error to access or invoke a static member by referencing it through an instance of the class, like a non-static member.

Software Engineering Observation 7.9

Static variables and methods exist, and can be used, even if no objects of that class have been instantiated.

Our next application declares two classes—Employee (Fig. 7.12) and EmployeeTest (Fig. 7.13). Class Employee declares private static variable count (Fig. 7.12, line 10), and public static property Count (lines 52–58). We omit the set accessor of property Count to make the property read-only—we do not want clients of the class to be able to

```csharp
1   // Fig. 7.12: Employee.cs
2   // Static variable used to maintain a count of the number of
3   // Employee objects in memory.
4   using System;
5
6   public class Employee
7   {
8      private string firstName;
9      private string lastName;
10     private static int count = 0; // number of objects in memory
11
12     // initialize employee, add 1 to static count and
13     // output string indicating that constructor was called
14     public Employee( string first, string last )
15     {
16        firstName = first;
17        lastName = last;
18        count++; // increment static count of employees
19        Console.WriteLine( "Employee constructor: {0} {1}; count = {2}",
20           FirstName, LastName, Count );
21     } // end Employee constructor
22
23     // subtract 1 from static count when the garbage collector
24     // calls destructor to clean up object;
25     // confirm that destructor was called
26     ~Employee()
27     {
28        count--; // decrement static count of employees
29        Console.WriteLine( "Employee destructor: {0} {1}; count = {2}",
30           FirstName, LastName, Count );
31     } // end destructor
32
```

Fig. 7.12 | static variable used to maintain a count of the number of Employee objects in memory. (Part 1 of 2.)

```
33          // read-only property that gets the first name
34          public string FirstName
35          {
36             get
37             {
38                return firstName;
39             } // end get
40          } // end property FirstName
41
42          // read-only property that gets the last name.
43          public string LastName
44          {
45             get
46             {
47                return lastName;
48             } // end get
49          } // end property LastName
50
51          // read-only property that gets the employee count
52          public static int Count
53          {
54             get
55             {
56                return count;
57             } // end get
58          } // end property Count
59       } // end class Employee
```

Fig. 7.12 | static variable used to maintain a count of the number of Employee objects in memory. (Part 2 of 2.)

modify count. The static variable count is initialized to 0 in line 10. If a static variable is not initialized, the compiler assigns a default value to the variable—in this case 0, the default value for type int. Variable count maintains a count of the number of objects of class Employee currently in memory. This includes objects that are already inaccessible from the application, but have not yet had their destructors invoked by the garbage collector.

When Employee objects exist, member count can be used in any method of an Employee object—this example increments count in the constructor (line 18) and decrements it in the destructor (line 28). When no objects of class Employee exist, member count can still be referenced, but only through a call to public static property Count (lines 52–58), as in Employee.Count, which evaluates to the number of Employee objects currently in memory.

Note that the Employee class has a destructor (lines 26–31). This destructor is included to decrement static variable count, then show when the garbage collector executes in this application. Unlike constructors and methods, the destructor cannot be invoked explicitly by any programmer-written code. It can only be invoked by the garbage collector, so it does not need an access modifier—in fact, it is a syntax error to include one.

EmployeeTest method Main (Fig. 7.13) instantiates two Employee objects (lines 14–15). When each Employee object's constructor is invoked, lines 16–17 of Fig. 7.12 assign the Employee's first name and last name to instance variables firstName and lastName. Note that these two statements do not make copies of the original string arguments. Actually, string objects in C# are immutable—they cannot be modified after they are created. Therefore, it is safe to have many references to one string object. This is not normally the case for objects of most other classes in C#. If string objects are immutable, you might wonder why we are able to use operators + and += to concatenate string objects. String concatenation operations actually result in a new string object containing the concatenated values. The original string objects are not modified.

```
1   // Fig. 7.13: EmployeeTest.cs
2   // Static member demonstration.
3   using System;
4
5   public class EmployeeTest
6   {
7       public static void Main( string[] args )
8       {
9           // show that count is 0 before creating Employees
10          Console.WriteLine( "Employees before instantiation: {0}",
11              Employee.Count );
12
13          // create two Employees; count should become 2
14          Employee e1 = new Employee( "Susan", "Baker" );
15          Employee e2 = new Employee( "Bob", "Blue" );
16
17          // show that count is 2 after creating two Employees
18          Console.WriteLine( "\nEmployees after instantiation: {0}",
19              Employee.Count );
20
21          // get names of Employees
22          Console.WriteLine( "\nEmployee 1: {0} {1}\nEmployee 2: {2} {3}\n",
23              e1.FirstName, e1.LastName,
24              e2.FirstName, e2.LastName );
25
26          // in this example, there is only one reference to each Employee,
27          // so the following statements cause the CLR to mark each
28          // Employee object as being eligible for destruction
29          e1 = null; // object e1 no longer needed
30          e2 = null; // object e2 no longer needed
31
32          GC.Collect(); // ask for garbage collection to occur now
33          // wait until the destructors
34          // finish writing to the console
35          GC.WaitForPendingFinalizers();
36
37          // show Employee count after calling garbage collector and
38          // waiting for all destructors to finish
39          Console.WriteLine( "\nEmployees after destruction: {0}",
40              Employee.Count );
41      } // end Main
42  } // end class EmployeeTest
```

Fig. 7.13 | static member demonstration. (Part I of 2.)

```
Employees before instantiation: 0
Employee constructor: Susan Baker; count = 1
Employee constructor: Bob Blue; count = 2

Employees after instantiation: 2

Employee 1: Susan Baker
Employee 2: Bob Blue

Employee destructor: Bob Blue; count = 1
Employee destructor: Susan Baker; count = 0

Employees after destruction: 0
```

Fig. 7.13 | static member demonstration. (Part 2 of 2.)

When Main has finished using the two Employee objects, references e1 and e2 are set to null at lines 29–30, so they no longer refer to the objects that were instantiated on lines 14–15. The objects become "eligible for garbage collection" because there are no more references to them in the application.

Eventually, the garbage collector might reclaim the memory for these objects (or the operating system will reclaim the memory when the application terminates). C# does not guarantee when, or even whether, the garbage collector will execute, so in line 32, this application explicitly calls the garbage collector using static method Collect of class GC to indicate that the garbage collector should make a "best-effort" attempt to reclaim objects that are inaccessible. This is just a best effort—it is possible that no objects or only a subset of the eligible objects will be collected. When method Collect returns, this does *not* indicate that the garbage collector has finished searching for memory to reclaim. The garbage collector may still, in fact, be executing. For this reason, we call static method **WaitForPendingFinalizers** of class GC. If the garbage collector has marked any objects eligible for destruction, invoking WaitforPendingFinalizers in line 35 stops the execution of the Main method until the destructors of these objects have been completely executed.

In Fig. 7.13's sample output, the garbage collector did reclaim the objects formerly referenced by e1 and e2 before lines 39–40 displayed the current Employee count. The last output line indicates that the number of Employee objects in memory is 0 after the call to GC.Collect(). The third- and second-to-last lines of the output show that the Employee object for Bob Blue was destructed before the Employee object for Susan Baker. The output on your system may differ, because the garbage collector is not guaranteed to execute when GC.Collect() is called, nor is it guaranteed to collect objects in a specific order. In fact, if you omit the call to WaitForPendingFinalizers, it is likely that lines 39–40 will execute before the garbage collector has a chance to call the destructors.

[*Note:* A method declared static cannot access non-static class members directly, because a static method can be called even when no objects of the class exist. For the same reason, the this reference cannot be used in a static method—the this reference must refer to a specific object of the class, and when a static method is called, there might not be any objects of its class in memory. The this reference is required to allow a method of a class to access non-static members of the same class.]

Common Programming Error 7.8

A compilation error occurs if a static method calls an instance (non-static) method in the same class by using only the method name. Similarly, a compilation error occurs if a static method attempts to access an instance variable in the same class by using only the variable name.

Common Programming Error 7.9

Referring to the this reference in a static method is a syntax error.

7.11 readonly Instance Variables

The *principle of least privilege* is fundamental to good software engineering. In the context of an application, the principle states that code should be granted only the amount of privilege and access needed to accomplish its designated task, but no more. Let us see how this principle applies to instance variables.

Some instance variables need to be modifiable, and some do not. In Section 6.4, we introduced keyword const for declaring constants. These constants must be initialized to a constant value when they are declared. Suppose, however, we want to initialize a constant belonging to an object in the object's constructor. C# provides keyword **readonly** to specify that an instance variable of an object is not modifiable and that any attempt to modify it after the object is constructed is an error. For example,

```
private readonly int INCREMENT;
```

declares readonly instance variable INCREMENT of type int. Like constants, readonly variables are declared with all capital letters by convention. Although readonly instance variables can be initialized when they are declared, this is not required. Readonly variables can be initialized by each of the class's constructors. The constructor can assign values to a readonly instance variable multiple times—the variable doesn't become unmodifiable until after the constructor completes execution.

Software Engineering Observation 7.10

Declaring an instance variable as readonly helps enforce the principle of least privilege. If an instance variable should not be modified after the object is constructed, declare it to be readonly to prevent modification.

Members that are declared as const must be assigned values at compile time. Therefore, const members can be initialized only with other constant values, such as integers, string literals, characters and other const members. Constant members with values that cannot be determined at compile time must be declared with keyword readonly, so they can be initialized at execution time. Variables that are readonly can be initialized with more complex expressions, such as an array initializer or a method call that returns a value or a reference to an object.

Our next example contains two classes—class Increment (Fig. 7.14) and class IncrementTest (Fig. 7.15). Class Increment contains a readonly instance variable of type int named INCREMENT (Fig. 7.14, line 6). Note that the readonly variable is not initialized in its declaration, so it should be initialized by the class's constructor (lines 10–13). If the class provides multiple constructors, every constructor should initialize the readonly variable. If a constructor does not initialize the readonly variable, the variable receives the same default value as any other instance variable (0 for numeric simple types, false for bool types and null for reference types), and the compiler generates a warning. In Fig. 7.14, the constructor receives int parameter incrementValue and assigns its value to INCREMENT (line 12). If class Increment's constructor does not initialize INCREMENT (if line 12 were omitted), the compiler would give the warning:

```
Field 'Increment.INCREMENT' is never assigned to, and will always
have its default value 0
```

Application class IncrementTest creates an object of class Increment (Fig. 7.15, line 9) and provides as the argument to the constructor the value 5, which is assigned to the readonly variable INCREMENT. Lines 11 and 16 implicitly invoke class Increment's ToString method, which returns a formatted string describing the value of private instance variable total.

Common Programming Error 7.10

Attempting to modify a readonly instance variable anywhere but its declaration or the object's constructors is a compilation error.

Error-Prevention Tip 7.2

Attempts to modify a readonly instance variable are caught at compilation time rather than causing execution-time errors. It is always preferable to get bugs out at compile time, if possible, rather than allowing them to slip through to execution time (where studies have found that repairing is often many times more costly).

```csharp
1   // Fig. 7.14: Increment.cs
2   // readonly instance variable in a class.
3   public class Increment
4   {
5       // readonly instance variable (uninitialized)
6       private readonly int INCREMENT;
7       private int total = 0; // total of all increments
8
9       // constructor initializes readonly instance variable INCREMENT
10      public Increment( int incrementValue )
11      {
12          INCREMENT = incrementValue; // initialize readonly variable (once)
13      } // end Increment constructor
14
15      // add INCREMENT to total
16      public void AddIncrementToTotal()
17      {
18          total += INCREMENT;
19      } // end method AddIncrementToTotal
20
21      // return string representation of an Increment object's data
22      public override string ToString()
23      {
24          return string.Format( "total = {0}", total );
25      } // end method ToString
26  } // end class Increment
```

Fig. 7.14 | readonly instance variable in a class.

```
 1   // Fig. 7.15: IncrementTest.cs
 2   // readonly instance variable initialized with a constructor argument.
 3   using System;
 4
 5   public class IncrementTest
 6   {
 7      public static void Main( string[] args )
 8      {
 9         Increment incrementer = new Increment( 5 );
10
11         Console.WriteLine( "Before incrementing: {0}\n", incrementer );
12
13         for ( int i = 1; i <= 3; i++ )
14         {
15            incrementer.AddIncrementToTotal();
16            Console.WriteLine( "After increment {0}: {1}", i, incrementer );
17         } // end for
18      } // end Main
19   } // end class IncrementTest
```

```
Before incrementing: total = 0

After increment 1: total = 5
After increment 2: total = 10
After increment 3: total = 15
```

Fig. 7.15 | readonly instance variable initialized with a constructor argument.

Software Engineering Observation 7.11

If a readonly instance variable is initialized to a constant only in its declaration, it is not necessary to have a separate copy of the instance variable for every object of the class. The variable should be declared const instead. Constants declared with const are implicitly static, so there will only be one copy for the entire class.

7.12 Software Reusability

Programmers concentrate on crafting new classes and reusing existing classes. Many class libraries exist, and others are being developed worldwide. Software is then constructed from existing, well-defined, carefully tested, well-documented, portable, performance-tuned, widely available components. This kind of software reusability speeds the development of powerful, high-quality software. *Rapid application development (RAD)* is of great interest today.

Microsoft provides C# programmers with thousands of classes in the .NET Framework Class Library to help them implement C# applications. The .NET Framework enables C# developers to work to achieve true reusability and rapid application development. C# programmers can focus on the task at hand when developing their applications and leave the lower-level details to the classes of the FCL. For example, to write an application that draws graphics, an FCL programmer does not require knowledge of graphics on every computer platform where the application will execute. Instead, the programmer can concentrate on learning .NET's graphics capabilities (which are quite substantial and growing) and write a C# application that draws the graphics, using FCL classes such as those in the System.Drawing namespace. When the application executes on a given computer, it is the job of the CLR to translate the MSIL commands compiled from the C# code into commands that the local computer can understand.

The FCL classes enable C# programmers to bring new applications to market faster by using preexisting, tested components. Not only does this reduce development time, it also improves the programmer's ability to debug and maintain applications. To take advantage of C#'s many capabilities, it is essential that programmers familiarize themselves with the variety of classes in the .NET Framework. There are many Web-based resources at msdn2.microsoft.com to help you with this task. The primary resource for learning about the FCL is the .NET Framework Reference in the MSDN library, which can be found at

msdn2.microsoft.com/en-us/library/ms229335

In addition, msdn2.microsoft.com provides many other resources, including tutorials, articles and sites specific to individual C# topics.

Good Programming Practice 7.1

Avoid reinventing the wheel. Study the capabilities of the FCL. If the FCL contains a class that meets your application's requirements, use that class rather than create your own.

To realize the full potential of software reusability, we need to improve cataloging schemes, licensing schemes, protection mechanisms that prevent master copies of classes from being corrupted, description schemes that system designers use to determine whether existing classes meet their needs, browsing mechanisms that determine what classes are available and how closely they meet software developer requirements, and the like. Many interesting research and development problems have been solved and many more need to be solved. These problems will likely be solved because the potential value of increased software reuse is enormous.

7.13   Data Abstraction and Encapsulation

Classes normally hide the details of their implementation from their clients. This is called *information hiding*. As an example, let us consider the stack data structure introduced in Section 5.6. Recall that a stack is a last-in, first-out (LIFO) data structure—the last item pushed (inserted) on the stack is the first item popped (removed) off the stack.

Stacks can be implemented with arrays and with other data structures, such as linked lists. A client of a stack class need not be concerned with the stack's implementation. The client knows only that when data items are placed in the stack, they will be recalled in last-in, first-out order. The client cares about what functionality a stack offers, not about how that functionality is implemented. This concept is referred to as *data abstraction*. Although programmers might know the details of a class's implementation, they should not write code that depends on these details. This enables a particular class (such as one that implements a stack and its *push* and *pop* operations) to be replaced with another version without affecting the rest of the system. As long as the public services of the class do not change (i.e., every original method still has the same name, return type and parameter list in the new class declaration), the rest of the system is not affected.

Most programming languages emphasize actions. In these languages, data exists to support the actions that applications must take. Data is "less interesting" than actions. Data is "crude." Only a few simple types exist, and it is difficult for programmers to create their own types. C# and the object-oriented style of programming elevate the importance of data. The primary activities of object-oriented programming in C# are the creation of types (e.g., classes) and the expression of the interactions among objects of those types. To create languages that emphasize data, the programming-languages community needed to formalize some notions about data. The formalization we consider here is the notion of *abstract data types (ADTs)*, which improve the application-development process.

Consider simple type int, which most people would associate with an integer in mathematics. Actually, an int is an abstract representation of an integer. Unlike mathematical integers, computer ints are fixed in size. For example, simple type int in C# is limited to the range –2,147,483,648 to +2,147,483,647. If the result of a calculation falls outside this range, an error occurs, and the computer responds in some manner. It might, for example, "quietly" produce an incorrect result, such as a value too large to fit in an int variable—commonly called *arithmetic overflow*. It also might throw an exception, called an OverflowException. (We discuss the two ways of dealing with arithmetic overflow in Section 10.8.) Mathematical integers do not have this problem. Therefore, the computer int is only an approximation of the real-world integer. The same is true of double and other simple types.

We have taken the notion of int for granted until this point, but we now consider it from a new perspective. Types like int, double, and char are all examples of abstract data types. They are representations of real-world concepts to some satisfactory level of precision within a computer system.

An ADT actually captures two notions: a *data representation* and the *operations* that can be performed on that data. For example, in C#, an int contains an integer value (data) and provides addition, subtraction, multiplication, division and remainder operations—division by zero is undefined. C# programmers use classes to implement abstract data types.

Software Engineering Observation 7.12

Programmers create types through the class mechanism. New types can be designed to be as convenient to use as the simple types. This marks C# as an extensible language. Although the language is easy to extend via new types, the programmer cannot alter the base language itself.

Another abstract data type we discuss is a *queue*, which is similar to a "waiting line." Computer systems use many queues internally. A queue offers well-understood behavior to its clients: Clients place items in a queue one at a time via an *enqueue* operation, then get them back one at a time via a *dequeue* operation. A queue returns items in *first-in, first-out (FIFO)* order, which means that the first item inserted in a queue is the first item removed from the queue. Conceptually, a queue can become infinitely long, but real queues are finite.

The queue hides an internal data representation that keeps track of the items currently waiting in line, and it offers operations to its clients (*enqueue* and *dequeue*). The clients are not concerned about the implementation of the queue—they simply depend on the queue to operate "as advertised." When a client enqueues an item, the queue should accept that item and place it in some kind of internal FIFO data structure. Similarly, when the client wants the next item from the front of the queue, the queue should remove the item from its internal representation and deliver it in FIFO order (i.e., the item that has been in the queue the longest should be returned by the next dequeue operation).

The queue ADT guarantees the integrity of its internal data structure. Clients cannot manipulate this data structure directly—only the queue ADT has access to its internal data. Clients are able to perform only allowable operations on the data representation—the ADT rejects operations that its public interface does not provide.

7.14 Time Class Case Study: Creating Class Libraries

In almost every example in the text, we have seen that classes from preexisting libraries, such as the .NET Framework Class Library, can be imported into a C# application. Each class in the FCL belongs to a namespace that contains a group of related classes. As applications become more complex, namespaces help you manage the complexity of application components. Class libraries and namespaces also facilitate software reuse by enabling applications to add classes from other namespaces (as we have done in most examples). This section introduces how to create your own class libraries.

Steps for Declaring and Using a Reusable Class

Before a class can be used in multiple applications, it must be placed in a class library to make it reusable. Figure 7.16 shows how to specify the namespace in which a class should be placed in the library. Figure 7.19 shows how to use our class library in an application. The steps for creating a reusable class are:

1. Declare a public class. If the class is not public, it can be used only by other classes in the same assembly.

2. Choose a namespace name and add a **namespace** *declaration* to the source-code file for the reusable class declaration.

3. Compile the class into a class library.

4. Add a reference to the class library in an application.

5. Specify a using directive for the namespace of the reusable class and use the class.

Step 1: Creating a public Class

For *Step 1* in this discussion, we use the public class Time1 declared in Fig. 7.1. No modifications have been made to the implementation of the class, so we will not discuss its implementation details again here.

Step 2: Adding the namespace Declaration

For *Step 2*, we add a namespace declaration to Fig. 7.1. The new version is shown in Fig. 7.16. Line 3 declares a namespace named Chapter09. Placing the Time1 class inside the namespace declaration indicates that the class is part of the specified namespace. The namespace name is part of the fully qualified class name, so the name of class Time1 is actually Chapter09.Time1. You can use this fully qualified name in your applications, or you can write a using directive (as we will see shortly) and use its *simple name* (the unqualified

```
 1   // Fig. 7.16: Time1.cs
 2   // Time1 class declaration in a namespace.
 3   namespace Chapter09
 4   {
 5      public class Time1
 6      {
 7         private int hour; // 0 - 23
 8         private int minute; // 0 - 59
 9         private int second; // 0 - 59
10
11         // set a new time value using universal time; ensure that
12         // the data remains consistent by setting invalid values to zero
13         public void SetTime( int h, int m, int s )
14         {
15            hour = ( ( h >= 0 && h < 24 ) ? h : 0 ); // validate hour
16            minute = ( ( m >= 0 && m < 60 ) ? m : 0 ); // validate minute
17            second = ( ( s >= 0 && s < 60 ) ? s : 0 ); // validate second
18         } // end method SetTime
19
20         // convert to string in universal-time format (HH:MM:SS)
21         public string ToUniversalString()
22         {
23            return string.Format( "{0:D2}:{1:D2}:{2:D2}",
24               hour, minute, second );
25         } // end method ToUniversalString
26
27         // convert to string in standard-time format (H:MM:SS AM or PM)
28         public override string ToString()
29         {
30            return string.Format( "{0}:{1:D2}:{2:D2} {3}",
31               ( ( hour == 0 || hour == 12 ) ? 12 : hour % 12 ),
32               minute, second, ( hour < 12 ? "AM" : "PM" ) );
33         } // end method ToString
34      } // end class Time1
35   } // end namespace Chapter09
```

Fig. 7.16 | Time1 class declaration in a namespace.

class name—Time1) in the application. If another namespace also contains a Time1 class, the fully qualified class names can be used to distinguish between the classes in the application and prevent a *name conflict* (also called a *name collision*).

Only namespace declarations, using directives, comments and C# attributes can appear outside the braces of a type declaration (e.g., classes and enumerations). Only class declarations declared public will be reusable by clients of the class library. Non-public classes are typically placed in a library to support the public reusable classes in that library.

Step 3: Compiling the Class Library
Step 3 is to compile the class into a class library. To create a class library in Visual C# Express, we must create a new project by clicking the **File** menu, selecting **New Project...** and choosing **Class Library** from the list of templates, as shown in Fig. 7.17. Then add the code from Fig. 7.16 into the new project (either by copying our code from the book's examples

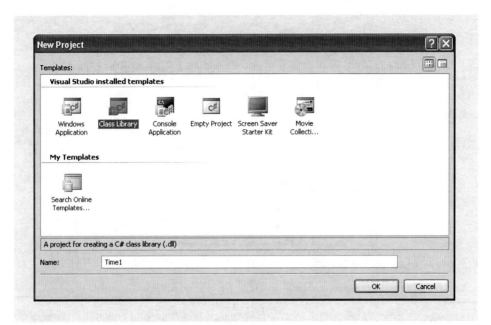

Fig. 7.17 | Creating a **Class Library** Project.

or by typing the code yourself). In the projects you've created so far, the C# compiler created an executable .exe containing the application. When you compile a **Class Library** project, the compiler creates a *.dll file*, known as a *dynamic link library*—a type of assembly that you can reference from other applications.

Step 4: Adding a Reference to the Class Library
Once the class is compiled and stored in the class library file, the library can be referenced from any application by indicating to the Visual C# Express IDE where to find the class library file (*Step 4*). Create a new (empty) project and right-click the project name in the **Solution Explorer** window. Select **Add Reference...** from the pop-up menu that appears. The dialog box that appears will contain a list of class libraries from the .NET Framework. Some class libraries, like the one containing the System namespace, are so common that they are added to your application implicitly. The ones in this list are not.

In the **Add Reference...** dialog box, click the **Browse** tab. Recall from Section 1.3 that when you build an application, Visual C# 2005 places the .exe file in the bin\Release folder in the directory of your application. When you build a class library, Visual C# places the .dll file in the same place. In the **Browse** tab, you can navigate to the directory containing the class library file you created in *Step 3*, as shown Fig. 7.18. Select the .dll file and click **OK**.

Step 5: Using the Class from an Application
Add a new code file to your application and enter the code for class Time1NamespaceTest (Fig. 7.19). Now that you've added a reference to your class library in this application, your Time1 class can be used by Time1NamespaceTest (*Step 5*) without adding the Time1.cs source code file to the project.

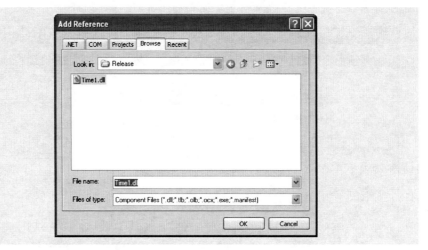

Fig. 7.18 | Adding a Reference.

In Fig. 7.19, the using directive in line 3 specifies that we'd like to use the class(es) of namespace Chapter09 in this file. Class Time1NamespaceTest is in the global namespace of this application because the class's file does not contain a namespace declaration. Since the two classes are in different namespaces, the using directive at line 3 allows class Time1NamespaceTest to use class Time1 as if it was in the same namespace.

Recall from Section 2.4 that we could omit the using directive in line 4 if we always referred to class Console by its fully qualified class name, System.Console. Similarly, we could omit the using directive in line 3 for namespace Chapter09 if we changed the Time1 declaration in line 11 of Fig. 7.19 to use class Time1's fully qualified name, as in:

```
Chapter09.Time1 time = new Chapter09.Time1();
```

```
1   // Fig. 7.19: Time1NamespaceTest.cs
2   // Time1 object used in an application.
3   using Chapter09;
4   using System;
5
6   public class Time1NamespaceTest
7   {
8      public static void Main( string[] args )
9      {
10        // create and initialize a Time1 object
11        Time1 time = new Time1(); // calls Time1 constructor
12
13        // output string representations of the time
14        Console.Write( "The initial universal time is: " );
15        Console.WriteLine( time.ToUniversalString() );
16        Console.Write( "The initial standard time is: " );
17        Console.WriteLine( time.ToString() );
18        Console.WriteLine(); // output a blank line
```

Fig. 7.19 | Time1 object used in an application. (Part 1 of 2.)

```
19
20        // change time and output updated time
21        time.SetTime( 13, 27, 6 );
22        Console.Write( "Universal time after SetTime is: " );
23        Console.WriteLine( time.ToUniversalString() );
24        Console.Write( "Standard time after SetTime is: " );
25        Console.WriteLine( time.ToString() );
26        Console.WriteLine(); // output a blank line
27
28        // set time with invalid values; output updated time
29        time.SetTime( 99, 99, 99 );
30        Console.WriteLine( "After attempting invalid settings:" );
31        Console.Write( "Universal time: " );
32        Console.WriteLine( time.ToUniversalString() );
33        Console.Write( "Standard time: " );
34        Console.WriteLine( time.ToString() );
35     } // end Main
36  } // end class Time1NamespaceTest
```

```
The initial universal time is: 00:00:00
The initial standard time is: 12:00:00 AM

Universal time after SetTime is: 13:27:06
Standard time after SetTime is: 1:27:06 PM

After attempting invalid settings:
Universal time: 00:00:00
Standard time: 12:00:00 AM
```

Fig. 7.19 | Time1 object used in an application. (Part 2 of 2.)

7.15 internal Access

Classes can be declared with only two access modifiers—public and internal. If there is no access modifier in the class declaration, the class defaults to *internal access*. This allows the class to be used by all code in the same assembly as the class, but not by code in other assemblies. Within the same assembly as the class, this is equivalent to public access. However, if a class library is referenced from an application, the library's internal classes will be inaccessible from the code of the application. Similarly, methods, instance variables and other members of a class declared internal are accessible to all code compiled in the same assembly, but not to code in other assemblies.

The application in Fig. 7.20 demonstrates internal access. The application contains two classes in one source-code file—the InternalAccessTest application class (lines 6–22) and the InternalData class (lines 25–43).

In the InternalData class declaration, lines 27–28 declare the instance variables number and message with the internal access modifier—class InternalData has access internal by default, so there is no need for an access modifier. The InternalAccessTest's static Main method creates an instance of the InternalData class (line 10) to demonstrate modifying the InternalData instance variables directly (as shown in lines 16–17). Within the same assembly, internal access is equivalent to public access. The

```
 1   // Fig. 7.20: InternalAccessTest.cs
 2   // Members declared internal in a class are accessible by other classes
 3   // in the same assembly.
 4   using System;
 5
 6   public class InternalAccessTest
 7   {
 8      public static void Main( string[] args )
 9      {
10         InternalData internalData = new InternalData();
11
12         // output string representation of internalData
13         Console.WriteLine( "After instantiation:\n{0}", internalData );
14
15         // change internal access data in internalData
16         internalData.number = 77;
17         internalData.message = "Goodbye";
18
19         // output string representation of internalData
20         Console.WriteLine( "\nAfter changing values:\n{0}", internalData );
21      } // end Main
22   } // end class InternalAccessTest
23
24   // class with internal access instance variables
25   class InternalData
26   {
27      internal int number; // internal-access instance variable
28      internal string message; // internal-access instance variable
29
30      // constructor
31      public InternalData()
32      {
33         number = 0;
34         message = "Hello";
35      } // end InternalData constructor
36
37      // return InternalData object string representation
38      public override string ToString()
39      {
40         return string.Format(
41            "number: {0}; message: {1}", number, message );
42      } // end method ToString
43   } // end class InternalData
```

```
After instantiation:
number: 0; message: Hello

After changing values:
number: 77; message: Goodbye
```

Fig. 7.20 | Members declared internal in a class are accessible by other classes in the same assembly.

results can be seen in the output window. If we compile this class into a `.dll` class library file and reference it from a new application, that application will have access to `public` class `InternalAccessTest`, but not to `internal` class `InternalData`, or its `internal` members.

7.16 Class View and Object Browser

Now that we have introduced key concepts of object-oriented programming, we present two features that Visual Studio provides to facilitate the design of object-oriented applications—**Class View** and **Object Browser**.

Using the Class View Window

The **Class View** displays the fields and methods for all classes in a project. To access this feature, select **Class View** from the **View** menu. Figure 7.21 shows the **Class View** for the `Time1` project of Fig. 7.1 (class `Time1`) and Fig. 7.2 (class `TimeTest1`). The view follows a hierarchical structure, positioning the project name (`Time1`) as the root and including a series of nodes that represent the classes, variables and methods in the project. If a plus sign (+) appears to the left of a node, that node can be expanded to show other nodes. If a minus sign (–) appears to the left of a node, that node can be collapsed. According to the **Class View**, project `Time1` contains class `Time1` and class `TimeTest1` as children. When class `Time1` is selected, the class's members appear in the lower half of the window. Class `Time1` contains methods `SetTime`, `ToString` and `ToUniversalString` (indicated by purple boxes) and instance variables `hour`, `minute` and `second` (indicated by blue boxes). The lock icons, placed to the left of the blue box icons for the instance variables, specify that the variables are `private`. Class `TimeTest1` contains method `Main`. Note that both class `Time1` and class `TimeTest1` contain the **Base Types** node. If you expand this node, you will see class `object` in each case, because each class inherits from class `System.Object` (discussed in Chapter 8).

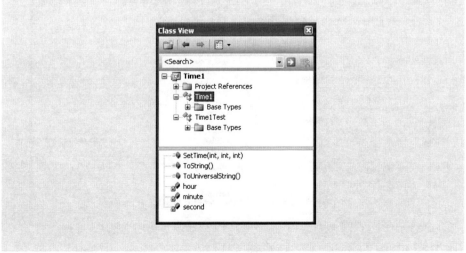

Fig. 7.21 | **Class View** of class `Time1` (Fig. 7.1) and class `TimeTest` (Fig. 7.2).

Using the Object Browser

Visual C# Express's **Object Browser** lists all classes in the C# library. You can use the **Object Browser** to learn about the functionality provided by a specific class. To open the **Object Browser**, select **Other Windows** from the **View** menu and click **Object Browser**. Figure 7.22 depicts the **Object Browser** when the user navigates to the Math class in namespace System in the assembly mscorlib (Microsoft Core Library). [*Note:* Be careful not to confuse the System namespace with the assembly named System. The System assembly describes other members of the System namespace, but class System.Math is in mscorlib.] The **Object Browser** lists all methods provided by class Math in the upper-right frame—this offers you "instant access" to information regarding the functionality of various objects. If you click the name of a member in the upper-right frame, a description of that member appears in the lower-right frame. Note also that the **Object Browser** lists in the left frame all classes of the FCL. The **Object Browser** can be a quick mechanism to learn about a class or a method of a class. Remember that you can also view the complete description of a class or a method in the online documentation available through the **Help** menu in Visual C# Express.

7.17 (Optional) Software Engineering Case Study: Starting to Program the Classes of the ATM System

In the Software Engineering Case Study sections in Chapters 1–6, we introduced the fundamentals of object orientation and developed an object-oriented design for our ATM system. In Chapters 2–5, we introduced object-oriented programming in C#. In Chapter 6, we took a deeper look at the details of programming with classes. We now begin implementing our object-oriented design by converting class diagrams to C# code. In the final Software Engineering Case Study section (Section 9.9), we modify the code to incorporate the object-oriented concepts of inheritance and polymorphism.

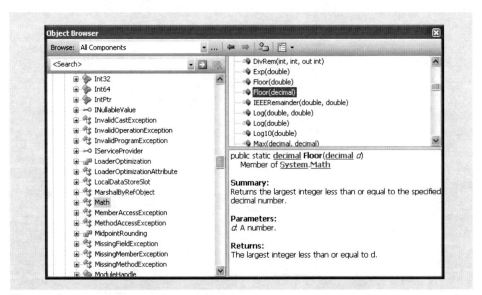

Fig. 7.22 | **Object Browser** for class Math.

Visibility

We now apply access modifiers to the members of our classes. In Chapter 2, we introduced access modifiers public and private. Access modifiers determine the *visibility*, or accessibility, of an object's attributes and operations to other objects. Before we can begin implementing our design, we must consider which attributes and methods of our classes should be public and which should be private.

In Chapter 2, we observed that attributes normally should be private and that methods invoked by clients of a class should be public. Methods that are called only by other methods of the class as "utility functions," however, should be private. The UML employs *visibility markers* for modeling the visibility of attributes and operations. Public visibility is indicated by placing a plus sign (+) before an operation or an attribute; a minus sign (–) indicates private visibility. Figure 7.23 shows our updated class diagram with visibility markers included. [*Note:* We do not include any operation parameters in Fig. 7.23. This is perfectly normal. Adding visibility markers does not affect the parameters already modeled in the class diagrams of Figs. 5.20–5.24.]

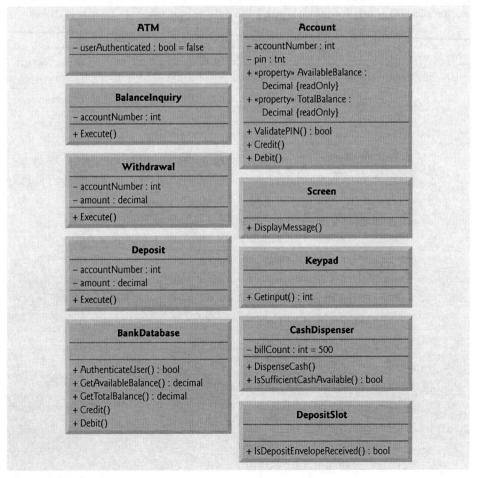

Fig. 7.23 | Class diagram with visibility markers.

Navigability

Before we begin implementing our design in C#, we introduce an additional UML notation. The class diagram in Fig. 7.24 further refines the relationships among classes in the ATM system by adding navigability arrows to the association lines. *Navigability arrows* (represented as arrows with stick arrowheads in the class diagram) indicate in which direction an association can be traversed and are based on the collaborations modeled in communication and sequence diagrams (see Section 6.14). When implementing a system designed using the UML, programmers use navigability arrows to help determine which objects need references to other objects. For example, the navigability arrow pointing from class ATM to class Bank-Database indicates that we can navigate from the former to the latter, thereby enabling the ATM to invoke the BankDatabase's operations. However, since Fig. 7.24 does not contain a navigability arrow pointing from class BankDatabase to class ATM, the BankDatabase cannot access the ATM's operations. Note that associations in a class diagram that have navigability arrows at both ends or do not have navigability arrows at all indicate *bidirectional navigability*—navigation can proceed in either direction across the association.

Like the class diagram of Fig. 2.24, the class diagram of Fig. 7.24 omits classes BalanceInquiry and Deposit to keep the diagram simple. The navigability of the associations in which these classes participate closely parallels the navigability of class Withdrawal's associations. Recall from Section 2.11 that BalanceInquiry has an association with class Screen. We can navigate from class BalanceInquiry to class Screen along this association, but we cannot navigate from class Screen to class BalanceInquiry. Thus, if we were to

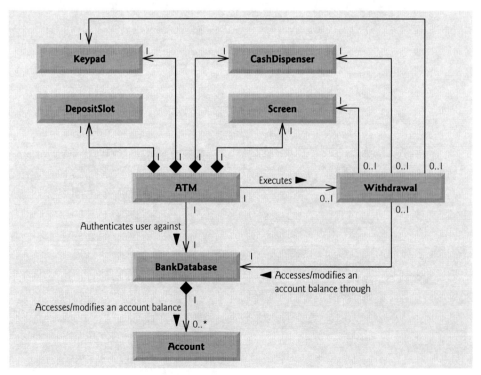

Fig. 7.24 | Class diagram with navigability arrows.

model class `BalanceInquiry` in Fig. 7.24, we would place a navigability arrow at class `Screen`'s end of this association. Also recall that class `Deposit` associates with classes `Screen`, `Keypad` and `DepositSlot`. We can navigate from class `Deposit` to each of these classes, but not vice versa. We therefore would place navigability arrows at the `Screen`, `Keypad` and `DepositSlot` ends of these associations. [*Note:* We model these additional classes and associations in our final class diagram in Section 9.9, after we have simplified the structure of our system by incorporating the object-oriented concept of inheritance.]

Implementing the ATM System from Its UML Design

We are now ready to begin implementing the ATM system. We first convert the classes in the diagrams of Fig. 7.23 and Fig. 7.24 into C# code. This code will represent the "skeleton" of the system. In Chapter 9, we modify the code to incorporate the object-oriented concept of inheritance.

As an example, we begin to develop the code for class `Withdrawal` from our design of class `Withdrawal` in Fig. 7.23. We use this figure to determine the attributes and operations of the class. We use the UML model in Fig. 7.24 to determine the associations among classes. We follow these four guidelines for each class:

1. Use the name located in the first compartment of a class in a class diagram to declare the class as a `public` class with an empty parameterless constructor. Class `Withdrawal` initially yields the code in Fig. 7.25. [*Note:* If we find that the class's instance variables require only default initialization, we will remove the empty parameterless constructor because it is unnecessary.]

2. Use the attributes located in the class's second compartment to declare the instance variables. The `private` attributes `accountNumber` and `amount` of class `Withdrawal` yield the code in Fig. 7.26.

3. Use the associations described in the class diagram to declare references to other objects. According to Fig. 7.24, `Withdrawal` can access one object of class `Screen`, one object of class `Keypad`, one object of class `CashDispenser` and one object of class `BankDatabase`. Class `Withdrawal` must maintain references to these objects to send messages to them, so lines 10–13 of Fig. 7.27 declare the appropriate references as `private` instance variables.

4. Use the operations located in the third compartment of Fig. 7.23 to declare the shells of the methods. If we have not yet specified a return type for an operation, we declare the method with return type `void`. Refer to the class diagrams of Figs. 5.20–5.24 to declare any necessary parameters. Adding the `public` operation `Execute` (which has an empty parameter list) in class `Withdrawal` yields the code in lines 23–26 of Fig. 7.28.

```
1  // Fig. 7.25: Withdrawal.cs
2  // Class Withdrawal represents an ATM withdrawal transaction
3  public class Withdrawal
4  {
5     // parameterless constructor
6     public Withdrawal()
7     {
8        // constructor body code
9     } // end constructor
10 } // end class Withdrawal
```

Fig. 7.25 | Initial C# code for class `Withdrawal` based on Figs. 7.23 and 7.24.

```
1  // Fig. 7.26: Withdrawal.cs
2  // Class Withdrawal represents an ATM withdrawal transaction
3  public class Withdrawal
4  {
5     // attributes
6     private int accountNumber; // account to withdraw funds from
7     private decimal amount; // amount to withdraw from account
8
9     // parameterless constructor
10    public Withdrawal()
11    {
12       // constructor body code
13    } // end constructor
14 } // end class Withdrawal
```

Fig. 7.26 | C# incorporating `private` variables for class `Withdrawal` based on Figs. 7.23 and 7.24.

```
1  // Fig. 7.27: Withdrawal.cs
2  // Class Withdrawal represents an ATM withdrawal transaction
3  public class Withdrawal
4  {
5     // attributes
6     private int accountNumber; // account to withdraw funds from
7     private decimal amount; // amount to withdraw
8
9     // references to associated objects
10    private Screen screen; // ATM's screen
11    private Keypad keypad; // ATM's keypad
12    private CashDispenser cashDispenser; // ATM's cash dispenser
13    private BankDatabase bankDatabase; // account information database
14
15    // parameterless constructor
16    public Withdrawal()
17    {
18       // constructor body code
19    } // end constructor
20 } // end class Withdrawal
```

Fig. 7.27 | C# code incorporating `private` reference handles for the associations of class `Withdrawal` based on Figs. 7.23 and 7.24.

```
 1   // Fig. 7.28: Withdrawal.cs
 2   // Class Withdrawal represents an ATM withdrawal transaction
 3   public class Withdrawal
 4   {
 5      // attributes
 6      private int accountNumber; // account to withdraw funds from
 7      private decimal amount; // amount to withdraw
 8
 9      // references to associated objects
10      private Screen screen; // ATM's screen
11      private Keypad keypad; // ATM's keypad
12      private CashDispenser cashDispenser; // ATM's cash dispenser
13      private BankDatabase bankDatabase; // account information database
14
15      // parameterless constructor
16      public Withdrawal()
17      {
18         // constructor body code
19      } // end constructor
20
21      // operations
22      // perform transaction
23      public void Execute()
24      {
25         // Execute method body code
26      } // end method Execute
27   } // end class Withdrawal
```

Fig. 7.28 | C# code incorporating method Execute in class Withdrawal based on Figs. 7.23 and 7.24.

Software Engineering Observation 7.13

Many UML modeling tools can convert UML-based designs into C# code, considerably speeding up the implementation process. For more information on these "automatic" code generators, refer to the Web resources listed at the end of Section 1.10.

This concludes our discussion of the basics of generating class files from UML diagrams. In the final Software Engineering Case Study section (Section 9.9), we demonstrate how to modify the code in Fig. 7.28 to incorporate the object-oriented concepts of inheritance and polymorphism, which we present in Chapters 8 and 9, respectively.

Software Engineering Case Study Self-Review Exercises

7.1 State whether the following statement is *true* or *false*, and if *false*, explain why: If an attribute of a class is marked with a minus sign (-) in a class diagram, the attribute is not directly accessible outside of the class.

7.2 In Fig. 7.24, the association between the ATM and the Screen indicates:
a) that we can navigate from the Screen to the ATM.
b) that we can navigate from the ATM to the Screen.
c) Both a and b; the association is bidirectional.
d) None of the above.

7.3 Write C# code to begin implementing the design for class Account.

Answers to Software Engineering Case Study Self-Review Exercises

7.1   True. The minus sign (–) indicates private visibility.

7.2   b.

7.3   The design for class Account yields the code in Fig. 7.29. Note that we include private instance variables availableBalance and totalBalance to store the data that properties Available-Balance and TotalBalance, and methods Credit and Debit, will manipulate.

```csharp
1   // Fig. 7.29: Account.cs
2   // Class Account represents a bank account.
3   public class Account
4   {
5      private int accountNumber; // account number
6      private int pin; // PIN for authentication
7      private decimal availableBalance; // available withdrawal amount
8      private decimal totalBalance; // funds available + pending deposit
9
10     // parameterless constructor
11     public Account()
12     {
13        // constructor body code
14     } // end constructor
15
16     // validates user PIN
17     public bool ValidatePIN()
18     {
19        // ValidatePIN method body code
20     } // end method ValidatePIN
21
22     // read-only property that gets the available balance
23     public decimal AvailableBalance
24     {
25        get
26        {
27           // AvailableBalance get accessor body code
28        } // end get
29     } // end property AvailableBalance
30
31     // read-only property that gets the total balance
32     public decimal TotalBalance
33     {
34        get
35        {
36           // TotalBalance get accessor body code
37        } // end get
38     } // end property TotalBalance
39
40     // credits the account
41     public void Credit()
42     {
43        // Credit method body code
44     } // end method Credit
```

Fig. 7.29 | C# code for class Account based on Figs. 7.23 and 7.24. (Part 1 of 2.)

```
45
46      // debits the account
47      public void Debit()
48      {
49          // Debit method body code
50      } // end method Debit
51 } // end class Account
```

Fig. 7.29 | C# code for class `Account` based on Figs. 7.23 and 7.24. (Part 2 of 2.)

7.18 Wrap-Up

In this chapter, we discussed additional class concepts. The `Time` class case study presented a complete class declaration consisting of `private` data, overloaded `public` constructors for initialization flexibility, properties for manipulating the class's data and methods that returned `string` representations of a `Time` object in two different formats. You learned that every class can declare a `ToString` method that returns a `string` representation of an object of the class and that this method can be invoked implicitly when an object of a class is output as a `string`.

You learned that the `this` reference is used implicitly in a class's non-`static` methods to access the class's instance variables and other non-`static` methods. You saw explicit uses of the `this` reference to access the class's members (including hidden fields) and learned how to use keyword `this` in a constructor to call another constructor of the class. You also learned how to declare indexers with the `this` keyword, allowing you to access the data of an object in much the same manner as you access the elements of an array.

You saw that a class can have references to objects of other classes as members—a concept known as composition. You learned about C#'s garbage collection capability and how it reclaims the memory of objects that are no longer used. We explained the motivation for `static` variables in a class, and demonstrated how to declare and use `static` variables and methods in your own classes. You also learned how to declare and initialize `readonly` variables.

We showed how to create a class library for reuse and how to use the classes of the library in an application. You learned that classes declared without an access modifier are given `internal` access by default. You saw that classes in an assembly can access the `internal`-access members of the other classes in the same assembly. We also showed how to use Visual Studio's **Class Library** and **Object Browser** windows to navigate the classes of the FCL and your own applications to discover information about those classes.

In the next chapter, you will learn another key object-oriented programming technology—inheritance. You will see that all classes in C# are related directly or indirectly to the `object` class. You will also begin to understand how inheritance enables you to build more powerful applications faster.

8

Object-Oriented Programming: Inheritance

OBJECTIVES

In this chapter you will learn:

- How inheritance promotes software reusability.

- The concepts of base classes and derived classes.

- To create a derived class that inherits attributes and behaviors from a base class.

- To use access modifier `protected` to give derived class methods access to base class members.

- To access base class members with `base`.

- How constructors are used in inheritance hierarchies.

- The methods of class `object`, the direct or indirect base class of all classes.

8.1 Introduction

This chapter continues our discussion of object-oriented programming (OOP) by introducing one of its primary features—*inheritance*, which is a form of software reuse in which a new class is created by absorbing an existing class's members and enhancing them with new or modified capabilities. With inheritance, programmers save time during application development by reusing proven and debugged high-quality software. This also increases the likelihood that a system will be implemented effectively.

When creating a class, rather than declaring completely new members, you can designate that the new class should inherit the members of an existing class. The existing class is called the *base class*, and the new class is the *derived class*. Each derived class can become the base class for future derived classes.

A derived class normally adds its own fields and methods. Therefore, a derived class is more specific than its base class and represents a more specialized group of objects. Typically, the derived class exhibits the behaviors of its base class and additional behaviors that are specific to the derived class.

The *direct base class* is the base class from which the derived class explicitly inherits. An *indirect base class* is any class above the direct base class in the *class hierarchy*, which defines the inheritance relationships among classes. The class hierarchy begins with class object (which is the C# alias for System.Object in the Framework Class Library), which *every* class directly or indirectly *extends* (or "inherits from"). Section 8.7 lists the methods of class object, which every other class inherits. In the case of *single inheritance,* a class is derived from one direct base class. C#, unlike C++, does not support multiple inheritance (which occurs when a class is derived from more than one direct base class). In Chapter 9,

Polymorphism, Interfaces & Operator Overloading, we explain how you can use interfaces to realize many of the benefits of multiple inheritance while avoiding the associated problems.

Experience in building software systems indicates that significant amounts of code deal with closely related special cases. When programmers are preoccupied with special cases, the details can obscure the big picture. With object-oriented programming, programmers can, when appropriate, focus on the commonalities among objects in the system rather than the special cases.

We distinguish between the *is-a relationship* and the *has-a relationship*. *Is-a* represents inheritance. In an *is-a* relationship, an object of a derived class can also be treated as an object of its base class. For example, a car *is a* vehicle, and a truck *is a* vehicle. By contrast, *has-a* represents composition (see Chapter 7). In a *has-a* relationship, an object contains as members references to other objects. For example, a car *has a* steering wheel, and a car object *has a* reference to a steering wheel object.

New classes can inherit from classes in *class libraries*. Organizations develop their own class libraries and can take advantage of others available worldwide. Some day, most new software likely will be constructed from *standardized reusable components*, just as automobiles and most computer hardware are constructed today. This will facilitate the development of more powerful, abundant and economical software.

8.2 Base Classes and Derived Classes

Often, an object of one class *is an* object of another class as well. For example, in geometry, a rectangle *is a* quadrilateral (as are squares, parallelograms and trapezoids). Thus, class Rectangle can be said to inherit from class Quadrilateral. In this context, class Quadrilateral is a base class and class Rectangle is a derived class. A rectangle *is a* specific type of quadrilateral, but it is incorrect to claim that every quadrilateral *is a* rectangle—the quadrilateral could be a parallelogram or some other shape. Figure 8.1 lists several simple examples of base classes and derived classes—note that base classes tend to be "more general," and derived classes tend to be "more specific."

Because every derived class object *is an* object of its base class, and one base class can have many derived classes, the set of objects represented by a base class is typically larger than the set of objects represented by any of its derived classes. For example, the base class Vehicle represents all vehicles—cars, trucks, boats, bicycles and so on. By contrast, derived class Car represents a smaller, more specific subset of vehicles.

Base class	Derived classes
Student	GraduateStudent, UndergraduateStudent
Shape	Circle, Triangle, Rectangle
Loan	CarLoan, HomeImprovementLoan, MortgageLoan
Employee	Faculty, Staff, HourlyWorker, CommissionWorker
BankAccount	CheckingAccount, SavingsAccount

Fig. 8.1 | Inheritance examples.

Inheritance relationships form tree-like hierarchical structures (Figs. 8.2 and 8.3). A base class exists in a hierarchical relationship with its derived classes. When classes participate in inheritance relationships, they become "affiliated" with other classes. A class becomes either a base class, supplying members to other classes, or a derived class, inheriting its members from another class. In some cases, a class is both a base class and a derived class.

Let us develop a sample class hierarchy, also called an ***inheritance hierarchy*** (Fig. 8.2). The UML class diagram of Fig. 8.2 shows a university community that has many types of members, including employees, students and alumni. Employees are either faculty members or staff members. Faculty members are either administrators (such as deans and department chairpersons) or teachers. Note that the hierarchy could contain many other classes. For example, students can be graduate or undergraduate students. Undergraduate students can be freshmen, sophomores, juniors or seniors.

Each arrow with a hollow triangular arrowhead in the hierarchy diagram represents an *is-a* relationship. As we follow the arrows in this class hierarchy, we can state, for instance, that "an Employee *is a* CommunityMember" and "a Teacher *is a* Faculty member." CommunityMember is the direct base class of Employee, Student and Alumnus, and is an indirect base class of all the other classes in the diagram. Starting from the bottom of the diagram, the reader can follow the arrows and apply the *is-a* relationship up to the topmost base class. For example, an Administrator *is a* Faculty member, *is an* Employee and *is a* CommunityMember.

Now consider the Shape inheritance hierarchy in Fig. 8.3. This hierarchy begins with base class Shape, which is extended by derived classes TwoDimensionalShape and ThreeDimensionalShape—Shapes are either TwoDimensionalShapes or ThreeDimensionalShapes. The third level of this hierarchy contains some specific TwoDimensionalShapes and ThreeDimensionalShapes. As in Fig. 8.2, we can follow the arrows from the bottom of the class diagram to the topmost base class in this class hierarchy to identify several *is-a* relationships. For instance, a Triangle *is a* TwoDimensionalShape and *is a* Shape, while a Sphere *is a* ThreeDimensionalShape and *is a* Shape. Note that this hierarchy could contain many other classes. For example, ellipses and trapezoids are TwoDimensionalShapes.

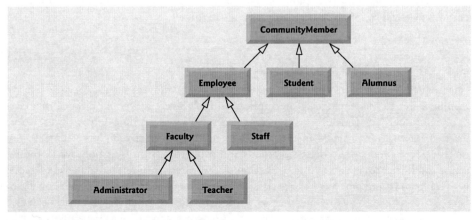

Fig. 8.2 | UML class diagram showing an inheritance hierarchy for university CommunityMembers.

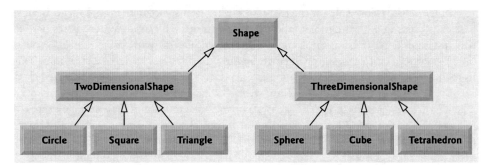

Fig. 8.3 | UML class diagram showing an inheritance hierarchy for Shapes.

Not every class relationship is an inheritance relationship. In Chapter 7, we discussed the *has-a* relationship, in which classes have members that are references to objects of other classes. Such relationships create classes by composition of existing classes. For example, given the classes Employee, BirthDate and TelephoneNumber, it is improper to say that an Employee *is a* BirthDate or that an Employee *is a* TelephoneNumber. However, an Employee *has a* BirthDate, and an Employee *has a* TelephoneNumber.

It is possible to treat base class objects and derived class objects similarly—their commonalities are expressed in the members of the base class. Objects of all classes that extend a common base class can be treated as objects of that base class (i.e., such objects have an *is-a* relationship with the base class). However, base class objects cannot be treated as objects of their derived classes. For example, all cars are vehicles, but not all vehicles are cars (the other vehicles could be trucks, planes or bicycles, for example). In this chapter and in Chapter 9, Polymorphism, Interfaces & Operator Overloading, we consider many examples of *is-a* relationships.

One problem with inheritance is that a derived class can inherit methods that it does not need or should not have. Even when a base class method is appropriate for a derived class, that derived class often needs a customized version of the method. In such cases, the derived class can *override* (redefine) the base class method with an appropriate implementation, as we will see often in the chapter's code examples.

8.3 protected Members

Chapter 7 discussed access modifiers public, private, and internal. A class's public members are accessible wherever the application has a reference to an object of that class or one of its derived classes. A class's private members are accessible only within the class itself. A base class's private members are inherited by its derived classes, but are not directly accessible by derived class methods and properties. In this section, we introduce access modifier protected. Using protected access offers an intermediate level of access between public and private. A base class's protected members can be accessed by members of that base class *and* by members of its derived classes. (Members of a class can also be declared *protected internal*. A base class's protected internal members can be accessed by members of that base class, by members of its derived classes *and* by any class in the same assembly.)

All non-private base class members retain their original access modifier when they become members of the derived class (i.e., public members of the base class become public members of the derived class, and protected members of the base class become protected members of the derived class).

Derived class methods can refer to public and protected members inherited from the base class simply by using the member names. When a derived class method overrides a base class method, the base class version of the method can be accessed from the derived class by preceding the base class method name with the keyword base and the dot (.) operator. We discuss accessing overridden members of the base class in Section 8.4.

Software Engineering Observation 8.1

Methods of a derived class cannot directly access private members of the base class. A derived class can change the state of private base class fields only through non-private methods and properties provided in the base class.

Software Engineering Observation 8.2

Declaring private fields in a base class helps you test, debug and correctly modify systems. If a derived class could access its base class's private fields, classes that inherit from that base class could access the fields as well. This would propagate access to what should be private fields, and the benefits of information hiding would be lost.

8.4 Relationship between Base Classes and Derived Classes

In this section, we use an inheritance hierarchy containing types of employees in a company's payroll application to discuss the relationship between a base class and its derived classes. In this company, commission employees (who will be represented as objects of a base class) are paid a percentage of their sales, while base-salaried commission employees (who will be represented as objects of a derived class) receive a base salary plus a percentage of their sales.

We divide our discussion of the relationship between commission employees and base-salaried commission employees into five examples. The first declares class CommissionEmployee, which directly inherits from class object and declares as private instance variables a first name, last name, social security number, commission rate and gross (i.e., total) sales amount.

The second example declares class BasePlusCommissionEmployee, which also directly inherits from class object and declares as private instance variables a first name, last name, social security number, commission rate, gross sales amount and base salary. We create the latter class by writing every line of code the class requires—we will soon see that it is much more efficient to create this class by inheriting from class CommissionEmployee.

The third example declares a separate BasePlusCommissionEmployee2 class that extends class CommissionEmployee (i.e., a BasePlusCommissionEmployee2 *is a* Commission-Employee who also has a base salary). We show that base class methods must be explicitly declared virtual if they are to be overridden by methods in derived classes. BasePlusCommissionEmployee2 attempts to access class CommissionEmployee's private members—this results in compilation errors, because a derived class cannot access its base class's private instance variables.

The fourth example shows that if base class CommissionEmployee's instance variables are declared as protected, a BasePlusCommissionEmployee3 class that extends class CommissionEmployee2 can access that data directly. For this purpose, we declare class CommissionEmployee2 with protected instance variables. All of the BasePlus-CommissionEmployee classes contain identical functionality, but we show how the class BasePlusCommissionEmployee3 is easier to create and manage.

After we discuss the convenience of using protected instance variables, we create the fifth example, which sets the CommissionEmployee instance variables back to private in class CommissionEmployee3 to enforce good software engineering. Then we show how a separate BasePlusCommissionEmployee4 class, which extends class Commission-Employee3, can use CommissionEmployee3's public methods to manipulate Commission-Employee3's private instance variables.

8.4.1 Creating and Using a CommissionEmployee Class

We begin by declaring class CommissionEmployee (Fig. 8.4). Line 3 begins the class declaration. The colon (:) followed by class name object at the end of the declaration header indicates that class CommissionEmployee extends class object (System.Object in the FCL). C# programmers use inheritance to create classes from existing classes. In fact, every class in C# (except object) extends an existing class. Because class CommissionEmployee extends class object, class CommissionEmployee inherits the methods of class object—class object does not have any fields. Every C# class directly or indirectly inherits object's methods. If a class does not specify that it inherits from another class, the new class implicitly inherits from object. For this reason, programmers typically do not include ": object" in their code—we do so in this example for demonstration purposes.

```
1    // Fig. 8.4: CommissionEmployee.cs
2    // CommissionEmployee class represents a commission employee.
3    public class CommissionEmployee : object
4    {
5       private string firstName;
6       private string lastName;
7       private string socialSecurityNumber;
8       private decimal grossSales; // gross weekly sales
9       private decimal commissionRate; // commission percentage
10
11      // five-parameter constructor
12      public CommissionEmployee( string first, string last, string ssn,
13         decimal sales, decimal rate )
14      {
15         // implicit call to object constructor occurs here
16         firstName = first;
17         lastName = last;
18         socialSecurityNumber = ssn;
19         GrossSales = sales; // validate gross sales via property
20         CommissionRate = rate; // validate commission rate via property
21      } // end five-parameter CommissionEmployee constructor
22
```

Fig. 8.4 | CommissionEmployee class represents a commission employee. (Part 1 of 3.)

```
23     // read-only property that gets commission employee's first name
24     public string FirstName
25     {
26        get
27        {
28           return firstName;
29        } // end get
30     } // end property FirstName
31
32     // read-only property that gets commission employee's last name
33     public string LastName
34     {
35        get
36        {
37           return lastName;
38        } // end get
39     } // end property LastName
40
41     // read-only property that gets
42     // commission employee's social security number
43     public string SocialSecurityNumber
44     {
45        get
46        {
47           return socialSecurityNumber;
48        } // end get
49     } // end property SocialSecurityNumber
50
51     // property that gets and sets commission employee's gross sales
52     public decimal GrossSales
53     {
54        get
55        {
56           return grossSales;
57        } // end get
58        set
59        {
60           grossSales = ( value < 0 ) ? 0 : value;
61        } // end set
62     } // end property GrossSales
63
64     // property that gets and sets commission employee's commission rate
65     public decimal CommissionRate
66     {
67        get
68        {
69           return commissionRate;
70        } // end get
71        set
72        {
73           commissionRate = ( value > 0 && value < 1 ) ? value : 0;
74        } // end set
75     } // end property CommissionRate
```

Fig. 8.4 | CommissionEmployee class represents a commission employee. (Part 2 of 3.)

```
76
77       // calculate commission employee's pay
78       public decimal Earnings()
79       {
80          return commissionRate * grossSales;
81       } // end method Earnings
82
83       // return string representation of CommissionEmployee object
84       public override string ToString()
85       {
86          return string.Format(
87             "{0}: {1} {2}\n{3}: {4}\n{5}: {6:C}\n{7}: {8:F2}",
88             "commission employee", FirstName, LastName,
89             "social security number", SocialSecurityNumber,
90             "gross sales", GrossSales, "commission rate", CommissionRate );
91       } // end method ToString
92    } // end class CommissionEmployee
```

Fig. 8.4 | CommissionEmployee class represents a commission employee. (Part 3 of 3.)

Software Engineering Observation 8.3

The compiler sets the base class of a class to object when the class declaration does not explicitly extend a base class.

The public services of class CommissionEmployee include a constructor (lines 12–21) and methods Earnings (lines 78–81) and ToString (lines 84–91). Lines 24–75 declare public properties for manipulating the class's instance variables firstName, lastName, socialSecurityNumber, grossSales and commissionRate (declared in lines 5–9). Class CommissionEmployee declares each of its instance variables as private, so objects of other classes cannot directly access these variables. Declaring instance variables as private and providing public properties to manipulate and validate them helps enforce good software engineering. The set accessors of properties GrossSales and CommissionRate, for example, validate their arguments before assigning the values to instance variables gross-Sales and commissionRate, respectively.

Constructors are not inherited, so class CommissionEmployee does not inherit class object's constructor. However, class CommissionEmployee's constructor calls class object's constructor implicitly. In fact, the first task of any derived class's constructor is to call its direct base class's constructor, either explicitly or implicitly (if no constructor call is specified), to ensure that the instance variables inherited from the base class are initialized properly. The syntax for calling a base class constructor explicitly is discussed in Section 8.4.3. If the code does not include an explicit call to the base class constructor, The compiler generates an implicit call to the base class's default or parameterless constructor. The comment in line 15 of Fig. 8.4 indicates where the implicit call to the base class object's default constructor is made (you do not write the code for this call). Class object's default (empty) constructor does nothing. Note that even if a class does not have constructors, the default constructor that the compiler implicitly declares for the class will call the base class's default or parameterless constructor. Class object is the only class that does not have a base class.

After the implicit call to object's constructor occurs, lines 16–20 of CommissionEmployee's constructor assign values to the class's instance variables. Note that we do not validate the values of arguments first, last and ssn before assigning them to the corresponding instance variables. We certainly could validate the first and last names—perhaps by ensuring that they are of a reasonable length. Similarly, a social security number could be validated to ensure that it contains nine digits, with or without dashes (e.g., 123-45-6789 or 123456789).

Method Earnings (lines 78–81) calculates a CommissionEmployee's earnings. Line 80 multiplies the commissionRate by the grossSales and returns the result.

Method ToString (lines 84–91) is special—it is one of the methods that every class inherits directly or indirectly from class object, which is the root of the C# class hierarchy. Section 8.7 summarizes class object's methods. Method ToString returns a string representing an object. This method is called implicitly by an application whenever an object must be converted to a string representation, such as in Console's Write method or string method Format using a format item. Class object's ToString method returns a string that includes the name of the object's class. It is primarily a placeholder that can be (and typically is) overridden by a derived class to specify an appropriate string representation of the data in a derived class object. Method ToString of class CommissionEmployee overrides (redefines) class object's ToString method. When invoked, CommissionEmployee's ToString method uses string method Format to return a string containing information about the CommissionEmployee. We use format specifier C to format grossSales as currency and the format specifier F2 to format the commissionRate with two digits of precision to the right of the decimal point. To override a base class method, a derived class must declare a method with keyword ***override*** and with the same signature (method name, number of parameters and parameter types) and return type as the base class method—object's ToString method takes no parameters and returns type string, so CommissionEmployee declares ToString with no parameters and return type string.

Common Programming Error 8.1

It is a compilation error to override a method with a different access modifier. Notice that overriding a method with a more restrictive access modifier would break the is-a relationship. If a public method could be overridden as a protected or private method, the derived class objects would not be able to respond to the same method calls as base class objects. Once a method is declared in a base class, the method must have the same access modifier for all that class's direct and indirect derived classes.

Figure 8.5 tests class CommissionEmployee. Lines 10–11 instantiate a CommissionEmployee object and invoke CommissionEmployee's constructor (lines 12–21 of Fig. 8.4)

```
1   // Fig. 8.5: CommissionEmployeeTest.cs
2   // Testing class CommissionEmployee.
3   using System;
4
5   public class CommissionEmployeeTest
6   {
7      public static void Main( string[] args )
8      {
9         // instantiate CommissionEmployee object
10        CommissionEmployee employee = new CommissionEmployee( "Sue",
11           "Jones", "222-22-2222", 10000.00M, .06M );
```

Fig. 8.5 | Testing class CommissionEmployee. (Part 1 of 2.)

```
12
13          // display commission employee data
14          Console.WriteLine(
15             "Employee information obtained by properties and methods: \n" );
16          Console.WriteLine( "{0} {1}", "First name is",
17             employee.FirstName );
18          Console.WriteLine( "{0} {1}", "Last name is",
19             employee.LastName );
20          Console.WriteLine( "{0} {1}", "Social security number is",
21             employee.SocialSecurityNumber );
22          Console.WriteLine( "{0} {1:C}", "Gross sales are",
23             employee.GrossSales );
24          Console.WriteLine( "{0} {1:F2}", "Commission rate is",
25             employee.CommissionRate );
26          Console.WriteLine( "{0} {1:C}", "Earnings are",
27             employee.Earnings() );
28
29          employee.GrossSales = 5000.00M; // set gross sales
30          employee.CommissionRate = .1M; // set commission rate
31
32          Console.WriteLine( "\n{0}:\n\n{1}",
33             "Updated employee information obtained by ToString", employee );
34          Console.WriteLine( "earnings: {0:C}", employee.Earnings() );
35       } // end Main
36    } // end class CommissionEmployeeTest
```

```
Employee information obtained by properties and methods:

First name is Sue
Last name is Jones
Social security number is 222-22-2222
Gross sales are $10,000.00
Commission rate is 0.06
Earnings are $600.00

Updated employee information obtained by ToString:

commission employee: Sue Jones
social security number: 222-22-2222
gross sales: $5,000.00
commission rate: 0.10
earnings: $500.00
```

Fig. 8.5 | Testing class CommissionEmployee. (Part 2 of 2.)

to initialize it with "Sue" as the first name, "Jones" as the last name, "222-22-2222" as the social security number, 10000.00M as the gross sales amount and .06M as the commission rate. We append the M suffix to the gross sales amount and the commission rate to indicate that these should be interpreted as decimal literals, rather than doubles. Lines 16–25 use CommissionEmployee's properties to retrieve the object's instance variable values for output. Lines 26–27 output the amount calculated by the Earnings method. Lines 29–30 invoke the set accessors of the object's GrossSales and CommissionRate properties to change the values of instance variables grossSales and commissionRate. Lines 32–33 output the string representation of the updated CommissionEmployee. Note that when an object is output using a format item, the object's ToString method is invoked implicitly to obtain the object's string representation. Line 34 outputs the earnings again.

8.4.2 Creating a BasePlusCommissionEmployee Class without Using Inheritance

We now discuss the second part of our introduction to inheritance by declaring and testing (completely new and independent) class BasePlusCommissionEmployee (Fig. 8.6), which contains a first name, last name, social security number, gross sales amount, commission rate and base salary. Class BasePlusCommissionEmployee's public services include a BasePlusCommissionEmployee constructor (lines 14–24) and methods Earnings (lines 99–102) and ToString (lines 105–113). Lines 28–96 declare public properties for the class's private instance variables firstName, lastName, socialSecurityNumber, grossSales, commissionRate and baseSalary (declared in lines 6–11). These variables, properties and methods encapsulate all the necessary features of a base-salaried commission employee. Note the similarity between this class and class CommissionEmployee (Fig. 8.4)—in this example, we do not yet exploit that similarity.

Note that class BasePlusCommissionEmployee does not specify that it extends object with the syntax ": object" in line 4, so the class implicitly extends object. Also note that, like class CommissionEmployee's constructor (lines 12–21 of Fig. 8.4), class BasePlusCommissionEmployee's constructor invokes class object's default constructor implicitly, as noted in the comment in line 17 of Fig. 8.6.

```csharp
1   // Fig. 8.6: BasePlusCommissionEmployee.cs
2   // BasePlusCommissionEmployee class represents an employee that receives
3   // a base salary in addition to a commission.
4   public class BasePlusCommissionEmployee
5   {
6      private string firstName;
7      private string lastName;
8      private string socialSecurityNumber;
9      private decimal grossSales; // gross weekly sales
10     private decimal commissionRate; // commission percentage
11     private decimal baseSalary; // base salary per week
12
13     // six-parameter constructor
14     public BasePlusCommissionEmployee( string first, string last,
15        string ssn, decimal sales, decimal rate, decimal salary )
16     {
17        // implicit call to object constructor occurs here
18        firstName = first;
19        lastName = last;
20        socialSecurityNumber = ssn;
21        GrossSales = sales; // validate gross sales via property
22        CommissionRate = rate; // validate commission rate via property
23        BaseSalary = salary; // validate base salary via property
24     } // end six-parameter BasePlusCommissionEmployee constructor
```

Fig. 8.6 | BasePlusCommissionEmployee class represents an employee that receives a base salary in addition to a commission. (Part 1 of 3.)

```
25
26      // read-only property that gets
27      // base-salaried commission employee's first name
28      public string FirstName
29      {
30         get
31         {
32            return firstName;
33         } // end get
34      } // end property FirstName
35
36      // read-only property that gets
37      // base-salaried commission employee's last name
38      public string LastName
39      {
40         get
41         {
42            return lastName;
43         } // end get
44      } // end property LastName
45
46      // read-only property that gets
47      // base-salaried commission employee's social security number
48      public string SocialSecurityNumber
49      {
50         get
51         {
52            return socialSecurityNumber;
53         } // end get
54      } // end property SocialSecurityNumber
55
56      // property that gets and sets
57      // base-salaried commission employee's gross sales
58      public decimal GrossSales
59      {
60         get
61         {
62            return grossSales;
63         } // end get
64         set
65         {
66            grossSales = ( value < 0 ) ? 0 : value;
67         } // end set
68      } // end property GrossSales
69
70      // property that gets and sets
71      // base-salaried commission employee's commission rate
72      public decimal CommissionRate
73      {
74         get
75         {
```

Fig. 8.6 | BasePlusCommissionEmployee class represents an employee that receives a base salary in addition to a commission. (Part 2 of 3.)

```
76          return commissionRate;
77       } // end get
78       set
79       {
80          commissionRate = ( value > 0 && value < 1 ) ? value : 0;
81       } // end set
82    } // end property CommissionRate
83
84    // property that gets and sets
85    // base-salaried commission employee's base salary
86    public decimal BaseSalary
87    {
88       get
89       {
90          return baseSalary;
91       } // end get
92       set
93       {
94          baseSalary = ( value < 0 ) ? 0 : value;
95       } // end set
96    } // end property BaseSalary
97
98    // calculate earnings
99    public decimal Earnings()
100   {
101      return BaseSalary + ( CommissionRate * GrossSales );
102   } // end method earnings
103
104   // return string representation of BasePlusCommissionEmployee
105   public override string ToString()
106   {
107      return string.Format(
108         "{0}: {1} {2}\n{3}: {4}\n{5}: {6:C}\n{7}: {8:F2}\n{9}: {10:C}",
109         "base-salaried commission employee", FirstName, LastName,
110         "social security number", SocialSecurityNumber,
111         "gross sales", GrossSales, "commission rate", CommissionRate,
112         "base salary", BaseSalary );
113   } // end method ToString
114 } // end class BasePlusCommissionEmployee
```

Fig. 8.6 | BasePlusCommissionEmployee class represents an employee that receives a base salary in addition to a commission. (Part 3 of 3.)

Class BasePlusCommissionEmployee's Earnings method (lines 99–102) computes the earnings of a base-salaried commission employee. Line 101 returns the result of adding the employee's base salary to the product of the commission rate and the employee's gross sales.

Class BasePlusCommissionEmployee overrides object method ToString to return a string containing the BasePlusCommissionEmployee's information (lines 105–113). Once again, we use format specifier C to format the gross sales and base salary as currency and format specifier F2 to format the commission rate with two digits of precision to the right of the decimal point (line 108).

Figure 8.7 tests class BasePlusCommissionEmployee. Lines 10–12 instantiate a Base-PlusCommissionEmployee object and pass "Bob", "Lewis", "333-33-3333", 5000.00M, .04M and 300.00M to the constructor as the first name, last name, social security number, gross sales, commission rate and base salary, respectively. Lines 17–30 use BasePlus-CommissionEmployee's properties and methods to retrieve the values of the object's instance variables and calculate the earnings for output. Line 32 invokes the object's BaseSalary property to change the base salary. Property BaseSalary's set accessor (Fig. 8.6, lines 92–95) ensures that instance variable baseSalary is not assigned a negative value, because an employee's base salary cannot be negative. Lines 34–35 of Fig. 8.7 invoke the object's ToString method implicitly to get the object's string representation.

```
1   // Fig. 8.7: BasePlusCommissionEmployeeTest.cs
2   // Testing class BasePlusCommissionEmployee.
3   using System;
4
5   public class BasePlusCommissionEmployeeTest
6   {
7      public static void Main( string[] args )
8      {
9         // instantiate BasePlusCommissionEmployee object
10        BasePlusCommissionEmployee employee =
11           new BasePlusCommissionEmployee( "Bob", "Lewis",
12           "333-33-3333", 5000.00M, .04M, 300.00M );
13
14        // display base-salaried commission employee data
15        Console.WriteLine(
16           "Employee information obtained by properties and methods: \n" );
17        Console.WriteLine( "{0} {1}", "First name is",
18           employee.FirstName );
19        Console.WriteLine( "{0} {1}", "Last name is",
20           employee.LastName );
21        Console.WriteLine( "{0} {1}", "Social security number is",
22           employee.SocialSecurityNumber );
23        Console.WriteLine( "{0} {1:C}", "Gross sales are",
24           employee.GrossSales );
25        Console.WriteLine( "{0} {1:F2}", "Commission rate is",
26           employee.CommissionRate );
27        Console.WriteLine( "{0} {1:C}", "Earnings are",
28           employee.Earnings() );
29        Console.WriteLine( "{0} {1:C}", "Base salary is",
30           employee.BaseSalary );
31
32        employee.BaseSalary = 1000.00M; // set base salary
33
34        Console.WriteLine( "\n{0}:\n\n{1}",
35           "Updated employee information obtained by ToString", employee );
36        Console.WriteLine( "earnings: {0:C}", employee.Earnings() );
37     } // end Main
38  } // end class BasePlusCommissionEmployeeTest
```

Fig. 8.7 | Testing class BasePlusCommissionEmployee. (Part 1 of 2.)

```
Employee information obtained by properties and methods:

First name is Bob
Last name is Lewis
Social security number is 333-33-3333
Gross sales are $5,000.00
Commission rate is 0.04
Earnings are $500.00
Base salary is $300.00

Updated employee information obtained by ToString:

base-salaried commission employee: Bob Lewis
social security number: 333-33-3333
gross sales: $5,000.00
commission rate: 0.04
base salary: $1,000.00
earnings: $1,200.00
```

Fig. 8.7 | Testing class BasePlusCommissionEmployee. (Part 2 of 2.)

Note that much of the code for class BasePlusCommissionEmployee (Fig. 8.6) is similar, if not identical, to the code for class CommissionEmployee (Fig. 8.4). For example, in class BasePlusCommissionEmployee, private instance variables firstName and lastName and properties FirstName and LastName are identical to those of class CommissionEmployee. Classes CommissionEmployee and BasePlusCommissionEmployee also both contain private instance variables socialSecurityNumber, commissionRate and grossSales, as well as properties to manipulate these variables. In addition, the BasePlusCommissionEmployee constructor is almost identical to that of class CommissionEmployee, except that BasePlusCommissionEmployee's constructor also sets the baseSalary. The other additions to class BasePlusCommissionEmployee are private instance variable baseSalary and property BaseSalary. Class BasePlusCommissionEmployee's ToString method is nearly identical to that of class CommissionEmployee, except that BasePlusCommissionEmployee's ToString also formats the value of instance variable baseSalary as currency.

We literally copied the code from class CommissionEmployee and pasted it into class BasePlusCommissionEmployee, then modified class BasePlusCommissionEmployee to include a base salary, and methods and properties that manipulate the base salary. This "copy-and-paste" approach is often error prone and time consuming. Worse yet, it can spread many physical copies of the same code throughout a system, creating a code-maintenance nightmare. Is there a way to "absorb" the members of one class in a way that makes them part of other classes without copying code? In the next several examples, we answer this question, using a more elegant approach to building classes, namely inheritance.

Error-Prevention Tip 8.1

Copying and pasting code from one class to another can spread errors across multiple source code files. To avoid duplicating code (and possibly errors) in situations where you want one class to "absorb" the members of another class, use inheritance rather than the "copy-and-paste" approach.

Software Engineering Observation 8.4

With inheritance, the common members of all the classes in the hierarchy are declared in a base class. When changes are required for these common features, you need only to make the changes in the base class—derived classes then inherit the changes. Without inheritance, changes would need to be made to all the source code files that contain a copy of the code in question.

8.4.3 Creating a CommissionEmployee– BasePlusCommissionEmployee Inheritance Hierarchy

Now we declare class BasePlusCommissionEmployee2 (Fig. 8.8), which extends class CommissionEmployee (Fig. 8.4). A BasePlusCommissionEmployee2 object *is a* CommissionEmployee (because inheritance passes on the capabilities of class CommissionEmployee), but class BasePlusCommissionEmployee2 also has instance variable baseSalary (Fig. 8.8, line 5). The colon (:) in line 3 of the class declaration indicates inheritance. As a derived class, BasePlusCommissionEmployee2 inherits the members of class CommissionEmployee and can access those members that are non-private. The constructor of class CommissionEmployee is not inherited. Thus, the public services of BasePlusCommissionEmployee2 include its constructor (lines 9–14), public methods and properties inherited from class CommissionEmployee, property BaseSalary (lines 18–28), method Earnings (lines 31–35) and method ToString (lines 38–47).

```csharp
1   // Fig. 8.8: BasePlusCommissionEmployee2.cs
2   // BasePlusCommissionEmployee2 inherits from class CommissionEmployee.
3   public class BasePlusCommissionEmployee2 : CommissionEmployee
4   {
5      private decimal baseSalary; // base salary per week
6
7      // six-parameter derived class constructor
8      // with call to base class CommissionEmployee constructor
9      public BasePlusCommissionEmployee2( string first, string last,
10        string ssn, decimal sales, decimal rate, decimal salary )
11        : base( first, last, ssn, sales, rate )
12     {
13        BaseSalary = salary; // validate base salary via property
14     } // end six-parameter BasePlusCommissionEmployee2 constructor
15
16     // property that gets and sets
17     // base-salaried commission employee's base salary
18     public decimal BaseSalary
19     {
20        get
21        {
22           return baseSalary;
23        } // end get
24        set
25        {
26           baseSalary = ( value < 0 ) ? 0 : value;
27        } // end set
28     } // end property BaseSalary
```

Fig. 8.8 | BasePlusCommissionEmployee2 inherits from class CommissionEmployee. (Part 1 of 2.)

```
29
30      // calculate earnings
31      public override decimal Earnings()
32      {
33          // not allowed: commissionRate and grossSales private in base class
34          return baseSalary + ( commissionRate * grossSales );
35      } // end method Earnings
36
37      // return string representation of BasePlusCommissionEmployee2
38      public override string ToString()
39      {
40          // not allowed: attempts to access private base class members
41          return string.Format(
42              "{0}: {1} {2}\n{3}: {4}\n{5}: {6:C}\n{7}: {8:F2}\n{9}: {10:C}",
43              "base-salaried commission employee", firstName, lastName,
44              "social security number", socialSecurityNumber,
45              "gross sales", grossSales, "commission rate", commissionRate,
46              "base salary", baseSalary );
47      } // end method ToString
48  } // end class BasePlusCommissionEmployee2
```

Error List					
⊗ 1 Error	⚠ 0 Warnings	ⓘ 0 Messages			
	Description	File	Line	Column	Project
⊗ 1	'BasePlusCommissionEmployee2.Earnings()': cannot override inherited member 'CommissionEmployee.Earnings()' because it is not marked virtual, abstract, or override	BasePlusComr	31	28	BasePlusCommissionEmployee2

Fig. 8.8 | BasePlusCommissionEmployee2 inherits from class CommissionEmployee. (Part 2 of 2.)

Each derived class constructor must implicitly or explicitly call its base class constructor to ensure that the instance variables inherited from the base class are initialized properly. BasePlusCommissionEmployee2's six-parameter constructor explicitly calls class CommissionEmployee's five-parameter constructor to initialize the base class portion of a BasePlusCommissionEmployee2 object (i.e., variables firstName, lastName, socialSecurityNumber, grossSales and commissionRate). Line 11 in the header of BasePlusCommissionEmployee2's six-parameter constructor invokes the CommissionEmployee's five-parameter constructor (declared at lines 12–21 of Fig. 8.4) by using a constructor initializer. In Section 7.6, we used constructor initializers with keyword this to call overloaded constructors in the same class. In line 11 of Fig. 8.8, we use a constructor initializer with keyword base to invoke the base class constructor. The arguments first, last, ssn, sales and rate are used to initialize base class members firstName, lastName, socialSecurityNumber, grossSales and commissionRate, respectively. If BasePlusCommissionEmployee2's constructor did not invoke CommissionEmployee's constructor explicitly, C# would attempt to invoke class CommissionEmployee's parameterless or default constructor—but the class does not have such a constructor, so the compiler would issue an error. When a base class contains a parameterless constructor, you can use base() in the constructor initializer to call that constructor explicitly, but this is rarely done.

Common Programming Error 8.2

A compilation error occurs if a derived class constructor calls one of its base class constructors with arguments that do not match the number and types of parameters specified in one of the base class constructor declarations.

Lines 31–35 of Fig. 8.8 declare method Earnings using keyword override to override the CommissionEmployee's Earnings method, as we did with method ToString in previous examples. Line 31 causes a compilation error indicating that we cannot override the base class's Earnings method because it was not explicitly "marked virtual, abstract, or override." The **virtual** and abstract keywords indicate that a base class method can be overridden in derived classes. (As you will learn in Section 9.4, abstract methods are implicitly virtual.) The override modifier declares that a derived class method overrides a virtual or abstract base class method. This modifier also implicitly declares the derived class method virtual and allows it to be overridden in derived classes further down the inheritance hierarchy.

If we add the keyword virtual to the declaration of method Earnings in Fig. 8.4 and recompile, other compilation errors appear. As shown in Fig. 8.9, the compiler generates additional errors for line 34 of Fig. 8.8 because base class CommissionEmployee's instance variables commissionRate and grossSales are private—derived class BasePlusCommissionEmployee2's methods are not allowed to access base class CommissionEmployee's private instance variables. Note that we used bold text in Fig. 8.8 to indicate erroneous code. The compiler issues additional errors at lines 43–45 of BasePlusCommissionEmployee2's ToString method for the same reason. The errors in BasePlusCommissionEmployee2 could have been prevented by using the public properties inherited from class CommissionEmployee. For example, line 34 could have invoked the get accessors of properties CommissionRate and GrossSales to access CommissionEmployee's private instance variables commissionRate and grossSales, respectively. Lines 43–45 also could have used appropriate properties to retrieve the values of the base class's instance variables.

		Description	File	Line	Column	Project
⊗	1	'CommissionEmployee.commissionRate' is inaccessible due to its protection level	BasePlusCc	34	29	BasePlusCommission Employee2
⊗	2	'CommissionEmployee.grossSales' is inaccessible due to its protection level	BasePlusCc	34	46	BasePlusCommission Employee2
⊗	3	'CommissionEmployee.firstName' is inaccessible due to its protection level	BasePlusCc	43	47	BasePlusCommission Employee2
⊗	4	'CommissionEmployee.lastName' is inaccessible due to its protection level	BasePlusCc	43	58	BasePlusCommission Employee2
⊗	5	'CommissionEmployee.socialSecurityNumber' is inaccessible due to its protection level	BasePlusCc	44	36	BasePlusCommission Employee2
⊗	6	'CommissionEmployee.grossSales' is inaccessible due to its protection level	BasePlusCc	45	25	BasePlusCommission Employee2
⊗	7	'CommissionEmployee.commissionRate' is inaccessible due to its protection level	BasePlusCc	45	56	BasePlusCommission Employee2

Error List — ⊗ 7 Errors — ⚠ 0 Warnings — ⓘ 0 Messages

Fig. 8.9 | Compilation errors generated by BasePlusCommissionEmployee2 (Fig. 8.8) after declaring the Earnings method in Fig. 8.4 with keyword virtual.

8.4.4 CommissionEmployee–BasePlusCommissionEmployee Inheritance Hierarchy Using protected Instance Variables

To enable class BasePlusCommissionEmployee to directly access base class instance variables firstName, lastName, socialSecurityNumber, grossSales and commissionRate, we can declare those members as protected in the base class. As we discussed in Section 8.3, a base class's protected members *are* inherited by all derived classes of that base class. Class CommissionEmployee2 (Fig. 8.10) is a modification of class CommissionEmployee (Fig. 8.4) that declares instance variables firstName, lastName, socialSecurityNumber, grossSales and commissionRate as protected rather than private (Fig. 8.10, lines 5–9). As discussed in Section 8.4.3, we also declare the Earnings method virtual in line 78 so that

```
1   // Fig. 8.10: CommissionEmployee2.cs
2   // CommissionEmployee2 with protected instance variables.
3   public class CommissionEmployee2
4   {
5      protected string firstName;
6      protected string lastName;
7      protected string socialSecurityNumber;
8      protected decimal grossSales; // gross weekly sales
9      protected decimal commissionRate; // commission percentage
10
11     // five-parameter constructor
12     public CommissionEmployee2( string first, string last, string ssn,
13        decimal sales, decimal rate )
14     {
15        // implicit call to object constructor occurs here
16        firstName = first;
17        lastName = last;
18        socialSecurityNumber = ssn;
19        GrossSales = sales; // validate gross sales via property
20        CommissionRate = rate; // validate commission rate via property
21     } // end five-parameter CommissionEmployee2 constructor
22
23     // read-only property that gets commission employee's first name
24     public string FirstName
25     {
26        get
27        {
28           return firstName;
29        } // end get
30     } // end property FirstName
31
32     // read-only property that gets commission employee's last name
33     public string LastName
34     {
35        get
36        {
37           return lastName;
38        } // end get
39     } // end property LastName
40
```

Fig. 8.10 | CommissionEmployee2 with protected instance variables. (Part 1 of 2.)

```
41      // read-only property that gets
42      // commission employee's social security number
43      public string SocialSecurityNumber
44      {
45         get
46         {
47            return socialSecurityNumber;
48         } // end get
49      } // end property SocialSecurityNumber
50
51      // property that gets and sets commission employee's gross sales
52      public decimal GrossSales
53      {
54         get
55         {
56            return grossSales;
57         } // end get
58         set
59         {
60            grossSales = ( value < 0 ) ? 0 : value;
61         } // end set
62      } // end property GrossSales
63
64      // property that gets and sets commission employee's commission rate
65      public decimal CommissionRate
66      {
67         get
68         {
69            return commissionRate;
70         } // end get
71         set
72         {
73            commissionRate = ( value > 0 && value < 1 ) ? value : 0;
74         } // end set
75      } // end property CommissionRate
76
77      // calculate commission employee's pay
78      public virtual decimal Earnings()
79      {
80         return commissionRate * grossSales;
81      } // end method Earnings
82
83      // return string representation of CommissionEmployee object
84      public override string ToString()
85      {
86         return string.Format(
87            "{0}: {1} {2}\n{3}: {4}\n{5}: {6:C}\n{7}: {8:F2}",
88            "commission employee", firstName, lastName,
89            "social security number", socialSecurityNumber,
90            "gross sales", grossSales, "commission rate", commissionRate );
91      } // end method ToString
92   } // end class CommissionEmployee2
```

Fig. 8.10 | CommissionEmployee2 with protected instance variables. (Part 2 of 2.)

BasePlusCommissionEmployee can override the method. Other than the change in the class name (and thus the change in the constructor name) to CommissionEmployee2, the rest of the class declaration in Fig. 8.10 is identical to that of Fig. 8.4.

We could have declared the base class CommissionEmployee2's instance variables firstName, lastName, socialSecurityNumber, grossSales and commissionRate as public to enable derived class BasePlusCommissionEmployee2 to access the base class instance variables. However, declaring public instance variables is poor software engineering, because it allows unrestricted access to the instance variables, greatly increasing the chance of errors. With protected instance variables, the derived class gets access to the instance variables, but classes that are not derived from the base class cannot access its variables directly.

Class BasePlusCommissionEmployee3 (Fig. 8.11) is a modification of class BasePlusCommissionEmployee2 (Fig. 8.8) that extends CommissionEmployee2 (line 4) rather than class CommissionEmployee. Objects of class BasePlusCommissionEmployee3 inherit CommissionEmployee2's protected instance variables firstName, lastName, socialSecurityNumber, grossSales and commissionRate—all these variables are now protected members of BasePlusCommissionEmployee3. As a result, the compiler does not generate errors when compiling line 34 of method Earnings and lines 42–44 of method ToString. If another class extends BasePlusCommissionEmployee3, the new derived class also inherits the protected members.

Class BasePlusCommissionEmployee3 does not inherit class CommissionEmployee2's constructor. However, class BasePlusCommissionEmployee3's six-parameter constructor (lines 10–15) calls class CommissionEmployee2's five-parameter constructor with a constructor initializer. BasePlusCommissionEmployee3's six-parameter constructor must explicitly call the five-parameter constructor of class CommissionEmployee2, because CommissionEmployee2 does not provide a parameterless constructor that could be invoked implicitly.

```
1   // Fig. 8.11: BasePlusCommissionEmployee3.cs
2   // BasePlusCommissionEmployee3 inherits from CommissionEmployee2 and has
3   // access to CommissionEmployee2's protected members.
4   public class BasePlusCommissionEmployee3 : CommissionEmployee2
5   {
6      private decimal baseSalary; // base salary per week
7
8      // six-parameter derived class constructor
9      // with call to base class CommissionEmployee constructor
10     public BasePlusCommissionEmployee3( string first, string last,
11        string ssn, decimal sales, decimal rate, decimal salary )
12        : base( first, last, ssn, sales, rate )
13     {
14        BaseSalary = salary; // validate base salary via property
15     } // end six-parameter BasePlusCommissionEmployee3 constructor
16
```

Fig. 8.11 | BasePlusCommissionEmployee3 inherits from CommissionEmployee2 and has access to CommissionEmployee2's protected members. (Part 1 of 2.)

```
17    // property that gets and sets
18    // base-salaried commission employee's base salary
19    public decimal BaseSalary
20    {
21       get
22       {
23          return baseSalary;
24       } // end get
25       set
26       {
27          baseSalary = ( value < 0 ) ? 0 : value;
28       } // end set
29    } // end property BaseSalary
30
31    // calculate earnings
32    public override decimal Earnings()
33    {
34       return baseSalary + ( commissionRate * grossSales );
35    } // end method Earnings
36
37    // return string representation of BasePlusCommissionEmployee3
38    public override string ToString()
39    {
40       return string.Format(
41          "{0}: {1} {2}\n{3}: {4}\n{5}: {6:C}\n{7}: {8:F2}\n{9}: {10:C}",
42          "base-salaried commission employee", firstName, lastName,
43          "social security number", socialSecurityNumber,
44          "gross sales", grossSales, "commission rate", commissionRate,
45          "base salary", baseSalary );
46    } // end method ToString
47 } // end class BasePlusCommissionEmployee3
```

Fig. 8.11 | BasePlusCommissionEmployee3 inherits from CommissionEmployee2 and has access to CommissionEmployee2's protected members. (Part 2 of 2.)

Figure 8.12 uses a BasePlusCommissionEmployee3 object to perform the same tasks that Fig. 8.7 performed on a BasePlusCommissionEmployee object (Fig. 8.6). Note that the outputs of the two applications are identical. Although we declared class BasePlus-CommissionEmployee without using inheritance and declared class BasePlus-CommissionEmployee3 using inheritance, both classes provide the same functionality. The source code for class BasePlusCommissionEmployee3, which is 47 lines, is considerably shorter than that for class BasePlusCommissionEmployee, which is 114 lines, because class BasePlusCommissionEmployee3 inherits most of its functionality from Commission-Employee2, whereas class BasePlusCommissionEmployee inherits only class object's functionality. Also, there is now only one copy of the commission employee functionality declared in class CommissionEmployee2. This makes the code easier to maintain, modify and debug, because the code related to a commission employee exists only in class CommissionEmployee2.

In this example, we declared base class instance variables as protected so that derived classes could inherit them. Inheriting protected instance variables slightly increases performance, because we can directly access the variables in the derived class without incurring the overhead of invoking the set or get accessors of the corresponding property. In most cases, however, it is better to use private instance variables to encourage proper software engineering, and leave code optimization issues to the compiler. Your code will be easier to maintain, modify and debug.

Using protected instance variables creates several potential problems. First, the derived class object can set an inherited variable's value directly without using the property's set accessor. Therefore, a derived class object can assign an invalid value to the variable, thus leaving the object in an inconsistent state. For example, if we were to declare CommissionEmployee3's instance variable grossSales as protected, a derived class object (e.g., BasePlusCommissionEmployee) could then assign a negative value to grossSales.

```csharp
// Fig. 8.12: BasePlusCommissionEmployeeTest3.cs
// Testing class BasePlusCommissionEmployee3.
using System;

public class BasePlusCommissionEmployeeTest3
{
   public static void Main( string[] args )
   {
      // instantiate BasePlusCommissionEmployee3 object
      BasePlusCommissionEmployee3 basePlusCommissionEmployee =
         new BasePlusCommissionEmployee3( "Bob", "Lewis",
         "333-33-3333", 5000.00M, .04M, 300.00M );

      // display base-salaried commission employee data
      Console.WriteLine(
         "Employee information obtained by properties and methods: \n" );
      Console.WriteLine( "{0} {1}", "First name is",
         basePlusCommissionEmployee.FirstName );
      Console.WriteLine( "{0} {1}", "Last name is",
         basePlusCommissionEmployee.LastName );
      Console.WriteLine( "{0} {1}", "Social security number is",
         basePlusCommissionEmployee.SocialSecurityNumber );
      Console.WriteLine( "{0} {1:C}", "Gross sales are",
         basePlusCommissionEmployee.GrossSales );
      Console.WriteLine( "{0} {1:F2}", "Commission rate is",
         basePlusCommissionEmployee.CommissionRate );
      Console.WriteLine( "{0} {1:C}", "Earnings are",
         basePlusCommissionEmployee.Earnings() );
      Console.WriteLine( "{0} {1:C}", "Base salary is",
         basePlusCommissionEmployee.BaseSalary );

      basePlusCommissionEmployee.BaseSalary = 1000.00M; // set base salary

      Console.WriteLine( "\n{0}:\n\n{1}",
         "Updated employee information obtained by ToString",
         basePlusCommissionEmployee );
      Console.WriteLine( "earnings: {0:C}",
         basePlusCommissionEmployee.Earnings() );
   } // end Main
} // end class BasePlusCommissionEmployeeTest3
```

Fig. 8.12 | Testing class BasePlusCommissionEmployee3. (Part 1 of 2.)

```
Employee information obtained by properties and methods:

First name is Bob
Last name is Lewis
Social security number is 333-33-3333
Gross sales are $5,000.00
Commission rate is 0.04
Earnings are $500.00
Base salary is $300.00

Updated employee information obtained by ToString:

base-salaried commission employee: Bob Lewis
social security number: 333-33-3333
gross sales: $5,000.00
commission rate: 0.04
base salary: $1,000.00
earnings: $1,200.00
```

Fig. 8.12 | Testing class `BasePlusCommissionEmployee3`. (Part 2 of 2.)

The second problem with using `protected` instance variables is that derived class methods are more likely to be written to depend on the base class's data implementation. In practice, derived classes should depend only on the base class services (i.e., non-private methods and properties) and not on the base class data implementation. With `protected` instance variables in the base class, we may need to modify all the derived classes of the base class if the base class implementation changes. For example, if for some reason we were to change the names of instance variables `firstName` and `lastName` to `first` and `last`, then we would have to do so for all occurrences in which a derived class directly references base class instance variables `firstName` and `lastName`. In such a case, the software is said to be *fragile* or *brittle*, because a small change in the base class can "break" derived class implementation. You should be able to change the base class implementation while still providing the same services to the derived classes. Of course, if the base class services change, we must reimplement our derived classes.

Software Engineering Observation 8.5

Declaring base class instance variables private *(as opposed to* protected*) enables the base class implementation of these instance variables to change without affecting derived class implementations.*

8.4.5 CommissionEmployee–BasePlusCommissionEmployee Inheritance Hierarchy Using `private` Instance Variables

We now reexamine our hierarchy once more, this time using the best software engineering practices. Class `CommissionEmployee3` (Fig. 8.13) declares instance variables `firstName`, `lastName`, `socialSecurityNumber`, `grossSales` and `commissionRate` as private (lines 5–9) and provides public properties `FirstName`, `LastName`, `SocialSecurityNumber`, `GrossSales` and `GrossSales` for manipulating these values. Note that methods `Earnings` (lines 78–81) and `ToString` (lines 84–91) use the class's properties to obtain the values of its instance variables. If we decide to change the instance variable names, the `Earnings` and

```
1    // Fig. 8.13: CommissionEmployee3.cs
2    // CommissionEmployee3 class represents a commission employee.
3    public class CommissionEmployee3
4    {
5       private string firstName;
6       private string lastName;
7       private string socialSecurityNumber;
8       private decimal grossSales; // gross weekly sales
9       private decimal commissionRate; // commission percentage
10
11      // five-parameter constructor
12      public CommissionEmployee3( string first, string last, string ssn,
13         decimal sales, decimal rate )
14      {
15         // implicit call to object constructor occurs here
16         firstName = first;
17         lastName = last;
18         socialSecurityNumber = ssn;
19         GrossSales = sales; // validate gross sales via property
20         CommissionRate = rate; // validate commission rate via property
21      } // end five-parameter CommissionEmployee3 constructor
22
23      // read-only property that gets commission employee's first name
24      public string FirstName
25      {
26         get
27         {
28            return firstName;
29         } // end get
30      } // end property FirstName
31
32      // read-only property that gets commission employee's last name
33      public string LastName
34      {
35         get
36         {
37            return lastName;
38         } // end get
39      } // end property LastName
40
41      // read-only property that gets
42      // commission employee's social security number
43      public string SocialSecurityNumber
44      {
45         get
46         {
47            return socialSecurityNumber;
48         } // end get
49      } // end property SocialSecurityNumber
50
51      // property that gets and sets commission employee's gross sales
52      public decimal GrossSales
53      {
```

Fig. 8.13 | CommissionEmployee3 class represents a commission employee. (Part 1 of 2.)

```
54          get
55          {
56              return grossSales;
57          } // end get
58          set
59          {
60              grossSales = ( value < 0 ) ? 0 : value;
61          } // end set
62      } // end property GrossSales
63
64      // property that gets and sets commission employee's commission rate
65      public decimal CommissionRate
66      {
67          get
68          {
69              return commissionRate;
70          } // end get
71          set
72          {
73              commissionRate = ( value > 0 && value < 1 ) ? value : 0;
74          } // end set
75      } // end property CommissionRate
76
77      // calculate commission employee's pay
78      public virtual decimal Earnings()
79      {
80          return CommissionRate * GrossSales;
81      } // end method Earnings
82
83      // return string representation of CommissionEmployee object
84      public override string ToString()
85      {
86          return string.Format(
87              "{0}: {1} {2}\n{3}: {4}\n{5}: {6:C}\n{7}: {8:F2}",
88              "commission employee", FirstName, LastName,
89              "social security number", SocialSecurityNumber,
90              "gross sales", GrossSales, "commission rate", CommissionRate );
91      } // end method ToString
92  } // end class CommissionEmployee3
```

Fig. 8.13 | CommissionEmployee3 class represents a commission employee. (Part 2 of 2.)

ToString declarations will not require modification—only the bodies of the properties that directly manipulate the instance variables will need to change. Note that these changes occur solely within the base class—no changes to the derived class are needed. Localizing the effects of changes like this is a good software engineering practice. Derived class BasePlusCommissionEmployee4 (Fig. 8.14) inherits CommissionEmployee3's non-private members and can access the private base class members via its public properties.

Class BasePlusCommissionEmployee4 (Fig. 8.14) has several changes to its method implementations that distinguish it from class BasePlusCommissionEmployee3 (Fig. 8.11). Methods Earnings (Fig. 8.14, lines 33–36) and ToString (lines 39–43) each invoke property BaseSalary's get accessor to obtain the base salary value, rather than

```
1   // Fig. 8.14: BasePlusCommissionEmployee4.cs
2   // BasePlusCommissionEmployee4 inherits from CommissionEmployee3 and has
3   // access to CommissionEmployee3's private data via
4   // its public properties.
5   public class BasePlusCommissionEmployee4 : CommissionEmployee3
6   {
7      private decimal baseSalary; // base salary per week
8
9      // six-parameter derived class constructor
10     // with call to base class CommissionEmployee3 constructor
11     public BasePlusCommissionEmployee4( string first, string last,
12        string ssn, decimal sales, decimal rate, decimal salary )
13        : base( first, last, ssn, sales, rate )
14     {
15        BaseSalary = salary; // validate base salary via property
16     } // end six-parameter BasePlusCommissionEmployee4 constructor
17
18     // property that gets and sets
19     // base-salaried commission employee's base salary
20     public decimal BaseSalary
21     {
22        get
23        {
24           return baseSalary;
25        } // end get
26        set
27        {
28           baseSalary = ( value < 0 ) ? 0 : value;
29        } // end set
30     } // end property BaseSalary
31
32     // calculate earnings
33     public override decimal Earnings()
34     {
35        return BaseSalary + base.Earnings();
36     } // end method Earnings
37
38     // return string representation of BasePlusCommissionEmployee4
39     public override string ToString()
40     {
41        return string.Format( "{0} {1}\n{2}: {3:C}",
42           "base-salaried", base.ToString(), "base salary", BaseSalary );
43     } // end method ToString
44  } // end class BasePlusCommissionEmployee4
```

Fig. 8.14 | BasePlusCommissionEmployee4 inherits from CommissionEmployee3 and has access to CommissionEmployee3's private data via its public properties.

accessing baseSalary directly. If we decide to rename instance variable baseSalary, only the body of property BaseSalary will need to change.

Class BasePlusCommissionEmployee4's Earnings method (Fig. 8.14, lines 33–36) overrides class CommissionEmployee3's Earnings method (Fig. 8.13, lines 78–81) to calculate the earnings of a base-salaried commission employee. The new version obtains the portion of the employee's earnings based on commission alone by calling CommissionEmployee3's Earnings method with the expression base.Earnings() (Fig. 8.14, line 35). BasePlusCommissionEmployee4's Earnings method then adds the base salary to this value to calculate the total earnings of the employee. Note the syntax used to invoke an overridden base class method from a derived class—place the keyword base and the dot (.) operator before the base class method name. This method invocation is a good software engineering practice—by having BasePlusCommissionEmployee4's Earnings method invoke CommissionEmployee3's Earnings method to calculate part of a BasePlusCommissionEmployee4 object's earnings, we avoid duplicating the code and reduce code-maintenance problems.

Common Programming Error 8.3

When a base class method is overridden in a derived class, the derived class version often calls the base class version to do a portion of the work. Failure to prefix the base class method name with the keyword base and the dot (.) operator when referencing the base class's method causes the derived class method to call itself, creating an error called infinite recursion. Recursion, used correctly, is a powerful capability, as you learned in Section 5.13, Recursion.

Common Programming Error 8.4

The use of "chained" base references to refer to a member (a method, property or variable) several levels up the hierarchy—as in base.base.Earnings()—is a compilation error.

Similarly, BasePlusCommissionEmployee4's ToString method (Fig. 8.14, lines 39–43) overrides class CommissionEmployee3's ToString method (Fig. 8.13, lines 84–91) to return a string representation that is appropriate for a base-salaried commission employee. The new version creates part of a BasePlusCommissionEmployee4 object's string representation (i.e., the string "commission employee" and the values of class CommissionEmployee3's private instance variables) by calling CommissionEmployee3's ToString method with the expression base.ToString() (Fig. 8.14, line 42). BasePlusCommissionEmployee4's ToString method then outputs the remainder of a BasePlusCommissionEmployee4 object's string representation (i.e., the value of class BasePlusCommissionEmployee4's base salary).

Figure 8.15 performs the same manipulations on a BasePlusCommissionEmployee4 object as did Fig. 8.7 and Fig. 8.12 on objects of classes BasePlusCommissionEmployee

```
1   // Fig. 8.15: BasePlusCommissionEmployeeTest4.cs
2   // Testing class BasePlusCommissionEmployee4.
3   using System;
4
5   public class BasePlusCommissionEmployeeTest4
6   {
7      public static void Main( string[] args )
8      {
9         // instantiate BasePlusCommissionEmployee3 object
10        BasePlusCommissionEmployee4 employee =
11           new BasePlusCommissionEmployee4( "Bob", "Lewis",
12           "333-33-3333", 5000.00M, .04M, 300.00M );
```

Fig. 8.15 | Testing class BasePlusCommissionEmployee4. (Part 1 of 2.)

```
13
14        // display base-salaried commission employee data
15        Console.WriteLine(
16          "Employee information obtained by properties and methods: \n" );
17        Console.WriteLine( "{0} {1}", "First name is",
18          employee.FirstName );
19        Console.WriteLine( "{0} {1}", "Last name is",
20          employee.LastName );
21        Console.WriteLine( "{0} {1}", "Social security number is",
22          employee.SocialSecurityNumber );
23        Console.WriteLine( "{0} {1:C}", "Gross sales are",
24          employee.GrossSales );
25        Console.WriteLine( "{0} {1:F2}", "Commission rate is",
26          employee.CommissionRate );
27        Console.WriteLine( "{0} {1:C}", "Earnings are",
28          employee.Earnings() );
29        Console.WriteLine( "{0} {1:C}", "Base salary is",
30          employee.BaseSalary );
31
32        employee.BaseSalary = 1000.00M; // set base salary
33
34        Console.WriteLine( "\n{0}:\n\n{1}",
35          "Updated employee information obtained by ToString", employee );
36        Console.WriteLine( "earnings: {0:C}", employee.Earnings() );
37     } // end Main
38  } // end class BasePlusCommissionEmployeeTest4
```

```
Employee information obtained by properties and methods:

First name is Bob
Last name is Lewis
Social security number is 333-33-3333
Gross sales are $5,000.00
Commission rate is 0.04
Earnings are $500.00
Base salary is $300.00

Updated employee information obtained by ToString:

base-salaried commission employee: Bob Lewis
social security number: 333-33-3333
gross sales: $5,000.00
commission rate: 0.04
base salary: $1,000.00
earnings: $1,200.00
```

Fig. 8.15 | Testing class `BasePlusCommissionEmployee4`. (Part 2 of 2.)

and `BasePlusCommissionEmployee3`, respectively. Although each "base-salaried commission employee" class behaves identically, class `BasePlusCommissionEmployee4` is the best engineered. By using inheritance and by using properties that hide the data and ensure consistency, we have efficiently and effectively constructed a well-engineered class.

In this section, you saw an evolutionary set of examples that was carefully designed to teach key capabilities for good software engineering with inheritance. You learned how to create a derived class using inheritance, how to use protected base class members to enable a derived class to access inherited base class instance variables and how to override base class methods to provide versions that are more appropriate for derived class objects. In addition, you applied software-engineering techniques from Chapter 2, Chapter 7 and this chapter to create classes that are easy to maintain, modify and debug.

8.5 Constructors in Derived Classes

As we explained in the preceding section, instantiating a derived class object begins a chain of constructor calls in which the derived class constructor, before performing its own tasks, invokes its direct base class's constructor either explicitly (via a constructor initializer with the base reference) or implicitly (calling the base class's default constructor or parameterless constructor). Similarly, if the base class is derived from another class (as every class except object is), the base class constructor invokes the constructor of the next class up in the hierarchy, and so on. The last constructor called in the chain is always the constructor for class object. The original derived class constructor's body finishes executing last. Each base class's constructor manipulates the base class instance variables that the derived class object inherits. For example, consider again the CommissionEmployee3–BasePlus-CommissionEmployee4 hierarchy from Fig. 8.13 and Fig. 8.14. When an application creates a BasePlusCommissionEmployee4 object, the BasePlusCommissionEmployee4 constructor is called. That constructor calls the constructor for class CommissionEmployee3, which in turn implicitly calls object's constructor. Class object's constructor has an empty body, so it immediately returns control to Commission-Employee3's constructor, which then initializes the private instance variables of CommissionEmployee3 that are part of the BasePlusCommissionEmployee4 object. When this constructor completes execution, it returns control to BasePlusCommission-Employee4's constructor, which initializes the BasePlusCommissionEmployee4 object's baseSalary.

Software Engineering Observation 8.6

When an application creates a derived class object, the derived class constructor immediately calls the base class constructor (explicitly, via base, or implicitly). The base class constructor's body executes to initialize the base class's instance variables that are part of the derived class object, then the derived class constructor's body executes to initialize the derived class-only instance variables. Even if a constructor does not assign a value to an instance variable, the variable is still initialized to its default value (i.e., 0 for simple numeric types, false for bools and null for references).

Our next example revisits the commission employee hierarchy by declaring a CommissionEmployee4 class (Fig. 8.16) and a BasePlusCommissionEmployee5 class (Fig. 8.17). Each class's constructor prints a message when invoked, enabling us to observe the order in which the constructors in the hierarchy execute.

Class CommissionEmployee4 (Fig. 8.16) contains the same features as the version of the class shown in Fig. 8.13. We modified the constructor (lines 14–25) to output text when it is invoked. Note that concatenating this with a string literal (line 24) implicitly invokes the ToString method of the object being constructed to obtain the object's string representation.

```
 1    // Fig. 8.16: CommissionEmployee4.cs
 2    // CommissionEmployee4 class represents a commission employee.
 3    using System;
 4
 5    public class CommissionEmployee4
 6    {
 7       private string firstName;
 8       private string lastName;
 9       private string socialSecurityNumber;
10       private decimal grossSales; // gross weekly sales
11       private decimal commissionRate; // commission percentage
12
13       // five-parameter constructor
14       public CommissionEmployee4( string first, string last, string ssn,
15          decimal sales, decimal rate )
16       {
17          // implicit call to object constructor occurs here
18          firstName = first;
19          lastName = last;
20          socialSecurityNumber = ssn;
21          GrossSales = sales; // validate gross sales via property
22          CommissionRate = rate; // validate commission rate via property
23
24          Console.WriteLine( "\nCommissionEmployee4 constructor:\n" + this );
25       } // end five-parameter CommissionEmployee4 constructor
26
27       // read-only property that gets commission employee's first name
28       public string FirstName
29       {
30          get
31          {
32             return firstName;
33          } // end get
34       } // end property FirstName
35
36       // read-only property that gets commission employee's last name
37       public string LastName
38       {
39          get
40          {
41             return lastName;
42          } // end get
43       } // end property LastName
44
45       // read-only property that gets
46       // commission employee's social security number
47       public string SocialSecurityNumber
48       {
49          get
50          {
51             return socialSecurityNumber;
52          } // end get
53       } // end property SocialSecurityNumber
```

Fig. 8.16 | CommissionEmployee4 class represents a commission employee. (Part 1 of 2.)

```
54
55       // property that gets and sets commission employee's gross sales
56       public decimal GrossSales
57       {
58          get
59          {
60             return grossSales;
61          } // end get
62          set
63          {
64             grossSales = ( value < 0 ) ? 0 : value;
65          } // end set
66       } // end property GrossSales
67
68       // property that gets and sets commission employee's commission rate
69       public decimal CommissionRate
70       {
71          get
72          {
73             return commissionRate;
74          } // end get
75          set
76          {
77             commissionRate = ( value > 0 && value < 1 ) ? value : 0;
78          } // end set
79       } // end property CommissionRate
80
81       // calculate commission employee's pay
82       public virtual decimal Earnings()
83       {
84          return CommissionRate * GrossSales;
85       } // end method Earnings
86
87       // return string representation of CommissionEmployee object
88       public override string ToString()
89       {
90          return string.Format(
91             "{0}: {1} {2}\n{3}: {4}\n{5}: {6:C}\n{7}: {8:F2}",
92             "commission employee", FirstName, LastName,
93             "social security number", SocialSecurityNumber,
94             "gross sales", GrossSales, "commission rate", CommissionRate );
95       } // end method ToString
96    } // end class CommissionEmployee4
```

Fig. 8.16 | CommissionEmployee4 class represents a commission employee. (Part 2 of 2.)

Class BasePlusCommissionEmployee5 (Fig. 8.17) is almost identical to BasePlus-CommissionEmployee4 (Fig. 8.14), except that BasePlusCommissionEmployee5's constructor outputs text when invoked. As in CommissionEmployee4 (Fig. 8.16), we concatenate this with a string literal to implicitly obtain the object's string representation.

Figure 8.18 demonstrates the order in which constructors are called for objects of classes that are part of an inheritance hierarchy. Method Main begins by instantiating CommissionEmployee4 object employee1 (lines 10–11). Next, lines 14–16 instantiate

BasePlusCommissionEmployee5 object employee2. This invokes the CommissionEmployee4 constructor, which prints output with the values passed from the BasePlusCommissionEmployee5 constructor, then performs the output specified in the BasePlusCommissionEmployee5 constructor. Lines 19–21 then instantiate BasePlusCommissionEmployee5 object employee3. Again, the CommissionEmployee4 and BasePlusCommissionEmployee5 constructors are both called. In each case, the body of the CommissionEmployee4 constructor executes before the body of the BasePlusCommissionEmployee5 constructor. Note that employee2 is constructed completely before construction of employee3 begins.

```
1   // Fig. 8.17: BasePlusCommissionEmployee5.cs
2   // BasePlusCommissionEmployee5 class declaration.
3   using System;
4
5   public class BasePlusCommissionEmployee5 : CommissionEmployee4
6   {
7      private decimal baseSalary; // base salary per week
8
9      // six-parameter derived class constructor
10     // with call to base class CommissionEmployee4 constructor
11     public BasePlusCommissionEmployee5( string first, string last,
12        string ssn, decimal sales, decimal rate, decimal salary )
13        : base( first, last, ssn, sales, rate )
14     {
15        BaseSalary = salary; // validate base salary via property
16
17        Console.WriteLine(
18           "\nBasePlusCommissionEmployee5 constructor:\n" + this );
19     } // end six-parameter BasePlusCommissionEmployee5 constructor
20
21     // property that gets and sets
22     // base-salaried commission employee's base salary
23     public decimal BaseSalary
24     {
25        get
26        {
27           return baseSalary;
28        } // end get
29        set
30        {
31           baseSalary = ( value < 0 ) ? 0 : value;
32        } // end set
33     } // end property BaseSalary
34
35     // calculate earnings
36     public override decimal Earnings()
37     {
38        return BaseSalary + base.Earnings();
39     } // end method Earnings
40
```

Fig. 8.17 | BasePlusCommissionEmployee5 class declaration. (Part 1 of 2.)

```
41      // return string representation of BasePlusCommissionEmployee5
42      public override string ToString()
43      {
44          return string.Format( "{0} {1}\n{2}: {3:C}",
45              "base-salaried", base.ToString(), "base salary", BaseSalary );
46      } // end method ToString
47   } // end class BasePlusCommissionEmployee5
```

Fig. 8.17 | BasePlusCommissionEmployee5 class declaration. (Part 2 of 2.)

8.6 Software Engineering with Inheritance

This section discusses customizing existing software with inheritance. When a new class extends an existing class, the new class inherits the members of the existing class. We can customize the new class to meet our needs by including additional members and by overriding base class members. Doing this does not require the derived class programmer to change the base class's source code. C# simply requires access to the compiled base class code, so it can compile and execute any application that uses or extends the base class. This powerful capability is attractive to independent software vendors (ISVs), who can develop proprietary classes for sale or license and make them available to users in class libraries. Users then can derive new classes from these library classes rapidly, without accessing the ISVs' proprietary source code.

```
1    // Fig. 8.18: ConstructorTest.cs
2    // Display order in which base class and derived class constructors
3    // are called.
4    using System;
5
6    public class ConstructorTest
7    {
8        public static void Main( string[] args )
9        {
10           CommissionEmployee4 employee1 = new CommissionEmployee4( "Bob",
11               "Lewis", "333-33-3333", 5000.00M, .04M );
12
13           Console.WriteLine();
14           BasePlusCommissionEmployee5 employee2 =
15               new BasePlusCommissionEmployee5( "Lisa", "Jones",
16               "555-55-5555", 2000.00M, .06M, 800.00M );
17
18           Console.WriteLine();
19           BasePlusCommissionEmployee5 employee3 =
20               new BasePlusCommissionEmployee5( "Mark", "Sands",
21               "888-88-8888", 8000.00M, .15M, 2000.00M );
22       } // end Main
23   } // end class ConstructorTest
```

Fig. 8.18 | Display order in which base class and derived class constructors are called. (Part 1 of 2.)

```
CommissionEmployee4 constructor:
commission employee: Bob Lewis
social security number: 333-33-3333
gross sales: $5,000.00
commission rate: 0.04


CommissionEmployee4 constructor:
base-salaried commission employee: Lisa Jones
social security number: 555-55-5555
gross sales: $2,000.00
commission rate: 0.06
base salary: $0.00

BasePlusCommissionEmployee5 constructor:
base-salaried commission employee: Lisa Jones
social security number: 555-55-5555
gross sales: $2,000.00
commission rate: 0.06
base salary: $800.00


CommissionEmployee4 constructor:
base-salaried commission employee: Mark Sands
social security number: 888-88-8888
gross sales: $8,000.00
commission rate: 0.15
base salary: $0.00

BasePlusCommissionEmployee5 constructor:
base-salaried commission employee: Mark Sands
social security number: 888-88-8888
gross sales: $8,000.00
commission rate: 0.15
base salary: $2,000.00
```

Fig. 8.18 | Display order in which base class and derived class constructors are called. (Part 2 of 2.)

Software Engineering Observation 8.7

Despite the fact that inheriting from a class does not require access to the class's source code, developers often insist on seeing the source code to understand how the class is implemented. They may, for example, want to ensure that they are extending a class that performs well and is implemented securely.

Sometimes, students have difficulty appreciating the scope of the problems faced by designers who work on large-scale software projects in industry. People experienced with such projects say that effective software reuse improves the software development process. Object-oriented programming facilitates software reuse, potentially shortening development time. The availability of substantial and useful class libraries delivers the maximum benefits of software reuse through inheritance. The FCL class libraries that are used by C#

tend to be rather general purpose. Many special-purpose class libraries exist and more are being created.

Software Engineering Observation 8.8

At the design stage in an object-oriented system, the designer often finds that certain classes are closely related. The designer should "factor out" common members and place them in a base class. Then the designer should use inheritance to develop derived classes, specializing them with capabilities beyond those inherited from the base class.

Software Engineering Observation 8.9

Declaring a derived class does not affect its base class's source code. Inheritance preserves the integrity of the base class.

Software Engineering Observation 8.10

Just as designers of non-object-oriented systems should avoid method proliferation, designers of object-oriented systems should avoid class proliferation. Such proliferation creates management problems and can hinder software reusability, because in a huge class library it becomes difficult for a client to locate the most appropriate classes. The alternative is to create fewer classes that provide more substantial functionality, but such classes might prove cumbersome.

Performance Tip 8.1

If derived classes are larger than they need to be (i.e., contain too much functionality), memory and processing resources might be wasted. Extend the base class that contains the functionality that is closest to what is needed.

Reading derived class declarations can be confusing, because inherited members are not declared explicitly in the derived classes, but are nevertheless present in them. A similar problem exists in documenting derived class members.

8.7 Class object

As we discussed earlier in this chapter, all classes inherit directly or indirectly from the object class (System.Object in the FCL), so its seven methods are inherited by all other classes. Figure 8.19 summarizes object's methods.

We discuss several of object's methods throughout this book (as indicated in the table). You can learn more about object's methods in object's online documentation in the Framework Class Library Reference at:

msdn2.microsoft.com/en-us/library/system.object_members

All array types implicitly inherit from class Array in the System namespace, which in turn extends class object. As a result, like all other objects, an array inherits the members of class object. For more information about the class Array, please see Array's documentation in the FCL Reference, at:

msdn2.microsoft.com/en-us/library/system.array_members

Method	Description
Equals	This method compares two objects for equality and returns true if they are equal and false otherwise. The method takes any object as an argument. When objects of a particular class must be compared for equality, the class should override method Equals to compare the contents of the two objects. The method's implementation should meet the following requirements: It should return false if the argument is null.
	• It should return true if an object is compared to itself, as in object1.Equals(object1).
	• It should return true only if both object1.Equals(object2) and object2.Equals(object1) would return true.
	• For three objects, if object1.Equals(object2) returns true and object2.Equals(object3) returns true, then object1.Equals(object3) should also return true.
	• A class that overrides the method Equals should also override the method GetHashCode to ensure that equal objects have identical hashcodes. The default Equals implementation determines only whether two references *refer to the same object* in memory.
Finalize	This method cannot be explicitly declared or called. When a class contains a destructor, the compiler implicitly renames it to override the protected method Finalize, which is called only by the garbage collector before it reclaims an object's memory. The garbage collector is not guaranteed to reclaim an object, thus it is not guaranteed that an object's Finalize method will execute. When a derived class's Finalize method executes, it performs its task, then invokes the base class's Finalize method. Finalize's default implementation is a placeholder that simply invokes the base class's Finalize method.
GetHashCode	A hashtable is a data structure that relates one object, called the key, to another object, called the value. When initially inserting a value into a hashtable, the key's GetHashCode method is called. The hashcode value returned is used by the hashtable to determine the location at which to insert the corresponding value. The key's hashcode is also used by the hashtable to locate the key's corresponding value.
GetType	Every object knows its own type at execution time. Method GetType (used in Section 9.5) returns an object of class Type (namespace System) that contains information about the object's type, such as its class name (obtained from Type property FullName).
Memberwise-Clone	This protected method, which takes no arguments and returns an object reference, makes a copy of the object on which it is called. The implementation of this method performs a *shallow copy*—instance variable values in one object are copied into another object of the same type. For reference types, only the references are copied..

Fig. 8.19 | object methods that are inherited directly or indirectly by all classes. (Part 1 of 2.)

Method	Description
Reference-Equals	This static method takes two object arguments and returns true if two objects are the same instance or if they are null references. Otherwise, it returns false.
ToString	This method (introduced in Section 5.4) returns a string representation of an object. The default implementation of this method returns the namespace followed by a dot and the class name of the object's class.

Fig. 8.19 | object methods that are inherited directly or indirectly by all classes. (Part 2 of 2.)

8.8 Wrap-Up

This chapter introduced inheritance—the ability to create classes by absorbing an existing class's members and enhancing them with new capabilities. You learned the notions of base classes and derived classes and created a derived class that inherits members from a base class. The chapter introduced access modifier protected; derived class methods can access protected base class members. You learned how to access base class members with base. You also saw how constructors are used in inheritance hierarchies. Finally, you learned about the methods of class object, the direct or indirect base class of all classes.

In Chapter 9, Polymorphism, Interfaces & Operator Overloading, we build on our discussion of inheritance by introducing polymorphism—an object-oriented concept that enables us to write applications that handle, in a more general manner, objects of a wide variety of classes related by inheritance. After studying Chapter 9, you will be familiar with classes, objects, encapsulation, inheritance and polymorphism—the most essential aspects of object-oriented programming.

9

Polymorphism, Interfaces & Operator Overloading

One Ring to rule them all,
One Ring to find them,
One Ring to bring them all
and in the darkness bind
them.
—John Ronald Reuel Tolkien

General propositions do not
decide concrete cases.
—Oliver Wendell Holmes

A philosopher of imposing
stature doesn't think in a
vacuum. Even his most
abstract ideas are, to some
extent, conditioned by
what is or is not known
in the time when he lives.
—Alfred North Whitehead

Why art thou cast down,
O my soul?
—Psalms 42:5

OBJECTIVES

In this chapter you will learn:

- The concept of polymorphism and how it enables you to "program in the general."
- To use overridden methods to effect polymorphism.
- To distinguish between abstract and concrete classes.
- To declare abstract methods to create abstract classes.
- How polymorphism makes systems extensible and maintainable.
- To determine an object's type at execution time.
- To create `sealed` methods and classes.
- To declare and implement interfaces.
- To overload operators to enable them to manipulate objects.

9.1 Introduction

We now continue our study of object-oriented programming by explaining and demonstrating *polymorphism* with inheritance hierarchies. Polymorphism enables us to "program in the general" rather than "program in the specific." In particular, polymorphism enables us to write applications that process objects that share the same base class in a class hierarchy as if they are all objects of the base class.

Consider the following example of polymorphism. Suppose we create an application that simulates the movement of several types of animals for a biological study. Classes Fish, Frog and Bird represent the three types of animals under investigation. Imagine that each of these classes extends base class Animal, which contains a method Move and maintains an animal's current location as *x-y* coordinates. Each derived class implements method Move.

Our application maintains an array of references to objects of the various Animal derived classes. To simulate the animals' movements, the application sends each object the same message once per second—namely, Move. However, each specific type of Animal responds to a Move message in a unique way—a Fish might swim three feet, a Frog might jump five feet and a Bird might fly 10 feet. The application issues the same message (i.e., Move) to each animal object generically, but each object knows how to modify its *x-y* coordinates appropriately for its specific type of movement. Relying on each object to know how to "do the right thing" (i.e., do what is appropriate for that type of object) in response to the same method call is the key concept of polymorphism. The same message (in this case, Move) sent to a variety of objects has "many forms" of results—hence the term polymorphism.

With polymorphism, we can design and implement systems that are easily extensible— new classes can be added with little or no modification to the general portions of the application, as long as the new classes are part of the inheritance hierarchy that the application processes generically. The only parts of an application that must be altered to accommodate new classes are those that require direct knowledge of the new classes that the programmer adds to the hierarchy. For example, if we extend class Animal to create class Tortoise (which might respond to a Move message by crawling one inch), we need to write only the Tortoise class and the part of the simulation that instantiates a Tortoise object. The portions of the simulation that process each Animal generically can remain the same.

This chapter has several parts. First, we discuss common examples of polymorphism. We then provide a live-code example demonstrating polymorphic behavior. As you will soon see, you will use base class references to manipulate both base class objects and derived class objects polymorphically.

We then present a case study that revisits the employee hierarchy of Section 8.4.5. We develop a simple payroll application that polymorphically calculates the weekly pay of several different types of employees using each employee's Earnings method. Though the earnings of each type of employee are calculated in a specific way, polymorphism allows us to process the employees "in the general." In the case study, we enlarge the hierarchy to include two new classes—SalariedEmployee (for people paid a fixed weekly salary) and HourlyEmployee (for people paid an hourly salary and "time-and-a-half" for overtime). We declare a common set of functionality for all the classes in the updated hierarchy in an "abstract" class, Employee, from which classes SalariedEmployee, HourlyEmployee and CommissionEmployee inherit directly and class BasePlusCommissionEmployee4 inherits indirectly. As you will soon see, when we invoke each employee's Earnings method off a base class Employee reference, the correct earnings calculation is performed due to C#'s polymorphic capabilities.

Occasionally, when performing polymorphic processing, we need to program "in the specific." Our Employee case study demonstrates that an application can determine the type of an object at execution time and act on that object accordingly. In the case study, we use these capabilities to determine whether a particular employee object *is a* BasePlus-CommissionEmployee. If so, we increase that employee's base salary by 10%.

The chapter continues with an introduction to C# interfaces. An interface describes a set of methods and properties that can be called on an object, but does not provide concrete implementations for them. Programmers can declare classes that *implement* (i.e., provide concrete implementations for the methods and properties of) one or more interfaces. Each interface member must be declared in all the classes that implement the interface. Once a class implements an interface, all objects of that class have an *is-a* relationship with the interface type, and all objects of the class are guaranteed to provide the functionality described by the interface. This is true of all derived classes of that class as well.

Interfaces are particularly useful for assigning common functionality to possibly unrelated classes. This allows objects of unrelated classes to be processed polymorphically—objects of classes that implement the same interface can respond to the same method calls. To demonstrate creating and using interfaces, we modify our payroll application to create a general accounts-payable application that can calculate payments due for the earnings of company employees and for invoice amounts to be billed for purchased goods. As you will see, interfaces enable polymorphic capabilities similar to those enabled by inheritance.

This chapter ends with an introduction to operator overloading. In previous chapters, we declared our own classes and used methods to perform tasks on objects of those classes. Operator overloading allows us to define the behavior of the built-in operators, such as +, - and <, when used on objects of our own classes. This provides a much more convenient notation than calling methods for performing tasks on objects.

9.2 Polymorphism Examples

We now consider several additional examples of polymorphism. If class Rectangle is derived from class Quadrilateral (a four-sided shape), then a Rectangle is a more specific version of a Quadrilateral. Any operation (e.g., calculating the perimeter or the area) that can be performed on a Quadrilateral object can also be performed on a Rectangle object. These operations also can be performed on other Quadrilaterals, such as Squares, Parallelograms and Trapezoids. The polymorphism occurs when an application invokes a method through a base class variable—at execution time, the correct derived class version of the method is called, based on the type of the referenced object. You will see a simple code example that illustrates this process in Section 9.3.

As another example, suppose we design a video game that manipulates objects of many different types, including objects of classes Martian, Venusian, Plutonian, SpaceShip and LaserBeam. Imagine that each class inherits from the common base class SpaceObject, which contains method Draw. Each derived class implements this method. A screen-manager application maintains a collection (e.g., a SpaceObject array) of references to objects of the various classes. To refresh the screen, the screen manager periodically sends each object the same message—namely, Draw. However, each object responds in a unique way. For example, a Martian object might draw itself in red with the appropriate number of antennae. A SpaceShip object might draw itself as a bright silver flying saucer. A LaserBeam object might draw itself as a bright red beam across the screen. Again, the same message (in this case, Draw) sent to a variety of objects has "many forms" of results.

A polymorphic screen manager might use polymorphism to facilitate adding new classes to a system with minimal modifications to the system's code. Suppose we want to add Mercurian objects to our video game. To do so, we must build a Mercurian class that extends SpaceObject and provides its own Draw method implementation. When objects of class Mercurian appear in the SpaceObject collection, the screen manager code invokes method Draw, exactly as it does for every other object in the collection, regardless of its type. So the new Mercurian objects simply "plug right in" without any modification of the screen manager code by the programmer. Thus, without modifying the system (other than to build new classes and modify the code that creates new objects), programmers can use polymorphism to include additional types that might not have been envisioned when the system was created.

Software Engineering Observation 9.1

Polymorphism promotes extensibility: Software that invokes polymorphic behavior is independent of the object types to which messages are sent. New object types that can respond to existing method calls can be incorporated into a system without requiring modification of the base system. Only client code that instantiates new objects must be modified to accommodate new types.

9.3 Demonstrating Polymorphic Behavior

Section 8.4 created a commission employee class hierarchy, in which class BasePlusCommissionEmployee inherited from class CommissionEmployee. The examples in that section manipulated CommissionEmployee and BasePlusCommissionEmployee objects by using references to them to invoke their methods. We aimed base class references at base class objects and derived class references at derived class objects. These assignments are natural and straightforward—base class references are intended to refer to base class objects, and derived class references are intended to refer to derived class objects. However, other assignments are possible.

In the next example, we aim a base class reference at a derived class object. We then show how invoking a method on a derived class object via a base class reference invokes the derived class functionality—the type of the *actual referenced object*, not the type of the *reference*, determines which method is called. This example demonstrates the key concept that an object of a derived class can be treated as an object of its base class. This enables various interesting manipulations. An application can create an array of base class references that refer to objects of many derived class types. This is allowed because each derived class object *is an* object of its base class. For instance, we can assign the reference of a BasePlusCommissionEmployee object to a base class CommissionEmployee variable because a BasePlusCommissionEmployee *is a* CommissionEmployee—so we can treat a BasePlusCommissionEmployee as a CommissionEmployee.

A base class object is not an object of any of its derived classes. For example, we cannot assign the reference of a CommissionEmployee object to a derived class BasePlusCommissionEmployee variable because a CommissionEmployee is not a BasePlusCommissionEmployee—a CommissionEmployee does not, for example, have a baseSalary instance variable and does not have a BaseSalary property. The *is-a* relationship applies from a derived class to its direct and indirect base classes, but not vice versa.

It turns out that the compiler does allow the assignment of a base class reference to a derived class variable if we explicitly cast the base class reference to the derived class type—a technique we discuss in greater detail in Section 9.5.6. Why would we ever want to perform such an assignment? A base class reference can be used to invoke only the methods declared in the base class—attempting to invoke derived-class-only methods through a base class reference results in compilation errors. If an application needs to perform a derived-class-specific operation on a derived class object referenced by a base class variable, the application must first cast the base class reference to a derived class reference through a technique known as ***downcasting***. This enables the application to invoke derived class methods that are not in the base class. We present a concrete example of downcasting in Section 9.5.6.

The example in Fig. 9.1 demonstrates three ways to use base class and derived class variables to store references to base class and derived class objects. The first two are straightforward—as in Section 8.4, we assign a base class reference to a base class variable, and we assign a derived class reference to a derived class variable. Then we demonstrate the relationship between derived classes and base classes (i.e., the *is-a* relationship) by assigning

```csharp
1   // Fig. 9.1: PolymorphismTest.cs
2   // Assigning base class and derived class references to base class and
3   // derived class variables.
4   using System;
5
6   public class PolymorphismTest
7   {
8      public static void Main( string[] args )
9      {
10        // assign base class reference to base class variable
11        CommissionEmployee3 commissionEmployee = new CommissionEmployee3(
12           "Sue", "Jones", "222-22-2222", 10000.00M, .06M );
13
14        // assign derived class reference to derived class variable
15        BasePlusCommissionEmployee4 basePlusCommissionEmployee =
16           new BasePlusCommissionEmployee4( "Bob", "Lewis",
17           "333-33-3333", 5000.00M, .04M, 300.00M );
18
19        // invoke ToString and Earnings on base class object
20        // using base class variable
21        Console.WriteLine( "{0} {1}:\n\n{2}\n{3}: {4:C}\n",
22           "Call CommissionEmployee3's ToString with base class reference",
23           "to base class object", commissionEmployee.ToString(),
24           "earnings", commissionEmployee.Earnings() );
25
26        // invoke ToString and Earnings on derived class object
27        // using derived class variable
28        Console.WriteLine( "{0} {1}:\n\n{2}\n{3}: {4:C}\n",
29           "Call BasePlusCommissionEmployee4's ToString with derived class",
30           "reference to derived class object",
31           basePlusCommissionEmployee.ToString(),
32           "earnings", basePlusCommissionEmployee.Earnings() );
33
34        // invoke ToString and Earnings on derived class object
35        // using base class variable
36        CommissionEmployee3 commissionEmployee2 =
37           basePlusCommissionEmployee;
38        Console.WriteLine( "{0} {1}:\n\n{2}\n{3}: {4:C}",
39           "Call BasePlusCommissionEmployee4's ToString with base class",
40           "reference to derived class object",
41           commissionEmployee2.ToString(), "earnings",
42           commissionEmployee2.Earnings() );
43     } // end Main
44  } // end class PolymorphismTest
```

Fig. 9.1 | Assigning base class and derived class references to base class and derived class variables. (Part 1 of 2.)

```
Call CommissionEmployee3's ToString with base class reference to base class
object:

commission employee: Sue Jones
social security number: 222-22-2222
gross sales: $10,000.00
commission rate: 0.06
earnings: $600.00

Call BasePlusCommissionEmployee4's ToString with derived class reference to
derived class object:

base-salaried commission employee: Bob Lewis
social security number: 333-33-3333
gross sales: $5,000.00
commission rate: 0.04
base salary: $300.00
earnings: $500.00

Call BasePlusCommissionEmployee4's ToString with base class reference to
derived class object:

base-salaried commission employee: Bob Lewis
social security number: 333-33-3333
gross sales: $5,000.00
commission rate: 0.04
base salary: $300.00
earnings: $500.00
```

Fig. 9.1 | Assigning base class and derived class references to base class and derived class variables. (Part 2 of 2.)

a derived class reference to a base class variable. [*Note:* This application uses classes CommissionEmployee3 and BasePlusCommissionEmployee4 from Fig. 8.13 and Fig. 8.14, respectively.]

In Fig. 9.1, lines 11–12 create a new CommissionEmployee3 object and assign its reference to a CommissionEmployee3 variable. Lines 15–17 create a new BasePlusCommissionEmployee4 object and assign its reference to a BasePlusCommissionEmployee4 variable. These assignments are natural—for example, a CommissionEmployee3 variable's primary purpose is to hold a reference to a CommissionEmployee3 object. Lines 21–24 use the reference commissionEmployee to invoke methods ToString and Earnings. Because commissionEmployee refers to a CommissionEmployee3 object, base class CommissionEmployee3's version of the methods are called. Similarly, lines 28–32 use basePlusCommissionEmployee to invoke the methods ToString and Earnings on the BasePlusCommissionEmployee4 object. This invokes derived class BasePlusCommissionEmployee4's version of the methods.

Lines 36–37 then assign the reference to derived class object basePlusCommissionEmployee to a base class CommissionEmployee3 variable, which lines 38–42 use to invoke methods ToString and Earnings. A base class variable that contains a reference to a derived class object and is used to call a virtual method actually calls the overriding derived class version of the method. Hence, commissionEmployee2.ToString() in line 41 actually calls class BasePlusCommissionEmployee4's ToString method. The compiler allows this "crossover" because an object of a derived class *is an* object of its base class (but not vice versa). When the compiler encounters a method call made through a variable, the compiler determines if the method can be called by checking the *variable's* class type. If that class contains the proper method declaration (or inherits one), the compiler allows the call to be compiled. At execution time, *the type of the object to which the variable refers* determines the actual method to use.

9.4 Abstract Classes and Methods

When we think of a class type, we assume that applications will create objects of that type. In some cases, however, it is useful to declare classes for which the programmer never intends to instantiate objects. Such classes are called *abstract classes*. Because they are used only as base classes in inheritance hierarchies, we refer to them as *abstract base classes*. These classes cannot be used to instantiate objects, because as you will soon see, abstract classes are incomplete—derived classes must declare the "missing pieces." We demonstrate abstract classes in Section 9.5.1.

The purpose of an abstract class is primarily to provide an appropriate base class from which other classes can inherit, and thus share a common design. In the Shape hierarchy of Fig. 8.3, for example, derived classes inherit the notion of what it means to be a Shape—common attributes such as location, color and borderThickness, and behaviors such as Draw, Move, Resize and ChangeColor. Classes that can be used to instantiate objects are called *concrete classes*. Such classes provide implementations of *every* method they declare (some of the implementations can be inherited). For example, we could derive concrete classes Circle, Square and Triangle from abstract base class TwoDimensionalShape. Similarly, we could derive concrete classes Sphere, Cube and Tetrahedron from abstract base class ThreeDimensionalShape. Abstract base classes are too general to create real objects—they specify only what is common among derived classes. We need to be more specific before we can create objects. For example, if you send the Draw message to abstract class TwoDimensionalShape, the class knows that two-dimensional shapes should be drawable, but it does not know what specific shape to draw, so it cannot implement a real Draw method. Concrete classes provide the specifics that make it reasonable to instantiate objects.

Not all inheritance hierarchies contain abstract classes. However, programmers often write client code that uses only abstract base class types to reduce client code's dependencies on a range of specific derived class types. For example, a programmer can write a method with a parameter of an abstract base class type. When called, such a method can be passed an object of any concrete class that directly or indirectly extends the base class specified as the parameter's type.

Abstract classes sometimes constitute several levels of the hierarchy. For example, the Shape hierarchy of Fig. 8.3 begins with abstract class Shape. On the next level of the hierarchy are two more abstract classes, TwoDimensionalShape and ThreeDimensionalShape. The next level of the hierarchy declares concrete classes for TwoDimensionalShapes (Circle, Square and Triangle) and for ThreeDimensionalShapes (Sphere, Cube and Tetrahedron).

You make a class abstract by declaring it with keyword abstract. An abstract class normally contains one or more *abstract methods*. An abstract method is one with keyword abstract in its declaration, as in

```
public abstract void Draw(); // abstract method
```

Abstract methods do not provide implementations. A class that contains abstract methods must be declared as an abstract class even if that class contains concrete (non-abstract) methods. Each concrete derived class of an abstract base class also must provide concrete implementations of the base class's abstract methods. We show an example of an abstract class with an abstract method in Fig. 9.4.

Properties can also be declared abstract, then overridden in derived classes with the override keyword, just like methods. This allows an abstract base class to specify common properties of its derived classes. Abstract property declarations have the form:

```
public abstract PropertyType MyProperty
{
    get;
    set;
} // end abstract property
```

The semicolons after the get and set keywords indicate that we provide no implementation for these accessors. An abstract property may omit implementations for the get accessor, the set accessor or both. Concrete derived classes must provide implementations for *every* accessor declared in the abstract property. When both get and set accessors are specified (as above), every concrete derived class must implement both. If one accessor is omitted, the derived class is not allowed to implement that accessor. Doing so causes a compilation error.

Constructors and static methods cannot be declared abstract. Constructors are not inherited, so an abstract constructor could never be implemented. Similarly, derived classes cannot override static methods, so an abstract static method could never be implemented.

Software Engineering Observation 9.2

An abstract class declares common attributes and behaviors of the various classes that inherit from it, either directly or indirectly, in a class hierarchy. An abstract class typically contains one or more abstract methods or properties that concrete derived classes must override. The instance variables, concrete methods and concrete properties of an abstract class are subject to the normal rules of inheritance.

Common Programming Error 9.1

Attempting to instantiate an object of an abstract class is a compilation error.

Common Programming Error 9.2

Failure to implement a base class's abstract methods and properties in a derived class is a compilation error unless the derived class is also declared abstract.

Although we cannot instantiate objects of abstract base classes, you will soon see that we *can* use abstract base classes to declare variables that can hold references to objects of any concrete classes derived from those abstract classes. Applications typically use such variables to manipulate derived class objects polymorphically. Also, you can use abstract base class names to invoke static methods declared in those abstract base classes.

Polymorphism is particularly effective for implementing so-called layered software systems. In operating systems, for example, each type of physical device could operate quite differently from the others. Even so, common commands can read or write data from and to the devices. For each device, the operating system uses a piece of software called a device driver to control all communication between the system and the device. The write message sent to a device driver object needs to be interpreted specifically in the context of that driver and how it manipulates a specific device. However, the write call itself really is no different from the write to any other device in the system: Place some number of bytes from memory onto that device. An object-oriented operating system might use an abstract base class to provide an "interface" appropriate for all device drivers. Then, through inheritance from that abstract base class, derived classes are formed that all behave similarly. The device driver methods are declared as abstract methods in the abstract base class. The implementations of these abstract methods are provided in the derived classes that correspond to the specific types of device drivers. New devices are always being developed, often long after the operating system has been released. When you buy a new device, it comes with a device driver provided by the device vendor. The device is immediately operational after you connect it to your computer and install the device driver. This is another elegant example of how polymorphism makes systems extensible.

It is common in object-oriented programming to declare an *iterator class* that can traverse all the objects in a collection, such as an array (Chapter 6) or an ArrayList. For example, an application can print an ArrayList of objects by creating an iterator object and using it to obtain the next list element each time the iterator is called. Iterators often are used in polymorphic programming to traverse a collection that contains references to objects of various classes in an inheritance hierarchy. An ArrayList of references to objects of class TwoDimensionalShape, for example, could contain references to objects from derived classes Square, Circle, Triangle and so on. Calling method Draw for each TwoDimensionalShape object off a TwoDimensionalShape variable would polymorphically draw each object correctly on the screen.

9.5 Case Study: Payroll System Using Polymorphism

This section reexamines the CommissionEmployee-BasePlusCommissionEmployee hierarchy that we explored throughout Section 8.4. Now we use an abstract method and polymorphism to perform payroll calculations based on the type of employee. We create an enhanced employee hierarchy to solve the following problem:

> *A company pays its employees on a weekly basis. The employees are of four types: Salaried employees are paid a fixed weekly salary regardless of the number of hours worked, hourly employees are paid by the hour and receive overtime pay for all hours worked in excess of 40 hours, commission employees are paid a percentage of their sales, and salaried-commission employees receive a base salary plus a percentage of their sales. For the current pay period, the company has decided to reward salaried-commission employees by adding 10% to their base salaries. The company wants to implement a C# application that performs its payroll calculations polymorphically.*

We use abstract class Employee to represent the general concept of an employee. The classes that extend Employee are SalariedEmployee, CommissionEmployee and HourlyEmployee. Class BasePlusCommissionEmployee—which extends CommissionEmployee—

represents the last employee type. The UML class diagram in Fig. 9.2 shows the inheritance hierarchy for our polymorphic employee payroll application. Note that abstract class Employee is italicized, as per the convention of the UML.

Abstract base class Employee declares the "interface" to the hierarchy—that is, the set of methods that an application can invoke on all Employee objects. We use the term "interface" here in a general sense to refer to the various ways applications can communicate with objects of any Employee derived class. Be careful not to confuse the general notion of an "interface" with the formal notion of a C# interface, the subject of Section 9.7. Each employee, regardless of the way his or her earnings are calculated, has a first name, a last name and a social security number, so private instance variables firstName, lastName and socialSecurityNumber appear in abstract base class Employee.

Software Engineering Observation 9.3

*A derived class can inherit "interface" or "implementation" from a base class. Hierarchies designed for **implementation inheritance** tend to have their functionality high in the hierarchy—each new derived class inherits one or more methods that were implemented in a base class, and the derived class uses the base class implementations. Hierarchies designed for **interface inheritance** tend to have their functionality lower in the hierarchy—a base class specifies one or more abstract methods that must be declared for each concrete class in the hierarchy, and the individual derived classes override these methods to provide derived-class-specific implementations.*

The following sections implement the Employee class hierarchy. The first section implements abstract base class Employee. The next four sections each implement one of the concrete classes. The sixth section implements a test application that builds objects of all these classes and processes those objects polymorphically.

9.5.1 Creating Abstract Base Class Employee

Class Employee (Fig. 9.4) provides methods Earnings and ToString, in addition to the properties that manipulate Employee's instance variables. An Earnings method certainly applies generically to all employees. But each earnings calculation depends on the employee's class. So we declare Earnings as abstract in base class Employee, because a default implementation does not make sense for that method—there is not enough information to determine what amount Earnings should return. Each derived class overrides Earnings with an appropriate implementation. To calculate an employee's earnings, the application

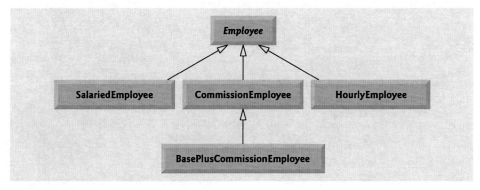

Fig. 9.2 | Employee hierarchy UML class diagram.

assigns a reference to the employee's object to a base class `Employee` variable, then invokes the `Earnings` method on that variable. We maintain an array of `Employee` variables, each of which holds a reference to an `Employee` object (of course, there cannot be `Employee` objects because `Employee` is an abstract class—because of inheritance, however, all objects of all derived classes of `Employee` may nevertheless be thought of as `Employee` objects). The application iterates through the array and calls method `Earnings` for each `Employee` object. C# processes these method calls polymorphically. Including `Earnings` as an abstract method in `Employee` forces every directly derived concrete class of `Employee` to override `Earnings` with a method that performs an appropriate pay calculation.

Method `ToString` in class `Employee` returns a `string` containing the first name, last name and social security number of the employee. Each derived class of `Employee` overrides method `ToString` to create a string representation of an object of that class containing the employee's type (e.g., `"salaried employee:"`), followed by the rest of the employee's information.

The diagram in Fig. 9.3 shows each of the five classes in the hierarchy down the left side and methods `Earnings` and `ToString` across the top. For each class, the diagram shows the desired results of each method. [*Note:* We do not list base class `Employee`'s properties because they are not overridden in any of the derived classes—each of these properties is inherited and used "as is" by each of the derived classes.]

	Earnings	ToString
Employee	abstract	*firstName lastName* social security number: *SSN*
Salaried-Employee	weeklySalary	salaried employee: *firstName lastName* social security number: *SSN* weekly salary: *weeklysalary*

Hourly-Employee	*If hours <= 40*
	  wage * hours
	If hours > 40
	  40 * wage +
	  (hours - 40) *
	  wage * 1.5
		hourly employee: *firstName lastName*
		social security number: *SSN*
		hourly wage: *wage*
		hours worked: *hours*

Commission-Employee	commissionRate * grossSales	commission employee: *firstName lastName* social security number: *SSN* gross sales: *grossSales* commission rate: *commissionRate*
BasePlus-Commission-Employee	(commissionRate * grossSales) + baseSalary	base salaried commission employee: *firstName lastName* social security number: *SSN* gross sales: *grossSales* commission rate: *commissionRate* base salary: *baseSalary*

Fig. 9.3 | Polymorphic interface for the `Employee` hierarchy classes.

Let us consider class Employee's declaration (Fig. 9.4). The class includes a constructor that takes the first name, last name and social security number as arguments (lines 10–15); read-only properties for obtaining the first name, last name and social security number (lines 18–24, 27–33 and 36–42, respectively); method ToString (lines 45–49), which uses properties to return the string representation of Employee; and abstract method Earnings (line 52), which must be implemented by concrete derived classes. Note that the Employee constructor does not validate the social security number in this example. Normally, such validation should be provided.

```
1   // Fig. 9.4: Employee.cs
2   // Employee abstract base class.
3   public abstract class Employee
4   {
5      private string firstName;
6      private string lastName;
7      private string socialSecurityNumber;
8
9      // three-parameter constructor
10     public Employee( string first, string last, string ssn )
11     {
12        firstName = first;
13        lastName = last;
14        socialSecurityNumber = ssn;
15     } // end three-parameter Employee constructor
16
17     // read-only property that gets employee's first name
18     public string FirstName
19     {
20        get
21        {
22           return firstName;
23        } // end get
24     } // end property FirstName
25
26     // read-only property that gets employee's last name
27     public string LastName
28     {
29        get
30        {
31           return lastName;
32        } // end get
33     } // end property LastName
34
35     // read-only property that gets employee's social security number
36     public string SocialSecurityNumber
37     {
38        get
39        {
40           return socialSecurityNumber;
41        } // end get
42     } // end property SocialSecurityNumber
```

Fig. 9.4 | Employee abstract base class. (Part 1 of 2.)

```
43
44        // return string representation of Employee object, using properties
45        public override string ToString()
46        {
47           return string.Format( "{0} {1}\nsocial security number: {2}",
48              FirstName, LastName, SocialSecurityNumber );
49        } // end method ToString
50
51        // abstract method overridden by derived classes
52        public abstract decimal Earnings(); // no implementation here
53     } // end abstract class Employee
```

Fig. 9.4 | Employee abstract base class. (Part 2 of 2.)

Why did we declare Earnings as an abstract method? It simply does not make sense to provide an implementation of this method in class Employee. We cannot calculate the earnings for a general Employee—we first must know the specific Employee type to determine the appropriate earnings calculation. By declaring this method abstract, we indicate that each concrete derived class *must* provide an appropriate Earnings implementation and that an application will be able to use base class Employee variables to invoke method Earnings polymorphically for any type of Employee.

9.5.2 Creating Concrete Derived Class SalariedEmployee

Class SalariedEmployee (Fig. 9.5) extends class Employee (line 3) and overrides Earnings (lines 28–31), which makes SalariedEmployee a concrete class. The class includes a constructor (lines 8–12) that takes a first name, a last name, a social security number and a weekly salary as arguments; property WeeklySalary to manipulate instance variable weeklySalary, including a set accessor that ensures we assign only non-negative values to weeklySalary (lines 15–25); method Earnings (lines 28–31) to calculate a SalariedEmployee's earnings; and method ToString (lines 34–38), which returns a string including the employee's type, namely, "salaried employee: ", followed by employee-specific information produced by base class Employee's ToString method and SalariedEmployee's WeeklySalary property. Class SalariedEmployee's constructor passes the first name, last name and social security number to the Employee constructor (line 9) via a constructor initializer to initialize the private instance variables not inherited from the base class. Method Earnings overrides Employee's abstract method Earnings to provide a concrete implementation that returns the SalariedEmployee's weekly salary. If we do not implement Earnings, class SalariedEmployee must be declared abstract—otherwise, a compilation error occurs (and, of course, we want SalariedEmployee to be a concrete class).

Method ToString (lines 34–38) of class SalariedEmployee overrides Employee method ToString. If class SalariedEmployee did not override ToString, SalariedEmployee would have inherited the Employee version of ToString. In that case, SalariedEmployee's ToString method would simply return the employee's full name and social security number, which does not adequately represent a SalariedEmployee. To produce a complete string representation of a SalariedEmployee, the derived class's ToString method returns "salaried employee: ", followed by the base class Employee-specific information (i.e., first name, last name and social security number) obtained by invoking

```
1   // Fig. 9.5: SalariedEmployee.cs
2   // SalariedEmployee class that extends Employee.
3   public class SalariedEmployee : Employee
4   {
5      private decimal weeklySalary;
6
7      // four-parameter constructor
8      public SalariedEmployee( string first, string last, string ssn,
9         decimal salary ) : base( first, last, ssn )
10     {
11        WeeklySalary = salary; // validate salary via property
12     } // end four-parameter SalariedEmployee constructor
13
14     // property that gets and sets salaried employee's salary
15     public decimal WeeklySalary
16     {
17        get
18        {
19           return weeklySalary;
20        } // end get
21        set
22        {
23           weeklySalary = ( ( value >= 0 ) ? value : 0 ); // validation
24        } // end set
25     } // end property WeeklySalary
26
27     // calculate earnings; override abstract method Earnings in Employee
28     public override decimal Earnings()
29     {
30        return WeeklySalary;
31     } // end method Earnings
32
33     // return string representation of SalariedEmployee object
34     public override string ToString()
35     {
36        return string.Format( "salaried employee: {0}\n{1}: {2:C}",
37           base.ToString(), "weekly salary", WeeklySalary );
38     } // end method ToString
39  } // end class SalariedEmployee
```

Fig. 9.5 | SalariedEmployee class that extends Employee.

the base class's ToString (line 37)—this is a nice example of code reuse. The string representation of a SalariedEmployee also contains the employee's weekly salary, obtained by using the class's WeeklySalary property.

9.5.3 Creating Concrete Derived Class HourlyEmployee

Class HourlyEmployee (Fig. 9.6) also extends class Employee (line 3). The class includes a constructor (lines 9–15) that takes as arguments a first name, a last name, a social security number, an hourly wage and the number of hours worked. Lines 18–28 and 31–42 declare properties Wage and Hours for instance variables wage and hours, respectively. The set accessor in property Wage (lines 24–27) ensures that wage is non-negative, and the set accessor in

```
1   // Fig. 9.6: HourlyEmployee.cs
2   // HourlyEmployee class that extends Employee.
3   public class HourlyEmployee : Employee
4   {
5      private decimal wage; // wage per hour
6      private decimal hours; // hours worked for the week
7
8      // five-parameter constructor
9      public HourlyEmployee( string first, string last, string ssn,
10        decimal hourlyWage, decimal hoursWorked )
11        : base( first, last, ssn )
12     {
13        Wage = hourlyWage; // validate hourly wage via property
14        Hours = hoursWorked; // validate hours worked via property
15     } // end five-parameter HourlyEmployee constructor
16
17     // property that gets and sets hourly employee's wage
18     public decimal Wage
19     {
20        get
21        {
22           return wage;
23        } // end get
24        set
25        {
26           wage = ( value >= 0 ) ? value : 0; // validation
27        } // end set
28     } // end property Wage
29
30     // property that gets and sets hourly employee's hours
31     public decimal Hours
32     {
33        get
34        {
35           return hours;
36        } // end get
37        set
38        {
39           hours = ( ( value >= 0 ) && ( value <= 168 ) ) ?
40                    value : 0; // validation
41        } // end set
42     } // end property Hours
43
44     // calculate earnings; override Employee's abstract method Earnings
45     public override decimal Earnings()
46     {
47        if ( Hours <= 40 ) // no overtime
48           return Wage * Hours;
49        else
50           return ( 40 * Wage ) + ( ( Hours - 40 ) * Wage * 1.5M );
51     } // end method Earnings
52
```

Fig. 9.6 | HourlyEmployee class that extends Employee. (Part 1 of 2.)

```
53        // return string representation of HourlyEmployee object
54        public override string ToString()
55        {
56           return string.Format(
57              "hourly employee: {0}\n{1}: {2:C}; {3}: {4:F2}",
58              base.ToString(), "hourly wage", Wage, "hours worked", Hours );
59        } // end method ToString
60     } // end class HourlyEmployee
```

Fig. 9.6 | HourlyEmployee class that extends Employee. (Part 2 of 2.)

property Hours (lines 37–41) ensures that hours is in the range 0–168 (the total number of hours in a week) inclusive. Class HourlyEmployee also includes method Earnings (lines 45–51) to calculate an HourlyEmployee's earnings; and method ToString (lines 54–59), which returns the employee's type, namely, "hourly employee: ", and employee-specific information. Note that the HourlyEmployee constructor, like the SalariedEmployee constructor, passes the first name, last name and social security number to the base class Employee constructor (line 11) to initialize the base class's private instance variables. Also, method ToString calls base class method ToString (line 58) to obtain the Employee-specific information (i.e., first name, last name and social security number)—this is another nice example of code reuse.

9.5.4 Creating Concrete Derived Class CommissionEmployee

Class CommissionEmployee (Fig. 9.7) extends class Employee (line 3). The class includes a constructor (lines 9–14) that takes a first name, a last name, a social security number, a sales amount and a commission rate; properties (lines 17–28 and 31–41) for instance variables commissionRate and grossSales, respectively; method Earnings (lines 44–47) to calculate a CommissionEmployee's earnings; and method ToString (lines 50–55), which returns the employee's type, namely, "commission employee: ", and employee-specific information.

```
1     // Fig. 9.7: CommissionEmployee.cs
2     // CommissionEmployee class that extends Employee.
3     public class CommissionEmployee : Employee
4     {
5        private decimal grossSales; // gross weekly sales
6        private decimal commissionRate; // commission percentage
7
8        // five-parameter constructor
9        public CommissionEmployee( string first, string last, string ssn,
10          decimal sales, decimal rate ) : base( first, last, ssn )
11       {
12          GrossSales = sales; // validate gross sales via property
13          CommissionRate = rate; // validate commission rate via property
14       } // end five-parameter CommissionEmployee constructor
15
16       // property that gets and sets commission employee's commission rate
17       public decimal CommissionRate
18       {
```

Fig. 9.7 | CommissionEmployee class that extends Employee. (Part 1 of 2.)

```
19            get
20            {
21               return commissionRate;
22            } // end get
23            set
24            {
25               commissionRate = ( value > 0 && value < 1 ) ?
26                              value : 0; // validation
27            } // end set
28         } // end property CommissionRate
29
30         // property that gets and sets commission employee's gross sales
31         public decimal GrossSales
32         {
33            get
34            {
35               return grossSales;
36            } // end get
37            set
38            {
39               grossSales = ( value >= 0 ) ? value : 0; // validation
40            } // end set
41         } // end property GrossSales
42
43         // calculate earnings; override abstract method Earnings in Employee
44         public override decimal Earnings()
45         {
46            return CommissionRate * GrossSales;
47         } // end method Earnings
48
49         // return string representation of CommissionEmployee object
50         public override string ToString()
51         {
52            return string.Format( "{0}: {1}\n{2}: {3:C}\n{4}: {5:F2}",
53               "commission employee", base.ToString(),
54               "gross sales", GrossSales, "commission rate", CommissionRate );
55         } // end method ToString
56      } // end class CommissionEmployee
```

Fig. 9.7 | CommissionEmployee class that extends Employee. (Part 2 of 2.)

The CommissionEmployee's constructor also passes the first name, last name and social security number to the Employee constructor (line 10) to initialize Employee's private instance variables. Method ToString calls base class method ToString (line 53) to obtain the Employee-specific information (i.e., first name, last name and social security number).

9.5.5 Creating Indirect Concrete Derived Class BasePlusCommissionEmployee

Class BasePlusCommissionEmployee (Fig. 9.8) extends class CommissionEmployee (line 3) and therefore is an indirect derived class of class Employee. Class BasePlusCommissionEmployee has a constructor (lines 8–13) that takes as arguments a first name, a last name, a social security number, a sales amount, a commission rate and a base salary. It then passes the first name, last name, social security number, sales amount and commission rate to the CommissionEmployee constructor (line 10) to initialize the base class's private data members. BasePlusCommissionEmployee also contains property BaseSalary (lines 17–27) to manipulate instance variable baseSalary. Method Earnings (lines 30–33) calculates a BasePlusCommissionEmployee's earnings. Note that line 32 in method Earnings calls base class CommissionEmployee's Earnings method to calculate the commission-based portion of the employee's earnings. This is another nice example of code reuse. BasePlusCommissionEmployee's ToString method (lines 36–40) creates a string representation of a BasePlusCommissionEmployee that contains "base-salaried", followed by the string obtained by invoking base class CommissionEmployee's ToString method (another example of code reuse), then the base salary. The result is a string beginning with "base-salaried commission employee", followed by the rest of the BasePlusCommissionEmployee's information. Recall that CommissionEmployee's ToString method obtains the employee's first name, last name and social security number by invoking the ToString method of its base class (i.e., Employee)—yet another example of code reuse. Note that BasePlusCommissionEmployee's ToString initiates a chain of method calls that span all three levels of the Employee hierarchy.

```
1   // Fig. 9.8: BasePlusCommissionEmployee.cs
2   // BasePlusCommissionEmployee class that extends CommissionEmployee.
3   public class BasePlusCommissionEmployee : CommissionEmployee
4   {
5      private decimal baseSalary; // base salary per week
6
7      // six-parameter constructor
8      public BasePlusCommissionEmployee( string first, string last,
9         string ssn, decimal sales, decimal rate, decimal salary )
10        : base( first, last, ssn, sales, rate )
11     {
12        BaseSalary = salary; // validate base salary via property
13     } // end six-parameter BasePlusCommissionEmployee constructor
14
15     // property that gets and sets
16     // base-salaried commission employee's base salary
17     public decimal BaseSalary
18     {
19        get
20        {
21           return baseSalary;
22        } // end get
23        set
24        {
25           baseSalary = ( value >= 0 ) ? value : 0; // validation
26        } // end set
27     } // end property BaseSalary
28
```

Fig. 9.8 | BasePlusCommissionEmployee class that extends CommissionEmployee. (Part 1 of 2.)

```
29        // calculate earnings; override method Earnings in CommissionEmployee
30        public override decimal Earnings()
31        {
32           return BaseSalary + base.Earnings();
33        } // end method Earnings
34
35        // return string representation of BasePlusCommissionEmployee object
36        public override string ToString()
37        {
38           return string.Format( "{0} {1}; {2}: {3:C}",
39              "base-salaried", base.ToString(), "base salary", BaseSalary );
40        } // end method ToString
41     } // end class BasePlusCommissionEmployee
```

Fig. 9.8 | BasePlusCommissionEmployee class that extends CommissionEmployee. (Part 2 of 2.)

9.5.6 Polymorphic Processing, Operator is and Downcasting

To test our Employee hierarchy, the application in Fig. 9.9 creates an object of each of the four concrete classes SalariedEmployee, HourlyEmployee, CommissionEmployee and BasePlusCommissionEmployee. The application manipulates these objects, first via variables of each object's own type, then polymorphically, using an array of Employee variables. While processing the objects polymorphically, the application increases the base salary of each BasePlusCommissionEmployee by 10% (this, of course, requires determining the

```
1     // Fig. 9.9: PayrollSystemTest.cs
2     // Employee hierarchy test application.
3     using System;
4
5     public class PayrollSystemTest
6     {
7        public static void Main( string[] args )
8        {
9           // create derived class objects
10          SalariedEmployee salariedEmployee =
11             new SalariedEmployee( "John", "Smith", "111-11-1111", 800.00M );
12          HourlyEmployee hourlyEmployee =
13             new HourlyEmployee( "Karen", "Price",
14             "222-22-2222", 16.75M, 40.0M );
15          CommissionEmployee commissionEmployee =
16             new CommissionEmployee( "Sue", "Jones",
17             "333-33-3333", 10000.00M, .06M );
18          BasePlusCommissionEmployee basePlusCommissionEmployee =
19             new BasePlusCommissionEmployee( "Bob", "Lewis",
20             "444-44-4444", 5000.00M, .04M, 300.00M );
21
22          Console.WriteLine( "Employees processed individually:\n" );
```

Fig. 9.9 | Employee hierarchy test application. (Part 1 of 3.)

```
23
24        Console.WriteLine( "{0}\n{1}: {2:C}\n",
25           salariedEmployee, "earned", salariedEmployee.Earnings() );
26        Console.WriteLine( "{0}\n{1}: {2:C}\n",
27           hourlyEmployee, "earned", hourlyEmployee.Earnings() );
28        Console.WriteLine( "{0}\n{1}: {2:C}\n",
29           commissionEmployee, "earned", commissionEmployee.Earnings() );
30        Console.WriteLine( "{0}\n{1}: {2:C}\n",
31           basePlusCommissionEmployee,
32           "earned", basePlusCommissionEmployee.Earnings() );
33
34        // create four-element Employee array
35        Employee[] employees = new Employee[ 4 ];
36
37        // initialize array with Employees of derived types
38        employees[ 0 ] = salariedEmployee;
39        employees[ 1 ] = hourlyEmployee;
40        employees[ 2 ] = commissionEmployee;
41        employees[ 3 ] = basePlusCommissionEmployee;
42
43        Console.WriteLine( "Employees processed polymorphically:\n" );
44
45        // generically process each element in array employees
46        foreach ( Employee currentEmployee in employees )
47        {
48           Console.WriteLine( currentEmployee ); // invokes ToString
49
50           // determine whether element is a BasePlusCommissionEmployee
51           if ( currentEmployee is BasePlusCommissionEmployee )
52           {
53              // downcast Employee reference to
54              // BasePlusCommissionEmployee reference
55              BasePlusCommissionEmployee employee =
56                 ( BasePlusCommissionEmployee ) currentEmployee;
57
58              employee.BaseSalary *= 1.10M;
59              Console.WriteLine(
60                 "new base salary with 10% increase is: {0:C}",
61                 employee.BaseSalary );
62           } // end if
63
64           Console.WriteLine(
65              "earned {0:C}\n", currentEmployee.Earnings() );
66        } // end foreach
67
68        // get type name of each object in employees array
69        for ( int j = 0; j < employees.Length; j++ )
70           Console.WriteLine( "Employee {0} is a {1}", j,
71              employees[ j ].GetType() );
72     } // end Main
73  } // end class PayrollSystemTest
```

Fig. 9.9 | Employee hierarchy test application. (Part 2 of 3.)

```
Employees processed individually:

salaried employee: John Smith
social security number: 111-11-1111
weekly salary: $800.00
earned: $800.00

hourly employee: Karen Price
social security number: 222-22-2222
hourly wage: $16.75; hours worked: 40.00
earned: $670.00

commission employee: Sue Jones
social security number: 333-33-3333
gross sales: $10,000.00
commission rate: 0.06
earned: $600.00

base-salaried commission employee: Bob Lewis
social security number: 444-44-4444
gross sales: $5,000.00
commission rate: 0.04; base salary: $300.00
earned: $500.00

Employees processed polymorphically:

salaried employee: John Smith
social security number: 111-11-1111
weekly salary: $800.00
earned $800.00

hourly employee: Karen Price
social security number: 222-22-2222
hourly wage: $16.75; hours worked: 40.00
earned $670.00

commission employee: Sue Jones
social security number: 333-33-3333
gross sales: $10,000.00
commission rate: 0.06
earned $600.00

base-salaried commission employee: Bob Lewis
social security number: 444-44-4444
gross sales: $5,000.00
commission rate: 0.04; base salary: $300.00
new base salary with 10% increase is: $330.00
earned $530.00

Employee 0 is a SalariedEmployee
Employee 1 is a HourlyEmployee
Employee 2 is a CommissionEmployee
Employee 3 is a BasePlusCommissionEmployee
```

Fig. 9.9 | Employee hierarchy test application. (Part 3 of 3.)

object's type at execution time). Finally, the application polymorphically determines and outputs the type of each object in the Employee array. Lines 10–20 create objects of each of the four concrete Employee derived classes. Lines 24–32 output the string representation and earnings of each of these objects. Note that each object's ToString method is called implicitly by Write when the object is output as a string with format items.

Line 35 declares employees and assigns it an array of four Employee variables. Lines 38–41 assign a SalariedEmployee object, an HourlyEmployee object, a Commission-Employee object and a BasePlusCommissionEmployee object to employees[0], employees[1], employees[2] and employees[3], respectively. Each assignment is allowed, because a SalariedEmployee *is an* Employee, an HourlyEmployee *is an* Employee, a CommissionEmployee *is an* Employee and a BasePlusCommissionEmployee *is an* Employee. Therefore, we can assign the references of SalariedEmployee, HourlyEmployee, CommissionEmployee and BasePlusCommissionEmployee objects to base class Employee variables, even though Employee is an abstract class.

Lines 46–66 iterate through array employees and invoke methods ToString and Earnings with Employee variable currentEmployee, which is assigned the reference to a different Employee in the array during each iteration. The output illustrates that the appropriate methods for each class are indeed invoked. All calls to method's ToString and Earnings are resolved at execution time, based on the type of the object to which currentEmployee refers. This process is known as *dynamic binding* or *late binding*. For example, line 48 implicitly invokes method ToString of the object to which currentEmployee refers. As a result of dynamic binding, the CLR decides which class's ToString method to call at execution time rather than at compile time. Note that only the methods of class Employee can be called via an Employee variable—and Employee, of course, includes the methods of class object, such as ToString. (Section 8.7 discussed the set of methods that all classes inherit from class object.) A base class reference can be used to invoke only methods of the base class.

We perform special processing on BasePlusCommissionEmployee objects—as we encounter them, we increase their base salary by 10%. When processing objects polymorphically, we typically do not need to worry about the "specifics," but to adjust the base salary, we do have to determine the specific type of each Employee object at execution time. Line 51 uses the is operator to determine whether a particular Employee object's type is BasePlusCommissionEmployee. The condition in line 51 is true if the object referenced by currentEmployee *is a* BasePlusCommissionEmployee. This would also be true for any object of a BasePlusCommissionEmployee derived class (if there were any) because of the *is-a* relationship a derived class has with its base class. Lines 55–56 downcast currentEmployee from type Employee to type BasePlusCommissionEmployee—this cast is allowed only if the object has an *is-a* relationship with BasePlusCommissionEmployee. The condition at line 51 ensures that this is the case. This cast is required if we are to use derived class BasePlusCommissionEmployee's BaseSalary property on the current Employee object—attempting to invoke a derived-class-only method directly on a base class reference is a compilation error.

 Common Programming Error 9.3

Assigning a base class variable to a derived class variable (without an explicit downcast) is a compilation error.

Software Engineering Observation 9.4

If at execution time the reference to a derived class object has been assigned to a variable of one of its direct or indirect base classes, it is acceptable to cast the reference stored in that base class variable back to a reference of the derived class type. Before performing such a cast, use the is operator to ensure that the object is indeed an object of an appropriate derived class type.

Common Programming Error 9.4

When downcasting an object, an InvalidCastException (of namespace System) occurs if at execution time the object does not have an is-a relationship with the type specified in the cast operator. An object can be cast only to its own type or to the type of one of its base classes.

If the is expression in line 51 is true, the if statement (lines 51–62) performs the special processing required for the BasePlusCommissionEmployee object. Using Base-PlusCommissionEmployee variable employee, line 58 uses the derived-class-only property BaseSalary to retrieve and update the employee's base salary with the 10% raise.

Lines 64–65 invoke method Earnings on currentEmployee, which calls the appropriate derived class object's Earnings method polymorphically. Note that obtaining the earnings of the SalariedEmployee, HourlyEmployee and CommissionEmployee polymorphically in lines 64–65 produces the same result as obtaining these employees' earnings individually in lines 24–32. However, the earnings amount obtained for the BasePlus-CommissionEmployee in lines 64–65 is higher than that obtained in lines 30–32, due to the 10% increase in its base salary.

Lines 69–71 display each employee's type as a string. Every object in C# knows its own class and can access this information through method **GetType**, which all classes inherit from class object. Method GetType returns an object of class Type (of namespace System), which contains information about the object's type, including its class name, the names of its public methods, and the name of its base class. Line 71 invokes method Get-Type on the object to get its runtime class (i.e., a Type object that represents the object's type). Then method ToString is implicitly invoked on the object returned by GetType. The Type class's ToString method returns the class name.

In the previous example, we avoid several compilation errors by downcasting an Employee variable to a BasePlusCommissionEmployee variable in lines 55–56. If we remove the cast operator (BasePlusCommissionEmployee) from line 56 and attempt to assign Employee variable currentEmployee directly to BasePlusCommissionEmployee variable employee, we receive a "Cannot implicitly convert type" compilation error. This error indicates that the attempt to assign the reference of base class object commis-sionEmployee to derived class variable basePlusCommissionEmployee is not allowed without an appropriate cast operator. The compiler prevents this assignment because a CommissionEmployee is not a BasePlusCommissionEmployee—again, the *is-a* relationship applies only between the derived class and its base classes, not vice versa.

Similarly, if lines 58 and 61 use base class variable currentEmployee, rather than derived class variable employee, to use derived-class-only property BaseSalary, we receive an "'Employee' does not contain a definition for 'BaseSalary'" compilation error on each of these lines. Attempting to invoke derived-class-only methods on a base class reference is not allowed. While lines 58 and 61 execute only if is in line 51 returns true to indicate that currentEmployee has been assigned a reference to a BasePlusCommission-Employee object, we cannot attempt to use derived class BasePlusCommissionEmployee property BaseSalary with base class Employee reference currentEmployee. The compiler would generate errors in lines 58 and 61, because BaseSalary is not a base class member and cannot be used with a base class variable. Although the actual method that is called depends on the object's type at execution time, a variable can be used to invoke only those methods that are members of that variable's type, which the compiler verifies. Using a base class Employee variable, we can invoke only methods and properties found in class Employee—methods Earnings and ToString, and properties FirstName, LastName and SocialSecurityNumber.

9.5.7 Summary of the Allowed Assignments Between Base Class and Derived Class Variables

Now that you have seen a complete application that processes diverse derived class objects polymorphically, we summarize what you can and cannot do with base class and derived class objects and variables. Although a derived class object also *is a* base class object, the two objects are nevertheless different. As discussed previously, derived class objects can be treated as if they are base class objects. However, the derived class can have additional derived-class-only members. For this reason, assigning a base class reference to a derived class variable is not allowed without an explicit cast—such an assignment would leave the derived class members undefined for a base class object.

We have discussed four ways to assign base class and derived class references to variables of base class and derived class types:

1. Assigning a base class reference to a base class variable is straightforward.

2. Assigning a derived class reference to a derived class variable is straightforward.

3. Assigning a derived class reference to a base class variable is safe, because the derived class object *is an* object of its base class. However, this reference can be used to refer only to base class members. If this code refers to derived-class-only members through the base class variable, the compiler reports errors.

4. Attempting to assign a base class reference to a derived class variable is a compilation error. To avoid this error, the base class reference must be cast to a derived class type explicitly. At execution time, if the object to which the reference refers is not a derived class object, an exception will occur. (For more on exception handling, see Chapter 10, Exception Handling.) The is operator can be used to ensure that such a cast is performed only if the object is a derived class object.

9.6 sealed Methods and Classes

We saw in Section 8.4 that only methods declared virtual, override or abstract can be overridden in derived classes. A method declared *sealed* in a base class cannot be overridden in a derived class. Methods that are declared private are implicitly sealed, because it is impossible to override them in a derived class (though the derived class can declare a new method with the same signature as the private method in the base class). Methods that are declared static also are implicitly sealed, because static methods cannot be overridden either. A derived class method declared both override and sealed can override a base class method, but cannot be overridden in derived classes further down the inheritance hierarchy.

A `sealed` method's declaration can never change, so all derived classes use the same method implementation, and calls to `sealed` methods are resolved at compile time—this is known as *static binding*. Since the compiler knows that `sealed` methods cannot be overridden, it can often optimize code by removing calls to `sealed` methods and replacing them with the expanded code of their declarations at each method-call location—a technique known as *inlining the code*.

Performance Tip 9.1

The compiler can decide to inline a `sealed` method call and will do so for small, simple `sealed` methods. Inlining does not violate encapsulation or information hiding, but does improve performance because it eliminates the overhead of making a method call.

A class that is declared `sealed` cannot be a base class (i.e., a class cannot extend a `sealed` class). All methods in a `sealed` class are implicitly `sealed`. Class `string` is a `sealed` class. This class cannot be extended, so applications that use `strings` can rely on the functionality of `string` objects as specified in the FCL.

Common Programming Error 9.5

Attempting to declare a derived class of a `sealed` class is a compilation error.

Software Engineering Observation 9.5

In the FCL, the vast majority of classes are not declared `sealed`. This enables inheritance and polymorphism—the fundamental capabilities of object-oriented programming.

9.7 Case Study: Creating and Using Interfaces

Our next example (Fig. 9.11–Fig. 9.15) reexamines the payroll system of Section 9.5. Suppose that the company involved wishes to perform several accounting operations in a single accounts-payable application—in addition to calculating the payroll earnings that must be paid to each employee, the company must also calculate the payment due on each of several invoices (i.e., bills for goods purchased). Though applied to unrelated things (i.e., employees and invoices), both operations have to do with calculating some kind of payment amount. For an employee, the payment refers to the employee's earnings. For an invoice, the payment refers to the total cost of the goods listed on the invoice. Can we calculate such different things as the payments due for employees and invoices polymorphically in a single application? Does C# offer a capability that requires that unrelated classes implement a set of common methods (e.g., a method that calculates a payment amount)? C# interfaces offer exactly this capability.

Interfaces define and standardize the ways in which people and systems can interact with one another. For example, the controls on a radio serve as an interface between a radio's users and its internal components. The controls allow users to perform a limited set of operations (e.g., changing the station, adjusting the volume, choosing between AM and FM), and different radios may implement the controls in different ways (e.g., using push buttons, dials, voice commands). The interface specifies *what* operations a radio must permit users to perform but does not specify *how* the operations are performed. Similarly, the interface between a driver and a car with a manual transmission includes the steering wheel, the gear shift, the clutch pedal, the gas pedal and the brake pedal. This same interface is found in nearly all manual-transmission cars, enabling someone who knows how to drive one particular manual-transmission car to drive just about any manual transmission car. The components of each individual car may look a bit different, but the general purpose is the same—to allow people to drive the car.

Software objects also communicate via interfaces. A C# interface describes a set of methods that can be called on an object, to tell the object to perform some task or return some piece of information, for example. The next example introduces an interface named IPayable that describes the functionality of any object that must be capable of being paid and thus must offer a method to determine the proper payment amount due. An *interface declaration* begins with the keyword interface and can contain only abstract methods, properties, indexers and events (events are discussed in Chapter 11, Graphical User Interface Concepts: Part 1.) All interface members are implicitly declared both public and abstract. In addition, each interface can extend one or more other interfaces to create a more elaborate interface that other classes can implement.

Common Programming Error 9.6

It is a compilation error to declare an interface member public or abstract explicitly, because they are redundant in interface member declarations. It is also a compilation error to specify any implementation details, such as concrete method declarations, in an interface.

To use an interface, a class must specify that it *implements* the interface by listing the interface after the colon (:) in the class declaration. Note that this is the same syntax used to indicate inheritance from a base class. A concrete class implementing the interface must declare each member of the interface with the signature specified in the interface declaration. A class that implements an interface but does not implement all the interface's members is an abstract class—it must be declared abstract and must contain an abstract declaration for each unimplemented member of the interface. Implementing an interface is like signing a contract with the compiler that states, "I will provide an implementation for all the members specified by the interface, or I will declare them abstract."

Common Programming Error 9.7

Failing to declare any member of an interface in a class that implements the interface results in a compilation error.

An interface is typically used when disparate (i.e., unrelated) classes need to share common methods. This allows objects of unrelated classes to be processed polymorphically—objects of classes that implement the same interface can respond to the same method calls. Programmers can create an interface that describes the desired functionality, then implement this interface in any classes requiring that functionality. For example, in the accounts-payable application developed in this section, we implement interface IPayable in any class that must be able to calculate a payment amount (e.g., Employee, Invoice).

An interface often is used in place of an abstract class when there is no default implementation to inherit—that is, no fields and no default method implementations. Like public abstract classes, interfaces are typically public types, so they are normally declared in files by themselves with the same name as the interface and the .cs filename extension.

9.7.1 Developing an IPayable Hierarchy

To build an application that can determine payments for employees and invoices alike, we first create an interface named IPayable. Interface IPayable contains method GetPaymentAmount that returns a decimal amount that must be paid for an object of any class that implements the interface. Method GetPaymentAmount is a general purpose version of method Earnings of the Employee hierarchy—method Earnings calculates a payment amount specifically for an Employee, while GetPaymentAmount can be applied to a broad range of unrelated objects. After declaring interface IPayable, we introduce class Invoice, which implements interface IPayable. We then modify class Employee such that it also implements interface IPayable. Finally, we update Employee derived class SalariedEmployee to "fit" into the IPayable hierarchy (i.e., rename SalariedEmployee method Earnings as GetPaymentAmount).

Good Programming Practice 9.1

By convention, the name of an interface begins with "I". This helps distinguish interfaces from classes, improving code readability.

Good Programming Practice 9.2

When declaring a method in an interface, choose a method name that describes the method's purpose in a general manner, because the method may be implemented by a broad range of unrelated classes.

Classes Invoice and Employee both represent things for which the company must be able to calculate a payment amount. Both classes implement IPayable, so an application can invoke method GetPaymentAmount on Invoice objects and Employee objects alike. This enables the polymorphic processing of Invoices and Employees required for our company's accounts-payable application.

The UML class diagram in Fig. 9.10 shows the interface and class hierarchy used in our accounts-payable application. The hierarchy begins with interface IPayable. The UML distinguishes an interface from a class by placing the word "interface" in guillemets («and ») above the interface name. The UML expresses the relationship between a class and an interface through a ***realization***. A class is said to "realize," or implement, an interface. A class diagram models a realization as a dashed arrow with a hollow arrowhead pointing from the implementing class to the interface. The diagram in Fig. 9.10 indicates that classes Invoice and Employee each realize (i.e., implement) interface IPayable. Note that as in the class diagram of Fig. 9.2, class Employee appears in italics, indicating that it is an abstract class. Concrete class SalariedEmployee extends Employee and inherits its base class's realization relationship with interface IPayable.

9.7.2 Declaring Interface IPayable

The declaration of interface IPayable begins in Fig. 9.11 at line 3. Interface IPayable contains public abstract method GetPaymentAmount (line 5). Note that the method cannot be explicitly declared public or abstract. Interface IPayable has only one method, but interfaces can have any number of members. In addition, method GetPaymentAmount has no parameters, but interface methods can have parameters.

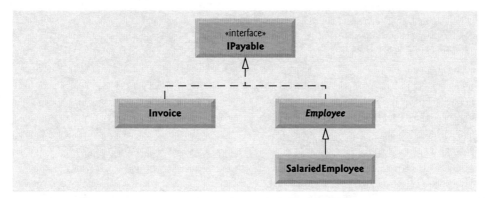

Fig. 9.10 | IPayable interface and class hierarchy UML class diagram.

```
1   // Fig. 9.11: IPayable.cs
2   // IPayable interface declaration.
3   public interface IPayable
4   {
5       decimal GetPaymentAmount(); // calculate payment; no implementation
6   } // end interface IPayable
```

Fig. 9.11 | IPayable interface declaration.

9.7.3 Creating Class Invoice

We now create class Invoice (Fig. 9.12) to represent a simple invoice that contains billing information for one kind of part. The class declares private instance variables partNumber, partDescription, quantity and pricePerItem (lines 5–8) that indicate the part number, the description of the part, the quantity of the part ordered and the price per item. Class Invoice also contains a constructor (lines 11–18), properties (lines 21–70) that manipulate the class's instance variables and a ToString method (lines 73–79) that returns a string representation of an Invoice object. Note that the set accessors of properties Quantity (lines 53–56) and PricePerItem (lines 66–69) ensure that quantity and pricePerItem are assigned only non-negative values.

Line 3 of Fig. 9.12 indicates that class Invoice implements interface IPayable. Like all classes, class Invoice also implicitly extends object. C# does not allow derived classes to inherit from more than one base class, but it does allow a class to inherit from a base class and implement any number of interfaces. All objects of a class that implement multiple interfaces have the *is-a* relationship with each implemented interface type. To implement more than one interface, use a comma-separated list of interface names after the colon (:) in the class declaration, as in:

> **public class** *ClassName* : *BaseClassName*, *FirstInterface*, *SecondInterface*, ...

When a class inherits from a base class and implements one or more interfaces, the class declaration must list the base class name before any interface names.

Class Invoice implements the one method in interface IPayable—method GetPaymentAmount is declared in lines 82–85. The method calculates the amount required

```
1   // Fig. 9.12: Invoice.cs
2   // Invoice class implements IPayable.
3   public class Invoice : IPayable
4   {
5      private string partNumber;
6      private string partDescription;
7      private int quantity;
8      private decimal pricePerItem;
9
10     // four-parameter constructor
11     public Invoice( string part, string description, int count,
12        decimal price )
13     {
14        PartNumber = part;
15        PartDescription = description;
16        Quantity = count; // validate quantity via property
17        PricePerItem = price; // validate price per item via property
18     } // end four-parameter Invoice constructor
19
20     // property that gets and sets the part number on the invoice
21     public string PartNumber
22     {
23        get
24        {
25           return partNumber;
26        } // end get
27        set
28        {
29           partNumber = value; // should validate
30        } // end set
31     } // end property PartNumber
32
33     // property that gets and sets the part description on the invoice
34     public string PartDescription
35     {
36        get
37        {
38           return partDescription;
39        } // end get
40        set
41        {
42           partDescription = value; // should validate
43        } // end set
44     } // end property PartDescription
45
46     // property that gets and sets the quantity on the invoice
47     public int Quantity
48     {
49        get
50        {
51           return quantity;
52        } // end get
```

Fig. 9.12 | Invoice class implements IPayable. (Part 1 of 2.)

```
53          set
54          {
55              quantity = ( value < 0 ) ? 0 : value; // validate quantity
56          } // end set
57      } // end property Quantity
58
59      // property that gets and sets the price per item
60      public decimal PricePerItem
61      {
62          get
63          {
64              return pricePerItem;
65          } // end get
66          set
67          {
68              pricePerItem = ( value < 0 ) ? 0 : value; // validate price
69          } // end set
70      } // end property PricePerItem
71
72      // return string representation of Invoice object
73      public override string ToString()
74      {
75          return string.Format(
76              "{0}: \n{1}: {2} ({3}) \n{4}: {5} \n{6}: {7:C}",
77              "invoice", "part number", PartNumber, PartDescription,
78              "quantity", Quantity, "price per item", PricePerItem );
79      } // end method ToString
80
81      // method required to carry out contract with interface IPayable
82      public decimal GetPaymentAmount()
83      {
84          return Quantity * PricePerItem; // calculate total cost
85      } // end method GetPaymentAmount
86  } // end class Invoice
```

Fig. 9.12 | Invoice class implements IPayable. (Part 2 of 2.)

to pay the invoice. The method multiplies the values of quantity and pricePerItem (obtained through the appropriate properties) and returns the result (line 84). This method satisfies the implementation requirement for the method in interface IPayable— we have fulfilled the interface contract with the compiler.

9.7.4 Modifying Class Employee to Implement Interface IPayable

We now modify class Employee to implement interface IPayable. Figure 9.13 contains the modified Employee class. This class declaration is identical to that of Fig. 9.4 with two exceptions. First, line 3 of Fig. 9.13 indicates that class Employee now implements interface IPayable. Second, since Employee now implements interface IPayable, we must rename Earnings to GetPaymentAmount throughout the Employee hierarchy. As with method Earnings in the version of class Employee in Fig. 9.4, however, it does not make sense to implement method GetPaymentAmount in class Employee, because we cannot calculate the earnings payment owed to a general Employee—first, we must know the specific type of

Employee. In Fig. 9.4, we declared method Earnings as abstract for this reason, and as a result, class Employee had to be declared abstract. This forced each Employee derived class to override Earnings with a concrete implementation.

In Fig. 9.13, we handle this situation the same way. Recall that when a class implements an interface, the class makes a contract with the compiler stating that the class either will implement each of the methods in the interface or will declare them abstract. If the latter option is chosen, we must also declare the class abstract. As we discussed in Section 9.4, any concrete derived class of the abstract class must implement the abstract

```csharp
1   // Fig. 9.13: Employee.cs
2   // Employee abstract base class.
3   public abstract class Employee : IPayable
4   {
5       private string firstName;
6       private string lastName;
7       private string socialSecurityNumber;
8
9       // three-parameter constructor
10      public Employee( string first, string last, string ssn )
11      {
12          firstName = first;
13          lastName = last;
14          socialSecurityNumber = ssn;
15      } // end three-parameter Employee constructor
16
17      // read-only property that gets employee's first name
18      public string FirstName
19      {
20          get
21          {
22              return firstName;
23          } // end get
24      } // end property FirstName
25
26      // read-only property that gets employee's last name
27      public string LastName
28      {
29          get
30          {
31              return lastName;
32          } // end get
33      } // end property LastName
34
35      // read-only property that gets employee's social security number
36      public string SocialSecurityNumber
37      {
38          get
39          {
40              return socialSecurityNumber;
41          } // end get
42      } // end property SocialSecurityNumber
```

Fig. 9.13 | Employee abstract base class. (Part 1 of 2.)

```
43
44        // return string representation of Employee object
45        public override string ToString()
46        {
47            return string.Format( "{0} {1}\nsocial security number: {2}",
48                FirstName, LastName, SocialSecurityNumber );
49        } // end method ToString
50
51        // Note: We do not implement IPayable method GetPaymentAmount here so
52        // this class must be declared abstract to avoid a compilation error.
53        public abstract decimal GetPaymentAmount();
54    } // end abstract class Employee
```

Fig. 9.13 | Employee abstract base class. (Part 2 of 2.)

methods of the base class. If the derived class does not do so, it too must be declared abstract. As indicated by the comments in lines 51–52, class Employee of Fig. 9.13 does not implement method GetPaymentAmount, so the class is declared abstract.

9.7.5 Modifying Class SalariedEmployee for Use in the IPayable Hierarchy

Figure 9.14 contains a modified version of class SalariedEmployee that extends Employee and implements method GetPaymentAmount. This version of SalariedEmployee is identical

```
1     // Fig. 9.14: SalariedEmployee.cs
2     // SalariedEmployee class that extends Employee.
3     public class SalariedEmployee : Employee
4     {
5         private decimal weeklySalary;
6
7         // four-parameter constructor
8         public SalariedEmployee( string first, string last, string ssn,
9             decimal salary ) : base( first, last, ssn )
10        {
11            WeeklySalary = salary; // validate salary via property
12        } // end four-parameter SalariedEmployee constructor
13
14        // property that gets and sets salaried employee's salary
15        public decimal WeeklySalary
16        {
17            get
18            {
19                return weeklySalary;
20            } // end get
21            set
22            {
23                weeklySalary = value < 0 ? 0 : value; // validation
24            } // end set
25        } // end property WeeklySalary
```

Fig. 9.14 | SalariedEmployee class that extends Employee. (Part 1 of 2.)

```
26
27      // calculate earnings; implement interface IPayable method
28      // that was abstract in base class Employee
29      public override decimal GetPaymentAmount()
30      {
31         return WeeklySalary;
32      } // end method GetPaymentAmount
33
34      // return string representation of SalariedEmployee object
35      public override string ToString()
36      {
37         return string.Format( "salaried employee: {0}\n{1}: {2:C}",
38            base.ToString(), "weekly salary", WeeklySalary );
39      } // end method ToString
40   } // end class SalariedEmployee
```

Fig. 9.14 | `SalariedEmployee` class that extends `Employee`. (Part 2 of 2.)

to that of Fig. 9.5 with the exception that the version here implements method GetPay-mentAmount (lines 29–32) instead of method Earnings. The two methods contain the same functionality but have different names. Recall that the IPayable version of the method has a more general name to be applicable to possibly disparate classes. The remaining Employee derived classes (e.g., HourlyEmployee, CommissionEmployee and BasePlusCommissionEm-ployee) also must be modified to contain method GetPaymentAmount in place of Earnings to reflect the fact that Employee now implements IPayable. We leave these modifications as an exercise and use only SalariedEmployee in our test application in this section.

When a class implements an interface, the same *is-a* relationship provided by inherit-ance applies. For example, class Employee implements IPayable, so we can say that an Employee *is an* IPayable, as are any classes that extend Employee. SalariedEmployee objects, for instance, are IPayable objects. As with inheritance relationships, an object of a class that implements an interface may be thought of as an object of the interface type. Objects of any classes derived from the class that implements the interface can also be thought of as objects of the interface type. Thus, just as we can assign the reference of a SalariedEmployee object to a base class Employee variable, we can assign the reference of a SalariedEmployee object to an interface IPayable variable. Invoice implements IPay-able, so an Invoice object also *is an* IPayable object, and we can assign the reference of an Invoice object to an IPayable variable.

Software Engineering Observation 9.6

Inheritance and interfaces are similar in their implementation of the is-a relationship. An object of a class that implements an interface may be thought of as an object of that interface type. An object of any derived classes of a class that implements an interface also can be thought of as an object of the interface type.

Software Engineering Observation 9.7

The is-a relationship that exists between base classes and derived classes, and between interfaces and the classes that implement them, holds when passing an object to a method. When a method parameter receives a variable of a base class or interface type, the method polymorphically processes the object received as an argument.

9.7.6 Using Interface `IPayable` to Process `Invoices` and `Employees` Polymorphically

`PayableInterfaceTest` (Fig. 9.15) illustrates that interface `IPayable` can be used to process a set of `Invoices` and `Employees` polymorphically in a single application. Line 10 declares payableObjects and assigns it an array of four `IPayable` variables. Lines 13–14 assign the references of `Invoice` objects to the first two elements of payableObjects. Lines 15–18 assign the references of `SalariedEmployee` objects to the remaining two elements of payableObjects. These assignments are allowed because an `Invoice` *is an* `IPayable`, a `SalariedEmployee` *is an* `Employee` and an `Employee` *is an* `IPayable`. Lines 24–29 use a foreach statement to process each `IPayable` object in payableObjects polymorphically, printing the object as a `string`, along with the payment due. Note that line 27 implicitly invokes method `ToString` off an `IPayable` interface reference, even though `ToString` is not declared in interface `IPayable`—all references (including those of interface types) refer to objects that extend `object` and therefore have a `ToString` method. Line 28 invokes `IPayable` method `GetPaymentAmount` to obtain the payment amount for each object in payableObjects, regardless of the actual type of the object. The output reveals that the method calls in lines 27–28 invoke the appropriate class's implementation of methods `ToString` and `GetPaymentAmount`. For instance, when currentEmployee refers to an `Invoice` during the first iteration of the foreach loop, class `Invoice`'s `ToString` and `GetPaymentAmount` methods execute.

Software Engineering Observation 9.8

All methods of class object *can be called by using a reference of an interface type—the reference refers to an object, and all objects inherit the methods of class* object.

```
1   // Fig. 9.15: PayableInterfaceTest.cs
2   // Tests interface IPayable with disparate classes.
3   using System;
4
5   public class PayableInterfaceTest
6   {
7      public static void Main( string[] args )
8      {
9         // create four-element IPayable array
10        IPayable[] payableObjects = new IPayable[ 4 ];
11
12        // populate array with objects that implement IPayable
13        payableObjects[ 0 ] = new Invoice( "01234", "seat", 2, 375.00M );
14        payableObjects[ 1 ] = new Invoice( "56789", "tire", 4, 79.95M );
15        payableObjects[ 2 ] = new SalariedEmployee( "John", "Smith",
16           "111-11-1111", 800.00M );
17        payableObjects[ 3 ] = new SalariedEmployee( "Lisa", "Barnes",
18           "888-88-8888", 1200.00M );
19
20        Console.WriteLine(
21           "Invoices and Employees processed polymorphically:\n" );
22
```

Fig. 9.15 | Tests interface `IPayable` with disparate classes. (Part 1 of 2.)

```
23          // generically process each element in array payableObjects
24          foreach ( IPayable currentPayable in payableObjects )
25          {
26             // output currentPayable and its appropriate payment amount
27             Console.WriteLine( "{0} \n{1}: {2:C}\n", currentPayable,
28                "payment due", currentPayable.GetPaymentAmount() );
29          } // end foreach
30       } // end Main
31    } // end class PayableInterfaceTest
```

```
Invoices and Employees processed polymorphically:

invoice:
part number: 01234 (seat)
quantity: 2
price per item: $375.00
payment due: $750.00

invoice:
part number: 56789 (tire)
quantity: 4
price per item: $79.95
payment due: $319.80

salaried employee: John Smith
social security number: 111-11-1111
weekly salary: $800.00
payment due: $800.00

salaried employee: Lisa Barnes
social security number: 888-88-8888
weekly salary: $1,200.00
payment due: $1,200.00
```

Fig. 9.15 | Tests interface IPayable with disparate classes. (Part 2 of 2.)

9.7.7 Common Interfaces of the .NET Framework Class Library

In this section, we overview several common interfaces in the .NET Framework Class Library. These interfaces are implemented and used in the same manner as those you create (e.g., interface IPayable in Section 9.7.2). The FCL's interfaces enable you to extend many important aspects of C# with your own classes. Figure 9.16 overviews several commonly used FCL interfaces.

9.8 Operator Overloading

Manipulations on class objects are accomplished by sending messages (in the form of method calls) to the objects. This method-call notation is cumbersome for certain kinds of classes, especially mathematical classes. For these classes, it would be convenient to use C#'s rich set of built-in operators to specify object manipulations. In this section, we show how to enable these operators to work with class objects—via a process called *operator overloading*.

Interface	Description
IComparable	As you learned in Chapter 1, C# contains several comparison operators (e.g., <, <=, >, >=, ==, !=) that allow you to compare simple-type values. In Section 9.8 you will see that these operators can be defined to compare two objects. Interface IComparable can also be used to allow objects of a class that implements the interface to be compared to one another. The interface contains one method, CompareTo, that compares the object that calls the method to the object passed as an argument to the method. Classes must implement CompareTo to return a value indicating whether the object on which it is invoked is less than (negative integer return value), equal to (0 return value) or greater than (positive integer return value) the object passed as an argument, using any criteria specified by the programmer. For example, if class Employee implements IComparable, its CompareTo method could compare Employee objects by their earnings amounts. Interface IComparable is commonly used for ordering objects in a collection such as an array.
IComponent	Implemented by any class that represents a component, including Graphical User Interface (GUI) controls (such as buttons or labels). Interface IComponent defines the behaviors that components must implement. We discuss IComponent and many GUI controls that implement this interface in Chapter 11, Graphical User Interface Concepts: Part 1, and Chapter 12, Graphical User Interface Concepts: Part 2.
IDisposable	Implemented by classes that must provide an explicit mechanism for releasing resources. Some resources can be used by only one program at a time. In addition, some resources, such as files on disk, are unmanaged resources that, unlike memory, cannot be released by the garbage collector. Classes that implement interface IDisposable provide a Dispose method that can be called to explicitly release resources. We discuss IDisposable briefly in Chapter 10, Exception Handling. You can learn more about this interface at msdn2.microsoft.com/en-us/library/aax125c9. The MSDN article *Implementing a Dispose Method* at msdn2.microsoft.com/en-us/library/fs2xkftw discusses the proper implementation of this interface in your classes.
IEnumerator	Used for iterating through the elements of a collection (such as an array) one element at a time. Interface IEnumerator contains method MoveNext to move to the next element in a collection, method Reset to move to the position before the first element and property Current to return the object at the current location.

Fig. 9.16 | Common interfaces of the .NET Framework Class Library.

Software Engineering Observation 9.9

Use operator overloading when it makes an application clearer than accomplishing the same operations with explicit method calls.

C# enables you to overload most operators to make them sensitive to the context in which they are used. Some operators are overloaded frequently, especially various arithmetic operators, such as + and -. The job performed by overloaded operators also can be performed by explicit method calls, but operator notation often is more natural. Figures 9.17–9.18 provide an example of using operator overloading with a Complex-Number class.

Class ComplexNumber (Fig. 9.17) overloads the plus (+), minus (-) and multiplication (*) operators to enable programs to add, subtract and multiply instances of class Complex-Number using common mathematical notation. Lines 8–9 declare instance variables for the real and imaginary parts of the complex number.

```
1   // Fig. 9.17: ComplexNumber.cs
2   // Class that overloads operators for adding, subtracting
3   // and multiplying complex numbers.
4   using System;
5
6   public class ComplexNumber
7   {
8      private double real; // real component of the complex number
9      private double imaginary; // imaginary component of the complex number
10
11     // constructor
12     public ComplexNumber( double a, double b )
13     {
14        real = a;
15        imaginary = b;
16     } // end constructor
17
18     // return string representation of ComplexNumber
19     public override string ToString()
20     {
21        return string.Format( "({0} {1} {2}i)",
22           Real, ( Imaginary < 0 ? "-" : "+" ), Math.Abs( Imaginary ) );
23     } // end method ToString
24
25     // read-only property that gets the real component
26     public double Real
27     {
28        get
29        {
30           return real;
31        } // end get
32     } // end property Real
33
```

Fig. 9.17 | Class that overloads operators for adding, subtracting and multiplying complex numbers. (Part 1 of 2.)

```
34        // read-only property that gets the imaginary component
35        public double Imaginary
36        {
37           get
38           {
39              return imaginary;
40           } // end get
41        } // end property Imaginary
42
43        // overload the addition operator
44        public static ComplexNumber operator+(
45           ComplexNumber x, ComplexNumber y )
46        {
47           return new ComplexNumber( x.Real + y.Real,
48              x.Imaginary + y.Imaginary );
49        } // end operator +
50
51        // overload the subtraction operator
52        public static ComplexNumber operator-(
53           ComplexNumber x, ComplexNumber y )
54        {
55           return new ComplexNumber( x.Real - y.Real,
56              x.Imaginary - y.Imaginary );
57        } // end operator -
58
59        // overload the multiplication operator
60        public static ComplexNumber operator*(
61           ComplexNumber x, ComplexNumber y )
62        {
63           return new ComplexNumber(
64              x.Real * y.Real - x.Imaginary * y.Imaginary,
65              x.Real * y.Imaginary + y.Real * x.Imaginary );
66        } // end operator *
67     } // end class ComplexNumber
```

Fig. 9.17 | Class that overloads operators for adding, subtracting and multiplying complex numbers. (Part 2 of 2.)

Lines 44–49 overload the plus operator (+) to perform addition of ComplexNumbers. Keyword *operator*, followed by an operator symbol, indicates that a method overloads the specified operator. Methods that overload binary operators must take two arguments. The first argument is the left operand, and the second argument is the right operand. Class ComplexNumber's overloaded plus operator takes two ComplexNumber references as arguments and returns a ComplexNumber that represents the sum of the arguments. Note that this method is marked public and static, which is required for overloaded operators. The body of the method (lines 47–48) performs the addition and returns the result as a new Complex-Number. Notice that we do not modify the contents of either of the original operands passed as arguments x and y. This matches our intuitive sense of how this operator should behave— adding two numbers does not modify either of the original numbers. Lines 52–66 provide similar overloaded operators for subtracting and multiplying ComplexNumbers.

Software Engineering Observation 9.10

Overload operators to perform the same function or similar functions on class objects as the operators perform on objects of simple types. Avoid non-intuitive use of operators.

Software Engineering Observation 9.11

At least one argument of an overloaded operator method must be a reference to an object of the class in which the operator is overloaded. This prevents programmers from changing how operators work on simple types.

Class ComplexTest (Fig. 9.18) demonstrates the overloaded operators for adding, subtracting and multiplying ComplexNumbers. Lines 14–27 prompt the user to enter two complex numbers, then use this input to create two ComplexNumbers and assign them to variables x and y.

```
1   // Fig 9.18: OperatorOverloading.cs
2   // Overloading operators for complex numbers.
3   using System;
4
5   public class ComplexTest
6   {
7      public static void Main( string[] args )
8      {
9         // declare two variables to store complex numbers
10        // to be entered by user
11        ComplexNumber x, y;
12
13        // prompt the user to enter the first complex number
14        Console.Write( "Enter the real part of complex number x: " );
15        double realPart = Convert.ToDouble( Console.ReadLine() );
16        Console.Write(
17           "Enter the imaginary part of complex number x: " );
18        double imaginaryPart = Convert.ToDouble( Console.ReadLine() );
19        x = new ComplexNumber( realPart, imaginaryPart );
20
21        // prompt the user to enter the second complex number
22        Console.Write( "\nEnter the real part of complex number y: " );
23        realPart = Convert.ToDouble( Console.ReadLine() );
24        Console.Write(
25           "Enter the imaginary part of complex number y: " );
26        imaginaryPart = Convert.ToDouble( Console.ReadLine() );
27        y = new ComplexNumber( realPart, imaginaryPart );
28
29        // display the results of calculations with x and y
30        Console.WriteLine();
31        Console.WriteLine( "{0} + {1} = {2}", x, y, x + y );
32        Console.WriteLine( "{0} - {1} = {2}", x, y, x - y );
33        Console.WriteLine( "{0} * {1} = {2}", x, y, x * y );
34     } // end method Main
35  } // end class ComplexTest
```

Fig. 9.18 | Overloading operators for complex numbers. (Part 1 of 2.)

```
Enter the real part of complex number x: 2
Enter the imaginary part of complex number x: 4

Enter the real part of complex number y: 4
Enter the imaginary part of complex number y: -2

(2 + 4i) + (4 - 2i) = (6 + 2i)
(2 + 4i) - (4 - 2i) = (-2 + 6i)
(2 + 4i) * (4 - 2i) = (16 + 12i)
```

Fig. 9.18 | Overloading operators for complex numbers. (Part 2 of 2.)

Lines 31–33 add, subtract and multiply x and y with the overloaded operators, then output the results. In line 31, we perform the addition by using the plus operator with ComplexNumber operands x and y. Without operator overloading, the expression x + y would not make sense—the compiler would not know how two objects should be added. This expression makes sense here because we've defined the plus operator for two ComplexNumbers in lines 44–49 of Fig. 9.17. When the two ComplexNumbers are "added" in line 31 of Fig. 9.18, this invokes the operator+ declaration, passing the left operand as the first argument and the right operand as the second argument. When we use the subtraction and multiplication operators in lines 32–33, their respective overloaded operator declarations are invoked similarly.

Notice that the result of each calculation is a reference to a new ComplexNumber object. When this new object is passed to the Console class's WriteLine method, its ToString method (lines 19–23 of Fig. 9.17) is implicitly invoked. We do not need to assign an object to a reference-type variable to invoke its ToString method. Line 31 of Fig. 9.18 could be rewritten to explicitly invoke the ToString method of the object created by the overloaded plus operator, as in:

```
Console.WriteLine( "{0} + {1} = {2}", x, y, ( x + y ).ToString() );
```

9.9 (Optional) Software Engineering Case Study: Incorporating Inheritance and Polymorphism into the ATM System

We now revisit our ATM system design to see how it might benefit from inheritance and polymorphism. To apply inheritance, we first look for commonality among classes in the system. We create an inheritance hierarchy to model similar classes in an elegant and efficient manner that enables us to process objects of these classes polymorphically. We then modify our class diagram to incorporate the new inheritance relationships. Finally, we demonstrate how to translate the inheritance aspects of our updated design into C# code.

In Section 2.11, we encountered the problem of representing a financial transaction in the system. Rather than create one class to represent all transaction types, we created three distinct transaction classes—BalanceInquiry, Withdrawal and Deposit—to represent the transactions that the ATM system can perform. The class diagram of Fig. 9.19 shows the attributes and operations of these classes. Note that they have one private attribute (accountNumber) and one public operation (Execute) in common. Each class requires attribute accountNumber to specify the account to which the transaction applies.

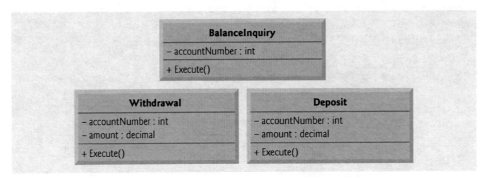

Fig. 9.19 | Attributes and operations of classes BalanceInquiry, Withdrawal and Deposit.

Each class contains operation Execute, which the ATM invokes to perform the transaction. Clearly, BalanceInquiry, Withdrawal and Deposit represent *types of* transactions. Figure 9.19 reveals commonality among the transaction classes, so using inheritance to factor out the common features seems appropriate for designing these classes. We place the common functionality in base class Transaction and derive classes BalanceInquiry, Withdrawal and Deposit from Transaction (Fig. 9.20).

The UML specifies a relationship called a ***generalization*** to model inheritance. Figure 9.20 is the class diagram that models the inheritance relationship between base class Transaction and its three derived classes. The arrows with triangular hollow arrowheads indicate that classes BalanceInquiry, Withdrawal and Deposit are derived from class Transaction by inheritance. Class Transaction is said to be a generalization of its derived classes. The derived classes are said to be ***specializations*** of class Transaction.

As Fig. 9.19 shows, classes BalanceInquiry, Withdrawal and Deposit share private int attribute accountNumber. We'd like to factor out this common attribute and place it in the base class Transaction. However, recall that a base class's private attributes are not accessible in derived classes. The derived classes of Transaction require access to attribute

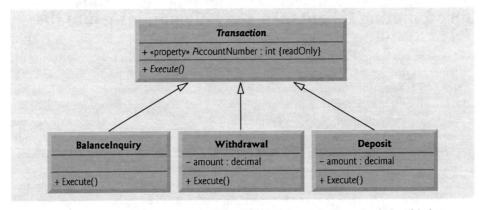

Fig. 9.20 | Class diagram modeling the generalization (i.e., inheritance) relationship between the base class Transaction and its derived classes BalanceInquiry, Withdrawal and Deposit.

accountNumber so that they can specify which Account to process in the BankDatabase. As you learned in Chapter 8, a derived class can access only the public, protected and protected internal members of its base class. However, the derived classes in this case do not need to modify attribute accountNumber—they need only to access its value. For this reason, we have chosen to replace private attribute accountNumber in our model with the public read-only property AccountNumber. Since this is a read-only property, it provides only a get accessor to access the account number. Each derived class inherits this property, enabling the derived class to access its account number as needed to execute a transaction. We no longer list accountNumber in the second compartment of each derived class, because the three derived classes inherit property AccountNumber from Transaction.

According to Fig. 9.19, classes BalanceInquiry, Withdrawal and Deposit also share operation Execute, so base class Transaction should contain public operation Execute. However, it does not make sense to implement Execute in class Transaction, because the functionality that this operation provides depends on the specific type of the actual transaction. We therefore declare Execute as an *abstract operation* in base class Transaction —it will become an abstract method in the C# implementation. This makes Transaction an abstract class and forces any class derived from Transaction that must be a concrete class (i.e., BalanceInquiry, Withdrawal and Deposit) to implement the operation Execute to make the derived class concrete. The UML requires that we place abstract class names and abstract operations in italics. Thus, in Fig. 9.20, Transaction and Execute appear in italics for the Transaction class; Execute is not italicized in derived classes BalanceInquiry, Withdrawal and Deposit. Each derived class overrides base class Transaction's Execute operation with an appropriate concrete implementation. Note that Fig. 9.20 includes operation Execute in the third compartment of classes BalanceInquiry, Withdrawal and Deposit, because each class has a different concrete implementation of the overridden operation.

As you learned in this chapter, a derived class can inherit interface and implementation from a base class. Compared to a hierarchy designed for implementation inheritance, one designed for interface inheritance tends to have its functionality lower in the hierarchy—a base class signifies one or more operations that should be defined by each class in the hierarchy, but the individual derived classes provide their own implementations of the operation(s). The inheritance hierarchy designed for the ATM system takes advantage of this type of inheritance, which provides the ATM with an elegant way to execute all transactions "in the general" (i.e., polymorphically). Each class derived from Transaction inherits some implementation details (e.g., property AccountNumber), but the primary benefit of incorporating inheritance into our system is that the derived classes share a common interface (e.g., abstract operation Execute). The ATM can aim a Transaction reference at any transaction, and when the ATM invokes the operation Execute through this reference, the version of Execute specific to that transaction runs (polymorphically) automatically (due to polymorphism). For example, suppose a user chooses to perform a balance inquiry. The ATM aims a Transaction reference at a new object of class BalanceInquiry, which the C# compiler allows because a BalanceInquiry *is a* Transaction. When the ATM uses this reference to invoke Execute, BalanceInquiry's version of Execute is called (polymorphically).

This polymorphic approach also makes the system easily extensible. Should we wish to create a new transaction type (e.g., funds transfer or bill payment), we would simply create an additional Transaction derived class that overrides the Execute operation with a version appropriate for the new transaction type. We would need to make only minimal changes to the system code to allow users to choose the new transaction type from the main menu and for the ATM to instantiate and execute objects of the new derived class. The ATM could execute transactions of the new type using the current code, because it executes all transactions identically (through polymorphism).

As you learned earlier in the chapter, an abstract class like Transaction is one for which the programmer never intends to (and, in fact, cannot) instantiate objects. An abstract class simply declares common attributes and behaviors for its derived classes in an inheritance hierarchy. Class Transaction defines the concept of what it means to be a transaction that has an account number and can be executed. You may wonder why we bother to include abstract operation Execute in class Transaction if Execute lacks a concrete implementation. Conceptually, we include this operation because it is the defining behavior of all transactions—executing. Technically, we must include operation Execute in base class Transaction so that the ATM (or any other class) can invoke each derived class's overridden version of this operation polymorphically via a Transaction reference.

Derived classes BalanceInquiry, Withdrawal and Deposit inherit property Account-Number from base class Transaction, but classes Withdrawal and Deposit contain the additional attribute amount that distinguishes them from class BalanceInquiry. Classes Withdrawal and Deposit require this additional attribute to store the amount of money that the user wishes to withdraw or deposit. Class BalanceInquiry has no need for such an attribute and requires only an account number to execute. Even though two of the three Transaction derived classes share the attribute amount, we do not place it in base class Transaction—we place only features common to *all* the derived classes in the base class, so derived classes do not inherit unnecessary attributes (and operations).

Figure 9.21 presents an updated class diagram of our model that incorporates inheritance and introduces abstract base class Transaction. We model an association between class ATM and class Transaction to show that the ATM, at any given moment, either is executing a transaction or is not (i.e., zero or one objects of type Transaction exist in the system at a time). Because a Withdrawal is a type of Transaction, we no longer draw an association line directly between class ATM and class Withdrawal—derived class Withdrawal inherits base class Transaction's association with class ATM. Derived classes BalanceInquiry and Deposit also inherit this association, which replaces the previously omitted associations between classes BalanceInquiry and Deposit, and class ATM. Note again the use of triangular hollow arrowheads to indicate the specializations (i.e., derived classes) of class Transaction, as indicated in Fig. 9.20.

We also add an association between class Transaction and the BankDatabase (Fig. 9.21). All Transactions require a reference to the BankDatabase so that they can access and modify account information. Each Transaction derived class inherits this reference, so we no longer model the association between class Withdrawal and the BankDatabase. Note that the association between class Transaction and the BankDatabase replaces the previously omitted associations between classes BalanceInquiry and Deposit, and the BankDatabase.

We include an association between class Transaction and the Screen because all Transactions display output to the user via the Screen. Each derived class inherits this association. Therefore, we no longer include the association previously modeled between

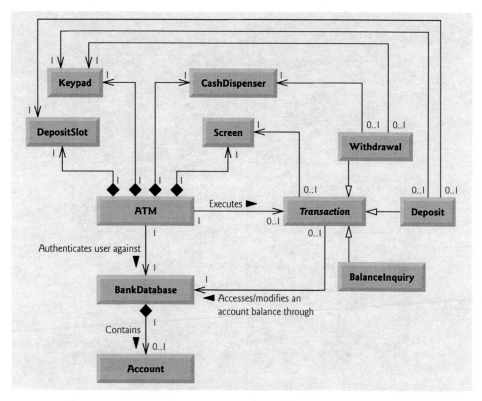

Fig. 9.21 | Class diagram of the ATM system (incorporating inheritance). Note that abstract class name Transaction appears in italics.

Withdrawal and the Screen. Class Withdrawal still participates in associations with the CashDispenser and the Keypad, however—these associations apply to derived class Withdrawal but not to derived classes BalanceInquiry and Deposit, so we do not move these associations to base class Transaction.

Our class diagram incorporating inheritance (Fig. 9.21) also models classes Deposit and BalanceInquiry. We show associations between Deposit and both the DepositSlot and the Keypad. Note that class BalanceInquiry takes part in only those associations inherited from class Transaction—a BalanceInquiry interacts only with the BankDatabase and the Screen.

The class diagram of Fig. 7.23 showed attributes, properties and operations with visibility markers. Now we present a modified class diagram in Fig. 9.22 that includes abstract base class Transaction. This abbreviated diagram does not show inheritance relationships (these appear in Fig. 9.21), but instead shows the attributes and operations after we have employed inheritance in our system. Note that abstract class name Transaction and abstract operation name Execute in class Transaction appear in italics. To save space, as we did in Fig. 3.16, we do not include those attributes shown by associations in Fig. 9.22. We also omit all operation parameters, as we did in Fig. 7.23—incorporating inheritance does not affect the parameters already modeled in Figs. 5.22–5.24.

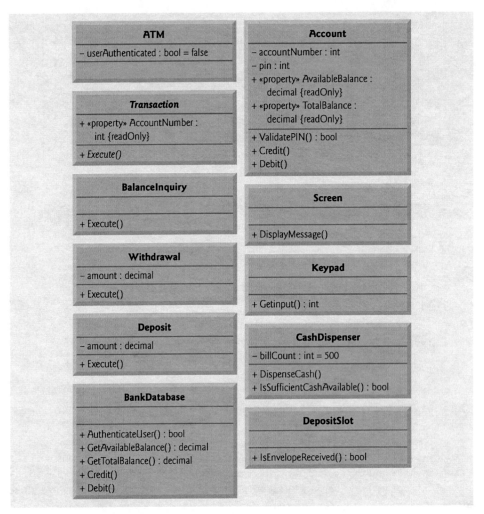

Fig. 9.22 | Class diagram after incorporating inheritance into the system.

Software Engineering Observation 9.12

A complete class diagram shows all the associations among classes, and all the attributes and operations for each class. When the number of class attributes, operations and associations is substantial (as in Fig. 9.21 and Fig. 9.22), a good practice that promotes readability is to divide this information between two class diagrams—one focusing on associations and the other on attributes and operations. When examining classes modeled in this fashion, it is crucial to consider both class diagrams to get a complete picture of the classes. For example, one must refer to Fig. 9.21 to observe the inheritance relationship between Transaction and its derived classes; that relationship is omitted from Fig. 9.22.

Implementing the ATM System Design Incorporating Inheritance

In Section 7.17, we began implementing the ATM system design in C# code. We now modify our implementation to incorporate inheritance, using class Withdrawal as an example.

1. If a class A is a generalization of class B, then class B is derived from (and is a specialization of) class A. For example, abstract base class Transaction is a generalization of class Withdrawal. Thus, class Withdrawal is derived from (and is a specialization of) class Transaction. Figure 9.23 contains the shell of class Withdrawal, in which the class definition indicates the inheritance relationship between Withdrawal and Transaction (line 3).

2. If class A is an abstract class and class B is derived from class A, then class B must implement the abstract operations of class A if class B is to be a concrete class. For example, class Transaction contains abstract operation Execute, so class Withdrawal must implement this operation if we want to instantiate Withdrawal objects. Figure 9.24 contains the portions of the C# code for class Withdrawal that can be inferred from Fig. 9.21 and Fig. 9.22. Class Withdrawal inherits property AccountNumber from base class Transaction, so Withdrawal does not declare this property. Class Withdrawal also inherits references to the Screen and the BankDatabase from class Transaction, so we do not include these references in our code. Figure 9.22 specifies attribute amount and operation Execute for class Withdrawal. Line 6 of Fig. 9.24 declares an instance variable for attribute amount. Lines 17–20 declare the shell of a method for operation Execute. Recall that derived class Withdrawal must provide a concrete implementation of the abstract method Execute from base class Transaction. The keypad and cash-Dispenser references (lines 7–8) are instance variables whose need is apparent from class Withdrawal's associations in Fig. 9.21—in the C# implementation of this class, a constructor initializes these references to actual objects.

```
1   // Fig 9.23: Withdrawal.cs
2   // Class Withdrawal represents an ATM withdrawal transaction.
3   public class Withdrawal : Transaction
4   {
5       // code for members of class Withdrawal
6   } // end class Withdrawal
```

Fig. 9.23 | C# code for shell of class Withdrawal.

```
1    // Fig 9.24: Withdrawal.cs
2    // Class Withdrawal represents an ATM withdrawal transaction.
3    public class Withdrawal : Transaction
4    {
5        // attributes
6        private decimal amount; // amount to withdraw
7        private Keypad keypad; // reference to keypad
8        private CashDispenser cashDispenser; // reference to cash dispenser
9
10       // parameterless constructor
11       public Withdrawal()
12       {
13           // constructor body code
14       } // end constructor
```

Fig. 9.24 | C# code for class Withdrawal based on Fig. 9.21 and Fig. 9.22. (Part 1 of 2.)

```
15
16      // method that overrides Execute
17      public override void Execute()
18      {
19          // Execute method body code
20      } // end method Execute
21  } // end class Withdrawal
```

Fig. 9.24 | C# code for class Withdrawal based on Fig. 9.21 and Fig. 9.22. (Part 2 of 2.)

ATM Case Study Wrap-Up

This concludes our object-oriented design of the ATM system. This working implementation uses most of the key object-oriented programming concepts that we have covered to this point in the book, including classes, objects, encapsulation, visibility, composition, inheritance and polymorphism. The code is abundantly commented and conforms to the coding practices you've learned so far. Mastering this code is a wonderful capstone experience for you after studying the nine Software Engineering Case Study sections in Chapters 1–7 and 9.

Software Engineering Case Study Self-Review Exercises

9.1 The UML uses an arrow with a _____ to indicate a generalization relationship.
   a) solid filled arrowhead
   b) triangular hollow arrowhead
   c) diamond-shaped hollow arrowhead
   d) stick arrowhead

9.2 State whether the following statement is *true* or *false*, and if *false*, explain why: The UML requires that we underline abstract class names and abstract operation names.

9.3 Write C# code to begin implementing the design for class Transaction specified in Fig. 9.21 and Fig. 9.22. Be sure to include private references based on class Transaction's associations. Also, be sure to include properties with public get accessors for any of the private instance variables that the derived classes must access to perform their tasks.

Answers to Software Engineering Case Study Self-Review Exercises

9.1 b.

9.2 False. The UML requires that we italicize abstract class names and operation names.

9.3 The design for class Transaction yields the code in Fig. 9.25.

9.10 Wrap-Up

This chapter introduced polymorphism—the ability to process objects that share the same base class in a class hierarchy as if they are all objects of the base class. The chapter discussed how polymorphism makes systems extensible and maintainable, then demonstrated how to use overridden methods to effect polymorphic behavior. We introduced the notion

```
 I   // Fig 9.25: Transaction.cs
 2   // Abstract base class Transaction represents an ATM transaction.
 3   public abstract class Transaction
 4   {
 5      private int accountNumber; // indicates account involved
 6      private Screen userScreen; // ATM's screen
 7      private BankDatabase database; // account info database
 8
 9      // parameterless constructor
10      public Transaction()
11      {
12         // constructor body code
13      } // end constructor
14
15      // read-only property that gets the account number
16      public int AccountNumber
17      {
18         get
19         {
20            return accountNumber;
21         } // end get
22      } // end property AccountNumber
23
24      // read-only property that gets the screen reference
25      public Screen UserScreen
26      {
27         get
28         {
29            return userScreen;
30         } // end get
31      } // end property UserScreen
32
33      // read-only property that gets the bank database reference
34      public BankDatabase Database
35      {
36         get
37         {
38            return database;
39         } // end get
40      } // end property Database
41
42      // perform the transaction (overridden by each derived class)
43      public abstract void Execute();
44   } // end class Transaction
```

Fig. 9.25 | C# code for class Transaction based on Fig. 9.21 and Fig. 9.22.

of an abstract class, which allows you to provide an appropriate base class from which other classes can inherit. You learned that an abstract class can declare abstract methods that each derived class must implement to become a concrete class, and that an application can use variables of an abstract class to invoke derived class implementations of abstract methods polymorphically. You also learned how to determine an object's type at execution time. We showed how to create sealed methods and classes. The chapter discussed declaring and implementing an interface as another way to achieve polymorphic behavior, often among objects of different classes. Finally, you learned how to define the behavior of the built-in operators on objects of your own classes with operator overloading.

You should now be familiar with classes, objects, encapsulation, inheritance, interfaces and polymorphism—the most essential aspects of object-oriented programming. In the next chapter, we take a deeper look at how to use exception handling to deal with errors during execution time.

10

Exception Handling

It is common sense to take a method and try it. If it fails, admit it frankly and try another. But above all, try something.
—Franklin Delano Roosevelt

O! throw away the worser part of it, And live the purer with the other half.
—William Shakespeare

If they're running and they don't look where they're going I have to come out from somewhere and catch them.
—J. D. Salinger

And oftentimes excusing of a fault Doth make the fault the worse by the excuse.
—William Shakespeare

O infinite virtue! com'st thou smiling from the world's great snare uncaught?
—William Shakespeare

OBJECTIVES

In this chapter you will learn:

- What exceptions are and how they are handled.
- When to use exception handling.
- To use `try` blocks to delimit code in which exceptions might occur.
- To `throw` exceptions to indicate a problem.
- To use `catch` blocks to specify exception handlers.
- To use the `finally` block to release resources.
- The .NET exception class hierarchy.
- `Exception` properties.
- To create user-defined exceptions.

10.1   Introduction

In this chapter, we introduce *exception handling*. An *exception* is an indication of a problem that occurs during a program's execution. The name "exception" comes from the fact that, although the problem can occur, it occurs infrequently. If the "rule" is that a statement normally executes correctly, then the occurrence of a problem represents the "exception to the rule." Exception handling enables programmers to create applications that can resolve (or handle) exceptions. In many cases, handling an exception allows a program to continue executing as if no problems were encountered. However, more severe problems may prevent a program from continuing normal execution, instead requiring the program to notify the user of the problem, then terminate in a controlled manner. The features presented in this chapter enable programmers to write clear, *robust* and more *fault-tolerant programs* (i.e., programs that are able to deal with problems that may arise and continue executing). The style and details of C# exception handling are based in part on the work of Andrew Koenig and Bjarne Stroustrup. "Best practices" for exception handling in Visual C# 2005 are specified in the Visual Studio documentation.[1]

Error-Prevention Tip 10.1

Exception handling helps improve a program's fault tolerance.

    This chapter begins with an overview of exception-handling concepts and demonstrations of basic exception-handling techniques. The chapter also overviews .NET's

---

1.   "Best Practices for Handling Exceptions [C#]," *.NET Framework Developer's Guide*, Visual Studio .NET Online Help. Available at msdn2.microsoft.com/library/seyhszts(en-us,vs.80).aspx.

exception-handling class hierarchy. Programs typically request and release resources (such as files on disk) during program execution. Often, the supply of these resources is limited, or the resources can be used by only one program at a time. We demonstrate a part of the exception-handling mechanism that enables a program to use a resource, then guarantee that the resource will be released for use by other programs, even if an exception occurs. The chapter demonstrates several properties of class System.Exception (the base class of all exception classes) and discusses how you can create and use your own exception classes.

10.2 Exception Handling Overview

Programs frequently test conditions to determine how program execution should proceed. Consider the following pseudocode:

> *Perform a task*
>
> *If the preceding task did not execute correctly*
> *Perform error processing*
>
> *Perform next task*
>
> *If the preceding task did not execute correctly*
> *Perform error processing*
>
> ...

In this pseudocode, we begin by performing a task; then we test whether that task executed correctly. If not, we perform error processing. Otherwise, we continue with the next task. Although this form of error handling works, intermixing program logic with error-handling logic can make programs difficult to read, modify, maintain and debug—especially in large applications.

Exception handling enables programmers to remove error-handling code from the "main line" of the program's execution, improving program clarity and enhancing modifiability. Programmers can decide to handle any exceptions they choose—all exceptions, all exceptions of a certain type or all exceptions of a group of related types (i.e., exception types that are related through an inheritance hierarchy). Such flexibility reduces the likelihood that errors will be overlooked, thus making programs more robust.

With programming languages that do not support exception handling, programmers often delay writing ***error-processing code*** and sometimes forget to include it. This results in less robust software products. C# enables programmers to deal with exception handling easily from the beginning of a project.

10.3 Example: Divide by Zero Without Exception Handling

First we demonstrate what happens when errors arise in a console application that does not use exception handling. Figure 10.1 inputs two integers from the user, then divides the first integer by the second using integer division to obtain an int result. In this example, we will see that an exception is ***thrown*** (i.e., an exception occurs) when a method detects a problem and is unable to handle it.

```
1    // Fig. 10.1: DivideByZeroNoExceptionHandling.cs
2    // An application that attempts to divide by zero.
3    using System;
4
5    class DivideByZeroNoExceptionHandling
6    {
7       static void Main()
8       {
9          // get numerator and denominator
10         Console.Write( "Please enter an integer numerator: " );
11         int numerator = Convert.ToInt32( Console.ReadLine() );
12         Console.Write( "Please enter an integer denominator: " );
13         int denominator = Convert.ToInt32( Console.ReadLine() );
14
15         // divide the two integers, then display the result
16         int result = numerator / denominator;
17         Console.WriteLine( "\nResult: {0:D} / {1:D} = {2:D}",
18            numerator, denominator, result );
19      } // end Main
20   } // end class DivideByZeroNoExceptionHandling
```

```
Please enter an integer numerator: 100
Please enter an integer denominator: 7

Result: 100 / 7 = 14
```

```
Please enter an integer numerator: 100
Please enter an integer denominator: 0

Unhandled Exception: System.DivideByZeroException:
   Attempted to divide by zero.
   at DivideByZeroNoExceptionHandling.Main()
      in C:\examples\ch12\Fig12_01\DivideByZeroNoExceptionHandling\
      DivideByZeroNoExceptionHandling.cs:line 16
```

```
Please enter an integer numerator: 100
Please enter an integer denominator: hello

Unhandled Exception: System.FormatException:
   Input string was not in a correct format.
   at System.Number.StringToNumber(String str, NumberStyles options,
      NumberBuffer& number, NumberFormatInfo info, Boolean parseDecimal)
   at System.Number.ParseInt32(String s, NumberStyles style,
      NumberFormatInfo info)
   at System.Convert.ToInt32(String value)
   at DivideByZeroNoExceptionHandling.Main()
      in C:\examples\ch12\Fig12_01\DivideByZeroNoExceptionHandling\
      DivideByZeroNoExceptionHandling.cs:line 13
```

Fig. 10.1 | Integer division without exception handling.

Running the Application

In most of the examples we have created so far, the application appears to run the same with or without debugging. As we discuss shortly, the example in Fig. 10.1 might cause errors, depending on the user's input. If you run this application using the **Debug > Start Debugging** menu option, the program pauses at the line where an exception occurs and displays the Exception Assistant, allowing you to analyze the current state of the program and debug it. We discuss the Exception Assistant in Section 10.4.3.

In this example, we do not wish to debug the application; we simply want to see what happens when errors arise. For this reason, we execute this application from a Command Prompt window. Select **Start > All Programs > Accessories > Command Prompt** to open a Command Prompt window, then use the `cd` command to change to the application's `Debug` directory. For example, if this application resides in the directory `C:\examples\ch12\Fig12_01\DivideByZeroNoExceptionHandling` on your system, you would type

```
cd /d C:\examples\ch12\Fig12_01\DivideByZeroNoExceptionHandling
\bin\Debug
```

in the Command Prompt, then press *Enter* to change to the application's `Debug` directory. To execute the application, type

```
DivideByZeroNoExceptionHandling.exe
```

in the Command Prompt, then press *Enter*. If an error arises during execution, a dialog is displayed indicating that the application has encountered a problem and needs to close. The dialog also asks whether you'd like to send information about this error to Microsoft. Since we are creating this error for demonstration purposes, you should click **Don't Send**. [*Note:* On some systems a **Just-In-Time Debugging** dialog is displayed instead. If this occurs, simply click the **No** button to dismiss the dialog.] At this point, an error message describing the problem is displayed in the Command Prompt. We formatted the error messages in Fig. 10.1 for readability. [*Note:* Selecting **Debug > Start Without Debugging** (or *<Ctrl> F5*) to run the application from Visual Studio executes the application's so-called release version. The error messages produced by this version of the application may differ from those shown in Fig. 10.1 due to optimizations that the compiler performs to create an application's release version.]

Analyzing the Results

The first sample execution in Fig. 10.1 shows a successful division. In the second sample execution, the user enters 0 as the denominator. Note that several lines of information are displayed in response to the invalid input. This information—known as a *stack trace*—includes the exception name (`System.DivideByZeroException`) in a descriptive message indicating the problem that occurred and the path of execution that led to the exception, method by method. This information helps you debug a program. The first line of the error message specifies that a `DivideByZeroException` has occurred. When *division by zero* in integer arithmetic occurs, the CLR throws a ***DivideByZeroException*** (namespace `System`). The text after the name of the exception, "`Attempted to divide by zero`," indicates that this exception occurred as a result of an attempt to divide by zero. Division by zero is not allowed in integer arithmetic. [*Note:* Division by zero with floating-point values is allowed. Such a calculation results in the value infinity, which is represented by either constant *Double.PositiveInfinity* or constant *Double.NegativeInfinity*, depending on whether the numerator is positive or negative. These values are displayed as Infinity or -Infinity. If both the numerator and denominator are zero, the result of the calculation is the constant *Double.NaN* ("not a number"), which is returned when a calculation's result is undefined.]

Each "at" line in the stack trace indicates a line of code in the particular method that was executing when the exception occurred. The "at" line contains the namespace, class name and method name in which the exception occurred (DivideByZeroNoException-Handling.Main), the location and name of the file in which the code resides (C:\examples\ch12\Fig12_01\DivideByZeroNoExceptionHandling\DivideByZeroNoException Handling.cs:line 16) and the line of code where the exception occurred. In this case, the stack trace indicates that the DivideByZeroException occurred when the program was executing line 16 of method Main. The first "at" line in the stack trace indicates the exception's *throw point*—the initial point at which the exception occurred (i.e., line 16 in Main). This information makes it easy for the programmer to see where the exception originated, and what method calls were made to get to that point in the program.

Now, let's look at a more detailed stack trace. In the third sample execution, the user enters the string "hello" as the denominator. This causes a FormatException, and another stack trace is displayed. Our earlier examples that read numeric values from the user assumed that the user would input an integer value. However, a user could erroneously input a noninteger value. A *FormatException* (namespace System) occurs, for example, when Convert method ToInt32 receives a string that does not represent a valid integer. Starting from the last "at" line in the stack trace, we see that the exception was detected in line 13 of method Main. The stack trace also shows the other methods that led to the exception being thrown—Convert.ToInt32, Number.ParseInt32 and Number.StringToNumber. To perform its task, Convert.ToInt32 calls method Number.ParseInt32, which in turn calls Number.StringToNumber. The throw point occurs in Number.StringToNumber, as indicated by the first "at" line in the stack trace.

Note that in the sample executions in Fig. 10.1, the program also terminates when exceptions occur and stack traces are displayed. This does not always happen—sometimes a program may continue executing even though an exception has occurred and a stack trace has been printed. In such cases, the application may produce incorrect results. The next section demonstrates how to handle exceptions to enable the program to run to normal completion.

10.4 Example: Handling DivideByZeroExceptions and FormatExceptions

Let us consider a simple example of exception handling. The application in Fig. 10.2 uses exception handling to process any DivideByZeroExceptions and FormatExceptions that might arise. The application displays two TextBoxes in which the user can type integers. When the user presses **Click To Divide**, the program invokes event handler DivideButton_Click (lines 17–48), which obtains the user's input, converts the input values to type int and divides the first number (numerator) by the second number (denominator). Assuming that the user provides integers as input and does not specify 0 as the

```csharp
1   // Fig. 10.2: DivideByZeroTest.cs
2   // Exception handlers for FormatException and DivideByZeroException.
3   using System;
4   using System.Windows.Forms;
5
6   namespace DivideByZeroTest
7   {
8      public partial class DivideByZeroTestForm : Form
9      {
10        public DivideByZeroTestForm()
11        {
12           InitializeComponent();
13        } // end constructor
14
15        // obtain 2 integers from the user
16        // and divide numerator by denominator
17        private void DivideButton_Click( object sender, EventArgs e )
18        {
19           OutputLabel.Text = ""; // clear Label OutputLabel
20
21           // retrieve user input and calculate quotient
22           try
23           {
24              // Convert.ToInt32 generates FormatException
25              // if argument is not an integer
26              int numerator = Convert.ToInt32( NumeratorTextBox.Text );
27              int denominator = Convert.ToInt32( DenominatorTextBox.Text );
28
29              // division generates DivideByZeroException
30              // if denominator is 0
31              int result = numerator / denominator;
32
33              // display result in OutputLabel
34              OutputLabel.Text = result.ToString();
35           } // end try
36           catch ( FormatException )
37           {
38              MessageBox.Show( "You must enter two integers.",
39                 "Invalid Number Format", MessageBoxButtons.OK,
40                 MessageBoxIcon.Error );
41           } // end catch
42           catch ( DivideByZeroException divideByZeroExceptionParameter )
43           {
44              MessageBox.Show( divideByZeroExceptionParameter.Message,
45                 "Attempted to Divide by Zero", MessageBoxButtons.OK,
46                 MessageBoxIcon.Error );
47           } // end catch
48        } // end method DivideButton_Click
49     } // end class DivideByZeroTestForm
50  } // end namespace DivideByZeroTest
```

Fig. 10.2 | Exception handlers for FormatException and DivideByZeroException. (Part 1 of 2.)

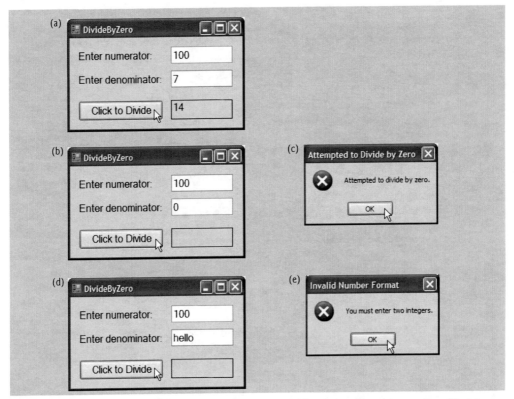

Fig. 10.2 | Exception handlers for `FormatException` and `DivideByZeroException`. (Part 2 of 2.)

denominator for the division, `DivideButton_Click` displays the division result in `Output-Label`. However, if the user inputs a noninteger value or supplies 0 as the denominator, an exception occurs. This program demonstrates how to *catch* and *handle* (i.e., deal with) such exceptions—in this case, displaying an error message and allowing the user to enter another set of values.

Before we discuss the details of the program, let's consider the sample output windows in Fig. 10.2. The window in Fig. 10.2(a) shows a successful calculation, in which the user enters the numerator 100 and the denominator 7. Note that the result (14) is an `int`, because integer division always yields an `int` result. The next two windows, Fig. 10.2(b) and Fig. 10.2(c), demonstrate the result of an attempt to divide by zero. In integer arithmetic, the CLR tests for division by zero and generates a `DivideByZeroException` if the denominator is zero. The program detects the exception and displays the error message dialog in Fig. 10.2(c) indicating the attempt to divide by zero. The last two output windows, Fig. 10.2(d) and Fig. 10.2(e), depict the result of inputting a non-`int` value—in this case, the user enters "hello" in the second `TextBox`, as shown in Fig. 10.2(d). When the user clicks **Click To Divide**, the program attempts to convert the input `strings` into `int` values using method `Convert.ToInt32` (lines 26–27). If an argument passed to `Convert.ToInt32` cannot be converted to an `int` value, the method throws a `FormatException`. The program catches the exception and displays the error message dialog in

Fig. 10.2(e) indicating that the user must enter two `int`s. Notice that we did not include a parameter name for the `catch` at line 36. In the `catch`'s block, we do not use any information from the `FormatException` object. Omitting the parameter name prevents the compiler from issuing a warning which indicates that we declared a variable, but did not use it in the `catch` block.

10.4.1 Enclosing Code in a `try` Block

Now we consider the user interactions and flow of control that yield the results shown in the sample output windows. The user inputs values into the `TextBox`es that represent the numerator and denominator, then presses **Click To Divide**. At this point, the program invokes method `DivideButton_Click`. Line 19 assigns the empty string to `OutputLabel` to clear any prior result in preparation for a new calculation. Lines 22–35 define a *try block* enclosing the code that might throw exceptions, as well as the code that is skipped when an exception occurs. For example, the program should not display a new result in `OutputLabel` (line 34) unless the calculation in line 31 completes successfully.

The two statements that read the `int`s from the `TextBox`es (lines 26–27) call method `Convert.ToInt32` to convert `string`s to `int` values. This method throws a `FormatException` if it cannot convert its `string` argument to an `int`. If lines 26–27 convert the values properly (i.e., no exceptions occur), then line 31 divides the `numerator` by the denominator and assigns the result to variable `result`. If denominator is 0, line 31 causes the CLR to throw a `DivideByZeroException`. If line 31 does not cause an exception to be thrown, then line 34 displays the result of the division.

10.4.2 Catching Exceptions

Exception-handling code appears in a ***catch block***. In general, when an exception occurs in a `try` block, a corresponding `catch` block catches the exception and handles it. The `try` block in this example is followed by two `catch` blocks—one that handles a `Format-Exception` (lines 36–41) and one that handles a `DivideByZeroException` (lines 42–47). A `catch` block specifies an exception parameter representing the exception that the `catch` block can handle. The `catch` block can use the parameter's identifier (which is chosen by the programmer) to interact with a caught exception object. If there is no need to use the exception object in the `catch` block, the exception parameter's identifier can be omitted. The type of the `catch`'s parameter is the type of the exception that the `catch` block handles. Optionally, programmers can include a `catch` block that does not specify an exception type or an identifier—such a `catch` block (known as a ***general catch clause***) catches all exception types. At least one `catch` block and/or a ***finally block*** (discussed in Section 10.6) must immediately follow a `try` block.

In Fig. 10.2, the first `catch` block catches `FormatExceptions` (thrown by method `Convert.ToInt32`), and the second `catch` block catches `DivideByZeroExceptions` (thrown by the CLR). If an exception occurs, the program executes only the first matching `catch` block. Both exception handlers in this example display an error message dialog. After either `catch` block terminates, program control continues with the first statement after the last `catch` block (the end of the method, in this example). We will soon take a deeper look at how this flow of control works in exception handling.

10.4.3 Uncaught Exceptions

An *uncaught exception* is an exception for which there is no matching catch block. You saw the results of uncaught exceptions in the second and third outputs of Fig. 10.1. Recall that when exceptions occur in that example, the application terminates early (after displaying the exception's stack trace). The result of an uncaught exception depends on how you execute the program—Fig. 10.1 demonstrated the results of an uncaught exception when an application is executed in a Command Prompt. If you run the application from Visual Studio with debugging and the runtime environment detects an uncaught exception, the application pauses, and a window called the ***Exception Assistant*** appears indicating where the exception occurred, the type of the exception and links to helpful information on handling the exception. Figure 10.3 shows the Exception Assistant that is displayed if the user attempts to divide by zero in the application of Fig. 10.1.

10.4.4 Termination Model of Exception Handling

When a method called in a program or the CLR detects a problem, the method or the CLR throws an exception. Recall that the point in the program at which an exception occurs is called the throw point—this is an important location for debugging purposes (as we demonstrate in Section 10.7). If an exception occurs in a try block (such as a Format-Exception being thrown as a result of the code in line 27 in Fig. 10.2), the try block terminates immediately, and program control transfers to the first of the following catch blocks in which the exception parameter's type matches the type of the thrown exception. In Fig. 10.2, the first catch block catches FormatExceptions (which occur if input of an invalid type is entered); the second catch block catches DivideByZeroExceptions (which occur if an attempt is made to divide by zero). After the exception is handled, program control does not return to the throw point because the try block has expired (which also causes any of its local variables to go out of scope). Rather, control resumes after the last catch block. This is known as the ***termination model of exception handling***. [*Note:* Some languages use the ***resumption model of exception handling***, in which after an exception is handled, control resumes just after the throw point.]

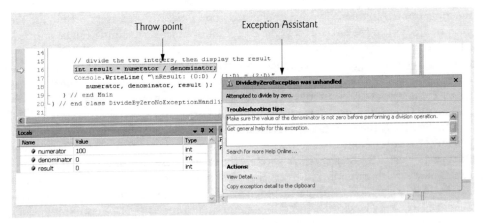

Fig. 10.3 | Exception Assistant.

Common Programming Error 10.1

Logic errors can occur if you assume that after an exception is handled, control will return to the first statement after the throw point.

If no exceptions occur in the `try` block, the program of Fig. 10.2 successfully completes the `try` block by ignoring the `catch` blocks in lines 36–41 and 42–47, and passing line 47. Then the program executes the first statement following the `try` and `catch` blocks. In this example, the program reaches the end of event handler `DivideButton_Click` (line 48), so the method terminates, and the program awaits the next user interaction.

The `try` block and its corresponding `catch` and `finally` blocks together form a ***try statement***. It is important not to confuse the terms "try block" and "try statement"—the term "try block" refers to the block of code following the keyword `try` (but before any `catch` or `finally` blocks), while the term "try statement" includes all the code from the opening `try` keyword to the end of the last `catch` or `finally` block. This includes the `try` block, as well as any associated `catch` blocks and `finally` block.

As with any other block of code, when a `try` block terminates, local variables defined in the block go out of scope. If a `try` block terminates due to an exception, the CLR searches for the first `catch` block that can process the type of exception that occurred. The CLR locates the matching `catch` by comparing the type of the thrown exception to each `catch`'s parameter type. A match occurs if the types are identical or if the thrown exception's type is a derived class of the `catch`'s parameter type. Once an exception is matched to a `catch` block, the code in that block executes and the other `catch` blocks in the `try` statement are ignored.

10.4.5 Flow of Control When Exceptions Occur

In the sample output of Fig. 10.2(b), the user inputs `hello` as the denominator. When line 27 executes, `Convert.ToInt32` cannot convert this `string` to an `int`, so `Convert.ToInt32` throws a `FormatException` object to indicate that the method was unable to convert the `string` to an `int`. When the exception occurs, the `try` block expires (terminates). Next, the CLR attempts to locate a matching `catch` block. A match occurs with the `catch` block in line 36, so the exception handler executes and the program ignores all other exception handlers following the `try` block.

Common Programming Error 10.2

Specifying a comma-separated list of parameters in a `catch` block is a syntax error. A `catch` block can have at most one parameter.

In the sample output of Fig. 10.2(d), the user inputs 0 as the denominator. When the division in line 31 executes, a `DivideByZeroException` occurs. Once again, the `try` block terminates, and the program attempts to locate a matching `catch` block. In this case, the first `catch` block does not match—the exception type in the `catch`-handler declaration is not the same as the type of the thrown exception, and `FormatException` is not a base class of `DivideByZeroException`. Therefore the program continues to search for a matching `catch` block, which it finds in line 42. Line 44 displays the value of property ***Message*** of class `Exception`, which contains the error message. Note that our program never "sets" this error message attribute. This is done by the CLR when it creates the exception object.

10.5 .NET Exception Hierarchy

In C#, the exception-handling mechanism allows only objects of class *Exception* (namespace System) and its derived classes to be thrown and caught. Note, however, that C# programs may interact with software components written in other .NET languages (such as C++) that do not restrict exception types. The general catch clause can be used to catch such exceptions.

This section overviews several of the .NET Framework's exception classes and focuses exclusively on exceptions that derived from class Exception. In addition, we discuss how to determine whether a particular method throws exceptions.

10.5.1 Classes ApplicationException and SystemException

Class *Exception* of namespace System is the base class of the .NET Framework exception class hierarchy. Two of the most important classes derived from Exception are *ApplicationException* and *SystemException*. ApplicationException is a base class that programmers can extend to create exception classes that are specific to their applications. We show how to create user-defined exception classes in Section 10.8. Programs can recover from most ApplicationExceptions and continue execution.

The CLR generates SystemExceptions, which can occur at any point during program execution. Many of these exceptions can be avoided if applications are coded properly. For example, if a program attempts to access an *out-of-range array index*, the CLR throws an exception of type *IndexOutOfRangeException* (a derived class of SystemException). Similarly, an exception occurs when a program uses an object reference to manipulate an object that does not yet exist (i.e., the reference has a value of null). Attempting to use a null reference causes a *NullReferenceException* (another derived class of SystemException). You saw earlier in this chapter that a DivideByZeroException occurs in integer division when a program attempts to divide by zero.

Other SystemException types thrown by the CLR include *OutOfMemoryException*, *StackOverflowException* and *ExecutionEngineException*. These are thrown when the something goes wrong that causes the CLR to become unstable. In some cases, such exceptions cannot even be caught. In general, it is best to simply log such exceptions then terminate your application.

A benefit of the exception class hierarchy is that a catch block can catch exceptions of a particular type or—because of the *is-a* relationship of inheritance—can use a base-class type to catch exceptions in a hierarchy of related exception types. For example, Section 10.4.2 discussed the catch block with no parameter, which catches exceptions of all types (including those that are not derived from Exception). A catch block that specifies a parameter of type Exception can catch all exceptions that derive from Exception, because Exception is the base class of all exception classes. The advantage of this approach is that the exception handler can access the caught exception's information via the parameter in the catch. We demonstrated accessing the information in an exception in line 44 of Fig. 10.2. We'll say more about accessing exception information in Section 10.7.

Using inheritance with exceptions enables an catch block to catch related exceptions using a concise notation. A set of exception handlers could catch each derived-class exception type individually, but catching the base-class exception type is more concise. However, this technique makes sense only if the handling behavior is the same for a base class and all derived classes. Otherwise, catch each derived-class exception individually.

Common Programming Error 10.3

It is a compilation error if a catch block that catches a base-class exception is placed before a catch block for any of that class's derived-class types. If this were allowed, the base-class catch block would catch all base-class and derived-class exceptions, so the derived-class exception handler would never execute.

10.5.2 Determining Which Exceptions a Method Throws

How do we determine that an exception might occur in a program? For methods contained in the .NET Framework classes, read the detailed descriptions of the methods in the online documentation. If a method throws an exception its description contains a section called **Exceptions** that specifies the types of exceptions the method throws and briefly describes possible causes for the exceptions. For example, search for "Convert.ToInt32 method" in the **Index** of the Visual Studio online documentation (use the **.NET Framework** filter). Select the document entitled **Convert.ToInt32 Method (System)**. In the document that describes the method, click the link **Convert.ToInt32(String)**. In the document that appears, the **Exceptions** section (near the bottom of the document) indicates that method Convert.ToInt32 throws two exception types—FormatException and OverflowException—and describes the reason why each might occur.

Software Engineering Observation 10.1

If a method throws exceptions, statements that invoke the method directly or indirectly should be placed in try blocks, and those exceptions should be caught and handled.

It is more difficult to determine when the CLR throws exceptions. Such information appears in the *C# Language Specification*. This document defines C#'s syntax and specifies cases in which exceptions are thrown. Figure 10.2 demonstrated that the CLR throws a DivideByZeroException in integer arithmetic when a program attempts to divide by zero. Section 5.7.2 of the language specification (12.7.2 in the ECMA version) discusses the division operator and when DivideByZeroExceptions occur.

10.6 finally Block

Programs frequently request and release resources dynamically (i.e., at execution time). For example, a program that reads a file from disk first makes a file-open request. If that request succeeds, the program reads the contents of the file. Operating systems typically prevent more than one program from manipulating a file at once. Therefore, when a program finishes processing a file, the program should close the file (i.e., release the resource) so other programs can use it. If the file is not closed, a ***resource leak*** occurs. In such a case, the file resource is not available to other programs, possibly because a program using the file has not closed it.

In programming languages such as C and C++, in which the programmer (not the language) is responsible for dynamic memory management, the most common type of resource leak is a ***memory leak***. A memory leak occurs when a program allocates memory (as C# programmers do via keyword new), but does not deallocate the memory when it is no longer needed. Normally, this is not an issue in C#, because the CLR performs garbage collection of memory that is no longer needed by an executing program (Section 7.10). However, other kinds of resource leaks (such as unclosed files) can occur.

Error-Prevention Tip 10.2

The CLR does not completely eliminate memory leaks. The CLR will not garbage collect an object until the program contains no more references to that object. Thus, memory leaks can occur if programmers inadvertently keep references to unwanted objects.

Moving Resource Release Code to a `finally` Block

Typically, exceptions occur when processing resources that require explicit release. For example, a program that processes a file might receive IOExceptions during the processing. For this reason, file processing code normally appears in a try block. Regardless of whether a program experiences exceptions while processing a file, the program should close the file when it is no longer needed. Suppose a program places all resource request and resource release code in a try block. If no exceptions occur, the try block executes normally and releases the resources after using them. However, if an exception occurs, the try block may expire before the resource-release code can execute. We could duplicate all the resource release code in each of the catch blocks, but this would make the code more difficult to modify and maintain. We could also place the resource release code after the try statement; however, if the try block terminates due to a return statement, code following the try statement would never execute.

To address these problems, C#'s exception handling mechanism provides the finally block, which is guaranteed to execute regardless of whether the try block executes successfully or an exception occurs. This makes the finally block an ideal location in which to place resource-release code for resources that are acquired and manipulated in the corresponding try block. If the try block executes successfully, the finally block executes immediately after the try block terminates. If an exception occurs in the try block, the finally block executes immediately after a catch block completes. If the exception is not caught by a catch block associated with the try block, or if a catch block associated with the try block throws an exception itself, the finally block executes before the exception is processed by the next enclosing try block (if there is one). By placing the resource release code in a finally block, we ensure that even if the program terminates due to an uncaught exception, the resource will be deallocated. Note that local variables in a try block cannot be accessed in the corresponding finally block. For this reason, variables that must be accessed in both a try block and its corresponding finally block should be declared before the try block.

Error-Prevention Tip 10.3

A `finally` block typically contains code to release resources acquired in the corresponding `try` block, which makes the `finally` block an effective mechanism for eliminating resource leaks.

Performance Tip 10.1

As a rule, resources should be released as soon as they are no longer needed in a program. This makes them available for reuse promptly.

If one or more catch blocks follow a try block, the finally block is optional. However, if no catch blocks follow a try block, a finally block must appear immediately after the try block. If any catch blocks follow a try block, the finally block (if there is one) appears after the last catch block. Only whitespace and comments can separate the blocks in a try statement.

Common Programming Error 10.4

Placing the finally block before a catch block is a syntax error.

Demonstrating the finally Block

The application in Fig. 10.4 demonstrates that the finally block always executes, regardless of whether an exception occurs in the corresponding try block. The program consists of method Main (lines 8–47) and four other methods that Main invokes to demonstrate finally. These methods are DoesNotThrowException (lines 50–67), ThrowException-WithCatch (lines 70–89), ThrowExceptionWithoutCatch (lines 92–108) and Throw-ExceptionCatchRethrow (lines 111–136).

```csharp
1   // Fig. 10.4: UsingExceptions.cs
2   // Using finally blocks.
3   // Demonstrate that finally always executes.
4   using System;
5
6   class UsingExceptions
7   {
8      static void Main()
9      {
10        // Case 1: No exceptions occur in called method
11        Console.WriteLine( "Calling DoesNotThrowException" );
12        DoesNotThrowException();
13
14        // Case 2: Exception occurs and is caught in called method
15        Console.WriteLine( "\nCalling ThrowExceptionWithCatch" );
16        ThrowExceptionWithCatch();
17
18        // Case 3: Exception occurs, but is not caught in called method
19        // because there is no catch block.
20        Console.WriteLine( "\nCalling ThrowExceptionWithoutCatch" );
21
22        // call ThrowExceptionWithoutCatch
23        try
24        {
25           ThrowExceptionWithoutCatch();
26        } // end try
27        catch
28        {
29           Console.WriteLine( "Caught exception from " +
30              "ThrowExceptionWithoutCatch in Main" );
31        } // end catch
32
33        // Case 4: Exception occurs and is caught in called method,
34        // then rethrown to caller.
35        Console.WriteLine( "\nCalling ThrowExceptionCatchRethrow" );
```

Fig. 10.4 | finally blocks always execute, regardless of whether an exception occurs. (Part 1 of 4.)

```
36
37          // call ThrowExceptionCatchRethrow
38          try
39          {
40              ThrowExceptionCatchRethrow();
41          } // end try
42          catch
43          {
44              Console.WriteLine( "Caught exception from " +
45                  "ThrowExceptionCatchRethrow in Main" );
46          } // end catch
47      } // end method Main
48
49      // no exceptions thrown
50      static void DoesNotThrowException()
51      {
52          // try block does not throw any exceptions
53          try
54          {
55              Console.WriteLine( "In DoesNotThrowException" );
56          } // end try
57          catch
58          {
59              Console.WriteLine( "This catch never executes" );
60          } // end catch
61          finally
62          {
63              Console.WriteLine( "finally executed in DoesNotThrowException" );
64          } // end finally
65
66          Console.WriteLine( "End of DoesNotThrowException" );
67      } // end method DoesNotThrowException
68
69      // throws exception and catches it locally
70      static void ThrowExceptionWithCatch()
71      {
72          // try block throws exception
73          try
74          {
75              Console.WriteLine( "In ThrowExceptionWithCatch" );
76              throw new Exception( "Exception in ThrowExceptionWithCatch" );
77          } // end try
78          catch ( Exception exceptionParameter )
79          {
80              Console.WriteLine( "Message: " + exceptionParameter.Message );
81          } // end catch
82          finally
83          {
84              Console.WriteLine(
85                  "finally executed in ThrowExceptionWithCatch" );
86          } // end finally
```

Fig. 10.4 | finally blocks always execute, regardless of whether an exception occurs. (Part 2 of 4.)

```
87
88          Console.WriteLine( "End of ThrowExceptionWithCatch" );
89       } // end method ThrowExceptionWithCatch
90
91       // throws exception and does not catch it locally
92       static void ThrowExceptionWithoutCatch()
93       {
94          // throw exception, but do not catch it
95          try
96          {
97             Console.WriteLine( "In ThrowExceptionWithoutCatch" );
98             throw new Exception( "Exception in ThrowExceptionWithoutCatch" );
99          } // end try
100         finally
101         {
102            Console.WriteLine( "finally executed in " +
103               "ThrowExceptionWithoutCatch" );
104         } // end finally
105
106         // unreachable code; logic error
107         Console.WriteLine( "End of ThrowExceptionWithoutCatch" );
108      } // end method ThrowExceptionWithoutCatch
109
110      // throws exception, catches it and rethrows it
111      static void ThrowExceptionCatchRethrow()
112      {
113         // try block throws exception
114         try
115         {
116            Console.WriteLine( "In ThrowExceptionCatchRethrow" );
117            throw new Exception( "Exception in ThrowExceptionCatchRethrow" );
118         } // end try
119         catch ( Exception exceptionParameter )
120         {
121            Console.WriteLine( "Message: " + exceptionParameter.Message );
122
123            // rethrow exception for further processing
124            throw;
125
126            // unreachable code; logic error
127         } // end catch
128         finally
129         {
130            Console.WriteLine( "finally executed in " +
131               "ThrowExceptionCatchRethrow" );
132         } // end finally
133
134         // any code placed here is never reached
135         Console.WriteLine( "End of ThrowExceptionCatchRethrow" );
136      } // end method ThrowExceptionCatchRethrow
137   } // end class UsingExceptions
```

Fig. 10.4 | finally blocks always execute, regardless of whether an exception occurs. (Part 3 of 4.)

```
Calling DoesNotThrowException
In DoesNotThrowException
finally executed in DoesNotThrowException
End of DoesNotThrowException

Calling ThrowExceptionWithCatch
In ThrowExceptionWithCatch
Message: Exception in ThrowExceptionWithCatch
finally executed in ThrowExceptionWithCatch
End of ThrowExceptionWithCatch

Calling ThrowExceptionWithoutCatch
In ThrowExceptionWithoutCatch
finally executed in ThrowExceptionWithoutCatch
Caught exception from ThrowExceptionWithoutCatch in Main

Calling ThrowExceptionCatchRethrow
In ThrowExceptionCatchRethrow
Message: Exception in ThrowExceptionCatchRethrow
finally executed in ThrowExceptionCatchRethrow
Caught exception from ThrowExceptionCatchRethrow in Main
```

Fig. 10.4 | `finally` blocks always execute, regardless of whether an exception occurs. (Part 4 of 4.)

Line 12 of `Main` invokes method `DoesNotThrowException`. The `try` block for this method outputs a message (line 55). Because the `try` block does not throw any exceptions, program control ignores the `catch` block (lines 57–60) and executes the `finally` block (lines 61–64), which outputs a message. At this point, program control continues with the first statement after the close of the `finally` block (line 66) which outputs a message indicating that the end of the method has been reached. Then, program control returns to `Main`.

Throwing Exceptions Using the throw Statement

Line 16 of `Main` invokes method `ThrowExceptionWithCatch` (lines 70–89), which begins in its `try` block (lines 73–77) by outputting a message. Next, the `try` block creates an `Exception` object and uses a ***throw statement*** to throw the exception object (line 76). Executing the `throw` statement indicates that an exception has occurred. So far you have only caught exceptions thrown by called methods. You can throw exceptions by using the `throw` statement. Just as with exceptions thrown by the FCL's methods and the CLR, this indicates to client applications that an error has occurred. A `throw` statement specifies an object to be thrown. The operand of a `throw` statement can be of type `Exception` or of any type derived from class `Exception`.

Common Programming Error 10.5

It is a compilation error if the argument of a throw—an exception object—is not of class Exception or one of its derived classes.

The `string` passed to the constructor becomes the exception object's error message. When a throw statement in a try block executes, the try block expires immediately, and program control continues with the first matching catch block (lines 78–81) following the try block. In this example, the type thrown (Exception) matches the type specified in the catch, so line 80 outputs a message indicating the exception that occurred. Then, the finally block (lines 82–86) executes and outputs a message. At this point, program control continues with the first statement after the close of the finally block (line 88), which outputs a message indicating that the end of the method has been reached. Program control then returns to Main. In line 80, note that we use the exception object's Message property to retrieve the error message associated with the exception (i.e., the message passed to the Exception constructor). Section 10.7 discusses several properties of class Exception.

Lines 23–31 of Main define a try statement in which Main invokes method Throw-ExceptionWithoutCatch (lines 92–108). The try block enables Main to catch any exceptions thrown by ThrowExceptionWithoutCatch. The try block in lines 95–99 of ThrowExceptionWithoutCatch begins by outputting a message. Next, the try block throws an Exception (line 98) and expires immediately.

Normally, program control would continue at the first catch following this try block. However, this try block does not have any catch blocks. Therefore, the exception is not caught in method ThrowExceptionWithoutCatch. Program control proceeds to the finally block (lines 100–104), which outputs a message. At this point, program control returns to Main—any statements appearing after the finally block (e.g., line 107) do not execute. In this example, such statements could cause logic errors, because the exception thrown in line 98 is not caught. In Main, the catch block in lines 27–31 catches the exception and displays a message indicating that the exception was caught in Main.

Rethrowing Exceptions

Lines 38–46 of Main define a try statement in which Main invokes method Throw-ExceptionCatchRethrow (lines 111–136). The try statement enables Main to catch any exceptions thrown by ThrowExceptionCatchRethrow. The try statement in lines 114–132 of ThrowExceptionCatchRethrow begins by outputting a message. Next, the try block throws an Exception (line 117). The try block expires immediately, and program control continues at the first catch (lines 119–127) following the try block. In this example, the type thrown (Exception) matches the type specified in the catch, so line 121 outputs a message indicating where the exception occurred. Line 124 uses the throw statement to *rethrow* the exception. This indicates that the catch block performed partial processing of the exception and now is passing the exception back to the calling method (in this case, Main) for further processing.

You can also rethrow an exception with a version of the throw statement which takes an operand that is the reference to the exception that was caught. It is important to note, however, that this form of throw statement resets the throw point, so the original throw point's stack trace information is lost. Section 10.7 demonstrates using a throw statement with an operand from a catch block. In that section, you will see that after an exception is caught, you can create and throw a different type of exception object from the catch block and you can include the original exception as part of the new exception object. Class library designers often do this to customize the exception types thrown from methods in their class libraries or to provide additional debugging information.

The exception handling in method ThrowExceptionCatchRethrow does not complete, because the program cannot run code in the catch block placed after the invocation of the throw statement in line 124. Therefore, method ThrowExceptionCatchRethrow terminates and returns control to Main. Once again, the finally block (lines 128–132) executes and outputs a message before control returns to Main. When control returns to Main, the catch block in lines 42–46 catches the exception and displays a message indicating that the exception was caught. Then the program terminates.

Returning After a finally Block

Note that the next statement to execute after a finally block terminates depends on the exception-handling state. If the try block successfully completes, or if a catch block catches and handles an exception, the program continues its execution with the next statement after the finally block. However, if an exception is not caught, or if a catch block rethrows an exception, program control continues in the next enclosing try block. The enclosing try could be in the calling method or in one of its callers. It also is possible to nest a try statement in a try block; in such a case, the outer try statement's catch blocks would process any exceptions that were not caught in the inner try statement. If a try block executes and has a corresponding finally block, the finally block executes even if the try block terminates due to a return statement. The return occurs after the execution of the finally block.

Common Programming Error 10.6

Throwing an exception from a finally block can be dangerous. If an uncaught exception is awaiting processing when the finally block executes, and the finally block throws a new exception that is not caught in the finally block, the first exception is lost, and the new exception is passed to the next enclosing try block.

Error-Prevention Tip 10.4

When placing code that can throw an exception in a finally block, always enclose the code in a try statement that catches the appropriate exception types. This prevents the loss of any uncaught and rethrown exceptions that occur before the finally block executes.

Software Engineering Observation 10.2

Do not place try blocks around every statement that might throw an exception, because this can make programs difficult to read. It is better to place one try block around a significant portion of code, and follow this try block with catch blocks that handle each of the possible exceptions. Then follow the catch blocks with a single finally block. Separate try blocks should be used when it is important to distinguish between multiple statements that can throw the same exception type.

using

Recall from earlier in this section that resource-release code should be placed in a finally block to ensure that a resource is released, regardless of whether there were exceptions when the resource was used in the corresponding try block. An alternative notation—the *using* statement (not to be confused with the using directive for using namespaces)—simplifies writing code in which you obtain a resource, use the resource in a try block and release the resource in a corresponding finally block. For example, a file processing application could process a file with a using statement to ensure that the file is closed properly when it is no longer needed. The resource must be an object that implements the

IDisposable interface and therefore has a Dispose method. The general form of a using statement would be

```
using ( ExampleObject exampleObject = new ExampleObject() )
{
    exampleObject.SomeMethod();
}
```

where ExampleObject is a class that implements the IDisposable interface. This code creates an object of type ExampleObject and uses it in a statement, then calls its Dispose method to release any resources used by the object. The using statement implicitly places the code in its body in a try block with a corresponding finally block that calls the object's Dispose method. For instance, the preceding code is equivalent to

```
{
    ExampleObject exampleObject = new ExampleObject();

    try
    {
        exampleObject.SomeMethod();
    }
    finally
    {
        if ( exampleObject != null )
            ( ( IDisposable ) exampleObject ).Dispose();
    }
}
```

Note that the if statement ensures that exampleObject still references an object; otherwise, a NullReferenceException might occur. You can read more about the using statement in the *C# Language Specification* Section 6.13.

10.7 Exception Properties

As we discussed in Section 10.5, exception types derive from class Exception, which has several properties. These frequently are used to formulate error messages indicating a caught exception. Two important properties are Message and **StackTrace**. Property Message stores the error message associated with an Exception object. This message can be a default message associated with the exception type or a customized message passed to an Exception object's constructor when the Exception object is thrown. Property Stack-Trace contains a string that represents the *method-call stack*. Recall that the runtime environment at all times keeps a list of open method calls that have been made but have not yet returned. The StackTrace represents the series of methods that have not finished processing at the time the exception occurs.

Error-Prevention Tip 10.5

A stack trace shows the complete method-call stack at the time an exception occurred. This enables the programmer to view the series of method calls that led to the exception. Information in the stack trace includes the names of the methods on the call stack at the time of the exception, the names of the classes in which the methods are defined and the names of the namespaces in which the classes are defined. If the program database (PDB) file that contains the debugging information for the method is available, the stack trace also includes line numbers; the first line number indicates the throw point, and subsequent line numbers indicate the locations from which the methods in the stack trace were called. PDB files are created by the IDE to maintain the debugging information for your projects.

Property InnerException

Another property used frequently by class-library programmers is ***InnerException***. Typically, class library programmers "wrap" exception objects caught in their code so that they then can throw new exception types that are specific to their libraries. For example, a programmer implementing an accounting system might have some account-number processing code in which account numbers are input as strings but represented as ints in the code. Recall that a program can convert strings to int values with Convert.ToInt32, which throws a FormatException when it encounters an invalid number format. When an invalid account number format occurs, the accounting system programmer might wish to employ a different error message than the default message supplied by FormatException or might wish to indicate a new exception type, such as InvalidAccountNumberFormatException. In such cases, the programmer would provide code to catch the FormatException, then create an appropriate type of Exception object in the catch block and pass the original exception as one of the constructor arguments. The original exception object becomes the InnerException of the new exception object. When an InvalidAccountNumberFormatException occurs in code that uses the accounting system library, the catch block that catches the exception can obtain a reference to the original exception via property InnerException. Thus the exception indicates both that the user specified an invalid account number and that the problem was an invalid number format. If the InnerException property is null, this indicates that the exception was not caused by another exception.

Other Exception Properties

Class Exception provides other properties, including ***HelpLink***, ***Source*** and ***TargetSite***. Property HelpLink specifies the location of the help file that describes the problem that occurred. This property is null if no such file exists. Property Source specifies the name of the application where the exception occurred. Property TargetSite specifies the method where the exception originated.

Demonstrating Exception Properties and Stack Unwinding

Our next example (Fig. 10.5) demonstrates properties Message, StackTrace and InnerException, and method ToString, of class Exception. In addition, the example introduces *stack unwinding*—when an exception is thrown but not caught in a particular scope, the method-call stack is "unwound," and an attempt is made to catch the exception in the next

```
 1   // Fig. 10.5: Properties.cs
 2   // Stack unwinding and Exception class properties.
 3   // Demonstrates using properties Message, StackTrace and InnerException.
 4   using System;
 5
```

Fig. 10.5 | Exception properties and stack unwinding. (Part 1 of 3.)

```
 6   class Properties
 7   {
 8      static void Main()
 9      {
10         // call Method1; any Exception generated is caught
11         // in the catch block that follows
12         try
13         {
14            Method1();
15         } // end try
16         catch ( Exception exceptionParameter )
17         {
18            // output the string representation of the Exception, then output
19            // properties InnerException, Message and StackTrace
20            Console.WriteLine( "exceptionParameter.ToString: \n{0}\n",
21               exceptionParameter.ToString() );
22            Console.WriteLine( "exceptionParameter.Message: \n{0}\n",
23               exceptionParameter.Message );
24            Console.WriteLine( "exceptionParameter.StackTrace: \n{0}\n",
25               exceptionParameter.StackTrace );
26            Console.WriteLine( "exceptionParameter.InnerException: \n{0}\n",
27               exceptionParameter.InnerException.ToString() );
28         } // end catch
29      } // end method Main
30
31      // calls Method2
32      static void Method1()
33      {
34         Method2();
35      } // end method Method1
36
37      // calls Method3
38      static void Method2()
39      {
40         Method3();
41      } // end method Method2
42
43      // throws an Exception containing an InnerException
44      static void Method3()
45      {
46         // attempt to convert string to int
47         try
48         {
49            Convert.ToInt32( "Not an integer" );
50         } // end try
51         catch ( FormatException formatExceptionParameter )
52         {
53            // wrap FormatException in new Exception
54            throw new Exception( "Exception occurred in Method3",
55               formatExceptionParameter );
56         } // end catch
57      } // end method Method3
58   } // end class Properties
```

Fig. 10.5 | Exception properties and stack unwinding. (Part 2 of 3.)

```
exceptionParameter.ToString:
System.Exception: Exception occurred in Method3 --->
   System.FormatException: Input string was not in a correct format.
   at System.Number.StringToNumber(String str, NumberStyles options,
      NumberBuffer& number, NumberFormatInfo info, Boolean parseDecimal)
   at System.Number.ParseInt32(String s, NumberStyles style,
      NumberFormatInfo info)
   at System.Convert.ToInt32(String value)
   at Properties.Method3() in C:\examples\ch12\Fig12_04\Properties\
      Properties.cs:line 49
   --- End of inner exception stack trace ---
   at Properties.Method3() in C:\examples\ch12\Fig12_04\Properties\
      Properties.cs:line 54
   at Properties.Method2() in C:\examples\ch12\Fig12_04\Properties\
      Properties.cs:line 40
   at Properties.Method1() in C:\examples\ch12\Fig12_04\Properties\
      Properties.cs:line 34
   at Properties.Main() in C:\examples\ch12\Fig12_04\Properties\
      Properties.cs:line 14

exceptionParameter.Message:
Exception occurred in Method3

exceptionParameter.StackTrace:
   at Properties.Method3() in C:\examples\ch12\Fig12_04\Properties\
      Properties.cs:line 54
   at Properties.Method2() in C:\examples\ch12\Fig12_04\Properties\
      Properties.cs:line 40
   at Properties.Method1() in C:\examples\ch12\Fig12_04\Properties\
      Properties.cs:line 34
   at Properties.Main() in C:\examples\ch12\Fig12_04\Properties\
      Properties.cs:line 14

exceptionParameter.InnerException:
System.FormatException: Input string was not in a correct format.
   at System.Number.StringToNumber(String str, NumberStyles options,
      NumberBuffer& number, NumberFormatInfo info, Boolean parseDecimal)
   at System.Number.ParseInt32(String s, NumberStyles style,
      NumberFormatInfo info)
   at System.Convert.ToInt32(String value)
   at Properties.Method3() in C:\examples\ch12\Fig12_04\Properties\
      Properties.cs:line 49
```

Fig. 10.5 | Exception properties and stack unwinding. (Part 3 of 3.)

outer try block. We keep track of the methods on the call stack as we discuss property StackTrace and the stack-unwinding mechanism. To see the proper stack trace, you should execute this program using steps similar to those presented in Section 10.3.

Program execution begins with Main, which becomes the first method on the method call stack. Line 14 of the try block in Main invokes Method1 (declared in lines 32–35), which becomes the second method on the stack. If Method1 throws an exception, the catch block in lines 16–28 handles the exception and outputs information about the exception that occurred. Line 34 of Method1 invokes Method2 (lines 38–41), which becomes the third method on the stack. Then line 40 of Method2 invokes Method3 (lines 44–57), which becomes the fourth method on the stack.

At this point, the method-call stack (from top to bottom) for the program is:

```
Method3
Method2
Method1
Main
```

The method called most recently (Method3) appears at the top of the stack; the first method called (Main) appears at the bottom. The try statement (lines 47–56) in Method3 invokes method Convert.ToInt32 (line 49), which attempts to convert a string to an int. At this point, Convert.ToInt32 becomes the fifth and final method on the call stack.

Throwing an *Exception* with an *InnerException*
Because the argument to Convert.ToInt32 is not in int format, line 49 throws a Format-Exception that is caught in line 51 of Method3. The exception terminates the call to Convert.ToInt32, so the method is removed (or unwound) from the method-call stack. The catch block in Method3 then creates and throws an Exception object. The first argument to the Exception constructor is the custom error message for our example, "Exception occurred in Method3." The second argument is the InnerException—the Format-Exception that was caught. The StackTrace for this new exception object reflects the point at which the exception was thrown (lines 54–55). Now Method3 terminates, because the exception thrown in the catch block is not caught in the method body. Thus, control returns to the statement that invoked Method3 in the prior method in the call stack (Method2). This removes, or *unwinds,* Method3 from the method-call stack.

When control returns to line 40 in Method2, the CLR determines that line 40 is not in a try block. Therefore the exception cannot be caught in Method2, and Method2 terminates. This unwinds Method2 from the call stack and returns control to line 28 in Method1.

Here again, line 34 is not in a try block, so Method1 cannot catch the exception. The method terminates and is unwound from the call stack, returning control to line 14 in Main, which *is* located in a try block. The try block in Main expires and the catch block (lines 16–28) catches the exception. The catch block uses method ToString and properties Message, StackTrace and InnerException to create the output. Note that stack unwinding continues until a catch block catches the exception or the program terminates.

Displaying Information About the *Exception*
The first block of output (which we reformatted for readability) in Fig. 10.5 contains the exception's string representation, which is returned from method ToString. The string begins with the name of the exception class followed by the Message property value. The next four items present the stack trace of the InnerException object. The remainder of the block of output shows the StackTrace for the exception thrown in Method3. Note that the StackTrace represents the state of the method-call stack at the throw point of the exception, rather than at the point where the exception eventually is caught. Each Stack-Trace line that begins with "at" represents a method on the call stack. These lines indicate the method in which the exception occurred, the file in which the method resides and the line number of the throw point in the file. Note that the inner-exception information includes the inner exception stack trace.

Error-Prevention Tip 10.6

When catching and rethrowing an exception, provide additional debugging information in the rethrown exception. To do so, create an Exception *object containing more specific debugging information, then pass the original caught exception to the new exception object's constructor to initialize the* InnerException *property.*

The next block of output (two lines) simply displays the Message property's value (Exception occurred in Method3) of the exception thrown in Method3.

The third block of output displays the StackTrace property of the exception thrown in Method3. Note that this StackTrace property contains the stack trace starting from line 54 in Method3, because that is the point at which the Exception object was created and thrown. The stack trace always begins from the exception's throw point.

Finally, the last block of output displays the string representation of the Inner-Exception property, which includes the namespace and class name of the exception object, as well as its Message and StackTrace properties.

10.8 User-Defined Exception Classes

In many cases, you can use existing exception classes from the .NET Framework Class Library to indicate exceptions that occur in your programs. However, in some cases, you might wish to create new exception classes specific to the problems that occur in your programs. *User-defined exception classes* should derive directly or indirectly from class ApplicationException of namespace System.

Good Programming Practice 10.1

Associating each type of malfunction with an appropriately named exception class improves program clarity.

Software Engineering Observation 10.3

Before creating a user-defined exception class, investigate the existing exceptions in the .NET Framework Class Library to determine whether an appropriate exception type already exists.

Figures 10.6 and 10.7 demonstrate a user-defined exception class. Class NegativeNumberException (Fig. 10.6) is a user-defined exception class representing exceptions that occur when a program performs an illegal operation on a negative number, such as attempting to calculate its square root.

According to "Best Practices for Handling Exceptions [C#]," user-defined exceptions should extend class ApplicationException, have a class name that ends with "Exception" and define three constructors: a parameterless constructor; a constructor that receives a string argument (the error message); and a constructor that receives a string argument and an Exception argument (the error message and the inner exception object). Defining these three constructors makes your exception class more flexible, allowing other programmers to easily use and extend it.

NegativeNumberExceptions most frequently occur during arithmetic operations, so it seems logical to derive class NegativeNumberException from class ArithmeticException. However, class ArithmeticException derives from class SystemException—the category of exceptions thrown by the CLR. Recall that user-defined exception classes should inherit from ApplicationException rather than SystemException.

```
 1   // Fig. 10.6: NegativeNumberException.cs
 2   // NegativeNumberException represents exceptions caused by
 3   // illegal operations performed on negative numbers.
 4   using System;
 5
 6   namespace SquareRootTest
 7   {
 8      class NegativeNumberException : ApplicationException
 9      {
10         // default constructor
11         public NegativeNumberException()
12            : base( "Illegal operation for a negative number" )
13         {
14            // empty body
15         } // end default constructor
16
17         // constructor for customizing error message
18         public NegativeNumberException( string messageValue )
19            : base( messageValue )
20         {
21            // empty body
22         } // end one-argument constructor
23
24         // constructor for customizing the exception's error
25         // message and specifying the InnerException object
26         public NegativeNumberException( string messageValue,
27            Exception inner )
28            : base( messageValue, inner )
29         {
30            // empty body
31         } // end two-argument constructor
32      } // end class NegativeNumberException
33   } // end namespace SquareRootTest
```

Fig. 10.6 | ApplicationException derived class thrown when a program performs an illegal operation on a negative number.

Class SquareRootForm (Fig. 10.7) demonstrates our user-defined exception class. The application enables the user to input a numeric value, then invokes method SquareRoot (lines 17–25) to calculate the square root of that value. To perform this calculation, SquareRoot invokes class Math's Sqrt method, which receives a double value as its argument. Normally, if the argument is negative, method Sqrt returns NaN. In this program, we would like to prevent the user from calculating the square root of a negative number. If the numeric value that the user enters is negative, method SquareRoot throws a NegativeNumberException (lines 21–22). Otherwise, SquareRoot invokes class Math's method Sqrt to compute the square root (line 24).

When the user inputs a value and clicks the **Square Root** button, the program invokes event handler SquareRootButton_Click (lines 28–53). The try statement (lines 33–52) attempts to invoke SquareRoot using the value input by the user. If the user input is not a valid number, a FormatException occurs, and the catch block in lines 40–45 processes the exception. If the user inputs a negative number, method SquareRoot throws a

NegativeNumberException (lines 21–22); the catch block in lines 46–52 catches and handles this type of exception.

```
1   // Fig. 10.7: SquareRootTest.cs
2   // Demonstrating a user-defined exception class.
3   using System;
4   using System.Windows.Forms;
5
6   namespace SquareRootTest
7   {
8      public partial class SquareRootForm : Form
9      {
10        public SquareRootForm()
11        {
12           InitializeComponent();
13        } // end constructor
14
15        // computes square root of parameter; throws
16        // NegativeNumberException if parameter is negative
17        public double SquareRoot( double value )
18        {
19           // if negative operand, throw NegativeNumberException
20           if ( value < 0 )
21              throw new NegativeNumberException(
22                 "Square root of negative number not permitted" );
23           else
24              return Math.Sqrt( value ); // compute square root
25        } // end method SquareRoot
26
27        // obtain user input, convert to double, calculate square root
28        private void SquareRootButton_Click( object sender, EventArgs e )
29        {
30           OutputLabel.Text = ""; // clear OutputLabel
31
32           // catch any NegativeNumberException thrown
33           try
34           {
35              double result =
36                 SquareRoot( Convert.ToDouble( InputTextBox.Text ) );
37
38              OutputLabel.Text = result.ToString();
39           } // end try
40           catch ( FormatException formatExceptionParameter )
41           {
42              MessageBox.Show( formatExceptionParameter.Message,
43                 "Invalid Number Format", MessageBoxButtons.OK,
44                 MessageBoxIcon.Error );
45           } // end catch
46           catch ( NegativeNumberException
47              negativeNumberExceptionParameter )
48           {
```

Fig. 10.7 | SquareRootForm class throws an exception if an error occurs when calculating the square root. (Part 1 of 2.)

```
49              MessageBox.Show( negativeNumberExceptionParameter.Message,
50                 "Invalid Operation", MessageBoxButtons.OK,
51                 MessageBoxIcon.Error );
52          } // end catch
53       } // end method SquareRootButton_Click
54    } // end class SquareRootForm
55 } // end namespace SquareRootTest
```

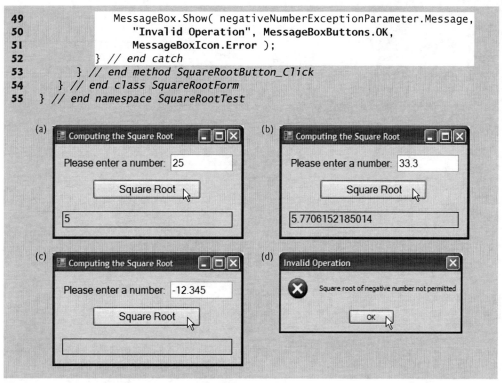

Fig. 10.7 | SquareRootForm class throws an exception if an error occurs when calculating the square root. (Part 2 of 2.)

10.9 Wrap-Up

In this chapter, you learned how to use exception handling to deal with errors in an application. We demonstrated that exception handling enables you to remove error-handling code from the "main line" of the program's execution. You saw exception handling in the context of a divide-by-zero example. You learned how to use try blocks to enclose code that may throw an exception, and how to use catch blocks to deal with exceptions that may arise. We discussed the termination model of exception handling, in which after an exception is handled, program control does not return to the throw point. We also discussed several important classes of the .NET Exception hierarchy, including ApplicationException (from which user-defined exception classes are derived) and SystemException. Next you learned how to use the finally block to release resources whether or not an exception occurs, and how to throw and rethrow exceptions with the throw statement. We also discussed how the using statement can be used to automate the process of releasing a resource. You then learned how to obtain information about an exception using Exception properties Message, StackTrace and InnerException, and method ToString. You learned how to create your own exception classes. In the next two chapters, we present an in-depth treatment of graphical user interfaces. In these chapters and throughout the rest of the book, we use exception handling to make our examples more robust, while still demonstrating new features of the language.

11

Graphical User Interface Concepts: Part 1

... the wisest prophets make sure of the event first.
—Horace Walpole

...The user should feel in control of the computer; not the other way around. This is achieved in applications that embody three qualities: responsiveness, permissiveness, and consistency.
—Apple Computer, Inc. 1985

All the better to see you with my dear.
—The Big Bad Wolf to Little Red Riding Hood

OBJECTIVES

In this chapter you will learn:

- Design principles of graphical user interfaces (GUIs).

- How to create graphical user interfaces.

- How to process events that are generated by user interactions with GUI controls.

- The namespaces that contain the classes for graphical user interface controls and event handling.

- How to create and manipulate `Button`, `Label`, `RadioButton`, `CheckBox`, `TextBox`, `Panel` and `NumericUpDown` controls.

- How to add descriptive `ToolTips` to GUI controls.

- How to process mouse and keyboard events.

11.1 Introduction

A graphical user interface (GUI) allows a user to interact visually with a program. A GUI (pronounced "GOO-ee") gives a program a distinctive "look" and "feel." Providing different applications with a consistent set of intuitive user-interface components enables users to become productive with each application faster.

Look-and-Feel Observation 11.1

Consistent user interfaces enable a user to learn new applications more quickly because the applications have the same "look" and "feel."

As an example of a GUI, consider Fig. 11.1, which shows an Internet Explorer Web browser window containing various GUI controls. Near the top of the window, there is a menu bar containing the menus **File**, **Edit**, **View**, **Favorites**, **Tools** and **Help**. Below the menu bar is a set of buttons, each of which has a defined task in Internet Explorer, such as going back to the previously viewed Web page, printing the current page or refreshing the page. Below these buttons lies a combobox, in which users can type the locations of Web sites that they wish to visit. To the left of the combobox is a label (**Address**) that indicates the combobox's purpose (in this case, entering the location of a Web site). Scrollbars are located at the right side and bottom of the window. Usually, scrollbars appear when a window contains more information than can be displayed in the window's viewable area. Scrollbars enable a user to view different portions of the window's contents. These controls form a user-friendly interface through which the user interacts with the Internet Explorer Web browser.

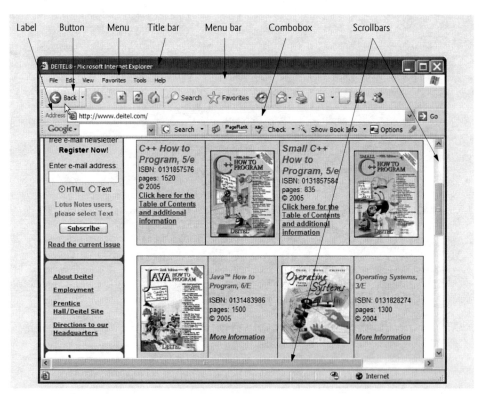

Fig. 11.1 | GUI controls in an Internet Explorer window.

GUIs are built from GUI controls (which are sometimes called *components* or *widgets*—short for *window gadgets*). GUI controls are objects that can display information on the screen or enable users to interact with an application via the mouse, keyboard or some other form of input (such as voice commands). Several common GUI controls are listed in Fig. 11.2—in the sections that follow and in Chapter 12, we discuss each of these in detail. Chapter 12 also explores the features and properties of additional GUI controls.

Control	Description
Label	Displays images or uneditable text.
TextBox	Enables the user to enter data via the keyboard. It can also be used to display editable or uneditable text.
Button	Triggers an event when clicked with the mouse.
CheckBox	Specifies an option that can be selected (checked) or unselected (not checked).
ComboBox	Provides a drop-down list of items from which the user can make a selection either by clicking an item in the list or by typing in a box.

Fig. 11.2 | Some basic GUI controls. (Part 1 of 2.)

Control	Description
ListBox	Provides a list of items from which the user can make a selection by clicking an item in the list. Multiple elements can be selected.
Panel	A container in which controls can be placed and organized.
NumericUpDown	Enables the user to select from a range of input values.

Fig. 11.2 | Some basic GUI controls. (Part 2 of 2.)

11.2 Windows Forms

Windows Forms are used to create the GUIs for programs. A Form is a graphical element that appears on your computer's desktop; it can be a dialog, a window or an *MDI window* (*multiple document interface window*)—discussed in Chapter 12, Graphical User Interface Concepts: Part 2. A *component* is an instance of a class that implements the *IComponent interface*, which defines the behaviors that components must implement, such as how the component is loaded. A control, such as a Button or Label, has a graphical representation at runtime. Some components lack graphical representations (e.g., class Timer of namespace System.Windows.Forms—see Chapter 12). Such, components are not visible at run time.

Figure 11.3 displays the Windows Forms controls and components from the C# **Toolbox**. The controls and components are organized into categories by functionality. Selecting the category **All Windows Forms** at the top of the **Toolbox** allows you to view all the controls and components from the other tabs in one list (as shown in Fig. 11.3). In this chapter and the next, we discuss many of these controls and components. To add a control or component to a Form, select that control component or from the **Toolbox** and drag it on the Form. To deselect a control or component, select the **Pointer** item in the **Toolbox** (the icon at the top of the list). When the **Pointer** item is selected, you cannot accidentally add a new control to the Form.

When there are several windows on the screen, the *active window* is the frontmost and has a highlighted title bar—typically darker blue than the other windows on the screen. A window becomes the active window when the user clicks somewhere inside it. The active window is said to "have the *focus*." For example, in Visual Studio the active window is the **Toolbox** when you are selecting an item from it, or the **Properties** window when you are editing a control's properties.

A Form is a *container* for controls and components. When you drag a control or component from the **Toolbox** on the Form, Visual Studio generates code that instantiates the object and sets its basic properties. This code is updated when the control or component's properties are modified in the IDE. If a control or component is removed from the Form, the generated code for that control is deleted. The generated code is placed by the IDE in a separate file using partial classes. Although we could write this code ourselves, it is much easier to create and modify controls and components using the **Toolbox** and **Properties** windows and allow Visual Studio to handle the details. In this chapter and the next, we use visual programming to build more substantial GUIs.

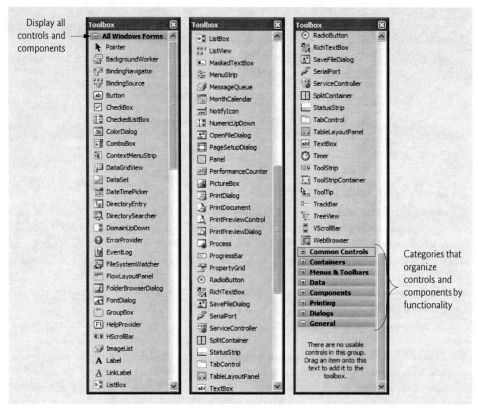

Fig. 11.3 | Components and controls for Windows Forms.

Each control or component we present in this chapter is located in namespace System.Windows.Forms. To create a Windows application, you generally create a Windows Form, set its properties, add controls to the Form, set their properties and implement event handlers (methods) that respond to events generated by the controls. Figure 11.4 lists common Form properties, methods and events.

Form properties, methods and events	Description
Common Properties	
AcceptButton	Button that is clicked when *Enter* is pressed.
AutoScroll	Boolean value that allows or disallows scrollbars when needed.
CancelButton	Button that is clicked when the *Escape* key is pressed.
FormBorderStyle	Border style for the Form (e.g., none, single, three-dimensional).

Fig. 11.4 | Common Form properties, methods and events. (Part 1 of 2.)

Form properties, methods and events	Description
Font	Font of text displayed on the Form, and the default font for controls added to the Form.
Text	Text in the Form's title bar.
Common Methods	
Close	Closes a Form and releases all resources, such as the memory used for the Form's controls and components. A closed Form cannot be reopened.
Hide	Hides a Form, but does not destroy the Form or release its resources.
Show	Displays a hidden Form.
Common Event	
Load	Occurs before a Form is displayed to the user. The handler for this event is displayed in the Visual Studio editor when you double click the Form in the Visual Studio designer.

Fig. 11.4 | Common Form properties, methods and events. (Part 2 of 2.)

When we create controls and event handlers, Visual Studio generates much of the GUI-related code. In visual programming, the IDE maintains GUI-related code and you write the bodies of the event handlers to indicate what actions the program should take when particular events occur.

11.3 Event Handling

Normally, a user interacts with an application's GUI to indicate the tasks that the application should perform. For example, when you write an e-mail in an e-mail application, clicking the **Send** button tells the application to send the e-mail to the specified e-mail addresses. GUIs are *event driven*. When the user interacts with a GUI component, the interaction—known as an *event*—drives the program to perform a task. Common events (user interactions) that might cause an application to perform a task include clicking a Button, typing in a TextBox, selecting an item from a menu, closing a window and moving the mouse. A method that performs a task in response to an event is called an *event handler*, and the overall process of responding to events is known as *event handling*.

11.3.1 A Simple Event-Driven GUI

The Form in the application of Fig. 11.5 contains a Button that a user can click to display a MessageBox. You have already created several GUI examples that execute an event handler in response to clicking a Button. In this example, we discuss Visual Studio's auto-generated code in more depth.

Using the techniques presented earlier in the book, create a Form containing a Button. First, create a new Windows application and add a Button to the Form. In the **Properties**

```
 1    // Fig. 11.5: SimpleEventExampleForm.cs
 2    // Using Visual Studio to create event handlers.
 3    using System;
 4    using System.Windows.Forms;
 5
 6    // Form that shows a simple event handler
 7    public partial class SimpleEventExampleForm : Form
 8    {
 9        // default constructor
10        public SimpleEventExampleForm()
11        {
12            InitializeComponent();
13        } // end constructor
14
15        // handles click event of Button clickButton
16        private void clickButton_Click( object sender, EventArgs e )
17        {
18            MessageBox.Show( "Button was clicked." );
19        } // end method clickButton_Click
20    } // end class SimpleEventExampleForm
```

Fig. 11.5 | Simple event-handling example using visual programming.

window for the Button, set the (Name) property to clickButton and the Text property to Click Me. You'll notice that we use a convention in which each variable name we create for a control ends with the control's type. For example, in the variable name clickButton, "Button" is the control's type.

When the user clicks the Button in this example, we' want the application to respond by displaying a MessageBox. To do this, you must create an event handler for the Button's Click event. You can create this event handler by double clicking the Button on the Form, which declares the following empty event handler in the program code:

```
private void clickButton_Click( object sender, EventArgs e )
{

} // end method clickButton_Click
```

By convention, C# names the event-handler method as *controlName_eventName* (e.g., clickButton_Click). The clickButton_Click event handler executes when the user clicks the clickButton control.

Each event handler receives two parameters when it is called. The first—an object reference named sender—is a reference to the object that generated the event. The second is a reference to an event arguments object of type EventArgs (or one of its derived classes), which is typically named e. This object contains additional information about the event that occurred. EventArgs is the base class of all classes that represent event information.

Software Engineering Observation 11.1

You should not expect return values from event handlers—event handlers are designed to execute code based on an action and return control to the main program.

Good Programming Practice 11.1

Use the event-handler naming convention controlName_eventName, *so method names are meaningful. Such names tell users what event a method handles for what control. This convention is not required, but it makes your code easier to read, understand, modify and maintain.*

To display a `MessageBox` in response to the event, insert the statement

```
MessageBox.Show( "Button was clicked." );
```

in the event handler's body. The resulting event handler appears in lines 16–19 of Fig. 11.5. When you execute the application and click the `Button`, a `MessageBox` appears displaying the text "`Button was clicked`".

11.3.2 Another Look at the Visual Studio Generated Code

Visual Studio generates the code that creates and initializes the GUI that you build in the GUI design window. This auto-generated code is placed in the `Designer.cs` file of the Form (`SimpleEventExampleForm.Designer.cs` in this example). You can open this file by expanding the node for the file you are currently working in (`SimpleEventExample-Form.cs`) and double clicking the file name that ends with `Designer.cs`. Figs. 11.6–11.7 show this file's contents. The IDE collapses the code in lines 21–53 of Fig. 11.7 by default.

Now that you have studied classes and objects in detail, this code will be easier to understand. Since this code is created and maintained by Visual Studio, you generally don't need to look at it. In fact, you do not need to understand most of the code shown here to build GUI applications. However, we now take a closer look to help you understand how GUI applications work.

```
SimpleEventExampleForm.Designer.cs
SimpleEventExampleForm                          components

 1  partial class SimpleEventExampleForm
 2  {
 3      /// <summary>
 4      /// Required designer variable.
 5      /// </summary>
 6      private System.ComponentModel.IContainer components = null;
 7
 8      /// <summary>
 9      /// Clean up any resources being used.
10      /// </summary>
11      /// <param name="disposing">true if managed resources should be disposed; otherwise,
12      protected override void Dispose(bool disposing)
13      {
14          if (disposing && (components != null))
15          {
16              components.Dispose();
17          }
18          base.Dispose(disposing);
19      }
20  }
```

Fig. 11.6 | First half of the Visual Studio generated code file.

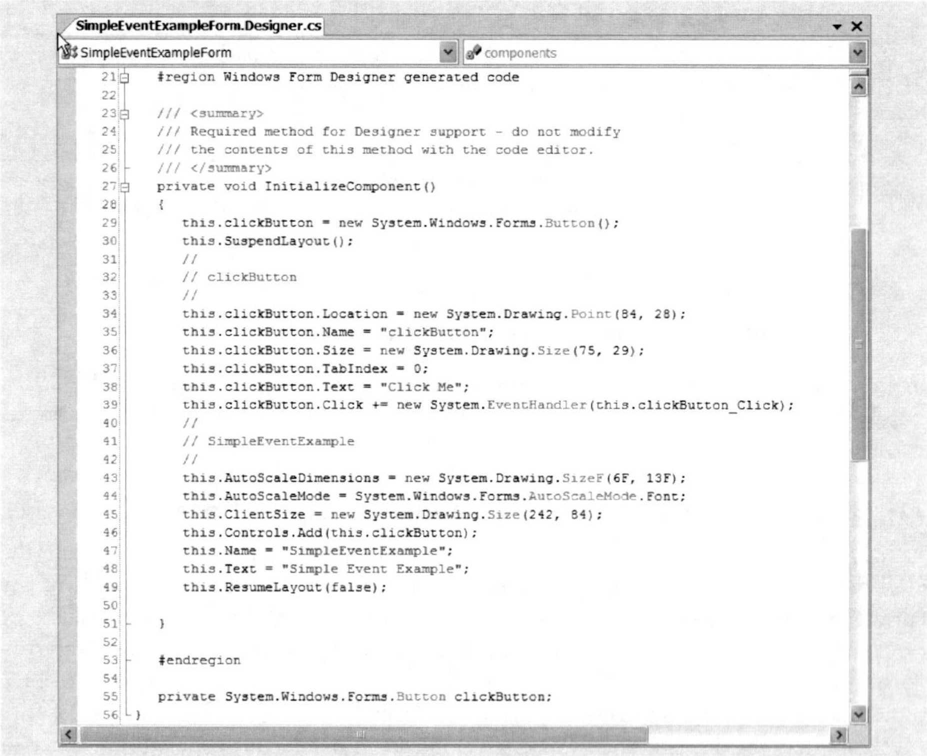


```
21 #region Windows Form Designer generated code
22
23     /// <summary>
24     /// Required method for Designer support - do not modify
25     /// the contents of this method with the code editor.
26     /// </summary>
27     private void InitializeComponent()
28     {
29        this.clickButton = new System.Windows.Forms.Button();
30        this.SuspendLayout();
31        //
32        // clickButton
33        //
34        this.clickButton.Location = new System.Drawing.Point(84, 28);
35        this.clickButton.Name = "clickButton";
36        this.clickButton.Size = new System.Drawing.Size(75, 29);
37        this.clickButton.TabIndex = 0;
38        this.clickButton.Text = "Click Me";
39        this.clickButton.Click += new System.EventHandler(this.clickButton_Click);
40        //
41        // SimpleEventExample
42        //
43        this.AutoScaleDimensions = new System.Drawing.SizeF(6F, 13F);
44        this.AutoScaleMode = System.Windows.Forms.AutoScaleMode.Font;
45        this.ClientSize = new System.Drawing.Size(242, 84);
46        this.Controls.Add(this.clickButton);
47        this.Name = "SimpleEventExample";
48        this.Text = "Simple Event Example";
49        this.ResumeLayout(false);
50
51     }
52
53     #endregion
54
55     private System.Windows.Forms.Button clickButton;
56 }
```

Fig. 11.7 | Second half of the Visual Studio generated code file.

The auto-generated code that defines the GUI is actually part of the `Form`'s class—in this case, `SimpleEventExampleForm`. Line 1 of Fig. 11.6 uses the `partial` modifier, which allows this class to be split among multiple files. Line 55 contains the declaration of the `Button` control `clickButton` that we created in **Design** mode. Note that the control is declared as an instance variable of class `SimpleEventExampleForm`. By default, all variable declarations for controls created through C#'s design window have a `private` access modifier. The code also includes the `Dispose` method for releasing resources (lines 12–19) and method `InitializeComponent` (lines 27–51), which contains the code that creates the `Button`, then sets some of the `Button`'s and the `Form`'s properties. The property values correspond to the values set in the **Properties** window for each control. Note that Visual Studio adds comments to the code that it generates, as in lines 31–33. Line 39 was generated when we created the event handler for the `Button`'s `Click` event.

Method `InitializeComponent` is called when the `Form` is created, and establishes such properties as the `Form` title, the `Form` size, control sizes and text. Visual Studio also uses the code in this method to create the GUI you see in design view. Changing the code in `InitializeComponent` may prevent Visual Studio from displaying the GUI properly.

Error-Prevention Tip 11.1

The code generated by building a GUI in **Design** *mode is not meant to be modified directly, and doing so can result in an application that functions incorrectly. You should modify control properties through the* **Properties** *window.*

11.3.3 Delegates and the Event-Handling Mechanism

The control that generates an event is known as the *event sender*. An event-handling method—known as the *event receiver*—responds to a particular event that a control generates. When the event occurs, the event sender calls its event receiver to perform a task (i.e., to "handle the event").

The .NET event-handling mechanism allows you to choose your own names for event-handling methods. However, each event-handling method must declare the proper parameters to receive information about the event that it handles. Since you can choose your own method names, an event sender such as a Button cannot know in advance which method will respond to its events. So, we need a mechanism to indicate which method is the event receiver for an event.

Delegates

Event handlers are connected to a control's events via special objects called *delegates*. A delegate object holds a reference to a method with a signature that is specified by the delegate type's declaration. GUI controls have predefined delegates that correspond to every event they can generate. For example, the delegate for a Button's Click event is of type EventHandler (namespace System). If you look at this type in the online help documentation, you will see that it is declared as follows:

```
public delegate void EventHandler( object sender, EventArgs e );
```

This uses the ***delegate*** keyword to declare a delegate type named EventHandler, which can hold references to methods that return void and receive two parameters—one of type object (the event sender) and one of type EventArgs. If you compare the delegate declaration with clickButton_Click's header (Fig. 11.5, line 16), you will see that this event handler indeed meets the requirements of the EventHandler delegate. Note that the preceding declaration actually creates an entire class for you. The details of this special class's declaration are handled by the compiler.

Indicating the Method that a Delegate Should Call

An event sender calls a delegate object like a method. Since each event handler is declared as a delegate, the event sender can simply call the appropriate delegate when an event occurs—a Button calls its EventHandler delegate in response to a click. The delegate's job is to invoke the appropriate method. To enable the clickButton_Click method to be called, Visual Studio assigns clickButton_Click to the delegate, as shown in line 39 of Fig. 11.7. This code is added by Visual Studio when you double click the Button control in **Design** mode. The expression

```
new System.EventHandler(this.clickButton_Click);
```

creates an EventHandler delegate object and initializes it with the clickButton_Click method. Line 39 uses the += operator to add the delegate to the Button's Click event. This indicates that clickButton_Click will respond when a user clicks the Button. Note that the += operator is overloaded by the delegate class that is created by the compiler.

You can actually specify that *several* different methods should be invoked in response to an event by adding other delegates to the Button's Click event with statements similar to line 39 of Fig. 11.7. Event delegates are ***multicast***—they represent a set of delegate objects that all have the same signature. Multicast delegates enable several methods to be called in response to a single event. When an event occurs, the event sender calls every method referenced by the multicast delegate. This is known as *event multicasting*. Event delegates derive from class ***MulticastDelegate***, which derives from class ***Delegate*** (both from namespace System).

11.3.4 Other Ways to Create Event Handlers

In all the GUI applications you have created so far, you double clicked a control on the Form to create an event handler for that control. This technique creates an event handler for a control's *default event*—the event that is most frequently used with that control. Typically, controls can generate many different types of events, and each type can have its own event handler. For instance, you already created Click event handlers for Buttons by double clicking a Button in design view (Click is the default event for a Button). However your application can also provide an event handler for a Button's MouseHover event, which occurs when the mouse pointer remains positioned over the Button. We now discuss how to create an event handler for an event that is not a control's default event.

Using the Properties Window to Create Event Handlers

You can create additional event handlers through the **Properties** window. If you select a control on the Form, then click the **Events** icon (the lightning bolt icon in Fig. 11.8) in the **Properties** window, all the events for that control are listed in the window. You can double click an event's name to display the event handler in the editor, if the event handler already exists, or to create the event handler. You can also select an event, then use the drop-down list to its right to choose an existing method that should be used as the event handler for that event. The methods that appear in this drop-down list are the class's methods that have the proper signature to be an event handler for the selected event. You can return to viewing the properties of a control by selecting the **Properties** icon (Fig. 11.8).

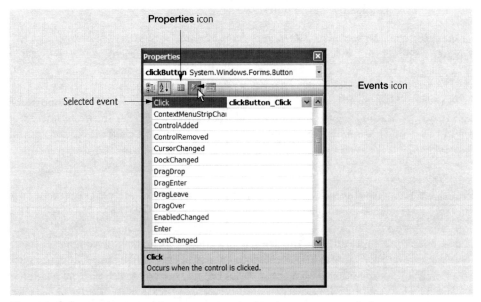

Fig. 11.8 | Viewing events for a Button control in the **Properties** window.

11.3.5 Locating Event Information

Read the Visual Studio documentation to learn about the different events raised by a control. To do this, select **Help > Index**. In the window that appears, select **.NET Framework** in the **Filtered by** drop-down list and enter the name of the control's class in the **Index** window. To ensure that you are selecting the proper class, enter the fully qualified class name as shown in Fig. 11.9 for class System.Windows.Forms.Button. Once you select a control's class in the documentation, a list of all the class's members is displayed. This list includes the events that the class can generate. In Fig. 11.9, we scrolled to class Button's events. Click the name of an event to view its description and examples of its use (Fig. 11.10). Notice that the Click event is listed as a member of class Control, because class Button's Click event is inherited from class Control.

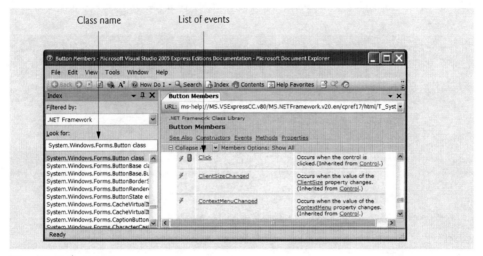

Fig. 11.9 | List of Button events.

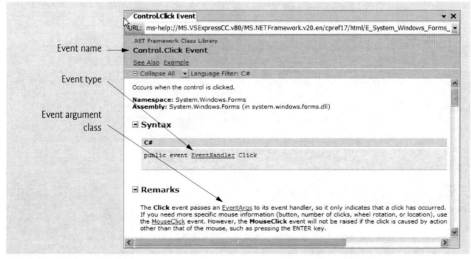

Fig. 11.10 | Click event details.

11.4 Control Properties and Layout

This section overviews properties that are common to many controls. Controls derive from class **Control** (namespace System.Windows.Forms). Figure 11.11 lists some of class Control's properties and methods. The properties shown here can be set for many controls. For example, the Text property specifies the text that appears on a control. The location of this text varies depending on the control. In a Windows Form, the text appears in the title bar, but the text of a Button appears on its face.

The **Focus** method transfers the focus to a control and makes it the **active control**. When you press the *Tab* key in an executing Windows application, controls receive the focus in the order specified by their **TabIndex** property. This property is set by Visual Studio based on the order in which controls are added to a Form, but you can change the tabbing order. TabIndex is helpful for users who enter information in many controls, such

Class Control properties and methods	Description
Common Properties	
BackColor	The control's background color.
BackgroundImage	The control's background image.
Enabled	Specifies whether the control is enabled (i.e., if the user can interact with it). Typically, portions of a disabled control appear "grayed out" as a visual indication to the user that the control is disabled.
Focused	Indicates whether the control has the focus.
Font	The Font used to display the control's text.
ForeColor	The control's foreground color. This usually determines the color of the text in the Text property.
TabIndex	The tab order of the control. When the *Tab* key is pressed, the focus transfers between controls based on the tab order. You can set this order.
TabStop	If true, then a user can give focus to this control via the *Tab* key.
Text	The text associated with the control. The location and appearance of the text vary depending on the type of control.
Visible	Indicates whether the control is visible.
Common Methods	
Focus	Acquires the focus.
Hide	Hides the control (sets the Visible property to false).
Show	Shows the control (sets the Visible property to true).

Fig. 11.11 | Class Control properties and methods.

as a set of TextBoxes that represent a user's name, address and telephone number. The user can enter information, then quickly select the next control by pressing the *Tab* key.

The **_Enabled_** property indicates whether the user can interact with a control to generate an event. Often, if a control is disabled, it is because an option is unavailable to the user at that time. For example, text editor applications often disable the "paste" command until the user copies some text. In most cases, a disabled control's text appears in gray (rather than in black). You can also hide a control from the user without disabling the control by setting the Visible property to false or by calling method Hide. In each case, the control still exists but is not visible on the Form.

You can use anchoring and docking to specify the layout of controls inside a container (such as a Form). *Anchoring* causes controls to remain at a fixed distance from the sides of the container even when the container is resized. Anchoring enhances the user experience. For example, if the user expects a control to appear in a particular corner of the application, anchoring ensures that the control will always be in that corner—even if the user resizes the Form. *Docking* attaches a control to a container such that the control stretches across an entire side. For example, a button docked to the top of a container stretches across the entire top of that container, regardless of the width of the container.

When parent containers are resized, anchored controls are moved (and possibly resized) so that the distance from the sides to which they are anchored does not vary. By default, most controls are anchored to the top-left corner of the Form. To see the effects of anchoring a control, create a simple Windows application that contains two Buttons. Anchor one control to the right and bottom sides by setting the **Anchor** property as shown in Fig. 11.12. Leave the other control unanchored. Execute the application and enlarge the Form. Notice that the Button anchored to the bottom-right corner is always the same distance from the Form's bottom-right corner (Fig. 11.13), but that the other control stays its original distance from the top-left corner of the Form.

Sometimes, it is desirable for a control to span an entire side of the Form, even when the Form is resized. For example, a control such as a status bar typically should remain at the bottom of the Form. Docking allows a control to span an entire side (left, right, top or bottom) of its parent container or to fill the entire container. When the parent control is resized, the docked control resizes as well. In Fig. 11.14, a Button is docked at the top of the Form (spanning the top portion). When the Form is resized, the Button is resized to the

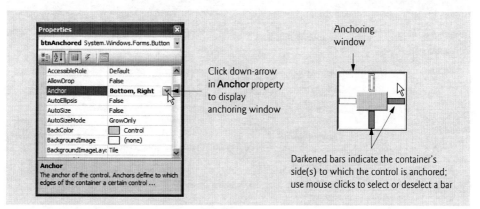

Fig. 11.12 | Manipulating the **Anchor** property of a control.

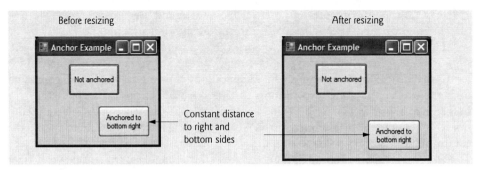

Fig. 11.13 | Anchoring demonstration.

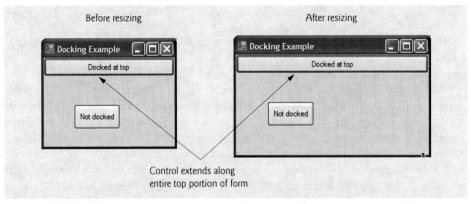

Fig. 11.14 | Docking a Button to the top of a Form.

Form's new width. Forms have a *Padding* property that specifies the distance between the docked controls and the Form edges. This property specifies four values (one for each side), and each value is set to 0 by default. Some common control layout properties are summarized in Fig. 11.15.

Control layout properties	Description
Anchor	Causes a control to remain at a fixed distance from the side(s) of the container even when the container is resized.
Dock	Allows a control to span one side of its container or to fill the entire container.
Padding	Sets the space between a container's edges and docked controls. The default is 0, causing the control to appear flush with the container's sides.
Location	Specifies the location (as a set of coordinates) of the upper-left corner of the control, in relation to its container.

Fig. 11.15 | Control layout properties. (Part 1 of 2.)

Control layout properties	Description
Size	Specifies the size of the control in pixels as a Size object, which has properties Width and Height.
MinimumSize, MaximumSize	Indicate the minimum and maximum size of a Control, respectively.

Fig. 11.15 | Control layout properties. (Part 2 of 2.)

The Anchor and Dock properties of a Control are set with respect to the Control's parent container, which could be a Form or another parent container (such as a Panel; discussed in Section 11.6). The minimum and maximum Form (or other Control) sizes can be set via properties *MinimumSize* and *MaximumSize*, respectively. Both are of type *Size*, which has properties *Width* and *Height* to specify the size of the Form. Properties MinimumSize and MaximumSize allow you to design the GUI layout for a given size range. The user cannot make a Form smaller than the size specified by property MinimumSize and cannot make a Form larger than the size specified by property MaximumSize. To set a Form to a fixed size (where the Form cannot be resized by the user), set its minimum and maximum size to the same value or set its FormBorderStyle property to FixedSingle.

Look-and-Feel Observation 11.2

For resizable Forms, ensure that the GUI layout appears consistent across various Form sizes.

Using Visual Studio To Edit a GUI's Layout

Visual Studio provides tools that help you with GUI layout. You may have noticed when dragging a control across a Form, that blue lines (known as *snap lines*) appear to help you position the control with respect to other controls (Fig. 11.16) and the Form's edges. This new feature of Visual Studio 2005 makes the control you are dragging appear to "snap into

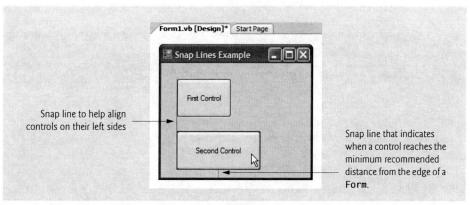

Fig. 11.16 | Snap lines in Visual Studio 2005.

place" alongside other controls. Visual Studio also provides the **Format** menu, which contains several options for modifying your GUI's layout. The **Format** menu does not appear in the IDE unless you select a control (or set of controls) in design view. When you select multiple controls, you can use the **Format** menu's **Align** submenu to align the controls. The **Format** menu also enables you to modify the amount of space between controls or to center a control on the Form.

11.5 Labels, TextBoxes and Buttons

Labels provide text information (as well as optional images) and are defined with class Label (a derived class of Control). A Label displays text that the user cannot directly modify. A Label's text can be changed programmatically by modifying the Label's Text property. Figure 11.17 lists common Label properties.

A textbox (class TextBox) is an area in which either text can be displayed by a program or the user can type text via the keyboard. A *password TextBox* is a TextBox that hides the information entered by the user. As the user types characters, the password TextBox masks the user input by displaying a character you specify (usually *). If you set the *Password-Char* property, the TextBox becomes a password TextBox. Users often encounter both types of TextBoxes, when logging into a computer or Web site—the username TextBox allows users to input their usernames; the password TextBox allows users to enter their passwords. Figure 11.18 lists the common properties and a common event of TextBoxes.

Common Label properties	Description
Font	The font of the text on the Label.
Text	The text on the Label.
TextAlign	The alignment of the Label's text on the control—horizontally (left, center or right) and vertically (top, middle or bottom).

Fig. 11.17 | Common Label properties.

TextBox properties and event	Description
Common Properties	
AcceptsReturn	If true in a multiline TextBox, pressing *Enter* in the TextBox creates a new line. If false, pressing *Enter* is the same as pressing the default Button on the Form. The default Button is the one assigned to a Form's AcceptButton property.
Multiline	If true, the TextBox can span multiple lines. The default value is false.

Fig. 11.18 | TextBox properties and event. (Part 1 of 2.)

TextBox properties and event	Description
PasswordChar	When this property is set to a character, the TextBox becomes a password box, and the specified character masks each character the user type. If no character is specified, the TextBox displays the typed text.
ReadOnly	If true, the TextBox has a gray background, and its text cannot be edited. The default value is false.
ScrollBars	For multiline textboxes, this property indicates which scrollbars appear (None, Horizontal, Vertical or Both).
Text	The TextBox's text content.
Common Event	
TextChanged	Generated when the text changes in a TextBox (i.e., when the user adds or deletes characters). When you double click the TextBox control in **Design** mode, an empty event handler for this event is generated.

Fig. 11.18 | TextBox properties and event. (Part 2 of 2.)

A button is a control that the user clicks to trigger a specific action or to select an option in a program. As you will see, a program can use several types of buttons, such as *checkboxes* and *radio buttons*. All the button classes derive from class ***ButtonBase*** (namespace System.Windows.Forms), which defines common button features. In this section, we discuss class Button, which typically enables a user to issue a command to an application. Figure 11.19 lists common properties and a common event of class Button.

Button properties and event	Description
Common Properties	
Text	Specifies the text displayed on the Button face.
FlatStyle	Modifies a Button's appearance—attribute Flat (for the Button to display without a three-dimensional appearance), Popup (for the Button to appear flat until the user moves the mouse pointer over the Button), Standard (three-dimensional) and System, where the Button's appearance is controlled by the operating system. The default value is Standard.
Common Event	
Click	Generated when the user clicks the Button. When you double click a Button in design view, an empty event handler for this event is created.

Fig. 11.19 | Button properties and event.

Look-and-Feel Observation 11.3

Although Labels, TextBoxes and other controls can respond to mouse clicks, Buttons are more natural for this purpose.

Figure 11.20 uses a TextBox, a Button and a Label. The user enters text into a password box and clicks the Button, causing the text input to be displayed in the Label. Normally, we would not display this text—the purpose of password TextBoxes is to hide the text being entered by the user. When the user clicks the **Show Me** Button, this application retrieves the text that the user typed in the password TextBox and displays it in another TextBox.

First, create the GUI by dragging the controls (a TextBox, a Button and a Label) on the Form. Once the controls are positioned, change their names in the **Properties** window from the default values—textBox1, button1 and label1—to the more descriptive displayPasswordLabel, displayPasswordButton and inputPasswordTextBox. The (Name) property in the **Properties** window enables us to change the variable name for a control. Visual Studio creates the necessary code and places it in method InitializeComponent of the partial class in the file LabelTextBoxButtonTestForm.Designer.cs.

```
1   // Fig. 11.20: LabelTextBoxButtonTestForm.cs
2   // Using a TextBox, Label and Button to display
3   // the hidden text in a password TextBox.
4   using System;
5   using System.Windows.Forms;
6
7   // Form that creates a password TextBox and
8   // a Label to display TextBox contents
9   public partial class LabelTextBoxButtonTestForm : Form
10  {
11     // default constructor
12     public LabelTextBoxButtonTestForm()
13     {
14        InitializeComponent();
15     } // end constructor
16
17     // display user input in Label
18     private void displayPasswordButton_Click(
19        object sender, EventArgs e )
20     {
21        // display the text that the user typed
22        displayPasswordLabel.Text = inputPasswordTextBox.Text;
23     } // end method displayPasswordButton_Click
24  } // end class LabelTextBoxButtonTestForm
```

Fig. 11.20 | Program to display hidden text in a password box.

We then set displayPasswordButton's Text property to "Show Me" and clear the Text of displayPasswordLabel and inputPasswordTextBox so that they are blank when the program begins executing. The BorderStyle property of displayPasswordLabel is set to Fixed3D, giving our Label a three-dimensional appearance. The BorderStyle property of all TextBoxes is set to Fixed3D by default. The password character for inputPassword-TextBox is set by assigning the asterisk character (*) to the PasswordChar property. This property accepts only one character.

We create an event handler for displayPasswordButton by double clicking this control in **Design** mode. We add line 22 to the event handler's body. When the user clicks the **Show Me** Button in the executing application, line 22 obtains the text entered by the user in inputPasswordTextBox and displays the text in displayPasswordLabel.

11.6 GroupBoxes and Panels

GroupBoxes and *Panels* arrange controls on a GUI. GroupBoxes and Panels are typically used to group several controls of similar functionality or several controls that are related in a GUI. All of the controls in a GroupBox or Panel move together when the GroupBox or Panel is moved.

The primary difference between these two controls is that GroupBoxes can display a caption (i.e., text) and do not include scrollbars, whereas Panels can include scrollbars and do not include a caption. GroupBoxes have thin borders by default; Panels can be set so that they also have borders by changing their BorderStyle property. Figures 11.21 and 11.22 list the common properties of GroupBoxes and Panels, respectively.

 Look-and-Feel Observation 11.4

Panels and GroupBoxes can contain other Panels and GroupBoxes for more complex layouts.

GroupBox properties	Description
Controls	The set of controls that the GroupBox contains.
Text	Specifies the caption text displayed at the top of the GroupBox.

Fig. 11.21 | GroupBox properties.

Panel properties	Description
AutoScroll	Indicates whether scrollbars appear when the Panel is too small to display all of its controls. The default value is false.
BorderStyle	Sets the border of the Panel. The default value is None; other options are Fixed3D and FixedSingle.
Controls	The set of controls that the Panel contains.

Fig. 11.22 | Panel properties.

Look-and-Feel Observation 11.5

You can organize a GUI by anchoring and docking controls inside a GroupBox or Panel. The GroupBox or Panel then can be anchored or docked inside a Form. This divides controls into functional "groups" that can be arranged easily.

To create a GroupBox, drag its icon from the **Toolbox** onto a Form. Then, drag new controls from the **Toolbox** into the GroupBox. These controls are added to the GroupBox's **Controls** property and become part of the GroupBox. The GroupBox's Text property specifies the caption.

To create a Panel, drag its icon from the **Toolbox** onto the Form. You can then add controls directly to the Panel by dragging them from the **Toolbox** onto the Panel. To enable the scrollbars, set the Panel's AutoScroll property to true. If the Panel is resized and cannot display all of its controls, scrollbars appear (Fig. 11.23). The scrollbars can be used to view all the controls in the Panel—both at design time and at execution time. In Fig. 11.23, we set the Panel's BorderStyle property to FixedSingle so that you can see the Panel in the Form.

Look-and-Feel Observation 11.6

Use Panels with scrollbars to avoid cluttering a GUI and to reduce the GUI's size.

The program in Fig. 11.24 uses a GroupBox and a Panel to arrange Buttons. When these Buttons are clicked, their event handlers change the text on a Label.

The GroupBox (named mainGroupBox) has two Buttons—hiButton (which displays the text **Hi**) and byeButton (which displays the text **Bye**). The Panel (named mainPanel) also has two Buttons, leftButton (which displays the text **Far Left**) and rightButton (which displays the text **Far Right**). The mainPanel has its AutoScroll property set to true, allowing scrollbars to appear when the contents of the Panel require more space

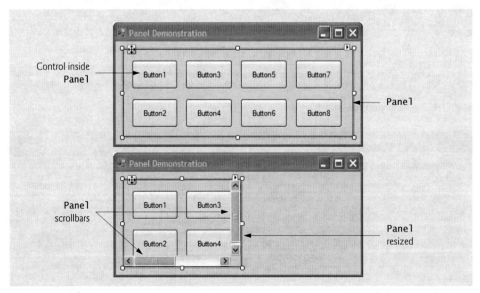

Fig. 11.23 | Creating a Panel with scrollbars.

```
 1   // Fig. 11.24: GroupboxPanelExampleForm.cs
 2   // Using GroupBoxes and Panels to hold Buttons.
 3   using System;
 4   using System.Windows.Forms;
 5
 6   // Form that displays a GroupBox and a Panel
 7   public partial class GroupBoxPanelExampleForm : Form
 8   {
 9      // default constructor
10      public GroupBoxPanelExampleForm()
11      {
12         InitializeComponent();
13      } // end constructor
14
15      // event handler for Hi Button
16      private void hiButton_Click( object sender, EventArgs e )
17      {
18         messageLabel.Text = "Hi pressed"; // change text in Label
19      } // end method hiButton_Click
20
21      // event handler for Bye Button
22      private void byeButton_Click( object sender, EventArgs e )
23      {
24         messageLabel.Text = "Bye pressed"; // change text in Label
25      } // end method byeButton_Click
26
27      // event handler for Far Left Button
28      private void leftButton_Click( object sender, EventArgs e )
29      {
30         messageLabel.Text = "Far left pressed"; // change text in Label
31      } // end method leftButton_Click
32
33      // event handler for Far Right Button
34      private void rightButton_Click( object sender, EventArgs e )
35      {
36         messageLabel.Text = "Far right pressed"; // change text in Label
37      } // end method rightButton_Click
38   } // end class GroupBoxPanelExampleForm
```

Fig. 11.24 | Using GroupBoxes and Panels to arrange Buttons.

than the Panel's visible area. The Label (named messageLabel) is initially blank. To add controls to mainGroupBox or mainPanel, Visual Studio calls method Add of each container's Controls property. This code is placed in the partial class located in the file Group-BoxPanelExampleForm.Designer.cs.

The event handlers for the four Buttons are located in lines 16–37. We added a line in each event handler (lines 18, 24, 30 and 36) to change the text of messageLabel to indicate which Button the user pressed.

11.7 CheckBoxes and RadioButtons

C# has two types of *state buttons* that can be in the on/off or true/false states—**CheckBoxes** and **RadioButtons**. Like class Button, classes CheckBox and RadioButton are derived from class ButtonBase.

CheckBoxes

A CheckBox is a small square that either is blank or contains a check mark. When the user clicks a CheckBox to select it, a check mark appears in the box. If the user clicks CheckBox again to deselect it, the check mark is removed. Any number of CheckBoxes can be selected at a time. A list of common CheckBox properties and events appears in Fig. 11.25.

CheckBox properties and events	Description
Common Properties	
Checked	Indicates whether the CheckBox is checked (contains a check mark) or unchecked (blank). This property returns a Boolean value.
CheckState	Indicates whether the CheckBox is checked or unchecked with a value from the CheckState enumeration (Checked, Unchecked or Indeterminate). Indeterminate is used when it is unclear whether the state should be Checked or Unchecked. For example, in Microsoft Word, when you select a paragraph that contains several character formats, then go to **Format > Font**, some of the CheckBoxes appear in the Indeterminate state. When CheckState is set to Indeterminate, the CheckBox is usually shaded.
Text	Specifies the text displayed to the right of the CheckBox.
Common Events	
CheckedChanged	Generated when the Checked property changes. This is a CheckBox's default event. When a user double clicks the CheckBox control in design view, an empty event handler for this event is generated.
CheckStateChanged	Generated when the CheckState property changes.

Fig. 11.25 | CheckBox properties and events.

The program in Fig. 11.26 allows the user to select CheckBoxes to change a Label's font style. The event handler for one CheckBox applies bold and the event handler for the other applies italic. If both CheckBoxes are selected, the font style is set to bold and italic. Initially, neither CheckBox is checked.

The boldCheckBox has its Text property set to Bold. The italicCheckBox has its Text property set to Italic. The Text property of outputLabel is set to Watch the font style change. After creating the controls, we define their event handlers. Double clicking the CheckBoxes at design time creates empty CheckedChanged event handlers.

To change the font style on a Label, you must set its Font property to a new *Font object* (lines 21–23 and 31–33). The Font constructor that we use here takes the font name, size and style as arguments. The first two arguments—outputLabel.Font.Name and outputLabel.Font.Size—use outputLabel's original font name and size. The style is specified with a member of the *FontStyle enumeration*, which contains Regular, Bold, Italic, Strikeout and Underline. (The Strikeout style displays text with a line through it.)

```
1   // Fig. 11.26: CheckBoxTestForm.cs
2   // Using CheckBoxes to toggle italic and bold styles.
3   using System;
4   using System.Drawing;
5   using System.Windows.Forms;
6
7   // Form contains CheckBoxes to allow the user to modify sample text
8   public partial class CheckBoxTestForm : Form
9   {
10     // default constructor
11     public CheckBoxTestForm()
12     {
13        InitializeComponent();
14     } // end constructor
15
16     // toggle the font style between bold and
17     // not bold based on the  current setting
18     private void boldCheckBox_CheckedChanged(
19        object sender, EventArgs e )
20     {
21        outputLabel.Font =
22           new Font( outputLabel.Font.Name, outputLabel.Font.Size,
23           outputLabel.Font.Style ^ FontStyle.Bold );
24     } // end metod boldCheckBox_CheckedChanged
25
26     // toggle the font style between italic and
27     // not italic based on the current setting
28     private void italicCheckBox_CheckedChanged(
29        object sender, EventArgs e )
30     {
31        outputLabel.Font =
32           new Font( outputLabel.Font.Name, outputLabel.Font.Size,
33           outputLabel.Font.Style ^ FontStyle.Italic );
34     } // end method italicCheckBox_CheckedChanged
35  } // end class CheckBoxTestForm
```

Fig. 11.26 | Using CheckBoxes to change font styles. (Part 1 of 2.)

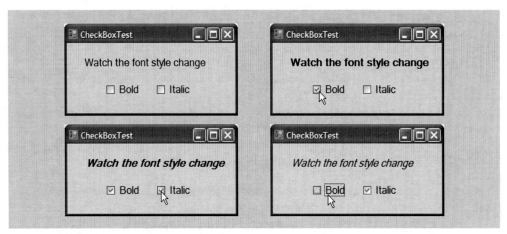

Fig. 11.26 | Using CheckBoxes to change font styles. (Part 2 of 2.)

A Font object's *Style* property is read-only, so it can be set only when the Font object is created.

Styles can be combined via *bitwise operators*—operators that perform manipulation on bits of information. All data is represented in the computer as combinations of 0s and 1s. Each 0 or 1 represents a bit. FontStyle has a System.FlagAttribute, meaning that the FontStyle bit values are selected in a way that allows us to combine different FontStyle elements to create compound styles, using bitwise operators. These styles are not mutually exclusive, so we can combine different styles and remove them without affecting the combination of previous FontStyle elements. We can combine these various font styles, using either the logical OR (|) operator or the logical exclusive OR (^) operator. When the logical OR operator is applied to two bits, if at least one bit of the two has the value 1, then the result is 1. Combining styles using the conditional OR operator works as follows. Assume that FontStyle.Bold is represented by bits 01 and that FontStyle.Italic is represented by bits 10. When we use the conditional OR (||) to combine the styles, we obtain the bits 11.

```
01  =   Bold
10  =   Italic
--
11  =   Bold and Italic
```

The conditional OR operator helps create style combinations. However, what happens if we want to undo a style combination, as we did in Fig. 11.26?

The logical exclusive OR operator enables us to combine styles and to undo existing style settings. When logical exclusive OR is applied to two bits, if both bits have the same value, then the result is 0. If both bits are different, then the result is 1.

Combining styles using logical exclusive OR works as follows. Assume, again, that FontStyle.Bold is represented by bits 01 and that FontStyle.Italic is represented by bits 10. When we use logical exclusive OR (^) on both styles, we obtain the bits 11.

```
01  =   Bold
10  =   Italic
--
11  =   Bold and Italic
```

Now, suppose that we would like to remove the FontStyle.Bold style from the previous combination of FontStyle.Bold and FontStyle.Italic. The easiest way to do so is to reapply the logical exclusive OR (∧) operator to the compound style and Font-Style.Bold.

```
11  =  Bold and Italic
01  =  Bold
--
10  =  Italic
```

This is a simple example. The advantages of using bitwise operators to combine FontStyle values become more evident when we consider that there are five different FontStyle values (Bold, Italic, Regular, Strikeout and Underline), resulting in 16 different Font-Style combinations. Using bitwise operators to combine font styles greatly reduces the amount of code required to check all possible font combinations.

In Fig. 11.26, we need to set the FontStyle so that the text appears in bold if it was not bold originally, and vice versa. Notice that line 23 uses the bitwise logical exclusive OR operator to do this. If outputLabel.Font.Style is bold, then the resulting style is not bold. If the text is originally italic, the resulting style is bold and italic, rather than just bold. The same applies for FontStyle.Italic in line 33.

If we did not use bitwise operators to compound FontStyle elements, we would have to test for the current style and change it accordingly. For example, in event handler boldCheckBox_CheckChanged, we could test for the regular style and make it bold; test for the bold style and make it regular; test for the italic style and make it bold italic; and test for the italic bold style and make it italic. This is cumbersome because, for every new style we add, we double the number of combinations. Adding a CheckBox for underline would require testing eight additional styles. Adding a CheckBox for strikeout would require testing 16 additional styles.

RadioButtons

Radio buttons (defined with class RadioButton) are similar to CheckBoxes in that they also have two states—*selected* and *not selected* (also called *deselected*). However, RadioButtons normally appear as a *group*, in which only one RadioButton can be selected at a time. Selecting one RadioButton in the group forces all the others to be deselected. Therefore, RadioButtons are used to represent a set of *mutually exclusive* options (i.e., a set in which multiple options cannot be selected at the same time).

Look-and-Feel Observation 11.7

Use RadioButtons when the user should choose only one option in a group.

Look-and-Feel Observation 11.8

Use CheckBoxes when the user should be able to choose multiple options in a group.

All RadioButtons added to a container become part of the same group. To separate RadioButtons into several groups, the RadioButtons must be added to GroupBoxes or Panels. The common properties and a common event of class RadioButton are listed in Fig. 11.27.

RadioButton properties and event	Description
Common Properties	
Checked	Indicates whether the RadioButton is checked.
Text	Specifies the RadioButton's text.
Common Event	
CheckedChanged	Generated every time the RadioButton is checked or unchecked. When you double click a RadioButton control in design view, an empty event handler for this event is generated.

Fig. 11.27 | RadioButton properties and event.

Software Engineering Observation 11.2

Forms, GroupBoxes, and Panels can act as logical groups for RadioButtons. The RadioButtons within each group are mutually exclusive to each other, but not to RadioButtons in different logical groups.

The program in Fig. 11.28 uses RadioButtons to enable users to select options for a MessageBox. After selecting the desired attributes, the user presses the **Display** Button to display the MessageBox. A Label in the lower-left corner shows the result of the MessageBox (i.e., which Button the user clicked—**Yes, No, Cancel**, etc.).

To store the user's choices, we create and initialize the iconType and buttonType objects (lines 11–12). Object iconType is of type MessageBoxIcon, and can have values Asterisk, Error, Exclamation, Hand, Information, None, Question, Stop and Warning. The sample output shows only Error, Exclamation, Information and Question icons.

Object buttonType is of type MessageBoxButtons, and can have values Abort-RetryIgnore, OK, OKCancel, RetryCancel, YesNo and YesNoCancel. The name indicates the options that are presented to the user in the MessageBox. The sample output windows show MessageBoxes for all of the MessageBoxButtons enumeration values.

We created two GroupBoxes, one for each set of enumeration values. The GroupBox captions are **Button Type** and **Icon**. The GroupBoxes contain RadioButtons for the corresponding enumeration options, and the RadioButtons' Text properties are set appropriately. Because the RadioButtons are grouped, only one RadioButton can be selected from each GroupBox. There is also a Button (displayButton) labeled **Display**. When a user clicks this Button, a customized MessageBox is displayed. A Label (displayLabel) displays which Button the user pressed within the MessageBox.

The event handler for the RadioButtons handles the CheckedChanged event of each RadioButton. When a RadioButton contained in the **Button Type** GroupBox is checked, the checked RadioButton's corresponding event handler sets buttonType to the appropriate value. Lines 21–45 contain the event handling for these RadioButtons. Similarly, when the user checks the RadioButtons belonging to the **Icon** GroupBox, the event handlers associated with these events (lines 48–80) set iconType to its corresponding value.

```
1    // Fig. 11.28: RadioButtonsTestForm.cs
2    // Using RadioButtons to set message window options.
3    using System;
4    using System.Windows.Forms;
5
6    // Form contains several RadioButtons--user chooses one
7    // from each group to create a custom MessageBox
8    public partial class RadioButtonsTestForm : Form
9    {
10      // create variables that store the user's choice of options
11      private MessageBoxIcon iconType;
12      private MessageBoxButtons buttonType;
13
14      // default constructor
15      public RadioButtonsTestForm()
16      {
17         InitializeComponent();
18      } // end constructor
19
20      // change Buttons based on option chosen by sender
21      private void buttonType_CheckedChanged( object sender, EventArgs e )
22      {
23         if ( sender == okButton ) // display OK Button
24            buttonType = MessageBoxButtons.OK;
25
26         // display OK and Cancel Buttons
27         else if ( sender == okCancelButton )
28            buttonType = MessageBoxButtons.OKCancel;
29
30         // display Abort, Retry and Ignore Buttons
31         else if ( sender == abortRetryIgnoreButton )
32            buttonType = MessageBoxButtons.AbortRetryIgnore;
33
34         // display Yes, No and Cancel Buttons
35         else if ( sender == yesNoCancelButton )
36            buttonType = MessageBoxButtons.YesNoCancel;
37
38         // display Yes and No Buttons
39         else if ( sender == yesNoButton )
40            buttonType = MessageBoxButtons.YesNo;
41
42         // only on option left--display Retry and Cancel Buttons
43         else
44            buttonType = MessageBoxButtons.RetryCancel;
45      } // end method buttonType_Changed
46
47      // change Icon based on option chosen by sender
48      private void iconType_CheckedChanged( object sender, EventArgs e )
49      {
50         if ( sender == asteriskButton ) // display asterisk Icon
51            iconType = MessageBoxIcon.Asterisk;
52
```

Fig. 11.28 | Using RadioButtons to set message-window options. (Part 1 of 4.)

```
53         // display error Icon
54         else if ( sender == errorButton )
55            iconType = MessageBoxIcon.Error;
56
57         // display exclamation point Icon
58         else if ( sender == exclamationButton )
59            iconType = MessageBoxIcon.Exclamation;
60
61         // display hand Icon
62         else if ( sender == handButton )
63            iconType = MessageBoxIcon.Hand;
64
65         // display information Icon
66         else if ( sender == informationButton )
67            iconType = MessageBoxIcon.Information;
68
69         // display question mark Icon
70         else if ( sender == questionButton )
71            iconType = MessageBoxIcon.Question;
72
73         // display stop Icon
74         else if ( sender == stopButton )
75            iconType = MessageBoxIcon.Stop;
76
77         // only one option left--display warning Icon
78         else
79            iconType = MessageBoxIcon.Warning;
80      } // end method iconType_CheckChanged
81
82      // display MessageBox and Button user pressed
83      private void displayButton_Click( object sender, EventArgs e )
84      {
85         // display MessageBox and store
86         // the value of the Button that was pressed
87         DialogResult result = MessageBox.Show(
88            "This is your Custom MessageBox.", "Custom MessageBox",
89            buttonType, iconType, 0, 0 );
90
91         // check to see which Button was pressed in the MessageBox
92         // change text displayed accordingly
93         switch (result)
94         {
95            case DialogResult.OK:
96               displayLabel.Text = "OK was pressed.";
97               break;
98            case DialogResult.Cancel:
99               displayLabel.Text = "Cancel was pressed.";
100               break;
101            case DialogResult.Abort:
102               displayLabel.Text = "Abort was pressed.";
103               break;
```

Fig. 11.28 | Using RadioButtons to set message-window options. (Part 2 of 4.)

```
104            case DialogResult.Retry:
105                displayLabel.Text = "Retry was pressed.";
106                break;
107            case DialogResult.Ignore:
108                displayLabel.Text = "Ignore was pressed.";
109                break;
110            case DialogResult.Yes:
111                displayLabel.Text = "Yes was pressed.";
112                break;
113            case DialogResult.No:
114                displayLabel.Text = "No was pressed.";
115                break;
116        } // end switch
117    } // end method displayButton_Click
118 } // end class RadioButtonsTestForm
```

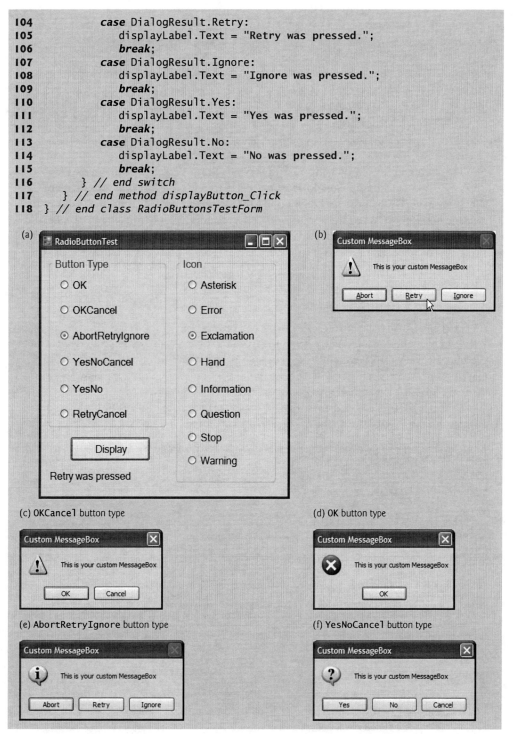

Fig. 11.28 | Using RadioButtons to set message-window options. (Part 3 of 4.)

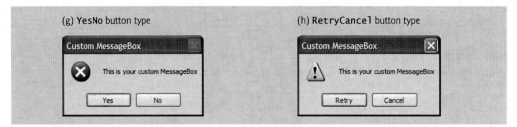

Fig. 11.28 | Using RadioButtons to set message-window options. (Part 4 of 4.)

The Click event handler for displayButton (lines 83–117) creates a MessageBox (lines 87–89). The MessageBox options are specified with the values stored in iconType and buttonType. When the user clicks one of the MessageBox's buttons, the result of the message box is returned to the application. This result is a value from the *DialogResult enumeration* that contains Abort, Cancel, Ignore, No, None, OK, Retry or Yes. The switch statement in lines 93–116 tests for the result and sets displayLabel.Text appropriately.

11.8 PictureBoxes

A PictureBox displays an image. The image can be one of several formats, such as bitmap, GIF (Graphics Interchange Format) and JPEG. A PictureBox's Image property specifies the image that is displayed, and the SizeMode property indicates how the image is displayed (Normal, StretchImage, Autosize or CenterImage). Figure 11.29 describes common PictureBox properties and a common event.

Figure 11.30 uses a PictureBox named imagePictureBox to display one of three bitmap images—image0, image1 or image2. These images are located in the images directory in the

PictureBox properties and event	Description
Common Properties	
Image	Sets the image to display in the PictureBox.
SizeMode	Enumeration that controls image sizing and positioning. Values are Normal (default), StretchImage, AutoSize and CenterImage. Normal places the image in the top-left corner of the PictureBox, and CenterImage puts the image in the middle. These two options truncate the image if it is too large. StretchImage resizes the image to fit in the PictureBox. AutoSize resizes the PictureBox to hold the image.
Common Event	
Click	Occurs when the user clicks the control. When you double click this control in the designer, an event handler is generated for this event.

Fig. 11.29 | PictureBox properties and event.

```
 1    // Fig. 11.30: PictureBoxTestForm.cs
 2    // Using a PictureBox to display images.
 3    using System;
 4    using System.Drawing;
 5    using System.Windows.Forms;
 6    using System.IO;
 7
 8    // Form to display different images when PictureBox is clicked
 9    public partial class PictureBoxTestForm : Form
10    {
11       private int imageNum = -1; // determines which image is displayed
12
13       // default constructor
14       public PictureBoxTestForm()
15       {
16          InitializeComponent();
17       } // end constructor
18
19       // change image whenever Next Button is clicked
20       private void nextButton_Click( object sender, EventArgs e )
21       {
22          imageNum = ( imageNum + 1 ) % 3; // imageNum cycles from 0 to 2
23
24          // create Image object from file, display in PicutreBox
25          imagePictureBox.Image = Image.FromFile(
26             Directory.GetCurrentDirectory() + @"\images\image" +
27             imageNum + ".bmp" );
28       } // end method nextButton_Click
29    } // end class PictureBoxTestForm
```

Fig. 11.30 | Using a PictureBox to display images. (Part 1 of 2.)

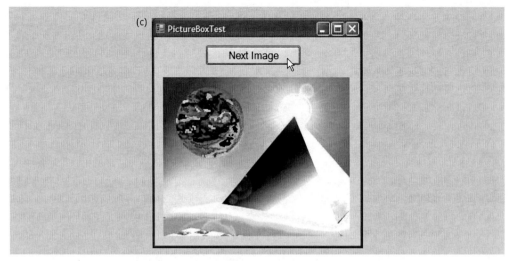

Fig. 11.30 | Using a `PictureBox` to display images. (Part 2 of 2.)

project's `bin/Debug` and `bin/Release` directories. Whenever a user clicks the **Next Image** Button, the image changes to the next image in sequence. When the last image is displayed and the user clicks the **Next Image** Button, the first image is displayed again. Inside event handler `nextButton_Click` (lines 20–28), we use an `int` (`imageNum`) to store the number of the image we want to display. We then set the `Image` property of `imagePictureBox` to an `Image` (lines 25–27).

11.9 ToolTips

We previously demonstrated tool tips—the helpful text that appears when the mouse hovers over an item in a GUI. Recall that the tool tips displayed in Visual Studio help you become familiar with the IDE's features and serve as useful reminders for each toolbar icon's functionality. Many programs use tool tips to remind users of each control's purpose. For example, Microsoft Word has tool tips that help users determine the purpose of the application's icons. This section demonstrates how use the ***ToolTip component*** to add tool tips to your applications. Figure 11.31 describes common properties and a common event of class `ToolTip`.

ToolTip properties and event	Description
Common Properties	
`AutoPopDelay`	The amount of time (in milliseconds) that the tool tip appears while the mouse is over a control.
`InitialDelay`	The amount of time (in milliseconds) that a mouse must hover over a control before a tool tip appears.

Fig. 11.31 | `ToolTip` properties and event. (Part 1 of 2.)

ToolTip properties and event	Description
ReshowDelay	The amount of time (in milliseconds) between which two different tool tips appear (when the mouse is moved from one control to another).
Common Event	
Draw	Raised when the tool tip is displayed. This event allows programmers to modify the appearance of the tool tip.

Fig. 11.31 | ToolTip properties and event. (Part 2 of 2.)

When you add a ToolTip component from the **Toolbox**, it appears in the *component tray*—the gray region below the Form in **Design** mode. Once a ToolTip is added to a Form, a new property appears in the **Properties** window for the Form's other controls. This property appears in the **Properties** window as **ToolTip on**, followed by the name of the ToolTip component. For instance, if our Form's ToolTip were named helpfulToolTip, you would set a control's **ToolTip on helpfulToolTip** property value to specify the control's tool tip text. Figure 11.32 demonstrates the ToolTip component. For this example, we create a GUI containing two Labels, so we can demonstrate different tool tip text for each Label. To make the sample outputs clearer, we set the BorderStyle property of each Label to FixedSingle, which displays a solid border. Since there is no event handling code in this example, the class in Fig. 11.32 contains only a constructor.

In this example, we named the ToolTip component labelsToolTip. Figure 11.33 shows the ToolTip in the component tray. We set the tool tip text for the first Label to "First Label" and the tool tip text for the second Label to "Second Label". Figure 11.34 demonstrates setting the tool tip text for the first Label.

```csharp
1   // Fig. 11.32: ToolTipExampleForm.cs
2   // Demonstrating the ToolTip component.
3   using System;
4   using System.Windows.Forms;
5
6   public partial class ToolTipExampleForm : Form
7   {
8      // default constructor
9      public ToolTipExampleForm()
10     {
11        InitializeComponent();
12     } // end constructor
13
14     // no event handlers needed for this example
15
16  } // end class ToolTipExampleForm
```

Fig. 11.32 | Demonstrating the ToolTip component. (Part 1 of 2.)

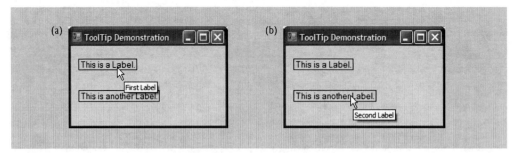

Fig. 11.32 | Demonstrating the ToolTip component. (Part 2 of 2.)

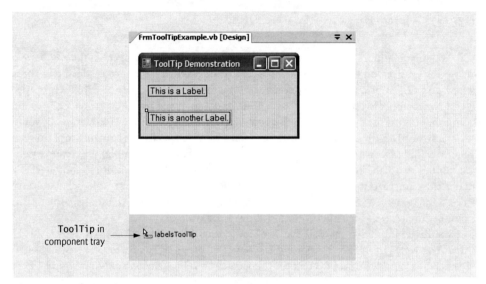

Fig. 11.33 | Demonstrating the component tray.

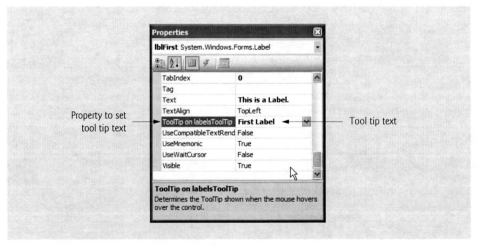

Fig. 11.34 | Setting a control's tool tip text.

11.10 NumericUpDown Control

At times, we will want to restrict a user's input choices to a specific range of numeric values. This is the purpose of the *NumericUpDown control*. This control appears as a TextBox, with two small Buttons on the right side—one with an up arrow and one with a down arrow. By default, a user can type numeric values into this control as if it were a TextBox or click the up and down arrows to increase or decrease the value in the control, respectively. The largest and smallest values in the range are specified with the *Maximum* and *Minimum* properties, respectively (both of type decimal). The *Increment* property (also of type decimal) specifies by how much the current number in the control changes when the user clicks the control's up and down arrows. Figure 11.35 describes common properties and a common event of class NumericUpDown.

NumericUpDown properties and event	Description
Common Properties	
Increment	Specifies by how much the current number in the control changes when the user clicks the control's up and down arrows.
Maximum	Largest value in the control's range.
Minimum	Smallest value in the control's range.
UpDownAlign	Modifies the alignment of the up and down Buttons on the NumericUpDown control. This property can be used to display these Buttons either to the left or to the right of the control.
Value	The numeric value currently displayed in the control.
Common Event	
ValueChanged	This event is raised when the value in the control is changed. This is the default event for the NumericUpDown control.

Fig. 11.35 | NumericUpDown properties and event.

Figure 11.36 demonstrates using a NumericUpDown control for a GUI that calculates interest rate. The calculations performed in this application are similar to those performed in Fig. 4.6. TextBoxes are used to input the principal and interest rate amounts, and a

```
1   // Fig. 11.36: interestCalculatorForm.cs
2   // Demonstrating the NumericUpDown control.
3   using System;
4   using System.Windows.Forms;
5
6   public partial class interestCalculatorForm : Form
7   {
```

Fig. 11.36 | Demonstrating the NumericUpDown control. (Part 1 of 2.)

```
 8      // default constructor
 9      public interestCalculatorForm()
10      {
11         InitializeComponent();
12      } // end constructor
13
14      private void calculateButton_Click(
15         object sender, EventArgs e )
16      {
17         // declare variables to store user input
18         decimal principal; // store principal
19         double rate; // store interest rate
20         int year; // store number of years
21         decimal amount; // store amount
22         string output; // store output
23
24         // retrieve user input
25         principal = Convert.ToDecimal( principalTextBox.Text );
26         rate = Convert.ToDouble( interestTextBox.Text );
27         year = Convert.ToInt32( yearUpDown.Value );
28
29         // set output header
30         output = "Year\tAmount on Deposit\r\n";
31
32         // calculate amount after each year and append to output
33         for ( int yearCounter = 1; yearCounter <= year;  yearCounter++ )
34         {
35            amount =  principal *
36               ( ( decimal ) Math.Pow( ( 1 + rate / 100 ), yearCounter ) );
37            output += ( yearCounter + "\t" +
38               string.Format( "{0:C}", amount ) + "\r\n" );
39         } // end for
40
41         displayTextBox.Text = output; // display result
42      } // end method calculateButton_Click
43   } // end class interestCalculatorForm
```

Fig. 11.36 | Demonstrating the NumericUpDown control. (Part 2 of 2.)

NumericUpDown control is used to input the number of years for which we want to calculate interest.

For the NumericUpDown control named yearUpDown, we set the Minimum property to 1 and the Maximum property to 10. We left the Increment property set to 1, its default value. These settings specify that users can enter a number of years in the range 1 to 10 in increments of 1. If we had set the Increment to 0.5, we could also input values such as 1.5 or 2.5. We set the NumericUpDown's **ReadOnly property** to true to indicate that the user can cannot type a number into the control to make a selection. Thus, the user must click the up and down arrows to modify the value in the control. By default, the ReadOnly property is set to false. The output for this application is displayed in a multiline read-only TextBox with a vertical scrollbar, so the user can scroll through the entire output.

11.11 Mouse-Event Handling

This section explains how to handle *mouse events*, such as *clicks*, *presses* and *moves*, which are generated when the user interacts with a control via the mouse. Mouse events can be handled for any control that derives from class System.Windows.Forms.Control. For most mouse events, information about the event is passed to the event-handling method through an object of class **MouseEventArgs**, and the delegate used to create the mouse-event handlers is **MouseEventHandler**. Each mouse-event-handling method for these events requires an object and a MouseEventArgs object as arguments.

Class MouseEventArgs contains information related to the mouse event, such as the mouse pointer's *x*- and *y*-coordinates, the mouse button pressed (Right, Left or Middle) and the number of times the mouse was clicked. Note that the *x*- and *y*-coordinates of the MouseEventArgs object are relative to the control that generated the event—i.e., point *(0,0)* represents the upper-left corner of the control where the mouse event occurred. Several common mouse events are described in Fig. 11.37.

Mouse events and event arguments	
Mouse Events with Event Argument of Type EventArgs	
MouseEnter	Occurs when the mouse cursor enters the control's boundaries.
MouseLeave	Occurs when the mouse cursor leaves the control's boundaries.
Mouse Events with Event Argument of Type MouseEventArgs	
MouseDown	Occurs when a mouse button is pressed while the mouse cursor is within a control's boundaries.
MouseHover	Occurs when the mouse cursor hovers within the control's boundaries.
MouseMove	Occurs when the mouse cursor is moved while in the control's boundaries.
MouseUp	Occurs when a mouse button is released when the cursor is over the control's boundaries.

Fig. 11.37 | Mouse events and event arguments. (Part 1 of 2.)

Mouse events and event arguments	
Class MouseEventArgs Properties	
Button	Specifies which mouse button was pressed (Left, Right, Middle or none).
Clicks	The number of times that the mouse button was clicked.
X	The *x*-coordinate within the control where the event occurred.
Y	The *y*-coordinate within the control where the event occurred.

Fig. 11.37 | Mouse events and event arguments. (Part 2 of 2.)

Figure 11.38 uses mouse events to draw on a Form. Whenever the user drags the mouse (i.e., moves the mouse while a mouse button is pressed), small circles appear on the Form at the position where each mouse event occurs during the drag operation.

In line 10, the program declares variable shouldPaint, which determines whether to draw on the Form. We want the program to draw only while the mouse button is pressed

```
1   // Fig 11.38: PainterForm.cs
2   // Using the mouse to draw on a Form.
3   using System;
4   using System.Drawing;
5   using System.Windows.Forms;
6
7   // creates a Form that is a drawing surface
8   public partial class PainterForm : Form
9   {
10     bool shouldPaint = false; // determines whether to paint
11
12     // default constructor
13     public PainterForm()
14     {
15        InitializeComponent();
16     } // end constructor
17
18     // should paint when mouse button is pressed down
19     private void PainterForm_MouseDown( object sender, MouseEventArgs e )
20     {
21        // indicate that user is dragging the mouse
22        shouldPaint = true;
23     } // end method PainterForm_MouseDown
24
25     // stop painting when mouse button is released
26     private void PainterForm_MouseUp( object sender, MouseEventArgs e )
27     {
28        // indicate that user released the mouse button
29        shouldPaint = false;
30     } // end method PainterForm_MouseUp
```

Fig. 11.38 | Using the mouse to draw on a Form. (Part 1 of 2.)

```
31
32       // draw circle whenever mouse moves with its button held down
33       private void PainterForm_MouseMove( object sender, MouseEventArgs e )
34       {
35          if ( shouldPaint ) // check if mouse button is being pressed
36          {
37             // draw a circle where the mouse pointer is present
38             Graphics graphics = CreateGraphics();
39             graphics.FillEllipse(
40                new SolidBrush( Color.BlueViolet ), e.X, e.Y, 4, 4 );
41             graphics.Dispose();
42          } // end if
43       } // end method PainterForm_MouseMove
44    } // end class PainterForm
```

Fig. 11.38 | Using the mouse to draw on a Form. (Part 2 of 2.)

(i.e., held down). Thus, when the user clicks or holds down a mouse button, the system generates a MouseDown event, and the event handler (lines 19–23) sets shouldPaint to true. When the user releases the mouse button, the system generates a MouseUp event, shouldPaint is set to false in the PainterForm_MouseUp event handler (lines 26–30) and the program stops drawing. Unlike MouseMove events, which occur continuously as the user moves the mouse, the system generates a MouseDown event only when a mouse button is first pressed and generates a MouseUp event only when a mouse button is released.

Whenever the mouse moves over a control, the MouseMove event for that control occurs. Inside the PainterForm_MouseMove event handler (lines 33–43), the program draws only if shouldPaint is true (i.e., a mouse button is pressed). Line 38 calls inherited Form method CreateGraphics to create a *Graphics* object that allows the program to draw on the Form. Class Graphics provides methods that draw various shapes. For example, lines 39–40 use method *FillEllipse* to draw a circle. The first parameter to method FillEllipse in this case is an object of class *SolidBrush*, which specifies the solid color that will fill the shape. The color is provided as an argument to class SolidBrush's constructor. Type *Color* contains numerous predefined color constants—we selected Color.BlueViolet. FillEllipse draws an oval in a bounding rectangle that is specified by the x- and y-coordinates of its upper-left corner, its width and its height—the final four arguments to the method. The x- and y-coordinates represent the location of the mouse event and can be taken from the mouse-event arguments (e.X and e.Y). To draw a circle, we set the width and height of the bounding rectangle so that they are equal—in this example, both are 4 pixels. `Graphics`, `SolidBrush` and `Color` are all part of the namespace `System.Drawing`.

11.12 Keyboard-Event Handling

Key events occur when keyboard keys are pressed and released. Such events can be handled for any control that inherits from `System.Windows.Forms.Control`. There are three key events—KeyPress, KeyUp and KeyDown. The **KeyPress** event occurs when the user presses a key that represents an ASCII character. The specific key can be determined with property **KeyChar** of the event handler's **KeyPressEventArgs** argument. ASCII is a 128-character set of alphanumeric symbols.

The KeyPress event does not indicate whether *modifier keys* (e.g., *Shift*, *Alt* and *Ctrl*) were pressed when a key event occurred. If this information is important, the **KeyUp** or **KeyDown** events can be used. The **KeyEventArgs** argument for each of these events contains information about modifier keys. Often, modifier keys are used in conjunction with the mouse to select or highlight information. Figure 11.39 lists important key event information. Several properties return values from the **Keys enumeration**, which provides constants that specify the various keys on a keyboard. Like the FontStyle enumeration (Section 11.7), the Keys enumeration is a `System.FlagAttribute`, so the enumeration's constants can be combined to indicate multiple keys pressed at the same time.

Keyboard events and event arguments	
Key Events with Event Arguments of Type `KeyEventArgs`	
KeyDown	Generated when a key is initially pressed.
KeyUp	Generated when a key is released.
Key Event with Event Argument of Type `KeyPressEventArgs`	
KeyPress	Generated when a key is pressed.
Class KeyPressEventArgs Properties	
KeyChar	Returns the ASCII character for the key pressed.
Handled	Indicates whether the KeyPress event was handled.
Class KeyEventArgs Properties	
Alt	Indicates whether the *Alt* key was pressed.
Control	Indicates whether the *Ctrl* key was pressed.
Shift	Indicates whether the *Shift* key was pressed.
Handled	Indicates whether the event was handled.
KeyCode	Returns the key code for the key as a value from the Keys enumeration. This does not include modifier-key information. It is used to test for a specific key.

Fig. 11.39 | Keyboard events and event arguments. (Part 1 of 2.)

Keyboard events and event arguments	
KeyData	Returns the key code for a key combined with modifier information as a Keys value. This property contains all information about the pressed key.
KeyValue	Returns the key code as an int, rather than as a value from the Keys enumeration. This property is used to obtain a numeric representation of the pressed key. The int value is known as a Windows virtual key code.
Modifiers	Returns a Keys value indicating any pressed modifier keys (*Alt*, *Ctrl* and *Shift*). This property is used to determine modifier-key information only.

Fig. 11.39 | Keyboard events and event arguments. (Part 2 of 2.)

Figure 11.40 demonstrates the use of the key-event handlers to display a key pressed by a user. The program is a Form with two Labels that displays the pressed key on one Label and modifier key information on the other.

```
 1   // Fig. 11.40: KeyDemoForm.cs
 2   // Displaying information about the key the user pressed.
 3       System;
 4       System.Windows.Forms;
 5
 6   // Form to display key information when key is pressed
 7                   KeyDemoForm : Form
 8   {
 9      // default constructor
10          KeyDemoForm()
11      {
12         InitializeComponent();
13      } // end constructor
14
15      // display the character pressed using KeyChar
16              KeyDemoForm_KeyPress(            sender, KeyPressEventArgs e )
17      {
18         charLabel.Text = "Key pressed: " + e.KeyChar;
19      } // end method KeyDemoForm_KeyPress
20
21      // display modifier keys, key code, key data and key value
22              KeyDemoForm_KeyDown(            sender, KeyEventArgs e )
23      {
24         keyInfoLabel.Text =
25            "Alt: " + ( e.Alt ? "Yes" : "No" ) + '\n' +
26            "Shift: " + ( e.Shift ? "Yes" : "No" ) + '\n' +
27            "Ctrl: " + ( e.Control ? "Yes" : "No" ) + '\n' +
28            "KeyCode: " + e.KeyCode + '\n' +
29            "KeyData: " + e.KeyData + '\n' +
30            "KeyValue: " + e.KeyValue;
31      } // end method KeyDemoForm_KeyDown
32
```

Fig. 11.40 | Demonstrating keyboard events. (Part 1 of 2.)

```
33      // clear Labels when key released
34               KeyDemoForm_KeyUp(        sender, KeyEventArgs e )
35      {
36          charLabel.Text = "";
37          keyInfoLabel.Text = "";
38      } // end method KeyDemoForm_KeyUp
39  } // end class KeyDemoForm
```

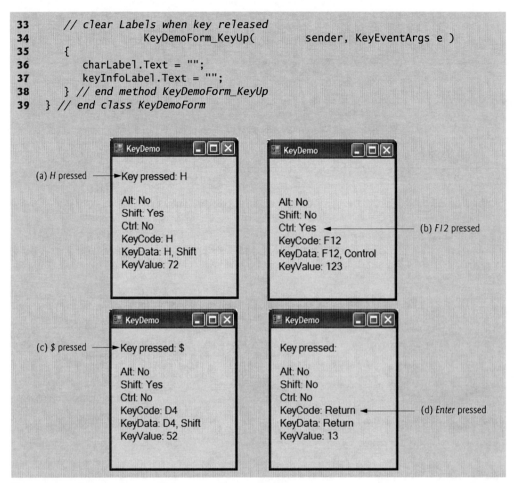

Fig. 11.40 | Demonstrating keyboard events. (Part 2 of 2.)

Initially, the two Labels (charLabel and keyInfoLabel) are empty. Control char-Label displays the character value of the key pressed, whereas keyInfoLabel displays information relating to the pressed key. Because the KeyDown and KeyPress events convey different information, the Form (KeyDemoForm) handles both.

The KeyPress event handler (lines 16–19) accesses the KeyChar property of the Key-PressEventArgs object. This returns the pressed key as a char and which we then display in charLabel (line 18). If the pressed key is not an ASCII character, then the KeyPress event will not occur, and charLabel will not display any text. ASCII is a common encoding format for letters, numbers, punctuation marks and other characters. It does not support keys such as the *function keys* (like *F1*) or the modifier keys (*Alt, Ctrl* and *Shift*).

The KeyDown event handler (lines 22–31) displays information from its KeyEventArgs object. The event handler tests for the *Alt, Shift* and *Ctrl* keys by using the Alt, Shift and Control properties, each of which returns a bool value—true if the corresponding key is pressed and false otherwise. The event handler then displays the KeyCode, KeyData and KeyValue properties.

The KeyCode property returns a Keys enumeration value (line 28). The KeyCode property returns the pressed key, but does not provide any information about modifier keys. Thus, both a capital and a lowercase "a" are represented as the *A* key.

The KeyData property (line 29) also returns a Keys enumeration value, but this property includes data about modifier keys. Thus, if "A" is input, the KeyData shows that both the *A* key and the *Shift* key were pressed. Lastly, KeyValue (line 30) returns the key code of the pressed key as an int. This int is the **key code**, which provides an int value for a wide range of keys and for mouse buttons. The Windows virtual key code is useful when one is testing for non-ASCII keys (such as *F12*).

The KeyUp event handler (lines 34–38) clears both Labels when the key is released. As we can see from the output, non-ASCII keys are not displayed in charLabel, because the KeyPress event is not generated. However, the KeyDown event still is generated, and keyInfoLabel displays information about the key that is pressed. The Keys enumeration can be used to test for specific keys by comparing the key pressed to a specific KeyCode.

Software Engineering Observation 11.3

To cause a control to react when a particular key is pressed (such as Enter*), handle a key event and test for the pressed key. To cause a* Button *to be clicked when the* Enter *key is pressed on a* Form, *set the* Form's *AcceptButton property.*

11.13 Wrap-Up

This chapter introduced several common GUI controls. We discussed event handling in detail, and showed how to create event handlers. We also discussed how delegates are used to connect event handlers to the events of specific controls. You learned how to use a control's properties and Visual Studio to specify the layout of your GUI. We then demonstrated several controls, beginning with Labels, Buttons and TextBoxes. You learned how to use GroupBoxes and Panels to organize other controls. We then demonstrated Check-Boxes and RadioButtons, which are state buttons that allow users to select among several options. We displayed images in PictureBox controls, displayed helpful text on a GUI with ToolTip components and specified a range of input values for users with a NumericUpDown control. We then demonstrated how to handle mouse and keyboard events. The next chapter introduces additional GUI controls. You will learn how to add menus to your GUIs and create Windows applications that display multiple Forms.

12

Graphical User Interface Concepts: Part 2

I claim not to have controlled events, but confess plainly that events have controlled me.
—Abraham Lincoln

Capture its reality in paint!
—Paul Cézanne

OBJECTIVES

In this chapter you will learn:

- To create menus, tabbed windows and multiple document interface (MDI) programs.

- To use the ListView and TreeView controls for displaying information.

- To create hyperlinks using the LinkLabel control.

- To display lists of information in ListBox and ComboBox controls.

- To input date and time data with the DateTimePicker.

- To create custom controls.

An actor entering through the door, you've got nothing. But if he enters through the window, you've got a situation.
—Billy Wilder

But, soft! what light through yonder window breaks? It is the east, and Juliet is the sun!
—William Shakespeare

12.1 Introduction

This chapter continues our study of GUIs. We begin our discussion with menus, which present users with logically organized commands (or options). Next, we discuss how to input and display dates and times using the MonthCalendar and DateTimePicker controls. We show how to develop menus with the tools provided by Visual Studio. We also introduce LinkLabels—powerful GUI components that enable the user to visit one of several destinations, such as a file on the current machine or a Web page, by simply clicking the mouse.

We demonstrate how to manipulate a list of values via a ListBox and how to combine several checkboxes in a CheckedListBox. We also create drop-down lists using ComboBoxes and display data hierarchically with a TreeView control. You will learn two other important GUI components—tab controls and multiple document interface (MDI) windows. These components enable you to create real-world programs with sophisticated GUIs.

Visual Studio provides a large set of GUI components, several of which are discussed in this (and the previous) chapter. Visual Studio also enables you to design custom controls and add those controls to the **ToolBox**, as we demonstrate in the last example of this chapter. The techniques presented in this chapter form the groundwork for creating more substantial GUIs and custom controls.

12.2 Menus

Menus provide groups of related commands for Windows applications. Although these commands depend on the program, some—such as **Open** and **Save**—are common to many applications. Menus are an integral part of GUIs, because they organize commands without "cluttering" the GUI.

In Fig. 12.1, an expanded menu from Visual Studio lists various commands (called *menu items*), plus *submenus* (menus within a menu). Notice that the top-level menus appear in the left portion of the figure, whereas any submenus or menu items are displayed to the right. The menu that contains a menu item is called that menu item's *parent menu*. A menu item that contains a submenu is considered to be the parent of that submenu.

All menu items can have *Alt* key shortcuts (also called *access shortcuts* or *hotkeys*), which are accessed by pressing *Alt* and the underlined letter (for example, *Alt F* typically expands the **File** menu). Menus that are not top-level menus can have shortcut keys as well (combinations of *Ctrl*, *Shift*, *Alt*, *F1*, *F2*, letter keys, etc.). Some menu items display check marks, usually indicating that multiple options on the menu can be selected at once.

To create a menu, open the **Toolbox** and drag a **MenuStrip** control onto the Form. This creates a menu bar across the top of the Form (below the title bar) and places a MenuStrip icon in the component tray. To select the MenuStrip, click this icon. You can now use **Design** mode to create and edit menus for your application. Menus, like other controls, have properties and events, which can be accessed through the **Properties** window.

To add menu items to the menu, click the **Type Here** TextBox (Fig. 12.2) and type the menu item's name. This action adds an entry to the menu of type **ToolStripMenuItem**. After you press the *Enter* key, the menu item name is added to the menu. Then more **Type Here** TextBoxes appear, allowing you to add items underneath or to the side of the original menu item (Fig. 12.3).

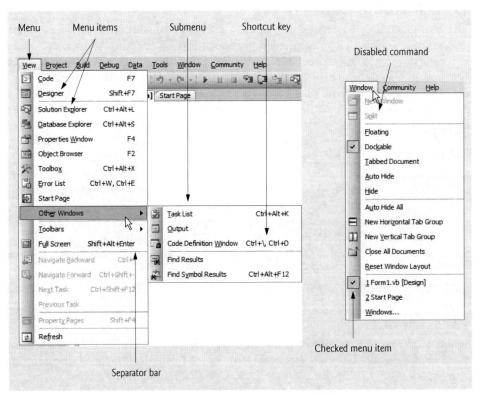

Fig. 12.1 | Menus, submenus and menu items.

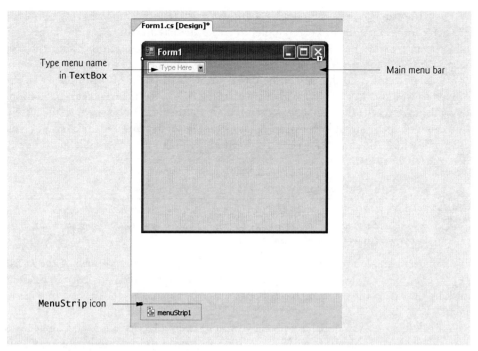

Type menu name in TextBox

Main menu bar

MenuStrip icon

Fig. 12.2 | Editing menus in Visual Studio.

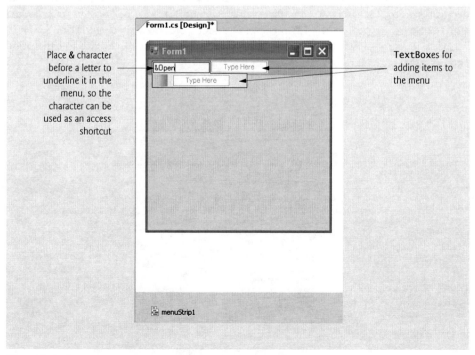

Place & character before a letter to underline it in the menu, so the character can be used as an access shortcut

TextBoxes for adding items to the menu

Fig. 12.3 | Adding ToolStripMenuItems to a MenuStrip.

To create an *access shortcut* (or *keyboard shortcut*), type an ampersand (&) before the character to be underlined. For example, to create the **File** menu item with the letter **F** underlined, type &File. To display an ampersand, type &&. To add other shortcut keys (e.g., *<Ctrl>-F9*) for menu items, set the ***ShortcutKeys*** property of the appropriate Tool-StripMenuItems. To do this, select the down arrow to the right of this property in the **Properties** window. In the window that appears (Fig. 12.4), use the CheckBoxes and drop-down list to select the shortcut keys. When you are finished, click elsewhere on the screen. You can hide the shortcut keys by setting property ***ShowShortcutKeys*** to false, and you can modify how the control keys are displayed in the menu item by modifying property ***ShortcutKeyDisplayString***.

Look-and-Feel Observation 12.1

Buttons can have access shortcuts. Place the & symbol immediately before the desired character in the Button's label. To press the button by using its access key in the running application, the user presses Alt and the underlined character.

You can remove a menu item by selecting it with the mouse and pressing the *Delete* key. Menu items can be grouped logically by ***separator bars***, which are inserted by right clicking the menu and selecting **Insert Separator** or by typing "-" for the text of a menu item.

In addition to text, Visual Studio allows you to easily add TextBoxes and ComboBoxes (drop-down lists) as menu items. When adding an item in **Design** mode, you may have noticed that before you enter text for a new item, you are provided with a drop-down list. Clicking the down arrow (Fig. 12.5) allows you to select the type of item to add—**Menu-Item** (of type ToolStripMenuItem, the default), **ComboBox** (of type ToolStripComboBox) and **TextBox** (of type ToolStripTextBox). We focus on ToolStripMenuItems. [*Note:* If you view this drop-down list for menu items that are not on the top level, a fourth option appears, allowing you to insert a separator bar.]

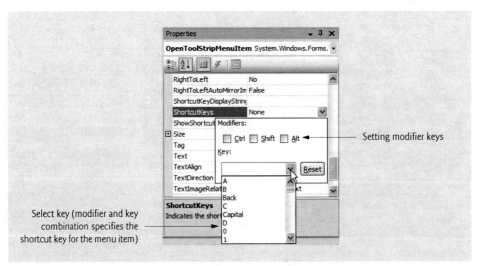

Fig. 12.4 | Setting a menu item's shortcut keys.

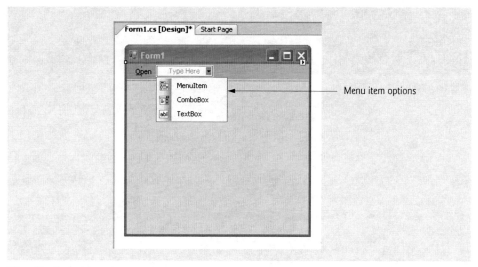

Fig. 12.5 | Menu item options.

ToolStripMenuItems generate a *Click* event when selected. To create an empty Click event handler, double click the menu item in **Design** mode. Common actions in response to these events include displaying dialogs and setting properties. Common menu properties and a common event are summarized in Fig. 12.6.

MenuStrip and ToolStripMenuItem properties and event	Description
MenuStrip Properties	
MenuItems	Contains the top-level menu items for this MenuStrip.
HasChildren	Indicates whether MenuStrip has any child controls (menu items).
RightToLeft	Causes text to display from right to left. This is useful for languages that are read from right to left.
ToolStripMenuItem Properties	
Checked	Indicates whether a menu item is checked. The default value is false, meaning that the menu item is unchecked.
CheckOnClick	Indicates that a menu item should appear checked or unchecked as the item is clicked.
Index	Specifies an item's position in its parent menu. A value of 0 places the MenuItem at the beginning of the menu.
MenuItems	Lists the submenu items for a particular menu item.

Fig. 12.6 | MenuStrip and ToolStripMenuItem properties and event. (Part 1 of 2.)

MenuStrip and ToolStripMenuItem properties and event	Description
ShortcutKey-DisplayString	Specifies text that should appear beside a menu item for a shortcut key. If left blank, the key names are displayed. Otherwise, the text in this property is displayed for the shortcut key.
ShortcutKeys	Specifies the shortcut key for the menu item (e.g., *<Ctrl>-F9* is equivalent to clicking a specific item).
ShowShortcutKeys	Indicates whether a shortcut key is shown beside menu item text. The default is true, which displays the shortcut key.
Text	Specifies the menu item's text. To create an *Alt* access shortcut, precede a character with & (e.g., &File to specify a menu named **File** with the letter **F** underlined).
Common ToolStripMenuItem Event	
Click	Generated when an item is clicked or a shortcut key is used. This is the default event when the menu is double clicked in the designer.

Fig. 12.6 | MenuStrip and ToolStripMenuItem properties and event. (Part 2 of 2.)

Look-and-Feel Observation 12.2

*It is a convention to place an ellipsis (...) after the name of a menu item that, when selected, displays a dialog (e.g. **Save As...**). Menu items that produce an immediate action without prompting the user for more information (e.g. **Save**) should not have an ellipsis following their name.*

Class MenuTestForm (Fig. 12.7) creates a simple menu on a Form. The Form has a top-level **File** menu with menu items **About** (which displays a MessageBox) and **Exit** (which terminates the program). The program also includes a **Format** menu, which contains menu items that change the format of the text on a Label. The **Format** menu has submenus **Color** and **Font**, which change the color and font of the text on a Label.

```
1   // Fig. 12.7: MenuTestForm.cs
2   // Using Menus to change font colors and styles.
3   using System;
4   using System.Drawing;
5   using System.Windows.Forms;
6
7   // our Form contains a Menu that changes the font color
8   // and style of the text displayed in Label
9   public partial class MenuTestForm : Form
10  {
11     // default constructor
12     public MenuTestForm()
13     {
```

Fig. 12.7 | Menus for changing text font and color. (Part 1 of 5.)

```
14        InitializeComponent();
15    } // end constructor
16
17    // display MessageBox when About ToolStripMenuItem is selected
18    private void aboutToolStripMenuItem_Click( object sender, EventArgs e )
19    {
20        MessageBox.Show(
21            "This is an example\nof using menus.",
22            "About", MessageBoxButtons.OK, MessageBoxIcon.Information );
23    } // end method aboutToolStripMenuItem_Click
24
25    // exit program when Exit ToolStripMenuItem is selected
26    private void exitToolStripMenuItem_Click( object sender, EventArgs e )
27    {
28        Application.Exit();
29    } // end method exitToolStripMenuItem_Click
30
31    // reset checkmarks for Color ToolStripMenuItems
32    private void ClearColor()
33    {
34        // clear all checkmarks
35        blackToolStripMenuItem.Checked = false;
36        blueToolStripMenuItem.Checked = false;
37        redToolStripMenuItem.Checked = false;
38        greenToolStripMenuItem.Checked = false;
39    } // end method ClearColor
40
41    // update Menu state and color display black
42    private void blackToolStripMenuItem_Click( object sender, EventArgs e )
43    {
44        // reset checkmarks for Color ToolStripMenuItems
45        ClearColor();
46
47        // set Color to Black
48        displayLabel.ForeColor = Color.Black;
49        blackToolStripMenuItem.Checked = true;
50    } // end method blackToolStripMenuItem_Click
51
52    // update Menu state and color display blue
53    private void blueToolStripMenuItem_Click( object sender, EventArgs e )
54    {
55        // reset checkmarks for Color ToolStripMenuItems
56        ClearColor();
57
58        // set Color to Blue
59        displayLabel.ForeColor = Color.Blue;
60        blueToolStripMenuItem.Checked = true;
61    } // end method blueToolStripMenuItem_Click
62
63    // update Menu state and color display red
64    private void redToolStripMenuItem_Click( object sender, EventArgs e )
65    {
```

Fig. 12.7 | Menus for changing text font and color. (Part 2 of 5.)

```
66        // reset checkmarks for Color ToolStripMenuItems
67        ClearColor();
68
69        // set Color to Red
70        displayLabel.ForeColor = Color.Red;
71        redToolStripMenuItem.Checked = true;
72     } // end method redToolStripMenuItem_Click
73
74     // update Menu state and color display green
75     private void greenToolStripMenuItem_Click( object sender, EventArgs e )
76     {
77        // reset checkmarks for Color ToolStripMenuItems
78        ClearColor();
79
80        // set Color to Green
81        displayLabel.ForeColor = Color.Green;
82        greenToolStripMenuItem.Checked = true;
83     } // end method greenToolStripMenuItem_Click
84
85     // reset checkmarks for Font ToolStripMenuItems
86     private void ClearFont()
87     {
88        // clear all checkmarks
89        timesToolStripMenuItem.Checked = false;
90        courierToolStripMenuItem.Checked = false;
91        comicToolStripMenuItem.Checked = false;
92     } // end method ClearFont
93
94     // update Menu state and set Font to Times New Roman
95     private void timesToolStripMenuItem_Click( object sender, EventArgs e )
96     {
97        // reset checkmarks for Font ToolStripMenuItems
98        ClearFont();
99
100       // set Times New Roman font
101       timesToolStripMenuItem.Checked = true;
102       displayLabel.Font = new Font(
103          "Times New Roman", 14, displayLabel.Font.Style );
104    } // end method timesToolStripMenuItem_Click
105
106    // update Menu state and set Font to Courier
107    private void courierToolStripMenuItem_Click(
108       object sender, EventArgs e )
109    {
110       // reset checkmarks for Font ToolStripMenuItems
111       ClearFont();
112
113       // set Courier font
114       courierToolStripMenuItem.Checked = true;
115       displayLabel.Font = new Font(
116          "Courier", 14, displayLabel.Font.Style );
117    } // end method courierToolStripMenuItem_Click
```

Fig. 12.7 | Menus for changing text font and color. (Part 3 of 5.)

```
118
119        // update Menu state and set Font to Comic Sans MS
120        private void comicToolStripMenuItem_Click( object sender, EventArgs e )
121        {
122           // reset checkmarks for Font ToolStripMenuItems
123           ClearFont();
124
125           // set Comic Sans font
126           comicToolStripMenuItem.Checked = true;
127           displayLabel.Font = new Font(
128              "Comic Sans MS", 14, displayLabel.Font.Style );
129        } // end method comicToolStripMenuItem_Click
130
131        // toggle checkmark and toggle bold style
132        private void boldToolStripMenuItem_Click( object sender, EventArgs e )
133        {
134           // toggle checkmark
135           boldToolStripMenuItem.Checked = !boldToolStripMenuItem.Checked;
136
137           // use logical exlusive OR to toggle bold, keep all other styles
138           displayLabel.Font = new Font(
139              displayLabel.Font.FontFamily, 14,
140              displayLabel.Font.Style ^ FontStyle.Bold );
141        } // end method boldToolStripMenuItem_Click
142
143        // toggle checkmark and toggle italic style
144        private void italicToolStripMenuItem_Click(
145           object sender, EventArgs e )
146        {
147           // toggle checkmark
148           italicToolStripMenuItem.Checked = !italicToolStripMenuItem.Checked;
149
150           // use logical exclusive OR to toggle italic, keep all other styles
151           displayLabel.Font = new Font(
152              displayLabel.Font.FontFamily, 14,
153              displayLabel.Font.Style ^ FontStyle.Italic );
154        } // end method italicToolStripMenuItem_Click
155    } // end class MenuTestForm
```

Fig. 12.7 | Menus for changing text font and color. (Part 4 of 5.)

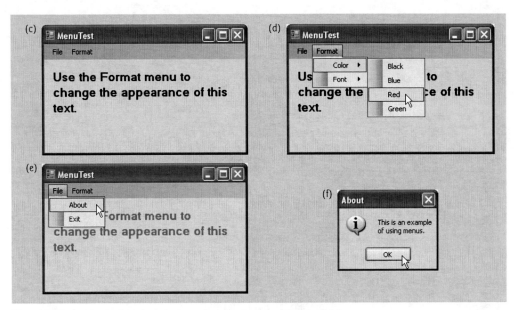

Fig. 12.7 | Menus for changing text font and color. (Part 5 of 5.)

To create this GUI, begin by dragging the MenuStrip from the **ToolBox** onto the Form. Then use **Design** mode to create the menu structure shown in the sample outputs. The **File** menu (fileToolStripMenuItem) has menu items **About** (aboutToolStripMenu-Item) and **Exit** (exitToolStripMenuItem); the **Format** menu (formatToolStripMenuItem) has two submenus. The first submenu, **Color** (colorToolStripMenuItem), contains menu items **Black** (blackToolStripMenuItem), **Blue** (blueToolStripMenuItem), **Red** (redTool-StripMenuItem) and **Green** (greenToolStripMenuItem). The second submenu, **Font** (fontToolStripMenuItem), contains menu items **Times New Roman** (timesToolStrip-MenuItem), **Courier** (courierToolStripMenuItem), **Comic Sans** (comicToolStripMenu-Item), a separator bar (dashToolStripMenuItem), **Bold** (boldToolStripMenuItem) and **Italic** (italicToolStripMenuItem).

The **About** menu item in the **File** menu displays a MessageBox when clicked (lines 18–23). The **Exit** menu item closes the application through static method *Exit* of class *Application* (line 28). Class Application's static methods control program execution. Method Exit causes our application to terminate.

We made the items in the **Color** submenu (**Black**, **Blue**, **Red** and **Green**) mutually exclusive—the user can select only one at a time (we explain how we did this shortly). To indicate that a menu item is selected, we will set each **Color** menu item's *Checked* property to true. This causes a check to appear to the left of a menu item.

Each **Color** menu item has its own Click event handler. The method handler for color **Black** is blackToolStripMenuItem_Click (lines 42–50). Similarly, the event handlers for colors **Blue**, **Red** and **Green** are blueToolStripMenuItem_Click (lines 53–61), redToolStripMenuItem_Click (lines 64–72) and greenToolStripMenuItem_Click (lines 75–83), respectively. Each **Color** menu item must be mutually exclusive, so each event handler calls method ClearColor (lines 32–39) before setting its corresponding Checked property to true. Method ClearColor sets the Checked property of each color MenuItem to `false`, effectively preventing more than one menu item from being selected at a time. In the designer, we initially set the **Black** menu item's `Checked` property to `true`, because at the start of the program, the text on the `Form` is black.

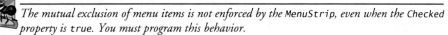

Software Engineering Observation 12.1

The mutual exclusion of menu items is not enforced by the `MenuStrip`, *even when the* `Checked` *property is* true. *You must program this behavior.*

The **Font** menu contains three menu items for fonts (**Courier**, **Times New Roman** and **Comic Sans**) and two menu items for font styles (**Bold** and **Italic**). We added a separator bar between the font and font-style menu items to indicate that these are separate options. A `Font` object can specify only one font at a time but can set multiple styles at once (e.g., a font can be both bold and italic). We set the font menu items to display checks. As with the **Color** menu, we must enforce mutual exclusion of these items in our event handlers.

Event handlers for font menu items **TimesRoman**, **Courier** and **ComicSans** are `timesToolStripMenuItem_Click` (lines 95–104), `courierToolStripMenuItem_Click` (lines 107–117) and `comicToolStripMenuItem_Click` (lines 120–129), respectively. These event handlers behave in a manner similar to that of the event handlers for the **Color** menu items. Each event handler clears the `Checked` properties for all font menu items by calling method `ClearFont` (lines 86–92), then sets the `Checked` property of the menu item that raised the event to `true`. This enforces the mutual exclusion of the font menu items. In the designer, we initially set the **Times New Roman** menu item's `Checked` property to `true`, because this is the original font for the text on the `Form`. The event handlers for the **Bold** and **Italic** menu items (lines 132–154) use the bitwise logical exclusive OR (^) operator to combine font styles, as we discussed in Chapter 11.

12.3 MonthCalendar Control

Many applications must perform date and time calculations. The .NET Framework provides two controls that allow an application to retrieve date and time information—the `MonthCalendar` and `DateTimePicker` (Section 12.4) controls.

The ***MonthCalendar*** (Fig. 12.8) control displays a monthly calendar on the `Form`. The user can select a date from the currently displayed month, or can use the provided links to navigate to another month. When a date is selected, it is highlighted. Multiple dates can be selected by clicking dates on the calendar while holding down the *Shift* key. The default event for this control is ***DateChanged***, which is generated when a new date is selected. Properties are provided that allow you to modify the appearance of the calendar, how many dates can be selected at once, and the minimum and maximum dates that may be selected. `MonthCalendar` properties and a common event are summarized in Fig. 12.9.

12.4 DateTimePicker Control

The ***DateTimePicker*** control (see output of Fig. 12.11) is similar to the `MonthCalendar` control, but displays the calendar when a down arrow is selected. The `DateTimePicker` can be used to retrieve date and time information from the user. The `DateTimePicker` is also more customizable than a `MonthCalendar` control—more properties are provided to edit the look and feel of the drop-down calendar. Property ***Format*** specifies the user's selection options using the ***DateTimePickerFormat*** enumeration. The values in this enumeration

Fig. 12.8 | MonthCalendar control.

MonthCalendar properties and event	Description
MonthCalendar Properties	
FirstDayOfWeek	Sets which day of the week is the first displayed for each week in the calendar.
MaxDate	The last date that can be selected.
MaxSelectionCount	The maximum number of dates that can be selected at once.
MinDate	The first date that can be selected.
MonthlyBoldedDates	An array of dates that will displayed in bold in the calendar.
SelectionEnd	The last of the dates selected by the user.
SelectionRange	The dates selected by the user.
SelectionStart	The first of the dates selected by the user.
Common MonthCalendar Event	
DateChanged	Generated when a date is selected in the calendar.

Fig. 12.9 | MonthCalendar properties and event.

are **Long** (displays the date in long format, as in **Friday, July 1, 2005**), **Short** (displays the date in short format, as in **7/1/2005**), **Time** (displays a time value, as in **11:48:02 PM**) and **Custom** (indicates that a custom format will be used). If value Custom is used, the display in the DateTimePicker is specified using property **CustomFormat**. The default event for this control is **ValueChanged**, which occurs when the selected value (whether a date or a time) is changed. DateTimePicker properties and a common event are summarized in Fig. 12.10.

Figure 12.11 demonstrates using the DateTimePicker control to select an item's drop-off time. Many companies use such functionality. For instance, several online DVD rental companies specify the day a movie is sent out, and the estimated time that the movie

DateTimePicker properties and event	Description
DateTimePicker Properties	
CalendarForeColor	Sets the text color for the calendar.
CalendarMonth-Background	Sets the calendar's background color.
CustomFormat	Sets the custom format string for the user's options.
Format	Sets the format of the date and/or time used for the user's options.
MaxDate	The maximum date and time that can be selected.
MinDate	The minimum date and time that can be selected.
ShowCheckBox	Indicates if a CheckBox should be displayed to the left of the selected date and time.
ShowUpDown	Used to indicate that the control should have up and down Buttons. This is helpful for instances when the DateTimePicker is used to select a time—the Buttons can be used to increase or decrease hour, minute and second values.
Value	The data selected by the user.
Common DateTimePicker Event	
ValueChanged	Generated when the Value property changes, including when the user selects a new date or time.

Fig. 12.10 | DateTimePicker properties and event.

will arrive at your home. In this application, the user selects a drop-off day, and then an estimated arrival date is displayed. The date is always two days after drop off, three days if a Sunday is reached (mail is not delivered on Sunday).

```
1   // Fig. 12.11: DateTimePickerForm.cs
2   // Using a DateTimePicker to select a drop off time.
3   using System;
4   using System.Windows.Forms;
5
6   public partial class DateTimePickerForm : Form
7   {
8      // default constructor
9      public DateTimePickerForm()
10     {
11        InitializeComponent();
12     } // end constructor
13
```

Fig. 12.11 | Demonstrating DateTimePicker. (Part 1 of 2.)

```
14      private void dateTimePickerDropOff_ValueChanged(
15         object sender, EventArgs e )
16      {
17         DateTime dropOffDate = dateTimePickerDropOff.Value;
18
19         // add extra time when items are dropped off around Sunday
20         if ( dropOffDate.DayOfWeek == DayOfWeek.Friday ||
21            dropOffDate.DayOfWeek == DayOfWeek.Saturday ||
22            dropOffDate.DayOfWeek == DayOfWeek.Sunday )
23
24            //estimate three days for delivery
25            outputLabel.Text = dropOffDate.AddDays( 3 ).ToLongDateString();
26         else
27            // otherwise estimate only two days for delivery
28            outputLabel.Text = dropOffDate.AddDays( 2 ).ToLongDateString();
29      } // end method dateTimePickerDropOff_ValueChanged
30
31      private void DateTimePickerForm_Load( object sender, EventArgs e )
32      {
33         // user cannot select days before today
34         dateTimePickerDropOff.MinDate = DateTime.Today;
35
36         // user can only select days of this year
37         dateTimePickerDropOff.MaxDate = DateTime.Today.AddYears( 1 );
38      } // end method DateTimePickerForm_Load
39   } // end class DateTimePickerForm
```

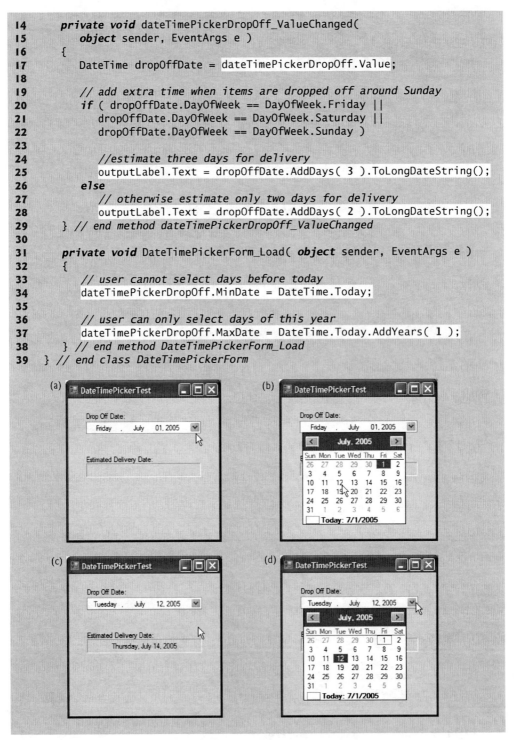

Fig. 12.11 | Demonstrating DateTimePicker. (Part 2 of 2.)

The DateTimePicker (dateTimePickerDropOff) has its Format property set to Long, so the user can select a date and not a time in this application. When the user selects a date, the ValueChanged event occurs. The event handler for this event (lines 14–29) first retrieves the selected date from the DateTimePicker's *Value* property (line 17). Lines 20–22 use the DateTime structure's *DayOfWeek* property to determine the day of the week on which the selected date falls. The day values are represented using the *DayOfWeek* enumeration. Lines 25 and 28 use DateTime's *AddDays* method to increase the date by two days or three days, respectively. The resulting date is then displayed in Long format using method *ToLongDateString*.

In this application, we do not want the user to be able to select a drop-off day before the current day, or one that is more than a year into the future. To enforce this, we set the DateTimePicker's *MinDate* and *MaxDate* properties when the Form is loaded (lines 34 and 37). Property Today returns the current day, and method *AddYears* (with an argument of 1) is used to specify a date one year in the future.

Let's take a closer look at the output. This application begins by displaying the current date (Fig. 12.11(a)). In Fig. 12.11(b), we selected the 12th of July. In Fig. 12.11(c), the estimated arrival date is displayed as the 14th. Figure 12.11(d) shows that the 12th, after it is selected, is highlighted in the calendar.

12.5 LinkLabel Control

The *LinkLabel* control displays links to other resources, such as files or Web pages (Fig. 12.12). A LinkLabel appears as underlined text (colored blue by default). When the mouse moves over the link, the pointer changes to a hand; this is similar to the behavior of a hyperlink in a Web page. The link can change color to indicate whether the link is new, previously visited or active. When clicked, the LinkLabel generates a *LinkClicked* event (see Fig. 12.13). Class LinkLabel is derived from class Label and therefore inherits all of class Label's functionality.

Look-and-Feel Observation 12.3

A LinkLabel is the preferred control for indicating that the user can click a link to jump to a resource such as a Web page, though other controls can perform similar tasks.

Class LinkLabelTestForm (Fig. 12.14) uses three LinkLabels to link to the C: drive, the Deitel Web site (www.deitel.com) and the Notepad application, respectively. The Text properties of the LinkLabel's driveLinkLabel, deitelLinkLabel and notepadLinkLabel describe each link's purpose.

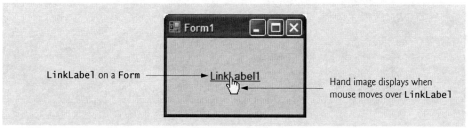

Fig. 12.12 | LinkLabel control in running program.

LinkLabel properties and event	Description
Common Properties	
ActiveLinkColor	Specifies the color of the active link when clicked.
LinkArea	Specifies which portion of text in the LinkLabel is part of the link.
LinkBehavior	Specifies the link's behavior, such as how the link appears when the mouse is placed over it.
LinkColor	Specifies the original color of all links before they have been visited. The default color is set by the system, but is usually blue.
LinkVisited	If true, the link appears as though it has been visited (its color is changed to that specified by property VisitedLinkColor). The default value is false.
Text	Specifies the control's text.
UseMnemonic	If true, the & character in the Text property acts as a shortcut (similar to the *Alt* shortcut in menus).
VisitedLinkColor	Specifies the color of visited links. The default color is set by the system, but is usually purple.
Common Event	*(Event arguments LinkLabelLinkClickedEventArgs)*
LinkClicked	Generated when the link is clicked. This is the default event when the control is double clicked in **Design** mode.

Fig. 12.13 | LinkLabel properties and event.

```
1   // Fig. 12.14: LinkLabelTestForm.cs
2   // Using LinkLabels to create hyperlinks.
3   using System;
4   using System.Windows.Forms;
5
6   // Form using LinkLabels to browse the C:\ drive,
7   // load a webpage and run Notepad
8   public partial class LinkLabelTestForm : Form
9   {
10     // default constructor
11     public LinkLabelTestForm()
12     {
13        InitializeComponent();
14     } // end constructor
15
```

Fig. 12.14 | LinkLabels used to link to a drive, a Web page and an application. (Part 1 of 3.)

```
16      // browse C:\ drive
17      private void driveLinkLabel_LinkClicked( object sender,
18         LinkLabelLinkClickedEventArgs e )
19      {
20         // change LinkColor after it has been clicked
21         driveLinkLabel.LinkVisited = true;
22
23         System.Diagnostics.Process.Start( @"C:\" );
24      } // end method driveLinkLabel_LinkClicked
25
26      // load www.deitel.com in web browser
27      private void deitelLinkLabel_LinkClicked( object sender,
28         LinkLabelLinkClickedEventArgs e )
29      {
30         // change LinkColor after it has been clicked
31         deitelLinkLabel.LinkVisited = true;
32
33         System.Diagnostics.Process.Start(
34            "IExplore", "http://www.deitel.com" );
35      } // end method deitelLinkLabel_LinkClicked
36
37      // run application Notepad
38      private void notepadLinkLabel_LinkClicked( object sender,
39         LinkLabelLinkClickedEventArgs e )
40      {
41         // change LinkColor after it has been clicked
42         notepadLinkLabel.LinkVisited = true;
43
44         // program called as if in run
45         // menu and full path not needed
46         System.Diagnostics.Process.Start( "notepad" );
47      } // end method driveLinkLabel_LinkClicked
48   } // end class LinkLabelTestForm
```

Fig. 12.14 | LinkLabels used to link to a drive, a Web page and an application. (Part 2 of 3.)

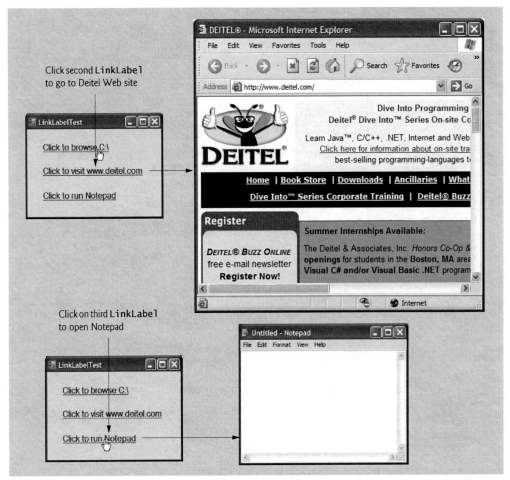

Fig. 12.14 | LinkLabels used to link to a drive, a Web page and an application. (Part 3 of 3.)

The event handlers for the LinkLabels call method **Start** of class **Process** (namespace **System.Diagnostics**), which allows you to execute other programs from an application. Method Start can take one argument, the file to open (a string), or two arguments, the application to run and its command-line arguments (two strings). Method Start's arguments can be in the same form as if they were provided for input to the Windows **Run** command (**Start > Run...**). For applications that are known to Windows, full path names are not needed, and the .exe extension often can be omitted. To open a file that has a file type that Windows recognizes, simply use the file's full path name. The Windows operating system must be able to use the application associated with the given file's extension to open the file.

The event handler for driveLinkLabel's LinkClicked event browses the C: drive (lines 17–24). Line 21 sets the LinkVisited property to true, which changes the link's color from blue to purple (the LinkVisited colors can be configured through the **Properties** window in Visual Studio). The event handler then passes @"C:\" to method Start (line 23), which opens a **Windows Explorer** window. The @ symbol that we placed before

"C:\" indicates that all characters in the string should be interpreted literally. Thus, the backslash within the string is not considered to be the first character of an escape sequence. This simplifies strings that represent directory paths, since you do not need to use \\ for each \ character in the path.

The event handler for deitelLinkLabel's LinkClicked event (lines 27–35) opens the Web page www.deitel.com in Internet Explorer. We achieve this by passing the Web page address as a string (lines 33–34), which opens Internet Explorer. Line 31 sets the LinkVisited property to true.

The event handler for notepadLinkLabel's LinkClicked event (lines 38–47) opens the Notepad application. Line 42 sets the LinkVisited property to true so the link appears as a visited link. Line 46 passes the argument "notepad" to method Start, which runs notepad.exe. Note that in line 46, the .exe extension is not required—Windows can determine whether it recognizes the argument given to method Start as an executable file.

12.6 ListBox Control

The *ListBox* control allows the user to view and select from multiple items in a list. List-Boxes are static GUI entities, which means that items must be added to the list programmatically. The user can be provided with TextBoxes and Buttons with which to specify items to be added to the list, but the actual additions must be performed in code. The *CheckedListBox* control (Section 12.7) extends a ListBox by including CheckBoxes next to each item in the list. This allows users to place checks on multiple items at once, as is possible with CheckBox controls. (Users also can select multiple items from a ListBox by setting the ListBox's *SelectionMode* property, which is discussed shortly.) Figure 12.15 displays a ListBox and a CheckedListBox. In both controls, scrollbars appear if the number of items exceeds the ListBox's viewable area.

Figure 12.16 lists common ListBox properties and methods, and a common event. The SelectionMode property determines the number of items that can be selected. This property has the possible values *None*, *One*, *MultiSimple* and *MultiExtended* (from the

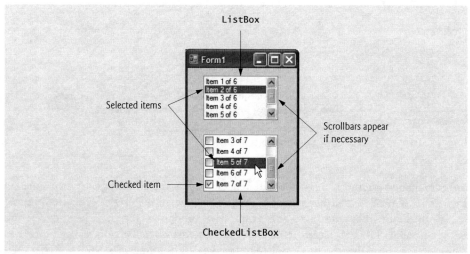

Fig. 12.15 | ListBox and CheckedListBox on a Form.

ListBox properties, methods and event	Description
Common Properties	
Items	The collection of items in the ListBox.
MultiColumn	Indicates whether the ListBox can break a list into multiple columns. Multiple columns eliminate vertical scrollbars from the display.
SelectedIndex	Returns the index of the selected item. If no items have been selected, the property returns -1. If the user selects multiple items, this property returns only one of the selected indices. For this reason, if multiple items are selected, you should use property SelectedIndices.
SelectedIndices	Returns a collection containing the indices for all selected items.
SelectedItem	Returns a reference to the selected item. If multiple items are selected, it returns the item with the lowest index number.
SelectedItems	Returns a collection of the selected item(s).
SelectionMode	Determines the number of items that can be selected, and the means through which multiple items can be selected. Values None, One, MultiSimple (multiple selection allowed) or MultiExtended (multiple selection allowed using a combination of arrow keys or mouse clicks and *Shift* and *Ctrl* keys).
Sorted	Indicates whether items are sorted alphabetically. Setting this property's value to true sorts the items. The default value is false.
Common Methods	
ClearSelected	Deselects every item.
GetSelected	Takes an index as an argument, and returns true if the corresponding item is selected.
Common Event	
SelectedIndexChanged	Generated when the selected index changes. This is the default event when the control is double clicked in the designer.

Fig. 12.16 | ListBox properties, methods and event.

SelectionMode enumeration)—the differences among these settings are explained in Fig. 12.16. The *SelectedIndexChanged* event occurs when the user selects a new item.

Both the ListBox and CheckedListBox have properties Items, SelectedItem and SelectedIndex. Property *Items* returns all the list items as a collection. Collections are a common way of managing lists of objects in the .NET framework. Many .NET GUI components (e.g., ListBoxes) use collections to expose lists of internal objects (e.g., items contained within a ListBox). The collection returned by property Items is represented as an object of type ***ObjectCollection***. Property ***SelectedItem*** returns the ListBox's currently selected item. If the user can select multiple items, use collection ***SelectedItems*** to return all the selected items as a collection. Property ***SelectedIndex*** returns the index of the selected item—if there could be more than one, use property ***SelectedIndices***. If no items are selected, property SelectedIndex returns -1. Method ***GetSelected*** takes an index and returns true if the corresponding item is selected.

To add items to a ListBox or to a CheckedListBox, we must add objects to its Items collection. This can be accomplished by calling method Add to add a string to the ListBox's or CheckedListBox's Items collection. For example, we could write

  myListBox.Items.Add(*myListItem*)

to add string *myListItem* to ListBox *myListBox*. To add multiple objects, you can either call method Add multiple times or call method AddRange to add an array of objects. Classes ListBox and CheckedListBox each call the submitted object's ToString method to determine the Label for the corresponding object's entry in the list. This allows you to add different objects to a ListBox or a CheckedListBox that later can be returned through properties SelectedItem and SelectedItems.

Alternatively, you can add items to ListBoxes and CheckedListBoxes visually by examining the Items property in the **Properties** window. Clicking the ellipsis button opens the **String Collection Editor**, which contains a text area for adding items; each item appears on a separate line (Fig. 12.17). Visual Studio then writes code to add these strings to the Items collection inside method InitializeComponent.

Figure 12.18 uses class ListBoxTestForm to add, remove and clear items from ListBox displayListBox. Class ListBoxTestForm uses TextBox inputTextBox to allow the user to type in a new item. When the user clicks the **Add** Button, the new item appears in displayListBox. Similarly, if the user selects an item and clicks **Remove**, the item is deleted. When clicked, **Clear** deletes all entries in displayListBox. The user terminates the application by clicking **Exit**.

The addButton_Click event handler (lines 18–22) calls method ***Add*** of the Items collection in the ListBox. This method takes a string as the item to add to displayListBox.

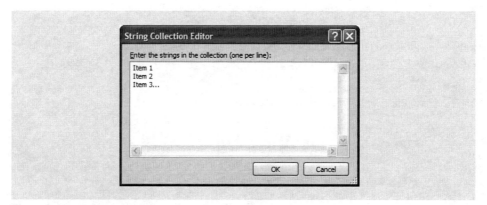

Fig. 12.17 | String Collection Editor.

In this case, the `string` used is the user-input text, or `inputTextBox.Text` (line 20). After the item is added, `inputTextBox.Text` is cleared (line 21).

The `removeButton_Click` event handler (lines 25–30) uses method **RemoveAt** to remove an item from the `ListBox`. Event handler `removeButton_Click` first uses property `SelectedIndex` to determine which index is selected. If `SelectedIndex` is not –1 (i.e., an item is selected) line 29 removes the item that corresponds to the selected index.

```
1   // Fig. 12.18: ListBoxTestForm.cs
2   // Program to add, remove and clear ListBox items
3   using System;
4   using System.Windows.Forms;
5
6   // Form uses a TextBox and Buttons to add,
7   // remove, and clear ListBox items
8   public partial class ListBoxTestForm : Form
9   {
10      // default constructor
11      public ListBoxTestForm()
12      {
13         InitializeComponent();
14      } // end constructor
15
16      // add new item to ListBox (text from input TextBox)
17      // and clear input TextBox
18      private void addButton_Click( object sender, EventArgs e )
19      {
20         displayListBox.Items.Add( inputTextBox.Text );
21         inputTextBox.Clear();
22      } // end method addButton_Click
23
24      // remove item if one is selected
25      private void removeButton_Click( object sender, EventArgs e )
26      {
27         // check if item is selected, remove if selected
28         if ( displayListBox.SelectedIndex != -1 )
29            displayListBox.Items.RemoveAt( displayListBox.SelectedIndex );
30      } // end method removeButton_Click
31
32      // clear all items in ListBox
33      private void clearButton_Click( object sender, EventArgs e )
34      {
35         displayListBox.Items.Clear();
36      } // end method clearButton_Click
37
38      // exit application
39      private void exitButton_Click( object sender, EventArgs e )
40      {
41         Application.Exit();
42      } // end method exitButton_Click
43   } // end class ListBoxTestForm
```

Fig. 12.18 | Program that adds, removes and clears `ListBox` items. (Part 1 of 2.)

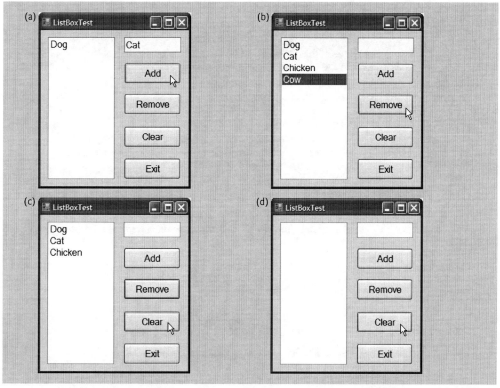

Fig. 12.18 | Program that adds, removes and clears ListBox items. (Part 2 of 2.)

The clearButton_Click event handler (lines 33–36) calls method **Clear** of the Items collection (line 35). This removes all the entries in displayListBox. Finally, event handler exitButton_Click (lines 39–42) terminates the application by calling method Application.Exit (line 41).

12.7 CheckedListBox Control

The CheckedListBox control derives from class ListBox and includes a CheckBox next to each item. As in ListBoxes, items can be added via methods Add and AddRange or through the **String Collection Editor**. CheckedListBoxes imply that multiple items can be selected, and the only possible values for the SelectionMode property are None and One. One allows multiple selection, because CheckBoxes imply that there are no logical restrictions on the items—the user can select as many items as required. Thus, the only choice is whether to give the user multiple selection or no selection at all. This keeps the CheckedListBox's behavior consistent with that of CheckBoxes. Common properties events and common method of CheckedListBoxes appear in Fig. 12.19.

Common Programming Error 12.1

*The IDE displays an error message if you attempt to set the SelectionMode property to Multi-Simple or MultiExtended in the **Properties** window of a CheckedListBox. If this value is set programmatically, a runtime error occurs.*

CheckedListBox properties, method and event	Description
Common Properties	*(All the ListBox properties, methods and events are inherited by CheckedListBox.)*
CheckedItems	Contains the collection of items that are checked. This is distinct from the selected item, which is highlighted (but not necessarily checked). [*Note:* There can be at most one selected item at any given time.]
CheckedIndices	Returns indices for all checked items.
SelectionMode	Determines how many items can be checked. The only possible values are One (allows multiple checks to be placed) or None (does not allow any checks to be placed).
Common Method	
GetItemChecked	Takes an index and returns true if the corresponding item is checked.
Common Event (Event arguments ItemCheckEventArgs)	
ItemCheck	Generated when an item is checked or unchecked.
ItemCheckEventArgs Properties	
CurrentValue	Indicates whether the current item is checked or unchecked. Possible values are Checked, Unchecked and Indeterminate.
Index	Returns the zero-based index of the item that changed.
NewValue	Specifies the new state of the item.

Fig. 12.19 | CheckedListBox properties, method and event.

Event ***ItemCheck*** occurs whenever a user checks or unchecks a CheckedListBox item. Event argument properties CurrentValue and NewValue return CheckState values for the current and new state of the item, respectively. A comparison of these values allows you to determine whether the CheckedListBox item was checked or unchecked. The CheckedListBox control retains the SelectedItems and SelectedIndices properties (it inherits them from class ListBox). However, it also includes properties CheckedItems and CheckedIndices, which return information about the checked items and indices.

In Fig. 12.20, class CheckedListBoxTestForm uses a CheckedListBox and a ListBox to display a user's selection of books. The CheckedListBox allows the user to select multiple titles. In the **String Collection Editor**, items were added for some Deitel books: C++, Java™, Visual Basic, Internet & WWW, Perl, Python, Wireless Internet and Advanced Java (the acronym HTP stands for "How to Program"). The ListBox (named display-ListBox) displays the user's selection. In the screenshots accompanying this example, the CheckedListBox appears to the left, the ListBox on the right.

```
 1   // Fig. 12.20: CheckedListBoxTestForm.cs
 2   // Using the checked ListBox to add items to a display ListBox
 3   using System;
 4   using System.Windows.Forms;
 5
 6   // Form uses a checked ListBox to add items to a display ListBox
 7   public partial class CheckedListBoxTestForm : Form
 8   {
 9      // default constructor
10      public CheckedListBoxTestForm()
11      {
12         InitializeComponent();
13      } // end constructor
14
15      // item about to change
16      // add or remove from display ListBox
17      private void inputCheckedListBox_ItemCheck(
18         object sender, ItemCheckEventArgs e )
19      {
20         // obtain reference of selected item
21         string item = inputCheckedListBox.SelectedItem.ToString();
22
23         // if item checked add to ListBox
24         // otherwise remove from ListBox
25         if ( e.NewValue == CheckState.Checked )
26            displayListBox.Items.Add( item );
27         else
28            displayListBox.Items.Remove( item );
29      } // end method inputCheckedListBox_ItemCheck
30   } // end class CheckedListBoxTestForm
```

Fig. 12.20 | CheckedListBox and ListBox used in a program to display a user selection. (Part I of 2.)

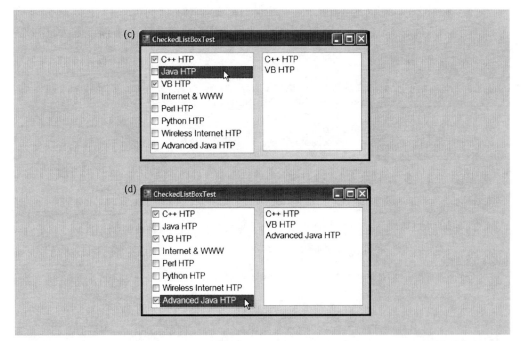

Fig. 12.20 | CheckedListBox and ListBox used in a program to display a user selection. (Part 2 of 2.)

When the user checks or unchecks an item in inputCheckedListBox, an ItemCheck event occurs and event handler inputCheckedListBox_ItemCheck (lines 17–29) executes. An if...else statement (lines 25–28) determines whether the user checked or unchecked an item in the CheckedListBox. Line 25 uses the NewValue property to determine whether the item is being checked (CheckState.Checked). If the user checks an item, line 26 adds the checked entry to the ListBox displayListBox. If the user unchecks an item, line 28 removes the corresponding item from displayListBox. This event handler was created by selecting the CheckedListBox in **Design** mode, viewing the control's events in the **Properties** window and double clicking the ItemCheck event.

12.8 ComboBox Control

The *ComboBox* control combines TextBox features with a *drop-down list*—a GUI component that contains a list from which a value can be selected. A ComboBox usually appears as a TextBox with a down arrow to its right. By default, the user can enter text into the TextBox or click the down arrow to display a list of predefined items. If a user chooses an element from this list, that element is displayed in the TextBox. If the list contains more elements than can be displayed in the drop-down list, a scrollbar appears. The maximum number of items that a drop-down list can display at one time is set by property *MaxDropDownItems*. Figure 12.21 shows a sample ComboBox in three different states.

As with the ListBox control, you can add objects to collection Items programmatically, using methods Add and AddRange, or visually, with the **String Collection Editor**. Figure 12.22 lists common properties and a common event of class ComboBox.

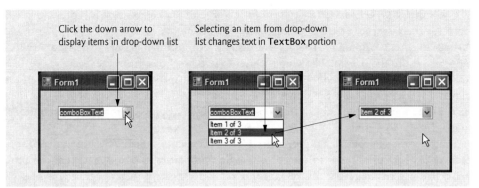

Fig. 12.21 | ComboBox demonstration.

Look-and-Feel Observation 12.4

Use a ComboBox to save space on a GUI. A disadvantage is that, unlike with a ListBox, the user cannot see available items without expanding the drop-down list.

ComboBox properties and event	Description
Common Properties	
DropDownStyle	Determines the type of ComboBox. Value Simple means that the text portion is editable, and the list portion is always visible. Value Drop-Down (the default) means that the text portion is editable, but the user must click an arrow button to see the list portion. Value Drop-DownList means that the text portion is not editable, and the user must click the arrow button to see the list portion.
Items	The collection of items in the ComboBox control.
MaxDropDownItems	Specifies the maximum number of items (between 1 and 100) that the drop-down list can display. If the number of items exceeds the maximum number of items to display, a scrollbar appears.
SelectedIndex	Returns the index of the selected item. If there is no selected item, -1 is returned.
SelectedItem	Returns a reference to the selected item.
Sorted	Indicates whether items are sorted alphabetically. Setting this property's value to true sorts the items. The default is false.
Common Event	
SelectedIndexChanged	Generated when the selected index changes (such as when a different item is selected). This is the default event when control is double clicked in the designer.

Fig. 12.22 | ComboBox properties and event.

Property ***DropDownStyle*** determines the type of ComboBox, and is represented as a value of the ***ComboBoxStyle*** enumeration, which contains values Simple, DropDown and DropDownList. Option ***Simple*** does not display a drop-down arrow. Instead, a scrollbar appears next to the control, allowing the user to select a choice from the list. The user also can type in a selection. Style ***DropDown*** (the default) displays a drop-down list when the down arrow is clicked (or the down-arrow key is pressed). The user can type a new item in the ComboBox. The last style is ***DropDownList***, which displays a drop-down list but does not allow the user to type in the TextBox.

The ComboBox control has properties ***Items*** (a collection), ***SelectedItem*** and ***SelectedIndex***, which are similar to the corresponding properties in ListBox. There can be at most one selected item in a ComboBox. If no items are selected, then SelectedIndex is -1. When the selected item changes, a ***SelectedIndexChanged*** event occurs.

Class ComboBoxTestForm (Fig. 12.23) allows users to select a shape to draw—circle, ellipse, square or pie (in both filled and unfilled versions)—by using a ComboBox. The ComboBox in this example is uneditable, so the user cannot type in the TextBox.

```
1   // Fig. 12.23: ComboBoxTestForm.cs
2   // Using ComboBox to select a shape to draw.
3   using System;
4   using System.Drawing;
5   using System.Windows.Forms;
6
7   // Form uses a ComboBox to select different shapes to draw
8   public partial class ComboBoxTestForm : Form
9   {
10      // default constructor
11      public ComboBoxTestForm()
12      {
13         InitializeComponent();
14      } // end constructor
15
16      // get index of selected shape, draw shape
17      private void imageComboBox_SelectedIndexChanged(
18         object sender, EventArgs e )
19      {
20         // create graphics object, Pen and SolidBrush
21         Graphics myGraphics = base.CreateGraphics();
22
23         // create Pen using color DarkRed
24         Pen myPen = new Pen( Color.DarkRed );
25
26         // create SolidBrush using color DarkRed
27         SolidBrush mySolidBrush = new SolidBrush( Color.DarkRed );
28
29         // clear drawing area setting it to color white
30         myGraphics.Clear( Color.White );
31
32         // find index, draw proper shape
33         switch ( imageComboBox.SelectedIndex )
34         {
```

Fig. 12.23 | ComboBox used to draw a selected shape. (Part 1 of 2.)

```
35              case 0: // case Circle is selected
36                 myGraphics.DrawEllipse( myPen, 50, 50, 150, 150 );
37                 break;
38              case 1: // case Rectangle is selected
39                 myGraphics.DrawRectangle( myPen, 50, 50, 150, 150 );
40                 break;
41              case 2: // case Ellipse is selected
42                 myGraphics.DrawEllipse( myPen, 50, 85, 150, 115 );
43                 break;
44              case 3: // case Pie is selected
45                 myGraphics.DrawPie( myPen, 50, 50, 150, 150, 0, 45 );
46                 break;
47              case 4: // case Filled Circle is selected
48                 myGraphics.FillEllipse( mySolidBrush, 50, 50, 150, 150 );
49                 break;
50              case 5: // case Filled Rectangle is selected
51                 myGraphics.FillRectangle( mySolidBrush, 50, 50, 150, 150 );
52                 break;
53              case 6: // case Filled Ellipse is selected
54                 myGraphics.FillEllipse( mySolidBrush, 50, 85, 150, 115 );
55                 break;
56              case 7: // case Filled Pie is selected
57                 myGraphics.FillPie( mySolidBrush, 50, 50, 150, 150, 0, 45 );
58                 break;
59           } // end switch
60
61           myGraphics.Dispose(); // release the Graphics object
62        } // end method imageComboBox_SelectedIndexChanged
63     } // end class ComboBoxTestForm
```

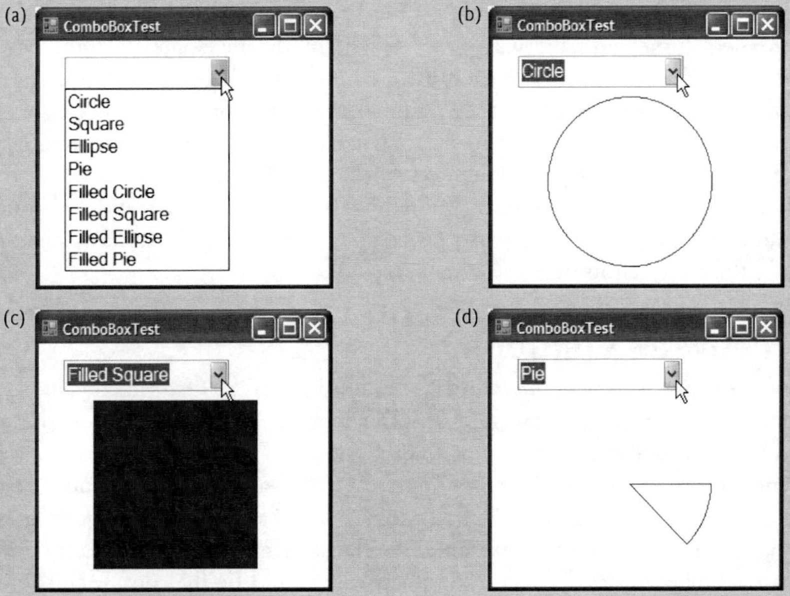

Fig. 12.23 | ComboBox used to draw a selected shape. (Part 2 of 2.)

Look-and-Feel Observation 12.5

Make lists (such as ComboBoxes) editable only if the program is designed to accept user-submitted elements. Otherwise, the user might try to enter a custom item that is improper for the purposes of your application.

After creating ComboBox imageComboBox, make it uneditable by setting its DropDown-Style to DropDownList in the **Properties** window. Next, add items Circle, Square, Ellipse, Pie, Filled Circle, Filled Square, Filled Ellipse and Filled Pie to the Items collection using the **String Collection Editor**. Whenever the user selects an item from imageComboBox, a SelectedIndexChanged event occurs and event handler imageComboBox_SelectedIndexChanged (lines 17–60) executes. Lines 21–27 create a Graphics object, a Pen and a SolidBrush, which are used to draw on the Form. The Graphics object (line 21) allows a pen or brush to draw on a component using one of several Graphics methods. The Pen object (line 24) is used by methods DrawEllipse, DrawRectangle and DrawPie (lines 36, 39, 42 and 45) to draw the outlines of their corresponding shapes. The SolidBrush object (line 27) is used by methods FillEllipse, FillRectangle and FillPie (lines 48, 51, 54 and 57) to fill their corresponding solid shapes. Line 30 colors the entire Form White, using Graphics method **Clear**.

The application draws a shape based on the selected item's index. The switch statement (lines 33–59) uses imageComboBox.SelectedIndex to determine which item the user selected. Graphics method **DrawEllipse** (line 36) takes a Pen, the *x*- and *y*-coordinates of the center and the width and height of the ellipse to draw. The origin of the coordinate system is in the upper-left corner of the Form; the *x*-coordinate increases to the right, and the *y*-coordinate increases downward. A circle is a special case of an ellipse (with the width and height equal). Line 36 draws a circle. Line 42 draws an ellipse that has different values for width and height.

Class Graphics method **DrawRectangle** (line 39) takes a Pen, the *x*- and *y*-coordinates of the upper-left corner and the width and height of the rectangle to draw. Method **DrawPie** (line 45) draws a pie as a portion of an ellipse. The ellipse is bounded by a rectangle. Method DrawPie takes a Pen, the *x*- and *y*-coordinates of the upper-left corner of the rectangle, its width and height, the start angle (in degrees) and the sweep angle (in degrees) of the pie. Angles increase clockwise. The **FillEllipse** (lines 48 and 54), **FillRectangle** (line 51) and **FillPie** (line 57) methods are similar to their unfilled counterparts, except that they take a SolidBrush instead of a Pen. Some of the drawn shapes are illustrated in the screen shots of Fig. 12.23.

12.9 TreeView Control

The **TreeView** control displays *nodes* hierarchically in a *tree*. Traditionally, nodes are objects that contain values and can refer to other nodes. A *parent node* contains *child nodes*, and the child nodes can be parents to other nodes. Two child nodes that have the same parent node are considered *sibling nodes*. A tree is a collection of nodes, usually organized in a hierarchical manner. The first parent node of a tree is the *root* node (a TreeView can have multiple roots). For example, the file system of a computer can be represented as a tree. The top-level directory (perhaps C:) would be the root, each subfolder of C: would be a child node and each child folder could have its own children. TreeView controls are useful for displaying hierarchal information, such as the file structure that we just mentioned. Figure 12.24 displays a sample TreeView control on a Form.

A parent node can be expanded or collapsed by clicking the plus box or minus box to its left. Nodes without children do not have these boxes.

The nodes in a TreeView are instances of class **TreeNode**. Each TreeNode has a **Nodes collection** (type **TreeNodeCollection**), which contains a list of other TreeNodes—known as its children. The Parent property returns a reference to the parent node (or null if the node is a root node). Figure 12.25 and Fig. 12.26 list the common properties of Tree-Views and TreeNodes, common TreeNode methods and a common TreeView event.

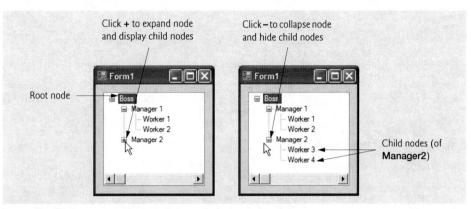

Fig. 12.24 | TreeView displaying a sample tree.

TreeView properties and event	Description
Common Properties	
CheckBoxes	Indicates whether CheckBoxes appear next to nodes. A value of true displays CheckBoxes. The default value is false.
ImageList	Specifies an ImageList object containing the node icons. An *ImageList* object is a collection that contains Image objects.
Nodes	Lists the collection of TreeNodes in the control. It contains methods Add (adds a TreeNode object), Clear (deletes the entire collection) and Remove (deletes a specific node). Removing a parent node deletes all of its children.
SelectedNode	The selected node.
*Common Event (Event arguments **TreeViewEventArgs**)*	
AfterSelect	Generated after selected node changes. This is the default event when the control is double clicked in the designer.

Fig. 12.25 | TreeView properties and event.

TreeNode properties and methods	Description
Common Properties	
Checked	Indicates whether the TreeNode is checked (CheckBoxes property must be set to true in the parent TreeView).
FirstNode	Specifies the first node in the Nodes collection (i.e., the first child in the tree).
FullPath	Indicates the path of the node, starting at the root of the tree.
ImageIndex	Specifies the index of the image shown when the node is deselected.
LastNode	Specifies the last node in the Nodes collection (i.e., the last child in the tree).
NextNode	Next sibling node.
Nodes	Collection of TreeNodes contained in the current node (i.e., all the children of the current node). It contains methods Add (adds a TreeNode object), Clear (deletes the entire collection) and Remove (deletes a specific node). Removing a parent node deletes all of its children.
PrevNode	Previous sibling node.
SelectedImageIndex	Specifies the index of the image to use when the node is selected.
Text	Specifies the TreeNode's text.
Common Methods	
Collapse	Collapses a node.
Expand	Expands a node.
ExpandAll	Expands all the children of a node.
GetNodeCount	Returns the number of child nodes.

Fig. 12.26 | TreeNode properties and methods.

To add nodes to the TreeView visually, click the ellipsis next to the Nodes property in the **Properties** window. This opens the **TreeNode Editor** (Fig. 12.27), which displays an empty tree representing the TreeView. There are Buttons to create a root, and to add or delete a node. To the right are the properties of current node. Here you can rename the node.

To add nodes programmatically, first create a root node. Create a new TreeNode object and pass it a string to display. Then call method Add to add this new TreeNode to the TreeView's Nodes collection. Thus, to add a root node to TreeView *myTreeView*, write

myTreeView.Nodes.Add(**new** TreeNode(*rootLabel*));

Delete current node

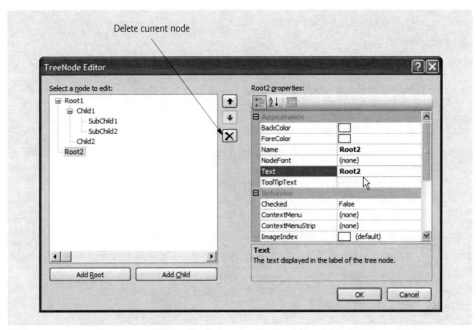

Fig. 12.27 | TreeNode Editor.

where *myTreeView* is the TreeView to which we are adding nodes, and *rootLabel* is the text to display in *myTreeView*. To add children to a root node, add new TreeNodes to its Nodes collection. We select the appropriate root node from the TreeView by writing

　　　myTreeView.Nodes[*myIndex*]

where *myIndex* is the root node's index in *myTreeView*'s Nodes collection. We add nodes to child nodes through the same process by which we added root nodes to *myTreeView*. To add a child to the root node at index *myIndex*, write

　　　myTreeView.Nodes[*myIndex*].Nodes.Add(**new** TreeNode(*ChildLabel*));

Class TreeViewDirectoryStructureForm (Fig. 12.28) uses a TreeView to display the contents of a directory chosen by the user. A TextBox and a Button are used to specify the directory. First, enter the full path of the directory you want to display. Then click the

```
1   // Fig. 12.28: TreeViewDirectoryStructureForm.cs
2   // Using TreeView to display directory structure.
3   using System;
4   using System.Windows.Forms;
5   using System.IO;
6
7   // Form uses TreeView to display directory structure
8   public partial class TreeViewDirectoryStructureForm : Form
9   {
```

Fig. 12.28 | TreeView used to display directories. (Part 1 of 3.)

```
10      string substringDirectory; // store last part of full path name
11
12      // default constructor
13      public TreeViewDirectoryStructureForm()
14      {
15         InitializeComponent();
16      } // end constructor
17
18      // populate current node with subdirectories
19      public void PopulateTreeView(
20         string directoryValue, TreeNode parentNode )
21      {
22         // array stores all subdirectories in the directory
23         string[] directoryArray =
24            Directory.GetDirectories( directoryValue );
25
26         // populate current node with subdirectories
27         try
28         {
29            // check to see if any subdirectories are present
30            if ( directoryArray.Length != 0 )
31            {
32               // for every subdirectory, create new TreeNode,
33               // add as a child of current node and recursively
34               // populate child nodes with subdirectories
35               foreach ( string directory in directoryArray )
36               {
37                  // obtain last part of path name from the full path name
38                  // by finding the last occurence of "\" and returning the
39                  // part of the path name that comes after this occurrence
40                  substringDirectory = directory.Substring(
41                     directory.LastIndexOf( '\\' ) + 1,
42                     directory.Length - directory.LastIndexOf( '\\' ) - 1 );
43
44                  // create TreeNode for current directory
45                  TreeNode myNode = new TreeNode( substringDirectory );
46
47                  // add current directory node to parent node
48                  parentNode.Nodes.Add( myNode );
49
50                  // recursively populate every subdirectory
51                  PopulateTreeView( directory, myNode );
52               } // end foreach
53            } // end if
54         } //end try
55
56         // catch exception
57         catch ( UnauthorizedAccessException )
58         {
59            parentNode.Nodes.Add( "Access denied" );
60         } // end catch
61      } // end method PopulateTreeView
```

Fig. 12.28 | TreeView used to display directories. (Part 2 of 3.)

```
62
63       // handles enterButton click event
64       private void enterButton_Click( object sender, EventArgs e )
65       {
66          // clear all nodes
67          directoryTreeView.Nodes.Clear();
68
69          // check if the directory entered by user exists
70          // if it does then fill in the TreeView,
71          // if not display error MessageBox
72          if ( Directory.Exists( inputTextBox.Text ) )
73          {
74             // add full path name to directoryTreeView
75             directoryTreeView.Nodes.Add( inputTextBox.Text );
76
77             // insert subfolders
78             PopulateTreeView(
79                inputTextBox.Text, directoryTreeView.Nodes[ 0 ] );
80          }
81          // display error MessageBox if directory not found
82          else
83             MessageBox.Show( inputTextBox.Text + " could not be found.",
84                "Directory Not Found", MessageBoxButtons.OK,
85                MessageBoxIcon.Error );
86       } // end method enterButton_Click
87    } // end class TreeViewDirectoryStructureForm
```

Fig. 12.28 | TreeView used to display directories. (Part 3 of 3.)

Button to set the specified directory as the root node in the TreeView. Each subdirectory of this directory becomes a child node. This layout is similar to that used in **Windows Explorer**. Folders can be expanded or collapsed by clicking the plus or minus boxes that appear to their left.

When the user clicks the enterButton, all the nodes in directoryTreeView are cleared (line 67). Then the path entered in inputTextBox is used to create the root node. Line 75 adds the directory to directoryTreeView as the root node, and lines 78–79 call method PopulateTreeView (lines 19–61), which takes a directory (a string) and a parent node. Method PopulateTreeView then creates child nodes corresponding to the subdirectories of the directory it receives as an argument.

Method PopulateTreeView (lines 19–61) obtains a list of subdirectories, using method **GetDirectories** of class Directory (namespace System.IO) in lines 23–24. Method GetDirectories takes a string (the current directory) and returns an array of strings (the subdirectories). If a directory is not accessible for security reasons, an UnauthorizedAccessException is thrown. Lines 57–60 catch this exception and add a node containing "Access Denied" instead of displaying the subdirectories.

If there are accessible subdirectories, lines 40–42 use the Substring method to increase readability by shortening the full path name to just the directory name. Next, each string in the directoryArray is used to create a new child node (line 45). We use method Add (line 48) to add each child node to the parent. Then method PopulateTreeView is called recursively on every subdirectory (line 51), which eventually populates the TreeView with the entire directory structure. Note that our recursive algorithm may cause a delay when the program loads large directories. However, once the folder names are added to the appropriate Nodes collection, they can be expanded and collapsed without delay. In the next section, we present an alternate algorithm to solve this problem.

12.10 ListView Control

The **ListView** control is similar to a ListBox in that both display lists from which the user can select one or more items (an example of a ListView can be found in Fig. 12.31). The important difference between the two classes is that a ListView can display icons next to the list items (controlled by its ImageList property). Property **MultiSelect** (a Boolean) determines whether multiple items can be selected. CheckBoxes can be included by setting property **CheckBoxes** (a Boolean) to true, making the ListView's appearance similar to that of a CheckedListBox. The **View** property specifies the layout of the ListBox. Property **Activation** determines the method by which the user selects a list item. The details of these properties and the ItemActivate event are explained in Fig. 12.29.

ListView properties and event	Description
Common Properties	
Activation	Determines how the user activates an item. This property takes a value in the ItemActivation enumeration. Possible values are OneClick (single-click activation), TwoClick (double-click activation, item changes color when selected) and Standard (double-click activation, item does not change color).
CheckBoxes	Indicates whether items appear with CheckBoxes. true displays CheckBoxes. The default is false.
LargeImageList	Specifies the ImageList containing large icons for display.

Fig. 12.29 | ListView properties and event. (Part 1 of 2.)

ListView properties and event	Description
Items	Returns the collection of ListViewItems in the control.
MultiSelect	Determines whether multiple selection is allowed. The default is true, which enables multiple selection.
SelectedItems	Gets the collection of selected items.
SmallImageList	Specifies the ImageList containing small icons for display.
View	Determines appearance of ListViewItems. Possible values are LargeIcon (large icon displayed, items can be in multiple columns), SmallIcon (small icon displayed, items can be in multiple columns), List (small icons displayed, items appear in a single column), Details (like List, but multiple columns of information can be displayed per item) and Tile (large icons displayed, information provided to right of icon, valid only in Windows XP or later).
Common Event	
ItemActivate	generated when an item in the ListView is activated. Does not contain the specifics of which item is activated.

Fig. 12.29 | ListView properties and event. (Part 2 of 2.)

ListView allows you to define the images used as icons for ListView items. To display images, an ImageList component is required. Create one by dragging it to a Form from the **ToolBox**. Then, select the ***Images*** property in the **Properties** window to display the **Image Collection Editor** (Fig. 12.30). Here you can browse for images that you wish to add to the ImageList, which contains an array of Images. Once the images have been defined, set property SmallImageList of the ListView to the new ImageList object. Property ***SmallImageList*** specifies the image list for the small icons. Property ***LargeImageList*** sets the ImageList for large icons. The items in a ListView are each of type ***ListViewItem***.

Fig. 12.30 | **Image Collection Editor** window for an ImageList component.

Icons for the ListView items are selected by setting the item's ***ImageIndex*** property to the appropriate index.

Class ListViewTestForm (Fig. 12.31) displays files and folders in a ListView, along with small icons representing each file or folder. If a file or folder is inaccessible because of permission settings, a MessageBox appears. The program scans the contents of the directory as it browses, rather than indexing the entire drive at once.

To display icons beside list items, create an ImageList for the ListView browser-ListView. First, drag and drop an ImageList on the Form and open the **Image Collection Editor**. Select our two simple bitmap images, provided in the bin\Release folder of this example—one for a folder (array index 0) and the other for a file (array index 1). Then set the object browserListView property SmallImageList to the new ImageList in the **Properties** window.

```
1   // Fig. 12.31: ListViewTestForm.cs
2   // Displaying directories and their contents in ListView.
3   using System;
4   using System.Drawing;
5   using System.Windows.Forms;
6   using System.IO;
7
8   // Form contains a ListView which displays
9   // folders and files in a directory
10  public partial class ListViewTestForm : Form
11  {
12     // store current directory
13     string currentDirectory = Directory.GetCurrentDirectory();
14
15     // default constructor
16     public ListViewTestForm()
17     {
18        InitializeComponent();
19     } // end constructor
20
21     // browse directory user clicked or go up one level
22     private void browserListView_Click( object sender, EventArgs e )
23     {
24        // ensure an item is selected
25        if ( browserListView.SelectedItems.Count != 0 )
26        {
27           // if first item selected, go up one level
28           if ( browserListView.Items[ 0 ].Selected )
29           {
30              // create DirectoryInfo object for directory
31              DirectoryInfo directoryObject =
32                 new DirectoryInfo( currentDirectory );
33
34              // if directory has parent, load it
35              if ( directoryObject.Parent != null )
36                 LoadFilesInDirectory( directoryObject.Parent.FullName );
37           } // end if
```

Fig. 12.31 | ListView displaying files and folders. (Part 1 of 4.)

```
38
39          // selected directory or file
40          else
41          {
42             // directory or file chosen
43             string chosen = browserListView.SelectedItems[ 0 ].Text;
44
45             // if item selected is directory, load selected directory
46             if ( Directory.Exists( currentDirectory + @"\" + chosen ) )
47             {
48                // if currently in C:\, do not need '\'; otherwise we do
49                if ( currentDirectory == @"C:\" )
50                   LoadFilesInDirectory( currentDirectory + chosen );
51                else
52                   LoadFilesInDirectory(
53                      currentDirectory + @"\" + chosen );
54             } // end if
55          } // end else
56
57          // update displayLabel
58          displayLabel.Text = currentDirectory;
59       } // end if
60    } // end method browserListView_Click
61
62    // display files/subdirectories of current directory
63    public void LoadFilesInDirectory( string currentDirectoryValue )
64    {
65       // load directory information and display
66       try
67       {
68          // clear ListView and set first item
69          browserListView.Items.Clear();
70          browserListView.Items.Add( "Go Up One Level" );
71
72          // update current directory
73          currentDirectory = currentDirectoryValue;
74          DirectoryInfo newCurrentDirectory =
75             new DirectoryInfo( currentDirectory );
76
77          // put files and directories into arrays
78          DirectoryInfo[] directoryArray =
79             newCurrentDirectory.GetDirectories();
80          FileInfo[] fileArray = newCurrentDirectory.GetFiles();
81
82          // add directory names to ListView
83          foreach ( DirectoryInfo dir in directoryArray )
84          {
85             // add directory to ListView
86             ListViewItem newDirectoryItem =
87                browserListView.Items.Add( dir.Name );
88
89             newDirectoryItem.ImageIndex = 0;  // set directory image
90          } // end foreach
```

Fig. 12.31 | ListView displaying files and folders. (Part 2 of 4.)

```
 91
 92          // add file names to ListView
 93          foreach ( FileInfo file in fileArray )
 94          {
 95             // add file to ListView
 96             ListViewItem newFileItem =
 97                browserListView.Items.Add( file.Name );
 98
 99             newFileItem.ImageIndex = 1;   // set file image
100          } // end foreach
101       } // end try
102
103       // access denied
104       catch ( UnauthorizedAccessException )
105       {
106          MessageBox.Show( "Warning: Some fields may not be " +
107             "visible due to permission settings",
108             "Attention", 0, MessageBoxIcon.Warning );
109       } // end catch
110    } // end method LoadFilesInDirectory
111
112    // handle load event when Form displayed for first time
113    private void ListViewTestForm_Load( object sender, EventArgs e )
114    {
115       // set Image list
116       Image folderImage = Image.FromFile(
117          currentDirectory + @"\images\folder.bmp" );
118
119       Image fileImage = Image.FromFile(
120          currentDirectory + @"\images\file.bmp" );
121
122       fileFolder.Images.Add( folderImage );
123       fileFolder.Images.Add( fileImage );
124
125       // load current directory into browserListView
126       LoadFilesInDirectory( currentDirectory );
127       displayLabel.Text = currentDirectory;
128    } // end method ListViewTestForm_Load
129 } // end class ListViewTestForm
```

Fig. 12.31 | ListView displaying files and folders. (Part 3 of 4.)

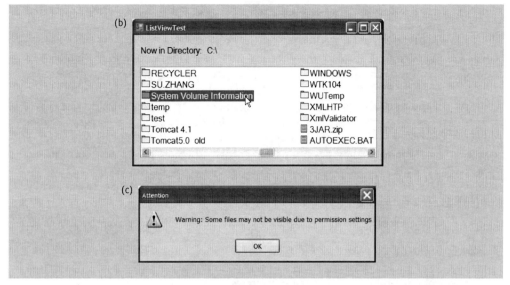

Fig. 12.31 | ListView displaying files and folders. (Part 4 of 4.)

Method LoadFilesInDirectory (lines 63–110) populates browserListView with the directory passed to it (currentDirectoryValue). It clears browserListView and adds the element "Go Up One Level". When the user clicks this element, the program attempts to move up one level (we see how shortly). The method then creates a DirectoryInfo object initialized with the string currentDirectory (lines 74–75). If permission is not given to browse the directory, an exception is thrown (and caught in line 104). Method Load-FilesInDirectory works differently from method PopulateTreeView in the previous program (Fig. 12.28). Instead of loading all the folders on the hard drive, method Load-FilesInDirectory loads only the folders in the current directory.

Class *DirectoryInfo* (namespace System.IO) enables us to browse or manipulate the directory structure easily. Method *GetDirectories* (line 79) returns an array of DirectoryInfo objects containing the subdirectories of the current directory. Similarly, method *GetFiles* (line 80) returns an array of class *FileInfo* objects containing the files in the current directory. Property *Name* (of both class DirectoryInfo and class FileInfo) contains only the directory or file name, such as temp instead of C:\myfolder\temp. To access the full name, use property *FullName*.

Lines 83–90 and lines 93–100 iterate through the subdirectories and files of the current directory and add them to browserListView. Lines 89 and 99 set the ImageIndex properties of the newly created items. If an item is a directory, we set its icon to a directory icon (index 0); if an item is a file, we set its icon to a file icon (index 1).

Method browserListView_Click (lines 22–60) responds when the user clicks control browserListView. Line 25 checks whether anything is selected. If a selection has been made, line 28 determines whether the user chose the first item in browserListView. The first item in browserListView is always **Go up one level**; if it is selected, the program attempts to go up a level. Lines 31–32 create a DirectoryInfo object for the current directory. Line 35 tests property Parent to ensure that the user is not at the root of the directory tree. Property *Parent* indicates the parent directory as a DirectoryInfo object; if no parent directory exists, `Parent` returns the value `null`. If a parent does directory exist, then line 36 passes the full name of the parent directory to method `LoadFilesInDirectory`.

If the user did not select the first item in `browserListView`, lines 40–55 allow the user to continue navigating through the directory structure. Line 43 creates `string chosen`, which receives the text of the selected item (the first item in collection `SelectedItems`). Line 46 determines whether the user has selected a valid directory (rather than a file). The program combines variables `currentDirectory` and `chosen` (the new directory), separated by a backslash (\), and passes this value to class `Directory`'s method *Exists*. Method `Exists` returns `true` if its `string` parameter is a directory. If this occurs, the program passes the `string` to method `LoadFilesInDirectory`. Because the `C:\` directory already includes a backslash, a backslash is not needed when combining `currentDirectory` and `chosen` (line 50). However, other directories must include the slash (lines 52–53). Finally, `displayLabel` is updated with the new directory (line 58).

This program loads quickly, because it indexes only the files in the current directory. This means that a small delay may occur when a new directory is loaded. In addition, changes in the directory structure can be shown by reloading a directory. The previous program (Fig. 12.28) may have a large initial delay as it loads an entire directory structure. This type of trade-off is typical in the software world.

Software Engineering Observation 12.2

When designing applications that run for long periods of time, you might choose a large initial delay to improve performance throughout the rest of the program. However, in applications that run for only short periods of time, developers often prefer fast initial loading times and small delays after each action.

12.11 TabControl Control

The *TabControl* control creates tabbed windows, such as the ones we have seen in Visual Studio (Fig. 12.32). This allows you to specify more information in the same space on a `Form`.

`TabControls` contain *TabPage* objects, which are similar to `Panels` and `GroupBoxes` in that `TabPages` also can contain controls. You first add controls to the `TabPage` objects, then add the `TabPages` to the `TabControl`. Only one `TabPage` is displayed at a time. To add objects to the `TabPage` and the `TabControl`, write

```
myTabPage.Controls.Add(myControl)
myTabControl.Controls.Add(myTabPage)
```

These statements call method `Add` of the `Controls` collection. The example adds `TabControl` *myControl* to `TabPage` *myTabPage*, then adds *myTabPage* to *myTabControl*. Alternatively, we can use method `AddRange` to add an array of `TabPages` or controls to a `TabControl` or `TabPage`, respectively. Figure 12.33 depicts a sample `TabControl`.

You can add `TabControls` visually by dragging and dropping them onto a `Form` in **Design** mode. To add `TabPages` in **Design** mode, right click the `TabControl` and select **Add Tab** (Fig. 12.34). Alternatively, click the *TabPages* property in the **Properties** window, and add tabs in the dialog that appears. To change a tab label, set the *Text* property of the `TabPage`. Note that clicking the tabs selects the `TabControl`—to select the `TabPage`, click the control area underneath the tabs. You can add controls to the `TabPage` by dragging and dropping

Tab windows

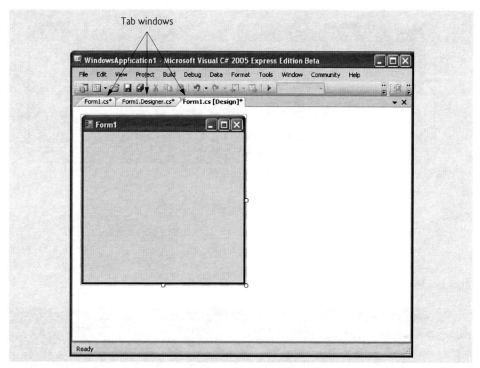

Fig. 12.32 | Tabbed windows in Visual Studio.

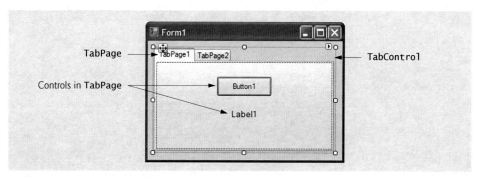

TabPage

TabControl

Controls in TabPage

Fig. 12.33 | TabControl with TabPages example.

items from the **ToolBox**. To view different TabPages, click the appropriate tab (in either design or run mode). Common properties and a common event of TabControls are described in Fig. 12.35.

Each TabPage generates a Click event when its tab is clicked. Event handlers for this event can be created by double clicking the body of the TabPage.

Class UsingTabsForm (Fig. 12.36) uses a TabControl to display various options relating to the text on a label (**Color**, **Size** and **Message**). The last TabPage displays an **About** message, which describes the use of TabControls.

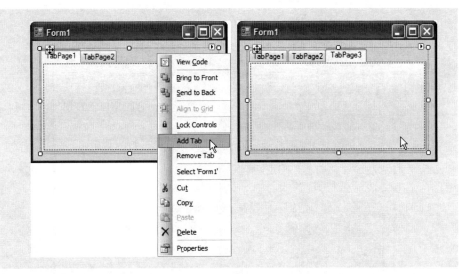

Fig. 12.34 | TabPages added to a TabControl.

TabControl properties and event	Description
Common Properties	
ImageList	Specifies images to be displayed on tabs.
ItemSize	Specifies the tab size.
Multiline	Indicates whether multiple rows of tabs can be displayed.
SelectedIndex	Index of the selected TabPage.
SelectedTab	The selected TabPage.
TabCount	Returns the number of tab pages.
TabPages	Collection of TabPages within the TabControl.
Common Event	
SelectedIndexChanged	Generated when SelectedIndex changes (i.e., another TabPage is selected).

Fig. 12.35 | TabControl properties and event.

```
1   // Fig. 12.36: UsingTabsForm.cs
2   // Using TabControl to display various font settings.
3   using System;
4   using System.Drawing;
```

Fig. 12.36 | TabControl used to display various font settings. (Part 1 of 3.)

```
 5    using System.Windows.Forms;
 6
 7    // Form uses Tabs and RadioButtons to display various font settings
 8    public partial class UsingTabsForm : Form
 9    {
10       // default constructor
11       public UsingTabsForm()
12       {
13          InitializeComponent();
14       } // end constructor
15
16       // event handler for Black RadioButton
17       private void blackRadioButton_CheckedChanged(
18          object sender, EventArgs e )
19       {
20          displayLabel.ForeColor = Color.Black; // change font color to black
21       } // end method blackRadioButton_CheckedChanged
22
23       // event handler for Red RadioButton
24       private void redRadioButton_CheckedChanged(
25          object sender, EventArgs e )
26       {
27          displayLabel.ForeColor = Color.Red; // change font color to red
28       } // end method redRadioButton_CheckedChanged
29
30       // event handler for Green RadioButton
31       private void greenRadioButton_CheckedChanged(
32          object sender, EventArgs e )
33       {
34          displayLabel.ForeColor = Color.Green; // change font color to green
35       } // end method greenRadioButton_CheckedChanged
36
37       // event handler for 12 point RadioButton
38       private void size12RadioButton_CheckedChanged(
39          object sender, EventArgs e )
40       {
41          // change font size to 12
42          displayLabel.Font = new Font( displayLabel.Font.Name, 12 );
43       } // end method size12RadioButton_CheckedChanged
44
45       // event handler for 16 point RadioButton
46       private void size16RadioButton_CheckedChanged(
47          object sender, EventArgs e )
48       {
49          // change font size to 16
50          displayLabel.Font = new Font( displayLabel.Font.Name, 16 );
51       } // end method size16RadioButton_CheckedChanged
52
53       // event handler for 20 point RadioButton
54       private void size20RadioButton_CheckedChanged(
55          object sender, EventArgs e )
56       {
```

Fig. 12.36 | TabControl used to display various font settings. (Part 2 of 3.)

```
57          // change font size to 20
58          displayLabel.Font = new Font( displayLabel.Font.Name, 20 );
59       } // end method size20RadioButton_CheckedChanged
60
61       // event handler for  Hello! RadioButton
62       private void helloRadioButton_CheckedChanged(
63          object sender, EventArgs e )
64       {
65          displayLabel.Text = "Hello!"; // change text to Hello!
66       } // end method helloRadioButton_CheckedChanged
67
68       // event handler for Goodbye! RadioButton
69       private void goodbyeRadioButton_CheckedChanged(
70          object sender, EventArgs e )
71       {
72          displayLabel.Text = "Goodbye!"; // change text to Goodbye!
73       } // end method goodbyeRadioButton_CheckedChanged
74    } // end class UsingTabsForm
```

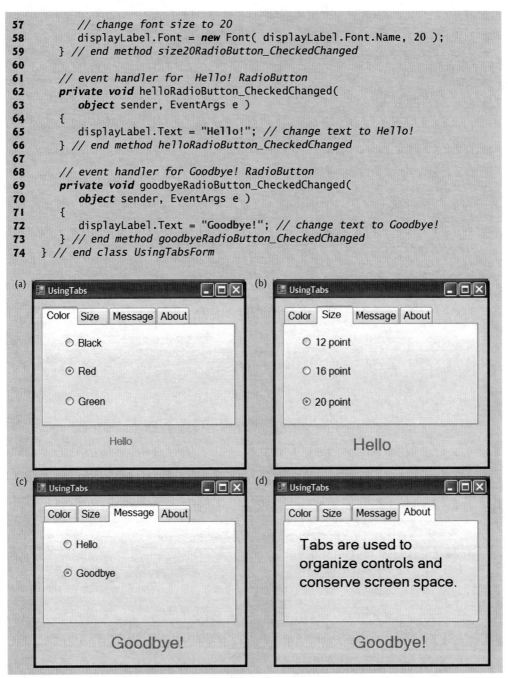

Fig. 12.36 | TabControl used to display various font settings. (Part 3 of 3.)

The textOptionsTabControl and the colorTabPage, sizeTabPage, messageTabPage and aboutTabPage are created in the designer (as described previously). The colorTabPage contains three RadioButtons for the colors black (blackRadioButton), red (redRadioButton) and green (greenRadioButton). This TabPage is displayed in Fig. 12.36(a). The Check-Changed event handler for each RadioButton updates the color of the text in displayLabel (lines 20, 27 and 34). The sizeTabPage (Fig. 12.36(b)) has three RadioButtons, corresponding to font sizes 12 (size12RadioButton), 16 (size16RadioButton) and 20 (size20RadioButton), which change the font size of displayLabel—lines 42, 50 and 58, respectively. The messageTabPage (Fig. 12.36(c)) contains two RadioButtons for the messages **Hello!** (helloRadioButton) and **Goodbye!** (goodbyeRadioButton). The two RadioButtons determine the text on displayLabel (lines 65 and 72, respectively). The aboutTabPage (Fig. 12.36(d)) contains a Label (messageLabel) describing the purpose of TabControls.

Software Engineering Observation 12.3

A TabPage can act as a container for a single logical group of RadioButtons, enforcing their mutual exclusivity. To place multiple RadioButton groups inside a single TabPage, you should group RadioButtons within Panels or GroupBoxes contained within the TabPage.

12.12 Multiple Document Interface (MDI) Windows

In previous chapters, we have built only *single document interface (SDI)* applications. Such programs (including Microsoft's Notepad and Paint) can support only one open window or document at a time. SDI applications usually have limited abilities—Paint and Notepad, for example, have limited image- and text-editing features. To edit multiple documents, the user must execute another instance of the SDI application.

Most recent applications are *multiple document interface (MDI)* programs, which allow users to edit multiple documents at once (e.g. Microsoft Office products). MDI programs also tend to be more complex—PaintShop Pro and Photoshop have a greater number of image-editing features than does Paint.

The main application window of an MDI program is called the *parent window*, and each window inside the application is referred to as a *child window*. Although an MDI application can have many child windows, each has only one parent window. Furthermore, a maximum of one child window can be active at once. Child windows cannot be parents themselves and cannot be moved outside their parent. Otherwise, a child window behaves like any other window (with regard to closing, minimizing, resizing, etc.). A child window's functionality can be different from the functionality of other child windows of the parent. For example, one child window might allow the user to edit images, another might allow the user to edit text and a third might display network traffic graphically, but all could belong to the same MDI parent. Figure 12.37 depicts a sample MDI application.

To create an MDI Form, create a new Form and set its ***IsMdiContainer*** property to true. The Form changes appearance, as in Fig. 12.38.

Next, create a child Form class to be added to the Form. To do this, right click the project in the **Solution Explorer**, select **Project > Add Windows Form...** and name the file. Edit the Form as you like. To add the child Form to the parent, we must create a new child Form object, set its ***MdiParent*** property to the parent Form and call the child Form's Show method. In general, to add a child Form to a parent, write

```
ChildFormClass childForm = New ChildFormClass();
childForm.MdiParent = parentForm;
childForm.Show();
```

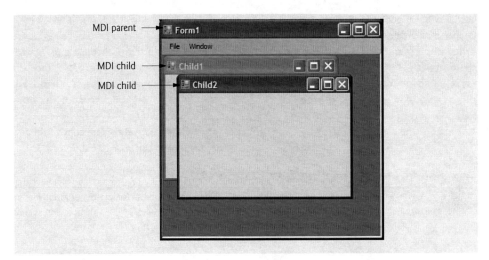

Fig. 12.37 | MDI parent window and MDI child windows.

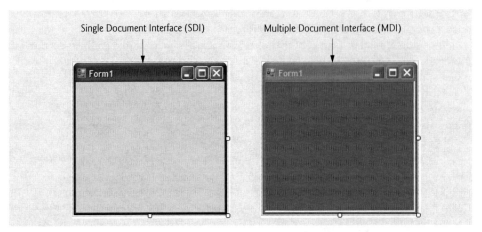

Fig. 12.38 | SDI and MDI forms.

In most cases, the parent Form creates the child, so the *parentForm* reference is this. The code to create a child usually lies inside an event handler, which creates a new window in response to a user action. Menu selections (such as **File**, followed by a submenu option of **New**, followed by a submenu option of **Window**) are common techniques for creating new child windows.

Class Form property **MdiChildren** returns an array of child Form references. This is useful if the parent window wants to check the status of all its children (for example, ensuring that all are saved before the parent closes). Property **ActiveMdiChild** returns a reference to the active child window; it returns Nothing if there are no active child windows. Other features of MDI windows are described in Fig. 12.39.

Child windows can be minimized, maximized and closed independently of each other and the parent window. Figure 12.40 shows two images: one containing two minimized child windows and a second containing a maximized child window. When the parent is

MDI Form properties, a method and event	Description
Common MDI Child Properties	
IsMdiChild	Indicates whether the Form is an MDI child. If true, Form is an MDI child (read-only property).
MdiParent	Specifies the MDI parent Form of the child.
Common MDI Parent Properties	
ActiveMdiChild	Returns the Form that is the currently active MDI child (returns null if no children are active).
IsMdiContainer	Indicates whether a Form can be an MDI parent. If true, the Form can be an MDI parent. The default value is false.
MdiChildren	Returns the MDI children as an array of Forms.
Common Method	
LayoutMdi	Determines the display of child forms on an MDI parent. The method takes as a parameter an MdiLayout enumeration with possible values ArrangeIcons, Cascade, TileHorizontal and TileVertical. Figure 12.42 depicts the effects of these values.
Common Event	
MdiChildActivate	Generated when an MDI child is closed or activated.

Fig. 12.39 | MDI parent and MDI child properties, method and event.

minimized or closed, the child windows are minimized or closed as well. Notice that the title bar in Fig. 12.40(b) is **Form1 - [Child2]**. When a child window is maximized, its title bar text is inserted into the parent window's title bar. When a child window is minimized or maximized, its title bar displays a restore icon, which can be used to return the child window to its previous size (its size before it was minimized or maximized).

C# provides a property that helps track which child windows are open in an MDI container. Property *MdiWindowListItem* of class MenuStrip specifies which menu, if any, displays a list of open child windows. When a new child window is opened, an entry is added to the list (as in the first screen of Figure 12.41). If nine or more child windows are open, the list includes the option **More Windows...**, which allows the user to select a window from a list in a dialog.

 Good Programming Practice 12.1

When creating MDI applications, include a menu that displays a list of the open child windows. This helps the user select a child window quickly, rather than having to search for it in the parent window.

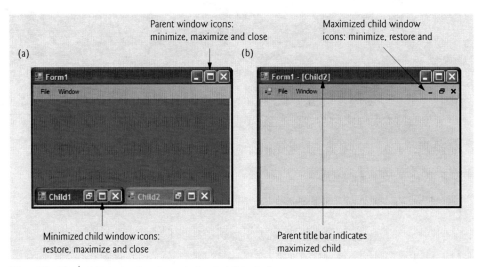

Fig. 12.40 | Minimized and maximized child windows.

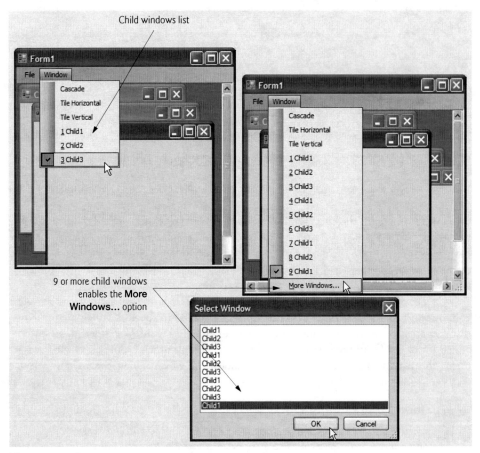

Fig. 12.41 | MenuItem property MdiList example.

MDI containers allow you to organize the placement ofs child windows. The child windows in an MDI application can be arranged by calling method **LayoutMdi** of the parent Form. Method LayoutMdi takes a **MdiLayout** enumeration, which can have values **ArrangeIcons**, **Cascade**, **TileHorizontal** and **TileVertical**. *Tiled windows* completely fill the parent and do not overlap; such windows can be arranged horizontally (value TileHorizontal) or vertically (value TileVertical). *Cascaded windows* (value Cascade) overlap—each is the same size and displays a visible title bar, if possible. Value ArrangeIcons arranges the icons for any minimized child windows. If minimized windows are scattered around the parent window, value ArrangeIcons orders them neatly at the bottom-left corner of the parent window. Figure 12.42 illustrates the values of the MdiLayout enumeration.

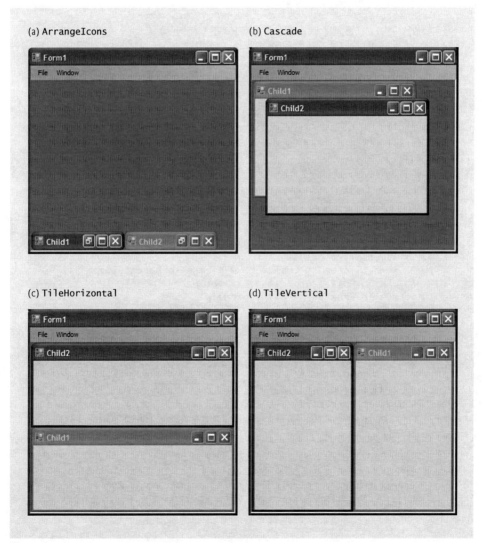

Fig. 12.42 | MdiLayout enumeration values.

Class `UsingMDIForm` (Fig. 12.43) demonstrates MDI windows. Class `UsingMDIForm` uses three instances of child `Form` `ChildForm` (Fig. 12.44), each containing a `PictureBox` that displays an image. The parent MDI `Form` contains a menu enabling users to create and arrange child `Form`s.

The program in Fig. 12.43 is the application. The MDI parent `Form`, which is created first, contains two top-level menus. The first of these menus, **File** (`fileToolStripMenu-Item`), contains both an **Exit** item (`exitToolStripMenuItem`) and a **New** submenu (`new-ToolStripMenuItem`) consisting of items for each child window. The second menu, **Window** (`windowToolStripMenuItem`), provides options for laying out the MDI children, plus a list of the active MDI children.

```csharp
1   // Fig. 12.43: UsingMDIForm.cs
2   // Demonstrating use of MDI parent and child windows.
3   using System;
4   using System.Windows.Forms;
5
6   // Form demonstrates the use of MDI parent and child windows
7   public partial class UsingMDIForm : Form
8   {
9      // default constructor
10     public UsingMDIForm()
11     {
12        InitializeComponent();
13     } // end constructor
14
15     // create Child 1 window when child1ToolStrip MenuItem is clicked
16     private void child1ToolStripMenuItem_Click(
17        object sender, EventArgs e )
18     {
19        // create new child
20        ChildForm formChild =
21           new ChildForm( "Child 1", @"\images\csharphtp1.jpg" );
22        formChild.MdiParent = this; // set parent
23        formChild.Show(); // display child
24     } // end method child1ToolStripMenuItem_Click
25
26     // create Child 2 window when child2ToolStripMenuItem is clicked
27     private void child2ToolStripMenuItem_Click(
28        object sender, EventArgs e )
29     {
30        // create new child
31        ChildForm formChild =
32           new ChildForm( "Child 2", @"\images\vbnethtp2.jpg" );
33        formChild.MdiParent = this; // set parent
34        formChild.Show(); // display child
35     } // end method child2ToolStripMenuItem_Click
36
37     // create Child 3 window when child3ToolStripMenuItem is clicked
38     private void child3ToolStripMenuItem_Click(
39        object sender, EventArgs e )
40     {
```

Fig. 12.43 | MDI parent-window class. (Part 1 of 3.)

```
41          // create new child
42          Child formChild =
43              new Child( "Child 3", @"\images\pythonhtp1.jpg" );
44          formChild.MdiParent = this; // set parent
45          formChild.Show(); // display child
46      } // end method child3ToolStripMenuItem_Click
47
48      // exit application
49      private void exitToolStripMenuItem_Click( object sender, EventArgs e )
50      {
51          Application.Exit();
52      } // end method exitToolStripMenuItem_Click
53
54      // set Cascade layout
55      private void cascadeToolStripMenuItem_Click(
56          object sender, EventArgs e )
57      {
58          this.LayoutMdi( MdiLayout.Cascade );
59      } // end method cascadeToolStripMenuItem_Click
60
61      // set TileHorizontal layout
62      private void tileHorizontalToolStripMenuItem_Click(
63          object sender, EventArgs e )
64      {
65          this.LayoutMdi( MdiLayout.TileHorizontal );
66      } // end method tileHorizontalToolStripMenuItem
67
68      // set TileVertical layout
69      private void tileVerticalToolStripMenuItem_Click(
70          object sender, EventArgs e )
71      {
72          this.LayoutMdi( MdiLayout.TileVertical );
73      } // end method tileVerticalToolStripMenuItem_Click
74  } // end class UsingMDIForm
```

Fig. 12.43 | MDI parent-window class. (Part 2 of 3.)

Fig. 12.43 | MDI parent-window class. (Part 3 of 3.)

In the **Properties** window, we set the Form's IsMdiContainer property to true, making the Form an MDI parent. In addition, we set the MenuStrip's MdiWindowListItem property to windowToolStripMenuItem. This enables the **Window** menu to contain the list of child MDI windows.

The **Cascade** menu item (cascadeToolStripMenuItem) has an event handler (cascadeToolStripMenuItem_Click, lines 55–59) that arranges the child windows in a cascading manner. The event handler calls method LayoutMdi with the argument Cascade from the MdiLayout enumeration (line 58).

The **Tile Horizontal** menu item (tileHorizontalToolStripMenuItem) has an event handler (tileHorizontalToolStripMenuItem_Click, lines 62–66) that arranges the child windows in a horizontal manner. The event handler calls method LayoutMdi with the argument TileHorizontal from the MdiLayout enumeration (line 65).

Finally, the **Tile Vertical** menu item (tileVerticalToolStripMenuItem) has an event handler (tileVerticalToolStripMenuItem_Click, lines 69–73) that arranges the child windows in a vertical manner. The event handler calls method LayoutMdi with the argument TileVertical from the MdiLayout enumeration (line 72).

At this point, the application is still incomplete—we must define the MDI child class. To do this, right click the project in the **Solution Explorer** and select **Add > Windows Form....** Then name the new class in the dialog as ChildForm (Fig. 12.44). Next, we add a PictureBox (picDisplay) to ChildForm. In the constructor, line 15 sets the title bar text. Lines 18–19 set ChildForm's Image property to an Image, using method FromFile.

```
1   // Fig. 12.44: ChildForm.cs
2   // Child window of MDI parent.
3   using System;
4   using System.Drawing;
5   using System.Windows.Forms;
6   using System.IO;
7
```

Fig. 12.44 | MDI child ChildForm. (Part 1 of 2.)

```
 8   public partial class ChildForm : Form
 9   {
10      public ChildForm( string title, string fileName )
11      {
12         // Required for Windows Form Designer support
13         InitializeComponent();
14
15         Text = title; // set title text
16
17         // set image to display in pictureBox
18         picDisplay.Image = Image.FromFile(
19            Directory.GetCurrentDirectory() + fileName );
20      } // end constructor
21   } // end class ChildForm
```

Fig. 12.44 | MDI child `ChildForm`. (Part 2 of 2.)

After the MDI child class is defined, the parent MDI Form (Fig. 12.43) can create new child windows. The event handlers in lines 16–46 create a new child Form corresponding to the menu item clicked. Lines 20–21, 31–32 and 42–43 create new instances of Child-Form. Lines 22, 33 and 44 set each Child's MdiParent property to the parent Form. Lines 23, 34 and 45 call method Show to display each child Form.

12.13 Visual Inheritance

Chapter 8 discussed how to create classes by inheriting from other classes. We have also used inheritance to create Forms that display a GUI, by deriving our new Form classes from class System.Windows.Forms.Form. This is an example of *visual inheritance*. The derived Form class contains the functionality of its Form base class, including any base-class properties, methods, variables and controls. The derived class also inherits all visual aspects—such as sizing, component layout, spacing between GUI components, colors and fonts—from its base class.

Visual inheritance enables you to achieve visual consistency across applications. For example, you could define a base Form that contains a product's logo, a specific background color, a predefined menu bar and other elements. You then could use the base Form throughout an application for uniformity and branding.

Class VisualInheritanceForm (Fig. 12.45) derives from Form. The output depicts the workings of the program. The GUI contains two Labels with text **Bugs, Bugs, Bugs** and **Copyright 2006, by deitel.com.**, as well as one Button displaying the text **Learn More**. When a user presses the **Learn More** Button, method learnMoreButton_Click (lines 16–22) is invoked. This method displays a MessageBox that provides some informative text.

```
 1   // Fig. 12.45: VisualInheritanceForm.cs
 2   // Base Form for use with visual inheritance.
 3   using System;
 4   using System.Windows.Forms;
```

Fig. 12.45 | Class VisualInheritanceForm, which inherits from class Form, contains a Button (**Learn More**). (Part 1 of 2.)

```
5
6    // base Form used to demonstrate visual inheritance
7    public partial class VisualInheritanceForm : Form
8    {
9        // default constructor
10       public VisualInheritanceForm()
11       {
12           InitializeComponent();
13       } // end constructor
14
15       // display MessageBox when Button is clicked
16       private void learnMoreButton_Click( object sender, EventArgs e )
17       {
18           MessageBox.Show(
19               "Bugs, Bugs, Bugs is a product of deitel.com",
20               "Learn More", MessageBoxButtons.OK,
21               MessageBoxIcon.Information );
22       } // end method learnMoreButton_Click
23   } // end class VisualInheritanceForm
```

Fig. 12.45 | Class VisualInheritanceForm, which inherits from class Form, contains a Button (**Learn More**). (Part 2 of 2.)

To allow other Forms to inherit from VisualInheritanceForm, we must package VisualInheritanceForm as a .dll (class library). Right click the project name in the **Solution Explorer** and select **Properties**, then choose the **Application** tab. In the **Output type** drop-down list, change **Windows Application** to **Class Library**. Building the project produces the .dll.

To visually inherit from VisualInheritanceForm, first create a new Windows application. In this application, add a reference to the .dll you just created (located in the previous application's bin/Release folder). Then open the file that defines the new application's GUI and modify the first line of the class so that it inherits from class VisualInheritanceForm. Note that you will only need to specify the class name. In design view, the new application's Form should now display the controls of the base Form (Fig. 12.46). We can still add more components to the Form.

Class VisualInheritanceTestForm (Fig. 12.47) is a derived class of VisualInheritanceForm. The output illustrates the functionality of the program. The GUI contains those components derived from class VisualInheritanceForm, as well as an additional Button with text **Learn The Program**. When a user presses this Button, method

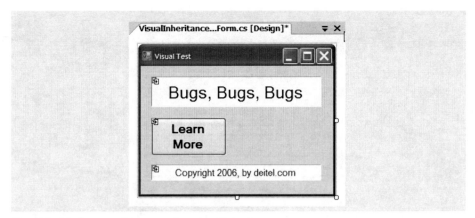

Fig. 12.46 | Form demonstrating visual inheritance.

learnProgramButton_Click (lines 17–22) is invoked. This method displays another MessageBox providing different informative text.

Figure 12.47 demonstrates that the components, their layouts and the functionality of base-class VisualInheritanceForm (Fig. 12.45) are inherited by VisualInheritanceTestForm. If a user clicks the button **Learn More**, the base class event handler learnMoreButton_Click displays a MessageBox. VisualInheritanceForm uses a private access modifier to declare its controls, so class VisualInheritanceTestForm cannot modify the controls inherited from class VisualInheritanceForm.

```
1   // Fig. 12.47: VisualInheritanceTestForm.cs
2   // Derived Form using visual inheritance.
3   using System;
4   using System.Windows.Forms;
5
6   // derived form using visual inheritance
7   public partial class VisualInheritanceTestForm :
8      VisualInheritanceForm   // code for inheritance
9   {
10     // default constructor
11     public VisualInheritanceTestForm()
12     {
13        InitializeComponent();
14     } // end constructor
15
16     // display MessageBox when Button is clicked
17     private void learnProgramButton_Click(object sender, EventArgs e)
18     {
19        MessageBox.Show( "This program was created by Deitel & Associates",
20           "Learn the Program", MessageBoxButtons.OK,
21           MessageBoxIcon.Information );
22     } // end method learnProgramButton_Click
23  } // end class VisualInheritanceTestForm
```

Fig. 12.47 | Class VisualInheritanceTestForm, which inherits from class VisualInheritanceForm, contains an additional Button. (Part 1 of 2.)

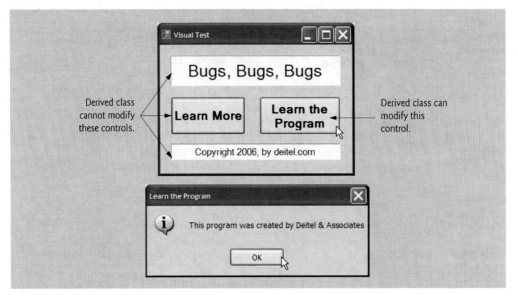

Fig. 12.47 | Class VisualInheritanceTestForm, which inherits from class VisualInheritanceForm, contains an additional Button. (Part 2 of 2.)

12.14 User-Defined Controls

The .NET Framework allows you to create *custom controls*. These custom controls appear in the user's **Toolbox** and can be added to Forms, Panels or GroupBoxes in the same way that we add Buttons, Labels and other predefined controls. The simplest way to create a custom control is to derive a class from an existing control, such as a Label. This is useful if you want to add functionality to an existing control, rather than having to reimplement the existing control to include the desired functionality. For example, you can create a new type of Label that behaves like a normal Label but has a different appearance. You accomplish this by inheriting from class Label and overriding method OnPaint.

All controls contain method *OnPaint*, which the system calls when a component must be redrawn (such as when the component is resized). Method OnPaint is passed a *PaintEventArgs* object, which contains graphics information—property *Graphics* is the graphics object used to draw, and property *ClipRectangle* defines the rectangular boundary of the control. Whenever the system raises the Paint event, our control's base class catches the event. Through polymorphism, our control's OnPaint method is called. Our base class's OnPaint implementation is not called, so we must call it explicitly from our OnPaint implementation before we execute our custom-paint code. In most cases, you want to do this to ensure that the original painting code executes in addition to the code you define in the custom control's class. Alternately, if we do not wish to let the base class OnPaint method execute, we do not call it.

To create a new control composed of existing controls, use class *UserControl*. Controls added to a custom control are called *constituent controls*. For example, a programmer could create a UserControl composed of a Button, a Label and a TextBox, each associated with some functionality (for example, the Button setting the Label's text to that contained in the TextBox). The UserControl acts as a container for the controls added to it. The UserControl contains constituent controls, so it does not determine how these constituent controls are displayed. Method OnPaint of the UserControl cannot be over-ridden. To control the appearance of each constituent control, you must handle each control's Paint event. The Paint event handler is passed a PaintEventArgs object, which can be used to draw graphics (lines, rectangles, etc.) on the constituent controls.

Using another technique, a programmer can create a brand new control by inheriting from class Control. This class does not define any specific behavior; that task is left to you. Instead, class Control handles the items associated with all controls, such as events and sizing handles. Method OnPaint should contain a call to the base class's OnPaint method, which calls the Paint event handlers. You must then add code that draws custom graphics inside the overridden OnPaint method when drawing the control. This technique allows for the greatest flexibility, but also requires the most planning. All three approaches are summarized in Fig. 12.48.

We create a "clock" control in Fig. 12.49. This is a UserControl composed of a Label and a Timer—whenever the Timer raises an event, the Label is updated to reflect the current time.

Timers (System.Windows.Forms namespace) are invisible components that reside on a Form, generating *Tick* events at a set interval. This interval is set by the Timer's *Interval*

Custom control techniques and PaintEventArgs properties	Description
Custom Control Techniques	
Inherit from Windows Forms control	You can do this to add functionality to a pre-existing control. If you override method OnPaint, call the base class's OnPaint method. Note that you only can add to the original control's appearance, not redesign it.
Create a UserControl	You can create a UserControl composed of multiple pre-existing controls (e.g., to combine their functionality). Note that you cannot override the OnPaint methods of custom controls. Instead, you must place drawing code in a Paint event handler. Again, note that you only can add to the original control's appearance, not redesign it
Inherit from class Control	Define a brand new control. Override method OnPaint, then call base class method OnPaint and include methods to draw the control. With this method you can customize control appearance and functionality.
PaintEventArgs Properties	
Graphics	The graphics object of the control. It is used to draw on the control.
ClipRectangle	Specifies the rectangle indicating the boundary of the control.

Fig. 12.48 | Custom control creation.

```
1   // Fig. 12.49: ClockUserControl.cs
2   // User-defined control with a timer and a Label.
3   using System;
4   using System.Windows.Forms;
5
6   // UserControl that displays the time on a Label
7   public partial class ClockUserControl : UserControl
8   {
9      // default constructor
10     public ClockUserControl()
11     {
12        InitializeComponent();
13     } // end constructor
14
15     // update Label at every tick
16     private void clockTimer_Tick(object sender, EventArgs e)
17     {
18        // get current time (Now), convert to string
19        displayLabel.Text = DateTime.Now.ToLongTimeString();
20     } // end method clockTimer_Tick
21  } // end class ClockUserControl
```

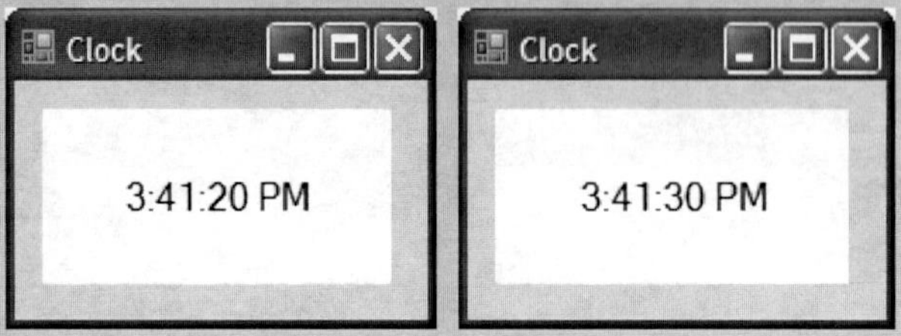

Fig. 12.49 | UserControl-defined clock.

property, which defines the number of milliseconds (thousandths of a second) between events. By default, timers are disabled and do not generate events.

This application contains a user control (ClockUserControl) and a Form that displays the user control. We begin by creating a Windows application. Next, we create a User-Control class for the project by selecting **Project > Add User Control...**. This displays a dialog from which we can select the type of control to add—user controls are already selected. We then name the file (and the class) ClockUserControl. Our empty Clock-UserControl is displayed as a grey rectangle.

You can treat this control like a Windows Form, meaning that you can add controls using the **ToolBox** and set properties using the **Properties** window. However, instead of creating an application, you are simply creating a new control composed of other controls. Add a Label (displayLabel) and a Timer (clockTimer) to the UserControl. Set the Timer interval to 1000 milliseconds and set displayLabel's text with each event (lines 16–20). To generate events, clockTimer must be enabled by setting property Enabled to true in the **Properties** window.

Structure *DateTime* (namespace System) contains property *Now*, which is the current time. Method *ToLongTimeString* converts Now to a string containing the current hour, minute and second (along with AM or PM). We use this to set the time in `displayLabel` in line 19.

Once created, our clock control appears as an item on the **ToolBox**. You may need to switch to the application's `Form` before the item appears in the **ToolBox**. To use the control, simply drag it to the `Form` and run the Windows application. We gave the `ClockUserControl` object a white background to make it stand out in the `Form`. Figure 12.49 shows the output of `ClockForm`, which contains our `ClockUserControl`. There are no event handlers in `ClockForm`, so we show only the code for `ClockUserControl`.

Visual Studio allows you to share custom controls with other developers. To create a `UserControl` that can be exported to other solutions, do the following:

1. Create a new **Class Library** project.

2. Delete `Class1.cs`, initially provided with the application.

3. Right click the project in the **Solution Explorer** and select **Add > User Control....** In the dialog that appears, name the user control file and click **Add**.

4. Inside the project, add controls and functionality to the `UserControl` (Fig. 12.50).

5. Build the project. Visual Studio creates a `.dll` file for the `UserControl` in the output directory (`bin/Release`). The file is not executable; class libraries are used to define classes that are reused in other executable applications.

6. Create a new Windows application.

7. In the new Windows application, right click the **ToolBox** and select **Choose Items....** In the **Choose Toolbox Items** dialog that appears, click **Browse....** Browse for the `.dll` file from the class library created in *Steps 1–5*. The item will then appear in the **Choose Toolbox Items** dialog (Fig. 12.51). If it is not already checked, check this item. Click **OK** to add the item to the **Toolbox**. This control can now be added to the `Form` as if it were any other control (Fig. 12.52).

12.15 Wrap-Up

Many of today's commercial applications provide GUIs that are easy to use and manipulate. Because of this demand for user-friendly GUIs, the ability to design sophisticated GUIs is an essential programming skill. Visual Studio's IDE makes GUI development quick and easy. In Chapters 11 and 12, we presented basic GUI development techniques. In Chapter 12, we demonstrated how to create menus, which provide users easy access to

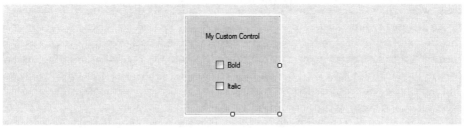

Fig. 12.50 | Custom-control creation.

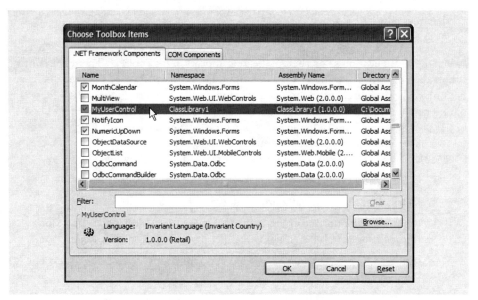

Fig. 12.51 | Custom control added to the **ToolBox**.

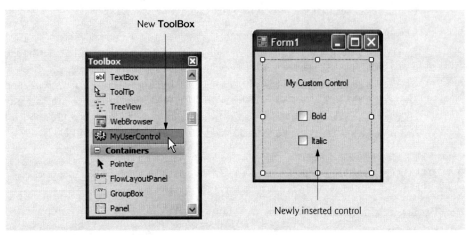

Fig. 12.52 | Custom control added to a Form.

an application's functionality. You learned the DateTimePicker and MonthCalendar controls, which allow users to input date and time values. We demonstrated LinkLabels, which are used to link the user to an application or a Web page. You used several controls that provide lists of data to the user—ListBoxes, CheckedListBoxes and ListViews. We used the ComboBox control to create drop-down lists, and the TreeView control to display data in hierarchical form. We then introduced complex GUIs that use tabbed windows and multiple document interfaces. The chapter concluded with demonstrations of visual inheritance and creating custom controls.

The next chapter explores multithreading. In many programming languages, you can create multiple threads, enabling several activities to proceed in parallel.

13

C# Text Manipulation and File I/O

OBJECTIVES

- *Characters and Unicode:* By default, .NET stores a character as a 16-bit Unicode character. This enables an application to support international character sets—a technique referred to as localization.

- *String Overview:* In .NET, strings are immutable. To use strings efficiently, it is necessary to understand what this means and how immutability affects string operations.

- *String Operations:* In addition to basic string operations, .NET supports advanced formatting techniques for numbers and dates.

- *StringBuilder:* The `StringBuilder` class offers an efficient alternative to concatenation for constructing screens.

- *Regular Expressions:* The .NET `Regex` class provides an engine that uses regular expressions to parse, match, and extract values in a string.

- *Text Streams:* Stream classes permit data to be read and written as a stream of bytes that can be encrypted and buffered.

- *Text Reading and Writing:* The `StreamReader` and `StreamWriter` classes make it easy to read from and write to physical files.

- *System.IO:* Classes in this namespace enable an application to work with underlying directory structure of the host operating system.

13.1   Introduction

This chapter introduces the string handling capabilities provided by the .NET classes. Topics include how to use the basic String methods for extracting and manipulating string content; the use of the String.Format method to display numbers and dates in special formats; and the use of regular expressions (regexes) to perform advanced pattern matching. Also included is a look at the underlying features of .NET that influence how an application works with text. Topics include how the Just-In-Time (JIT) compiler optimizes the use of literal strings; the importance of Unicode as the cornerstone of character and string representations in .NET; and the built-in *localization* features that permit applications to automatically take into account the culture-specific characteristics of languages and countries.

This chapter is divided into two major topics. The first topic focuses on how to create, represent, and manipulate strings using the System.Char, System.String, and Regex classes; the second takes up a related topic of how to store and retrieve string data. It begins by looking at the Stream class and how to use it to process raw bytes of data as streams that can be stored in files or transmitted across a network. The discussion then moves to using the TextReader/TextWriter classes to read and write strings as lines of text. The chapter concludes with examples of how members of the System.IO namespace are used to access the Microsoft Windows directory and file structure.

13.2   Characters and Unicode

One of the watershed events in computing was the introduction of the ASCII 7-bit character set in 1968 as a standardized encoding scheme to uniquely identify alphanumeric characters and other common symbols. It was largely based on the Latin alphabet and contained 128 characters. The subsequent ANSI standard doubled the number of characters—primarily to include symbols for European alphabets and currencies. However, because it was still based on Latin characters, a number of incompatible encoding schemes sprang up to represent non-Latin alphabets such as the Greek and Arabic languages.

Recognizing the need for a universal encoding scheme, an international consortium devised the Unicode specification. It is now a standard, accepted worldwide, that defines a unique number for every character "no matter what the platform, no matter what the program, no matter what the language."[1]

13.2.1 Unicode

NET fully supports the Unicode standard. Its internal representation of a character is an unsigned 16-bit number that conforms to the Unicode encoding scheme. Two bytes enable a character to represent up to 65,536 values. Figure 13.1 illustrates why two bytes are needed.

The uppercase character on the left is a member of the Basic Latin character set that consists of the original 128 ASCII characters. Its decimal value of 75 can be depicted in 8 bits; the unneeded bits are set to zero. However, the other three characters have values that range from 310 (0x0136) to 56,609 (0xDB05), which can be represented by no less than two bytes.

Unicode characters have a unique identifier made up of a name and value, referred to as a *code point*. The current version 4.0 defines identifiers for 96,382 characters. These characters are grouped in over 130 character sets that include language scripts, symbols for math, music, OCR, geometric shapes, Braille, and many other uses.

Because 16 bits cannot represent the nearly 100,000 characters supported worldwide, more bytes are required for some character sets. The Unicode solution is a mechanism by which two sets of 16-bit units define a character. This pair of code units is known as a *surrogate pair*. Together, this *high surrogate* and *low surrogate* represent a single 32-bit *abstract* character into which characters are mapped. This approach supports over 1,000,000 characters. The surrogates are constructed from values that reside in a reserved area at the high end of the Unicode code space so that they are not mistaken for actual characters.

As a developer, you can pretty much ignore the details of whether a character requires 16 or 32 bits because the .NET API and classes handle the underlying details of representing Unicode characters. One exception to this—discussed later in this section—occurs if you parse individual bytes in a stream and need to recognize the surrogates. For this, .NET provides a special object to iterate through the bytes.

> ### Core Note 13.1
>
> *Unicode characters can only be displayed if your computer has a font supporting them. On a Windows operating system, you can install a font extension (ttfext.exe) that displays the supported Unicode ranges for a .ttf font. To use it, right-click the .ttf font name and select Properties. Console applications cannot print Unicode characters because console output always displays in a non-proportional typeface.*

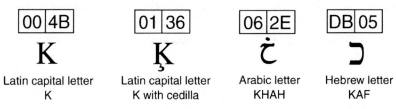

00 4B	01 36	06 2E	DB 05
K	Ķ	خ	כ
Latin capital letter K	Latin capital letter K with cedilla	Arabic letter KHAH	Hebrew letter KAF

Fig. 13.1 | Unicode memory layout of a character.

---

1. Unicode Consortium—www.unicode.org.

13.2.2 Working with Characters

A single character is represented in .NET as a char (or Char) structure. The char structure defines a small set of members that can be used to inspect and transform its value. Here is a brief review of some standard character operations.

Assigning a Value to a Char Type

The most obvious way to assign a value to a char variable is with a literal value. However, because a char value is represented internally as a number, you can also assign it a numeric value. Here are examples of each:

```
string klm = "KLM";
byte    b = 75;
char k;
// Different ways to assign 'K' to variable K
k = 'K';
k = klm[0];                  // Assign "K" from first value in klm
k = (char) 75;              // Cast decimal
k = (char) b;              // cast byte
k = Convert.ToChar(75);    // Converts value to a char
```

Converting a Char Value to a Numeric Value

When a character is converted to a number, the result is the underlying Unicode (ordinal) value of the character. Casting is the most efficient way to do this, although Convert methods can also be used. In the special case where the char is a digit and you want to assign the linguistic value—rather than the Unicode value—use the static GetNumericValue method.

```
// '7' has Unicode value of 55
char k = '7';
int n = (int) k;                // n = 55
n = (int) char.GetNumericValue(k);   // n = 7
```

Characters and Localization

One of the most important features of .NET is the capability to automatically recognize and incorporate culture-specific rules of a language or country into an application. This process, known as localization, may affect how a date or number is formatted, which currency symbol appears in a report, or how string comparisons are carried out. In practical terms, localization means a single application would display the date May 9, 2004 as 9/5/2004 to a user in Paris, France and as 5/9/2004 to a user in Paris, Texas. The Common Language Runtime (CLR) automatically recognizes the local computer's culture and makes the adjustments.

The .NET Framework provides more than a hundred *culture names* and identifiers that are used with the CultureInfo class to designate the language/country to be used with culture sensitive operations in a program. Although localization has a greater impact when working with strings, the Char.ToUpper method in this example is a useful way to demonstrate the concept.

```
// Include the System.Globalization namespace
// Using CultureInfo - Azerbaijan
char i = 'i';
// Second parameter is false to use default culture settings
// associated with selected culture
CultureInfo myCI = new CultureInfo("az", false );
i = Char.ToUpper(i,myCI);
```

An overload of ToUpper() accepts a CultureInfo object that specifies the culture (language and country) to be used in executing the method. In this case, az stands for the Azeri language of the country Azerbaijan (more about this follows). When the Common Language Runtime sees the CultureInfo parameter, it takes into account any aspects of the culture that might affect the operation. When no parameter is provided, the CLR uses the system's default culture.

Core Note 13.2

On a Windows operating system, the .NET Framework obtains its default culture information from the system's country and language settings. It assigns these values to the Thread.Current-Thread.CurrentCulture property. You can set these options by choosing Regional Options in the Control Panel.

So why choose Azerbaijan, a small nation on the Caspian Sea, to demonstrate localization? Among all the countries in the world that use the Latin character set, only Azerbaijan and Turkey capitalize the letter i not with I (U+0049), but with an I that has a dot above it (U+0130). To ensure that ToUpper() performs this operation correctly, we must create an instance of the CultureInfo class with the Azeri culture name—represented by az—and pass it to the method. This results in the correct Unicode character—and a satisfied population of 8.3 million Azerbaijani.

Characters and Their Unicode Categories

The Unicode Standard classifies Unicode characters into one of 30 categories. .NET provides a UnicodeCategory enumeration that represents each of these categories and a Char.GetUnicodecategory() method to return a character's category. Here is an example:

```
Char k  = 'K';
int iCat = (int) char.GetUnicodeCategory(k);   // 0
Console.WriteLine(char.GetUnicodeCategory(k)); // UppercaseLetter
char cr = (Char)13;
iCat = (int) char.GetUnicodeCategory(cr);      // 14
Console.WriteLine(char.GetUnicodeCategory(cr)); // Control
```

The method correctly identifies K as an UppercaseLetter and the carriage return as a Control character. As an alternative to the unwieldy GetUnicodeCategory, char includes a set of static methods as a shortcut for identifying a character's Unicode category. They are nothing more than wrappers that return a true or false value based on an internal call to GetUnicodeCategory. The table in Fig. 13.2 lists these methods.

Method	Unicode Category	Description
IsControl	4	Control code whose Unicode value is U+007F, or in the range U+0000 through U+001F, or U+0080 through U+009F.
IsDigit	8	Is in the range 0–9.
IsLetter	0, 1, 2, 4	Letter.
IsLetterorDigit	0, 1, 8	Union of letters and digits.

Fig. 13.2 | Char Methods That Verify Unicode Categories. (Part 1 of 2.)

Method	Unicode Category	Description
IsLower	1	Lowercase letter.
IsUpper	0	Uppercase letter.
IsPunctuation	18, 19, 20, 21, 22, 23, 24	Punctuation symbol—for example, DashPunctuation(19) or OpenPunctuation(20), OtherPunctuation(24).
IsSeparator	11, 12, 13	Space separator, line separator, paragraph separator.
IsSurrogate	16	Value is a high or low surrogate.
IsSymbol	25, 26, 28	Symbol.
IsWhiteSpace	11	Whitespace can be any of these characters: space (0x20), carriage return (0x0D), horizontal tab (0x09), line feed (0x0A), form feed (0x0C), or vertical tab (0x0B).

Fig. 13.2 | Char Methods That Verify Unicode Categories. (Part 2 of 2.)

Using these methods is straightforward. The main point of interest is that they have overloads that accept a single char parameter, or two parameters specifying a string and index to the character within the string.

```
Console.WriteLine(Char.IsSymbol('+'));          // true
Console.WriteLine(Char.IsPunctuation('+')):     // false
string str = "black magic";
Console.WriteLine(Char.IsWhiteSpace(str, 5));   // true
char p = '.';
Console.WriteLine(Char.IsPunctuation(p));       // true
Int iCat = (int) char.GetUnicodeCategory(p);    // 24
Char p = '(';
Console.WriteLine(Char.IsPunctuation(p));       // true
int iCat = (int) char.GetUnicodeCategory(p);    // 20
```

13.3 The String Class

This section discusses the System.String class and provides a detailed look at creating, comparing, and formatting strings. Before proceeding to this discussion, let's first review the basics:

- The System.String class is a reference type having value semantics. This means that unlike most reference types, string comparisons are based on the value of the strings and not their location.

- A string is a sequence of Char types. Any reference to a character within a string is treated as a char.

- Strings are *immutable*. This means that after a string is created, it cannot be changed at its current memory location: You cannot shorten it, append to it, or change a character within it. The string value can be changed, of course, but the modified string is stored in a new memory location. The original string remains until the Garbage Collector removes it.

- The System.Text.StringBuilder class provides a set of methods to construct and manipulate strings within a buffer. When the operations are completed, the contents are converted to a string. StringBuilder should be used when an application makes extensive use of concatenation and string modifications.

13.3.1 Creating Strings

A string is created by declaring a variable as a string type and assigning a value to it. The value may be a literal string or dynamically created using concatenation. This is often a perfunctory process and not an area that most programmers consider when trying to improve code efficiency. In .NET, however, an understanding of how literal strings are handled can help a developer improve program performance.

String Interning

One point to emphasize is to distinguish how value and reference types are stored in memory. Recall that value types are stored on a stack, whereas reference types are placed on a managed heap. It turns out that that the CLR also sets aside a third area in memory called the *intern pool*, where it stores all the string literals during compilation. The purpose of this pool is to eliminate duplicate string values from being stored.

Consider the following code:

```
string poem1 = "Kubla Khan";
string poem2 = "Kubla Khan";
string poem3 = String.Copy(poem2); // Create new string object
string poem4 = "Christabel";
```

Figure 13.3 shows a simplified view of how the strings and their values are stored in memory.

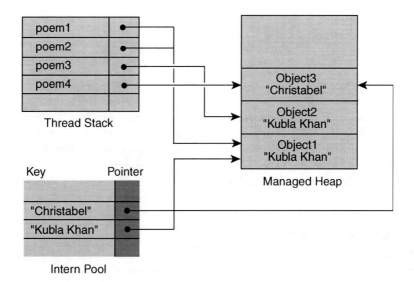

Fig. 13.3 | String interning.

The intern pool is implemented as a hash table. The hash table *key* is the actual string and its *pointer* references the associated string object on the managed heap. When the JIT compiler compiles the preceding code, it places the first instance of "Kubla Khan" (poem1) in the pool and creates a reference to the string object on the managed heap. When it encounters the second string reference to "Kubla Khan" (poem2), the CLR sees that the string already exists in memory and, instead of creating a new string, simply assigns poem2 to the same object as poem1. This process is known as string interning. Continuing with the example, the String.Copy method creates a new string poem3 and creates an object for it in the managed heap. Finally, the string literal associated with poem4 is added to the pool.

To examine the practical effects of string interning, let's extend the previous example. We add code that uses the equivalence (==) operator to compare string values and the Object.ReferenceEquals method to compare their addresses.

```
Console.WriteLine(poem1 == poem2);                    // true
Console.WriteLine(poem1 == poem3);                    // true
Console.WriteLine(ReferenceEquals(poem1, poem3)); // false
Console.WriteLine(ReferenceEquals(poem1,
                "Kubla Khan"));                        // true
```

The first two statements compare the value of the variables and—as expected—return a true value. The third statement compares the memory location of the variables poem3 and poem2. Because they reference different objects in the heap, a value of false is returned.

The .NET designers decided to exclude dynamically created values from the intern pool because checking the intern pool each time a string was created would hamper performance. However, they did include the String.Intern method as a way to selectively add dynamically created strings to the literal pool.

```
string khan = " Khan";
string poem5 = "Kubla" + khan;
Console.WriteLine(ReferenceEquals(poem5, poem1)); // false
// Place the contents of poem5 in the intern pool-if not there
poem5 = String.Intern(poem5);
Console.WriteLine(ReferenceEquals(poem5, poem1)); // true
```

The String.Intern method searches for the value of poem5 ("Kubla Khan") in the intern pool; because it is already in the pool, there is no need to add it. The method returns a reference to the already existing object (Object1) and assigns it to poem5. Because poem5 and poem1 now point to the same object, the comparison in the final statement is true. Note that the original object created for poem5 is released and swept up during the next Garbage Collection.

Core Recommendation 13.1

Use the String.Intern method to allow a string variable to take advantage of comparison by reference, but only if it is involved in numerous comparisons.

13.3.2 Overview of String Operations

The System.String class provides a large number of static and instance methods, most of which have several overload forms. For discussion purposes, they can be grouped into four major categories based on their primary function:

- **String Comparisons.** The String.Equals, String.Compare, and String.CompareOrdinal methods offer different ways to compare string values. The choice depends on whether an ordinal or lexical comparison is needed, and whether case or culture should influence the operation.

- **Indexing and Searching.** A string is an array of Unicode characters that may be searched by iterating through it as an array or by using special index methods to locate string values.

- **String Transformations.** This is a catchall category that includes methods for inserting, padding, removing, replacing, trimming, and splitting character strings.

- **Formatting.** NET provides format specifiers that are used in conjunction with String.Format to represent numeric and DateTime values in a number of standard and custom formats.

Many of the string methods—particularly for formatting and comparisons—are culture dependent. Where applicable, we look at how culture affects the behavior of a method.

13.4 Comparing Strings

The most efficient way to determine if two string variables are equal is to see if they refer to the same memory address. We did this earlier using the ReferenceEquals method. If two variables do not share the same memory address, it is necessary to perform a character-by-character comparison of the respective values to determine their equality. This takes longer than comparing addresses, but is often unavoidable.

.NET attempts to optimize the process by providing the String.Equals method that performs both reference and value comparisons automatically. We can describe its operation in the following pseudo-code:

```
If string1 and string2 reference the same memory location
    Then strings must be equal
Else
    Compare strings character by character to determine equality
```

This code segment demonstrates the static and reference forms of the Equals method:

```
string poem1 = "Kubla Khan";
string poem2 = "Kubla Khan";
string poem3 = String.Copy(poem2);
string poem4 = "kubla khan";
//
Console.WriteLine(String.Equals(poem1,poem2));  // true
Console.WriteLine(poem1.Equals(poem3));          // true
Console.WriteLine(poem1 == poem3);       // equivalent to Equals
Console.WriteLine(poem1 == poem4);       // false - case differs
```

Note that the == operator, which calls the Equals method underneath, is a more convenient way of expressing the comparison.

Although the Equals method satisfies most comparison needs, it contains no overloads that allow it to take case sensitivity and culture into account. To address this shortcoming, the string class includes the Compare method.

13.4.1 Using String.Compare

String.Compare is a flexible comparison method that is used when culture or case must be taken into account. Its many overloads accept culture and case-sensitive parameters, as well as supporting substring comparisons.

Syntax:

```
int Compare (string str1, string str2)
Compare (string str1, string str2, bool IgnoreCase)
Compare (string str1, string str2, bool IgnoreCase,
        CultureInfo ci)
Compare (string str1, int index1, string str2, int index2,
        int len)
```

Parameters:

str1 and str2	Specify strings to be compared.
IgnoreCase	Set true to make comparison case-insensitive (default is false).
index1 and index2	Starting position in str1 and str2.
ci	A CultureInfo object indicating the culture to be used.

Compare returns an integer value that indicates the results of the comparison. If the two strings are equal, a value of 0 is returned; if the first string is less than the second, a value less than zero is returned; if the first string is greater than the second, a value greater than zero is returned.

The following segment shows how to use Compare to make case-insensitive and case-sensitive comparisons:

```
int result;
string stringUpper = "AUTUMN";
string stringLower = "autumn";
// (1) Lexical comparison: "A" is greater than "a"
result = string.Compare(stringUpper,stringLower);        // 1
// (2) IgnoreCase set to false
result = string.Compare(stringUpper,stringLower,false); // 1
// (3)Perform case-insensitive comparison
result = string.Compare(stringUpper,stringLower,true);  // 0
```

Perhaps even more important than case is the potential effect of culture information on a comparison operation. .NET contains a list of comparison rules for each culture that it supports. When the Compare method is executed, the CLR checks the culture associated with it and applies the rules. The result is that two strings may compare differently on a computer with a US culture vis-à-vis one with a Japanese culture. There are cases where it may be important to override the current culture to ensure that the program behaves the same for all users. For example, it may be crucial that a sort operation order items exactly the same no matter where the application is run.

By default, the Compare method uses culture information based on the Thread.CurrentThread.CurrentCulture property. To override the default, supply a CultureInfo object as a parameter to the method. This statement shows how to create an object to represent the German language and country:

```
CultureInfo ci = new CultureInfo("de-DE");  // German culture
```

To explicitly specify a default culture or no culture, the CultureInfo class has two properties that can be passed as parameters—CurrentCulture, which tells a method to use the culture of the current thread, and InvariantCulture, which tells a method to ignore any culture.

Let's look at a concrete example of how culture differences affect the results of a Compare() operation.

```
using System.Globalization;   // Required for CultureInfo

// Perform case-sensitive comparison for Czech culture
string s1 = "circle";
string s2 = "chair";
result = string.Compare(s1, s2,
         true, CultureInfo.CurrentCulture));       // 1
result = string.Compare(s1, s2,
         true, CultureInfo.InvariantCulture));     // 1
// Use the Czech culture
result = string.Compare(s1, s2,
         true, new CultureInfo("cs-CZ"));          // -1
```

The string values "circle" and "chair" are compared using the US culture, no culture, and the Czech culture. The first two comparisons return a value indicating that "circle" > "chair", which is what you expect. However, the result using the Czech culture is the opposite of that obtained from the other comparisons. This is because one of the rules of the Czech language specifies that "ch" is to be treated as a single character that lexically appears after "c".

Core Recommendation 13.2

When writing an application that takes culture into account, it is good practice to include an explicit CultureInfo parameter in those methods that accept such a parameter. This provides a measure of self-documentation that clarifies whether the specific method is subject to culture variation.

13.4.2 Using String.CompareOrdinal

To perform a comparison that is based strictly on the ordinal value of characters, use String.CompareOrdinal. Its simple algorithm compares the Unicode value of two strings and returns a value less than zero if the first string is less than the second; a value of zero if the strings are equal; and a value greater than zero if the first string is greater than the second. This code shows the difference between it and the Compare method:

```
string stringUpper = "AUTUMN";
string stringLower = "autumn";
//
result = string.Compare(stringUpper,stringLower,
        false, CultureInfo.InvariantCulture);        // 1
result = string.CompareOrdinal(stringUpper,stringLower);  // -32
```

Compare performs a lexical comparison that regards the uppercase string to be greater than the lowercase. CompareOrdinal examines the underlying Unicode values. Because A (U+0041) is less than a (U+0061), the first string is less than the second.

13.5 Searching, Modifying, and Encoding a String's Content

This section describes string methods that are used to perform diverse but familiar tasks such as locating a substring within a string, changing the case of a string, replacing or removing text, splitting a string into delimited substrings, and trimming leading and trailing spaces.

13.5.1 Searching the Contents of a String

A string is an implicit zero-based array of chars that can be searched using the array syntax string[n], where n is a character position within the string. For locating a substring of one or more characters in a string, the string class offers the IndexOf and IndexOfAny methods. The table in Fig. 13.4 summarizes these.

13.5.2 Searching a String That Contains Surrogates

All of these techniques assume that a string consists of a sequence of 16-bit characters. Suppose, however, that your application must work with a Far Eastern character set of 32-bit characters. These are represented in storage as a *surrogate pair* consisting of a high and low 16-bit value. Clearly, this presents a problem for an expression such as poem[ndx], which would return only half of a surrogate pair.

For applications that must work with surrogates, .NET provides the StringInfo class that treats all characters as *text elements* and can automatically detect whether a character is 16 bits or a surrogate. Its most important member is the GetTextElementEnumerator method, which returns an enumerator that can be used to iterate through text elements in a string.

```
TextElementEnumerator tEnum =
        StringInfo.GetTextElementEnumerator(poem) ;
while (tEnum.MoveNext())  // Step through the string
{
    Console.WriteLine(tEnum.Current);  // Print current char
}
```

MoveNext() and Current are members implemented by all enumerators.

String Member	Description

[n]	Indexes a 16-bit character located at position n within a string.
	
	`int ndx= 0;`
	`while (ndx < poem.Length)`
	`{`
	    `Console.Write(poem[ndx]); //Kubla Khan`
	    `ndx += 1;`
	`}`

IndexOf/LastIndexOf
 	
(string, [int start],
[int count])
 	
count. Number of chars to examine.
	Returns the index of the first/last occurrence of a specified string within an instance. Returns –1 if no match.
	
	`string poem = "Kubla Khan";`
	`int n = poem.IndexOf("la");   // 3`
	`n = poem.IndexOf('K');       // 0`
	`n = poem.IndexOf('K',4);     // 6`

IndexOfAny/LastIndexOfAny	Returns the index of the first/last character in an array of Unicode characters.
	
	`string poem = "Kubla Khan";`
	`char[] vowels = new char[5]`
	    `{'a', 'e', 'i', 'o', 'u'};`
	`n = poem.IndexOfAny(vowels);       // 1`
	`n = poem.LastIndexOfAny(vowels); // 8`
	`n = poem.IndexOfAny(vowels,2);   // 4`

Fig. 13.4 | Ways to Examine Characters Within a String.

13.5.3 String Transformations

The table in Fig. 13.5 summarizes the most important string class methods for modifying a string. Because the original string is immutable, any string constructed by these methods is actually a new string with its own allocated memory.

Most of these methods have analogues in other languages and behave as you would expect. Somewhat surprisingly, as we see in the next section, most of these methods are not available in the StringBuilder class. Only Replace, Remove, and Insert are included.

13.5.4 String Encoding

Encoding comes into play when you need to convert between strings and bytes for operations such as writing a string to a file or streaming it across a network. Character encoding and decoding offer two major benefits: efficiency and interoperability. Most strings read in English consist of characters that can be represented by 8 bits. Encoding can be used to strip an extra byte (from the 16-bit Unicode memory representation) for transmission and storage. The flexibility of encoding is also important in allowing an application to interoperate with legacy data or third-party data encoded in different formats.

Tag	Description

Insert (int, string)	Inserts a string at the specified position.
	
	``csharp
	string mariner = "and he stoppeth three";
	string verse = mariner.Insert(
	    mariner.IndexOf(" three")," one of");
	// verse --> "and he stoppeth one of three"
	``

PadRight/PadLeft	Pads a string with a given character until it is a specified width. If no character is specified, whitespace is used.
	
	``csharp
	string rem = "and so on";
	rem = rem.PadRight(rem.Length+3,'.');
	// rem --> "and so on..."
	``

Remove(p , n)	Removes n characters beginning at position p.
	
	``csharp
	string verse = "It is an Ancient Mariner";
	string newverse = (verse.Remove(0,9));
	// newverse --> "Ancient Mariner"
	``

Replace (A , B)	Replaces all occurrences of A with B, where A and B are chars or strings.
	
	``csharp
	string aString = "nap ace sap path";
	string iString = aString.Replace('a','i');
	// iString --> "nip ice sip pith"
	``

Split(char[])	The char array contains delimiters that are used to break a string into substrings that are returned as elements in a string array.
	
	``csharp
	string words = "red,blue orange ";
	string [] split = words.Split(new Char []
	                {' ', ','});
	Console.WriteLine(split[2]); // orange
	``

ToUpper()
ToUpper(CultureInfo)
ToLower()
ToLower(CultureInfo)
	Returns an upper- or lowercase copy of the string.
	
	``csharp
	string poem2="Kubla Khan";
	poem2= poem2.ToUpper(
	        CultureInfo.InvariantCulture);
	``

Trim()
Trim(params char[])
	Removes all leading and trailing whitespaces. If a char array is provided, all leading and trailing characters in the array are removed.
	
	``csharp
	string name = " Samuel Coleridge";
	name = name.Trim(); // "Samuel Coleridge"
	``

TrimEnd (params char[])
TrimStart(params char[])
	Removes all leading or trailing characters specified in a char array. If null is specified, whitespaces are removed.
	
	``csharp
	string name = " Samuel Coleridge";
	trimName = name.TrimStart(null);
	shortname = name.TrimEnd('e','g','i');
	// shortName --> "Samuel Colerid"
	``

Fig. 13.5 | Methods for Manipulating and Transforming Strings. (Part 1 of 2.)

Tag	Description
Substring(n) Substring(n, 1)	Extracts the string beginning at a specified position (n) and of length l, if specified.
	```string title="Kubla Khan";``` ```Console.WriteLine(title.Substring(2,3)); //bla```
ToCharArray() ToCharArray(n, 1)	Extracts characters from a string and places in an array of Unicode characters.

	```string myVowels = "aeiou";```
	```char[] vowelArr;```
	```vowelArr = myVowels.ToCharArray();```
	```Console.WriteLine(vowelArr[1]); // "e"```

Fig. 13.5 | Methods for Manipulating and Transforming Strings. (Part 2 of 2.)

The .NET Framework supports many forms of character encoding and decoding. The most frequently used include the following:

- **UTF-8.** Each character is encoded as a sequence of 1 to 4 bytes, based on its underlying value. ASCII compatible characters are stored in 1 byte; characters between 0x0080 and 0x07ff are stored in 2 bytes; and characters having a value greater than or equal to 0x0800 are converted to 3 bytes. Surrogates are written as 4 bytes. UTF-8 (which stands for UCS Transformation Format, 8-bit form) is usually the default for .NET classes when no encoding is specified.

- **UTF-16.** Each character is encoded as 2 bytes (except surrogates), which is how characters are represented internally in .NET. This is also referred to as Unicode encoding.

- **ASCII.** Encodes each character as an 8-bit ASCII character. This should be used when all characters are in the ASCII range (0x00 to 0x7F). Attempting to encode a character outside of the ACII range yields whatever value is in the character's low byte.

Encoding and decoding are performed using the Encoding class found in the System.Text namespace. This abstract class has several static properties that return an object used to implement a specific encoding technique. These properties include ASCII, UTF8, and Unicode. The latter is used for UTF-16 encoding.

An encoding object offers several methods—each having several overloads—for converting between characters and bytes. Here is an example that illustrates two of the most useful methods: GetBytes, which converts a text string to bytes, and GetString, which reverses the process and converts a byte array to a string.

```
string text= "In Xanadu did Kubla Khan";
Encoding UTF8Encoder = Encoding.UTF8;
byte[] textChars = UTF8Encoder.GetBytes(text);
Console.WriteLine(textChars.Length);        // 24
// Store using UTF-16
textChars = Encoding.Unicode.GetBytes(text);
Console.WriteLine(textChars.Length);        // 48
```

```
// Treat characters as two bytes
string decodedText = Encoding.Unicode.GetString(textChars);
Console.WriteLine(decodedText); // "In Xanadu did ...  "
```

You can also instantiate the encoding objects directly. In this example, the UTF-8 object could be created with

```
UTF8Encoding UTF8Encoder = new UTF8Encoding();
```

With the exception of ASCIIEncoding, the constructor for these classes defines parameters that allow more control over the encoding process. For example, you can specify whether an exception is thrown when invalid encoding is detected.

13.6 StringBuilder

The primary drawback of strings is that memory must be allocated each time the contents of a string variable are changed. Suppose we create a loop that iterates 100 times and concatenates one character to a string during each iteration. We could end up with a hundred strings in memory, each differing from its preceding one by a single character.

The StringBuilder class addresses this problem by allocating a work area (buffer) where its methods can be applied to the string. These methods include ways to append, insert, delete, remove, and replace characters. After the operations are complete, the ToString method is called to convert the buffer to a string that can be assigned to a string variable. Figure 13.6 introduces some of the StringBuilder methods in an example that creates a comma delimited list.

All operations occur in a single buffer and require no memory allocation until the final assignment to csv. Let's take a formal look at the class and its members.

```
using System;
using System.Text;
public class MyApp
{
    static void Main()
    {
        // Create comma delimited string with quotes around names
        string namesF = "Jan Donna Kim ";
        string namesM = "Rob James";
        StringBuilder sbCSV = new StringBuilder();
        sbCSV.Append(namesF).Append(namesM);
        sbCSV.Replace(" ","','");
        // Insert quote at beginning and end of string
        sbCSV.Insert(0,"'").Append("'");
        string csv = sbCSV.ToString();
        // csv = 'Jan','Donna','Kim','Rob','James'
    }
}
```

Fig. 13.6 | Introduction to StringBuilder.

13.6.1 StringBuilder Class Overview

Constructors for the StringBuilder class accept an initial string value as well as integer values that specify the initial space allocated to the buffer (in characters) and the maximum space allowed.

```
// Stringbuilder(initial value)
StringBuilder sb1 = new StringBuilder("abc");
// StringBuilder(initial value, initial capacity)
StringBuilder sb2 = new StringBuilder("abc", 16);
// StringBuiler(Initial Capacity, maximum capacity)
StringBuilder sb3 = new StringBuilder(32,128);
```

The idea behind StringBuilder is to use it as a buffer in which string operations are performed. Here is a sample of how its Append, Insert, Replace, and Remove methods work:

```
int i = 4;
char[] ch = {'w','h','i','t','e'};
string myColor = " orange";
StringBuilder sb = new StringBuilder("red blue green");
sb.Insert(0, ch);                    // whitered blue green
sb.Insert(5," ");                    // white red blue green
sb.Insert(0,i);                      // 4white red blue green
sb.Remove(1,5);                      // 4 red blue green
sb.Append(myColor);                  // 4 red blue green orange
sb.Replace("blue","violet");         // 4 red violet green orange
string colors = sb.ToString();
```

13.6.2 StringBuilder Versus String Concatenation

Figure 13.7 tests the performance of StringBuilder versus the concatenation operator. The first part of this program uses the + operator to concatenate the letter a to a string in each of a loop's 50,000 iterations. The second half does the same, but uses the String-Builder.Append method. The Environment.TickCount provides the beginning and ending time in milliseconds.

Executing this program results in the following output:

```
String routine
Start: 1422091687
Stop: 1422100046
Difference: 9359
StringBuilder routine
Start: 1422100046
Stop: 1422100062
Difference: 16
```

The results clearly indicate the improved performance StringBuilder provides: The standard concatenation requires 9,359 milliseconds versus 16 milliseconds for String-Builder. When tested with loops of 1,000 iterations, StringBuilder shows no significant advantage. Unless your application involves extensive text manipulation, the standard concatenation operator should be used.

```
using System;
using System.Text;
public class MyApp
{
    static void Main()
    {
        Console.WriteLine("String routine");
        string a = "a";
        string str = string.Empty;
        int istart, istop;
        istart = Environment.TickCount & Int32.MaxValue;
        Console.WriteLine("Start: "+istart);
        // Use regular C# concatenation operator
        for(int i=0; i<50000; i++)
        {
            str += a;
        }
        istop = Environment.TickCount;
        Console.WriteLine("Stop: "+istop);
        Console.WriteLine("Difference: " + (istop-istart));
        // Perform concatenation with StringBuilder
        Console.WriteLine("StringBuilder routine");
        StringBuilder builder = new StringBuilder();
        istart = Environment.TickCount;
        Console.WriteLine("Start: "+istart);
        for(int i=0; i<50000; i++)
        {
            builder.Append(a);
        }
        istop = Environment.TickCount;
        str = builder.ToString();
        Console.WriteLine("Stop: "+Environment.TickCount);
        Console.WriteLine("Difference: "+ (istop-istart));
    }
}
```

Fig. 13.7 | Comparison of StringBuilder and Regular Concatenation.

13.7 Formatting Numeric and DateTime Values

The String.Format method is the primary means of formatting date and numeric data for display. It accepts a string composed of text and embedded format items followed by one or more data arguments. Each format item references a data argument and specifies how it is to be formatted. The CLR creates the output string by converting each data value to a string (using ToString), formatting it according to its corresponding format item, and then replacing the format item with the formatted data value. Here is a simple example:

```
String s= String.Format("The square root of {0} is {1}.",64,8);
// output: The square root of 64 is 8.
```

The method has several overloads, but this is the most common and illustrates two features common to all: a format string and a list of data arguments. Note that `Console.WriteLine` accepts the same parameters and can be used in place of `String.Format` for console output.

13.7.1 Constructing a Format Item

Figure 13.8 breaks down a `String.Format` example into its basic elements. The most interesting of these is the format item, which defines the way data is displayed.

As we can see, each format item consists of an index and an optional alignment and format string. All are enclosed in brace characters:

1. The *index* is a zero-based integer that indicates the argument to which it is to be applied. The index can be repeated to refer to the same argument more than once.

2. The optional *alignment* is an integer that indicates the minimum width of the area that contains the formatted value. If alignment value is positive, the argument value is right justified; if the value is negative, it is left justified.

3. The optional *format string* contains the formatting codes to be applied to the argument value. If it is not specified, the output of the argument's `ToString` method is used. .NET provides several standard format codes to be used with numbers and dates as well as codes that are used to create custom format strings.

13.7.2 Formatting Numeric Values

Nine characters, or format specifiers, are available to format numbers into currency, scientific, hexadecimal, and other representations. Each character can have an integer appended to it that specifies a precision particular to that format—usually this indicates the number of decimal places. C# recognizes the standard format specifiers[2] shown in Fig. 13.9.

The patterns in this table can also be used directly with `Console.Write` and `Console.WriteLine`:

```
Console.WriteLine("The Hex value of {0} is {0:X} ",31); //1F
```

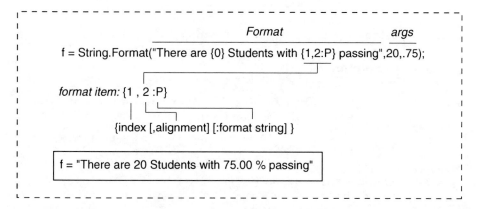

Fig. 13.8 | `String.Format` example.

---

2. Microsoft Windows users can set formats using the Control Panel — Regional Options settings.

Format Specifier	Description	Pattern	Output
C or c	Currency. Number is represented as a currency amount. The precision specifies the number of decimal places.	{0:C2}, 1458.75	$ 1,458.75
D or d	Decimal. Applies to integral values. The precision indicates the total number of spaces the number occupies; is padded with zeros on left if necessary.	{0:D5}, 455 {0:D5}, -455	00455 -00455
E or e	Scientific. The number is converted to a scientific notation: ddddE+nnn. The precision specifies the number of digits after the decimal point.	{0,10:E2}, 3298.78 {0,10:E4}, -54783.4	3.30+E003 -5.4783+E004
F or f	Fixed Point. The number is converted to format of: ddd.ddd. The precision indicates the number of decimal places.	{0,10:F0}, 162.57 {0,10:F2}, 8162.57	162 8162.57
G or g	General. The number is converted to fixed point or scientific notation based on the precision and type of number. Scientific is used if the exponent is greater than or equal to the specified precision or less than −4.	{0,10:G}, .0000099 {0,10:G2}, 455.89 {0,10:G3}, 455.89 {0,10:G}, 783229.34	9.9E-06 4.6E+02 456 783229.34
N or n	Number. Converts to a string that uses commas as thousands separators. The precision specifies the number of decimal places.	{0,10:N}, 1045.78 {0,10:N1}, 45.98	1,045.78 45.9
P or p	Percent. Number is multiplied by 100 and presented as percent with number of decimal places specified by precision.	{0,10:P}, 0.78 {0,10:P3}, 0.7865	78.00 % 78.650 %
R or r	Round-trip. Converts to a string that retains all decimal place accuracy. Then number to be converted must be floating point.	{0,10:R}, 1.62736	1.62736
X or x	Hexadecimal. Converts the number to its hex representation. The precision indicates the minimum number of digits shown. Number is padded with zeros if needed.	{0,10:X}, 25 {0,10:X4}, 25 {0,10:x4}, 31	19 0019 001f

Fig. 13.9 | Formatting Numeric Values with Standard Numeric Format Strings.

The format specifiers can be used alone to enhance output from the `ToString` method:

```
decimal pct = .758M;
Console.Write("The percent is "+pct.ToString("P2")); // 75.80 %
```

.NET also provides special formatting characters that can be used to create custom numeric formats. The most useful characters are pound sign (#), zero (0), comma (,), period (.), percent sign (%), and semi-colon (;). The following code demonstrates their use:

```
decimal dVal = 2145.88M;    // decimal values require M suffix
string myFormat;
myFormat = dVal.ToString("#####");           //   2146
myFormat = dVal.ToString("#,###.00");        //   2,145.88
myFormat = String.Format("Value is {0:#,###.00; (#,###.00)}",-4567);
// semicolon specifies alternate formats. (4,567.00)
myFormat = String.Format("Value is {0:$#,###.00}", 4567);
                                             //   $4,567.00
Console.WriteLine("{0:##.00%}",.18);         //   18.00 %
```

The role of these characters should be self-explanatory except for the semicolon (;), which deserves further explanation. It separates the format into two groups: the first is applied to positive values and the second to negative. Two semicolons can be used to create three groups for positive, negative, and zero values, respectively.

13.7.3 Formatting Dates and Time

Date formatting requires a `DateTime` object. As with numbers, this object has its own set of standard format specifiers. The table in Fig. 13.10 summarizes these.

Here are some concrete examples that demonstrate date formatting. In each case, an instance of a `DateTime` object is passed an argument to a format string.

```
DateTime curDate = DateTime.Now;  // Get Current Date
Console.Writeline("Date: {0:d} ", curDate);    // 1/19/2004
// f: --> Monday, January 19, 2004 5:05 PM
Console.Writeline("Date: {0:f} ", curDate);
// g: --> 1/19/2004 5:05 PM
Console.Writeline("Date: {0:g} ", curDate);
```

If none of the standard format specifiers meet your need, you can construct a custom format from a set of character sequences designed for that purpose. The table in Fig. 13.11 lists some of the more useful ones for formatting dates.

Here are some examples of custom date formats:

```
DateTime curDate = DateTime.Now;
f = String.Format("{0:dddd} {0:MMM} {0:dd}", curDate);
// output: Monday Jan 19

f = currDate.ToString("dd MMM yyyy")
// output: 19 Jan 2004

// The standard short date format (d) is equivalent to this:
Console.WriteLine(currDate.ToString("M/d/yyyy"));  // 1/19/2004
Console.WriteLine(currDate.ToString("d"));         // 1/19/2004
```

```
CultureInfo ci = new CultureInfo("de-DE");          // German
f = currDate.ToString("dd-MMMM-yyyy HH:mm", ci)
// output: 19-Januar-2004 23:07
```

ToString is recommended over String.Format for custom date formatting. It has a more convenient syntax for embedding blanks and special separators between the date elements; in addition, its second parameter is a culture indicator that makes it easy to test different cultures.

Dates and Culture

Dates are represented differently throughout the world, and the ability to add culture as a determinant in formatting dates shifts the burden to .NET from the developer. For example, if the culture on your system is German, dates are automatically formatted to reflect a European format: the day precedes the month; the day, month, and year are

Format Specifier	Description	Example—English	Example—German
d	Short date pattern	1/19/2004	19.1.2004
D	Long date pattern	Monday, January 19, 2004	Montag, 19 Januar, 2004
f	Full date/time pattern (short time)	Monday, January 19, 2004 4:05 PM	Montag, 19 Januar, 2004 16:05
F	Full date/time pattern (full time)	Monday, January 19, 2004 4:05:20 PM	Montag, 19 Januar, 2004 16:05:20
g	General date/time pattern (short time)	1/19/2004 4:05 PM	19/1/2004 16:05
G	General date/time pattern (long time)	1/19/2004 4:05:20 PM	19/1/2004 16:05:20
M, m	Month day pattern	January 19	19 Januar
Y, y	Year month pattern	January, 2004	Januar, 2004
t	Short time pattern	4:05 PM	16:05
T	Long time pattern	4:05:20 PM	16:05:20
s	Universal Sortable Date-Time pattern. Conforms to ISO 8601. Uses local time.	2004-01-19T16:05:20	2004-01-19T16:05:20
u	Universal Sortable Date-Time pattern	2004-01-19 16:05:20Z	2004-01-19 16:05:20Z
U	Universal Sortable Date-Time pattern. Uses universal time.	Monday, January 19, 2004 21:05:20 PM	Montag, 19. Januar, 2004 21:05:20

Fig. 13.10 | Formatting Dates with Standard Characters.

Format	Description	Example
d	Day of month. No leading zero.	5
dd	Day of month. Always has two digits.	05
ddd	Day of week with three-character abbreviation.	Mon
dddd	Day of week full name.	Monday
M	Month number. No leading zero.	1
MM	Month number with leading zero if needed.	01
MMM	Month name with three-character abbreviation.	Jan
MMMM	Full name of month.	January
y	Year. Last one or two digits.	5
yy	Year. Last one or two digits with leading zero if needed.	05
yyyy	Four-digit year.	2004
HH	Hour in 24-hour format.	15
mm	Minutes with leading zero if needed.	20

Fig. 13.11 | Character Patterns for Custom Date Formatting.

separated by periods (.) rather than slashes (/); and the phrase Monday, January 19 becomes Montag, 19. Januar. Here is an example that uses ToString with a German CultureInfo parameter:

```
CultureInfo ci = new CultureInfo("de-DE");        // German
Console.WriteLine(curDate.ToString("D",ci));
// output ---> Montag, 19. Januar 2004
Console.WriteLine(curDate.ToString("dddd",ci));   // -->Montag
```

The last statement uses the special custom format "dddd" to print the day of the week. This is favored over the DateTime.DayofWeek enum property that returns only an English value.

NumberFormatInfo and DateTimeFormatInfo Classes

These two classes govern how the previously described format patterns are applied to dates and numbers. For example, the NumberFormatInfo class includes properties that specify the character to be used as a currency symbol, the character to be used as a decimal separator, and the number of decimal digits to use when displaying a currency value. Similarly, DateTimeFormatInfo defines properties that correspond to virtually all of the standard format specifiers for dates. One example is the FullDateTimePattern property that defines the pattern returned when the character F is used to format a date.

NumberFormatInfo and DateTimeFormatInfo are associated with specific cultures, and their properties are the means for creating the unique formats required by different cultures. .NET provides a predefined set of property values for each culture, but they can be overridden.

Their properties are accessed in different ways depending on whether the current or non-current culture is being referenced (current culture is the culture associated with the current thread). The following statements reference the current culture:

```
NumberFormatInfo.CurrentInfo.<property>
CultureInfo.CurrentCulture.NumberFormat.<property>
```

The first statement uses the static property CurrentInfo and implicitly uses the current culture. The second statement specifies a culture explicitly (CurrentCulture) and is suited for accessing properties associated with a non-current CultureInfo instance.

```
CultureInfo ci = new CultureInfo("de-DE");
string f = ci.NumberFormat.CurrencySymbol;
```

NumberFormatInfo and DateTimeFormatInfo properties associated with a non-current culture can be changed; those associated with the current thread are read-only. Figure 13.12 offers a sampling of how to work with these classes.

In summary, .NET offers a variety of standard patterns that satisfy most needs to format dates and numbers. Behind the scenes, there are two classes, NumberFormatInfo and DateTimeFormatInfo, that define the symbols and rules used for formatting. .NET provides each culture with its own set of properties associated with an instance of these classes.

```
using System
using System.Globalization
Class MyApp
{
    // NumberFormatInfo
    string curSym = NumberFormatInfo.CurrentInfo.CurrencySymbol;
    int dd  = NumberFormatInfo.CurrentInfo.CurrencyDecimalDigits;
    int pdd = NumberFormatInfo.CurrentInfo.PercentDecimalDigits;
    // --> curSym = "$"   dd = 2   pdd = 2
    // DateTimeFormatInfo
    string ldp= DateTimeFormatInfo.CurrentInfo.LongDatePattern;
    // --> ldp = "dddd, MMMM, dd, yyyy"
    string enDay = DateTimeFormatInfo.CurrentInfo.DayNames[1];
    string month = DateTimeFormatInfo.CurrentInfo.MonthNames[1];
    CultureInfo ci = new CultureInfo("de-DE");
    string deDay = ci.DateTimeFormat.DayNames[1];
    // --> enDay = "Monday"  month = February  deDay = "Montag"
    // Change the default number of decimal places
    // in a percentage
    decimal passRate = .840M;
    Console.Write(passRate.ToString("p",ci));  // 84,00%
    ci.NumberFormat.PercentDecimalDigits = 1;
    Console.Write(passRate.ToString("p",ci));  // 84,0%
}
```

Fig. 13.12 | Using NumberFormatInfo and DateTimeFormatInfo.

13.8 Regular Expressions

The use of strings and expressions to perform pattern matching dates from the earliest programming languages. In the mid-1960s SNOBOL was designed for the express purpose of text and string manipulation. It influenced the subsequent development of the *grep* tool in the Unix environment that makes extensive use of regular expressions. Those who have worked with grep or Perl or other scripting languages will recognize the similarity in the .NET implementation of regular expressions.

Pattern matching is based on the simple concept of applying a special pattern string to some text source in order to match an instance or instances of that pattern within the text. The pattern applied against the text is referred to as a regular expression, or *regex*, for short.

Entire books have been devoted to the topic of regular expressions. This section is intended to provide the essential knowledge required to get you started using regular expressions in the .NET world. The focus is on using the Regex class, and creating regular expressions from the set of characters and symbols available for that purpose.

13.8.1 The Regex Class

You can think of the Regex class as the engine that evaluates regular expressions and applies them to target strings. It provides both static and instance methods that use regexes for text searching, extraction, and replacement. The Regex class and all related classes are found in the System.Text.RegularExpressions namespace.

Syntax:

```
Regex( string pattern )
Regex( string pattern, RegexOptions)
```

Parameters:

pattern	Regular expression used for pattern matching.
RegexOptions	An enum whose values control how the regex is applied. Values include:
	CultureInvariant—Ignore culture.
	IgnoreCase—Ignore upper- or lowercase.
	RightToLeft—Process string right to left.

Example:

```
Regex r1 = new Regex(" ");   // Regular expression is a blank
String words[] = r1.Split("red blue orange yellow");
// Regular expression matches upper- or lowercase "at"
Regex r2 = new Regex("at", RegexOptions.IgnoreCase);
```

As the example shows, creating a Regex object is quite simple. The first parameter to its constructor is a regular expression. The optional second parameter is one or more (separated by |) RegexOptions enum values that control how the regex is applied.

Regex Methods

The Regex class contains a number of methods for pattern matching and text manipulation. These include IsMatch, Replace, Split, Match, and Matches. All have instance and static overloads that are similar, but not identical.

Core Recommendation 13.3

If you plan to use a regular expression repeatedly, it is more efficient to create a Regex object. When the object is created, it compiles the expression into a form that can be used as long as the object exists. In contrast, static methods recompile the expression each time they are used.

Let's now examine some of the more important `Regex` methods. We'll keep the regular expressions simple for now because the emphasis at this stage is on understanding the methods—not regular expressions.

IsMatch()

This method matches the regular expression against an input string and returns a boolean value indicating whether a match is found.

```
string searchStr = "He went that a way";
Regex myRegex = new Regex("at");
// instance methods
bool match = myRegex.IsMatch(searchStr);          // true
// Begin search at position 12 in the string
match = myRegex.IsMatch(searchStr,12);            // false
// Static Methods - both return true
match = Regex.IsMatch(searchStr,"at");
match = Regex.IsMatch(searchStr,"AT",RegexOptions.IgnoreCase);
```

Replace()

This method returns a string that replaces occurrences of a matched pattern with a specified replacement string. This method has several overloads that permit you to specify a start position for the search or control how many replacements are made.

Syntax:

```
static Replace (string input, string pattern, string replacement
              [,RegexOptions])

Replace(string input, string replacement)
Replace(string input, string replacement, int count)
Replace(string input, string replacement, int count, int startat)
```

The count parameter denotes the maximum number of matches; `startat` indicates where in the string to begin the matching process. There are also versions of this method—which you may want to explore further—that accept a `MatchEvaluator` delegate parameter. This delegate is called each time a match is found and can be used to customize the replacement process.

Here is a code segment that illustrates the static and instance forms of the method:

```
string newStr;
newStr = Regex.Replace("soft rose","o","i");   // sift rise
// instance method
Regex myRegex = new Regex("o");                 // regex = "o"
// Now specify that only one replacement may occur
newStr = myRegex.Replace("soft rose","i",1);   // sift rose
```

Split()

This method splits a string at each point a match occurs and places that matching occurrence in an array. It is similar to the `String.Split` method, except that the match is based on a regular expression rather than a character or character string.

Syntax:

```
String[] Split(string input)
String[] Split(string input, int count)
String[] Split(string input, int count, int startat)
Static String[] Split(string input, string pattern)
```

Parameters:

input	The string to split.
count	The maximum number of array elements to return. A count value of 0 results in as many matches as possible. If the number of matches is greater than count, the last match consists of the remainder of the string.
startat	The character position in *input* where the search begins.
pattern	The regex pattern to be matched against the input string.

This short example parses a string consisting of a list of artists' last names and places them in an array. A comma followed by zero or more blanks separates the names. The regular expression to match this delimiter string is: ", [ ]*". You will see how to construct this later in the section.

```
string impressionists = "Manet,Monet, Degas, Pissarro,Sisley";
// Regex to match a comma followed by 0 or more spaces
string patt = @",[ ]*";
// Static method
string[] artists = Regex.Split(impressionists, patt);
// Instance method is used to accept maximum of four matches
Regex myRegex = new Regex(patt);
string[] artists4 = myRegex.Split(impressionists, 4);
foreach (string master in artists4)
   Console.Write(master);
// Output --> "Manet" "Monet" "Degas" "Pissarro,Sisley"
```

Match() and Matches()

These related methods search an input string for a match to the regular expression. `Match()` returns a single `Match` object and `Matches()` returns the object `MatchCollection`, a collection of all matches.

Syntax:

```
Match Match(string input)
Match Match(string input, int startat)
Match Match(string input, int startat, int numchars)
static Match(string input, string pattern, [RegexOptions])
```

The Matches method has similar overloads but returns a MatchCollection object.

Match and Matches are the most useful Regex methods. The Match object they return is rich in properties that expose the matched string, its length, and its location within the target string. It also includes a Groups property that allows the matched string to be further broken down into matching substrings. The table in Fig. 13.13 shows selected members of the Match class.

The following code demonstrates the use of these class members. Note that the dot (.) in the regular expression functions as a wildcard character that matches any single character.

```
string verse = "In Xanadu did Kubla Khan";
string patt = ".an...";          // "." matches any character
Match verseMatch = Regex.Match(verse, patt);
Console.WriteLine(verseMatch.Value);   // Xanadu
Console.WriteLine(verseMatch.Index);   // 3
//
string newPatt = "K(..)";                //contains group(..)
Match kMatch = Regex.Match(verse, newPatt);
while (kMatch.Success) {
    Console.Write(kMatch.Value);         // -->Kub -->Kha
    Console.Write(kMatch.Groups[1]);     // -->ub  -->ha
    kMatch = kMatch.NextMatch();
}
```

This example uses NextMatch to iterate through the target string and assign each match to kMatch (if NextMatch is left out, an infinite loop results). The parentheses surrounding the two dots in newPatt break the pattern into *groups* without affecting the actual pattern matching. In this example, the two characters after K are assigned to group objects that are accessed in the Groups collection.

Sometimes, an application may need to collect all of the matches before processing them—which is the purpose of the MatchCollection class. This class is just a container for holding Match objects and is created using the Regex.Matches method discussed earlier. Its most useful properties are Count, which returns the number of captures, and Item,

Member	Description
Index	Property returning the position in the string where the first character of the match is found.
Groups	A collection of groups within the class. Groups are created by placing sections of the regex with parentheses. The text that matches the pattern in parentheses is placed in the Groups collection.
Length	Length of the matched string.
Success	True or False depending on whether a match was found.
Value	Returns the matching substring.
NextMatch()	Returns a new Match with the results from the next match operation, beginning with the character after the previous match, if any.

Fig. 13.13 | Selected Members of the Match Class.

which returns an individual member of the collection. Here is how the NextMatch loop in the previous example could be rewritten:

```
string verse = "In Xanadu did Kubla Khan";
String newpatt = "K(..)";
foreach (Match kMatch in Regex.Matches(verse, newpatt))
   Console.Write(kMatch.Value);   // -->Kub  -->Kha
// Could also create explicit collection and work with it.
MatchCollection mc = Regex.Matches(verse, newpatt);
Console.WriteLine(mc.Count);      // 2
```

13.8.2 Creating Regular Expressions

The examples used to illustrate the Regex methods have employed only rudimentary regular expressions. Now, let's explore how to create regular expressions that are genuinely useful. If you are new to the subject, you will discover that designing Regex patterns tends to be a trial-and-error process; and the endeavor can yield a solution of simple elegance— or maddening complexity. Fortunately, almost all of the commonly used patterns can be found on one of the Web sites that maintain a searchable library of Regex patterns (www.regexlib.com is one such site).

A regular expression can be broken down into four different types of metacharacters that have their own role in the matching process:

- **Matching characters.** These match a specific type of character—for example, \d matches any digit from 0 to 9.

- **Repetition characters.** Used to prevent having to repeat a matching character or item—for example, \d{3} can be used instead of \d\d\d to match three digits.

- **Positional characters.** Designate the location in the target string where a match must occur—for example, ^\d{3} requires that the match occur at the beginning of the string.

- **Escape sequences.** Use the backslash (\) in front of characters that otherwise have special meaning—for example, \} permits the right brace to be matched.

The table in Fig. 13.14 summarizes the most frequently used patterns.

13.8.3 A Pattern Matching Example

Let's apply these character patterns to create a regular expression that matches a Social Security Number (SSN):

```
bool iMatch = Regex.IsMatch("245-09-8444",
                     @"\d\d\d-\d\d-\d\d\d\d");
```

This is the most straightforward approach: Each character in the Social Security Number matches a corresponding pattern in the regular expression. It's easy to see, however, that simply repeating symbols can become unwieldy if a long string is to be matched. Repetition characters improve this:

```
bool iMatch = Regex.IsMatch("245-09-8444",
                     @"\d{3}-\d{2}-\d{4}");
```

Pattern	Matching Criterion	Example
+	Match one or more occurrences of the previous item.	to+ matches too and tooo. It does not match t.
*	Match zero or more occurrences of the previous item.	to* matches t or too or tooo.
?	Match zero or one occurrence of the previous item. Performs "non-greedy" matching.	te?n matches ten or tn. It does not match teen.
{n}	Match exactly n occurrences of the previous character.	te{2}n matches teen. It does not match ten or teeen.
{n,}	Match at least n occurrences of the previous character.	te{1,}n matches ten and teen. It does not match tn.
{n,m}	Match at least n and no more than m occurrences of the previous character.	te{1,2}n matches ten and teen.
\	Treat the next character literally. Used to match characters that have special meaning such as the patterns +, *, and ?.	A\+B matches A+B. The slash (\) is required because + has special meaning.
\d \D	Match any digit (\d) or non-digit (\D). This is equivalent to [0-9] or [^0-9], respectively.	\d\d matches 55. \D\D matches xx.
\w \W	Match any word plus underscore (\w) or non-word (\W) character. \w is equivalent to [a-zA-Z0-9_]. \W is equivalent to [^a-zA-Z0-9_] .	\w\w\w\w matches A_19 . \W\W\W matches ($).
\n \r \t \v \f	Match newline, carriage return, tab, vertical tab, or form feed, respectively.	N/A
\s \S	Match any whitespace (\s) or non-whitespace (\S). A whitespace is usually a space or tab character.	\w\s\w\s\w matches A B C.
. (dot)	Matches any single character. Does not match a newline.	a.c matches abc. It does not match abcc.
|	Logical OR.	"in|en" matches enquiry.
[. . .]	Match any single character between the brackets. Hyphens may be used to indicate a range.	[aeiou] matches u. [\d\D] matches a single digit or non-digit.
[^. . .]	All characters except those in the brackets.	[^aeiou] matches x.

Fig. 13.14 | Regular Expression Patterns.

Another consideration in matching the Social Security Number may be to restrict where it exists in the text. You may want to ensure it is on a line by itself, or at the beginning or end of a line. This requires using *position characters* at the beginning or end of the matching sequence.

Let's alter the pattern so that it matches only if the Social Security Number exists by itself on the line. To do this, we need two characters: one to ensure the match is at the beginning of the line, and one to ensure that it is also at the end. According to Fig. 13.15, ^ and $ can be placed around the expression to meet these criteria. The new string is

```
@"^\d{3}-\d{2}-\d{4}$"
```

These positional characters do not take up any space in the expression—that is, they indicate where matching may occur but are not involved in the actual matching process.

As a final refinement to the SSN pattern, let's break it into *groups* so that the three sets of numbers separated by dashes can be easily examined. To create a group, place parentheses around the parts of the expression that you want to examine independently. Here is a simple code example that uses the revised pattern:

```
string ssn = "245-09-8444";
string ssnPatt = @"^(\d{3})-(\d{2})-(\d{4})$";
Match ssnMatch = Regex.Match(ssn, ssnPatt);
if (ssnMatch.Success){
    Console.WriteLine(ssnMatch.Value);          // 245-09-8444
    Console.WriteLine(ssnMatch.Groups.Count);   // 4
    // Count is 4 since Groups[0] is set to entire SSN
    Console.Write(ssnMatch.Groups[1]);          // 245
    Console.Write(ssnMatch.Groups[2]);          // 09
    Console.Write(ssnMatch.Groups[3]);          // 8444
}
```

We now have a useful pattern that incorporates position, repetition, and group characters. The approach that was used to create this pattern—started with an obvious pattern and refined it through multiple stages—is a useful way to create complex regular expressions (see Fig. 13.16).

13.8.4 Working with Groups

As we saw in the preceding example, the text resulting from a match can be automatically partitioned into substrings or groups by enclosing sections of the regular expression in parentheses. The text that matches the enclosed pattern becomes a member of the

Position Character	Description
^	Following pattern must be at the start of a string or line.
$	Preceding pattern must be at end of a string or line.
\A	Preceding pattern must be at the start of a string.
\b \B	Move to a word boundary (\b), where a word character and non-word character meet, or a non-word boundary.
\z \Z	Pattern must be at the end of a string (\z) or at the end of a string before a newline.

Fig. 13.15 | Characters That Specify Where a Match Must Occur.

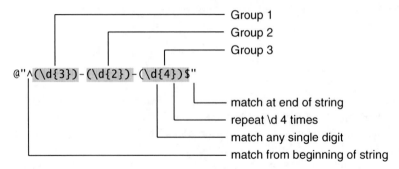

Fig. 13.16 | Regular expression.

`Match.Groups[]` collection. This collection can be indexed as a zero-based array: the 0 element is the entire match, element 1 is the first group, element 2 the second, and so on.

Groups can be named to make them easier to work with. The name designator is placed adjacent to the opening parenthesis using the syntax ?*<name>*. To demonstrate the use of groups, let's suppose we need to parse a string containing the forecasted temperatures for the week (for brevity, only two days are included):

```
string txt ="Monday Hi:88 Lo:56 Tuesday Hi:91 Lo:61";
```

The regex to match this includes two groups: day and `temps`. The following code creates a collection of matches and then iterates through the collection, printing the content of each group:

```
string rgPatt = @"(?<day>[a-zA-Z]+)\s*(?<temps>Hi:\d+\s*Lo:\d+)";
MatchCollection mc = Regex.Matches(txt, rgPatt); //Get matches
foreach(Match m in mc)
{
    Console.WriteLine("{0} {1}",
                    m.Groups["day"],m.Groups["temps"]);
}
//Output:    Monday Hi:88 Lo:56
//           Tuesday Hi:91 Lo:61
```

 Core Note 13.3

There are times when you do not want the presence of parentheses to designate a group that captures a match. A common example is the use of parentheses to create an OR expression—for example, (an|in|on). To make this a non-capturing group, place ?: inside the parentheses—for example, (?:an|in|on).

Backreferencing a Group

It is often useful to create a regular expression that includes matching logic based on the results of previous matches within the expression. For example, during a grammatical check, word processors flag any word that is a repeat of the preceding word(s). We can create a regular expression to perform the same operation. The secret is to define a group that matches a word and then uses the matched value as part of the pattern. To illustrate, consider the following code:

```
string speech = "Four score and and seven years";
patt = @"(\b[a-zA-Z]+\b)\s\1";              // Match repeated words
MatchCollection mc = Regex.Matches(speech, patt);
foreach(Match m in mc) {
       Console.WriteLine(m.Groups[1]);   // --> and
}
```

This code matches only the repeated words. Let's examine the regular expression:

Text/Pattern	Description
and and @"(\b[a-zA-Z]+\b)\s	Matches a word bounded on each side by a word boundary (\b) and followed by a whitespace.
and **and** \1	The backreference indicator. Any group can be referenced with a slash (\) followed by the group number. The effect is to insert the group's matched value into the expression.

A group can also be referenced by name rather than number. The syntax for this back-reference is \k followed by the group name enclosed in <>:

```
patt = @"(?<word>\b[a-zA-Z]+\b)\s\k<word>";
```

13.8.5 Examples of Using Regular Expressions

This section closes with a quick look at some patterns that can be used to handle common pattern matching challenges. Two things should be clear from these examples: There are virtually unlimited ways to create expressions to solve a single problem, and many pattern matching problems involve nuances that are not immediately obvious.

Using Replace to Reverse Words

```
string userName = "Claudel, Camille";
userName = Regex.Replace( userName, @"(\w+),\s*(\w+)", "$2 $1" );
Console.WriteLine(userName);   // Camille Claudel
```

The regular expression assigns the last and first name to groups 1 and 2. The third parameter in the Replace method allows these groups to be referenced by placing $ in front of the group number. In this case, the effect is to replace the entire matched name with the match from group 2 (first name) followed by the match from group 1 (last name).

Parsing Numbers

```
String myText = "98, 98.0, +98.0, +98";
string numPatt = @"\d+";                        // Integer
numPatt = @"(\d+\.?\d*)|(\.\d+)";               // Allow decimal
numPatt = @"([+-]?\d+\.?\d*)|([+-]?\.\d+)";     // Allow + or -
```

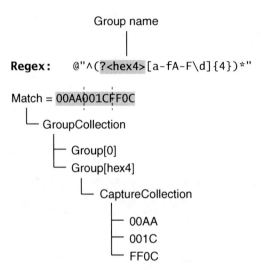

Group name

Regex: @"^(?<hex4>[a-fA-F\d]{4})*"

Match = 00AA001CFF0C

└─ GroupCollection

├─ Group[0]
└─ Group[hex4]

└─ CaptureCollection

├─ 00AA
├─ 001C
└─ FF0C

Fig. 13.17 | Hex numbers captured by regular expression.

Note the use of the OR (|) symbol in the third line of code to offer alternate patterns. In this case, it permits an optional number before the decimal.

The following code uses the ^ character to anchor the pattern to the beginning of the line. The regular expression contains a group that matches four bytes at a time. The * character causes the group to be repeated until there is nothing to match. Each time the group is applied, it captures a 4-digit hex number that is placed in the CaptureCollection object.

```
string hex = "00AA001CFF0C";
string hexPatt =  @"^(?<hex4>[a-fA-F\d]{4})*";
Match hexMatch = Regex.Match(hex,hexPatt);
Console.WriteLine(hexMatch.Value); // --> 00AA001CFF0C
CaptureCollection cc = hexMatch.Groups["hex4"].Captures;
foreach (Capture c in cc)
    Console.Write(c.Value); // --> 00AA 001C FF0C
```

Figure 13.17 shows the hierarchical relationship among the Match, GroupCollection, and CaptureCollection classes.

13.9 System.IO: Classes to Read and Write Streams of Data

The System.IO namespace contains the primary classes used to move and process streams of data. The data source may be in the form of text strings, as discussed in this chapter, or raw bytes of data coming from a network or device on an I/O port. Classes derived from the Stream class work with raw bytes; those derived from the TextReader and TextWriter classes operate with characters and text strings (see Fig. 13.18). We'll begin the discussion with the Stream class and look at how its derived classes are used to manipulate byte streams of data. Then, we'll examine how data in a more structured text format is handled using the TextReader and TextWriter classes.

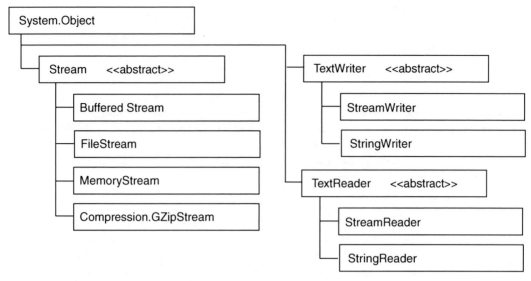

Fig. 13.18 | Selected System.IO classes.

13.9.1 The Stream Class

This class defines the generic members for working with raw byte streams. Its purpose is to abstract data into a stream of bytes independent of any underlying data devices. This frees the programmer to focus on the data stream rather than device characteristics. The class members support three fundamental areas of operation: reading, writing, and seeking (identifying the current byte position within a stream). The table in Fig. 13.19 summarizes some of its important members. Not included are methods for asynchronous I/O.

These methods and properties provide the bulk of the functionality for the FileStream, MemoryStream, and BufferedStream classes, which we examine next.

13.9.2 FileStreams

A FileStream object is created to process a stream of bytes associated with a *backing store*—a term used to refer to any storage medium such as disk or memory. The following code segment demonstrates how it is used for reading and writing bytes:

```
try
{
    // Create FileStream object
    FileStream fs = new FileStream(@"c:\artists\log.txt",
        FileMode.OpenOrCreate, FileAccess.ReadWrite);
    byte[] alpha = new byte[6] {65,66,67,68,69,70}; //ABCDEF
    // Write array of bytes to a file
    // Equivalent to: fs.Write(alpha,0, alpha.Length);
    foreach (byte b in alpha) {
        fs.WriteByte(b);}
    // Read bytes from file
    fs.Position = 0;          // Move to beginning of file
```

```
        for (int i = 0; i< fs.Length; i++)
            Console.Write((char) fs.ReadByte()); //ABCDEF
        fs.Close();
    catch(Exception ex)
    {
        Console.Write(ex.Message);
    }
```

As this example illustrates, a stream is essentially a byte array with an internal pointer that marks a current location in the stream. The ReadByte and WriteByte methods process stream bytes in sequence. The Position property moves the internal pointer to any position in the stream. By opening the FileStream for ReadWrite, the program can intermix reading and writing without closing the file.

Creating a FileStream

The FileStream class has several constructors. The most useful ones accept the path of the file being associated with the object and optional parameters that define file mode, access rights, and sharing rights. The possible values for these parameters are shown in Fig. 13.20.

The FileMode enumeration designates how the operating system is to open the file and where to position the file pointer for subsequent reading or writing. The table in Fig. 13.21 is worth noting because you will see the enumeration used by several classes in the System.IO namespace.

Member	Description
CanRead CanSeek CanWrite	Indicates whether the stream supports reading, seeking, or writing.
Length	Length of stream in bytes; returns long type.
Position	Gets or sets the position within the current stream; has long type.
Close()	Closes the current stream and releases resources associated with it.
Flush()	Flushes data in buffers to the underlying device—for example, a file.
Read(byte array, offset, count) ReadByte()	Reads a sequence of bytes from the stream and advances the position within the stream to the number of bytes read. ReadByte reads one byte. Read returns number of bytes read; ReadByte returns −1 if at end of the stream.
SetLength()	Sets the length of the current stream. It can be used to extend or truncate a stream.
Seek()	Sets the position within the current stream.
Write(byte array, offset, count) WriteByte()	Writes a sequence of bytes (Write) or one byte (WriteByte) to the current stream. Neither has a return value.

Fig. 13.19 | Selected Stream Members.

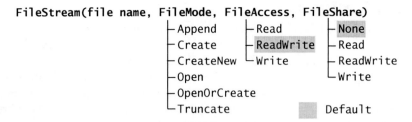

Fig. 13.20 | Options for `FileStream` constructors.

Value	Description
Append	Opens an existing file or creates a new one. Writing begins at the end of the file.
Create	Creates a new file. An existing file is overwritten.
CreateNew	Creates a new file. An exception is thrown if the file already exists.
Open	Opens an existing file.
OpenOrCreate	Opens a file if it exists; otherwise, creates a new one.
Truncate	Opens an existing file, removes its contents, and positions the file pointer to the beginning of the file.

Fig. 13.21 | `FileMode` Enumeration Values.

The `FileAccess` enumeration defines how the current `FileStream` may access the file; `FileShare` defines how file streams in other processes may access it. For example, `FileShare.Read` permits multiple file streams to be created that can simultaneously read the same file.

13.9.3 MemoryStreams

As the name suggests, this class is used to stream bytes to and from memory as a substitute for a temporary external physical store. To demonstrate, here is an example that copies a file. It reads the original file into a memory stream and then writes this to a `FileStream` using the `WriteTo` method:

```
FileStream fsIn = new FileStream(@"c:\manet.bmp",
            FileMode.Open, FileAccess.Read);
FileStream fsOut = new FileStream(@"c:\manetcopy.bmp",
            FileMode.OpenOrCreate, FileAccess.Write);
MemoryStream ms = new MemoryStream();
// Input image byte-by-byte and store in memory stream
int imgByte;
while ((imgByte = fsIn.ReadByte())!=-1){
   ms.WriteByte((byte)imgByte);
}
ms.WriteTo(fsOut);              // Copy image from memory to disk
byte[] imgArray = ms.ToArray(); // Convert to array of bytes
fsIn.Close();
fsOut.Close();
ms.Close();
```

13.9.4 BufferedStreams

One way to improve I/O performance is to limit the number of reads and writes to an external device—particularly when small amounts of data are involved. Buffers have long offered a solution for collecting small amounts of data into larger amounts that could then be sent more efficiently to a device. The BufferedStream object contains a buffer that performs this role for an underlying stream. You create the object by passing an existing stream object to its constructor. The BufferedStream then performs the I/O operations, and when the buffer is full or closed, its contents are flushed to the underlying stream. By default, the BufferedStream maintains a buffer size of 4096 bytes, but passing a size parameter to the constructor can change this.

Buffers are commonly used to improve performance when reading bytes from an I/O port or network. Here is an example that associates a BufferedStream with an underlying FileStream. The heart of the code consists of a loop in which FillBytes (simulating an I/O device) is called to return an array of bytes. These bytes are written to a buffer rather than directly to the file. When fileBuffer is closed, any remaining bytes are flushed to the FileStream fsOut1. A write operation to the physical device then occurs.

```
private void SaveStream() {
    Stream fsOut1 = new FileStream(@"c:\captured.txt",
        FileMode.OpenOrCreate, FileAccess.Write);
    BufferedStream fileBuffer = new BufferedStream(fsOut1);
    byte[] buff;          // Array to hold bytes written to buffer
    bool readMore=true;
    while(readMore) {
        buff = FillBytes();          // Get array of bytes
        for (int j = 0;j<buff[16];j++){
            fileBuffer.WriteByte(buff[j]);   // Store bytes in buffer
        }
        if(buff[16]< 16) readMore=false;    // Indicates no more data
    }
    fileBuffer.Close();   // Flushes all remaining buffer content
    fsOut1.Close();       // Must close after bufferedstream
}
// Method to simulate I/O device receiving data
private static byte[] FillBytes() {
    Random rand = new Random();
    byte[] r = new Byte[17];
    // Store random numbers to return in array
    for (int j=0;j<16;j++) {
        r[j]= (byte) rand.Next();
        if(r[j]==171)          // Arbitrary end of stream value
        {
            r[16]=(byte)(j);  // Number of bytes in array
            return r;
        }
    }
    System.Threading.Thread.Sleep(500);  // Delay 500ms
    return r;
}
```

13.9.5 Using StreamReader and StreamWriter to Read and Write Lines of Text

Unlike the Stream derived classes, StreamWriter and StreamReader are designed to work with text rather than raw bytes. The abstract TextWriter and TextReader classes from which they derive define methods for reading and writing text as lines of characters. Keep in mind that these methods rely on a FileStream object underneath to perform the actual data transfer.

Writing to a Text File

StreamWriter writes text using its Write and WriteLine methods. Note their differences:

- WriteLine works only with strings and automatically appends a newline (carriage return\linefeed).

- Write does not append a newline character and can write strings as well as the textual representation of any basic data type (int32, single, and so on) to the text stream.

The StreamWriter object is created using one of several constructors:

Syntax (partial list):

```
public StreamWriter(string path)
public StreamWriter(stream s)
public StreamWriter(string path, bool append)
public StreamWriter(string path, bool append, Encoding encoding)
```

Parameters:

path	Path and name of file to be opened.
s	Previously created Stream object—typically a FileStream.
append	Set to true to append data to file; false overwrites.
encoding	Specifies how characters are encoded as they are written to a file. The default is UTF-8 (UCS Transformation Format) that stores characters in the minimum number of bytes required.

This example creates a StreamWriter object from a FileStream and writes two lines of text to the associated file:

```
string filePath = @"c:\cup.txt";
// Could use: StreamWriter sw = new StreamWriter(filePath);
// Use FileStream to create StreamWriter
FileStream fs = new FileStream(filePath, FileMode.OpenOrCreate,
                FileAccess.ReadWrite);
StreamWriter sw2 = new StreamWriter(fs);
// Now that it is created, write to the file
sw2.WriteLine("The world is a cup");
sw2.WriteLine("brimming\nwith water.");
sw2.Close();  // Free resources
```

Reading from a Text File

A `StreamReader` object is used to read text from a file. Much like `StreamWriter`, an instance of it can be created from an underlying `Stream` object, and it can include an encoding specification parameter. When it is created, it has several methods for reading and viewing character data (see Fig. 13.22).

This code creates a `StreamReader` object by passing an explicit `FileStream` object to the constructor. The `FileStream` is used later to reposition the reader to the beginning of the file.

```
String path= @"c:\cup.txt";
if(File.Exists(path))
{
   FileStream fs = new FileStream(path,
         FileMode.OpenOrCreate, FileAccess.ReadWrite);
   StreamReader reader = new StreamReader(fs);
   // or StreamReader reader = new StreamReader(path);
   // (1) Read first line
   string line = reader.ReadLine();
   // (2) Read four bytes on next line
   char[] buff  = new char[4];
   int count = reader.Read(buff,0,buff.Length);
   // (3) Read to end of file
   string cup = reader.ReadToEnd();
   // (4) Reposition to beginning of file
   //     Could also use reader.BaseStream.Position = 0;
   fs.Position = 0;
   // (5) Read from first line to end of file
   line = null;
   while ((line = reader.ReadLine()) != null){
      Console.WriteLine(line);
   }
   reader.Close();
}
```

Member	Description
Peek()	Returns the next available character without moving the position of the reader. Returns an int value of the character or −1 if none exists.
Read() Read(char buff, int ndx, int count)	Reads next character (`Read()`) from a stream or reads next count characters into a character array beginning at ndx.
ReadLine()	Returns a string comprising one line of text.
ReadToEnd()	Reads all characters from the current position to the end of the `TextReader`. Useful for downloading a small text file over a network stream.

Fig. 13.22 | Selected `StreamReader` Methods.

Core Note 13.4

A StreamReader *has an underlying* FileStream *even if it is not created with an explicit one. It is accessed by the* BaseStream *property and can be used to reposition the reader within the stream using its* Seek *method. This example moves the reader to the beginning of a file:*

```
reader.BaseStream.Seek(0, SeekOrigin.Begin);
```

13.9.6 StringWriter and StringReader

These two classes do not require a lot of discussion, because they are so similar in practice to the StreamWriter and StreamReader. The main difference is that these streams are stored in memory, rather than in a file. The following example should be self-explanatory:

```
StringWriter writer = new StringWriter();
writer.WriteLine("Today I have returned,");
writer.WriteLine("after long months ");
writer.Write("that seemed like centuries");
writer.Write(writer.NewLine);
writer.Close();
// Read String just written from memory
string myString = writer.ToString();
StringReader reader = new StringReader(myString);
string line = null;
while ((line = reader.ReadLine()) !=null) {
    Console.WriteLine(line);
}
reader.Close();
```

The most interesting aspect of the StringWriter is that it is implemented underneath as a StringBuilder object. In fact, StringWriter has a GetStringBuilder method that can be used to retrieve it:

```
StringWriter writer = new StringWriter();
writer.WriteLine("Today I have returned,");
// Get underlying StringBuilder
StringBuilder sb = writer.GetStringBuilder();
sb.Append("after long months ");
Console.WriteLine(sb.ToString());
writer.Close();
```

Core Recommendation 13.4

Use the StringWriter *and* StringBuilder *classes to work with large strings in memory. A typical approach is to use the* StreamReader.ReadToEnd *method to load a text file into memory where it can be written to the* StringWriter *and manipulated by the* StringBuilder.

13.9.7 Encryption with the CryptoStream Class

An advantage of using streams is the ability to layer them to add functionality. We saw earlier how the BufferedStream class performs I/O on top of an underlying FileStream. Another class that can be layered on a base stream is the CryptoStream class that enables data in the underlying stream to be encrypted and decrypted. This section describes how to use this class in conjunction with the StreamWriter and StreamReader classes to read and write encrypted text in a FileStream. Figure 13.23 shows how each class is composed from the underlying class.

CryptoStream is located in the System.Security.Cryptography namespace. It is quite simple to use, requiring only a couple of lines of code to apply it to a stream. The .NET Framework provides multiple cryptography algorithms that can be used with this class. Later, you may want to investigate the merits of these algorithms, but for now, our interest is in how to use them with the CryptoStream class.

Two techniques are used to encrypt data: assymmetric (or *public key*) and symmetric (or *private key*). Public key is referred to as asymmetric because a public key is used to decrypt data, while a different private key is used to encrypt it. Symmetric uses the same private key for both purposes. In our example, we are going to use a private key algorithm. The .NET Framework Class Library contains four classes that implement symmetric algorithms:

- DESCryptoServiceProvider—Digital Encryption Standard (DES) algorithm

- RC2CryptoServiceProvider—RC2 algorithm

- RijndaelManaged—Rijndael algorithm

- TrippleDESCryptoServiceProvider—TripleDES algorithm

We use the DES algorithm in our example, but we could have chosen any of the others because implementation details are identical. First, an instance of the class is created. Then, its key and IV (Initialization Vector) properties are set to the same key value. DES requires these to be 8 bytes; other algorithms require different lengths. Of course, the key is used to encrypt and decrypt data. The IV ensures that repeated text is not encrypted identically. After the DES object is created, it is passed as an argument to the constructor of the CryptoStream class. The CryptoStream object simply treats the object encapsulating the algorithm as a black box.

The example shown here includes two methods: one to encrypt and write data to a file stream, and the other to decrypt the same data while reading it back. The encryption is performed by WriteEncrypt, which receives a FileStream object parameter encapsulating the output file and a second parameter containing the message to be encrypted; ReadEncrypt receives a FileStream representing the file to be read.

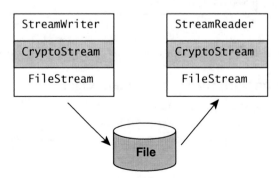

Fig. 13.23 | Layering streams for encryption/decryption.

```
fs = new FileStream("C:\\test.txt", FileMode.Create,
                FileAccess.Write);
MyApp.WriteEncrypt(fs, "Selected site is in Italy.");
fs= new FileStream("C:\\test.txt",FileMode.Open,
                FileAccess.Read);
string msg = MyApp.ReadEncrypt(fs);
Console.WriteLine(msg);
fs.Close();
```

WriteEncrypt encrypts the message and writes it to the file stream using a Stream-Writer object that serves as a wrapper for a CrytpoStream object. CryptoStream has a lone constructor that accepts the file stream, an object encapsulating the DES algorithm logic, and an enumeration specifying its mode.

```
// Encrypt FileStream
private static void WriteEncrypt(FileStream fs, string msg) {
    // (1) Create Data Encryption Standard (DES) object
    DESCryptoServiceProvider crypt = new
            DESCryptoServiceProvider();
    // (2) Create a key and Initialization Vector -
    // requires 8 bytes
    crypt.Key = new byte[] {71,72,83,84,85,96,97,78};
    crypt.IV  = new byte[] {71,72,83,84,85,96,97,78};
    // (3) Create CryptoStream stream object
    CryptoStream cs = new CryptoStream(fs,
        crypt.CreateEncryptor(),CryptoStreamMode.Write);
    // (4) Create StreamWriter using CryptoStream
    StreamWriter sw = new StreamWriter(cs);
    sw.Write(msg);
    sw.Close();
    cs.Close();
}
```

ReadEncrypt reverses the actions of WriteEncrypt. It decodes the data in the file stream and returns the data as a string object. To do this, it layers a CryptoStream stream on top of the FileStream to perform decryption. It then creates a StreamReader from the CryptoStream stream that actually reads the data from the stream.

```
// Read and decrypt a file stream.
private static string ReadEncrypt(FileStream fs) {
    // (1) Create Data Encryption Standard (DES) object
    DESCryptoServiceProvider crypt =
            new DESCryptoServiceProvider();
    // (2) Create a key and Initialization Vector
    crypt.Key = new byte[] {71,72,83,84,85,96,97,78};
    crypt.IV  = new byte[] {71,72,83,84,85,96,97,78};
    // (3) Create CryptoStream stream object
    CryptoStream cs = new CryptoStream(fs,
            crypt.CreateDecryptor(),CryptoStreamMode.Read);
    // (4) Create StreamReader using CryptoStream
    StreamReader sr = new StreamReader(cs);
    string msg = sr.ReadToEnd();
    sr.Close();
    cs.Close();
    return msg;
}
```

13.10 System.IO: Directories and Files

The System.IO namespace includes a set of system-related classes that are used to manage files and directories. Figure 13.24 shows a hierarchy of the most useful classes. Directory and DirectoryInfo contain members to create, delete, and query directories. The only significant difference in the two is that you use Directory with static methods, whereas a DirectoryInfo object must be created to use instance methods. In a parallel manner, File and FileInfo provide static and instance methods for working with files.

13.10.1 FileSystemInfo

The FileSystemInfo class is a base class for DirectoryInfo and FileInfo. It defines a range of members that are used primarily to provide information about a file or directory. The abstract FileSystemInfo class takes advantage of the fact that files and directories share common features. Its properties include CreationTime, LastAccessTime, Last-WriteTime, Name, and FullName. It also includes two important methods: Delete to delete a file or directory and Refresh that updates the latest file and directory information.

Here is a quick look at some of the FileSystemInfo members using DirectoryInfo and FileInfo objects. Note the use of the Refresh method before checking the directory and file attributes.

```csharp
// DirectoryInfo
string dir  = @"c:\artists";
DirectoryInfo di = new DirectoryInfo(dir);
di.Refresh();
DateTime IODate = di.CreationTime;
Console.WriteLine("{0:d}",IODate)              // 10/9/2001
// FileInfo
string file = @"C:\artists\manet.jpg";
FileInfo fi = new FileInfo(file);
```

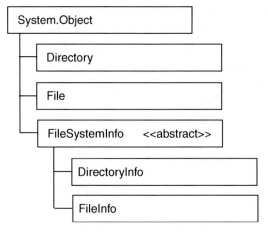

Fig. 13.24 | Directory and File classes in the System.IO namespace.

```
if (fi.Exists) {
    fi.Refresh();
    IODate = fi.CreationTime;
    Console.WriteLine("{0:d}",IODate);        // 5/15/2004
    Console.WriteLine(fi.Name);               // monet.txt
    Console.WriteLine(fi.Extension);          // .txt
    FileAttributes attrib = fi.Attributes;
    Console.WriteLine((int) attrib);          // 32
    Console.WriteLine(attrib);                // Archive
}
```

13.10.2 Working with Directories Using the DirectoryInfo, Directory, and Path Classes

When working with directories, you usually have a choice between using the instance methods of DirectoryInfo or the corresponding static methods of Directory. As a rule, if you are going to refer to a directory in several operations, use an instance of Directory-Info. The table in Fig. 13.25 provides a comparison summary of the available methods.

Let's look at some examples using both static and instance methods to manipulate and list directory members. The sample code assumes the directory structure shown in Fig. 13.26.

Create a Subdirectory
This code adds a subdirectory named cubists below expressionists:

```
// Directory static method to create directory
string newPath =
      @"c:\artists\expressionists\cubists";
if (!Directory.Exists(newPath))
   Directory.CreateDirectory(newPath);

// DirectoryInfo
string curPath= @"c:\artists\expressionists";
di = new DirectoryInfo(curPath);
if (di.Exists) di.CreateSubdirectory(newPath);
```

Delete a Subdirectory
This code deletes the cubists subdirectory just created:

```
string newPath = @"c:\artists\expressionists\cubists";
// Directory
if (Directory.Exists(newPath)) Directory.Delete(newPath);
// The following fails because the directory still contains files
Directory.Delete(@"c:\artists\expressionists");
// The following succeeds because true is passed to the method
Directory.Delete(@"c:\artists\expressionists",true);

// DirectoryInfo
DirectoryInfo di = new DirectoryInfo(newPath);
If (di.Exists) di.Delete();
```

DirectoryInfo		Directory	
Member	**Description**	**Member**	**Description**
Create() CreateSubdirectory()	Create a directory or subdirectory.	CreateDirectory()	Pass the string path to the method. Failure results in an exception.
Delete()	Delete a directory.	Delete(string) Delete(string, bool)	First version deletes an empty directory. Second version deletes a directory and all subdirectories if boolean value is true.
GetDirectories()	Returns an array of DirectoryInfo type containing all subdirectories in the current directory.	GetDirectories(string) GetDirectories(string, string filter)	Returns a string array containing the names of directories in the path. A filter may be used to specify directory names.
GetFiles()	Returns an array of FileInfo types containing all files in the directory.	GetFiles(string) GetFiles(string, filter)	Returns string array of files in directory. A filter may be used to match against file names. The filter may contain wildcard characters ? or * to match a single character or zero or more characters.
Parent	Retrieves parent directory of current path.	GetParent()	Retrieves parent directory of specified path.
N/A		GetLogicalDrives()	Returns string containing logical drives on system. Format: <drive>:\

Fig. 13.25 | Comparison of Selected DirectoryInfo and Directory Members.

```
C:\
   \artists
   \impressionists
       monet.txt
       monet.htm
       sisley.txt
   \expressionists
       scheile.txt
       wollheim.txt
```

Fig. 13.26 | Directory structure used in Directory examples.

List Directories and Files
This code defines a method that recursively loops through and lists the subdirectories and selected files on the C:\artists path. It uses the static Directory methods GetDirectories and GetFiles. Both of these return string values.

```
static readonly int Depth=4; // Specify directory level to search
ShowDir (@"c:\artists\", 0); // Call method to list files
// Display directories and files using recursion
public static void ShowDir(string sourceDir, int recursionLvl)
{
    if (recursionLvl<= Depth) // Limit subdirectory search depth
    {
        // Process the list of files found in the directory
        Console.WriteLine(sourceDir);
        foreach( string fileName in
                Directory.GetFiles(sourceDir,"s*.*"))
        {
            Console.WriteLine("  "+Path.GetFileName(fileName));

        // Use recursion to process subdirectories
        foreach(string subDir in
                Directory.GetDirectories(sourceDir))
            ShowDir(subDir,recursionLvl+1);  // Recursive call
    }
}
```

GetFiles returns a full path name. The static Path.GetFileName method is used to extract the file name and extension from the path. For demonstration purposes, a filter has been added to the GetFiles method to have it return only the path of files that begins with s.

Here is the same operation using the DirectoryInfo class. Its GetDirectories and GetFiles methods behave differently than the Directory versions: They return objects rather than strings, and they return the immediate directory or file name rather than the entire path.

```
// DirectoryInfo
public static void ShowDir(DirectoryInfo sourceDir,
                            int recursionLvl)
{
    if (recursionLvl<= Depth)  // Limit subdirectory search depth
```

```
        {
            // Process the list of files found in the directory
            Console.WriteLine(sourceDir.FullName);
            foreach( FileInfo fileName in
                    sourceDir.GetFiles("s*.*"))
                Console.WriteLine("  "+fileName);
            // Use recursion to process subdirectories
            foreach(DirectoryInfo subDir in sourceDir.GetDirectories())
                ShowDir2(subDir,recursionLvl+1);  // Recursive call
        }
    }
```

The method is called with two parameters: a `DirectoryInfo` object that encapsulates the path and an initial depth of 0.

```
    DirectoryInfo dirInfo = new DirectoryInfo(@"c:\artists\");
    ShowDir(dirInfo, 0);
```

Using the Path Class to Operate on Path Names

To eliminate the need for developers to create code that manipulates a path string, .NET provides a `Path` class that consists of static methods designed to operate on a path string. The methods—a shortcut for Regex patterns—extract selected parts of a path or return a boolean value indicating whether the path satisfies some criterion. Note that because the format of a path is platform dependent (a Linux path is specified differently than a Windows path), the .NET implementation of this class is tailored to the platform on which it runs.

To illustrate the static `Path` methods, let's look at the results of applying selected methods to this path:

```
    string fullPath = @"c:\artists\impressionists\monet.htm";
```

Method	Returns
Path.GetDirectoryName(fullPath)	c:\artists\impressionists
Path.GetExtension(fullPath)	.htm
GetFileName(fullPath)	monet.htm
GetFullPath(fullPath)	c:\artists\impressionists\monet.htm
GetPathRoot(fullPath)	c:\
Path.HasExtension(fullPath)	true

13.10.3 Working with Files Using the FileInfo and File Classes

The `FileInfo` and `File` classes are used for two purposes: to provide descriptive information about a file and to perform basic file operations. The classes include methods to copy, move, and delete files, as well as open files for reading and writing. This short segment uses a FileInfo object to display a file's properties, and the static File.Copy method to copy a file:

```
string fname= @"c:\artists\impressionists\degas.txt";
// Using the FileInfo class to print file information
FileInfo fi = new FileInfo(fname);  // Create FileInfo object
if (fi.Exists)
{
    Console.Write("Length: {0}\nName: {1}\nDirectory: {2}",
    fi.Length, fi.Name, fi.DirectoryName);
    // output: --> 488  degas.txt  c:\artists\impressionists
}
// Use File class to copy a file to another directory
if (File.Exists(fname))
{
    try
    {
        // Exception is thrown if file exists in target directory
        // (source, destination, overwrite=false)
        File.Copy(fname,@"c:\artists\19thcentury\degas.txt",false);
    }
    catch(Exception ex)
    {
        Console.Write(ex.Message);
    }
}
```

Using FileInfo and File to Open Files

The File and FileInfo classes offer an alternative to creating FileStream, StreamWriter, and StreamReader objects directly. The table in Fig. 13.27 summarizes the FileInfo methods used to open a file. The static File methods are identical except that their first parameter is always a string containing the name or path of the file to open.

The FileInfo.Open method is the generic and most flexible way to open a file:

```
public FileStream Open(FileMode mode, FileAccess access,
                       FileShare share)
```

Create, OpenRead, and OpenWrite are specific cases of Open that offer an easy-to-use method that returns a FileStream object and requires no parameters. Similarly, the OpenText, AppendText, and CreateText methods return a StreamReader or StreamWriter object.

The decision to create a FileStream (or StreamReader/StreamWriter) using FileInfo or the FileStream constructor should be based on how the underlying file is used in the application. If the file is being opened for a single purpose, such as for input by a StreamReader, creating a FileStream directly is the best approach. If multiple operations are required on the file, a FileInfo object is better. This example illustrates the advantages of using FileInfo. First, it creates a FileStream that is used for writing to a file; then, another FileStream is created to read the file's contents; finally, FileInfo.Delete is used to delete the file.

```
FileInfo     fi = new FileInfo(@"c:\temp.txt");
FileStream   fs = fi.Create();          // Create file
```

Member	Returns	Description
Open(mode) Open(mode,access) Open(mode,access,share)	FileStream	Opens a file with access and sharing privileges. The three overloads take FileMode, FileAccess, and FileShare enumerations.
Create()	FileStream	Creates a file and returns a FileStream object. If file exists, returns reference to it.
OpenRead()	FileStream	Opens the file in read mode.
OpenWrite()	FileStream	Opens a file in write mode.
AppendText()	StreamWriter	Opens the file in append mode. If file does not exist, it is created. Equivalent to Stream-Writer(string, true).
CreateText()	StreamWriter	Opens a file for writing. If the file exists, its contents are overwritten. Equivalent to StreamWriter(string, false).
OpenText()	StreamReader	Opens the file in read mode. Equivalent to StreamReader(string).

Fig. 13.27 | Selected FileInfo Methods for Opening a File.

```
StreamWriter sw= new StreamWriter(fs);  // Create StreamWriter
sw.Write("With my crossbow\nI shot the Albatross. ");
sw.Close();                    // Close StreamWriter
// Now use fi to create a StreamReader
fs = fi.OpenRead();            // Open for reading
StreamReader sr = new StreamReader(fs);
while(( string l = sr.ReadLine())!= null)
{
    Console.WriteLine(l);      // --> With my crossbow
}                              // --> I shot the Albatross.
sr.Close();
fs.Close();
fi.Delete();                   // Delete temporary file
```

13.11 Summary

The demands of working with text have increased considerably from the days when it meant dealing with 7-bit ASCII or ANSII characters. Today, the Unicode standard defines the representation of more than 90,000 characters comprising the world's alphabets. We've seen that .NET fully embraces this standard with its 16-bit characters. In addition, it supports the concept of localization, which ensures that a machine's local culture information is taken into account when manipulating and representing data strings.

String handling is facilitated by a rich set of methods available through the String and StringBuilder classes. A variety of string comparison methods are available with options to include case and culture in the comparisons. The String.Format method is of particular note with its capacity to display dates and numbers in a wide range of standard and custom formats. String manipulation and concatenation can result in an inefficient use of memory. We saw how the `StringBuilder` class is an efficient alternative for basic string operations. Applications that require sophisticated pattern matching, parsing, and string extraction can use regular expressions in conjunction with the `Regex` class.

The `System.IO` namespace provides a number of classes for reading and writing data: The `FileStream` class is used to process raw bytes of data; `MemoryStream` and `Buffered-Stream` allow bytes to be written to memory or buffered; the `StreamReader` and `Stream-Writer` classes support the more traditional line-oriented I/O. Operations related to managing files and directories are available as methods on the `File`, `FileInfo`, `Directory`, and `DirectoryInfo` classes. These are used to create, copy, delete, and list files and directories.

13.12 Test Your Understanding

1. Which class encapsulates information about a specific culture?

2. Name two ways to access the default culture within an application.

3. Match each regular expression:

   a) `@"(\b[^\Wa-z0-9_][^\WA-Z0-9_]*\b)"`

   b) `@"(\b[^\Wa-z0-9_]+\b)"`

   c) `@"(\b[^\WA-Z0-9_]+\b)"`

   with the function it performs:

   a) Find all capitalized words.

   b) Find all lowercase words.

   c) Find all words with the initial letter capitalized.

4. When is it more advantageous to use the instance methods of `Regex` rather than the static ones?

5. Which string comparison method(s) is (are) used to implement this statement:

   ```
   if (myString == "Monday") bool sw = true;
   ```

6. Match each statement:

   a) `curdt.ToString("D")`

   b) `curdt.ToString("M")`

   c) `curdt.ToString("ddd MMM dd")`

   with its output:

   a) March 9

   b) Tuesday, March 9, 2004

   c) Tue Mar 09

7. Which of these objects is not created from an existing `FileStream`?

   a) `FileInfo`

   b) `StreamReader`

   c) `BufferedStream`

8. You can create a `FileStream` object with this statement:

```
FileStream fs = new FileStream(fname,
                    FileMode.OpenOrCreate,
                    FileAccess.Write,FileShare.None);
```

Which one of the following statements creates an identical `FileStream` using an existing `FileInfo` object, `fi`?

a) `fs = fi.OpenWrite();`

b) `fs = fi.Create();`

c) `fs = fi.CreateText();`

9.   Indicate whether the following comparisons are true or false:

a) `(string.Compare("Alpha","alpha") >0)`

b) `(string.Compare("Alpha","alpha",true) ==0)`

c) `(string.CompareOrdinal("Alpha","alpha")>0)`

d) `(string.Equals("alpha","Alpha"))`

14

Working with XML in .NET

14.1 Introduction

Extensible Markup Language (XML) plays a key role in the .NET universe. Configuration files that govern an application or Web page's behavior are deployed in XML; objects are stored or streamed across the Internet by serializing them into an XML representation; Web Services intercommunication is based on XML; and .NET methods support the interchange of data between an XML and relational data table format.

XML describes data as a combination of markup language and content that is analogous to the way HTML describes a Web page. Its flexibility permits it to easily represent flat, relational, or hierarchical data. To support one of its design goals—that it "should be human-legible and reasonably clear"[1]—it is represented in a text-only format. This gives it the significant advantage of being platform independent, which has made it the de facto standard for transmitting data over the Internet.

This chapter focuses on pure XML and the classes that reside in the System.Xml namespace hierarchy. It begins with basic background information on XML: how schemas are used to validate XML data and how style sheets are used to alter the way XML is displayed. The remaining sections present the .NET classes that are used to read, write, update, and search XML documents. If you are unfamiliar with .NET XML, you may surprised how quickly you become comfortable with reading and searching XML data. Extracting information from even a complex XML structure is refreshingly easy with the XPath query language—and far less tedious than the original search techniques that

---

1. W3C Extensible Markup Language (XML), 1.0 (Third Edition), http://www.w3.org/TR/REC-xml/

required traversing each node of an XML tree. In many ways, it is now as easy to work with XML as it is to work with relational data.

14.2 Working with XML

Being literate in one's spoken language is defined as having the basic ability to read and write that language. In XML, functional literacy embraces more than reading and writing XML data. In addition to the XML data document, there is an XML Schema document (.xsd) that is used to validate the content and structure of an XML document. If the XML data is to be displayed or transformed, one or more XML style sheets (.xsl) can be used to define the transformation. Thus, we can define our own form of XML literacy as the ability to do five things:

1. Create an XML file.

2. Read and query an XML file.

3. Create an XML Schema document.

4. Use an XML Schema document to validate XML data.

5. Create and use an XML style sheet to transform XML data.

The purpose of this section is to introduce XML concepts and terminology, as well as some .NET techniques for performing the preceding tasks. Of the five tasks, all are covered in this section, with the exception of reading and querying XML data, which is presented in later sections.

14.2.1 Using XML Serialization to Create XML Data

Serialization is a convenient way to store objects so they can later be deserialized into the original objects. If the natural state of your data allows it to be represented as objects, or if your application already has it represented as objects, XML serialization often offers a good choice for converting it into an XML format. However, there are some restrictions to keep in mind when applying XML serialization to a class:

- The class must contain a `public` default (parameterless) constructor.

- Only a `public` property or field can be serialized.

- A read-only property cannot be serialized.

- To serialize the objects in a custom collection class, the class must derive from the `System.Collections.CollectionBase` class and include an indexer. The easiest way to serialize multiple objects is usually to place them in a strongly typed array.

An Example Using the XmlSerializer Class

Figure 14.1 shows the XML file that we're going to use for further examples in this section. It was created by serializing instances of the class shown in Fig. 14.2.

In comparing Fig. 14.1 and 14.2, it should be obvious that the XML elements are a direct rendering of the public properties defined for the `movies` class. The only exceptional feature in the code is the `XmlElement` attribute, which will be discussed shortly.

To transform the class in Fig. 14.2 to the XML in Fig. 14.1, we follow the three steps shown in the code that follows. First, the objects to be serialized are created and stored in

```
<?xml version="1.0" standalone="yes"?>
   <films>
      <movies>
         <movie_ID>5</movie_ID>
         <movie_Title>Citizen Kane </movie_Title>
         <movie_Year>1941</movie_Year>
         <movie_DirectorID>Orson Welles</movie_DirectorID>
         <bestPicture>Y</bestPicture>
         <AFIRank>1</AFIRank>
      </movies>
      <movies>
         <movie_ID>6</movie_ID>
         <movie_Title>Casablanca </movie_Title>
         <movie_Year>1942</movie_Year>
         <movie_Director>Michael Curtiz</movie_Director>
         <bestPicture>Y</bestPicture>
         <AFIRank>1</AFIRank>
      </movies>
   </films>
```

Fig. 14.1 | Sample XML File.

```
using System.Xml;
using System.Xml.Serialization;
// other code here ...
public class movies
{
   public movies()  // Parameterless constructor is required
   {  }
   public movies(int ID, string title, string dir,string pic,
                 int yr, int movierank)
   {
      movieID = ID;
      movie_Director = dir;
      bestPicture = pic;
      rank = movierank;
      movie_Title = title;
      movie_Year = yr;
   }
   // Public properties that are serialized
   public int movieID
   {
      get { return mID; }
      set { mID = value; }
   }
   public string movie_Title
   {
      get { return mTitle; }
      set { mTitle = value; }
   }
```

Fig. 14.2 | Using XmlSerializer to Create an XML File. (Part 1 of 2.)

```
    public int movie_Year
    {
       get { return mYear; }
       set { mYear = value; }
    }
    public string movie_Director
    {
       get { return mDirector; }
       set { mDirector = value; }
    }
    public string bestPicture
    {
       get { return mbestPicture; }
       set { mbestPicture = value; }
    }
    [XmlElement("AFIRank")]
    public int rank
    {
       get { return mAFIRank; }
       set { mAFIRank = value; }
    }
    private int mID;
    private string mTitle;
    private int mYear;
    private string mDirector;
    private string mbestPicture;
    private int mAFIRank;
}
```

Fig. 14.2 | Using `XmlSerializer` to Create an XML File. (Part 2 of 2.)

an array. Second, an `XmlSerializer` object is created. Its constructor (one of many con-structor overloads) takes the object type it is serializing as the first parameter and an attribute as the second. The attribute enables us to assign "films" as the name of the root element in the XML output. The final step is to execute the `XmlSerializer.Serialize` method to send the serialized output to a selected stream—a file in this case.

```
// (1) Create array of objects to be serialized
movies[] films = {new movies(5,"Citizen Kane","Orson Welles",
                        "Y", 1941,1 ),
                    new movies(6,"Casablanca","Michael Curtiz",
                        "Y", 1942,2)};
// (2) Create serializer
//     This attribute is used to assign name to XML root element
XmlRootAttribute xRoot = new XmlRootAttribute();
   xRoot.ElementName = "films";
   xRoot.Namespace = "http://www.corecsharp.net";
   xRoot.IsNullable = true;
// Specify that an array of movies types is to be serialized
XmlSerializer xSerial = new XmlSerializer(typeof(movies[]),
                                    xRoot);
string filename=@"c:\oscarwinners.xml";
// (3) Stream to write XML into
TextWriter writer = new StreamWriter(filename);
xSerial.Serialize(writer,films);
```

Serialization Attributes

By default, the elements created from a class take the name of the property they represent. For example, the `movie_Title` property is serialized as a `<movie_Title>` element. However, there is a set of serialization attributes that can be used to override the default serialization results. Figure 14.2 includes an `XmlElement` attribute whose purpose is to assign a name to the XML element that is different than that of the corresponding property or field. In this case, the `rank` property name is replaced with `AFIRank` in the XML.

There are more than a dozen serialization attributes. Here are some other commonly used ones:

`XmlAttribute`	Is attached to a property or field and causes it to be rendered as an attribute within an element.
	Example: `XmlAttribute("movieID")]`
	Result: `<movies movieID="5">`
`XmlIgnore`	Causes the field or property to be excluded from the XML.
`XmlText`	Causes the value of the field or property to be rendered as text. No elements are created for the member name.
	Example: `[XmlText]`
	`public string movie_Title{`
	Result: `<movies movieID="5">Citizen Kane`

14.2.2 XML Schema Definition (XSD)

The XML Schema Definition document is an XML file that is used to validate the contents of another XML document. The schema is essentially a template that defines in detail what is permitted in an associated XML document. Its role is similar to that of the BNF (Backus-Naur Form) notation that defines a language's syntax for a compiler.

.NET provides several ways (others are included in Chapter 15, "ADO.NET") to create a schema from an XML data document. One of the easiest ways is to use the XML Schema Definition tool (`Xsd.exe`). Simply run it from a command line and specify the XML file for which it is to produce a schema:

```
C:/ xsd.exe  oscarwinners.xml
```

The output, `oscarwinners.xsd`, is shown in Fig. 14.3.

As should be evident from this small sample, the XML Schema language has a rather complex syntax. Those interested in all of its details can find them at the URL shown in the first line of the schema. For those with a more casual interest, the most important thing to note is that the heart of the document is a description of the valid types that may be contained in the XML data that the schema describes. In addition to the `string` and `int` types shown here, other supported types include `boolean`, `double`, `float`, `dateTime`, and `hexBinary`.

The types specified in the schema are designated as simple or complex. The `complextype` element defines any node that has children or an attribute; the `simpletype` has no attribute or child. You'll encounter many schemas where the simple types are defined at the beginning of the schema, and complex types are later defined as a combination of simple types.

```
<xs:schema id="films" xmlns=""
      xmlns:xs=http://www.w3.org/2001/XMLSchema
      xmlns:msdata="urn:schemas-microsoft-com:xml-msdata">
  <xs:element name="films" msdata:IsDataSet="true">
    <xs:complexType>
      <xs:choice minOccurs="0" maxOccurs="unbounded">
        <xs:element name="movies">
          <xs:complexType>
            <xs:sequence>
              <xs:element name="movie_ID" type="xs:int"
                    minOccurs="0" />
              <xs:element name="movie_Title" type="xs:string"
                    minOccurs="0" />
              <xs:element name="movie_Year" type="xs:int"
                    minOccurs="0" />
              <xs:element name="movie_Director" type="xs:string"
                    minOccurs="0" />
              <xs:element name="bestPicture" type="xs:string"
                    minOccurs="0" />
              <xs:element name="AFIRank" type="xs:int"
                    minOccurs="0"
              />
            </xs:sequence>
          </xs:complexType>
        </xs:element>
      </xs:choice>
    </xs:complexType>
  </xs:element>
</xs:schema>
```

Fig. 14.3 | XML Schema to Apply Against XML in Fig. 14.1.

XML Schema Validation

A schema is used by a validator to check an XML document for conformance to the layout and content defined by the schema. .NET implements validation as a read and check process. As a class iterates through each node in an XML tree, the node is validated. Figure 14.4 illustrates how the XmlValidatingReader class performs this operation.

First, an XmlTextReader is created to stream through the nodes in the data document. It is passed as an argument to the constructor for the XmlValidatingReader. Then, the ValidationType property is set to indicate a schema will be used for validation. This property can also be set to XDR or DTD to support older validation schemas.

The next step is to add the schema that will be used for validating to the reader's schema collection. Finally, the XmlValidatingReader is used to read the stream of XML nodes. Exception handling is used to display any validation error that occurs.

Note that the XmlValidatingReader class implements the XmlReader class underneath. We'll demonstrate using XmlReader to perform validation in the next section. In fact, in most cases, XmlReader (.NET 2.0 implmentation) now makes XmlValidating-Reader obsolete.

```
private static bool ValidateSchema(string xml, string xsd)
{
   // Parameters: XML document and schemas
   // (1) Create a validating reader
   XmlTextReader tr = new XmlTextReader(xml");
   XmlValidatingReader xvr = new XmlValidatingReader(tr);
   // (2) Indicate schema validation
   xvr.ValidationType= ValidationType.Schema;
   // (3) Add schema to be used for validation
   xvr.Schemas.Add(null, xsd);
   try
   {
      Console.WriteLine("Validating: ");
      // Loop through all elements in XML document
      while(xvr.Read())
      {
         Console.Write(".");
      }
   }catch (Exception ex)
   { Console.WriteLine( "\n{0}",ex.Message); return false;}
   return true;
}
```

Fig. 14.4 | XML Schema Validation.

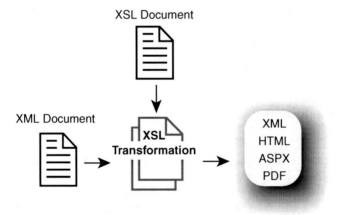

Fig. 14.5 | Publishing documents with XSLT.

14.2.3 Using an XML Style Sheet

A style sheet is a document that describes how to transform raw XML data into a different format. The mechanism that performs the transformation is referred to as an XSLT (Extensible Style Language Transformation) processor. Figure 14.5 illustrates the process: The XSLT processor takes as input the XML document to be transformed and the XSL document that defines the transformation to be applied. This approach permits output to be generated dynamically in a variety of formats. These include XML, HTML or ASPX for a Web page, and a PDF document.

The XslTransform Class

The .NET version of the XSLT processor is the XslTransform class found in the System
.Xml.Xsl namespace. To demonstrate its use, we'll transform our XML movie data into
an HTML file for display by a browser (see Fig. 14.6).

Before the XslTransform class can be applied, an XSLT style sheet that describes the
transformation must be created. Figure 14.7 contains the style sheet that will be used. As
you can see, it is a mixture of HTML markup, XSL elements, and XSL commands that
displays rows of movie information with three columns. The XSL elements and functions
are the key to the transformation. When the XSL style sheet is processed, the XSL elements
are replaced with the data from the original XML document.

Movie Title	Movie Year	AFI Rank	Director
Casablanca	1942	2	Michael Curtiz
Citizen Kane	1941	1	Orson Welles

Fig. 14.6 | XML data is transformed into this HTML output.

```
<?xml version="1.0"?>
<xsl:stylesheet version="1.0"
    xmlns:xsl="http://www.w3.org/1999/XSL/Transform">
  <xsl:template match="/">
   <HTML>
      <TITLE>Movies</TITLE>
      <Table border="0" padding="0" cellspacing="1">
      <THEAD>
        <TH>Movie Title</TH>
        <TH>Movie Year </TH>
        <TH>AFI Rank    </TH>
        <TH>Director    </TH>
      </THEAD>
      <xsl:for-each select="//movies">
         <xsl:sort select="movie_Title" />
         <tr>
           <td><xsl:value-of select="movie_Title"/> </td>
           <td align="center"><xsl:value-of select=
               "movie_Year"/></td>
           <td align="center"><xsl:value-of select=
               "AFIRank" /></td>
         <td><xsl:value-of select="movie_Director" /></td>
         </tr>
      </xsl:for-each>
      </Table>
   </HTML>
  </xsl:template>
</xsl:stylesheet>
```

Fig. 14.7 | XML Style Sheet to Create HTML Output.

Some points of interest:

- The URL in the namespace of the `<xsl:stylesheet>` element must be exactly as shown here.

- The `match` attribute is set to an XPath query that indicates which elements in the XML file are to be converted. Setting `match="/"` selects all elements.

- The `for-each` construct loops through a group of selected nodes specified by an XPath expression following the `select` attribute. XPath is discussed in Section 14.4, "Using XPath to Search XML."

- The `value-of` function extracts a selected value from the XML document and inserts it into the output.

- The `<xsl:sort>` element is used to sort the incoming data and is used in conjunction with the `for-each` construct. Here is its syntax:

```
select = XPath expression
order = {"ascending" | "descending"}
data-type = {"text" | "number"}
case-order = {"upper-first" | "lower-first"}
```

After a style sheet is created, using it to transform a document is a breeze. As shown by the following code, applying the `XslTransform` class is straightforward. After creating an instance of it, you use its `Load` method to specify the file containing the style sheet. The `XslTransform.Transform` method performs the transformation. This method has several overloads. The version used here requires an `XpathDocument` object that represents the XML document, as a parameter, and an `XmlWriter` parameter that designates where the output is written—an HTML file in this case.

```
// Transform XML into HTML and store in movies.htm
XmlWriter writer = new
      XmlTextWriter("c:\\movies.htm",Encoding.UTF8);
XslTransform xslt = new XslTransform();
XPathDocument xpd = new
      XPathDocument("c:\\oscarwinners.xml");
xslt.Load("movies.xsl");
xslt.Transform(xpd, null, writer,null);
```

Core Note 14.1

You can link a style sheet to an XML document by placing an href *statement in the XML document on the line preceding the root element definition:*

```
<?xml:stylesheet type="text/xsl" href="movies.xsl" ?>
```

If a document is linked to a style sheet that converts XML to HTML, most browsers automatically perform the transformation and display the HTML. This can be a quick way to perform trial-and-error testing when developing a style sheet.

It takes only a small leap from this simple XSLT example to appreciate the potential of being able to transform XML documents dynamically. It is a natural area of growth for Web Services and Web pages that now on demand accept input in one format, transform it, and serve the output up in a different format.

14.3 Techniques for Reading XML Data

XML can be represented in two basic ways: as the familiar external document containing embedded data, or as an in-memory tree structure know as a Document Object Model (DOM). In the former case, XML can be read in a forward-only manner as a stream of tokens representing the file's content. The object that performs the reading stays connected to the data source during the read operations. The XmlReader and XmlTextReader shown in Fig. 14.8 operate in this manner.

More options are available for processing the DOM because it is stored in memory and can be traversed randomly. For simply reading a tree, the XmlNodeReader class offers an efficient way to traverse a tree in a forward, read-only manner. Other more sophisticated approaches that also permit tree modification are covered later in this section.

14.3.1 XmlReader Class

XmlReader is an abstract class possessing methods and properties that enable an application to pull data from an XML file one node at a time in a forward-only, read-only manner. A depth-first search is performed, beginning with the root node in the document. Nodes are inspected using the Name, NodeType, and Value properties.

XmlReader serves as a base class for the concrete classes XmlTextReader and XmlNodeReader. As an abstract class, XmlReader cannot be directly instantiated; however, it has a static Create method that can return an instance of the XmlReader class. This feature became available with the release of .NET Framework 2.0 and is recommended over the XmlTextReader class for reading XML streams.

Figure 14.9 illustrates how to create an XmlReader object and use it to read the contents of a short XML document file. The code is also useful for illustrating how .NET converts the content of the file into a stream of node objects. It's important to understand the concept of nodes because an XML or HTML document is defined (by the official W3C Document Object Model (DOM) specification[2]) as a hierarchy of node objects.

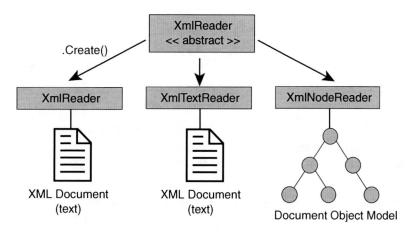

Fig. 14.8 | Classes to read XML data.

---

2. W3C Document Object Model (DOM) Level 3 Core Specification, April, 2004,
    http://www.w3.org/TR/2004/REC-DOM-Level-3-Core-20040407/core.html

```
// Include these namespaces:
// using System.Xml;
// using System.Xml.XPath;
public void ShowNodes()
{
    //(1) Settings object enables/disables features on XmlReader
    XmlReaderSettings settings = new XmlReaderSettings();
    settings.ConformanceLevel = ConformanceLevel.Fragment;
    settings.IgnoreWhitespace = true;
    try
    {
        //(2) Create XmlReader object
        XmlReader rdr = XmlReader.Create("c:\\oscarsshort.xml",
                                         settings);
        while (rdr.Read())
        {
            Format(rdr);
        }
        rdr.Close();
    }
    catch (Exception e)
    {
        Console.WriteLine ("Exception: {0}", e.ToString());
    }
}
private static void Format(XmlTextReader reader)
{
    //(3) Print Current node properties
    Console.Write( reader.NodeType+ "<" + reader.Name + ">" +
                   reader.Value);
    Console.WriteLine();
}
```

Fig. 14.9 │ Using XmlReader to Read an XML Document.

Before creating the XmlReader, the code first creates an XmlReaderSettings object. This object sets features that define how the XmlReader object processes the input stream. For example, the ConformanceLevel property specifies how the input is checked. The statement

```
settings.ConformanceLevel = ConformanceLevel.Fragment;
```

specifies that the input must conform to the standards that define an XML 1.0 *document fragment*—an XML document that does not necessarily have a root node.

This object and the name of the XML document file are then passed to the Create method that returns an XmlReader instance:

```
XmlReader rdr = XmlReader.Create("c:\\oscarsshort.xml,settings);
```

The file's content is read in a node at a time by the XmlReader.Read method, which prints the NodeType, Name, and Value of each node. Figure 14.10 shows the input file and a portion of the generated output. Line numbers have been added so that an input line and its corresponding node information can be compared.

Input File: oscarsshort.xml

```
(1)  <?xml version="1.0" standalone="yes"?>
(2)  <films>
(3)    <movies>
(4)      <!-- Selected by AFI as best movie -->
(5)      <movie_ID>5</movie_ID>
(6)      <![CDATA[<a href="http://www.imdb.com/tt0467/">Kane</a>]]>
(7)      <movie_Title>Citizen Kane </movie_Title>
(8)      <movie_Year>1941</movie_Year>
(9)      <movie_Director>Orson Welles</movie_Director>
(10)     <bestPicture>Y</bestPicture>
(11)   </movies>
(12) </films>
```

Program Output (NodeType, <Name>, Value):

```
(1)  XmlDeclaration<xml>version="1.0" standalone="yes"
(2)  Element<films>
(3)  Element<movies>
(4)  Comment<> Selected by AFI as best movie
(5)  Element<movie_ID>
        Text<>5
     EndElement<movie_ID>
(6)  CDATA<><a href="http://www.imdb.com/tt0467/">Kane</a>
(7)  Element<movie_Title>
        Text<>Citizen Kane
     EndElement<movie_Title>
        ...
(12) EndElement<films>
```

Fig. 14.10 | XML Input and Corresponding Nodes.

Programs that use XmlReader typically implement a logic pattern that consists of an outer loop that reads nodes and an inner switch statement that identifies the node using an XMLNodeType enumeration. The logic to process the node information is handled in the case blocks:

```
while (reader.Read())
{
   switch (reader.NodeType)
   {
      case XmlNodeType.Element:
      // Attributes are contained in elements
         while(reader.MoveToNextAttribute())
         {
            Console.WriteLine(reader.Name+reader.Value);
         }
      break;
      case XmlNodeType.Text:
      // Process ..
      break;
      case XmlNodeType.EndElement
      // Process ..
      break;
   }
}
```

The Element, Text, and Attribute nodes mark most of the data content in an XML document. Note that the Attribute node is regarded as metadata attached to an element and is the only one not exposed directly by the XmlReader.Read method. As shown in the preceding code segment, the attributes in an Element can be accessed using the MoveTo-NextAttribute method.

The table in Fig. 14.11 summarizes the node types. It is worth noting that these types are not an arbitrary .NET implementation. With the exception of Whitespace and XmlDeclaration, they conform to the DOM Structure Model recommendation.

Option	Description and Use

Attribute	An attribute or value contained within an element. Example:
	
	`<movie_title genre="comedy">The Lady Eve`
	`</movie_title>`
	
	Attribute is genre="comedy". Attributes must be located within an element.
	
	`if(reader.NodeType==XmlNodeType.Element){`
	`  while(reader.MoveToNextAttribute())`
	`  {`
	`    Console.WriteLine(reader.Name+reader.Value);`
	`  }`

CData	Designates that the element is not to be parsed. Markup characters are treated as text:
	
	`![CDATA[<ELEMENT>`
	`<a href="http://www.imdb.com">movies</a>`
	`</ELEMENT>]]>`

Comment	To make a comment:
	
	`<!-- comment -->`
	
	To have comments ignored:
	
	`XmlReaderSettings.IgnoreComment = true;`

Document	A document root object that provides access to the entire XML document.
DocumentFragment	A document fragment. This is a node or subtree with a document. It provides a way to work with part of a document.
DocumentType	Document type declaration indicated by <!DOCTYPE ... >. Can refer to an external Document Type Definition (DTD) file or be an inline block containing Entity and Notation declarations.
Element	An XML element. Designated by the < > brackets: `<movie_Title>`
EndElement	An XML end element tag. Marks the end of an element: `</movie_Title>`
EndEntity	End of an Entity declaration.

Fig. 14.11 | XmlNodeType Enumeration. (Part 1 of 2.)

Option	Description and Use

Entity	Defines text or a resource to replace the entity name in the XML. An entity is defined as a child of a document type node:
	
	`<!DOCTYPE movies[`
	`    <!ENTITY leadingactress "stanwyck">`
	`]>`
	
	XML would then reference this as:
	
	`<actress>&leadingactress;</actress>`

EntityReference	A reference to the entity. In the preceding example, `&leadingactress;` is an `EntityReference`.
Notation	A notation that is declared within a `DocumentType` declaration. Primary use is to pass information to the XML processor. Example: `<!NOTATION homepage="www.sci.com" !>`
ProcessingInstruction	Useful for providing information about how the data was generated or how to process it. Example: `<?pi1 Requires IE 5.0 and above ?>`
Text	The text content of a node.
Whitespace	Whitespace refers to formatting characters such as tabs, line feeds, returns, and spaces that exist between the markup and affect the layout of a document.
XmlDeclaration	The first node in the document. It provides version information. `<?xml version="1.0" standalone="yes"?>`

Fig. 14.11 | XmlNodeType Enumeration. (Part 2 of 2.)

14.3.2 XmlNodeReader Class

The XmlNodeReader is another forward-only reader that processes XML as a stream of nodes. It differs from the XmlReader class in two significant ways:

- It processes nodes from an in-memory DOM tree structure rather than a text file.

- It can begin reading at any subtree node in the structure—not just at the root node (beginning of the document).

In Figure 14.12, an XmlNodeReader object is used to list the movie title and year from the XML-formatted movies database. The code contains an interesting twist: The XmlNodeReader object is not used directly, but instead is passed as a parameter to the constructor of an XmlReader object. The object serves as a wrapper that performs the actual reading. This approach has the advantage of allowing the XmlSettings values to be assigned to the reader.

The parameter passed to the XmlNodeReader constructor determines the first node in the tree to be read. When the entire document is passed—as in this example—reading

```
private void ListMovies()
{
    // (1) Specify XML file to be loaded as a DOM
    XmlDocument doc = new XmlDocument();
    doc.Load("c:\\oscarwinners.xml");
    // (2) Settings for use with XmlNodeReader object
    XmlReaderSettings settings = new XmlReaderSettings();
    settings.ConformanceLevel = ConformanceLevel.Fragment;
    settings.IgnoreWhitespace = true;
    settings.IgnoreComments = true;
    // (3) Create a nodereader object
    XmlNodeReader noderdr = new XmlNodeReader(doc);
    // (4) Create an XmlReader as a wrapper around node reader
    XmlReader reader = XmlReader.Create(noderdr, settings);
    while (reader.Read())
    {
        if(reader.NodeType==XmlNodeType.Element){
            if (reader.Name == "movie_Title")
            {
                reader.Read();  // next node is text for title
                Console.Write(reader.Value);    // Movie Title
            }
            if (reader.Name == "movie_Year")
            {
                reader.Read();  // next node is text for year
                Console.WriteLine(reader.Value); // year
            }
        }
    }
}
```

Fig. 14.12 | Using XmlNodeReader to Read an XML Document.

begins with the top node in the tree. To select a specific node, use the XmlDocument .SelectSingleNode method as illustrated in this segment:

```
XmlDocument doc = new XmlDocument();
doc.Load("c:\\oscarwinners.xml");  // Build tree in memory
XmlNodeReader noderdr = new
        XmlNodeReader(doc.SelectSingleNode("films/movies[2]"));
```

Refer to Fig. 14.1 and you can see that this selects the second movies element group, which contains information on *Casablanca*.

If your application requires read-only access to XML data and the capability to read selected subtrees, the XmlNodeReader is an efficient solution. When updating, writing, and searching become requirements, a more sophisticated approach is required; we'll look at those techniques later in this section.

14.3.3 The XmlReaderSettings Class

A significant advantage of using an XmlReader object—directly or as a wrapper—is the presence of the XmlReaderSettings class as a way to define the behavior of the XmlReader object. Its most useful properties specify which node types in the input stream are ignored and whether XML validation is performed. The table in Fig. 14.13 lists the XmlReader-Settings properties.

Property	Default Value	Description
CheckCharacters	true	Indicates whether characters and XML names are checked for illegal XML characters. An exception is thrown if one is encountered.
CloseInput	false	An XmlReader object may be created by passing a stream to it. This property indicates whether the stream is closed when the reader object is closed.
ConformanceLevel	Document	Indicates whether the XML should conform to the standards for a Document or DocumentFragment.
DtdValidate	false	Indicates whether to perform DTD validation.
IgnoreComments IgnoreInlineSchema IgnoreProcessingInstructions IgnoreSchemaLocation IgnoreValidationWarnings IgnoreWhitespace	false true false true true false	Specify whether a particular node type is processed or ignored by the XmlReader.Read method.
LineNumberOffset LinePositionOffset	0 0	XmlReader numbers lines in the XML document beginning with 0. Set this property to change the beginning line number and line position values.
Schemas	is empty	Contains the XmlSchemaSet to be used for XML Schema Definition Language (XSD) validation.
XsdValidate	false	Indicates whether XSD validation is performed.

Fig. 14.13 | Properties of the XmlReaderSettings Class.

14.3.4 Using an XML Schema to Validate XML Data

The final two properties listed in Fig. 14.13—Schemas and XsdValidate—are used to validate XML data against a schema. Recall that a schema is a template that describes the permissible content in an XML file or stream. Validation can be (should be) used to ensure that data being read conforms to the rules of the schema. To request validation, you must add the validating schema to the XmlSchemaSet collection of the Schemas property; next, set XsdValidate to true; and finally, define an event handler to be called if a validation error occurs. The following code fragment shows the code used with the schema and XML data in Fig. 14.1 and 14.3:

```
XmlReaderSettings settings = new XmlReaderSettings();
// (1) Specify schema to be used for validation
settings.Schemas.Add(null,"c:\\oscarwinners.xsd");
```

```
// (2) Must set this to true
settings.XsdValidate = true;
// (3) Delegate to handle validation error event
settings.ValidationEventHandler += new
    System.Xml.Schema.ValidationEventHandler(SchemaValidation);
// (4) Create reader and pass settings to it
XmlReader rdr = XmlReader.Create("c:\\oscarwinners.xml",
    settings);
// process XML data ...
...
// Method to handle errors detected during schema validation
private void SchemaValidation(object sender, System.Xml.Schema
.ValidationEventArgs e)
{
    MessageBox.Show(e.Message);
}
```

Note that a detected error does not stop processing. This means that all the XML data can be checked in one pass without restarting the program.

14.3.5 Options for Reading XML Data

All the preceding examples that read XML data share two characteristics: data is read a node at a time, and a node's value is extracted as a string using the XmlReader.Value property. This keeps things simple, but ignores the underlying XML data. For example, XML often contains numeric data or data that is the product of serializing a class. Both cases can be handled more efficiently using other XmlReader methods.

XmlReader has a suite of ReadValueAsxxx methods that can read the contents of a node in its native form. These include ReadValueAsBoolean, ReadValueAsDateTime, ReadValueAsDecimal, ReadValueAsDouble, ReadValueAsInt32, ReadValueAsInt64, and ReadValueAsSingle. Here's an example:

```
int age;
if(reader.Name == "Age") age= reader.ReadValueAsInt32();
```

XML that corresponds to the public properties or fields of a class can be read directly into an instance of the class with the ReadAsObject method. This fragment reads the XML data shown in Fig. 14.1 into an instance of the movies class. Note that the name of the field or property must match an element name in the XML data.

```
// Deserialize XML into a movies object
if (rdr.NodeType == XmlNodeType.Element && rdr.Name == "movies")
{
    movies m = (movies)rdr.ReadAsObject(typeof(movies));
    // Do something with object
}
// XML data is read directly into this class
public class movies
{
    public int movie_ID;
    public string movie_Title;
    public string movie_Year;
    private string director;
```

```
        public string bestPicture;
        public string movie_Director
        {
            set { director = value; }
            get { return (director); }
        }
    }
```

14.4 Techniques for Writing XML Data

In many cases, the easiest way to present data in an XML format is to use .NET serialization. As demonstrated in Section 14.1, if the data is in a collection class, it can be serialized using the XmlSerializer class; as we see in the next chapter, if it's in a DataSet, the DataSet.WriteXml method can be applied. The advantages of serialization are that it is easy to use, generates well-formed XML, and is symmetrical—the XML that is written can be read back to create the original data objects.

For cases where serialization is not an option—a comma delimited file, for instance—or where more control over the XML layout is needed, the XmlWriter class is the best .NET solution.

Writing XML with the XmlWriter Class

The XmlWriter class offers precise control over each character written to an XML stream or file. However, this flexibility does require a general knowledge of XML and can be tedious to code, because a distinct Writexxx method is used to generate each node type. On the positive side, it offers several compliance checking features, and the ability to write CLR typed data directly to the XML stream:

- XmlWriterSettings.CheckCharacters property configures the XmlWriter to check for illegal characters in text nodes and XML names, as well as check the validity of XML names. An exception is thrown if an invalid character is detected.

- XmlWriterSettings.ConformanceLevel property configures the XmlWriter to guarantee that the stream complies with the conformance level that is specified. For example, the XML may be set to conform to a document or document fragment.

- XmlWriter.WriteValue method is used to write data to the XML stream as a CLR type (int, double, and so on) without having to first convert it to a string.

Figure 14.14 illustrates the basic principles involved in using the XmlWriter class. Not surprisingly, there are a lot of similarities to the closely related XmlReader class. Both use the Create method to create an object instance, and both have constructor overloads that accept a settings object—XmlWriterSettings, in this case—to define the behavior of the reader or writer. The most important of these setting properties is the conformance level that specifies either document or fragment (a subtree) conformance.

A series of self-describing methods, which support all the node types listed in Fig. 14.11, generate the XML. Note that exception handling should always be enabled to trap any attempt to write an invalid name or character.

Before leaving the topic of XML writing, note that .NET also provides XmlText-Writer and XmlNodeWriter classes as concrete implementations of the abstract XmlWriter

```
private void WriteMovie()
{
    string[,] movieList = { { "Annie Hall", "Woody Allen" },
                            { "Lawrence of Arabia", "David Lean" } };
    // (1) Define settings to govern writer actions
    XmlWriterSettings settings = new XmlWriterSettings();
    settings.Indent = true;
    settings.IndentChars = ("    ");
    settings.ConformanceLevel = ConformanceLevel.Document;
    settings.CloseOutput = false;
    settings.OmitXmlDeclaration = false;
    // (2) Create XmlWriter object
    XmlWriter writer = XmlWriter.Create("c:\\mymovies.xml", settings);
    writer.WriteStartDocument();
    writer.WriteComment("Output from xmlwriter class");
    writer.WriteStartElement("films");
    for (int i = 0; i <= movieList.GetUpperBound(0) ; i++)
    {
        try
        {
            writer.WriteStartElement("movie");
            writer.WriteElementString("Title", movieList[i, 0]);
            writer.WriteElementString("Director", movieList[i, 1]);
            writer.WriteStartElement("Movie_ID");
            writer.WriteValue(i); // No need to convert to string
            writer.WriteEndElement();
            writer.WriteEndElement();
        }
        catch (Exception ex)
        {
            MessageBox.Show(ex.Message);
        }
    }
    writer.WriteEndElement();
    writer.Flush();  // Flush any remaining content to XML stream
    writer.Close();
    /*
        Output:
        <?xml version="1.0" encoding="utf-8"?>
        <!--Output from xmlwriter class-->
        <films>
            <movie>
                <Title>Annie Hall</Title>
                <Director>Woody Allen</Director>
                <Movie_ID>0</Movie_ID>
            </movie>
            <movie>
                <Title>Lawrence of Arabia</Title>
                <Director>David Lean</Director>
                <Movie_ID>1</Movie_ID>
            </movie>
        </films>
    */
}
```

Fig. 14.14 | Write XML Using XmlWriter Class.

class. The former does not offer any significant advantages over the XmlWriter. The node writer is a bit more useful. It creates a DOM tree in memory that can be processed using the many classes and methods designed for that task. Refer to .NET documentation for XmlNodeWriter details.

14.5 Using XPath to Search XML

A significant benefit of representing XML in a tree model—as opposed to a data stream—is the capability to query and locate the tree's content using XML Path Language (XPath). This technique is similar to using a SQL command on relational data. An XPath expression (query) is created and passed to an engine that evaluates it. The expression is parsed and executed against a data store. The returned value(s) may be a set of nodes or a scalar value.

XPath is a formal query language defined by the XML Path Language 2.0 specification (www.w3.org/TR/xpath). Syntactically, its most commonly used expressions resemble a file system path and may represent either the absolute or relative position of nodes in the tree.

In the .NET Framework, XPath evaluation is exposed through the XPathNavigator abstract class. The navigator is an XPath processor that works on top of any XML data source that exposes the IXPathNavigable interface. The most important member of this interface is the CreateNavigator method, which returns an XPathNavigator object. Figure 14.15 shows three classes that implement this interface. Of these, XmlDocument and XmlDataDocument are members of the System.Xml namespace; XPathDocument (as well as the XmlNavigator class) resides in the System.Xml.XPath namespace.

- XmlDocument. Implements the W3C Document Object Model (DOM) and supports XPath queries, navigation, and editing.

- XmlDataDocument. In addition to the features it inherits from XmlDocument, it provides the capability to map XML data to a DataSet. Any changes to the DataSet are reflected in the XML tree and vice versa.

- XPathDocument. This class is optimized to perform XPath queries and represents XML in a tree of read-only nodes that is more streamlined than the DOM.

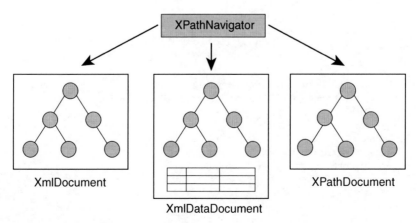

Fig. 14.15 | XML classes that support XPath navigation.

14.5.1 Constructing XPath Queries

Queries can be executed against each of these classes using either an XPathNavigator object or the SelectNodes method implemented by each class. Generic code looks like this:

```
// XPATHEXPRESSION is the XPath query applied to the data
// (1) Return a list of nodes
XmlDocument doc = new XmlDocument();
doc.Load("movies.xml");
XmlNodeList selection = doc.SelectNodes(XPATHEXPRESSION);
// (2) Create a navigator and execute the query
XPathNavigator nav = doc.CreateNavigator();
XPathNodeIterator iterator = nav.Select(XPATHEXPRESSION);
```

The XpathNodeIterator class encapsulates a list of nodes and provides a way to iterate over the list.

As with regular expressions (refer to Chapter 13, "C# Text Manipulation and File I/O"), an XPath query has its own syntax and operators that must be mastered in order to efficiently query an XML document. To demonstrate some of the fundamental XPath operators, we'll create queries against the data in Fig. 14.16.

The table in Fig. 14.17 summarizes commonly used XPath operators and provides an example of using each.

Note that the filter operator permits nodes to be selected by their content. There are a number of functions and operators that can be used to specify the matching criteria. The table in Fig. 14.18 lists some of these.

Refer to the XPath standard (http://www.w3.org/TR/xpath) for a comprehensive list of operators and functions.

Let's now look at examples of using XPath queries to search, delete, and add data to an XML tree. Our source XML file is shown in Fig. 14.16. For demonstration purposes, examples are included that represent the XML data as an XmlDocument, XPathDocument, and XmlDataDocument.

```
<films>
  <directors>
    <director_id>54</director_id>
    <first_name>Martin</first_name>
    <last_name>Scorsese</last_name>
    <movies>
      <movie_ID>30</movie_ID>
      <movie_Title>Taxi Driver</movie_Title>
      <movie_DirectorID>54</movie_DirectorID>
      <movie_Year>1976</movie_Year>
    </movies>
    <movies>
      <movie_ID>28</movie_ID>
      <movie_Title>Raging Bull </movie_Title>
      <movie_DirectorID>54</movie_DirectorID>
      <movie_Year>1980</movie_Year>
    </movies>
  </directors>
</films>
```

Fig. 14.16 | XML Representation of Directors/Movies Relationship.

Operator	Description
Child operator (/)	References the root of the XML document, where the expression begins searching. The following expression returns the last_name node for each director in the table: `/films/directors/last_name`

Recursive descendant operator (//)	This operator indicates that the search should include descendants along the specified path. The following all return the same set of last_name nodes. The difference is that the first begins searching at the root, and second at each directors node:
	
	`//last_name`
	`//directors//last_name`

Wildcard operator (*)	Returns all nodes below the specified path location. The following returns all nodes that are descendants of the movies node: `//movies/*`
Current operator (.)	Refers to the currently selected node in the tree, when navigating through a tree node-by-node. It effectively becomes the root node when the operator is applied. In this example, if the current node is a directors node, this will find any last_name child nodes: `.//last_name`
Parent operator (..)	Used to represent the node that is the parent of the current node. If the current node were a movies node, this would use the directors node as the start of the path: `../last_name`
Attribute operator (@)	Returns any attributes specified. The following example would return the movie's runtime assuming there were attributes such as `<movie_ID time="98">` included in the XML. `//movies//@time`

Filter operator ([ ])	Allows nodes to be filtered based on a matching criteria. The following example is used to retrieve all movie titles directed by Martin Scorsese:
	
	`//directors[last_name='Scorsese']`
	`    /movies/movie_Title`

Collection operator ([ ])	Uses brackets just as the filter, but specifies a node based on an ordinal value. Is used to distinguish among nodes with the same name. This example returns the node for the second movie, *Raging Bull*: `//movies[2]` (Index is not 0 based.)
Union operator (|)	Returns the union of nodes found on specified paths. This example returns the first and last name of each director: `//last_name	//first_name`

Fig. 14.17 | XPath Operators.

Function/Operator	Description
and, or	Logical operators.
Example: "directors[last_name= 'Scorsese' and first_name= 'Martin']"	
position( )	Selects node(s) at specified position.
Example: "//movies[position()=2]"	
contains(node,string)	Matches if node value contains specified string.
Example: "//movies[contains(movie_Title,'Tax')]"	
starts-with(node,string)	Matches if node value begins with specified string.
Example: "//movies[starts-with(movie_Title,'A')]"	
substring-after(string,string)	Extracts substring from the first string that follows occurrence of second string.
Example: "//movies[substring-after('The Graduate','The ')='Graduate']"	
substring(string, pos,length)	Extracts substring from node value.
Example: "//movies[substring(movie_Title,2,1)='a']"	

Fig. 14.18 | Functions and Operators used to Create an XPath Filter.

14.5.2 XmlDocument and XPath

The expression in this example extracts the set of last_name nodes. It then prints the associated text. Note that underneath, SelectNodes uses a navigator to evaluate the expression.

```
string exp = "/films/directors/last_name";
XmlDocument doc = new XmlDocument();
doc.Load("directormovies.xml");  // Build DOM tree
XmlNodeList directors = doc.SelectNodes(exp);
foreach(XmlNode n in directors)
    Console.WriteLine(n.InnerText);  // Last name or director
```

The XmlNode.InnerText property concatenates the values of child nodes and displays them as a text string. This is a convenient way to display tree contents during application testing.

14.5.3 XPathDocument and XPath

For applications that only need to query an XML document, the XPathDocument is the recommended class. It is free of the overhead required for updating a tree and runs 20 to 30 percent faster than XmlDocument. In addition, it can be created using an XmlReader to load all or part of a document into it. This is done by creating the reader, positioning it to a desired subtree, and then passing it to the XPathDocument constructor. In this example, the XmlReader is positioned at the root node, so the entire tree is read in:

```
string exp = "/films/directors/last_name";
// Create method was added with .NET 2.0
XmlReader rdr = XmlReader.Create("c:\\directormovies.xml");
// Pass XmlReader to the constructor
```

```
xDoc = new XPathDocument(rdr);
XPathNavigator nav= xDoc.CreateNavigator();
XPathNodeIterator iterator;
iterator = nav.Select(exp);
// List last name of each director
while (iterator.MoveNext())
    Console.WriteLine(iterator.Current.Value);
// Now, list only movies for Martin Scorsese
string exp2 =
    "//directors[last_name='Scorsese']/movies/movie_Title";
iterator = nav.Select(exp2);
while (iterator.MoveNext())
    Console.WriteLine(iterator.Current.Value);
```

Core Note 14.2

Unlike the SelectNodes method, the navigator's Select method accepts XPath expressions as both plain text and precompiled objects. The following statements demonstrate how a compiled expression could be used in the preceding example:

```
string exp = "/films/directors/last_name";
// use XmlNavigator to create XPathExpression object
XPathExpression compExp = nav.Compile(exp);
iterator = nav.Select(compExp);
```

Compiling an expression improves performance when the expression (query) is used more than once.

14.5.4 XmlDataDocument and XPath

The XmlDataDocument class allows you to take a DataSet (an object containing rows of data) and create a replica of it as a tree structure. The tree not only represents the DatSet, but is synchronized with it. This means that changes made to the DOM or DataSet are automatically reflected in the other.

Because XmlDataDocument is derived from XmlDocument, it supports the basic methods and properties used to manipulate XML data. To these, it adds methods specifically related to working with a DataSet. The most interesting of these is the GetRowFromElement method that takes an XmlElement and converts it to a corresponding DataRow.

A short example illustrates how XPath is used to retrieve the set of nodes representing the movies associated with a selected director. The nodes are then converted to a DataRow, which is used to print data from a column in the row.

```
// Create document by passing in associated DataSet
XmlDataDocument xmlDoc = new XmlDataDocument(ds);
string exp = "//directors[last_name='Scorsese']/movies";
XmlNodeList nodeList =
      xmlDoc.DocumentElement.SelectNodes(exp);
DataRow myRow;
foreach (XmlNode myNode in nodeList)
{
   myRow = xmlDoc.GetRowFromElement((XmlElement)myNode);
   if (myRow != null){
      // Print Movie Title from a DataRow
      Console.WriteLine(myRow["movie_Title"].ToString());
   }
}
```

This class should be used only when its hybrid features add value to an application. Otherwise, use XmlDocument if updates are required or XPathDocument if the data is read-only.

Adding and Removing Nodes on a Tree

Besides locating and reading data, many applications need to add, edit, and delete information in an XML document tree. This is done using methods that edit the content of a node and add or delete nodes. After the changes have been made to the tree, the updated DOM is saved to a file.

To demonstrate how to add and remove nodes, we'll operate on the subtree presented as text in Fig. 14.19 and as a graphical tree in Fig. 14.20.

```
Public void UseXPath()
{
   XmlDocument doc = new XmlDocument();
   doc.Load("c:\\directormovies.xml");
   // (1) Locate movie to remove
   string exp = "//directors[last_name='Scorsese']/
         movies[movie_Title='Raging Bull']";
   XmlNode movieNode = doc.SelectSingleNode(exp);
   // (2) Delete node and child nodes for movie
   XmlNode directorNode = movieNode.ParentNode;
   directorNode.RemoveChild(movieNode);
   // (3) Add new movie for this director
   //     First, get and save director's ID
   string directorID =
         directorNode.SelectSingleNode("director_id").InnerText;
   // XmlElement is dervied from XmlNode and adds members
   XmlElement movieEl = doc.CreateElement("movies");
   directorNode.AppendChild(movieEl);
   // (4) Add Movie Description
   AppendChildElement(movieEl, "movie_ID", "94");
   AppendChildElement(movieEl, "movie_Title", "Goodfellas");
   AppendChildElement(movieEl, "movie_Year", "1990");
   AppendChildElement(movieEl, "movie_DirectorID",
                                directorID);
   // (5) Save updated XML Document
   doc.Save("c:\\directormovies2.xml");
}
// Create node and append to parent
public void AppendChildElement(XmlNode parent, string elName,
                                string elValue)
{
   XmlElement newEl =
         parent.OwnerDocument.CreateElement(elName);
   newEl.InnerText = elValue;
   parent.AppendChild(newEl);
}
```

Fig. 14.19 │ Using XmlDocument and XPath to Add and Remove Nodes.

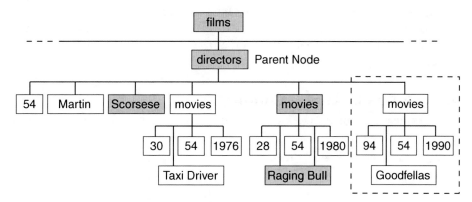

Fig. 14.20 | Subtree used to delete and remove nodes.

This example uses the XmlDocument class to represent the tree for which we will remove one movies element and add another one. XPath is used to locate the movies node for Raging Bull along the path containing Scorsese as the director:

```
"//directors[last_name='Scorsese']/movies[movie_Title=
    'Raging Bull']"
```

This node is deleted by locating its parent node, which is on the level directly above it, and executing its RemoveChild method.

Adding a node requires first locating the node that will be used to attach the new node. Then, the document's Createxxx method is used to generate an XmlNode or XmlNode-derived object that will be added to the tree. The node is attached using the current node's AppendChild, InsertAfter, or InsertBefore method to position the new node in the tree. In this example, we add a movies element that contains information for the movie *Goodfellas*.

14.6 Summary

To work with XML, a basic understanding of the XML document, schema, and style sheet is required. An XML document, which is a representation of information based on XML guidelines, can be created in numerous ways. The XmlSerializer class can be used when the data takes the form of an object or objects within a program. After the XML document is created, a schema can be derived from it using the XML Schema Definition (XSD) tool. Several classes use the schema to provide automatic document validation. The usefulness of XML data is extended by the capability to transform it into virtually any other format using an XML style sheet. The style sheet defines a set of rules that are applied during XML Style Sheet Transformation (XSLT).

XML data can be processed as a stream of nodes or an in-memory tree known as a Document Object Model (DOM). The XmlReader and XmlNodeReader classes provide an efficient way to process XML as a read-only, forward-only stream. The XmlReader, XPathDocument, and XmlDataReader classes offer methods for processing nodes in the tree structure.

In many cases, data extraction from an XML tree can be best achieved using a query, rather than traversing the tree nodes. The XPath expression presents a rich, standardized syntax that is easily used to specify criteria for extracting a node, or multiple nodes, from an XML tree.

14.7 Test Your Understanding

1. XmlReader is an abstract class. How do you create an instance of it to read an XML document?

2. What is the purpose of the XmlReaderSettings class?

3. Which of these classes cannot be used to update an XML document?

   a) XmlDocument

   b) XmlDataDocument

   c) XmlPathDocument

4. Using the XML data from Fig. 14.16, show the node values returned by the following XPath expressions:

   a) //movies[substring(movie_Title,2,1)='a']

   b) //movies[2]

   c) //movies[movie_Year >= 1978]

   d) //directors[last_name='Scorsese']
       /movies/movie_Title

5. Describe two ways to perform schema validation on an XML document.

15

ADO.NET

OBJECTIVES

- *ADO.NET Architecture:* ADO.NET provides access to data using custom or generic data providers. This section looks at the classes a provider must supply that enable an application to connect to a data source and interact with it using SQL commands.

- *Introduction to Using ADO.NET:* ADO.NET supports data access using a connected or disconnected connectivity model. An introduction and comparison of the two architectures is provided.

- *The Connected Model:* Use of the connected model requires an understanding of the role that `Connection` and `Command` classes have in retrieving data. Examples illustrate how to create a connection and use the `Command` class to issue SQL commands, invoke stored procedures, and manage multi-command transactions.

- *The Disconnected Model:* Disconnected data is stored in an in-memory `DataTable` or `DataSet`. The latter is usually made up of multiple `DataTables` that serve as a local relational data store for an application. A `DataAdapter` is typically used to load this data and then apply updates to the original data source. Techniques are introduced for handling synchronization issues that arise when updating disconnected data.

- *XML Data Access:* Although it does not provide intrinsic XML classes, ADO.NET supports XML integration through properties and methods of the `DataSet` class. Examples show how to use `WriteXml` and `ReadXml` to create an XML file from a `DataSet` and populate a `DataSet` from an XML file, respectively.

15.1 Introduction

ADO.NET is based on a flexible set of classes that allow data to be accessed from within the managed environment of .NET. These classes are used to access a variety of data sources including relational databases, XML files, spreadsheets, and text files. Data access is through an API, known as a managed data provider. This provider may be written specifically for a database, or may be a more generic provider such as OLE DB or ODBC (Open DataBase Connectivity). Provider classes expose a connection object that binds an application to a data source, and a command object that supports the use of standard SQL commands to fetch, add, update, or delete data.

ADO.NET supports two broad models for accessing data: disconnected and connected. The disconnected model downloads data to a client's machine where it is encapsulated as an in-memory `DataSet` that can be accessed like a local relational database. The connected model relies on record-by-record access that requires an open and sustained connection to the data source. Recognizing the most appropriate model to use in an application is at the heart of understanding ADO.NET. This chapter examines both models—offering code examples that demonstrate the classes used to implement each.

15.2 Overview of the ADO.NET Architecture

The ADO.NET architecture is designed to make life easier for both the application developer and the database provider. To the developer, it presents a set of abstract classes that define a common set of methods and properties that can be used to access any data source. The data source is treated as an abstract entity, much like a drawing surface is to the GDI+ classes. Figure 15.1 depicts this concept.

For database providers, ADO.NET serves as a blueprint that describes the base API classes and interface specifications providers must supply with their product. Beneath the surface, the vendor implements the custom code for connecting to their database, processing SQL commands, and returning the results. Many database products, such as MySQL and Oracle, have custom .NET data provider implementations available. In addition, they have generic OLE DB versions. The .NET data provider should always be the first choice because it offers better performance and often supports added custom features. Let's look at both the OLE DB and native .NET data providers.

15.2.1 OLE DB Data Provider in .NET

An OLE DB provider is the code that sits between the data consumer and the native API of a data source. It maps the generic OLE DB API to the data source's native APIs. It is a COM-based solution in which the data consumer and provider are COM objects that communicate through COM interfaces. Database vendors and third parties have written OLE DB providers for just about every significant data source. In contrast, far fewer .NET data providers exist. To provide a bridge to these preexisting OLE DB interfaces, .NET includes an OleDB data provider that functions as a thin wrapper to route calls into the native OLE DB. Because interoperability with COM requires switching between managed and unmanaged code, performance can be severely degraded.[1]

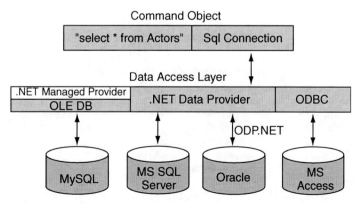

Fig. 15.1 | ADO.NET data access options.

---

1. Test results for .NET 1.1 have shown the SQL Client provider to be up to 10 times faster than OLE DB.

As we see in the next section, writing code to use OLE DB is essentially the same as working with a .NET data provider. In fact, new .NET classes provide a "factory" that can dynamically produce code for a selected provider. Consequently, responding to a vendor's upgrade from OLE DB to a custom provider should have no appreciable effect on program logic.

15.2.2 .NET Data Provider

The .NET data provider provides the same basic service to the client as the OLE DB provider: exposing a data source's API to a client. Its advantage is that it can directly access the native API of the data source, rather than relying on an intermediate data access bridge. Native providers may also include additional features to manipulate data types native to the data source and improve performance. For example, the Oracle provider, ODP.NET, includes adjustable settings to control connection pooling, the number of rows to be prefetched, and the size of non-scalar data being fetched.

Data Provider Objects for Accessing Data

A managed data provider exposes four classes that enable a data consumer to access the provider's data source. Although these classes are specific to the provider, they derive from abstract ADO.NET classes:

- `DbConnection`. Establishes a connection to the data source.

- `DbCommand`. Used to query or send a command to the data source.

- `DbDataReader`. Provides read-only and forward-only access to the data source.

- `DBDataAdapter`. Serves as a channel through which a `DataSet` connects to a provider.

Because these are abstract classes, the developer is responsible for specifying the vendor's specific implementation within the code. As we see next, the object names can be hard coded or provided generically by a provider factory class.

Provider Factories

Each data provider registers a `ProviderFactory` class and a provider string in the `machine.config` file. The available providers can be listed using the static `GetFactory-Classes` method of the `DbProviderFactories` class. As this code shows, the method returns a `DataTable` containing four columns of information about the provider.

```
DataTable tb = DbProviderFactories.GetFactoryClasses();
foreach (DataRow drow in tb.Rows )
{
    StringBuilder sb = new StringBuilder("");
    for (int i=0; i<tb.Columns.Count; i++)
    {
        sb.Append((i+1).ToString()).Append(drow[i].ToString());
        sb.Append("\n");
    }
    Console.WriteLine(sb.ToString());
}
```

```
1 SqlClient Data Provider
2 .Net Framework Data Provider for SqlServer
3 System.Data.SqlClient
4 System.Data.SqlClient.SqlClientFactory, System.Data,
   Version=2.0.3600.0, Culture=neutral,
   PublicKeyToken=b77a5c561934e089
```

Fig. 15.2 | Data provider information returned by GetFactoryClasses().

Running this code for ADO.NET 2.0 lists four Microsoft written providers: Odbc, OleDb, OracleClient, and SqlClient. Figure 15.2 shows output for the SqlClient provider.

To use these providers, your code must create objects specific to the provider. For example, the connection object for each would be an OdbcConnection, OleDbConnection, OracleConnection, or SqlConnection type. You can create the objects supplied by the providers directly:

```
SqlConnection conn = new SqlConnection();
SqlCommand cmd     = new SqlCommand();
SqlDataReader dr   = cmd.ExecuteReader();
```

However, suppose your application has to support multiple data sources. A switch/case construct could be used, but a better—and more flexible—approach is to use a class factory to create these objects dynamically based on the provider selected. ADO.NET provides just that—a DbProviderFactory class that is used to return objects required by a specific data provider. It works quite simply. A string containing the provider name is passed to the GetFactory method of the DbProviderFactories class. The method returns a factory object that is used to create the specific objects required by the provider. Figure 15.3 demonstrates using a factory.

This approach requires only that a provider and connection string be provided. For example, we can easily switch this to an ODBC provider by changing two statements:

```
string provider= "System.Data.Odbc";
// The DSN (Data Source Name) is defined using an ODBC utility
string connstr = "DSN=movies;Database=films";
```

Note that the factory class provides a series of Create methods that returns the objects specific to the data provider. These methods include CreateCommand, CreateConnection, and CreateDataAdapter.

15.3 Data Access Models: Connected and Disconnected

This section offers an overview of using ADO.NET to access data stored in relational tables. Through simple examples, it presents the classes and concepts that distinguish the connected and disconnected access models.

All examples in this section—as well as the entire chapter—use data from the Films database defined in Figure 15.4. It consists of a movies table containing the top 100 movies

```
// System.Data.Common namespace is required
DbProviderFactory factory ;
string provider = "System.Data.SqlClient";  // data provider
string connstr = "Data Source=MYSERVER;Initial Catalog=films;
         User Id=filmsadmin;Password=bogart;";
// Get factory object for SQL Server
factory = DbProviderFactories.GetFactory(provider);
// Get connection object. using ensures connection is closed.
using (DbConnection  conn = factory.CreateConnection())
{
   conn.ConnectionString = connstr;
   try
   {
      conn.Open();
      DbCommand cmd = factory.CreateCommand(); // Command object
      cmd.CommandText = "SELECT * FROM movies WHERE movie_ID=8" ;
      cmd.Connection = conn;
      DbDataReader dr;
      dr = cmd.ExecuteReader();
      dr.Read();
      MessageBox.Show((string)dr["movie_Title"]);
      conn.Close();
   }
   catch (DbException ex)
   { MessageBox.Show(ex.ToString()); }
   catch (Exception ex)
   { MessageBox.Show(ex.ToString()); }
   finally { conn.Close(); }
}
```

Fig. 15.3 | Using the DbProviderFactory Class.

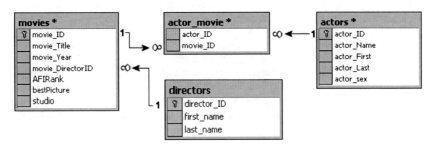

Fig. 15.4 | Films database tables.

as selected by the American Film Institute (AFI) in 1996, an actors table that lists the principal actors who performed in the movies, and an actor-movie helper table that links the two. The data is downloadable as a Microsoft Access (.mdb) file and an XML text (.xml) file.

15.3.1 Connected Model

In the ADO.NET connected mode, an active connection is maintained between an application's DataReader object and a data source. A row of data is returned from the data source each time the object's Read method is executed. The most important characteristic of the connected model is that it reads data from a resultset (records returned by a SQL command) one record at a time in a forward-only, read-only manner. It provides no direct way to update or add data. Figure 15.5 depicts the relationship between the DataReader, Command, and Connection classes that comprise the connected model.

Working with the DataReader typically involves four steps:

1. The connection object is created by passing a connection string to its constructor.

2. A string variable is assigned the SQL command that specifies the data to fetch.

3. A command object is created. Its overloads accept a connection object, a query string, and a transaction object (for executing a group of commands).

4. The DataReader object is created by executing the Command.ExecuteReader() method. This object is then used to read the query results one line at a time over the active data connection.

The following code segment illustrates these steps with a SqlClient data provider. The code reads movie titles from the database and displays them in a ListBox control. Note that the DataReader, Command, and Connection objects are described in detail later in this chapter.

```
//System.Data.SqlClient namespace is required
// (1) Create Connection
SqlConnection conn = new SqlConnection(connstr);
conn.Open();
// (2) Query string
string sql = "SELECT movie_Title FROM movies ORDER BY movie_Year";
// (3) Create Command object
SqlCommand cmd = new SqlCommand(sql, conn);
DbDataReader rdr;
// (4) Create DataReader
rdr = cmd.ExecuteReader(CommandBehavior.CloseConnection);
while (rdr.Read())
{
    listBox1.Items.Add(rdr["movie_Title"]);  // Fill ListBox
}
rdr.Close();  // Always close datareader
```

The parameter to ExecuteReader specifies that the connection is closed when the data reader object is closed.

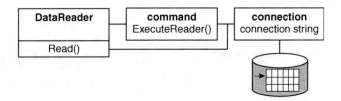

Fig. 15.5 | DataReader is used in ADO.NET connected mode.

15.3.2 Disconnected Model

The concept behind the disconnected model is quite simple: Data is loaded—using a SQL command—from an external source into a memory cache on the client's machine; the resultset is manipulated on the local machine; and any updates are passed from data in memory back to the data source.

The model is "disconnected" because the connection is only open long enough to read data from the source and make updates. By placing data on the client's machine, server resources—data connections, memory, processing time—are freed that would otherwise be required to manipulate the data. The drawback is the time required to load the resultset, and the memory used to store it.

As Figure 15.6 illustrates, the key components of the disconnected model are the DataApdapter and DataSet. The DataAdapter serves as a bridge between the data source and the DataSet, retrieving data into the tables that comprise the DataSet and pushing changes back to the data source. A DataSet object functions as an in-memory relational database that contains one or more DataTables, along with optional relationships that bind the tables. A DataTable contains rows and columns of data that usually derive from a table in the source database.

Among the numerous methods and properties exposed by the DataAdapter class, the Fill and Update methods are the two most important. Fill passes a query to a database and stores the returned set of data in a selected DataTable; Update performs a deletion, insertion, or update operation based on changes within the DataSet. The actual update commands are exposed as DataAdapter properties. The DataAdapter is presented in much more detail in Section 15.4, "DataSets, DataTables, and the Disconnected Model."

Core Note 15.1

Each data provider supplies its own data adapter. Thus, if you look through the System.Data child namespaces (SqlClient, OracleClient, Oledb), you'll find a SqlDataAdapter, Oracle-DataAdapter, and OleDbDataAdapter, among others. An easy way to acquire the desired adapter in your application is to call the DbProviderFactory.CreateDataAdapter method to return an instance of it.

As a simple introduction to how a DataAdapter and DataSet work together, Figure 15.7 shows how to create a DataTable, fill it with data from a database, and add it to a DataSet.

The first step is to create an instance of a SqlDataAdapter by passing the select command and the connection string to its constructor. The data adapter takes care of creating the Connection object and opening and closing the connection as needed. After an empty DataSet is created, the DataAdapter's Fill method creates a table movies in the DataSet

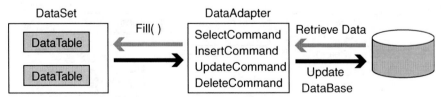

Fig. 15.6 | DataAdapter is used in ADO.NET disconnected mode.

```
string sql = "SELECT movie_Title, movie_Year FROM movies";
string connStr = " Data Source=MYSERVER;Initial Catalog=films;
                   User Id=filmsadmin;Password=bogart;";
// (1) Create data adapter object
SqlDataAdapter da = new SqlDataAdapter(sql,connStr);
// (2) Create dataset
DataSet ds = new DataSet();
// (3) Create table in dataset and fill with data
da.Fill(ds, "movies");  // Fill table with query results
DataTable dt = ds.Tables["movies"];
// (4) Add movie titles to list box
for (int i=0; i< dt.Rows.Count;i++)
{
   DataRow row = dt.Rows[i];
   listBox1.Items.Add(row["movie_Title"]);
}
```

Fig. 15.7 | Using a DataAdapter to Load Data from a Database.

and fills it with rows of data returned by the SQL command. Each column of the table corresponds to a column in the source data table. Behind the scenes, the data transfer is performed by creating a SqlDataReader that is closed after the transfer is complete.

The data in the table is then used to populate a list box by looping through the rows of the table. As we see in the next chapter, we could achieve the same effect by binding the list control to the table—a mechanism for automatically filling a control with data from a bound source.

15.4 ADO.NET Connected Model

As described earlier, the connected model is based on establishing a connection to a database and then using commands to update, delete, or read data on the connected source. The distinguishing characteristic of this model is that commands are issued directly to the data source over a live connection—which remains open until the operations are complete. Whether working with a connected or disconnected model, the first step in accessing a data source is to create a connection object to serve as a communications pathway between the application and database.

15.4.1 Connection Classes

There are multiple connection classes in ADO.NET—each specific to a data provider. These include SqlConnection, OracleConnection, OleDBConnection, and OdbcConnection. Although each may include custom features, ADO.NET compatibility requires that a connector class implement the IDbConnection interface. The table in Fig. 15.8 summarizes the members defined by this interface.

Core Note 15.2

Even though connection classes implement the IDbConnection interface, they do not necessarily have to provide meaningful functionality. For example, the OracleConnection class does not support the ConnectionTimeOut, Database, or ChangeDatabase members.

Category	Name	Description
Property	ConnectionString	Gets or sets the string used to connect to a data source.
Property	ConnectionTimeout	The number of seconds to wait while trying to establish a connection to a data source before timing out.
Property	Database	Name of the database associated with the current connection.
Property	State	Current state of the connection. Returns a ConnectionState enumeration name: Broken, Closed, Connecting, Executing, Fetching, or Open.
Method	Open Close	Opens a connection. Rolls back any pending operations and closes the connection—returning it to a connection pool, if one is used.
Method	BeginTransaction	Initiates a database transaction.
Method	ChangeDatabase	Changes the current database for an open connection. The new database name is passed as string to the method.
Method	CreateCommand	Creates a command object to be associated with connection.

Fig. 15.8 | Members of the IDbConnection Interface.

Connection String
The connection string specifies the data source and necessary information required to access the data source, such as password and ID. In addition to this basic information, the string can include values for fields specific to a data provider. For example, a SQL Server connection string can include values for Connection Timeout and Packet Size (size of network packet).

The table in Fig. 15.9 offers a representative list of commonly used connection strings.

The connection string is used to create the connection object. This is typically done by passing the string to the constructor of the connection object.

```
string cn= "Data Source=MYSERVER;Initial Catalog=films;
        User Id=filmsadmin;Password=bogart;";
SqlConnection conn = new SqlConnection(cn);
conn.Open();   // Open connection
```

A connection string can also be built using a safer, object-oriented manner using one of the ConnectionStringBuilder classes supplied by a managed data provider.[2] As this code demonstrates, the values comprising the connection string are assigned to properties

2. SqlClient, Oracle, OleDB, and ODBC implementations are available with ADO.NET 2.0.

Connection Type	Description and Use

SqlConnection
Using SQL Server authentication.
	"server=MYSERVER;
	uid=filmsadmin;
	pwd=bogart;
	database=films;"
	Or
	"Data Source=MYSERVER;User ID=filmsadmin;
	password=bogart;Initial Catalog=films;"

SqlConnection Using Windows authentication.	"server=MYSERVER; database=films; Trusted_Connection=yes"
OleDbConnection Connects to a Microsoft Access database.	"Provider=Microsoft.Jet.OLEDB.4.0; Data Source=c:\\movies.mdb;" For Internet applications, you may not be able to specify a physical path. Use MapPath to convert a virtual path into a physical path: string path= Server.MapPath("/data/movies.mdb"); Data Source="+path+";"
ODBC (DSN)	"DSN=movies;".

Fig. 15.9 | Connection String Examples.

of this class. Internally, the object constructs a string from these properties and exposes it as a ConnectionString property.

```
SqlConnectionStringBuilder sqlBldr = new
    SqlConnectionStringBuilder();
scb.DataSource    = "MYSERVER";
// Or scp["Data Source"] = "MYSERVER";
sqlBldr.Password  = "bogart";
sqlBldr.UserID    = "filmsadmin";
sqlBldr.InitialCatalog = "films";
SqlConnection conn = new
SqlConnection(sqlBldr.ConnectionString);
conn.Open();
```

The ConnectionStringBuilder object is also useful for applications that input the connection string from a configuration file or other source. Setting the ConnectionString property to the connection string value exposes members that control the behavior of the connection. The table in Fig. 15.10 lists selected properties of the SqlConnectionString-Builder class.

Method	Description
Asynchronous-Processing	Boolean value that indicates whether asynchronous process is permitted on the connection. The command object is responsible for making asynchronous requests.
ConnectionTimeout	Corresponds to the ConnectionTimeout property of the Connection object.
DataSource	Name or address of the SQL Server to connect to.
MaxPoolSize MinPoolSize	Sets or returns the maximum and minimum number of connections in the connection pool for a specific connection string.
Password	Password for accessing SQL Server account.
Pooling	A boolean value that indicates whether connection pooling is used.
UserID	User ID required to access a SQL Server account.

Fig. 15.10 | Selected Properties of the SqlConnectionStringBuilder Class.

Core Note 15.3

For demonstration purposes, the connection strings in these examples are shown as cleartext within the application's code. In reality, a connection string should be stored outside of an application's assembly. For Web applications, the Web.Config file is often a reasonable choice. .NET includes a special configuration section to hold connection strings and supports techniques to encrypt the configuration information.

Desktop applications that access a central database can store the information on the client's machine (in the registry or a configuration file) or have it downloaded as part of an application's startup. The latter approach provides better scalability and security, particularly if the server returns a connection object rather than the string.

Connection Pooling

Creating a connection is a time-consuming process—in some cases taking longer than the subsequent commands take to execute. To eliminate this overhead, ADO.NET creates a pool of identical connections for each unique connection string request it receives. This enables future requests with that connection string to be satisfied from the pool, rather than by reconnecting to the server and performing the overhead to validate the connection.

There are several rules governing connection pooling that you should be aware of:

- Connection pooling is turned on by default. It can be disabled for a SqlConnection by including "Pooling=false" in the connection string; an OleDbConnection requires "OLE DB Services=-4".

- Each connection pool is associated with a distinct connection string. When a connection is requested, the pool handler compares the connection string with those of existing pools. If it matches, a connection is allocated from the pool.

- If all connections in a pool are in use when a request is made, the request is queued until a connection becomes free. Connections are freed when the Close or Dispose method on a connection is called.

- The connection pool is closed when all connections in it are released by their owners and have timed out.

Under SQL Server, you control the behavior of connection pooling by including key-value pairs in the connection string. These keywords can be used to set minimum and maximum numbers of connections in the pool, and to specify whether a connection is reset when it is taken from the pool. Of particular note is the Lifetime keyword that specifies how long a connection may live until it is destroyed. This value is checked when a connection is returned to the pool. If the connection has been open longer than its Lifetime value, it is destroyed.

This code fragment demonstrates the use of these keywords for SqlClient:

```
cnString = "Server=MYSERVER;Trusted_Connection=yes;
      database=films;"          +
      "connection reset=false;" +
      "connection Lifetime=60;" +  // Seconds
      "min pool size=1;"        +
      "max pool size=50";          // Default=100
SqlConnection conn = new SqlConnection(cnString);
```

15.4.2 The Command Object

After a connection object is created, the next step in accessing a database—for the connected model—is to create a command object that submits a query or action command to a data source. Command classes are made available by data providers and must implement the IDbCommand interface.

Creating a Command Object
You can use one of its several constructors to create a command object directly, or use the ProviderFactory approach mentioned in Section 15.1.

This segment demonstrates how to create a command object and explicitly set its properties:

```
SqlConnection conn = new SqlConnection(connstr);
Conn.open();
string sql = "insert into movies(movie_Title,movie_Year,
      movie_Director) values(@title,@yr,@bestpicture)";
SqlCommand cmd = new SqlCommand();
// Assign connection object and sql query to command object
cmd.Connection = conn;
cmd.commandText = sql;
// Fill in parameter values in query
// This is recommended over concatenation in a query string
cmd.Parameters.AddWithValue ("@title", "Schindler's List");
cmd.Parameters.AddWithValue ("@yr", "1993");
cmd.Parameters.AddWithValue ("@bestpic", "Y");
```

In situations where multiple data providers may be used, a provider factory provides a more flexible approach. The factory is created by passing its constructor a string containing the data provider. The factory's `CreateCommand` method is used to return a command object.

```
string provider = "System.Data.SqlClient";
DBProviderFactory factory =
    DbProviderFactories.GetFactory(provider);
DbCommand cmd    = factory.CreateCommand();
cmd.CommandText = sql;      // Query or command
cmd.Connection  = conn;     // Connection object
```

Note that `DbCommand` is an abstract class that implements the `IDbCommand` interface. It assumes the role of a generic command object. This can eliminate the need to cast the returned command object to a specific provider's command object such as `SqlCommand`. However, casting is required if you need to access custom features of a provider's command class—for example, only `SqlCommand` has an `ExecuteXmlReader` method.

Executing a Command

The SQL command assigned to the `CommandText` property is executed using one of the four command methods in Fig. 15.11.

The `ExecuteReader` method is the most important of these methods. It returns a `DataReader` object that exposes the rows returned by the query. The behavior of this method can be modified by using its overload that accepts a `CommandBehavior` type parameter. As an example, the following statement specifies that a single row of data is to be returned:

```
rdr = cmd.ExecuteReader(CommandBehavior.SingleResult);
```

Method	Description

ExecuteNonQuery	Executes an action query and returns the number of rows affected:
	
	`cmd.CommandText = "DELETE movies WHERE movie_ID=220";`
	`int ct = cmd.ExecuteNonQuery();`

ExecuteReader	Executes a query and returns a `DataReader` object that provides access to the query's resultset. This method accepts an optional `CommandBehavior` object that can improve execution efficiency.
	
	`cmd.CommandText="SELECT * FROM movies`
	`    WHERE movie_year > '1945';`
	`SqlDataReader rdr= cmd.ExecuteReader();`

ExecuteScalar	Executes a query and returns the value of the first column in the first row of the resultset as a scalar value.
	
	`cmd.CommandText="SELECT COUNT(movie_title)`
	`    FROM movies";`
	`int movieCt = (int) cmd.ExecuteScalar();`

ExecuteXmlReader	Available for SQL Server data provider only. Returns an `XmlReader` object that is used to access the resultset. `XmlReader` is discussed in Chapter 14, "Working with XML in .NET."

Fig. 15.11 | Command `Executexxx` Methods.

Some data providers take advantage of this parameter to optimize query execution. The list of values for the CommandBehavior enumeration includes the following:

- SingleRow. Indicates that the query should return one row. Default behavior is to return multiple resultsets.

- SingleResult. The query is expected to return a single scalar value.

- KeyInfo. Returns column and primary key information. It is used with a data reader's GetSchema method to fetch column schema information.

- SchemaOnly. Used to retrieve column names for the resultset.
  Example:

  ```
  dr=cmd.ExecuteReader(CommandBehavior.SchemaOnly);
  string col1= dr.GetName(0);  // First column name
  ```

- SequentialAccess. Permits data in the returned row to be accessed sequentially by column. This is used with large binary (BLOB) or text fields.

- CloseConnection. Close connection when reader is closed.

Executing Stored Procedures with the Command Object

A stored procedure is a set of SQL code stored in a database that can be executed as a script. It's a powerful feature that enables logic to be encapsulated, shared, and reused among applications. ADO.NET supports the execution of stored procedures for OleDb , SqlClient, ODBC, and OracleClient data providers.

Executing a stored procedure is quite simple: set the SqlCommand.CommandText property to the name of the procedure; set the CommandType property to the enumeration CommandType.StoredProcedure; and then call the ExecuteNonQuery method.

```
cmd.CommandText = "SP_AddMovie";  // Stored procedure name
cmd.CommandType = CommandType.StoredProcedure;
cmd.ExecuteNonQuery();
```

When a stored procedure contains input or output parameters, they must be added to the command object's Parameters collection before the procedure is executed. To demonstrate, let's execute the stored procedure shown in Fig. 15.12. This procedure allows records to be fetched from the movies table as pages containing 10 rows of data. Input to the procedure is the desired page; the output parameter is the total number of pages available. This code fragment illustrates how parameters are set and how the procedure is invoked to return the first page:

```
SqlCommand cmd  = new SqlCommand();
cmd.CommandText = "SPMOVIES_LIST";  // Stored procedure name
cmd.CommandType = CommandType.StoredProcedure;
cmd.Parameters.Add(@PageRequest", SqlDbType.Int);
cmd.Parameters.Add(@TotalPages", SqlDbType.Int);
cmd.Parameters[0].Direction= ParameterDirection.Input;
cmd.Parameters[0].Value= 1;             // Retrieve first page
cmd.Parameters[1].Direction=ParameterDirection.Output;
cmd.CommandTimeout=10;  // Give command 10 seconds to execute
SqlDataReader rdr = cmd.ExecuteReader();
while (rdr.Read()){
//   do something with results
}
rdr.Close();  // Must close before reading parameters
int totpages= cmd.Parameters[1].Value;
```

```
CREATE PROCEDURE SPMOVIES_LIST
   @PageRequest int,
   @TotalPages int output
AS
   /*
      Procedure to return a resultset of movies ordered
      by title.
      Resultset contains 10 movies for the specified page.
   */
   SET NOCOUNT ON
   select @TotalPages = CEILING(COUNT(*)/10) from movies
   if @PageRequest = 1 or @PageRequest <1
   begin
      select top 10 * from movies order by movie_Title
      set @PageRequest = 1
      return 0
   end
   begin
      if @PageRequest > @TotalPages
         set @PageRequest = @TotalPages
      declare @RowCount int
      set @RowCount = (@PageRequest * 10)
      exec ('SELECT * FROM
   (SELECT TOP 10 a.* FROM
   (SELECT TOP ' + @RowCount + ' * FROM movies ORDER BY
         movie_Title) a
    ORDER BY movie_Title desc) b
    ORDER BY Movie_Title')

      return 0
   end
```

Fig. 15.12 | Stored SQL Server Procedure to Return a Page of Records.

This example uses the SqlClient data provider. With a couple of changes, OleDb can be used just as easily. The primary difference is in the way they handle parameters. SqlClient requires that the parameter names match the names in the stored procedure; OleDb passes parameters based on position, so the name is irrelevant. If the procedure sends back a return code, OleDB must designate the first parameter in the list to handle it. SqlClient simply adds a parameter—the name is unimportant—that has its direction set to ReturnValue.

Using Parameterized Commands Without Stored Procedures

An earlier example (See "Creating a Command Object" on page 609.) used this statement to create a SQL command to store a movie in the Films database:

```
string sql = "insert into movies(movie_Title,movie_Year,
      bestpicture) values(@title,@yr,@bestpic)";
// Parameters set values to be stored
cmd.Parameters.AddWithValue ("@title", "Schindler's List");
cmd.Parameters.AddWithValue ("@yr", "1993");
cmd.Parameters.AddWithValue ("@bestpic", "Y");
```

The alternative, which uses concatenation, looks like this:

```
string title = "Schindler''s List";  // Two single quotes needed
string yr = "1993";
string pic = "Y";
sql = "insert into movies(movie_Title,movie_Year,
        bestpicture) values";
sql += "('"+title+"','"+yr+"','"+pic+"') ";
```

Not only is the parameterized version more readable and less prone to syntactical error, but it also provides a significant benefit: It automatically handles the problem of placing double single quotes ('') in a SQL command. This problem occurs when attempting to store a value such as O'Quinn, which has an embedded quote that conflicts with SQL syntax. Parameters eliminate the usual approach to search each string and replace an embedded single quote with a pair of single quotes.

15.4.3 DataReader Object

As we have seen in several examples, a DataReader exposes the rows and columns of data returned as the result of executing a query. Row access is defined by the IDataReader interface that each DataReader must implement; column access is defined by the IDataRecord interface. We'll look at the most important members defined by these interfaces as well as some custom features added by data providers.

Accessing Rows with DataReader

A DataReader returns a single row from a resultset each time its Read method is executed. If no rows remain, the method returns false. The reader should be closed after row processing is completed in order to free system resources. You can check the Data-Reader.IsClosed property to determine if a reader is closed.

Although a DataReader is associated with a single command, the command may contain multiple queries that return multiple resultsets. This code fragment demonstrates how a DataReader processes the rows returned by two queries.

```
string q1 = "SELECT * FROM movies WHERE movie_Year < 1940";
string q2 = "SELECT * FROM movies WHERE movie_Year > 1980";
cmd.CommandText = q1 + ";" + q2;
DbDataReader rdr = cmd.ExecuteReader();
bool readNext = true;
while (readNext)
{
    while (rdr.Read())
    {
        MessageBox.Show(rdr.GetString(1));
    }
    readNext = rdr.NextResult(); // Another resultset?
}
rdr.Close();
conn.Close();
```

The two things to note are the construction of the CommandString with multiple queries and the use of the NextResult method to determine if results from another query are present.

Core Note 15.4

The DataReader has no property or method that provides the number of rows returned in its resultset. Because data is received one row at a time, the resultset could be altered by additions and deletions to the database as records are read. However, there is a HasRows property that returns true if the data reader contains one or more rows.

Accessing Column Values with DataReader

There are numerous ways to access data contained in the columns of the current Data-Reader row: as an array with column number (zero-based) or name used as an index; using the GetValue method by passing it a column number; and using one of the strongly typed Getxxx methods that include GetString, GetInt32, GetDateTime, and GetDouble. The following code segment contains an example of each technique:

```
cmd.CommandText="SELECT movie_ID, movie_Title FROM movies";
rdr = cmd.ExecuteReader();
rdr.Read();
string title;
// Multiple ways to access data in a column
title = rdr.GetString(1);
title = (string)rdr.GetSqlString(1); // SqlClient provider
title = (string)rdr.GetValue(1);
title = (string)rdr["movie_Title"];  // Implicit item
title = (string)rdr[1];              // Implicit item
```

The GetString method has the advantage of mapping the database contents to a native .NET data type. The other approaches return object types that require casting. For this reason, use of the Get methods is recommended. Note that although GetString does not require casting, it does not perform any conversion; thus, if the data is not of the type expected, an exception is thrown.

Many applications rely on a separate data access layer to provide a DataReader. In such cases, the application may require metadata to identify column names, data types, and other columnar information. Column names, which are useful for generating report headings, are readily available through the GetName method:

```
// List column names for a DataReader
DbDataReader rdr = GetReader();        // Get a DataReader
for (int k = 0; k < rdr.FieldCount; k++)
{
    Console.WriteLine(rdr.GetName(k));  // Column name
}
rdr.Close();
```

Complete column schema information is available through the GetSchemaTable method. It returns a DataTable in which there is one row for each field (column) in the resultset. The columns in the table represent schema information. This code segment demonstrates how to access all the column information for a resultset. For brevity, only three of the 24 columns of information are shown:

```
DataTable schemaTable = rdr.GetSchemaTable();
int ict = 0;
foreach (DataRow r in schemaTable.Rows)
```

```
    {
        foreach (DataColumn c in schemaTable.Columns){
            Console.WriteLine(ict.ToString()+"
                              "+c.ColumnName + ": "+r[c]);
            ict++;
        }
    }
    // Selected Output:
    //        0 ColumnName: movie_ID
    //        1 ColumnOrdinal: 0
    //        12 DataType: System.Int32
```

15.5 DataSets, DataTables, and the Disconnected Model

The ADO.NET disconnected model is based on using a DataSet object as an in-memory cache. A DataAdapter serves as the intermediary between the DataSet and the data source that loads the cache with data. After it has completed its task, the DataAdapter returns the connection object to the pool, thus disconnecting the data from the data source. Interestingly, the DataAdapter is actually a wrapper around a data provider's DataReader, which performs the actual data loading.

15.5.1 The DataSet Class

In many ways, a DataSet object plays the role of an in-memory database. Its Tables property exposes a collection of DataTables that contain data and a data schema describing the data. The Relations property returns a collection of DataRelation objects that define how tables are interrelated. In addition, DataSet methods are available to Copy, Merge, and Clear the contents of the DataSet.

Keep in mind that the DataSet and DataTable are core parts of ADO.NET and—unlike the Connection, DataReader, and DataAdapter—they are not tied to a specific data provider. An application can create, define, and populate a DataSet with data from any source.

Besides tables and their relations, a DataSet can also contain custom information defined by the application. A look at Fig. 15.13 shows the major collection classes in the DataSet hierarchy. Among these is PropertyCollection, which is a set of custom properties stored in a hash table and exposed through the DataSet.ExtendedProperties property. It is often used to hold a time stamp or descriptive information such as column validation requirements for tables in the data set.

The discussion of the DataSet class begins with its most important member—the DataTable collection.

15.5.2 DataTables

One step below the DataSet in the disconnected model hierarchy is the DataTable collection. This collection—accessed through the DataSet.Tables property—stores data in a row-column format that mimics tables in a relational database. The DataTable class has a rich set of properties and methods that make it useful as a stand-alone data source or as part of a table collection in a DataSet. The most important of these are the Columns and Rows properties, which define the layout and content of a table.

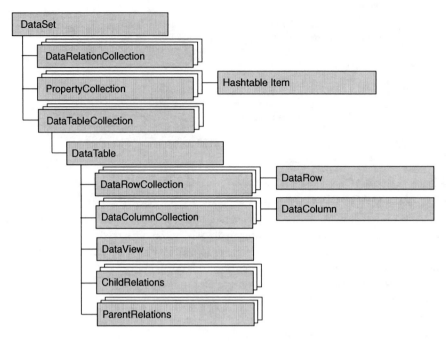

Fig. 15.13 | DataSet class hierarchy.

DataColumns

The DataTable.Columns property exposes a collection of DataColumn objects that represent each data field in the DataTable. Taken together, the column properties produce the data schema for the table. The table in Fig. 15.14 summarizes the most important properties.

DataTable columns are created automatically when the table is filled with the results of a database query or from reading an XML file. However, for applications that fill a table dynamically—such as from user input or real-time data acquisition—it may be necessary to write the code that defines the table structure. It's a worthwhile exercise in its own right that enhances a developer's understanding of the DataSet hierarchy.

The following segment creates a DataTable object, creates DataColumn objects, assigns property values to the columns, and adds them to the DataTable. To make things interesting, a calculated column is included.

```
DataTable tb = new DataTable("Order");
DataColumn dCol = new DataColumn("ID",
      Type.GetType("System.Int16"));
dCol.Unique = true;  // ID must be unique for each data row
dCol.AllowDBNull = false;
tb.Columns.Add(dCol);
dCol= new DataColumn("Price", Type.GetType("System.Decimal"));
tb.Columns.Add(dCol);
dCol=new DataColumn("Quan",Type.GetType("System.Int16"));
tb.Columns.Add(dCol);
dCol= new DataColumn("Total",Type.GetType("System.Decimal"));
dCol.Expression= "Price * Quan";
tb.Columns.Add(dCol);
```

```
// List column names and data type
foreach (DataColumn dc in tb.Columns)
{
    Console.WriteLine(dc.ColumnName);
    Console.WriteLine(dc.DataType.ToString());
}
```

Note that the ID column is defined to contain unique values. This constraint qualifies the column to be used as a key field in establishing a parent-child relationship with another table in a DataSet. To qualify, the key must be unique—as in this case—or defined as a *primary key* for the table. You assign a primary key to a table by setting its PrimaryKey field to the value of an array containing the column(s) to be used as the key. Here is an example that specifies the ID field a primary key:

```
DataColumn[] col = {tb.Columns["ID"]};
tb.PrimaryKey = col;
```

We'll see how to use a primary key to create table relationships and merge data later in this section.

Core Note 15.5

If a primary key consists of more than one column—such as a first and last name—you can enforce a unique constraint on these columns in three steps: by creating an array to hold the columns, creating a UniqueConstraint object by passing the array to its constructor; and adding the constraint to the data table's Constraints collection:

```
DataColumn[] cols = {tb.Columns["fname"]
                     tb.Columns["lname"]};
tb.Constraints.Add(new UniqueConstraint("nameKey", cols));
```

Method	Description
ColumnName	Name of the column.
DataType	Type of data contained in this column.
Example: col1.DataType = System.Type.GetType("System.String")	
MaxLength	Maximum length of a text column. –1 if there is no maximum length.
ReadOnly	Indicates whether the values in the column can be modified.
AllowDBNull	Boolean value that indicates whether the column may contain null values.
Unique	Boolean value that indicates whether the column may contain duplicate values.
Expression	An expression defining how the value of a column is calculated.
Example: colTax.Expression = "colSales * .085";	
Caption	The caption displayed in the user interface.
DataTable	The name of the DataTable containing this column.

Fig. 15.14 | Properties of the DataColumn Class.

DataRows

Data is added to a table by creating a new DataRow object, filling it with column data, and adding the row to the table's DataRow collection. Here is an example that places data in the table created in the preceding example.

```
DataRow row;
row = tb.NewRow();          // Create DataRow
row["Title"] = "Casablanca";
row["Price"] = 22.95;
row["Quan"] = 2;
row["ID"] = 12001;
tb.Rows.Add(row);          // Add row to Rows collection
Console.WriteLine(tb.Rows[0]["Total"].ToString()); // 45.90
```

A DataTable has methods that allow it to commit and roll back changes made to the table. In order to do this, it keeps the status of each row in the DataRow.RowState property. This property is set to one of five DataRowState enumeration values: Added, Deleted, Detached, Modifed, or Unchanged. Let's extend the preceding example to demonstrate how these values are set:

```
tb.Rows.Add(row);                       // Added
tb.AcceptChanges();                     // ...Commit changes
Console.Write(row.RowState);            // Unchanged
tb.Rows[0].Delete();                    // Deleted
// Undo deletion
tb.RejectChanges();                     // ...Roll back
Console.Write(tb.Rows[0].RowState);     // Unchanged
DataRow myRow;
MyRow = tb.NewRow();                    // Detached
```

The two DataTable methods AcceptChanges and RejectChanges are equivalent to the commit and rollback operations in a database. These apply to all changes made from the time the table was loaded or since AcceptChanges was previously invoked. In this example, we are able to restore a deleted row because the deletion is not committed before RejectChanges is called. Note that the changes are to the data table—not the original data source.

For each column value in a row, ADO.NET maintains a current and original value. When RejectChanges is called, the current values are set to the original values. The opposite occurs if AcceptChanges is called. The two sets of values can be accessed concurrently through the DataRowVersion enumerations Current and Original:

```
DataRow r = tb.Rows[0];
r["Price"]= 14.95;
r.AcceptChanges();
r["Price"]= 16.95;
Console.WriteLine("Current: {0} Original: {1} ",
        r["Price",DataRowVersion.Current],
        r["Price",DataRowVersion.Original]);
// output:  Current: 16.95  Original: 14.95
```

Keeping track of table row changes takes on added importance when the purpose is to update an underlying data source. We'll see later in this section how the DataAdapter updates database tables with changes made to DataTable rows.

15.5.3 Loading Data into a DataSet

Now that we have seen how to construct a `DataTable` and punch data into it row-by-row, let's look at how data and a data schema can be automatically loaded from a relational database into tables in a `DataSet`. For details on loading XML data, refer to Section 15.6, "XML and ADO.NET," on page 626.

Using the DataReader to Load Data into a DataSet

A `DataReader` object can be used in conjunction with a `DataSet` or `DataTable` to fill a table with the rows generated by a query. This requires creating a `DataReader` object and passing it as a parameter to the `DataTable.Load` method:

```
cmd.CommandText = "SELECT * FROM movies WHERE movie_Year < 1945";
DBDataReader rdr =
        cmd.ExecuteReader(CommandBehavior.CloseConnection);
DataTable dt = new DataTable("movies");
dt.Load(rdr);    // Load data and schema into table
Console.WriteLine(rdr.IsClosed);   // True
```

The `DataReader` is closed automatically after all of the rows have been loaded. The `CloseConnection` parameter ensures that the connection is also closed.

If the table already contains data, the `Load` method merges the new data with the existing rows of data. Merging occurs only if rows share a primary key. If no primary key is defined, rows are appended. An overloaded version of `Load` takes a second parameter that defines how rows are combined. This parameter is a `LoadOption` enumeration type having one of three values: `OverwriteRow`, `PreserveCurrentValues`, or `UpdateCurrentValues`. These options specify whether the merge operation overwrites the entire row, original values only, or current values only. This code segment illustrates how data is merged with existing rows to overwrite the current column values:

```
cmd.CommandText = "SELECT * FROM movies WHERE movie_Year < 1945";
DBDataReader rdr = cmd.ExecuteReader( );
DataTable dt = new DataTable("movies");
dt.Load(rdr);                        // Load rows into table
Console.Write(dt.Rows[0]["movie_Title"]);  // Casablanca

// Assign primary key so rows can be merged
DataColumn[] col = new DataColumn[1];
col[0] = dt.Columns["movie_ID"];
dt.PrimaryKey = col;
DataRow r = dt.Rows[0];              // Get first row of data
r["movie_Title"] = "new title";     // Change current column value
// Since reader is closed, must fill reader again
rdr = cmd.ExecuteReader(CommandBehavior.CloseConnection);
// Merge data with current rows. Overwrites current values
dt.Load(rdr, LoadOption.UpdateCurrentValues );
// Updated value has been overwritten
Console.Write(dt.Rows[0]["movie_Title"]);  // Casablanca
```

Using the DataAdapter to Load Data into a DataSet

A `DataAdapter` object can be used to fill an existing table, or create and fill a new table, with the results from a query. The first step in this process is to create an instance of the

DataAdapter for a specific data provider. As the following code shows, several constructor overloads are available:

```
// (1) The easiest: a query and connection string as arguments
String sql = "SELECT * FROM movies";
SqlDataAdapter da = new SqlDataAdapter(sql, connStr);

// (2) Assign a command object to the SelectCommand property
SqlDataAdapter da = new SqlDataAdapter();
SqlConnection conn = new SqlConnection(connStr);
da.SelectCommand = new SqlCommand(sql,conn);

// (3) Pass in a query string and connection object
SqlConnection conn = new SqlConnection(connStr);
SqlDataAdapter da = new SqlDataAdapter(sql, conn);
```

Of these, the first version is the simplest. It accepts two strings containing the query and connection. From these, it constructs a SqlCommand object that is assigned internally to its SelectCommand property. Unlike the other constructors, there is no need to write code that explicitly creates a SqlCommand or SqlConnection object.

In the overloads that accept a connection object as a parameter, the opening and closing of the connection is left to the DataAdapter. If you add a statement to explicitly open the connection, you must also include code to close it. Otherwise, the DataAdapter leaves it open, which locks the data in the database.

After the DataAdapter object is created, its Fill method is executed to load data into a new or existing table. In this example, a new table is created and assigned the default name Table:

```
DataSet ds = new DataSet();
// Create DataTable, load data, and add to DataSet
// Could use da.Fill(ds,"movies") to specify table name.
int numrecs = da.Fill(ds);   // Returns number of records loaded
```

For an existing table, the behavior of the Fill command depends on whether the table has a primary key. If it does, those rows having a key that matches the key of the incoming data are replaced. Incoming rows that do not match an existing row are appended to the DataTable.

15.5.4 Using the DataAdapter to Update a Database

After a DataAdapter has loaded data into a table, the underlying connection is closed, and subsequent changes made to the data are reflected only in the DataSet—not the underlying data source. To apply changes to the data source, a DataAdapter is used to restore the connection and send the changed rows to the database. The same DataAdapter used to fill the DataSet can be used to perform this task.

The DataAdapter has three properties—InsertCommand, DeleteCommand, and UpdateCommand—that are assigned the actual SQL commands to perform the tasks that correspond to the property name. These commands are executed when the Upate method of the DataAdapter is invoked. The challenge lies in creating the SQL commands that post the changes and assigning them to the appropriate DataAdapter properties. Fortunately, each data provider implements a CommandBuilder class that can be used to handle this task automatically.

The CommandBuilder Object

A CommandBuilder object generates the commands necessary to update a data source with changes made to a DataSet. It's amazingly self-sufficient. You create an instance of it by passing the related DataAdapter object to its constructor; then, when the DataAdapter.Update method is called, the SQL commands are generated and executed. The following segment shows how changes to a DataTable are flushed to the database associated with the DataAdapter:

```
DataTable dt= ds.Tables["movies"]; // Shortcut to reference table

// (1) Use command builder to generate update commands
SqlCommandBuilder sb = new SqlCommandBuilder(da);

// (2) Add movie to table
DataRow drow = dt.NewRow();
drow["movie_Title"] = "Taxi Driver";
drow["movie_Year"] = "1976";
dt.Rows.Add(drow);

// (3) Delete row from table
dt.Rows[4].Delete();

// (4) Edit Column value
dt.Rows[5]["movie_Year"] = "1944";

// (5) Update underlying Sql Server table
int updates = da.Update(ds, "movies");
MessageBox.Show("Rows Changed: " +updates.ToString());   // 3
```

There are a couple of restrictions to be aware of when using the CommandBuilder: The Select command associated with the DataAdapter must refer to a single table, and the source table in the database must include a primary key or a column that contains unique values. This column (or columns) must be included in the original Select command.

Core Note 15.6

You can create your own update commands without using a CommandBuilder. Although it can be a lengthy process, it can also yield more efficient commands. For applications that require considerable database updates, you may want to consult an ADO.NET book for details on coding update logic directly.

Synchronizing the DataSet and the DataBase

As demonstrated in this example, the use of a DataAdapter simplifies and automates the process of updating a database—or any data store. However, there is a rock in this snowball: the problem of multi-user updates. The disconnected model is based on *optimistic concurrency,* an approach in which the rows of the underlying data source are not locked between the time they are read and the time updates are applied to the data source. During this interval, another user may update the data source. Fortunately, the Update method recognizes if changes have occurred since the previous read and fails to apply changes to a row that has been altered.

There are two basic strategies for dealing with a concurrency error when multiple updates are being applied: roll back all changes if a violation occurs, or apply the updates that do not cause an error and identify the ones that do so they can be reprocessed.

Using Transactions to Roll Back Multiple Updates

When the `DataAdapter.ContinueUpdateonErrors` property is set to `false`, an exception is thrown when a row update cannot be completed. This prevents subsequent updates from being attempted, but does not affect updates that occurred prior to the exception. Because updates may be interdependent, applications often require an all-or-none strategy. The easiest way to implement this strategy is to create a .NET transaction in which all of the update commands execute. To do so, create a `SqlTransaction` object and associate it with the `SqlDataAdapter.SelectCommand` by passing it to its constructor. If an exception occurs, the transaction's `Rollback` method is used to undo any changes; if no exceptions occur, the `Commit` method is executed to apply all the update commands. Figure 15.15 is an example that wraps the updates inside a transaction.

```
SqlDataAdapter da = new SqlDataAdapter();
SqlCommandBuilder sb = new SqlCommandBuilder(da);
SqlTransaction tran;
SqlConnection conn = new SqlConnection(connStr);
conn.Open();      // Must open to use with transaction
// (1) Create a transaction
SqlTransaction tran = conn.BeginTransaction();
// (2) Associate the SelectCommand with the transaction
da.SelectCommand = new SqlCommand(sql, conn, tran);
DataSet ds = new DataSet();
da.Fill(ds, "movies");
//
// Code in this section makes updates to DataSet rows
try
{
    int updates = da.Update(ds, "movies");
    MessageBox.Show("Updates: "+updates.ToString());
}
// (3) If exception occurs, roll back all updates in transaction
catch (Exception ex)
{
    MessageBox.Show(ex.Message);   // Error updating
    if (tran != null)
    {
        tran.Rollback();        // Roll back any updates
        tran = null;
        MessageBox.Show("All updates rolled back.");
    }
}
finally
{
// (4) If no errors, commit all updates
    if (tran != null)
    {
        tran.Commit();
        MessageBox.Show("All updates successful. ");
        tran = null;
    }
}
conn.Close();
```

Fig. 15.15 | Using Transaction to Roll Back Database Updates.

Identifying Rows That Cause Update Errors

When DataAdapter.ContinueUpdateonErrors is set to true, processing does not halt if a row cannot be updated. Instead, the DataAdapter updates all rows that do not cause an error. It is then up to the programmer to identify the rows that failed and determine how to reprocess them.

Rows that fail to update are easily identified by their DataRowState property (discussed earlier in the description of DataRows). Rows whose update succeeds have a value of Unchanged; rows that fail have their original Added, Deleted, or Modified value. A simple code segment demonstrates how to loop through the rows and identify those that are not updated (see Fig. 15.16).

Note that even though the delete occurs first, it does not affect the other operations. The SQL statement that deletes or updates a row is based on a row's primary key value—not relative position. Also, be aware that updates on the same row are combined and

```
// SqlDataAdapter da loads movies table
da.ContinueUpdateOnError = true;
DataSet ds = new DataSet();
try
{
   da.Fill(ds, "movies");
   DataTable dt = ds.Tables["movies"];
   SqlCommandBuilder sb = new SqlCommandBuilder(da);
   // ... Sample Update operations
   dt.Rows[29].Delete();                        // Delete
   dt.Rows[30]["movie_Year"] = "1933";          // Update
   dt.Rows[30]["movie_Title"] = "King Kong";    // Update
   dt.Rows[31]["movie_Title"] = "Fantasia";     // Update
   DataRow drow = dt.NewRow();
   drow["movie_Title"] = "M*A*S*H";
   drow["movie_Year"] = "1970";
   dt.Rows.Add(drow);                           // insert
   // Submit updates
   int updates = da.Update(ds, "movies");
   // Following is true if any update failed
   if (ds.HasChanges())
   {
      // Load rows that failed into a DataSet
      DataSet failures = ds.GetChanges();
      int rowsFailed = failures.Rows.Count;
      Console.WriteLine("Update Failures: "+rowsFailed);
      foreach (DataRow r in failures.Tables[0].Rows )
      {
         string state = r.RowState.ToString());
         // Have to reject changes to show deleted row
         if (r.RowState == DataRowState.Deleted)
              r.RejectChanges();
         string ID= ((int)r["movie_ID"]).ToString();
         string msg= state + " Movie ID: "+ID;
         Console.WriteLine(msg);
      }
   }
}
```

Fig. 15.16 | Identify Attempts to Update a Database That Fails.

counted as a single row update by the Update method. In this example, updates to row 30 count as one update.

Handling concurrency issues is not a simple task. After you identify the failures, the next step—how to respond to the failures—is less clear, and depends on the application. Often times, it is necessary to re-read the rows from the database and compare them with the rows that failed in order to determine how to respond. The ability to recognize RowState and the current and original values of rows is the key to developing code that resolves update conflicts.

15.5.5 Defining Relationships Between Tables in a DataSet

A DataRelation is a parent/child relationship between two DataTables. It is defined on matching columns in the two tables. The columns must be the same DataType, and the column in the parent table must have unique values. The syntax for its constructor is

```
public DataRelation(
    string relationName,
    DataColumn parentColumn,
    DataColumn childColumn)
```

A DataSet has a Relations property that provides access to the collection of DataRelations defined for tables contained in the DataSet. Use the Relations.Add method to place relations in the collection. Figure 15.17 illustrates these ideas. It contains code to set up a parent/child relationship between the directors and movies tables in order to list movies by each director.

Relations and Constraints
When a relationship is defined between two tables, it has the effect of adding a Foreign-KeyConstraint to the Constraints collections of the child DataTable. This constraint determines how the child table is affected when rows in a parent table are changed or deleted. In practical terms, this means that if you delete a row in the parent table, you can have the related child row(s) deleted—or optionally, have their key value set to null. Similarly, if a key value is changed in the parent table, the related rows in the child can have their key value changed or set to null.

The rule in effect is determined by the value of the DeleteRule and UpdateRule properties of the constraint. These can take one of four Rule enumeration values:

- Cascade. Deletes or updates related rows in child table. This is the default.
- None. Takes no action.
- SetDefault. Sets key values in child rows to column's default value.
- SetNull. Sets key values in child rows to null.

This code segment illustrates how constraints affect the capability to add a row to a child table and delete or change a row in the parent table. The tables from the preceding example are used.

```
// (1) Try to add row with new key to child table
DataRow row = child.NewRow();
row["movie_directorID"] = 999;
child.Rows.Add(row);    // Fails - 999 does not exist in parent
```

```
// (2) Delete row in parent table
row = parent.Rows[0];
row.Delete();          // Deletes rows in child having this key
// (3) Relax constraints and retry adding row
ds.EnforceConstraints = false;
row["movie_directorID"] = 999;
child.Rows.Add(row);   // Succeeds
ds.EnforceConstraints = true;      // Turn back on
// (4) Change constraint to set rows to null if parent changed
((ForeignKeyConstraint)child.Constraints[0]).DeleteRule =
    Rule.SetNull ;
```

```
DataSet ds = new DataSet();
// (1) Fill table with movies
string sql = "SELECT movie_ID,movie_Title,movie_DirectorID,
    movie_Year FROM movies";
SqlConnection conn = new SqlConnection(connStr);
SqlCommand cmd = new SqlCommand();
SqlDataAdapter da = new SqlDataAdapter(sql, conn);
da.Fill(ds, "movies");
// (2) Fill table with directors
sql = "SELECT director_id,(first_name + ' '+ last_name) AS
    fullname FROM directors";
da.SelectCommand.CommandText = sql;
da.Fill(ds, "directors");
// (3) Define relationship between directors and movies
DataTable parent = ds.Tables["directors"];
DataTable child = ds.Tables["movies"];
DataRelation relation = new DataRelation("directormovies",
    parent.Columns["director_ID"],
    child.Columns["movie_DirectorID"]);
// (4) Add relation to DataSet
ds.Relations.Add(relation);
// (5) List each director and his or her movies
foreach (DataRow r in parent.Rows)
{
    Console.WriteLine(r["fullname"];       // Director name
    foreach (DataRow rc in
    r.GetChildRows("directormovies"))
    {
        Console.WriteLine("  "+rc["movie_title"]);
    }
}
/*
    Sample Output:
        David Lean
            Lawrence of Arabia
            Bridge on the River Kwai, The
        Victor Fleming
            Gone with the Wind
            Wizard of Oz, The
*/
```

Fig. 15.17 | Create a Relationship Between the Directors and Movies Tables.

Note that setting the EnforceConstraints property to false turns off all constraints—which in database terms eliminates the check for *referential integrity*.[3] This allows a movie to be added even though its movie_DirectorID column (foreign key) does not have a corresponding row in the directors table. It also permits a director to be deleted even though a movie by that director exists in the movies table. This clearly compromises the integrity of the database and should be used only when testing or populating individual tables in a database.

15.5.6 Choosing Between the Connected and Disconnected Model

The DataReader and DataSet offer different approaches to processing data—each with its advantages and disadvantages. The DataReader provides forward-only, read-only access to data. By processing a row at a time, it minimizes memory requirements. A DataSet, on the other hand, offers read/write access to data, but requires enough memory to hold a copy of the data fetched from a data source. From this, you can derive a couple of general rules: If the application does not require the capability to update the data source and is used merely for display and selection purposes, a DataReader should be the first consideration; if the application requires updating data, a DataSet should be considered.

Of course, the general rules have to be weighed against other factors. If the data source contains a large number of records, a DataSet may require too many resources; or if the data requires only a few updates, the combination of DataReader and Command object to execute updates may make more sense. Despite the gray areas, there are many situations where one is clearly preferable to the other.

A DataSet is a good choice when the following apply:

* Data need to be serialized and/or sent over the wire using HTTP.
* Multiple read-only controls on a Windows Form are bound to the data source.
* A Windows Form control such as a GridView or DataView is bound to an updatable data source.
* A desktop application must edit, add, and delete rows of data.

A DataReader is a good choice when the following apply:

* A large number of records must be handled so that the memory requirements and time to load make a DataSet impracticable.
* The data is read-only and bound to a Windows or Web Form list control.
* The database is highly volatile, and the contents of a DataSet might be updated often.

15.6 XML and ADO.NET

Just as relational data has a schema that defines its tables, columns, and relationships, XML uses a Schema Definition language (XSD) to define the layout of an XML document. Its main use is to validate the content of XML data. See Section 10.1, "Working with XML," for a discussion of XML Schema.

---

3.   The foreign key in any referencing table must always refer to a valid row in the referenced table.

The XML classes reside in the System.Xml namespace hierarchy and are not part of ADO.NET. However, the ADO.NET DataSet class provides a bridge between the two with a set of methods that interacts with XML data and schemas:

- ReadXML. Loads XML data into a DatSet.

- WriteXml and GetXml. Writes the DataSet's contents to an XML formatted stream.

- WriteXmlSchema and GetXmlSchema. Generates an XML Schema from the DataSet schema.

- ReadXmlSchema. Reads an XML Schema file and creates a database schema.

- InferXmlSchema. Creates a DataSet schema from XML data.

- GetXml and GetXmlSchema, Returns a string containing the XML representation of the data or the XSD schema for XML representation.

We'll first look at examples that show how to write XML from a DataSet. This XML output is then used as input in subsequent examples that create a DataSet from XML.

15.6.1 Using a DataSet to Create XML Data and Schema Files

When working with XML, the DataSet is used as an intermediary to convert between XML and relational data. For this to work, the XML data should be structured so that it can be represented by the relationships and row-column layout that characterizes relational data.

The following code segment illustrates how easy it is to create an XML data file and schema from a DataSet's contents. A DataAdapter is used to populate a DataSet with a subset of the movies table. The WriteXml and WriteXmlSchema methods are then used to translate this to XML output.

```
DataSet ds = new DataSet("films");
DataTable dt = ds.Tables.Add("movies");
string sql = "SELECT * FROM movies WHERE bestPicture='Y'";
SqlDataAdapter da = new SqlDataAdapter(sql, conn);
da.Fill(dt);
// Write Schema representing DataTable to a file
ds.WriteXmlSchema("c:\\oscars.xsd");   // create schema
// Write Table data to an XML file
ds.WriteXml("c:\\oscarwinners.xml");   // data in xml format
/* To place schema inline with XML data in same file:
    ds.WriteXml(("c:\\oscarwinners.xml",
             XmlWriteMode.WriteSchema);
*/
```

The schema output shown in Fig. 15.18 defines the permissible content of an XML document (file). If you compare this with Fig. 15.4 on page 602, you can get a general feel for how it works. For example, each field in the movies table is represented by an element containing the permissible field name and type.

```
<?xml version="1.0" encoding="utf-16"?>
<xs:schema id="films" xmlns=""
xmlns:xs="http://www.w3.org/2001/XMLSchema"
xmlns:msdata="urn:schemas-microsoft-com:xml-msdata">
  <xs:element name="films" msdata:IsDataSet="true">
    <xs:complexType>
      <xs:choice minOccurs="0" maxOccurs="unbounded">
        <xs:element name="movies">
          <xs:complexType>
            <xs:sequence>
              <xs:element name="movie_ID" type="xs:int"
                        minOccurs="0" />
              <xs:element name="movie_Title" type="xs:string"
                        minOccurs="0" />
              <xs:element name="movie_Year" type="xs:int"
                        minOccurs="0" />
              <xs:element name="movie_DirectorID" type="xs:int"
                        minOccurs="0" />
              <xs:element name="AFIRank" type="xs:int"
                        minOccurs="0" />
              <xs:element name="bestPicture" type="xs:string"
                        minOccurs="0" />
            </xs:sequence>
          </xs:complexType>
        </xs:element>
      </xs:choice>
    </xs:complexType>
  </xs:element>
</xs:schema>
```

Fig. 15.18 | XML Schema from Movies Table—oscars.xsd.

Figure 15.19 displays an abridged listing of the XML version of the relational data. The name of the DataSet is the root element. Each row in the table is represented by a child element (movies) containing elements that correspond to the columns in the data table.

15.6.2 Creating a DataSet Schema from XML

Each ADO.NET DataSet has a schema that defines the tables, table columns, and table relationships that comprise the DataSet. As we saw in the preceding example, this schema can be translated into an XML schema using the WriteXmlSchema method. ReadXmlSchema mirrors the process—adding tables and relationships to a DataSet. In this example, the XML schema for the movies table (refer to Fig. 15.18) is used to create a DataSet schema:

```
DataSet ds = new DataSet();
ds.ReadXmlSchema("c:\\oscars.xsd");
DataTable tb = ds.Tables[0];
// List Columns for table
string colList = tb.TableName +": ";
for (int i = 0; i < tb.Columns.Count; i++)
   { colList += tb.Columns[i].Caption + "  "; }
Console.WriteLine(colList);
/* output is:
movies: movie_ID  movie_Title  movie_Year movie_DirectorID
        bestpicture AFIRank
*/
```

```
<?xml version="1.0" encoding="utf-16"?>
<?xml version="1.0" standalone="yes"?>
<films>
  <movies>
    <movie_ID>5</movie_ID>
    <movie_Title>Citizen Kane </movie_Title>
    <movie_Year>1941</movie_Year>
       <movie_DirectorID>1</movie_Director>
    <AFIRank>1</AFIRank>
    <bestPicture>Y</bestPicture>
  </movies>
  <movies>
    <movie_ID>6</movie_ID>
    <movie_Title>Casablanca </movie_Title>
    <movie_Year>1942</movie_Year>
    <movie_DirectorID>2</movie_Director>
    <AFIRank>2</AFIRank>
    <bestPicture>Y</bestPicture>
  </movies>
  ...
</films>
```

Fig. 15.19 | Movies Data as an XML Document—`oscarwinners.xml`.

It is also possible to create a schema by inferring its structure from the XML data or using a `DataAdapter` to configure the schema:

```
// (1) Create schema by inferring it from XML data
ds.Tables.Clear();   // Remove tables from DataSet
ds.InferXmlSchema("c:\\oscarwinners.xml",null);

// (2) Create schema using Data Adapter
ds.Tables.Clear();
string sql = "SELECT * FROM movies";
SqlDataAdapter da = new SqlDataAdapter(sql, connStr);
// Creates DataTable named "movies"
da.FillSchema(ds, SchemaType.Source, "movies");
```

Core Note 15.7

By creating the `DataSet` schema(s) in a separate step from reading in XML data, you can control the data that is read from the source XML file. Only data for the columns defined by the schema are read in. Conversely, if the schema defines more columns than are in the XML file, these columns are empty in the `DataSet`.

15.6.3 Reading XML Data into a DataSet

The `DataSet.ReadXml` method provides a way to read either data only or both the data and schema into a `DataSet`. The method has several overloads that determine whether a schema is also created. The two overloads used with files are

```
XmlReadMode ReadXml(string XMLfilename);
XmlReadMode ReadXml(string XMLfilename, XmlReadMode mode);
```

Parameters:

XMLfilename   Name of file (.xml) containing XML data.
mode   One of the XmlReadMode enumeration values.

The XmlReadMode parameter merits special attention. Its value specifies how a schema is derived for the table(s) in a DataSet. It can specify three sources for the schema: from a schema contained (inline) in the XML file, from the schema already associated with the DataSet, or by inferring a schema from the contents of the XML file. The table in Fig. 15.20 summarizes how selected enumeration members specify the schema source. The numbers in the table indicate the order in which a schema is selected. For example, ReadSchema specifies that the inline schema is the first choice; if it does not exist, the schema associated with the DataSet is used; if neither exists, a data table is not built.

The code segment in Fig. 15.21 loads an XML file into a DataSet and then calls a method to display the contents of each row in the table created. Because the DataSet does not have a predefined schema, and the file does not include an inline schema, ReadXml infers it from the contents of the file.

Note the use of ExtendedProperties to store the name of the data source in the data set. Because this collection of custom properties is implemented as a Hashtable, it is accessed using that syntax:

```
string src = (string)ds.ExtendedProperties["source"];
ds.ExtendedProperties.Clear(); // clear hash table
```

Using ReadXml with Nested XML Data

The XML file used in the preceding example has a simple structure that is easily transformed into a single table: The <movies> tag (refer to Fig. 15.19) represents a row in a table, and the elements contained within it become column values. Most XML is more complex than this example and requires multiple tables to represent it. Although ReadXml

	Schema Source			
XmlReadMode	**Inline**	**DataSet**	**Infer**	**Comment**
Auto	1	2	3	The default when no XmlReadMode is provided.
IgnoreSchema		1		Uses only the DataSet's schema. Data in the file that is not in the schema is ignored.
InferSchema			1	Ignores inline schema, and builds tables by inference from XML file. Error occurs if DataSet already contains conflicting schema.
ReadSchema	1	2		If tables created from inline schema already exist in DataSet, an exception is thrown.

Fig. 15.20 | XmlReadMode Values Determine How a Schema Is Derived for a DataSet.

```
//  Load XML data into dataset and create schema if one does
//  not exist
DataSet ds = new DataSet();
ds.ReadXml("c:\\oscarwinners.xml");
// Save source of data in dataset
ds.ExtendedProperties.Add("source", "c:\\oscarwinners.xml");
ShowTable(ds.Tables[0]);

// Display each row in table
private void ShowTable(DataTable t)
{
    foreach(DataRow dr in t.Rows)
    {
        StringBuilder sb = new StringBuilder("Table: ");
        sb.Append(t.TableName).Append("\n");
        foreach(DataColumn c in t.Columns)
        {
            sb.Append(c.Caption).Append(": ");
            sb.Append(dr[c.ColumnName].ToString()).Append("\n");
        }
        Console.WriteLine(sb.ToString());
    }
}
```

Fig. 15.21 | Using ReadXml to Load XML Data into a DataSet.

has limitations (it cannot handle attributes), it can recognize nested XML and render multiple tables from it. As an example, let's alter the oscarwinners.xml file to include a <director> tag within each <movies> block.

```
<films>
  <movies>
    <movie_ID>5</movie_ID>
    <movie_Title>Citizen Kane </movie_Title>
    <movie_Year>1941</movie_Year>
    <director>
      <first_name>Orson</first_name>
      <last_name>Welles</last_name>
    </director>
    <bestPicture>Y</bestPicture>
    <AFIRank>1</AFIRank>
  </movies>
  ... more movies here
</films>
```

Next, run this code to display the contents of the table(s) created:

```
DataSet ds = new DataSet();
ds.ReadXml("c:\\oscarwinnersv2.xml");
foreach (DataTable dt in ds.Tables)
    ShowTable(dt);
```

Figure 15.22 depicts the DataSet tables created from reading the XML file. It creates two tables, automatically generates a movies_ID key for each table, and assigns values to this key, which link a row in the movies table to an associated row in the director table.

DataTable

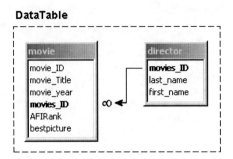

Fig. 15.22 | DataSet tables and relationship created from XML.

15.7 Summary

ADO.NET supports two database connectivity models: connected and disconnected. The connected model remains connected to the underlying database while traversing a resultset in a forward-only read-only manner; the disconnected model can retrieve a resultset into an in-memory cache and disconnect itself from the source data. Two distinctly separate data storage objects are available for implementing these models: the DataReader and the DataSet. The DataReader serves up data a row at a time; the DataSet functions as an in-memory relational database. Changes to the contents of the DataSet can be posted back to the original data source using the DataAdapter object. This object includes properties and methods designed to address synchronization issues that arise when disconnected data is used to update a database.

Although XML classes are not part of the ADO.NET namespaces, a level of interaction between relational and XML data is provided through the ADO.NET DataSet class. This class includes WriteXmlSchema and WriteXml methods that are used to create an XML schema and document. The versatile DataSet.ReadXml method has several overloads that are used to construct a DataSet from an XML data file or schema.

15.8 Test Your Understanding

1. What four classes must a .NET data provider supply?

2. Given the following code:

```
SqlCommand cmd = new SqlCommand();
cmd.Connection = conn;
string s = "insert into movies(movie_title, movie_year,
           bestpicture)values(&p1,&p2,&p3); "
cmd.CommandText= s;
```

which of the following code segments completes the SQL query string to insert the movie row?

a) `string p1="Star Wars";`
   `int p2 = 1977;`
   `string p3= "N";`

b) ```
cmd.Parameters.AddWithValue ("@p1","Star Wars");
cmd.Parameters.AddWithValue ("@p2", "1977");
cmd.Parameters.AddWithValue ("@p3", "N");
```

c) ```
cmd.Parameters.Add("@p1", SqlDbType.NVarChar, 100);
cmd.Parameters.Add("@p2", SqlDbType.NVarChar, 4);
cmd.Parameters.Add("@p3", SqlDbType.NVarChar, 1);
p1.Value = "Star Wars";
p2.Value = "1977";
p3.Value = "N";
```

3. Describe the purpose of these three command object methods:

```
ExecuteNonQuery
ExecuteReader
ExecuteScalar
```

4. Compare the role of the DataReader and the DataAdapter.

5. What is the difference between a DataSet and a DataTable?

6. The DataRowState property maintains the status of a row. Which of these is not a valid DataRowState value?

   a) Added

   b) Deleted

   c) Rejected

   d) Changed

7. You have an XML file and want to create a DataSet that has rows and columns that match the layout of the XML file. The XML file does not have a schema (.xsd) file associated with it. What DataSet method is used to create the DataSet schema?

16

Data Binding with Windows Forms Controls

OBJECTIVES

- *DataBinding Overview:* Associating data with a control is easy on the surface; however, it is important to understand what's going on underneath. This section provides an overview of simple and complex data binding, one-way and two-way data binding, and the role of the `Binding` and `BindingManagerBase` classes.

- *A Data Binding Application:* A Windows Forms application illustrates how to bind data in a `DataSet` and `DataTable` to simple and complex controls.

- *The DataGridView:* The `DataGridView` introduced with .NET 2.0 has a rich set of features that enable it to display and manipulate relational data. Examples illustrate how to create a master-detail grid and a virtual mode grid.

16.1 Introduction

Chapter 15, "ADO.NET." discussed how to access data using ADO.NET. This chapter extends the discussion to describe the techniques by which data is "bound" to the Windows Forms controls that display data. Because all controls derive their data binding capabilities from the base Control class, knowledge of its properties and methods can be applied to all controls.

Data binding comes in two flavors: simple and complex. Controls that contain one value, such as a label or Textbox, rely on simple binding. Controls populated with rows of data, such as a ListBox, DataGrid, or DataGridView, require complex binding. We'll look at how both are implemented.

Of the Windows Forms controls that bind to data, the DataGridView is the most complex and useful. Its layout maps directly to the rows and columns of a relational database or similarly structured XML document. This chapter takes a detailed look at the properties and methods of this control, and provides examples of how this control can be used to implement common database applications.

16.2 Overview of Data Binding

Data binding provides a way to link the contents of a control with an underlying data source. The advantage to this linkage or "binding" is that changes to the immediate data source can be reflected automatically in data controls bound to it, and changes in the data control are posted automatically to the intermediate data source. The term *intermediate data source* is used to distinguish it from the original data source, which may be an external database. The controls cannot be bound directly to a data source over an active connection. Binding is restricted to the in-memory representation of the data. Figure 16.1 shows the basic components of the binding model: the original data source, the intermediate storage, and the Form controls that are bound to values in the local storage through a binding object. Let's examine the model in more detail.

16.2.1 Simple Data Binding

Simple data binding, which is available to all controls, links a data source to one or more properties of a control. A good example is the Textbox control that exposes easily recognizable properties such as Text, Width, and BackColor. An application can set these dynamically by binding them to a data source. Here is a code segment that creates an object whose public properties are mapped to the properties on the TextBox.

```
// Create object (width, text, color)
TextParms tp = new TextParms(200, "Casablanca", Color.Beige);
// Bind text and BackColor properties of control
txtMovie.DataBindings.Add("Text", tp, "Tb_Text");
txtMovie.DataBindings.Add("BackColor", tp, "Tb_Background");

// Or create binding and then add in two steps
Binding binding = new Binding("Width", tp, "Tb_Width");
txtMovie.DataBindings.Add(binding);
```

The DataBindings.Add method creates a collection of bindings that links the data source to the control's properties. The method's syntax is

```
DataBindings.Add( control property, data source, data member)
```

control property	Property on the control that is being bound.
data source	Object that contains data being bound to control.
data member	Data member on the data source that is being used. Set this to null if the data source's ToString() method provides the value.

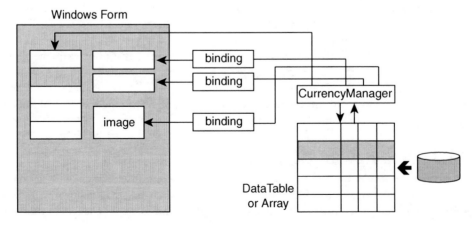

Fig. 16.1 | Multiple controls bound to a single data source.

A control may have multiple bindings associated with it, but only one per property. This means that the code used to create a binding can be executed only once; a second attempt would generate an exception. To avoid this, each call to add a binding should be preceded with code that checks to see if a binding already exists; if there is a binding, it should be removed.

```
if (txtMovie.DataBindings["Text"] != null)
    txtMovie.DataBindings.Remove(txtMovie.DataBindings["Text"]);
txtMovie.DataBindings.Add("Text", tp, "Tb_Text");
```

Binding to a List

The true value of data binding becomes obvious when the data source contains multiple items to be displayed. In the preceding example, the control was bound to a single object. Let's now create an array of these objects—each representing a different movie. Instead of binding to a single object, the control is bound to the array (see Fig. 16.2). The control can still only display a single movie title at a time, but we can scroll through the array and display a different title that corresponds to the current array item selected. This scrolling is accomplished using a *binding manager*, which is discussed shortly.

This example creates an ArrayList of objects that are used to set the TextBox properties on the fly.

```
ArrayList tbList = new ArrayList();
// Beige color indicated movie won oscar as best picture
tbList.Add(new TextParms(200,"Casablanca",Color.Beige));
tbList.Add(new TextParms(200, "Citizen Kane", Color.White));
tbList.Add(new TextParms(200, "King Kong", Color.White));
// Bind to properties on the Textbox
txtMovie.DataBindings.Add("Text", tbList, "Tb_Text");
txtMovie.DataBindings.Add("BackColor", tbList,
                          "Tb_Background");
txtMovie.DataBindings.Add("Width", tbList, "Tb_Width");
```

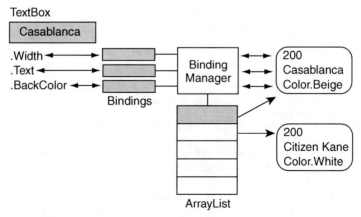

Fig. 16.2 | Binding TextBox properties to objects in a list.

The one difference in the bindings from the preceding example is that the data source now refers to the `ArrayList`. By default, the `TextBox` takes the values associated with the first item in the array. When the index of the array points to the second row, the displayed value changes to "Citizen Kane."

Simple Binding with ADO.NET

Binding to a table in a `DataSet` is basically the same as binding to a list. In this example, the `Text` property of the control is bound to the `movie_Year` column in a `DataTable`.

```
ds = new DataSet("films");
string sql = "select * from movies order by movie_Year";
da = new SqlDataAdapter(sql, conn);
da.Fill(ds,"movies");        // create datatable "movies"
// Bind text property to movie_Year column in movies table
txtYr.DataBindings.Add("Text", ds,"movies.movie_Year");
```

Although the control could be bound directly to a `DataTable`, the recommended approach is to bind the property to a `DataSet` and use the `DataTable` name as a qualifier to specify the column that provides the data. This makes it clear which table the value is coming from.

16.2.2 Complex Data Binding with List Controls

Complex binding is only available on controls that include properties to specify a data source and data members on the data source. This select group of controls is limited to the `ListBox`, `CheckedListBox`, `ComboBox`, `DataGrid`, and `DataGridView`. Complex binding allows each control to bind to a collection of data—the data source must support the `IList` interface—and display multiple items at once. Because the `DataGridView` is discussed at length in the last half of this chapter, let's look at how complex binding is implemented on the `ListBox` control. The details also apply to other `List` controls.

Binding a list control to a data source requires setting a minimum of two properties: `DataSource`, which specifies the source, and `DisplayMember`, which describes the member—usually a data column or property—in the data source that is displayed in the control. This code segment illustrates how a `ListBox` bound to a `DataSet` displays movie titles:

```
da.Fill(ds,"movies");
DataTable dt = ds.Tables[0];
// Minimum properties to bind listbox to a DataTable
listBox1.DataSource = ds;
listBox1.DisplayMember = "movies.movie_Title";

// Optional property that assigns a value to each item row
listBox1.ValueMember = "movies.movie_ID";
```

After these values are set, the list box is automatically filled. The `DataSource` property can be changed programmatically to fill the control with a different set of data, or it can be set to `null` to clear the control's content. Note also that although no `Binding` object is explicitly created, a `DataBindings` collection is created underneath and is accessible through code.

The bound list box control is often grouped with other controls, such as a text box or label, in order to display multiple values from a row of data. When the controls are bound to the same data source, scrolling through the list box causes each control to display a value from the same data row. To illustrate, let's add the following simple bindings to the preceding code:

```
txtStudio.DataBindings.Add("Text", ds,"movies.studio");
txtYear.DataBindings.Add("Text", ds,"movies.movie_Year");
```

These text boxes display the studio name and year of the movie currently selected in the list box (see Fig. 16.3).

16.2.3 One-Way and Two-Way Data Binding

The data bound to a control can be changed in two ways: by updating the underlying data source, such as adding a row to a table, or by modifying the visible contents of the control. In both cases, the changes should be reflected in the associated control or data source—a process referred to as two-way data binding. In general, that is what happens. However, a control may be bound to a data source in read-only mode when its only purpose is to present data. To understand how these techniques are implemented, let's look at how updating occurs—from the perspective of the control and the data source.

Effects on the Data Source of Updating a Control Value

By default, changes made to data in a control are also made to the underlying in-memory data source. If the year value in Fig. 16.3 is changed, the value in the corresponding row and column of the DataTable is also changed. Note that if the year is represented as an integer in the table, the value entered in the control must be an integer value. Data binding automatically checks types and rejects values (keeps the same value in the control) that do not match the type of the underlying data.

In the case where a control is bound to a property on an object, the property must provide write support in order for its value to be updated. For example, if the year and studio list boxes in the preceding example were bound to the following properties,

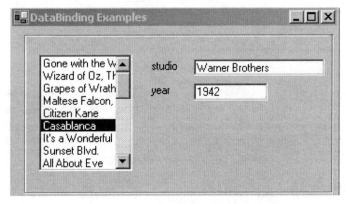

Fig. 16.3 | Using data binding to populate controls on a form.

respectively, only year could be updated; changes made to the studio control would be ignored and it would revert to its original value.

```
public int Movie_Year { set { myYear = value;  }
                        get { return myYear;   } }

// Read only property. Control cannot update this.
public string Studio  { get { return myStudio; } }
```

Note that changes in a control are not propagated to the data source until the user moves to another item in the GUI control. Underneath, this changes the current position within the binding manager—firing an event that causes the data to be updated.

Effects on a Control of Updating the Data Source

When a DataSet is used as the data source for controls, any additions, deletions, or changes made to the data are automatically reflected in the associated bound control(s). Custom data sources require some programming assistance to accomplish this.

If a control is bound to an object property, a change to the value of that property is not automatically sent to the control. Instead, the binding manager looks for an event named propertyChanged on the data source. If found, it provides a handler for this event to receive notice when that property's value changes. To enable the binding manager to handle a changed value, you must define a propertyChanged event on the data source class, and fire the event when a change occurs. To illustrate, let's extend the previous example to add the event to the class containing the Movie_Year property, and add code to fire the event when the property changes.

```
// Event to notify bound control that value has changed
public event EventHandler Movie_YearChanged;

// Property control is bound to year value
public int Movie_Year {
    set {
            myYear = value;
            // Notify bound control(s) of change
            if (Movie_YearChanged != null)
                Movie_YearChanged(this, EventArgs.Empty);
    }
    get { return myYear; }
}
```

The other situation to handle is when a data item is deleted from or added to the data source. Controls that are bound to the source using simple binding are updated automatically; controls using complex binding are not. In the latter case, the update can be forced by executing the Refresh method of a CurrencyManager object. As we see next, the CurrencyManager is a binding manager especially designed for list data sources.

16.2.4 Using Binding Managers

As illustrated in Fig. 16.4, each data source has a binding manager that keeps track of all connections to it. When the data source is updated, the binding manager is responsible for synchronizing the values in all controls bound to the data. Conversely, if a value is changed

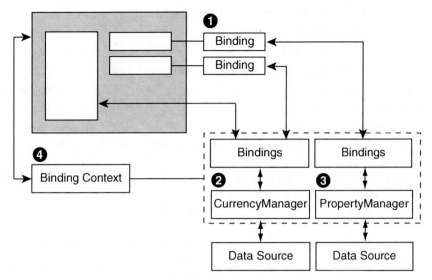

Fig. 16.4 | Binding managers synchronize the data source and controls.

on one of the bound controls, the manager updates the source data accordingly. A binding manager is associated with only one data source. Thus, if an application has controls bound to multiple data sources, each will have its own manager.

Binding requires the interaction of several objects to coordinate the two-way flow of data between a data source and control. Let's look at the four most important objects, which are denoted by numbers in Fig. 16.4.

1. Binding. Maintains a simple binding between a property on a control and a property on a single object. The following statements demonstrate how to create a binding and gain access to it:

    ```
    txtYr.DataBindings.Add("Text", ds,
                        "movies.movie_Year");
    Binding binding = txtYr.DataBindings["Text"];
    // "txtYr"
    MessageBox.Show(binding.Control.ToString());
    // Create a binding manager object
    BindingManagerBase mgr= binding.BindingManagerBase;
    ```

2. CurrencyManager. This class derives from the abstract BindingManagerBase class and serves as a binding manager for list data sources such as a DataTable or Array. This object provides five members that an application can use to manage the relationship between a data source and control:

    -   Bindings. Returns the collection of bindings being managed.

    -   Count. The number of rows in the list that is being managed.

    -   Current. Returns the current item (such as a row) in the data source as an object.

- **Position.** Gets/sets the position in the data source currently indexed by the control.

- **PositionChanged.** Fires when the Position in the list changes.

- **CurrentChanged.** Is triggered when the bound value changes.

3. **PropertyManager.** This class, which also derives from BindingManagerBase, maps the properties on an object to properties on a bound control.

4. **BindingContext.** Observe in Fig. 16.4 that the BindingContext is linked to a form and a collection of BindingManagerBase objects. Its job is to manage a collection of binding managers for a specific control—in this case, a Form. The control could just as well be a Panel or GroupBox on a form. A program's main interest in the BindingContext is to use it to gain access to the binding manager for a data source. These statements, for example, return the manager for the table movies.

```
BindingManagerBase mgr = this.BindingContext[ds,"movies"];
// Or use casting to get specific manager.
CurrencyManager mgr= (CurrencyManager)
                    this.BindingContext[ds,"movies"];
```

Using the BindingManagerBase to Navigate a List

Let's now look at how the members of the BindingManagerBase class are used to move through the items in a source data list and simultaneously update the contents of controls bound to the list. The example binds a list box and text box to the familiar movies data table.

```
// Bind listbox to a dataset.datatable
listBox1.DataSource = ds;
listBox1.DisplayMember = "movies.movie_Title";

// Bind to TextBox
txtStudio.DataBindings.Add("text", ds, "movies.studio");
// BindingManagerBase bmb has class-wide scope
bmb = this.BindingContext[ds, "movies"];
// Create delegate pointing to event handler
bmb.PositionChanged += new
        EventHandler(bmb_PositionChanged);
```

The following method moves to the next item in the data source list when a button is clicked. It would typically be paired with a method to move backward in the list.

```
// This method moves to the next row in the table.
// If at the end of the table it moves to the beginning.
private void Forward_Click (object sender, EventArgs e)
{
    if (listBox1.Items.Count > 0)
    {
        bmb.Position = bmb.Position >= bmb.Count - 1 ? 0 :
            ++bmb.Position;
    }
}
```

The PositionChanged event is fired each time the binding manager moves to a new position in the list. This could be triggered programmatically or by the user clicking a row in the list box control.

```
private void bmb_PositionChanged(object sender,
                                 EventArgs e)
{
    BindingManagerBase bmb = (BindingManagerBase)sender;
    // Item should be a DataRowView if from a table
    object ob = bmb.Current.GetType();
    if (ob == typeof(System.Data.DataRowView))
    {
        DataRowView view = (DataRowView)bmb.Current;
        // Could access: ((string)view["movie_Title"]);
    }
}
```

Note that the Current property is used to return an object representing the current item. The data source in this example is a data table, but the object returned is not the expected DataRow—it is a DataRowView object. It is up to the code to provide the proper casting to access properties in the selected item.

16.3 Using Simple and Complex Data Binding in an Application

Several concepts were introduced in the first section. Let's bring them together in an application that relies on data binding to display and update information from the Films database. Figure 16.5 shows a screen shot of the application's user interface.

Each control on the Windows Form—except buttons—is bound to a data source. A ListBox and ComboBox illustrate complex binding; two text boxes, a CheckBox, and a

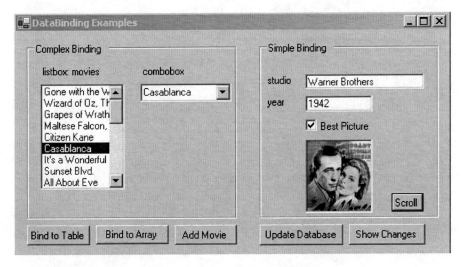

Fig. 16.5 | Application combining complex and simple binding.

PictureBox, are bound using simple binding. The controls can be bound dynamically to either a data table or an array that contains custom objects. The Scroll button moves down the list box by internally using a binding manager to advance to the next item in the data source list. Let's dissect the program by looking at code associated with the buttons. Much of the code should be familiar from code segments in the previous section and does not require further explanation.

16.3.1 Binding to a DataTable

The code in Fig. 16.6 is executed when the Bind to Table button is clicked. It loads the necessary data from the Films database into a table and binds the controls on the form to it. This populates the ListBox and ComboBox with a list of movie titles. The value in the other controls is derived from the content of the current row (highlighted in the list box). The most interesting of these is the PictureBox, which has its BackgroundImage property bound to a column in the table containing images. Because the database does not contain images, the program adds this column to the data table and fills it with images for the movie in each row.

```
// Bind control to data from a database
private void btnTableBind_Click(object sender, EventArgs e)
{
    SqlConnection conn = new SqlConnection(GetString());
    conn.Open();
    ds = new DataSet("films");
    string sql = "SELECT movie_ID, movie_title, movie_year,
        studio, afi_rank, CASE WHEN bestpicture ='Y'
        THEN 1 ELSE 0 END as BestPicture FROM movies ORDER BY
        movie_Year";
    da = new SqlDataAdapter(sql, conn);
    // Command builder keeps track of changes to data
    SqlCommandBuilder sb = new SqlCommandBuilder(da);
    da.Fill(ds,"movies");
    DataTable dt = ds.Tables[0];
    Data Column dCol = new DataColumn("movie_Image",
        Type.GetType("System.Object"));
    dt.Columns.Add(dCol);
    // Place image in new column. Name is based on movie ranking.
    Image defaultImage = Image.FromFile(@"c:\defaultimg.jpg");
    foreach (DataRow dRow in dt.Rows)
    {
        string rank = ((int)dRow["afi_rank"]).ToString();
        string imgFile = "c:\\afi" + rank + ".gif";
        try
        {
            Image imgObject = Image.FromFile(imgFile);
            dRow["movie_Image"] = imgObject;
        }
        catch (Exception ex)
        {
            dRow["movie_Image"] = defaultImage;
        }
    }
}
```

Fig. 16.6 | Binding Controls to a DataSet. (Part 1 of 2.)

```
   // Nothing to this point should be considered a change
   dt.AcceptChanges();
// Bind listbox and combobox to datasource
   listBox1.DataSource = ds;
   listBox1.DisplayMember = "movies.movie_Title";
   listBox1.ValueMember = "movies.movie_ID";
   comboBox1.DataSource = ds;
   comboBox1.DisplayMember = "movies.movie_Title";
   // Binding manager has global scope
   bmb = this.BindingContext[ds, "movies"];
 bmb.PositionChanged += new
        EventHandler(bmb_PositionChanged);
    try
  {
    // TextBox.Text  - binds to studio name
    if(txtStudio.DataBindings["text"] != null)
         txtStudio.DataBindings.Remove(
             txtStudio.DataBindings["Text"]);
    txtStudio.DataBindings.Add("text", ds, "movies.studio");

    // TextBox.Text - binds to year movie released
    if(txtYear.DataBindings["text"] != null)
         txtYear.DataBindings.Remove(
              txtYear.DataBindings["Text"]);
    txtYear.DataBindings.Add("text", ds,
                             "movies.movie_year");

    // CheckBox.Checked - binds to best picture value (0 or 1)
    if (checkBox1.DataBindings["Checked"] != null)
         checkBox1.DataBindings.Remove(
             checkBox1.DataBindings["Checked"]);
    checkBox1.DataBindings.Add("Checked", ds,
         "movies.BestPicture");

    // PictureBox.BackgroundImage - Binds to image
    if (pictureBox1.DataBindings["BackgroundImage"] != null)
         pictureBox1.DataBindings.Remove(
             pictureBox1.DataBindings["BackgroundImage"]);
    pictureBox1.DataBindings.Add("BackgroundImage", ds,
         "movies.movie_Image");
  }
  catch (Exception ex)
  {
    MessageBox.Show(ex.Message);
  }
}
```

Fig. 16.6 | Binding Controls to a DataSet. (Part 2 of 2.)

16.3.2 Binding Controls to an ArrayList

Clicking the Bind to Array button, binds the controls to an ArrayList that is filled with instances of the custom class MyMovie (see Fig. 16.7). After the data source is created, the binding process is identical to that followed with the data set.

```
// Bind control to array populated with instances of custom class
private void BindToArray()
{
    movieList = new ArrayList();
    Image movieImg = Image.FromFile(@"c:\defaultimg.jpg");
    // Create objects and add to array
    movieList.Add(new MyMovie("2","Casablanca",1942,
            "Warner Bros.",true, Image.FromFile("c:\afi2.gif")));
    movieList.Add(new MyMovie("1","Citizen Kane", 1941,
            "RKO", false,
            Image.FromFile("c:\afi1.gif")));
    movieList.Add(new MyMovie("4","Gone with the Wind", 1941,
            "Selznick International", true,
            Image.FromFile("c:\afi4.gif")));
    //
    listBox1.DataSource = movieList;
    listBox1.DisplayMember = "Movie_Title";
    //
    comboBox1.DataSource = movieList;
    comboBox1.DisplayMember = "Movie_Title";
    bmb = this.BindingContext[movieList]; ;
    bmb.PositionChanged += new
            EventHandler(bmb_PositionChanged);
    if (txtStudio.DataBindings["Text"] != null)
        txtStudio.DataBindings.Remove(
                txtStudio.DataBindings["Text"]);
    txtStudio.DataBindings.Add("Text", movieList, "Studio");
    //
    if (txtYear.DataBindings["Text"] != null)
        txtYear.DataBindings.Remove(
                txtYear.DataBindings["Text"]);
    txtYear.DataBindings.Add("Text", movieList, "Movie_Year");
    //
    if (checkBox1.DataBindings["Checked"] != null)
        checkBox1.DataBindings.Remove(
            checkBox1.DataBindings["Checked"]);
    checkBox1.DataBindings.Add("Checked", movieList,
                                "BestPicture");
    //
    if (pictureBox1.DataBindings["BackgroundImage"] != null)
        pictureBox1.DataBindings.Remove(
            pictureBox1.DataBindings["BackgroundImage"]);
    pictureBox1.DataBindings.Add("BackgroundImage", movieList,
            "Movie_Image");
}
```

Fig. 16.7 | Binding Controls to an Array of Objects.

When designing a custom class to be used as a data source, the primary consideration is whether the bindable properties provide read-only or read/write access. If they are read-only, the only requirement is that they be `public`. For properties that can be updated, the class must expose and fire an event to which the binding can subscribe. Recall that the name of this event is `propertynameChanged`. This event is fired in the `Set` block of the property (see Fig. 16.8).

```
// Bind control to array populated with instances of
// custom class
public class MyMovie
{
   private string myID;
   private string myTitle;
   private int myYear;
   private string myStudio;
   private bool myBestPicture;
   private Image myImage;
   //
   public event EventHandler Movie_YearChanged;
   public event EventHandler StudioChanged;
   public MyMovie(string id, string title, int year,
                  string studio,
         bool bp, Image img)
 {
      myTitle = title;
      myYear = year;
      myStudio = studio;
      myBestPicture = bp;
      myImage = img;
      myID = id;
   }
   // Only public properties can be bound to control
   public string Movie_Title  { get { return myTitle; } }
   // Make read/write so update can occur
   public int Movie_Year {
      get { return myYear; }
      set {
         myYear = value;
         if (Movie_YearChanged != null)
            Movie_YearChanged(this, EventArgs.Empty);
      }
   }

   public string Studio {
      get { return myStudio; }
      set {
         myStudio = value;
         if (StudioChanged != null) StudioChanged(this,
            EventArgs.Empty);
      }
   }
   public Image  Movie_Image  { get { return myImage; } }
   public bool   BestPicture  { get { return myBestPicture; } }
}
```

Fig. 16.8 | Custom Data Source Class.

16.3.3 Adding an Item to the Data Source

Clicking the Add Movie button causes information about a single movie to be added to the data source (see Fig. 16.9). If the source is a table, a row is added; if an array, an object is created and inserted. An addition to a data table is automatically pushed to the control

```
// Test effects of adding a new item to the data source
private void button2_Click(object sender, EventArgs e)
{
    if (ds != null)
    {
        // Add a row to the table
        DataTable dt = ds.Tables[0];
        DataRow dRow = dt.NewRow();
        dRow["movie_ID"] = 99;
        dRow["movie_Title"] = "Rear Window";
        dRow["movie_Year"] = "1954";
        dRow["studio"] = "Paramount";
        dRow["BestPicture"] = 0;
        dRow["afi_rank"] = 42;
        Image defaultImage = Image.FromFile(@"c:\afi42.gif");
        dRow["movie_Image"] = defaultImage;
        dt.Rows.Add(dRow);
    }
    else
    {
        Image movieImg = Image.FromFile(@"c:\afi42.gif");
        movieList.Add(new MyMovie("42", "Rear Window", 1954,
                "Paramount", false, movieImg));
        // Refresh() is needed to display item in ListBox/ComboBox
        CurrencyManager cm =
                (CurrencyManager)this.BindingContext[movieList];
        cm.Refresh();
    }
}
```

Fig. 16.9 | Add an Item to a Data Source.

and made visible. When a custom object is added, the Refresh method of the Currency-Manager must be executed to synchronize the control. Note that Refresh is specific to the CurrencyManager class and not available on BindingManagerBase.

16.3.4 Identifying Updates

The rows in a table have a RowState property that can be used to determine if a value in the row has been changed (discussed in Chapter 15). This method checks the value of that property for each row in the data source table. If the value is DataRowState.Modified, each column in the row is checked to determine which values have changed (see Fig. 16.10). This routine can be used to determine whether an update to the original database is necessary. Observe that the method checks only for data changes. You can easily extend it to check for deletions and additions.

16.3.5 Update Original Database with Changes

When the modifiable data source is a data table, the Update method of its associated Data-Adapter can be used to flush changes to the database. This topic is discussed in detail in Section 11.4, "DataSets, DataTables, and the Disconnected Model."

```
// Checks status of each row in data table to identify any
// changes. This works only when data source is a Data Table.
private bool DataIsDirty(DataTable dt){
   bool result = false;
   foreach(DataRow drw in dt.Rows){
      // Check all rows in the table for a modified state
      if(drw.RowState == DataRowState.Modified)
      {
          string msg = (string)drw["movie_Title"]+":";
          string curr;
          string orig;
          // Examine each column in the row for a change
          foreach(DataColumn col in dt.Columns)
          {
              curr= drw[col,
                 DataRowVersion.Current].ToString().Trim();
              orig= drw[col,
                 DataRowVersion.Original].ToString().Trim();
              if(!curr.Equals(orig) || curr != orig ||
                 string.CompareOrdinal(curr,orig) !=0)
              {
                  msg += "\r\n" + orig + " " + curr;
                  result=true;
              }
          }
          MessageBox.Show(msg);    // Display changes in a row
      }
   }
   return result;
}
```

Fig. 16.10 | Check Data Source for Any Updates.

```
try
{
    int updates = da.Update(ds, "movies");
    MessageBox.Show("Updates: "+updates.ToString());
}
catch (Exception ex)
{
    MessageBox.Show(ex.Message);
}
```

16.4 The DataGridView Class

The DataGridView control, introduced with .NET 2.0, supersedes the DataGrid—which now exists primarily for legacy purposes. With more than a hundred properties and methods, the DataGridView is by far the most complex Windows Forms control for displaying data. Accordingly, it is also the most flexible. Styles that govern appearance can be applied on a cell-by-cell basis, by rows, by columns, or across all cells in the grid. Cells are not limited to text. They may contain a TextBox, Image, CheckBox, Link, or Button control.

Data binding is supported by the DataSource property, just as with the controls defined in the previous section. In addition, the DataGridView provides a unique *virtual* mode that permits it to handle more than 100,000 rows of data. DataGridView methods, events, and properties allow an application to easily manage the mapping between virtual and physical storage.

All of these features are discussed in this section. We'll look at selected properties and events along with code examples that illustrate their use.

16.4.1 Properties

Despite its myriad features, the DataGridView has an elegantly simple structure. As shown in Fig. 16.11, in its most elemental form, it consists of column headers, row headers, and cells. To these, we can add the Columns and Rows collections that allow an application to access the grid by indexing a row or column. That is the foundation. Each property and event discussed in this section relates to one of these five classes.

The DataGridView class inherits many of its properties from the Control class; to these, it adds properties required to support its own special characteristics and behavior. The properties listed in Fig. 16.12 are primarily in this latter category. The list is not meant to be exhaustive; instead, it presents those properties you'll refer to most frequently when implementing a grid.

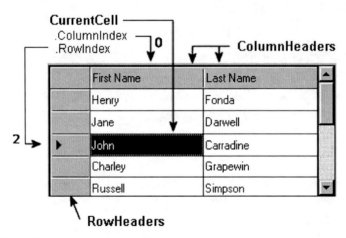

Fig. 16.11 | Basic DataGridView elements.

Category	Property Name	Description
User functionality	AllowUserToAddRows AllowUserToDeleteRows	Indicates whether a user may add/delete rows. Default: true.
	AllowUserToOrderColumns	Indicates whether user can rearrange columns.
	ColumnHeadersHeightResizable	Indicates whether the user can change the height of the column headers. Default: true.

Fig. 16.12 | Selected Properties of the DataGridView Class. (Part 1 of 3.)

Category	Property Name	Description
User functionality *(continued)*	MultiSelect	Indicates whether user may select one or more rows at a time.
	SelectionMode	Indicates the cells selected when clicking any individual or header cell.
		enum DataGridViewSelectionMode values: ColumnHeaderSelect RowHeaderSelect FullColumnSelect FullRowSelect CellSelect
	ReadOnly	Indicates whether user can modify data in cells. Values: true or false.
Appearance	AlternatingRows-Default-CellStyle	Gets or sets the default cell style applied to the odd numbered rows in the grid.
	BackColor	The background color of the grid.
	BackgroundColor	Gets or sets the background color for the area of the grid not containing data cells or column/row headers.
	BorderStyle	Gets or sets the border style for the DataGridView. enum BorderStyle values: BorderStyle.Fixed3D BorderStyle.FixedSingle BorderStyle.None
	CellBorderStyle	Gets or sets the border style used for cells in the grid. enum DataGridViewCellBorderStyle values: (to draw between rows) SingleHorizontal SunkenHorizontal RaisedHorizontal (to draw between columns) SingleVertical SunkenVertical RaisedVertical (to place a border between rows and columns) SingleSunken Raised

Fig. 16.12 | Selected Properties of the DataGridView Class. (Part 2 of 3.)

Category	Property Name	Description
Appearance (*continued*)	ColumnCount	Gets or sets the number of columns in the DataGridView.
	ColumnHeadersBorder-Style RowHeadersBorderStyle	Border style applied to to column/row headers. enum DataGridViewHeaderBorderStyle values: Custom Raised Sunk None Single
	ColumnHeadersVisible RowHeadersVisible	Displays or suppresses headers. Values: true or false.
	ColumnHeaderDefault-Cell-Style	Defines cell style properties for column header cells.
	DefaultCellStyle	DataGridViewCellStyle object that defines the default cell style properties for cells. Note that this includes column header cells.
	FirstDisplayedCell	The first cell displayed in the grid, usually upper-left corner.
	GridColor	The color of the lines separating the cells.
Collections	Columns	Collection of all grid columns. Individual columns are accessed by an index: Columns[iI].
	Rows	Collection of all grid rows. Individual rows are accessed by an index: Rows[i].
	SelectedColumns	Collection of columns selected.
	SelectedRows	Collection of rows selected.
	SelectedCells	Collection of cells selected.

Fig. 16.12 | Selected Properties of the DataGridView Class. (Part 3 of 3.)

Constructing a DataGridView

Figure 16.13 shows how to define columns for a DataGridView, set properties to define its appearance and behavior, and add rows of data. (We'll see in the succeeding example how to use the more common approach of loading data from a database.)

Note that the column header cells and data cells have different styles. If a style is not set for the header, it uses the same DefaultCellStyle as the data cells.

Figure 16.14 shows the DataGridView created by this code.

DataBinding with a DataGridView

A DataGridView is bound to a data source using complex binding. As in our list box example, the DataSource property specifies the data source. The similarity ends there, however, because a DataGridView must display multiple data values. To do so, the DataMember property is set to the name of a table within the data source. The data to be displayed in

```
// Set properties of a DataGridView and fill with data
private void CreateGrid()
{
   // (1) Define column headers
   dataGridView1.ColumnCount = 3;
   dataGridView1.Columns[0].HeaderText = "Movie Title";
   dataGridView1.Columns[1].HeaderText = "Year";
   dataGridView1.Columns[2].HeaderText = "Director";
   dataGridView1.Columns[1].Name  = "Year";
   dataGridView1.Columns[0].Width = 150;
   dataGridView1.Columns[1].Width = 40;
   dataGridView1.Columns[2].Width = 110;
   // (2) Define style for data cells
   DataGridViewCellStyle style = new DataGridViewCellStyle();
   style.BackColor = Color.Bisque;
   style.Font = new Font("Arial", 8, FontStyle.Bold);
   style.ForeColor = Color.Navy;
   //                        (left,top,right,bottom)
   style.Padding = new Padding(5, 2, 5, 5);
   style.SelectionBackColor = Color.LightBlue;
   dataGridView1.DefaultCellStyle = style;
   // (3) Define style for column headers
   DataGridViewCellStyle styleHdr = new
         DataGridViewCellStyle();
   styleHdr.Padding = new Padding(1, 1, 1, 1);
   styleHdr.BackColor = Color.OldLace;
   styleHdr.ForeColor = Color.Black;
   dataGridView1.ColumnHeadersDefaultCellStyle = styleHdr;
   // (4) Define user capabilities
   dataGridView1.AllowUserToAddRows      = false;
   dataGridView1.AllowUserToOrderColumns = false;
   dataGridView1.AllowUserToDeleteRows   = false;
   // (5) Place data in grid manually (datasource is better)
   object[] row1 = {"Casablanca", "1942","Michael Curtiz"};
   dataGridView1.Rows.Add(row1);
   object[] row2 = {"Raging Bull","1980","Martin Scorsese"};
   dataGridView1.Rows.Add(row2);
   object[] row3 = {"On the Waterfront","1954","Elia Kazan"};
   dataGridView1.Rows.Add(row3);
   object[] row4 = {"Some Like it Hot","1959","Billy Wilder"};
   dataGridView1.Rows.Add(row4);
}
```

Fig. 16.13 | Setting DataGridView Properties and Adding Rows of Data.

each column is specified by setting the column's DataPropertyName property to the name of the underlying data table column.

```
// Turn this off so column names do not come from data source
dataGridView1.AutoGenerateColumns = false;
// Specify table as data source
dataGridView1.DataSource = ds;       // Dataset
dataGridView1.DataMember = "movies"; // Table in dataset
```

Movie Title	Year	Director
Casablanca	1942	Michael Curtiz
Raging Bull	1980	Martin Scorsese
On the Waterfront	1954	Elia Kazan
Some Like it Hot	1959	Billy Wilder

Fig. 16.14 | DataGridView built from code in Listing 16.6.

```
// Tie the columns in the grid to column names in the data table
dataGridView1.Columns[0].DataPropertyName = "Title";
dataGridView1.Columns[1].DataPropertyName = "Year";
dataGridView1.Columns[2].DataPropertyName = "director";
```

The DataGridView supports two-way data binding for ADO.NET data sources: Changes made to the grid are reflected in the underlying table, and changes made to the table are reflected in the grid. For example, this code responds to a button click by adding a new row to the grid's data source. The addition is immediately reflected in the control. However, if we try to add a row directly to the DataGridView, an exception occurs because adding directly to a bound control is not permitted.

```
private void buttonAdd_Click(object sender, EventArgs e)
{
    // Adding to underlying table is okay
    r[0] = "TAXI";
    r[1] = "1976";
    r[2] = "Martin Scorsese";
    dt.Rows.Add(r);
    // Adding directly to DataGridView does not work
    object[] row = {"The Third Man", "1949", "Orson Welles"};
    DataRow r = dt.NewRow();
    DataGridView1.Rows.Add(row4);  // Fails!
}
```

Updating the original database from which a grid is loaded can be done by issuing individual SQL commands or using a DataAdapter. The discussion in the previous section applies.

Core Note 16.1

A DataGridView may have a mixture of bound and non-bound columns. Thus, columns can be added to a bound control, but rows cannot.

Setting the Row Height
The default height of rows in a DataGridView is based on accommodating a single line of text. If the row contains large sized fonts or images, they are truncated. It is usually better

to force the grid to take the size of each cell in the row into account and base the overall height on the tallest cell. That's the role of the grid's AutoSizeRows method. Its simplest overloaded version takes a single parameter—a DataGridViewAutoSizeRowsMode enumeration value—that indicates the criterion used for setting row height. The two most useful enumeration members are ColumnAllRows, which bases the row height on all columns in the row, and ColumnsDisplayedRows, which applies the same criterion, but to visible rows only.

```
dataGridView1.AutoSizeRows(
    DataGridViewAutoSizeRowsMode.ColumnsAllRows);
```

The AutoSizeRows method sets the row size when it is executed. If subsequent updates cause the height of cells in a row to change, the row height does not adjust to the changes. Also, if a row is sortable, clicking a column header to sort the grid causes all rows to revert to the default row height. Fortunately, the DataGridView has an AutoSizeRows-Mode property that causes row heights to automatically adjust to changes in grid content.

```
dataGridView1.AutoSizeRowsMode =
    DataGridViewAutoSizeRowsMode.HeaderAndColumnsAllRows;
```

Note that this statement does not take effect until the AutoSizeRows method is executed, and that it prevents users from manually resizing rows.

Working with Columns and Column Types

The DataGridView is not a full-blown spreadsheet, but it does offer some features a user expects from a spreadsheet. These include the following:

- **Frozen Column(s).** For a grid that requires horizontal scrolling, it is often useful to "freeze" columns so that they always remain on the screen. Setting a column's Frozen property to true has the effect of freezing it and all columns to its left.

  ```
  dataGridView1.Columns[0].Frozen = true;
  ```

- **ReadOnly Columns.** Selected column can be made read-only.

  ```
  dataGridView1.Columns[2].ReadOnly = true;
  ```

- **Minimum Width.** By default, a user can widen and narrow columns in a grid. The minimum size permitted for a column can be controlled by setting the MinimumWidth property to a value in pixels:

  ```
  dataGridView1.Columns[0].MinimumWidth=100;
  ```

- **Sorting.** By default, clicking a column header sorts the rows based on values in that column—if the column contains sortable values. It's SortMode property can be used to disable sorting:

  ```
  dataGridView1.Columns[0].SortMode =
          DataGridViewColumnSortMode.NotSortable;
  ```

- **Multiple Column Types.** Six predefined column classes are available that can be used to represent information in a grid, using the familiar formats of the TextBox, CheckBox, Image, Button, ComboBox, and Link. The name for each of these controls follows the format DataGridView**Controlname**Column.

This code segment adds a column of buttons to a grid. The first step is to create an instance of the column class. Its characteristics and data values—if any—are then set. Finally, the Columns.Add method is used to add the column to the grid's column collection.

```
// (1) Create instance of column type
DataGridViewButtonColumn buttons = new
        DataGridViewButtonColumn();
// Text to place in column header
buttons.HeaderText = "Delete";
// (2) Set characteristics of control
buttons.Text = "Delete";    // Default text for button
buttons.FlatStyle = FlatStyle.Standard;
// Create a datagridview cell to use as a template to set
// all buttons in the column to the same style.
buttons.CellTemplate = new DataGridViewButtonCell();
buttons.CellTemplate.Style.BackColor = Color.Yellow ;
buttons.CellTemplate.Style.Font = new Font("Arial", 8);
// Specify column position on grid
buttons.DisplayIndex = 1;
// (3) Add column to grid
dataGridView.Columns.Add(buttons);
```

Any of the column types may be bound to a data source. Although a button is usually set manually, it can be bound to a property in the grid's data source in two ways:

```
// Use the DataGridviewButtonColumn class
buttons.DataPropertyName = "Title";
// Use the Columns class (button is in column 1 of the grid)
dataGridView3.Columns[1].DataPropertyName = "Title";
```

Buttons provide a convenient way for a user to select a grid row and trigger an action such as a pop-up form that displays further information related to the row. Buttons located in grid cells, however, have no direct event, such as a Click, associated with them. Instead, events are associated with an action on the overall grid or specific cells on the grid. By identifying a cell for instance, an event handler can determine which button is clicked.

16.4.2 Events

Just about every mouse and cursor movement that can occur over a DataGridView can be detected by one of its events. In addition, events signify when data is changed, added, or deleted. The table in Fig. 16.15 provides a summary of the most useful events. Accompanying the table is a list of the delegate used to implement these events.

The following are delegates associated with events in Fig. 16.15:

```
(1) public sealed delegate void DataGridViewCellEventHandler(
        object sender, DataGridViewCellEventArgs e)

(2) public sealed delegate void DataGridViewCellMouseEventHandler(
        object sender, DataGridViewCellMouseEventArgs e)

(3) public sealed delegate void EventHandler(
        object sender, EventHandlerArgs e)
```

```
(4) public sealed delegate void DataGridViewRowEventHandler (
        object sender, DataGridViewRowEventArgs e)

(5) public sealed delegate void
        DataGridViewCellFormattingEventHandler(
            object sender, DataGridViewCellFormattingEventArgs e)

(6) public sealed delegate void
        DataGridViewCellPaintingEventHandler(
            object sender, DataGridViewCellPaintingEventArgs e)

(7) public sealed delegate void
        DataGridViewDataErrorEventHandler(
            object sender, DataGridViewDataErrorEventArgs e)
```

Let's look at some common uses for these events.

Category	Event (Delegate)	Description
Cell actions	CellValueChanged (1)	Occurs when the value of a cell changes.
	CurrentCellChanged (3)	Occurs when the value of the current cell changes
	CellClick (1)	Occurs when any part of the cell is clicked. This includes cell borders and padding.
	CellContentClick (1)	Occurs only if the cell content is clicked.
	CellEnter (1) CellLeave (1)	Occurs when cell receives/loses input focus.
	CellFormatting (5)	Occurs prior to formatting a cell for display.
	CellMouseClick (2) CellMouseDoubleClick (2)	Occurs whenever a mouse clicks/double clicks anywhere on a cell.
	CellMouseDown (2) CellMouseUp (2)	Occurs when a mouse button is pressed/raised while it is over a cell.
	CellMouseEnter (1) CellMouseLeave (1)	Occurs when the mouse pointer enters or leaves a cell's area.
	CellPainting (6)	Raised when a cell is to be painted.
Column actions	ColumnHeaderMouseClick (2) ColumnHeaderMouseDouble-Click (2)	Occurs when a column header is clicked/double clicked.
Row actions	RowEnter (1) RowLeave (1)	Occurs when a row receives/loses the input focus.

Fig. 16.15 | Selected DataGridView Events. (Part 1 of 2.)

Category	Event (Delegate)	Description
Row actions *(continued)*	RowHeaderMouseClick (2) RowHeaderDoubleMouse-Click (2)	Occurs when a user clicks/double clicks a row header.
	UserAddedRow (4) UserDeletedRow (4)	Occurs when a user adds/deletes a row in the grid.
Data error	DataError (7)	Occurs when an external data parsing or validation operations fails. Typically occurs due to an attempt to load invalid data into a data grid cell.

Fig. 16.15 | Selected DataGridView Events. (Part 2 of 2.)

Cell Formatting

The CellFormatting event gives you the opportunity to format a cell before it is rendered. This comes in handy if you want to distinguish a subset of cells by some criteria. For example, the grid in Fig. 16.14 contains a column indicating the year a movie was released. Let's change the background color of cells in that column to red if the year is less than 1950.

```
// Set cells in year column to red if year is less than 1950
private void Grid3_CellFormatting(object sender,
    DataGridViewCellFormattingEventArgs e)
{
    if (this.dataGridView3.Columns[e.ColumnIndex].Name == "Year")
    {
        string yr = (string)e.Value;
        if (Int32.Parse(yr) < 1950)
        {
            e.CellStyle.ForeColor = Color.Red;
            e.CellStyle.SelectionForeColor = Color.Red;
            // Indicate that event was handled
            e.FormattingApplied = true;
        }
    }
}
```

The ColumnIndex property of the EventArgs parameter is used to determine if the year column is being formatted. If so, the code checks the year and formats the cell accordingly. Note that the FormattingApplied property must be set if custom formatting is performed.

Recognizing Selected Rows, Columns, and Cells

As shown in Fig. 16.15, selecting a cell in a grid can trigger any number of events that can be used to indicate the current cell or the cell just left. Some of the events are almost over-engineered. For example, there seems little to distinguish CellContentClick and CellClick. Others exist to recognize grid navigation using both the mouse and keyboard: The CellClick is not triggered by arrow keys; however, the CellEnter event is fired no matter how a cell is selected. All of these cell-related events have a consistent event handler signature. The `EventArgs` parameter provides column and row index properties to identify the cell. Here is an example:

```
private void Grid1_CellEnter(object sender,
      DataGridViewCellEventArgs e)
{
    // Both of these display the column index of the selected cell
    MessageBox.Show("enter "+e.ColumnIndex.ToString());
    MessageBox.Show(
          DataGridView1.CurrentCell.ColumnIndex.ToString());
}
```

Core Note 16.2

Although row and column header cells cannot become "current cells," they are assigned a column and row index value. Row headers always have a column index of −1, and column headers have row index of −1.

The cell events can be used to recognize a single row and column selection. However, a grid may also permit multiple row, column, and cell selections. In these cases, it is necessary to use the `SelectedRows`, `SelectedColumns`, and `SelectedCells` collections to access the selected grid values.

Multiple row selection is made available on a `DataGridView` by setting its `MultiSelect` property to `true`—which is the default value. A row is selected by clicking its row header. It can also be selected by clicking any cell in the row if the grid's `SelectionMode` property is set to `DataGridViewSelectionMode.FullRowSelect`. The property can also be set to `FullColumnSelect`, which causes a cell's column to be selected. Note that column and row selection are mutually exclusive: only one can be in effect at a time.

This segment illustrates how to iterate through the collection of selected rows. The same approach is used for columns and cells.

```
// Display selected row numbers and content of its column 1
if (dataGridView1.SelectedRows.Count > 0)
{
    StringBuilder sb = new StringBuilder();
    for (int i = 0; i < dataGridView1.SelectedRows.Count; i++)
    {
        sb.Append("Row: ");
        sb.Append(
              dataGridView1.SelectedRows[i].Index.ToString() );
        sb.Append( dataGridView1.SelectedRows[i].Cells[1].Value);
        sb.Append(Environment.NewLine);
    }
    MessageBox.Show (sb.ToString(), "Selected Rows");
}
```

Data Error Handling

The `DataError` event fires when a problem occurs loading data into a grid or posting data from the grid to the underlying data store. The error is quite easy to detect: compare the value of the Context property of the ErrorEventArgs parameter with the DataGridView-DataErrorContext enumeration values. Here is an example:

```
// Define event handler
DataGridView1.DataError += new
        DataGridViewDataErrorEventHandler(DataGridView1_DataError);

// DataError Event Handler
private void dataGridView1_DataError(object sender,
        DataGridViewDataErrorEventArgs dgError)
{
    // Context provides information about the grid when the
    // error occurred.
    MessageBox.Show("Error: " + dgError.Context.ToString());
    // Problem committing grid data to underlying data source
    if (dgError.Context == DataGridViewDataErrorContext.Commit)
    {
        MessageBox.Show("Commit error");
    }
    // Occurs when selection cursor moves to another cell
    if (dgError.Context ==
            DataGridViewDataErrorContext.CurrentCellChange)
    {
        MessageBox.Show("Cell change");
    }
    if (dgError.Context ==
            DataGridViewDataErrorContext.Parsing)
    {
        MessageBox.Show("parsing error");
    }
    // Could not format data coming from/going to data source
    if (dgError.Context ==
            DataGridViewDataErrorContext.Formatting)
    {
        MessageBox.Show("formatting error");
    }
}
```

16.4.3 Setting Up Master-Detail DataGridViews

One of the more common relationships between tables in a database is that of the master-detail relationship, where the records in the master table have multiple associated records in the detail table. DataGridViews provide a natural way of displaying this relationship. To illustrate, let's create an application based on the Films database that displays a master grid containing a list of movies and a detail grid that display actors who played in the movie selected in the first grid. To make it interesting, we'll include an image column in the movie grid that contains a picture of the Oscar statuette for movies that won for best picture.

The master grid is bound to the movies table; the details grid is bound to the actors table. Both tables, as shown in Fig. 16.16, contain the columns that are bound to their respective DataGridView columns. In addition, they contain a movieID column that links the two in the master-detail relationship.

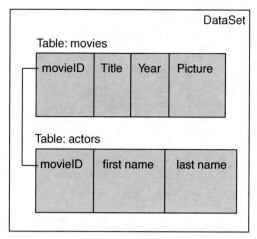

Fig. 16.16 | Master-detail tables.

The tables and their relationships are created using the techniques described in Chapter 15:

```
ds = new DataSet();
DataTable dt = new DataTable("movies");  // Master
DataTable da = new DataTable("actors");  // Detail
da.Columns.Add("movieID");
da.Columns.Add("firstname");
da.Columns.Add("lastname");
//
dt.Columns.Add("movieID");
dt.Columns.Add("Title");
dt.Columns.Add("Year");
dt.Columns.Add("picture", typeof(Bitmap));  // To hold image
ds.Tables.Add(dt);
ds.Tables.Add(da);
// Define master-detail relationship
DataRelation rel = new DataRelation("movieactor",
    dt.Columns["movieID"], da.Columns["movieID"]);
ds.Relations.Add(rel);
```

After defining the table schemas, they are populated from the database using a DataReader object. Because the database does not contain an image—although it could—the image is inserted based on the value of the bestPicture field.

```
Bitmap oscar   = new Bitmap(@"c:\oscar.gif");   // Oscar image
Bitmap nooscar = new Bitmap(@"c:\nooscar.gif"); // Blank image
// Populate movies table from datareader
while (dr.Read())
{
   DataRow drow = dt.NewRow();
   drow["Title"] = (string)(dr["movie_Title"]);
   drow["Year"]  = ((int)dr["movie_Year"]).ToString();
```

```
        drow["movieID"] = (int)dr["movie_ID"];
        if ((string)dr["bestPicture"] == "Y") drow["picture"] =
            oscar; else drow["picture"] = nooscar;
        dt.Rows.Add(drow);
    }
```

The actors table is filled with the results of the query:

```
    sql = "SELECT am.movie_ID, actor_first,actor_last FROM actors a
        JOIN actor_movie am ON a.actor_ID = am.actor_ID";
```

After the tables are created and populated, the final steps are to define the grids and bind their columns to the tables. This segment adds three columns to the master grid—one of which is an image type column.

```
    DataGridViewImageColumn vic = new DataGridViewImageColumn();
    dataGridView1.Columns.Add(vic);    // Add image type column
    //
    dataGridView1.ColumnCount = 3;
    dataGridView1.Columns[0].Name = "Oscar";
    dataGridView1.Columns[1].HeaderText = "Movie Title";
    dataGridView1.Columns[2].HeaderText = "Year";
```

Then, the binding is performed:

```
    // Bind grids to dataset
    dataGridView1.DataSource = ds;
    dataGridView1.DataMember = "movies";
    dataGridView2.DataSource = ds;
    // ***Set to DataRelation for detail
    dataGridView2.DataMember = dt.TableName+".movieactor";
    // Bind grid columns to table columns
    dataGridView1.Columns[0].DataPropertyName = "picture";
    dataGridView1.Columns[1].DataPropertyName = "Title";
    dataGridView1.Columns[2].DataPropertyName = "Year";
    dataGridView1.Columns[3].DataPropertyName = "director";
    dataGridView2.Columns[0].DataPropertyName = "firstname";
    dataGridView2.Columns[1].DataPropertyName = "lastname";
```

Pay close attention to the binding of dataGridView2. It is bound to the relationship defined between the tables, rather than directly to the actors table. This binding causes the names of the movie's cast to be displayed in the grid when a movie is selected.

Figure 16.17 shows a sample screen. Much of the excluded code in this example deals with setting grid styles and capabilities. A full code listing is available in the book's code download. (See the Preface for the download URL addresses and instructions.)

16.4.4 Virtual Mode

When a DataGridView is bound to a data source, the entire data source must exist in memory. This enables quick refreshing of the control's cells as a user navigates from row to row. The downside is that a large data store may have prohibitive memory requirements. To handle excessive memory requirements, a DataGridView can be run in virtual mode by setting its VirtualMode property to true. In this mode, the application takes

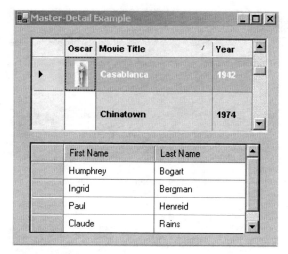

Fig. 16.17 | Master-detail relationship.

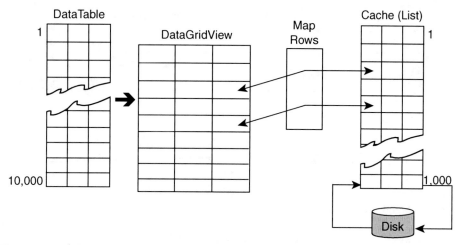

Fig. 16.18 | Data binding versus virtual mode.

responsibility for maintaining an underlying data cache to handle the population, editing, and deletion of DataGridView cells based on actions of the user. The cache contains data for a selected portion of the grid. If a row in the grid cannot be satisfied from cache, the application must load the cache with the necessary data from the original data source. Figure 16.18 compares virtual storage with binding to a DataTable.

Virtual mode implementation requires that an application handle two special virtual mode events: CellValueNeeded, which occurs when a cell value must be displayed; and CellValuePushed, which occurs when a cell's value is edited. Other events are also required to manage the data cache. These are summarized in Fig. 16.19.

To illustrate the fundamentals of implementing a DataGridView in virtual mode, let's look at the code used to create the DataGridView shown in Fig. 16.20.

Event	Description
NewRowsNeeded	Virtual mode event. Occurs when a row is appended to the `Data-GridView`.
CellValueNeeded	Virtual mode event. Occurs when cell in grid needs to be displayed.
CellValuePushed	Virtual mode event. Occurs when a cell value is edited by the user.
RowValidated	Occurs when another row is selected.
UserDeletingRow	Occurs when a row is selected and the Delete key is pressed.

Fig. 16.19 | `DataGridView` Events Used to Implement Virtual Mode.

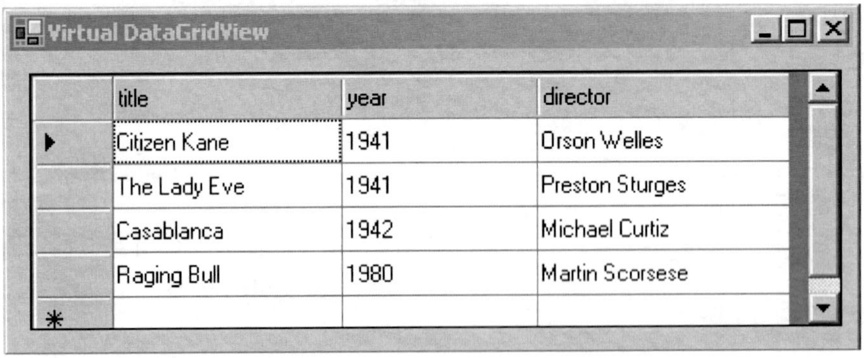

Fig. 16.20 | `DataGridView` using virtual mode.

The variables having class scope are shown here. Note that the data cache is implemented as a generics `List` object that holds instances of the `movie` class. The `movie` class exposes three properties that are displayed on the grid: `Title`, `Movie_Year`, and `Director`.DataGridView dgv;

```
List<movie> movieList = new List<movie>(20);  // cache
bool rowNeeded;   // True when new row appended to grid
int storeRow = 0;
int currRow = -1; // Set to row being added
movie currMovie;  // Holds movie object for current row
```

Figure 16.21 shows the overhead code to initialize the `DataGridView`, register the event handlers, and populate the data cache (this would usually come from a database).

The heart of the application is represented by the event handler methods shown in Fig. 16.22. To summarize them:

- `RowNeeded`. Is triggered when the user begins to add a new row at the bottom of the grid. `currRow` is set to the row number of any row being added.

- `CellNeeded`. Is triggered when a cell needs to be redrawn. This does not require that a row be selected, but occurs as you move the cursor over cells in the grid. This routine identifies the column the cell is in and displays the data from the cache or the object that is created for new rows. Note that the `MapRow()` is called

```
// Set properties of a DataGridView and fill with data
dgv = new DataGridView();
// Event handlers for virtual mode events
dgv.CellValueNeeded += new
    DataGridViewCellValueEventHandler(CellNeeded);
dgv.CellValuePushed += new
    DataGridViewCellValueEventHandler(CellPushed);
dgv.NewRowNeeded += new
    DataGridViewRowEventHandler(RowNeeded);
// Event handlers always available for DataGridView
dgv.UserDeletingRow += new
    DataGridViewRowCancelEventHandler (RowDeleting);
dgv.RowValidated += new
    DataGridViewCellEventHandler( RowValidated);
dgv.VirtualMode = true;
dgv.RowCount = 5;
dgv.ColumnCount = 3;
// Headers for columns
dgv.Columns[0].HeaderText = "title";
dgv.Columns[1].HeaderText = "year";
dgv.Columns[2].HeaderText = "director";
// Fill cache. In production, this would come from database.
movieList.Add(new movie("Citizen Kane",1941,"Orson Welles"));
movieList.Add(new movie("The Lady Eve",1941,"
                        "Preston Sturges"));
// ... Add other movies here
```

Fig. 16.21 | Virtual DataGridView: Initialization.

```
// Called when a new row is appended to grid
private void RowNeeded(object sender,
                    DataGridViewRowEventArgs e)
{
   rowNeeded = true;
   currRow = dgv.Rows.Count - 1;
}

// Called when a cell must be displayed/refreshed
private void CellNeeded(object sender,
                    DataGridViewCellValueEventArgs e)
{
   if (rowNeeded)
   {
      rowNeeded = false;
      currMovie = new movie();
      return;
   }
   storeRow = MapRow(e.RowIndex);
   if(storeRow >=0 && currRow  ==-1)
        currMovie =  movieList[storeRow];
   string colName = dgv.Columns[e.ColumnIndex].HeaderText;
   if(storeRow>=0)  // Refresh cell from cache
```

Fig. 16.22 | Virtual DataGridView: Event Handlers. (Part 1 of 3.)

```
      {
         if (colName == "title")e.Value =
             movieList[storeRow].Title;
         if (colName == "year") e.Value =
             movieList[storeRow].Movie_Year.ToString();
         if (colName == "director") e.Value =
             movieList[storeRow].Director;
      } else            // refresh cell from object for new row
      {
         if (colName == "title")e.Value = currMovie.Title;
         if (colName == "year")e.Value =
             currMovie.Movie_Year.ToString();
         if (colName == "director") e.Value = currMovie.Director;
      }
   }
   // Cell has been updated
   private void CellPushed(object sender,
                          DataGridViewCellValueEventArgs e)
   {
      // Update property on movie object for this row
      storeRow = MapRow(e.RowIndex);
      string colName = dgv.Columns[e.ColumnIndex].HeaderText;
      if (colName == "title") currMovie.Title = (string)e.Value;
      if (colName == "year")
      {
         int retval;
         if(int.TryParse((string)e.Value,out retval))
             currMovie.Movie_Year = retval;
      }
      if (colName == "director") currMovie.Director =
          (string)e.Value;
   }
   // Occurs when user changes current row
   // Update previous row in cache when this occurs
   private void RowValidated(object sender,
                          DataGridViewCellEventArgs e)
   {
      storeRow = MapRow(e.RowIndex);
      if (storeRow < 0) storeRow = movieList.Count;
      currRow = -1;
      if (currMovie != null)
      {
         // Save the modified Customer object in the data store.
         storeRow = MapRow(e.RowIndex);
         if (storeRow >= 0)
             movieList[storeRow] = currMovie;
         else movieList.Add(currMovie);
             currMovie = null;
      }
   }
   // Row selected and Del key pushed
   private void RowDeleting(object sender,
                          DataGridViewRowCancelEventArgs e)
```

Fig. 16.22 | Virtual `DataGridView`: Event Handlers. (Part 2 of 3.)

```
{
    if (MapRow(e.Row.Index)>=0)
    { movieList.RemoveAt(e.Row.Index); }
    if (e.Row.Index == currRow)
    {
        currRow = -1;
        currMovie = null;
    }
}
// Maps grid row to row in cache. More logic would be added
// for application that refreshes cache from database.
private int MapRow(int dgvRow)
{
    if (dgvRow < movieList.Count)return dgvRow;
        else return -1;
}
```

Fig. 16.22 | Virtual `DataGridView`: Event Handlers. (Part 3 of 3.)

to translate a row in the grid to its corresponding row in the cache. In this simple example, there is always a one-to-one relationship because the cache and grid contain the same number of rows. In a production application, row 5000 in a grid might map to row 1 in the cache.

- `CellPushed`. Called when a cell value is edited. This routine updates a movie object that represents the selected row with the new value.

- `RowValidated`. Signals that a different row has been selected and is used to update the previous row. If the row exists in the cache, it is updated; a new row is added to the cache.

- `RowDeleting`. Called when user selects a row to delete. If the row exists in the cache, it is removed.

This example provides only the basic details for implementing a virtual `DataGrid-View`. The next step is to extend it to include a virtual memory manager that reloads the cache when data must be fetched from disk to display a cell.

16.5 **Summary**

Data binding is used to link the data displayed in a control with an underlying data source. In many cases, it can eliminate the manual code required to populate controls. There are two basic types of binding: simple and complex. Simple is used with controls that display only one value; complex is used to display multiple data values in selected controls such as a list box or data grid.

Each data source has a binding manager that keeps track of all connections to it. This manager is responsible for synchronizing values in the data store and controls bound to it. For list data sources such as an array or data table, the binding manager is a `CurrencyManager` object; for a property on an object, the binding manager is a `PropertyManger` object. Both of these objects expose methods that allow them to be used to navigate through their data source.

Of the data bound controls, the DataGridView offers the richest interface. It permits data to be displayed and manipulated in a grid format. Style classes and appearance properties enable almost all of its features to be customized. Its event members allow virtually any action involving the grid to be detected—from a click on a cell to the addition of a row. It also permits control types such as a button, image, or ComboBox to be inserted into any of its cells. Although data binding is typically used to populate a DataGridView, the control also supports a virtual mode that allows an application to manage the grid's content using a custom data cache.

16.6 Test Your Understanding

1. Indicate whether the following are true or false:

   a) A TextBox supports complex binding.

   b) The width of a control can be bound to a data source.

   c) All controls support simple binding.

   d) A data source can only be bound to one control at a time.

   e) A data source may have multiple binding managers.

   f) Changes made to the value of a control are always propagated to the data source.

   g) Controls can be bound to custom data objects.

   h) The PropertyManager class inherits from the CurrencyManager class.

   i) Only public properties may be bound to a control.

2. What is the difference between simple and complex binding? One-way and two-way binding?

3. Describe how to allow a custom data source to support two-way binding.

4. Which property and enumeration cause the entire row in a DataGridView to be highlighted when a single cell in the row is selected?

5. Which of these cannot be included in a DataGridView cell?

   a) TextBox

   b) ListBox

   c) Button

   d) ComboBox

6. How do you ensure that a column in a DataGridView is always displayed on the screen?

Index

[*Note:* Page references for defining occurrences appears in ***bold italic***.]